THE CONDITION OF MAN

Books by Lewis Mumford

THE STORY OF UTOPIAS 1922

STICKS AND STONES 1924

THE GOLDEN DAY 1926

HERMAN MELVILLE 1929

THE BROWN DECADES 1931

TECHNICS AND CIVILIZATION 1934

THE CULTURE OF CITIES 1938

MEN MUST ACT 1939

FAITH FOR LIVING 1940

THE SOUTH IN ARCHITECTURE 1941

THE CONDITION OF MAN 1944

CITY DEVELOPMENT 1945

VALUES FOR SURVIVAL 1946

GREEN MEMORIES 1947

THE CONDUCT OF LIFE 1951

ART AND TECHNICS 1952

IN THE NAME OF SANITY 1954

FROM THE GROUND UP 1956

THE TRANSFORMATIONS OF MAN 1956

THE CITY IN HISTORY 1961

THE HIGHWAY AND THE CITY 1963

THE URBAN PROSPECT 1968

THE MYTH OF THE MACHINE:
I. TECHNICS AND HUMAN DEVELOPMENT 1967
II. THE PENTAGON OF POWER 1970

INTERPRETATIONS AND FORECASTS:
1922-1972 1973

FINDINGS AND KEEPINGS 1975

MY WORKS AND DAYS 1979

THE CONDITION OF MAN

LEWIS MUMFORD

A Harvest/HBJ Book
Harcourt Brace Jovanovich, Publishers
New York and London

ISBN 0-15-621550-0

Library of Congress Catalog Card Number: 72-91160

Printed in the United States of America

B C D E F G H I J

PREFACE

Since 'The Condition of Man' appeared in 1944, the condition of man has worsened. What were once only local demoralizations or disasters now threaten to turn into planetary calamities. That fact should not surprise earlier readers of this work: but the book's acceptance during the difficult war years, when it attracted more readers than either 'Technics and Civilization' or 'The Culture of Cities,' the first two volumes in 'The Renewal of Life' series, is easier to explain than its later neglect. Many who are reasonably familiar with my work have by now not even heard of 'The Condition of Man' or else confuse it with a companion volume, 'The Conduct of Life,' first published in 1951 and long available in paperback. Ironically, both the failures and the ambivalent, if not spurious, successes of Western civilization have updated 'The Condition of Man.'

Re-reading the text of 'The Condition of Man' today, with the cold sobriety that comes from long absence, I find little that I would care to change either in the tone or the contents of that work, though there is much that with further years of experience I would add—and in fact have added in 'The Conduct of Life,' 'The Transformations of Man,' and 'The Myth of the Machine.' If this book, after more than a decade of neglect, now returns to life, it is probably because its more unwelcome interpretations of the weaknesses of modern civilization have been confirmed, and because it nevertheless offers a more hopeful view of the nature of man and the potentials of human development than the nihilists, the existentialists, and the brutalists—the current prophets of anti-life—have made fashionable.

Unlike the followers of Oswald Spengler, I have not urged submission to the 'men of fact,' those guardians of the 'Pentagon of Power' who now dominate political, military, and economic affairs. Unlike the existentialist followers of the Nazi philosopher Heidegger, I have not taken our contemporary nausea and despair as the ultimate revelation of all human experience. Unlike those who cling to older religious orthodoxies, I have not counseled retreat into a bat-infested ideological cave, where in the darkness the faithful may somnolently alleviate their anxieties and fears, consoled by dreams that anesthetize the nightmares of waking life. The appeal of this book is to the 'awakened ones'; and the fact that it is again available is perhaps evidence that the circle of 'awakened ones' is widening: I mean those who know that salvation, like charity, begins at home.

In this now-favorable social climate, I am content to let 'The Condition of Man' speak for itself; all the more because so many of its statements about the prospects of our civilization which seemed dubious, presumptuous, or wantonly pessimistic have now been all too amply confirmed. But toward the end of the book there is one matter to which I would call the reader's attention, lest he suppose that the evidence and the conclusions I drew from it were more at fault than they have proved to be. In the final chapter I observed that, in contrast to the past three centuries of expansion and rapid change, a period of stabilization on a planetary basis was now at hand. This assumption was based on the statistical fact that in the more industrialized Western countries—except the Netherlands—the rate of population increase was steadily slowing down, so that a balance of births and deaths, or even a lowering of peak numbers, was already in sight. At the same time, a similar closing of territorial and economic expansion seemed at hand.

Though this view of stabilization contradicted the Victorian faith in the possibility of indefinite progress, I indicated that it was the very condition for genuine improvements in the condition of man. When this equilibrium would be reached, John Stuart Mill had pointed out in the 1874 edition of the 'Principles of Political Economy,' the offices of leisure, education, and public service, once confined to a dominant minority, would be open to the entire population. These happy prospects have obviously still to be realized. But the continued advance of the Welfare State, even in countries drained by extravagant Cold War expenditures, reveals how necessary and socially beneficent this change toward vertical expansion—equalizing advantages between the lower and upper strata of society—would be.

If my projection of a stabilized, internally balanced economy proved premature, my immediate error resulted from causes I had not overlooked but rather had definitely taken into account. On page 408 I pointed out that the now-obsolete economy based on a yearly increase of the gross national product could be maintained only by war or augmented preparations for war, which would absorb by sheer waste the inflated surplus that the capitalist economy had never learned to distribute equitably—or to liquidate without bringing on an economic depression. Furthermore, a pseudo-stabilization by "finance, insurance, and corporate monopolies" might frustrate a more viable social method for achieving dynamic equilibrium. Both these anticipated possibilities have come to pass.

Being only a social diagnostician, not a clairvoyant or an Old Testament prophet, I did not foresee, even in 1944, the imminent invention of the atom bomb, still less its immediate use; nor did I suspect that with the invention of intercontinental and interplanetary rockets even more massive forms of Keynesian pyramid building would be exploited to give the illusion of limitless power and prosperity. Certainly I did not suppose that the atrocious fascist strategy of mass genocide would be taken over in 1942 by our own 'democratic' government and would not be either publicly challenged or renounced when the pressures of war had lifted. Finally, I could not suspect that our temporary American monopoly of 'absolute' nuclear weapons would create a huge vested interest—military, industrial, and scientific—in preparations for random human extermination and indiscriminate ecological destruction by atomic, bacterial, and chemical means. All these perversions have temporarily reinstated the obsolete ideological premises and objectives of a compulsively expanding and affluent economy, with its obsessive 'pecuniary-pleasure' motivation. (See 'The Pentagon of Power.')

While I did not foresee the pressure toward super-military expansion that the Cold War would exert, I may nevertheless claim credit for taking into account the possibility of a fresh increase in population and even for pointing to the very conditions that might bring about such a reversal. As early as 1938, at a moment when population experts were almost unanimous in supposing that the current decline in the net reproduction rate would continue at least among Westernized nations, I had noted in 'The Culture of Cities' that "one can easily imagine, for instance, a new cult of family life, growing up in the face of some decimating catastrophe, which would necessitate a swift [upward] revision in plans for housing and city development: a generous urge toward procreation might clash in policy with the view of the prudent, bent on preserving a barely achieved equilibrium." That hypothetical catastrophe all too quickly became a reality in the Second World War, and the possibility of still more decimating massacres has been with us for the last quarter of a century. So as concerns the postwar population explosion, I was not nearly as surprised as the demographic specialists whose statistical curves rested on more limited observations. I was indeed mistaken in supposing that the forces making for a general societal stabilization were already in operation, for they had been abruptly thrown into reverse by the pressures of the power complex making for further uncontrolled expansion.

But now it turns out that my error was only a temporary one, at least as concerns the United States. For the latest official population statistics (1972) indicate that if the current level of 2.1 children per young woman of child-bearing age continues, within two generations—other things being equal—the number of births and deaths will balance. If such stabilization takes place in population, the area least open to governmental regulation, it should be easier to achieve by rational measures in other areas of expansion, once the necessity for establishing a dynamic equilibrium is recognized.

In any event, I was a generation in advance of most contemporaries in accepting Mill's description of the social desirability of such stabilization. Mill's forecast of such an economy was so contrary to current expectations of automatic progress that he never troubled—or dared!—to elaborate it; and the unfortunately misleading name he had chosen for this chapter, 'The Stationary State,' failed to emphasize the dynamic nature of any organic equilibrium, which must allow for contraction as well as growth.

My citation of Mill's forgotten theorem has nevertheless brought to 'The Condition of Man' the attention of the present generation of economists. Already an officially chartered research group in the State of New York, The Institute on Man and Science, has been exploring the implications of a "steady state" economy. And Ezra J. Mishan's 'Costs of Economic Growth' (1967) has opened up a whole new cycle of thought, concentrated on the ecological problems of human survival. So the chief effect of the regressive transformations that have taken place in the last quarter of a century has been to change my conclusions from the indicative to the imperative mood: not "We shall" achieve a dynamic equilibrium, but "*We must*"—if we are not to destroy the delicate ecological balance upon which all life depends. To work toward this end has now become not only a test of political sagacity, but an inescapable moral obligation.

In short, events have only sharpened the sense of urgency under which this book was originally written. If mankind should succeed in overcoming the forces of disintegration, it will be because millions of men and women all over the planet have at last been sufficiently moved by their dismaying experiences and by the prospects of premature debility and death to change their minds, alter their conduct, and transform their daily lives and their institutions so as to ensure the survival and renewal of human culture. With those possibilities and prospects I have dwelt at length in the two volumes of 'The Myth of the Machine.' Toward the full understanding of these works, 'The Condition of Man' should prove a useful introduction.

—L. M.

CONTENTS

ILLUSTRATIONS

NOTE: *Illustrations and captions are an integral part of the book: designed to be consulted separately without breaking the flow of the text.*

THE CONDITION OF MAN

INTRODUCTION

What is man? What meaning has his life? What is his origin, his condition, his destiny? To what extent is he a creature of forces beyond his knowledge and his control, the plaything of nature and the sport of the gods? To what extent is he a creator who takes the raw materials of existence, the heat of the sun, the stones and the trees and the soil, his very body and its organs, and refashions the world to which nature has bound him, so that a good part of it reflects his own image and responds to his will and his ideal? These questions are as old as the ability to put them in so many words; perhaps older. And in framing its answer each epoch in human culture, each generation, leaves its characteristic mark.

All the questions man asks about his life are multiplied by the fact of death: for man differs from all other creatures, it would seem, in being aware of his own death and in never being fully reconciled to sharing the natural fate of all living organisms. The tree of knowledge, with its apple that gave man awareness of good and evil, also grew a more bitter fruit man wrenched from its branches: the consciousness of the shortness of the individual life and the finality of death. In his resistance to death man has often achieved a maximum assertion of life: like a child at the sea's edge, working desperately to build up the walls of his sand castle before the next wave breaks over it, man has often made death the center of his most valued efforts, cutting temples out of the rock, heaping pyramids high above the desert, transposing the mockeries of human power into visions of godlike omnipotence, translating human beauty into everlasting stone, human experience into printed words, and time itself, arrested in art, into a simulacrum of eternity.

Death happens to all living things; but man alone has created out of the constant threat of death a will-to-endure, and out of the desire for continuity and immortality in all their many conceivable forms, a more meaningful kind of life, in which Man redeems the littleness of individual men.

To achieve knowledge of himself and his place in the world man has from the earliest appearance of civilization scanned the heavens above and looked into his own heart. Like every other animal, he survives because he plays nature's game: he, too, seizes food and seeks shelter, he mates and reproduces; he learns to kill dangerous rivals and to avoid poisons: he schools himself to co-operate with his own kind and to wage war against all hostile, or seemingly hostile, forms of life. So well did he master these primitive arts, with his free hands, his upright posture, his discriminating, self-controlling forebrain, that he finally dominated every other species on the planet; and in this very process accomplished an even greater miracle—he domesticated himself. Here was a new form of life-play; and out of it most of the life-conserving, life-furthering processes of civilization have grown.

During the last century the nature of man has been redefined by scientific investigation: much that was in the realm of myth or poetry hitherto has now been substantiated by detailed analysis and united to broader generalizations than any single myth or religious intuition had established.

With Charles Darwin, we understand that man's nature is continuous with that of animal creation: the biological past of many contributing organisms has shaped the organs of his own body: their needs, their impulses, their urges have laid channels for his own conduct. Every fresh emergent that man has made always runs the risk of being dragged back to the norm of his animal past: that is the "original sin" whose burden he can never escape, though it carries with it as compensation all the vitalities of the animal world and all those primitive processes of co-operation, loyalty, and sexual love which have been the foundations of his higher life.

Again, like every other organism, man is in constant interaction with his environment, mainly by his daily effort to protect himself against danger, to nourish his body, and to secure his future survival. Karl Marx's stress on the fact that work conditions all of man's other activities, his belief that changing processes of production result in cultural transformations that affect seemingly remote parts of man's social life, are now integral parts of our knowledge of man's nature.

Man's capacity to impose work on himself not merely gave him greater security and freedom but made possible a more highly organized kind of society: not by accident perhaps was the original step from tribal societies to civilization accompanied for long by the enslavement of large groups, until all men were ready to submit to the slavery of work itself for the purpose of the wider and completer liberation that results from the economic division of labor. But in origin work and play have the same common trunk and cannot be detached: every mastery of the economic conditions of life lightens the burdens of servile work and opens up new possibilities for art and play; and in these realms man gains a fuller insight into his surroundings, his community, and himself. Thus man's released activities grow out of his conditioned activities: the esthetic flower out of the economic leaf.

Without compulsory labor, civilizations would not originally have produced enough spare energy to maintain their higher activities. Without freedom from compulsory labor, man cannot enjoy these higher activities.

Man is pre-eminently the handy animal: his meeting thumb and forefinger and his free arms have given him a power to manipulate his environment that no other creature possesses. No organic view of man can, accordingly, ignore the weight and significance of man's technics: the first book in the present series, Technics and Civilization, is devoted wholly to this subject. But this is not the same as saying that economic needs and technical processes are self-perpetuating and self-transforming, and that man's life in work constitutes his only essential reality. Those who believe in economic determinism, as the single clue to history, ascribe an independent life to mechanisms and conceive of the human community as being passively molded by them. To hold that man is completely conditioned by his agents of production is as false as to hold that he can completely escape their pervasive effects.

Man gains, through work, the insight into nature he needs to transmute work into artifacts and symbols that have a use beyond ensuring his immediate animal survival. The ultimate justification of work lies not alone in the performance and the product but in the realm of the arts and sciences. The *role* of work is to make man a master of the conditions of life: hence its constant discipline is essential to his grasp of the real world. The *function* of work is to provide man with a living: not for the purpose of enlarging his capacities to consume but of liberating his capacities to create. The social *meaning* of work derives from the acts of creation it makes possible.

If work is the chief of man's self-maintaining activities, every act that he performs has the same underlying purpose: to effect within the organism a dynamic equilibrium and to enable it to continue the processes of growth and to postpone those that make for death. A succession of physiologists, from Claude Bernard to J. S. Haldane and Walter Cannon, have established the importance of man's internal environment: its delicately maintained stability is the condition of his being set free to think and feel and exercise his senses without keeping too sharp an eye upon the bare necessities of survival. Disturbances in this internal environment affect the psyche long before they cast a burden on man's other organs; and there is much reason to think that the opposite process also takes place: a succession of investigators from Janet and Freud onward have established the fact that psychic disharmony may disrupt the equilibrium of the whole physical organism and even cause drastic disturbances of function in one or another organ.

Man's sanity and health consist, in fact, in his maintaining this double balance: an even internal environment that frees the mind for independent explorations and a balance of mind that enables the body to function as an effective whole, despite continued changes of circumstance, changes of occupation, and changes of physiological equilibrium through growth itself. Change is a constant factor in all these processes: but not indefinite change, for all life-maintaining changes are in the direction of equilibrium: those old standards of the Greek philosophers, harmony and composure under all circumstances, as in Socrates' imperturbable conduct at Potidea, have the sanction of scientific wisdom. That equilibrium is itself dynamic: for it is only by accepting and controlling change that man can maintain his organism at its full capacity to function.

As with other organisms man is subject to arrests, fixations, lapses into inertness. In his desire to avoid physical danger, he may imitate the errors of the armored reptiles; in trying to achieve a stable social order, he may be tempted to imitate the ants, which have achieved complete social harmony at the price of going no farther in their development; in his desire for an easy physical life, he may resort to parasitism, and in his effort to overcome pain he may deliberately choose insensibility, which is a living death.

All these temptations are vices because they are denials of the essential nature of the living organism: denials of its capacity for variation, in which it differs from insensate matter; its capacity for experimental life-play, seeking a fuller mastery of its circumstances and its very self; and finally, its capacity for insurgence, its unwillingness to take things lying down. Variation, experiment, and insurgence are all of them attributes of freedom; and though all organisms seem to make a bid for freedom, it is man who has strained hardest to achieve it and to keep it as an essential attribute of at least some part of his society: even when he denied it to a whole community, he reserved it for a favored group or class.

Man's extraordinary biological success has been due to the fact that he was, in an extreme degree, the free and adventurous animal, with insatiable curiosity that was stronger than that of the elephant's child, with a desire for mobility that has finally given him command of every medium of locomotion, even the air, with an audacity that gave him control over fire and now promises to release intra-atomic energy. But he was also the self-nurturing, the self-domesticating animal, who prolonged his own mating season past the period of rut and prolonged the infancy of his children long enough to turn random infantile vocalizations into the orderly associations and symbolisms of language. Man's freedom has always been achieved within the co-operative patterns of his culture: not freedom to reject his social heritage, to depart from the human norm, but to select, to modify, to augment that heritage, and to raise the norm.

So much for the elemental nature of man. It is an essential part of his history; but there is another part that it is even more important to reckon with: that which he shares with the other social animals, and above all, that which emerged through the development of man's specifically human traits.

Man's life differs from that of most other organisms in that individuation has become more important to him than strict conformity to type: he participates in all the characters of his species, and yet, by the very complexity of his needs, each individual makes over the life-course of the species and achieves a character and becomes a person. The more fully he organizes his environment, the more skillfully he associates in groups, the more constantly he draws on his social heritage, the more does the person emerge from society as its fulfillment and perfection. But that process is never finished. Every other animal but man is a complete representative of his species: man remains the unfinished animal, like the measuring worm at the end of a twig, in Albert Pinkham Ryder's illustration, ever reaching out into the unknown. Man's growth, therefore, is not completed by his biological fulfillment as a mate and a parent: nor is it completed by his death. Man's nature is a self-surpassing and a self-transcending one: his utmost achievements are always beginnings and his fullest growth must still leave him unsatisfied.

This quality of self-transcendence must be joined to another fact about the nature of man: namely, that above his instinctive and automatic activities lies a whole stratum where purpose and meaning have full play. A meaningless life and a purposeless life belong to the not-yet-human. Man does not, therefore, merely function toward survival, his own or that of his species, like other animals: he functions towards ends, which he himself becomes progressively conscious of and progressively able to define. Outside such meanings and ends, the bitter words of the Preacher will hold: All is vanity. Man's purposes are not alone given in nature, but superimposed on nature through his social heritage: man's ecologic partnership with the earth and all other living forms must—as Patrick Geddes elaborated—be complemented by man's special creations, art, culture, and polity, the processes through which he has made over every aspect of his natural environment, turning love-calls into music and stone quarries into cities.

Like the social insects man has found a way of strengthening certain useful individual traits through the social division of labor: a further working out of the original biological division of tasks between the sexes. Because of the element of compulsion and exploitation that was present in the passage from primitive tribal co-operation to organized communities, these functional divisions have often tended historically to harden into castes. But the real justification for the social division of labor lies in the fact that it gives the individual personality the benefit of the whole community's heightened capacities. It is in and through the community that the individual person finds himself enlarged, energized—and completed. In society man faces himself and realizes himself; and in a free society, mobile and democratic, like Athens in the fifth century B.C., each citizen has an opportunity to plumb all his potentialities: the specialized fragments are re-united in the whole man. At that point the human person becomes an emergent from the community, embodying it and transcending it: rejecting complete "adjustment" for the sake of growth.

The social division of labor found in some degree in all human societies was made possible by an even earlier human advance: the invention of symbolization and the development of language. This is the most specifically human characteristic; and it has given a special kind of cohesion to the human community: that which results from a common response to a common group of symbols. Man's natural environment is complemented by his *idolum:* and by idolum I mean a symbolic milieu composed of images, sounds, words, fabrications, and even natural objects to which man has attached a representative value. Symbolic representation makes possible an interchange of experiences without respect to immediate limitations of time and space. As man found ways of creating "permanent" symbols in stone or reproducing his symbols by manifolding and copying, he has been able to make larger and larger areas of his otherwise private experience available to other men, though they are separated from him by birth or distance.

The ability to create symbols and respond to symbols is an essential difference between the world of brutes and the world of men. Without symbols, man's life would be one of immediate appetites, immediate sensations; limited to a past shorter than his own lifetime, at the mercy of a future he could never anticipate, never prepare for. In such a world out of hearing would be out of reach, and out of sight would be out of mind. By means of symbols man builds a coherent world out of patches of sense-data and gleams of individual experience.

The failure to understand the role of symbolization in human life has been responsible for a grave misunderstanding of the nature of man. Because symbols are subjective in origin, in that they are not found in nature outside man, many people fancy that they are unreal, mischievous, or that a more sound existence would be possible if all symbols were excluded except those that could be reduced to quantities or visible operations. Those who have advocated this view lack an understanding of man's essence and true aptitude. On this subject Jean Calvin, for example, is a safer guide than many current behaviorists. "The manifold agility of the soul, which enables it to take a survey of heaven and earth; to join the past and the present; to retain the memory of things heard long ago; to conceive of whatever it chooses by the help of imagination: its ingenuity, also, in the invention of such admirable arts, are certain proofs of the divinity of man." Thus Calvin. This agility of the soul is the result of man's development of the symbol: a more miraculous tool than the fire that Prometheus stole from heaven.

Communication, communion, and co-operation, the three essential attributes of human society, are all dependent upon the acceptance of common symbols to which the same meanings, functions, and values are attached. Without those symbols there may be cohabitation; there may even be a primitive kind of co-operation confined to the visible object and the passing moment: but no more. And in turn, the deepening humanization of man in society depends upon his capacity to turn experiences into symbols and symbols into life-experiences. With limited symbols, he lives in a closed world, closed in time, closed in space: a world without distances, perspectives, alternatives, prospects. Only by means of symbols can man widen the powers of discrimination and the acts of choice: only by symbols can he release himself from immediate pressures and cast the events of his life into an order he has pre-ordained and shaped in the mind. Thus symbols are not vicarious substitutes for experience but a means of enhancing it and enlarging its domain.

Ritual, art, poesy, drama, music, dance, philosophy, science, myth, religion, are accordingly all as essential to man as his daily bread: man's true life consists not alone in the work activities that directly sustain him, but in the symbolic activities which give significance both to the processes of work and their ultimate products and consummations. There is no poverty worse than that of being excluded, by ignorance, by insensibility, or by a failure to master the language, from the meaningful symbols of one's culture: those forms of social deafness or blindness are truly death to the human personality. For it is through the effort to achieve meaning, form, and value that the potentialities of man are realized, and his actual life in turn is raised to a higher potential.

The three studies in this series attempt to give full weight to all the essential conditions for man's development; but in this survey of The Condition of Man it becomes important to redress the conventional contemporary unbalance, by giving emphasis precisely to those aspects of man's life that are usually neglected: his dreams, his purposes, his ideals, his utopias. Many and various are the products of man's art: but his final work of art is himself.

To achieve a more organic view of man's nature and prospects we must reverse the conventional metaphysics, which looks upon the so-called physical universe as basic and ultimate, and which regards the facts of human existence as derivative. This metaphysics became popular because uniformities and mathematical certainties were first established in the physical sciences and first applied to the heavenly bodies, remote from this man-infected world. But man is not born into that bare physical universe: rather, he is born into a world of human values, human purposes, human instruments, human designs; and all that he knows or believes about the physical world is the result of his own personal and social development. The very language he uses for neutral scientific description is a social product that antedates his science. Indeed, the tendency to look upon processes in the physical world as more important, more fundamental, than the processes of organisms, societies, and personalities is itself a by-product of a particular moment of human history: the outcome of a systematic self-deflation.

The path of human development has been from sensation to significance, from the externally conditioned to the internally conditioned, from herdlike cohesion to rational co-operation, from automatism to freedom. Thus the poor beplagued creature of circumstances who greets us at the beginning of history becomes progressively the shaper of his own character, the creator of his own destiny. But only up to a point. . . . For this increase of self-control is subject to numerous hazards and setbacks: man is the sport of natural forces both outside and within himself, forces he sometimes circumvents but never entirely sets at naught. Pride trips him; reason unnerves him. Even man's cunningest efforts to escape nature's dominion may recoil against him: has he not, at this moment of apparent triumph over nature, seen himself slip helplessly back from freedom to automatism, from civilization to barbarism? In short, man's creativeness is always subject to his creatureliness; in the end, as Robert Frost says, he must leave something to God.

Man's higher development has been due to his unwillingness to accept the limits of the outer world as his own ultimate boundaries. Dreams, impulses, intuitions, welling up within him, have helped man to give part of that world the dimensions of his own being: a Kantian discovery that positivism unreasonably condemns. Man sees God, as the theologians say, and seeks to walk with Him in righteousness. Against the naked wishes of his own ego he sets the super-ego: on one side a collective censor and mentor, a judge and a moral conscience, bringing the private self into relation with the public self, uniting the wishes of the moment with the needs of a lifetime; and on the other side, the gods and muses, ministers of grace, urging him to goodness and beauty, beguiling him with visions that surpass the ego's most exalted private dreams.

Often man's imagination has led him into error and his search for light has plunged him into deeper darkness, even as his will-to-perfection has sometimes made him inhuman, cruel, life-denying. It was easier for myth and religion to personify subjects than for science to objectify objects. But the final outcome of these efforts has been a deeper insight into his condition and destiny than his practical activities by themselves would ever have called forth. For it is by means of his ideal fabrications that man circumvents his animal fate: his idolum and his super-ego help him to transcend the narrow pragmatic limits of human society.

Thus, deviously but persistently, man has developed into a person: tied to a local community, yet seeking brotherhood with all like-minded men; bound to his own tribe, yet seeking a common tongue which others can share and a wider purpose in which they can cooperate; tethered to his biological destiny, yet most deeply human when he is detached and released, when, "counting gain or loss as one," he accepts Krishna's call to face battle and death. Man comes into the world, he struggles, he triumphs, he dies, not in order merely to perpetuate his species but to give it a new destiny—that which his own cumulative culture makes possible: a destiny that gives to the cosmos itself, perhaps, an emergent end, only latent in matter and life till man himself appeared. A monad that can think and feel is more important than a galaxy of impassive stars. The soul, as Whitman well says, stands cool and composed before a million universes.

Man's subjective and his objective world are in constant interplay: nothing that he knows about the universe can be dissociated from the facts of his own life; and no product of his culture is so detached from the larger groundwork of existence that he can impute to his individual powers what alone has been made possible by countless generations of men and by the underlying co-operation of the entire system of nature. Nature has helped man to model his very self, and in turn, his own idolum has become a second nature, fulfilling more completely his latent powers. Such historic accumulations of culture form the topsoil and humus in which the higher life of man has flourished. Let the historic roots of a culture be plowed up, let the dust storms scatter the loose soil, and what is left is a bare surface of non-historic experience which will not sustain human life or thought.

Man alone lives in a time-world that transcends the limitations of his local environment: the world of the past, the present, and the possible; or, if you will, the real, the realizing, and the realizable. Once he loses hold on any of these dimensions of his experience, he cuts himself off from a part of reality.

The slogan of the political reformers of the eighteenth century was—The past has nothing to teach us; history is only the record of superstitions, frauds, miseries, and lies. But the actions of these reformers were usually more rational than their doctrines: they were not so indifferent to human experience as to deny that honesty was better than fraud or justice better than crime. Only in our own age have the final consequences of their anti-historic nihilism shown themselves. During the last generation, particularly in the United States, it became popular to say that only contemporary history was important; whereas the truth is that all history is important *because* it is contemporary and nothing is perhaps more so than those hidden parts of the past that still survive without our being aware of their daily impact. He who knows only the events of the last generation or the last century knows less than nothing about what is actually happening now or what is about to take place.

So far from being overwhelmed by the accumulations of history, the fact is that mankind has never consciously carried enough of its past along with it. Hence a tendency to stereotype a few sorry moments of the past, instead of perpetually re-thinking it, re-valuating it, re-living it in the mind. It is only by this act of deliberately recapturing the past that one can escape its unconscious influence; and this ordering of man's real experience is, as Croce has well said, the true groundwork of philosophy. By lengthening the historic perspective, one gains power to throw off the partialities and relativities of one's immediate society; likewise, by facing the totality of human experience, one becomes aware of elements that the fashion or habit of one's own particular epoch may arbitrarily have neglected: archaic elements, primal elements, irrational elements, neglected mutations and concealed survivals, often overlooked by the wise in their too narrow wisdom.

In this sense, history is a reservoir of human creativeness. Without the perpetual rediscovery and reinterpretation of history, without free access to that reservoir, the life of any single generation would be but a trickle of water in a desert.

The limited conventions of historians have made us forget, however, that history has an anticipatory side: it is the domain of the possible, the starting point of the ideal. The real future is no mechanical continuation of the present, which can be projected by a simple curve on a graph. From moment to moment the inertia of the past may be altered by new factors springing from both inside and outside the human personality. The creation and selection of new potentialities, the projection of ideal goals is, with reference to the future, the counterpart of an intelligent commerce with the past. The neglect of the ideal leads only to the covert practice of giving to the present an ideal significance it does not possess. Utopia, as the expression of rational possibilities, is an integral feature of purposive living; for no human life is fully rational unless it anticipates its own life-course and controls its present actions and present needs in the light of some more general plan, some larger system of values, into which all the parts of its existence tend to fit.

History is the dynamic working out of the drama of a culture; and in the drama of a culture, the nature of man defines itself and realizes itself in partial detachment from the world common to other living organisms. If nature is the theater of human life, the historic cultures provide the scenery against which men act their parts. Much of the activity that goes into a drama is preparatory and instrumental: but who would go to the theater if all that went on was the raising and lowering of the curtain or a perpetual change of scene—no matter with what mechanical adroitness those tasks might be carried on? The combined efforts of the architects, builders, mechanics, scene shifters and spectators would not, in themselves, produce a significant drama.

The drama itself is not a mere repetitive doing and acting: it consists in symbolic deeds and actions and words through which the characters who participate in it realize their fullest potentialities as men and women, in a significant and purposive performance. Only when the drama is enacted are the struggle and sweat of the preparatory workers justified. All our questions as to the condition of man, then, remain bottomless until one places man in the frame of a particular culture and a particular historic moment: for his nature reveals itself only in the acting out of his particular drama; and it cannot be understood by a static external analysis, since time and purpose and development are of its essence.

With such basic notions as to the nature of man we now approach the present crisis in modern civilization and attempt to bring to it a fresh understanding.

In the present book I purpose to deal at length with the tangled elements of Western man's spiritual history. People whose course of life has reached a crisis must confront their collective past as fully as a neurotic patient must unbury his personal life: long-forgotten traumas in history may have a disastrous effect upon millions who remain unaware of them. If we have not time to understand the past, we will not have the insight to control the future; for the past never leaves us, and the future is already here.

The period through which we are living presents itself as one of unmitigated confusion and disintegration: a period of paralyzing economic depressions, of unrestrained butcheries and enslavements, and of world-ravaging wars: a period whose evil fulfillments have betrayed all its beneficent promises. But behind all these phenomena of physical destruction we can detect an earlier and perhaps more fundamental series of changes: a loss of communion between classes and peoples, a breakdown in stable behavior, a loss of form and purpose in many of the arts, with a growing emphasis on the accidental and the trivial: in short, the earliest form of this crisis was an internal "schism of the soul," as Toynbee calls it, and a break up of the over-all pattern of meaning.

The drama our civilization had presented during the last four centuries was played to its end: it was in fact played out; and the continued presence of the actors on the same stage, babbling the same parts, repeating gestures too well learned, resulted only in a confusion that covered their general emptiness of purpose.

The time has come for a new drama to be conceived and enacted. Each of us has his part to play in that renewal. And first of all, we must understand the formative forces that are still at work in our civilization: by such fuller and deeper knowledge of our own living past, we will refashion the actors themselves and give them new parts to perform. Now, as once before in the disintegrating classic and medieval worlds, the achievement of a new personality, a new attitude toward man and nature and the cosmos, are matters of life and death. We must recapture once more our sense of what it is to be a man: we must fashion a fresh way of life, which will give to every man a new value and meaning in his daily activities. A crisis that has been faced and mastered gives the survivor a new confidence in his powers: thereby he reaches a higher point than he might have achieved through a more normal line of growth. There lies our hope.

In an attempt to control the disintegrating forces that are at work in our society, we must resume the search for unity; and to this end, we must explore the historic nature of the modern personality and the community, in all their richness, variety, complication, and depth, as both the means and the end of our effort. As the processes of unity take form in the mind, we may expect to see a similar integration take place in institutions. But this change is not an automatic one. Only those who daily seek to renew and perfect themselves will be capable of transforming our society; while only those who are eager to share their highest goods with the whole community—indeed, with all humanity—will be capable of transforming themselves.

CHAPTER I. PRELUDE TO AN ERA

1: Anticipations of Dissolution

Modern man in the West first took shape in a period of cultural disintegration: a slow, painful, largely unconscious process whose meaning did not become plain to him until all hope of arresting it had disappeared.

Some of the best traits in our character are the product of a grand retreat that took place within the very heart of classic civilization, at a time when all its values seemed secure. If pity and love have had a larger part to play in our life than they did in the ancient world, it is mainly because they nourished man during a period when he was dying of starvation while sitting at a feast. To understand our present selves, we must understand the central core which formed the primitive Christian: not because we can live again within that archaic mold, but because we can then see into the nature of our own plight and direct our efforts towards an even more positive renewal.

For more than fifteen hundred years, our Western World has been dominated by the personality and the myth of Jesus of Nazareth. The prophecies that announced him, the words attributed to him, the rites that enthroned him, the myths that magnified him, the institutions that supplanted him, have all left their imprint even on seemingly remote parts of Western man's existence. Any interpretation of contemporary events which neglects the parallel between the Roman order and the modern world, and which fails to understand the path taken by the Christian communities, lacks a possible guide to the future. If we are to find a straighter path, we must at least recognize the historic reasons for Christianity's success.

One of the most convenient of Western man's fictions is his habit of dating the events of world history before and after the birth of Jesus Christ. But this mode of reckoning produces a false perspective: it shows time shrinking, year by year, from six thousand to one thousand, down to unity; and then beginning to increase once more. This produces the illusion of a waning and waxing of events: a steep descent and a steady upward rise. No one can doubt that the turning point itself was a decisive one. But there was a long underground germination. The Christian era did not begin with the birth of Christ: it began five or six hundred years before. We know far less about the immediate mission of Christ than we do about the prelude and the aftermath. Isaiah, Hesiod, Lao-tse, Buddha, Confucius, Solon, Zoroaster were activators in a far-spreading ethical and mystical movement that set the stage for the Christian drama.

In a curious way, the illusion of dwindling years gives a fairly accurate picture of the course of life among the Greeks and the Jews from the fifth and fourth century B.C. onwards. Christianity took possession of a world in decay. The Jews had reached their high point in culture and religion by the end of the sixth century: their supreme figure was the prophet Isaiah. From that point on the voice of the prophets was underlined by events: their dark predictions and warnings were justified in a succession of catastrophes, until these harried people, no longer able to hold their own in a world of military rapine, fell at last under the yoke of the Romans. The period of their downfall was marked by an end of the old prophecies, which had been filled with somber determination and rational hope, calling for an heroic discipline in the community. Human effort would no longer save these people from misfortune. Something superhuman was required.

The coming of Christ marked a definite turning point in Judaism. He is the last of the great line of prophets; after him come the Rabbis, the commentators, the philosophers, the moralists; and as the Jews themselves were further dispersed over the earth, reaching China, traveling down into darkest Africa, making their way across the bleak wastes of Russia, they carried with them the limitations that Christianity presently transcended: their tribalism, their racialism, the venerable customs that sealed them up in their own self-sufficient world. Yet this people became the catalytic agent in the new transformation of society: their presence was necessary, but they were unaffected by the change that took place. Without them, nothing so significant might have happened on the world stage: yet everything that Christianity formulated and did was accomplished, so to say, saving their presence. Judaism, translated into Christianity, lost itself to gain a world. That loss and that gain can be understood only in the light of the disruption of the classic order itself.

2: Attic Fulfillment

Another important part of the story of modern man begins for us among a people far different from the motley mass of Africans, Syrians,

Romans, Teutons, who were finally to crave the Gospel and create the structure of the Christian Church: it begins with the Greeks.

By the sixth century, this people had long been settled among the islands in the Aegean Sea and the adjacent mainlands: through colonization and trade, their culture extended over into Sicily on the West and up along the shores of the Black Sea on the East. They were hunters, farmers, herdsmen: eventually sailors and merchants and craftsmen. Their soil was thin, even before the goats had ravaged the undergrowth of the forests and the woodman's ax cut down the live oaks, the plane trees, and the pines. They lived in a land of contrasts and extremes, with teeming winter rains and dry summers that turn raging rivers into stone-bottomed creeks. Here a continent life prevailed: the hard routine of the farm, fairly described by Hesiod: bread, milk, honey, olives, an occasional goat or sheep: almost always enough, almost never too much. But occasionally there was luxury in the seaports as the products of the potter and the smith found markets in distant lands, the little black ships bringing back purple dye from Tyre and papyrus from Egypt, even as the Yankee merchant captain brought back to Salem the silks of Calcutta and the porcelain of China.

Sparta and Ionia were the poles of this life: Sparta with its rigor and its abstinence, self-commanded even when necessity was lacking: Ionia, an outpost of the East, with its perfumes and its gay silken clothes, its incense and its luxury. A land of keen outlines: headlands and temples etched, knife-sharp, against a sapphire blue sky. Cities occupied the foreground: small, friendly, almost parochial, based upon family and tribe, filled with neighbors who met face to face, and who kept one foot in their ancestral village.

By the sixth century B.C. the experience of these peoples had begun to bear fruit. Their struggles and jealousies, their adventures and hardships and wars, had taken shape in the Homeric poems, the Odyssey and the Iliad in particular: the fighting man who uses his muscles superbly, and the curious, restless man who uses his wits, assumed ideal forms in Achilles and Odysseus. In Hesiod, the voice of the village came forth: denouncing injustice, hating war, picturing the descent of man from the Golden Age of the past to the Iron Age of the present, but celebrating with pious confidence man's Works and Days. Misfortune was common but life was sweet: though the gods avenged Prometheus's theft of fire from heaven, they left man Hope.

Swiftly comes the creative moment in this civilization. The mind remains delicately suspended: the eye looks around, discriminates, inquires, beholds the natural world and passes at a bound from sprawling fantasy to continent, self-defining knowledge. In Thales and Anaximander natural science is born: in Parmenides and his successors, logic. Sport lifts the trammels of material necessity even in thinking: the mind has its own Olympic celebration; and for a moment the highest good lies not in making or in doing, but in quietly seeing: theory and esthetics are the dominant modes of Greek experience. Theory means reflective contemplation; esthetics, ordered perception. Over all spread the new doctrines of logic: an attempt to bring the order of thought and the order of being into a single realm. Kalakogathia, beautiful goodness, is the Hellenic expression for this unity. Beauty spreads from the body in the gymnasium to the statue that stands at the entrance: the rhythm of gesture and movement flows from the dancer and the discus thrower to the black outlines of the figures on vase, cup, and bowl.

Above all, the reign of law begins: caked and clotted custom, which had established the limited brotherhood of family and tribe, which had given the old warrior nobles their pre-eminence in the community, must now submit to criticism, revaluation, revision. Law brings with it a widening sense of order, which includes both the physical universe and the social structure: it is no accident that the first great natural philosopher, Thales, and the first great Greek law-giver, Solon, appear in the sixth century and correspond with each other.

In the fourth century, Plato laid down the ideal conditions for government: that a philosopher should become a king, or that a king should acquire philosophy: furthermore, a reluctance to assume office was one of the marks of the true ruler. All these conditions had been fulfilled in the person of Solon. When he became the archon, or temporary ruler, he effected a series of bold reforms: he wiped out the accumulated burden of debts, brought about by the introduction of a money economy into a simple agricultural society; he prevented men from selling themselves desperately into bondage; he reduced the privileges and voting power of the landed aristocracy; he established a democratic polity in which free citizens became the active administrators of the laws, took part in judicial decisions, participated in military service. Not merely did Solon refuse to assume exclusive power himself: he retired from the scene and went traveling, in order to test the strength and efficacy of his reforms. His individual actions were courageous, his detachment exemplary. What might not a group of Solons accomplish?

Though Solon established the rule of law, to supplant the rule of customs or individuals, the latter came back, almost immediately, in the tyranny of Pisistratus. But the democratic experiment was well started; and the experience of the Athenians, during the next two centuries, was to demonstrate its advantages and drawbacks. In the full tide of law, civic responsibility, communal participation in the arts, common sacrifice in the defense of the country, the human person flourished, with a free creativeness it had never probably shown on such a scale before. If custom passed into law, ritual and myth passed into religious drama in the tragedies of Aeschylus and Sophocles; and the ribald eroticism of the village, in the capering license of the springtide, became the comedies of Aristophanes, in which healthy smut was mixed with wit, intellectual criticism, political reprimand.

In the world of thought, as in the domain of action, law was the foundation of freedom: a method of overcoming the irrational and the unpredictable. The legal meaning of law plays into the scientific meaning from Anaximander down to Ostwald in our own day. Without order there can be no freedom and without defining the limits of obligation one cannot achieve them or pass beyond them. In time, the impersonal equity of Nature became, with the Stoic philosophers, the pattern for human society: orderly government based itself upon the primal laws of nature, reborn in the human heart.

Law, order, continuity: these conditions are fundamental to freedom, variety, and novelty, and are thus the very basis of social creativeness: for freedom without law is irresponsible anarchy, variety without order is chaos, and novelty without continuity is empty distraction. We who live in an age of tyranny and disorder can recapture, perhaps, a little of the breathless wonder and delight that the people of Athens felt when they established a written constitution and engraved it on columns in the market place, so that all might read, bear witness, and understand the principles upon which their political life was based.

The important thing to notice about Greek culture in its heyday is that nature and society were understood as a unity: Heraclitus' Treatise on Nature was divided into three parts, on the universe, on politics, and on theology. Had he added a fourth part, on medicine, he would have embraced the full contribution of Hellenic thought to the molding of personality.

While the personality was thus unified, it was possible for a statesman like Solon to be a distinguished poet; for a stonecutter like Socrates to be a doughty soldier and a supreme teacher; for a tragic dramatist like Sophocles to take his turn as a general in command of Athens' armies. Out of an organic society arises an equally organic sense of the person. The test of this unified view of man, society, and nature comes in the treatment of disease. If one knew nothing of Greek law, science, or architecture, one might deduce much of what I have been describing from the teachings of Hippocrates and his school.

What were the specific contributions of the School of Hippocrates—a special cure, an infallible diagnostic? Not in the least: Hippocrates' great discovery lay in the perception that the cure of disease and the maintenance of health belonged to the same branch of knowledge and practice: disease was not an aberration, but a fulfillment of the order of nature.

Hippocrates' merit was to begin with the patient instead of the disorder: to see him in his environment, and to understand the effect of air, climate, water, soil, situation, and food upon the internal equilibrium of the body. Exercise, regimen, and diet were, with change of scene, the secrets of medical cure, because they were originally the secret of man's own improvement of his physical condition. The Hippocratic tracts point out that the work of the physician is not a whit different, with respect to diet, from the original work of mankind in finding out what sorts of food could be digested, and what are unfitted for human use. Man was not an isolated body; and his disease was no mysterious possession of the body by an evil spirit, but an event in the order of nature, to be followed patiently and to be rectified, not by a single remedy, but by every means that is available for producing health.

In The Laws Plato called the true physician an educator, and contrasted him with the quack who tends to slaves and who applies his quick and ready remedies, after a diagnosis equally brief. It is as educators that one must consider the School of Hippocrates: physicians whose wisdom consisted in understanding nature and co-operating with her, making the patient take his own share in this co-operation, even to the point of accepting death with resignation. *Know thyself* runs through this whole culture: Thales utters it: Hippocrates formulates it: the Delphic Oracle has it written over the gates of the Temple: Socrates repeats it. The essential element in this regimen of self-knowledge is leisure and patience; and that applies to both the bodily and the spiritual conditions of man. But in practice this meant that only a limited group, the free citizens—or at least the wealthy—could live a fully human life.

"If anyone, regardless of the appointed time, tries to subdue diseases by medicine," observes Plato in the Timaeus, "he only aggravates and multiplies them. Wherefore we ought always to manage them by regimen, as far as we can spare the time, and not provoke a disagreeable enemy by medicine." This counsel of patience was not a foreign one to Greek culture, so long as it kept its agricultural connections, and continued to live by the olive tree, which bears no fruit for the first fifteen or twenty years of its existence. It was only when this agricultural tie was weakened by extensive trade and imperialist exploitation that patience gave out. Then people looked for short-cuts to happiness, to success, or to personal perfection. Some of Plato's contempt for the Sophists must have been due to the fact that they not only taught wisdom for pay but promised that it would quickly bear fruit.

When one surveys Hellas at the beginning of the fifth century it would seem as if the Greeks were on the brink of a permanently happy dispensation: fear quieted, pain under control, disease gently diverted to health, human relationships passing from force and custom to justice and rational ethics—with beauty rising, in the painted images or marble temples of the Acropolis, above the simple dwellings, still unpretentious as in a village, huddled together below. If the shield of Homer presented an idyll of the early life of the village, the Panathenaic frieze represented the ideal consummation of the polis. Was the smile on the face of the sixth century statues, that smile we now call archaic, not more than an inane convention? Life was good. Reason and measure had appeared.

Reason, as Parmenides observed, delivers one from the aimless government of the eye, the echoing of the ear, the bondage of habit: it is truer than the senses. Measurement frees one from confusion and muddle: the builder with his rule and his compass achieves accuracy and geometric beauty, which Plato calls the highest form of beauty: in shipbuilding, in temple building, in all manner of carpentry and masonry, in pottery and in plastic art, these subtle craftsmen work out ideal proportions. Practical men, if they do not develop the new mathematical theorems, take advantage of them: the properties of a triangle and a circle become known: mathematical order and organic order are both present in the Parthenon.

But reason, measure, balance, depend for their existence upon the continuity of the life that they order. From the fifth century on two forces were at work that upset this life: an inner repression and division, and a series of outer pressures and calamities. Let us examine them.

3: Twilight at Noon

The fierce sunlight of the sixth century awakening did not last long. Indeed, a cloud passed over the sun, chilling the landscape, when the sun itself was still near zenith. Man does not live by day alone; and when reason attempts to supplant man's instincts and organic reflexes and dumb feelings, instead of utilizing them to better ends, man stumbles and falters, as he does when he attempts by use of his conscious mind to put one foot before another in going down stairs.

Mystery and darkness envelop man, and night to him has many forms, the night of his animal past, the night of his unconscious urges, the night of an ignorance whose circumference seems to widen with every expansion of his conscious knowledge, and finally, the night of non-existence and death, which encloses his personal life at both ends. Reason could gently laugh the Homeric gods out of existence, because they were inferior in their sudden angers and exorbitant lecheries to the self-control practiced by living men: but reason could not exorcise the demons that rose out of man's unconscious, nor could it extricate man from a chain of events in which both determinism and chance sometimes mocked the efforts of the human will.

At their height, the Greeks were conscious of many unresolved dilemmas in man's life: Aeschylus and Sophocles wrestled with these mysteries and uttered repeated warnings against the pride of the conscious intellect and the reliance upon man's conscious powers. Traditional religion had taught men to walk warily. Oedipus is destined to kill his father and marry his mother: the more he attempts to escape his destiny, the more fatally he finds himself enmeshed in it: those who have not faced this abiding irrationality have not dared to look reality in the face. The very obscurity of man's unconscious impulses, their uncontrollable character, upset both reason and measure. Violence, curbed by constitutions and deliberations in the Assembly, did not disappear: hatred, passion, injustice did not yield as easily to a sound regimen as tuberculosis or gastritis. Indeed, sophisticated thinkers, like Thrasymachus in The Republic, argued for the rights of the strong and the justice of the unjust. Athens, boasting of her freedom and enlightenment, exacted tributes from her allies, so that Pericles' great public works program might be sumptuously fulfilled: in the name of her old religion, she put to death the most religious man in Athens. Reason? . . . Measure? . . .

But this was not all. The entire Greek polity was built upon an institution that defied reason: the institution of slavery. Though slavery had originated, perhaps, as an alternative to putting to death a conquered foe, and so once represented a moral advance, now it had become just the opposite: warfare became a means of increasing the number of slaves. To justify the inhuman relationship, the Greeks insisted that the slave was an inferior species of being, meant by nature for base and servile tasks—as if those who had lost in battle were not often the superior of those who had captured them. To challenge slavery, the whole character of the polis must have altered: the easier choice was to rationalize this irrationality and repress the sense of guilt its existence unconsciously produced. This failure to carry reason into the practical details of life discredited its pretensions.

But reason showed still another weakness: pushed too far it undermined life at its source. Henri Bergson considered that religion is a self-preservative effort to keep man from suicide at the moment he becomes fully conscious of the fact of death: only the acceptance of a mystery beyond the compass of his reason keeps his life from becoming devaluated and his spirit from becoming discouraged over the reports of reason.

In sexual life if love were a purposeless welling forth of appetites, homosexual love might seem as reasonable as heterosexual love—and in turn heterosexual love might become as unashamedly sterile. All the irrationalities of human love, however, move eventually toward a goal more imperative than pleasure: the conception and nurture of children, the perpetuation of the race. The very mechanisms of sex are adapted to that higher reason: the mystery of life itself, seeking its own extension and perpetuation. Even when the love of a man and a woman has no direct biological issue, their passion and their deepening loyalty symbolize and anticipate that final outcome: the triumph of life. And as long as the ancient forms of fertility are not violated, the relationship may be a fruitful and life-exalting one.

In Greece the practice of homosexuality and infanticide might seem to have cold reason on their side; yet they were profoundly hostile to life. Sexual play is the greatest of all forms of play; but when the person is reduced to a mere plaything, even the body feels degraded and cheated. By man's very freedom from animal periodicity, by the fact that sexual impulses may be evoked at every season, and know no limit short of physical exhaustion or impotence, instinctive controls are weakened and the need for a deeper biological wisdom becomes greater. The rejection of woman, reducing her to a stunted role as ignorant wife and house-bound mother, seriously undermined the integrity of Greek culture: the freedom of the hetaira did not redeem her sister's state.

In the end, Hellenic woman restored the balance of life, by bringing back the irrational and the mysterious: the wild cry of the Bacchae rang through the woods, and the saviour appeared, the Wine-God, Dionysus himself. The Apollonian religion of measure had never taken the full measure of man.

Frustration and a sense of guilt appeared in Hellenic culture in the second half of the fifth century. And one fact makes it plain that this guilt was almost universally shared: a religious cult, or a series of them, came into existence and attempted to lift the heavy burden, bringing the excluded classes and the rejected impulses back into the circle of the human. Salvation by *birth* as a freeman gave place to salvation by *belief* in a redeeming god who could elevate even the slave.

Just as the monasteries of a later age were situated apart, far from the old cities and circuses, so these new mystery cults had no connection with the cults of the city gods or the household gods, the banal deities that presided over family and civic duties. The new god came from afar: a stranger to Olympus. The rites performed in his name belonged to a world apart from the cities: they restored the unrestrained animality of the vineyard and the primeval terrors of the forest. Every year Bacchus flourished and died: and every year he was born again. The initiation into the mystery religions differed from the ephebic oath of the new citizen, a daylight ritual: now the mystery was a real mystery, performed in darkness and in secrecy: a demonic glimpse into the darkness of hell, an angelic swooning into heaven.

The new believer in the mystery suffered in life from guilt, defilement, debasement, exclusion: in his initiation he was terrified and humiliated and finally, at the proper moment, he was purified. At the end he saw light, and became a creature of light: one of the elect. He had felt the burden of sin, and now he had found salvation. The kinship of the damned gave place to the fellowship of the saved, those whose true life would begin in the afterworld.

The Orphic, Bacchic, and Eleusinian mysteries kept their secrets too well to leave a sufficient record behind; but it is plain that they represented a new element in this Greek world which cut across its habitual ways of thinking and feeling: an essay into the obscure, the irrational, the incommensurable. From Orpheus, the explorer of the underworld, from Dionysus, God of wine and women and demonic inspiration, loosener of inhibitions, came the embryonic shape of a new personality.

This personality was not so much at home in the daylight world as the sixth century Greek: but he was more acutely aware of his own turbid depths, and was already living in a dimension of experience neither reason nor measure had effectually touched. Toward the end of his life, the great exponent of rationalism, Euripides, wrote a play in celebration of Bacchus that was almost an act of renunciation and self-dethronement: an elevation of life at the expense of reason. That play was prophetic of things to come. In the fifth century the cloud of unconscious impulses and repressed vitalities was no larger than a man's hand: by the first century A.D. it almost covered the sky.

4: The Idolization of a Dead Self

The failure of Hellenic civilization had many causes; but one of them was its unreadiness to control the processes of economic expansion. The self that the Athenian admired was that enshrined in the polis; but this self had been formed by hardship and restraint: it could not survive financial prosperity and the ease and luxury that went with it. The Athens that Pericles praised in his famous Funeral Oration perished in the war brought on by his extravagant policies: the words Thucydides put in his mouth showed blind complacence.

Maritime trade brought a great variety of goods into Athens; and since its citizens were addicted to the arts of politics and war, much commerce fell into the hands of overseas merchants, coming from Phoenicia and Carthage and other distant lands. These foreigners swelled the numbers of the trading cities; they brought in riches; they made and displayed their new-gotten wealth; in general, they were excluded from the burden of military service and the duties of self-government. Riches begot the desire for riches: the sparse abstemious life of the sixth century now remained only in the villages of the hinterland; and the contempt of the landed aristocracy was sometimes not unmixed with envy. Now money had intervened and the old balance was upset: money counted for more than land. By the fourth century Aristotle had seen enough of the results to say that timocracy, or the rule of the moneyed classes, was of all forms of government the worst.

One of the surviving fragments of Solon's writings bears three words: "covetousness and insolence." They sound like words of prophecy: no words could have better summed up the causes of Greece's external decline. The Delphic Oracle, the universal church of the Hellenic World, added to its treasuries and lost claim to spiritual authority: the Olympic Games, the great means for political comity, the occasion of poetic contests that aroused a Pindar, became a vehicle for sordid professionalism: wandering from celebration to celebration—for the Olympic Games had many imitators—Theagenes of Thasos was reputed to have won some 1400 prizes. Covetousness and insolence: stigmata of decline.

Commercial intercourse and rivalry had brought new political problems to the Greek cities. For good and bad, commerce made them interdependent. Their chance for survival, in a world threatened by the Persian, the Macedonian, and finally the Roman Empire, depended almost wholly upon their talent for co-operation: one by one they could be exterminated. Unfortunately, Greater Greece was only a geographic conception: in spite of the amphictyonic council, it never achieved political reality; and

Athens' leadership was on a basis of a cunning exploitation of her allies, not co-operation. Hence the archaic pattern of an earlier day prevailed: land-locked minds attempted to preserve each harbor and valley as an independent unit: rejecting the logic of federal union, the cities of Hellas invited unification by conquest.

Demosthenes made a bold attempt to persuade his countrymen to recognize their true situation and unite; but their minds and wills were frozen in the image of the past. They did not even have the strength of purpose to draw on the Festival funds till 338, the year of Chaeronea. So Demosthenes uttered the last cry of anguish over their failure. Soon after, Greece became a colonial dependency: then a connoisseur's paradise. Perhaps the ultimate stage in degradation came when Corinth sold off the mementoes of its great past as curios for Roman sightseers and art dealers.

The disintegration of Hellenic civilization came with such heart-breaking swiftness that even the wisest of the Greeks did not know what had happened to them. The collapse was all the more shocking because it occurred during a period of intense cultural vitality. Corruption from within and violence from without shattered the organic structure of life; but all the visible signs of greatness remained: indeed the statues, the theaters, the gymnasia, a good part of the art we now behold in museums, were a product of the period of retreat: men sought to live out in art alone a life they had once partly translated into action, as neighbors, friends, lovers.

Though the outward shell seemed whole, the spirit underwent a radical change. To Plato, in his youth, all things seemed possible: The Republic witnesses that belief in perfection. Toward the end of his life a sobered and saddened man writes The Laws. He still cannot believe that all is over: but his demands are more modest. His own failure to regenerate Syracuse, under the tyrant Dionysius, had chastened him. How could reason prevail if men remained unteachable?

The crisis that the Greeks faced has an obvious parallel in our own culture, not least in the fact that it came so unexpectedly on the heels of their superb achievements in every department of art and thought; and we can gain some insight into our own position, perhaps, if we interpret correctly the situation in which Plato found himself, as a representative Old Athenian, at the end of the Peloponnesian War. Both his insight and his blindness, his achievements and his failures, are instructive.

Plato, nearer to the high fifth century culture than his pupil, Aristotle, was profoundly moved by it: in both his thought and his personality it took living form, though the Athenian polity, while momentarily recovering from the Rule of the Thirty, was already on the downgrade, exhausted by the great plague, undermined by war, tempted by the facile, false solutions of dictatorship, tempted even more by those fleshpots which had played such a minor role in the fifth century scheme. Plato's whole life was in effect an effort to find a means to restore order and purpose in a community that was becoming progressively disorganized, banal, and purposeless: in which the divine was succumbing to the all-too-human. He sought to conceive a commonwealth that could survive in a disintegrating world; and to this end he strove to unite the virtues of the Athenian and the Spartan: the pliant individualist culture of the first with the self-abnegating discipline of the second.

Not the least significant thing about Plato's utopias, however, was that he did not go to any pains to restore the arts and humanities to the place they had occupied in fifth century Athens: he sought rather to subordinate them and regulate them, even to banish some of them from his ideal commonwealth. Was this a perverse judgment on Plato's part? To generations of later humanists it has often seemed so. But what forced Plato to this hard choice? The answer should be plain: Athens needed men, and the humanities by themselves did not produce them. Indeed, for lack of political discipline and moral responsibility, the teachers of the humanities hindered rather than aided the making of men: they were producing facile rhetoricians, glib orators, clever teachers, connoisseurs, not men capable of living robustly on every plane of existence. Citizens who would serve in the law courts or on the battlefield as readily as they would write a poem or pursue an abstract truth, men of the stature of Sophocles or Socrates, were no longer being created. Plato, the artist, was ready to reduce the scope and influence of the arts in order to save the civilization that had created them. Nothing bears better evidence of the crisis he faced or the terrible sincerity he brought to its understanding.

Though Aristotle is generally looked upon as the seasoned man of the world, and Plato as the more poetic kind of idealist, who demanded the impossible, the fact is that Plato's intuitions saw more deeply into the dilemmas of Athens and the Greeks generally.

Plato's balanced man had four outstanding virtues: wisdom, which was the gift of philosophy, and which gave an insight into the ultimate nature of things; courage, the aristocratic virtue, of which the Spartans were the exemplars, not in battle alone but also in that daily training and toughening which makes men ready to forego pleasure, comfort, even life; temperance, which was the bequest of Hippocratic medicine; and finally justice, which was a combination of wisdom and courage. Each of these virtues Plato attempted to fix forever in a definite caste of society: wisdom, being the highest, formed the ruling group of philosophers; courage, which was next needed, was the property of the military guardians of the state. Temperance was a virtue that related to all classes. Justice itself was the principle of function: each man in his place, doing the work nature and wise training had fitted him for; autonomous within his own department—for men work best when minding their own business—but subordinate in relation to the social organization as a whole. Finally, Plato sought to redeem woman's lot by following the Spartan mode of according women equality with the men and by freeing both sexes from the burdens of restrictive domesticity. The guardians had all things in common, even their wives, their husbands, their children.

Such a static order, unfortunately, left no place for freedom; and therefore, though Plato failed to realize this, no place for continued growth and development, the essential processes of life. His pedagogy, so admirable in its insight into the requirements of the very young—for he said that play was the best of teachers for them—overlooked the need for a continued process of trial and selection, and had no insight into the role of error as an educative force. His prescription for goodness was to lay down a perfect constitution and enforce it with kindly ruthlessness: the poet was banished, music was censored, old classics like Homer were taught with discretion: political power rested in the hands of mathematicians used to applying the inflexible rules of geometry.

In a word, Plato sought to restore and transfix the archaic ideal self of Athens: his thought was the victim of a cultural narcissism. Hence he did not realize that the most stable rule is always a composition of active forces, with perpetual shifts and changes, re-alignments and re-balances, for the sake of maintaining equilibrium; and he failed to understand that if every organism and every society must seek order and continuity it must also transcend itself and transform itself by unceasing acts of growth. For the Greek, perfect movement was circular: it returned on itself. While the spiral was a familiar figure in Ionic decoration, it left no image of progressive evolution on the Greek mind. The belief in the Eternal Return, of endless cycles of history repeating themselves minutely, was the metaphysical form of this Greek self-worship.

The highest possibility of life, for the Greeks, was a static one: life arrested meant art perfected: for them the community itself, the polis, was a work of art. Unfortunately, art perfected may also *in time* mean life denied. No mere work of man deserves that homage.

No one has given a better description of individual excellences than Plato; no one else has shown more clearly the weakness of de-moralized power and of an impotent morality. He knew that strength needed the sanction of virtue and reasonable purpose; he knew that goodness needed the support of disciplined strength. "From the cruel, or hardly curable, or altogether incurable acts of injustice done to him by others, a man can escape only by fighting and defending himself and conquering, and by never ceasing to punish them . . . wherefore I say that good men ought, when occasion demands, to be both gentle and passionate." This was a side of goodness that Christianity, as Renan pointed out, neglected at its peril: the realm of civic virtue. The meek may *see* heaven; only the strong are capable of establishing it on earth. Plato wrote when he could still dare to hope for that triumph in his own world: a generation or two later philosophy posed a different question to her adepts.

What hampered Plato's social ideas? What made him place a premium upon a fixed and immobilized social order? Why, though he was acutely aware of the crisis the Greeks were passing through, did he seek, not the way beyond, but the way backward, to a more primitive innocence and a more simple order? His real problem was one he did not even consider as a logical possibility: how to create a commonwealth capable of overcoming the limitations of Hellenic society, bridging the division between the slave and the free; the gap between the Hellenes and the Barbarians, that is, all other groups; the disparity between a continent rural life and an expansive mercantile economy tending toward mechanical uniformity.

The problem, in other words, was how to put military power and money power in their place, by a form of co-operation and union that had no foundation in Plato's philosophy: one capable of embracing territories and peoples outside the Greek polis. If Sparta was not the answer, neither was Solon's Athens. A new form of fellowship was required, capable of breaking down the walls that separated city from city, race from race, class from class. How to turn the new fellowship of the religious mystery into a universal fellowship for political mastery: that was the problem of problems.

To his dying day, Plato never conceived that transformation. The most illumined mind in Greece, the ripest fruit on the ancient tree of Hellas, reduced the problem of political wisdom to this: how can a community of 5040 citizens—at most forty or fifty thousand people, including slaves and children—survive in a hostile world? There was no answer to that question. Was it not, indeed, an egotistic denial of the very values that the Greeks had created: values to which other peoples had contributed, and in which they were entitled to share?

If that was the best ideal of the fourth century one need not be surprised at the worst reality of the third century. Aristotle, though more familiar with the spread of empires and more remote from the small, still

"Homeric" world of the sixth century, nevertheless provided no better answer than Plato. He was not so definite as Plato as to the size of his ideal commonwealth; but the problem he sought to solve was just as limited: what size of territory, what numbers, will enable a people to live *to* itself and survive *by* itself? That question can only be answered on a precivilized level; for it is the capacity for entering into a wider world in time and space, through linguistic communication, religious communion, political co-operation, that permits men to pass from the closed society of the tribe to the open society of the commonwealth.

The question that neither Plato nor Aristotle had asked themselves was how self-sufficient the polis had been at any period. Their self-contained world was illusion. Attica had been fructified by Ionia and even Boeotia: Ionia by Crete and Egypt: both had built into their new structures the polished fragments of a great past. Where had the alphabet come from? Stone-cutting and sculpture? The chariot, the horse, the plow, the potter's wheel? The form of the Temple and many of their gods? Eventually the Greeks were to have commerce with the wider world that had helped to form them: as a result of their political humiliation they participated in the common life by means of their language: their very conquerors adopted it and spread it farther. But by this time body and spirit could no longer be united. After the third century, the lot of the Greek was to be the teacher of the peoples who had conquered him. In that sense, Aristotle's own life forecast the fate of Hellas; and it is no accident that Hellenistic thought burgeoned in the Egyptian city his Macedonian pupil founded: Alexandria.

We can now see why Plato failed so completely to regenerate his own culture or to lay down even an ideological basis for renewal. What undermined him, what undermined the Greeks, was their failure to embrace humanity: their failure to be concerned with the whole life of man and with every member of human society, to address the soldier, the sailor, the craftsman, the farmer, and to give hope and faith to the common man in every region. Plato's message was addressed solely to his class and his culture. It called for a radical re-orientation to life, and yet it left the chief sacred cows of his world, slavery and class rule, contentedly chewing their cud. Pride of family, pride of city, pride of intellect were all self-defeating. Failing to embrace humanity, the philosophers could not even save themselves.

So much for the vain and fatal parochialism of Hellenic men. But there was another bequest, born of the land, the climate, the experience of these peoples: one that must still be reckoned with and absorbed. This was the doctrine of the mean. It made a fresh contribution to ethics, and it helped to shape a new personality.

The sources of the Greek doctrine of the mean are so multifold that one can scarcely touch an occupation that does not bear witness to it. Aristotle even explained that the political wisdom of the Hellenes was due to their territorial mean: they existed between the peoples of the cold countries of the North, who have courage but no political sagacity and no arts, and the peoples of warm Asia, who are adepts in the arts but lack the virtue of courage. The Greeks sought the temperate zone of morality: enough of everything, but not even the good in excess. Wine is good but it must be watered; exercise is good but only vulgar fellows have bunchy muscles and devote their lives to sport. Everything was good in due measure.

Aristotle's emphasis on the mean served Western man as Confucius' similar doctrine served the Chinese. This essential Greek doctrine differed from that of the Persians, with their eternal battle between darkness and light, between evil and good. For the Greek, the good was the midway point between extremes which, because they were extremes, were bad. Thus the Greeks introduced into the conception of virtue a mathematical element: the mean was the measured: reason was in essence ratio, a sense of proportion. Even virtue and restraint might be overdone; so one must picture the symposium, the intellectual drinking party to which Plato and Xenophon introduce us, as an attempt to establish a balance between the rational and the sensual.

Unfortunately, people often suffer through their virtues, even more than by their vices: precisely because they seem good, they throw one off guard: more people die from indigestion than from poisoning. Even the doctrine of the mean may be intemperately pursued; for the balance must sometimes be weighted down heavily on one side or the other. The mean is good for the long run, but not in equal measure at every moment. One cannot live a balanced life in an earthquake, a shipwreck, or a fire: instead, all one's energies must be focused on the swift acts of rescue, escape, or salvage. After the doctrine of the mean had been enunciated with lucid finality in Aristotle's Ethics and his Politics, there to start on a long independent career, catastrophe threatened Hellas: all it was, all it might be, were challenged by the spreading might of Macedonia and Rome.

At that moment, the cities of Greece were caught by the temperate and even-balanced ideals they had held before themselves. Their very love of the polis tied them to a dead self. They sought to evade their obligations, to slip out of the situation, to attempt by trickery or evasion to deny the need for struggle. They spent money for public festivals and ancient ceremonies that should have gone into naval armaments: see Demosthenes' address On the Symmories. They disputed vivaciously and open-mindedly; they practiced art; they went to the theater and the gymnasium; they dwelt hopefully on the good qualities of the approaching conqueror: above all, they shut their eyes tightly to the danger, trusted promises made by Philip that were almost at once broken; and one by one they abandoned potential allies to the enemy in the hope that his appetite for conquest would be appeased, and they would find themselves overlooked.

In short, the Greeks acted as if their pleasant, temperate, esthetically balanced life would last forever. But in fact, it robbed them of the strength they needed for a decisive effort: they appeased Philip too soon and resisted him too late. The defeat at Chaeronea in 338 B.C. marked the beginning of the end.

5: The Greek Diaspora

From the end of the Peloponnesian War, uncertainty, trouble, and disaster crowded in on the cities of the Aegean. Violence broke out everywhere: Athens itself had set the precedent in the cold, insolent brutality of its attack upon little Melos: a deed which provoked the wrath and indignation of Euripides, and must have profoundly shocked many of his fellow citizens. At that moment, a retreat began: first in the mind, then in every department of life. Art became "psychological," portraying anguish, pain, anger, terror; by the third century portraiture had almost descended to the inessential grimace of the candid camera. Sculpture recorded struggle, not poise: or if not struggle, the passing impression rather than the composed form.

In becoming "human" both drama and sculpture became little: they denied the highest dignity of man: his capacity for impersonality and detachment. Moments of lyric tenderness remain: a wistful epitaph, a Tanagra figurine, a third century torso whose breasts and belly are still almost tremulous under the touch of love; but all that arose out of greatness and that demands greatness in response slowly disappeared: when the Romans wished to draw on the sources again, they could only copy the ancient models.

Even before the decisive blow was struck by military might, there were those who were ready to haul down the flag: not only ambitious traitors like Socrates' favorite pupil, Alcibiades, but humble ones, like Antisthenes, who was twenty years older than Plato. Antisthenes proclaimed an open retreat from Periclean ideals. He was the son of a Thracian slave woman; remembering her lot, he deserted his well-born friends and set himself up in a gymnasium built for the "base-born," that is, for non-citizens. He dressed like a common workman, made friends with the disreputable, welcomed hardship and sacrifice.

With Antisthenes, philosophy entered the dog-house; indeed his disciple, Diogenes, exulted in this fact and proclaimed that human life was no better than a dog's life: hence the Greek name for this doggish philosophy, Cynicism. Antisthenes, Diogenes Laertius tells us, gave the impulse to the indifference of Diogenes, the continence of Crates, and the hardihood of Zeno. Diogenes spewed out the old ideals of life: the son of a man who debased the coinage, he boasted his ignoble forebear and proclaimed that his own purpose was to deface all the coinage current in the world: rejecting tradition, rejecting the customs of the temple, along with marriage and the care of the body. No fine theories: no bodily shame: in short, no super-ego; he even masturbated in the marketplace to prove his indifference to convention. Eat only vegetables: drink cold water: content yourself with a single garment: spurn money. "It is the privilege of the Gods to want nothing, and of godlike men to want little." Thus spake Diogenes.

Crates declared that Ignominy and Poverty were his country. Diogenes, captured by pirates on a voyage to Aegina, was taken to Crete and sold as a slave. Here was a philosophy that rationalized this bitter fate: a creed the slave could embrace no less than the citizen. Embracing it, the citizen was prepared in advance for violence, the loss of home, the sack of his city, the depletion of his worldly goods. By anticipating the worst, cynicism sought to dull the actual shock: by elaborating the thema of rejection, the Cynic gave the rejected a title role in the new drama. There is a connection between the indigenous Greeks who turned their backs on this dying world and the cosmopolitan Greeks who, six or seven hundred years later, flocked out to the edge of the desert in Egypt. And Diogenes, with his staff, his cup, his wallet, his hood, even created the classic costume of the Christian pilgrim. But his toplofty humility rejected the mystery cults: "It would be ludicrous," he said, "if Agesilaus and Epaminondas are to dwell in the mire while certain folk of no account will live in the Isles of the Blest because they have been initiated."

The struggle between the free spirit of Hellas and the tyranny that enveloped it was a long one: a procession of heroes lined the avenue of retreat. In sheer intellectual vigor and resolute statesmanship, Demosthenes was the greatest of these rear-guard fighters; but individual dignity, individual intrepidity were not lacking elsewhere. Zeno the Eleatic bit off the ear or nose of Nearchus, according to one account; or caused this tyrant to be stoned by a mob, according to another. But in the Garden of Epicurus another doctrine was preached.

Epicurus was a true figure of the Diaspora. He was born in a colony in Samos, in 321, and his family, after spending thirty years on the land, were driven off by the Thracians. His own education was interrupted; indeed, he went through the typical experiences of the broken refugee's life. Epicurus did not pretend that one can be indifferent to natural sorrows; he pointed out that those who sought to survive by indifference were either hard of heart or full of vanity. But as a refugee he had found the true secret for survival under such conditions: live in the moment and banish the morbid luxury of anticipation. Hide yourself!

Epicurus's disciples, enamored of his doctrine, presented him with a garden in Athens; and there his school, almost a community, held forth, with men and women meeting as equals in discourse. They were not the first women to share the company of a philosopher; but one feels their personal presence more definitely than in Socrates' communion with Diotima. From now on, indeed, in trouble and sorrow, woman reconquers a place for herself in public life: heretofore only the courtesans had such an opportunity. Woman displaced the monosexual society of the camp, the gymnasium, the stadium: her breast warmth was needed when the wounds of life became otherwise unbearable. She possessed what was lacking in this warring, man-ridden world: a sense of the continuity of life and the perpetual need for sympathy, fellow-feeling, consolation. In the shadow of the philosopher's garden, no less than in a deeper midnight retreat in the mountains, woman trims her lamp and waits. Bacchus has come! And one greater than Bacchus approaches.

Epicurus's philosophy was falsely identified, even by contemporary defamers, with the mere pursuit of pleasure. He himself sometimes gave grounds for that interpretation, for he said: "I invite you to continuous pleasures, not to virtues that unsettle the mind with vain and empty hopes of fruition." But continuous pleasures are also a vain and empty hope for the refugee: he wants tranquillity, freedom from want, freedom from pain, freedom from fear. Suffering can be borne; do not fear death; keep life moving smoothly, neither expecting too much nor dreading too much. This philosophy is not one of pleasure but of prudence: if one gathers a few rosebuds one must be sure to avoid the thorns. To disinfect the world of the stench of inhumanity, one must study nature: atoms alone are real and there is nought beyond these ultimate particles. "Their professed ideals," observes Gilbert Murray ". . . seem to result in rather a low tension, in a life that is only half alive." The observation is just; but what more could a refugee ask for? This is a world of diminishing prospects and fading hopes. Even the power of Rome cannot replenish it.

6: Fin de Millennium

The breakup of a civilization is often accompanied by a deceptive amount of social activity. As in a bodily fever, the pulse becomes more rapid, the rate of oxidation faster, even the flush on the patient's cheek may give the deceptive appearance of health: only the glassy eye will indicate that the patient is unconscious of what is going on about him: his mind instead is grappling with phantoms.

In this Hellenistic world, so rational in its surface activities, phantoms and visions appeared in growing numbers, precisely at the moment when the Museum of Alexandria was supporting a vast corps of savants and professors who were carrying exact science beyond the realms Aristotle had explored. Theophrastus developed a systematic botany. Hero of Alexandria invented the reaction steam turbine: the first groping toward the modern steam engine. Archimedes founded the science of hydrostatics and made decisive contributions to mechanics. But these inventions and discoveries did little to lighten labor: steam or clockwork was used merely to open temple doors without human hand—and thus superstitiously heighten the religious awe of the worshiper. Slave labor, which undermined the ancient polity, also reduced the province of the machine. And though the scholars of Alexandria collected, collated, classified, made accessible to other scholars, a growing body of knowledge, the results did not flow out into life: after Aristotle's synthesis, learning tended to fill books and deflate men. Frustrated, cheated, the ordinary man descended to new depths of irrational impulse and superstitious habit. Have we not seen a similar reaction in our own time?

Meanwhile, the Romans took over. To understand the limited nature of their success we must examine the cultural medium in which the eventual conquerors and organizers of the Mediterranean lands lived. We shall see that it not merely made Christianity possible, but in some form made it almost inevitable. Our languages, our laws, our forms of thought, our ethical principles all received an indelible imprint from these people.

During the three centuries before Christ, Rome had conquered the circuit of lands around it. In Central Italy a new people, solid compact peasants, wielders of a mighty spade, had widened their domains: thrifty, abstemious, sensible people, men of the earth earthy, who planted trees, built aqueducts and arcades, drained swamps, and dressed the land to a high degree of perfection: their sword and their spade were as their right and their left hands. A rural people with their eyes on the earth: the greatest of their poets, at the height of their glory, wrote a series of verses on farming and the pleasures of rural life: their proudest generals, like

Cincinnatus or Scipio, lived a hard farmer's life, close to their country homes and their household gods, gods of the hearth, gods of fertility.

To plant, to build, to mate, to fight, to govern: this made a Roman. But the conquest of cities ensured the enslavement of men: the greater the success of this conquest, the more rapidly the Roman lost his self-sufficiency and the need for rigorous, purposive living. Men cannot be trusted with easy alternatives. At the moment they fancy that they are at last living like gods, they often cease even to be able to live like men.

Around Rome, a series of great cultures were in a state of dissolution and decay: their still healthy tissue fed the young body of Rome and their infected organs poisoned it. Babylonia had long seen its day; Egypt, that one-horse shay of cultures, was about to collapse; the world of the Hellenes was rapidly crumbling. The very facilities for travel and intercourse which the imperial conquest made possible, only quickened this process. Trade never flourishes alone. From Syria, with its busy workshops for textiles and dyes, the merchants sent out dancers, courtesans, acrobats to every rich port or market. Chaldea exported its soothsayers and astrologists: Berôssos set up a school of Chaldean philosophy at Cos as early as Alexander's time. Egypt, no longer self-contained, gave Isis and Serapis to Rome; and the foreign cult of Kybele, the Great Mother, rising in the mountains of Thrace, was called in by Roman augurs at a critical moment to ensure the conquest of Carthage. Persia, home of Mazdism, brought forth a younger religion, that of Mithra and the Bull: the God of Light, the beast of blood and potency.

All these cults and philosophies, no longer closely bound to their cultures, migrated to Rome. Trade flourished, or if not trade, loot: ideas followed cargoes. Rome became a vast maw into which goods of all kinds were indiscriminately thrown: silks and dyes, rare foods and subtle thoughts, epicurean feasts and epicurean philosophies. By the first century B.C. some Romans were even attracted to Judaism: lured by its rigorous ethics, its noble theology, its vision of a just God, working in and through history.

But where was the power to digest all these offerings? Rome held neither a unified religion nor a body of scientific thought that was equal to the task of transforming the debris of these dying cultures into a unified and living organism, capable of further growth. Rome's very rapacity injured its power of selection. Read Plutarch and Lucian, men of the most generous capacities and the widest culture: the Fenélon and the Voltaire of a mature age. These admirable writers have, alas! one great defect: they know too much for their own good. The connoisseur has replaced the creator. Such a community faces too many incompatible choices; and as a result, fashion takes the place of organic necessity, and novelty becomes a substitute for rational development. Roman power covered an ever wider orbit: Roman law, Roman administration, Roman sanitation, Roman engineering were everywhere. But the inner logic that held all these parts together, the structure of meaning, collapsed: as life became mechanically disciplined it became spiritually incoherent. Presently the inner life of the Roman was peopled by demons, fantasies, chimeras, philosophies, created by other people than themselves, swallowed whole: an indigestible mass. By attempting to grab everything, the Roman lost the power to pick and choose.

Politically the new Roman order accomplished in time what the individual polis had never been able to do: it unified the peoples of this world and brought them the boon of peace and orderly administration: eventually it gave them a common language for intercourse, namely, Greek. But this unification was superimposed and therefore one-sided: not a partnership of equals but a system of patrol. Traders, speculators, curiosity seekers, tax collectors, and art collectors swarmed everywhere on the heels of the military arm. Pausanias wrote a guidebook to the antiquities and works of art in Greece as useful as Baedeker today. With all Rome's generous show of law, justice, order, the underlying economic fact was pillage and extortion, and the cornerstone of the whole system was human slavery.

The order achieved by Rome was real but repressive: no wonder that Pliny the Naturalist, contrasting the fertile scientific thought of the earlier Greeks with the barrenness of his own age, was puzzled by the result; he sought to account for the fact that "at this day, in the blessed peace which we enjoy, under a prince who so greatly encourages the advancement of the arts, no new inquiries are set on foot, nor do we even make ourselves masters of the discoveries of the ancients." He attributed the failure to the fact that "the manners of men have degenerated, not that the advantages are diminished"; but he had no clue to the mode of this degeneration, though his own works demonstrated it. His curiosity was literally all-devouring; but it made him a colossal collector of scientific odds-and-ends, not a rational experimenter. Roman culture was choked by its material advantages.

Rome's power of organization concealed the decay that accompanied it. The engineering system, though ponderous, was magnificent: aqueducts, water-mains, sewers, water closets, paved streets, spacious baths, colonnaded avenues, spread from one end to another of this Roman world, from Trier to Timgad. A Roman camp, thanks to the legionary's spade, became overnight a city: with trenches, walls, sanitary facilities, mechanical order. The paved roads, the solid posting inns, built of stone, the mechanical order and regularity that prevailed everywhere, impressed a contemporary Chinese visitor: even at the extreme edge of the Empire, in Britain, the remains of the Roman road, crossing hill and dale in a straight line, still awaken one's admiration—though the very inflexibility of this order also gives rise to skepticism as to its intelligence. Unfortunately at the very moment all these physical triumphs were achieved, there were disorder and malaise in the human spirit.

The larger Rome's cities became, the farther away did its citizens withdraw from daily contact with the soil; the greater the conquests on the borders of the empire, the more numerous were the civic defeats at the center; the more justice appeared in the daily transactions of men, the more unjust seemed the foundations upon which the whole fabric of administration and law were founded. Symptoms of devitalization, discouragement, bitter self-disgust, appeared long before Rome's active disintegration: indeed, in the midst of the so-called Golden Age which preceded the birth of Jesus.

7: Discouragement and Decline

Admirable historian that he was, Gibbon's view of the decline of the classic world, as following the introduction of Christianity, scarcely does justice to the facts. The symptoms of the decline were felt long before this; and the creative power of Rome, concentrated upon the arts of war and government, was unable to arrest the disintegration that took place in other departments. Rome's active Time of Troubles was preceded by a long period of discouragement: the characteristic signs, which first appeared in the Hellenic world, were described by Polybius, who died in 124 B.C., while Rome was still a Republic and all its energies were apparently on the upgrade.

"We have not had to suffer either epidemics or prolonged wars," wrote Polybius, "and yet the towns are deserted and the lands barren. We lack men because we lack children. People are too fond of money and comfort, and not enough of work. Consequently they are no longer willing to marry, or, if they marry, they try to have no more than one or two children, in order to bring them up in luxury and to leave them a finer inheritance." But what of those who supplied the luxuries and comforts? What of those from whose harvests or cargoes the money for taxes came?

Long before Christianity entered the world, a desperate *fin de millennium* atmosphere enveloped this whole culture. Jewish literature, in particular, was filled with apocalyptic visions: the Messiah was coming. In the apocalypse of Enoch, time was described as a week of seven days, each day a thousand years in length. Six thousand had passed: a new millennium was coming during which the elect would live in happiness, free from the influence of evil. This was the Sabbath of rest in the cosmic week: after that would follow the eighth day, the beginning of a timeless order. This collection of prophecies, composed by Orthodox Jews between 170 and 64 B.C., did not stand alone. Even worldly princes attempted to cash in on the grim desperation of their subjects by giving themselves the title of "The Saviour."

Daniel read the dreams of his conquerors: in turn he prophesied a greater conqueror, a Messiah, who would unloose the bonds of Israel and redeem the world. Out of gnawing disillusion rose these illusions: hope became immense because it had no legitimate expectation of fulfillment. When one is starving, one might as well dream of a banquet as of a crust of bread.

The common mark of the Jewish apocalyptic writings is their dismal vision of the present and their radiant hopes for the future: they welcome the night because it appears to bring the dawn nearer. The vision of death spread over this world; and the sense of foreboding was not confined to the Jews; for it showed itself no less clearly in the philosophers of the covered arcade, or Stoa, whose first leader, Zeno of Citium, flourished between 350 and 260 B.C. The doctrine of Stoicism, if one must sum it up in a sentence, is "Nothing can hurt me." Its method was to anticipate death by inuring the body to pain and by preparing the spirit, if necessary, to commit suicide. By emptying out his pockets beforehand, the Stoic protected himself from robbery. The price of that insurance was perpetual penury.

Observe that this sense of sardonic despair was not confined to the most miserable of the conquered peoples: violence had been steadily gaining the upper hand, in the clash and conflict of empires; and the possibilities of slavery and sudden death had multiplied. Even to hold the empire down, once it had been conquered, required painful efforts: the jailor was confined by the same prison that held his captive and showed the same prison pallor. Helpless refugees and homeless aliens were everywhere: they carried their own fears, fear of torture, fear of sudden death, into the very homes of their masters.

Stoicism deliberately disparaged the external triumphs of life, in order to find an equal power to belittle its humiliations. What cannot be mended must not be minded: only inner freedom counts. The Stoic began by guarding against life's evils and ended by being insensible to life's goods. The philosophy that made a slave's life tolerable had the paradoxical effect of making a master's intolerable; for if indifference and insensibility were the final counsels of wisdom, why should anyone bear the heat and burden of the day? This philosophy of cosmic negation reached its climax in Marcus Aurelius, whose reign closed the great Silver Age of the Antonines in the second century A.D. The Emperor's chilly sentences repeat the old burden of Diogenes; but by now even an emperor's life is a dog's life. In all things he found only "decay—nothing but water, dust, bones, stench."

"Consider in thy mind, for example's sake, the times of Vespasian," the resolute Emperor soliloquizes, "thou shalt see but the same things: some marrying, some bringing up children, some sick, some dying, some fighting, some feasting, some merchandising, some tilling, some flattering, some boasting, some suspecting, some undermining, some wishing to die, some fretting and murmuring at their present, some wooing, some hoarding, some seeking after magistracies, and some after kingdoms. And is not their age quite over, and ended? . . . In the like manner consider other periods, both of times and of whole nations, and see how many men, after they had with all their might and main intended and prosecuted some worldly thing or other, did soon drop away and were resolved into the elements." That morbid refrain echoes on almost every page. "Death hangs over thee."

"What is life?" asks Marcus Aurelius; and he answers: "A bone thrown to a company of hungry curs; a bait for greedy fishes; the painfulness and continual burden-bearing of wretched ants, the running to and fro of mice: little puppets drawn up and down with wires and nerves: these be the objects of the world." None of the Christians whose persecution this emperor ordered could add a word to this black indictment. And these were not the sentiments of a galled slave or a weak neurotic: they were the mature beliefs of a man nurtured in kindness, adequate to all his public duties, the head of a mighty state organization, honorable in the performance of every heavy task: the beliefs of a man who had, if anyone had, "everything to live for." If life was as repulsive as this at the top, what must it have been at the bottom?

Naturally Stoicism, with its military sense of duty and public service, was not the creed of the easygoing multitude; nor was it the philosophy of those who sought to ease the perplexities of the spirit by giving fuller reign to the desires of the body. The true answer to a meaningless existence is to conceive a pattern of life that possesses meaning and purpose: the false answer is to look for solace in a fuller preoccupation with those very activities that result in this meaninglessness. Some historians have denied that Rome's downfall was caused in any degree by the exclusive concentration on wealth and luxury, pointing out that only a minority of

Romans enjoyed such luxury: but they have overlooked the fact that the economic practices of the minority debilitated the entire social organism.

Caught by the demands of their appetites in a predatory economy, the Romans finally became parasitic upon the peoples they ruled; and they sought to fill their emptiness by elaborating a ritual of conspicuous waste and increasing the number and variety of sensations derivable from eating, drinking, bathing, and sexual intercourse. Soldiers, senators, magnates, tax gatherers, and common citizens were all partners in an ever-spreading conspiracy to get something for nothing. The name for this miscarriage of life is parasitism.

Since the nineteenth century, parasitism has become a term with a definite biological significance: one organism living on another, effortlessly sustaining its life, often losing its organs of sight or locomotion, suffering visible bodily deterioration—all this is now familiar in natural history. But the word and the practice have their origin in the Roman world: here predatory voracity was finally limited only by parasitic sloth. Sponging in Rome was reduced to a science: bribes, gifts, tips, gratuities, extortions supplemented the economic rewards of the market. The philosopher, Seneca, wrote his longest treatise On Benefits: on the proper relations between the giver of gifts and the recipient.

Trade and rational commercial calculation had a secondary place in this system: the more chancy economy of extortion and donation was responsible for no small part of the traffic. Capitalism in the modern sense could not flourish here—not as Marx thought, because the classic world was more humane than the Victorian Age but because this economy lacked both an adequate system of arithmetic and a just method of accountancy. It was the incalculable that flourished, and the unforeseen that became the expected. Whether a client ate well or poorly would depend upon whether or not his patron awoke with a headache and an upset stomach. Chance became God: anything might happen.

"Throughout the world," wrote Pliny in his Natural History, "at every place and hour, by every voice, Fortune alone is invoked and her name spoken: she is the one defendant, the one culprit, the one thought in men's minds, the one object of praise, the one cause. She is worshiped with insults, counted as fickle and often as blind, wandering, inconsistent, elusive, changeful, and friend of the unworthy. . . . We are so much at the mercy of chance that Chance is our God."

That says everything; it even says much about the boasted triumphs of civil engineering and the reign of law. Peace and order had proved disappointing; or rather, peace and order in society did not guarantee peace and order in the mind. The Imperial Age was an age of the colossal:

the longest road in the world, the highest lighthouse, the strongest bridge, the biggest monument, the most luxurious banquet. Everywhere the human scale was lost; and everywhere men were bridled by things. The Greek motto of "Nothing too much" met in Rome its logical opposite: "Even everything is not enough." Pillage and pilfer, grab and gorge: fill to repletion and vomit and fill again! In the rich man's house the vomitorium became an essential chamber: the place where the guzzler of rich food emptied his stomach, so that he might come back to the feast for more.

If one seeks an explanation for the excesses of Christian asceticism, one must look for it in the surfeits that marked this upper-class economy of abundance: it arises from the natural self-disgust that follows a prolonged debauch, and constitutes a kind of protective starvation that ensures the return of normal appetite. To explain the triumph of Paul and Augustine, one must read the description of Trimalchio's feast in the Satyricon of Petronius Arbiter. What had the Roman made of the body? Corrupted meat. And what was the soul? A polluted dream.

8: Bread and Circuses

Stoicism was essentially the creed of the soldier, who marches in the ranks, takes orders, has no control over his actions, knows that death may come at any moment: his impassiveness is the positive achievement of drill. But Stoicism lacked the soldier's compensations: his silent scorn for his dashing superiors and the easy unbuckling of his moral armor when the march is over or the battle won. Legs and arms submitted, so to say, to discipline; but to offset this inhuman automatism, the belly and genitals evolved a life of their own: mystical, public, orgiastic, all-absorbing.

In contrast to the Greeks, who before the fourth century had been unified and liberated by the cult of the body, the Romans worked out a religion of the body on a purely muscular and sensational basis: instead of feeding the super-ego, the Roman cult supported a materialistic ritual. In the institutions of the circus, the arena, and the pantomime, the Romans created a special engine for relieving the tension of military and civic repression. Here the spectator was supreme: master of an effortless existence. Here he encountered death without undergoing danger; contemplated danger without having to display skill; practiced cruelty without the possibility of retaliation; or participated in a collective orgasm for nothing more than the price of admission.

Rome under the Antonines may have harbored a million people. At least one-third and possibly one-half of the population of the city, according to Carcopino, lived on public charity. But it was not merely by the free distribution of bread or by filling the servile client's little carryall or *sportula* with the leftovers of last night's feast, that the gross inequalities of Roman life were maintained. Even in Rome, men did not live by bread alone: the circus and the arena were no less necessary. As early as the Republic, the Circus Maximus was in existence; presently, during the imperial era, the number of circuses, arenas, and hippodromes increased in Rome, and more or less in every other important municipality. In the arena there were chariot races: competition, excitement, opportunities for betting; despite dangers to the overturned charioteers, this was perhaps the most innocent of Roman amusements.

But in the circus there arose a different kind of spectacle. Here criminals were punished; here military captives were made to fight with each other until one or both were killed; here other prisoners were thrown to the wild beasts, to be torn apart and devoured alive. Punishment was originally a public spectacle, presumably to serve as a warning for the spectator: now it served another purpose—it provided outright pleasure. The Roman populace, frustrated and humiliated, many of them compelled to live in huge tenements, so recklessly built by speculative landlords that every now and then they collapsed and buried their denizens in the ruins, projected their own terrors and humiliations upon their helpless victims. Their oppressors were unassailable: the army knew who paid them. So the populace turned on their fellow men and battened on their sufferings. Out of a revolting exploitation, came this equally revolting revenge.

Terrorism, violence, lust were organized and systematized on a scale that passes belief: people lived from day to day in the vicarious enjoyment of the most ingenious brutalities that have ever depraved the human soul. The Romans became esthetes of torture. The demand for victims even increased the scope and purview of crime: as if sins were not frequent enough, fantastic breaches were invented, such as that of showing disrespect for the holy image of the emperor by carrying into a latrine or a house of ill-fame a coin or a ring impressed with his sacred features.

One need not go to the Christian apologists for a damning description of this public debasement: Seneca, a Roman of the Romans, will serve as witness. "Nothing is so damaging to good character," he remarked, "as the habit of lounging at games. . . . I come home more greedy, more ambitious, more voluptuous, and even more cruel and inhuman because I have been among other human beings. By chance I attended a mid-day exhibition, expecting some fun, wit, and relaxation—an exhibition at which men's eyes might have respite from the slaughter of their fellow men. But it was quite the reverse. . . . It is pure murder. . . . You may retort: 'But he was a highway robber; he killed a man!' And what of it? Granted that, as a murderer, he deserved punishment, what crime have you committed, poor fellow, that you should deserve to sit and see this show?"

Would you know the exact character of these spectacles? It requires almost as strong a stomach as to read about the tortures in a Nazi concentration camp. Behold the "retinue of swords and fire and chains and a mob of beasts . . . let loose upon the disemboweled entrails of men. Picture to yourself under this head the prison, the cross, the rack, the hook, and the stake which they drive straight through a man until it protrudes from his throat. Think of human limbs torn apart by chariots driven in opposite directions, of the terrible shirt smeared with and interwoven with inflammable materials, and of all the other contrivances devised by cruelty. . . . It is not surprising, then, if our greatest terror is of such a fate." Is it surprising, either, that the man who wrote these lines, one of the fortunate classes, with a country estate, a place at court, riches and fame, committed suicide in order to avoid the daily anticipation of being assassinated at command of his emperor?

Even now Seneca is worth reading; for he is a connecting link, in a far more direct fashion than Epictetus, Marcus Aurelius, or Plotinus, between Roman and Christian philosophy: a symbol that even the hard Roman soul could not endure forever these rites of cruelty and torture, greed and lust. His attack on slavery, indeed, was a turning point in pagan morality: it rang out with a clarity that many Christian apologists for long lacked. " 'They are slaves,' people declare. Nay, rather they are men. 'Slaves!' No, they are unpretentious friends. 'Slaves!' No, they are our fellow slaves, if one reflects that Fortune has equal rights over slaves and freemen alike." No matter how painfully one might school oneself to accept the inhumanities of this society, in the end it cast a sickening shadow over the heart.

If sadism became an engrossing collective ritual, eroticism remained an obsessive itch. There had once been a time in Rome when license existed under a religious sanction, in the Saturnalia: the mysteries of sex are close to the heart of every religion. Augustus, at the foundation of the Empire, introduced the celebration of the *ludi seculares.* Sacrifices were offered for three nights, to the fates, to the goddesses of procreation, and to mother earth. "It was impossible to ask the Gods more clearly," Ferrero remarks, "for an age purified from destructive vice, fruitful in men, and happy in well-merited prosperity." But the Gods did not answer his plea. Despite severe censorship and drastic legal regulations, adultery became fashionable and abortions necessary. Sexual intercourse became ever more easy and ubiquitous. Slaves, whores, pederasts were at hand for the asking. When the body was sated, the imagination whipped it up again: when the genitals failed to respond, the eye glutted itself on revolting exhibitions of carnality, such as that which Petronius describes at one of his feasts in the Satyricon.

The circus released inhibitions and heightened sexual excitement: assignations would begin there, as often as not. When the pantomime was introduced by Pylades of Cilicia and Bathyllus of Alexandria in 18 B.C., a new form of theater was devised for the bored Roman citizen. Here invisible voices accompanied by music sang a story, while the actor or mime interpreted it in action and gesture. This sounds a little like a modern opera; but as the pantomime worked out, the favorite plots were those in which disrobing—the strip tease—and copulation were enacted. The kind of sentimental erotic entertainment described by Xenophon in The Banquet—genteel but debilitating—was now produced on a wholesale plan.

Circus, pantomime, feast, spectacle, public bath, must have kept the sexual organs in a state of swollen expectation. Can one doubt that in this state of sexual over-stimulation and fatigue there was a withdrawal of interest from sex itself and a weakening of sexual tension? Obscenity took the place of desire, and exhibitionism and voyeurism did duty for potency and delight. What we loosely call perversion is often only the arrest of sexual courtship at some half-way point in its development: a passing moment is singled out from the entire act and made the chief object of play. Whereas sublimation, when it is successfully pursued, utilizes sexual energy and even raises it to a higher pitch, perversion turns it aside and drains it off. In this sense, it is no paradox to speak of deficient sexuality in a world given over to the promotion of lust.

Speaking of the saturnalian aspects of his society, Seneca remarked: "Once December was a month, now it is a year." That was true in more than the erotic aspect. Holidays multiplied. After Sulla there were 93 days devoted to public holidays when the Romans were entertained at the expense of the State. At the time of Marcus Aurelius there were 155 days devoted to spectacles. By 354 A.D. there were 175 days of games out of some 200 public holidays. These figures give some notion of how debilitating this regime must have been for the majority of Roman citizens, especially when one remembers that the serious business of the day stopped at noon. Perhaps the slaves were lucky: their work kept them busy.

Here again one understands why idleness came to be looked on, in Christianity, as the parent of sin: the chief device of Satan. In a society like that of the United States in the nineteenth century, working under the pressure of puritanic convictions and capitalistic method, work might easily be overdone and idleness, sportiveness, impulsiveness might be demanded in the interest of health and balance. Not so in Rome. Here an empty life was made emptier by a routine that almost reversed the normal roles of work and play. And here self-contempt deepened into life-contempt. Suicide was almost the only honorable refuge of a manly soul.

Such a wholesale diversion of energy possibly accounts for the failure of inventiveness in Roman society: this held true, according to Seeck, even for war. In literature and philosophy the old themes were re-tailored until they were threadbare. Even in the arts of sexual enjoyment, where one would have thought Roman ingenuity might have stretched itself, there were no critical improvements: contraception, for example, remained an empirical and unreliable art; and even in the contraceptives listed by Souranos of Ephesus, those of dubious efficacy mingled with well-tried inventions like the occlusive pessary: water from the firebucket of a smith, drunk after every menstrual period, was supposed to cause sterility. Roman women paid the penalty for these hazy prescriptions in the frequent practice of abortion. In reckoning with the reaction against sexual indulgence which was to take place, one must count the peculiar psychological malaise that follows abortion as a contributing factor: a reaction almost the opposite of that sense of relaxation and fulfillment that usually follows a happy birth.

9: The New Realm of Inventiveness

The slowing down of invention in the major departments of practical life only emphasizes an extraordinary change that took place from the second century B.C. onward. For there was one realm in which steady changes and modifications took place: changes which were to re-shape the world. That was in the domain of religion.

At no point did the dry formalisms of the old Roman religion give a fresh shape to the human personality. Most of the gods and goddesses Rome placed in her Pantheon were second-hand importations: the Roman priest had as much connection with ethical duties as a surrogate of wills; the most typical of religious ceremonies was the augury, a form of pious prognostication based on the examination of the entrails of animals. The lesser deities were little more than personifications of functions: a superstitious turning of processes into people. According to Tertullian, the Romans imagined that Alemona nourished the foetus, Nona and Decina watched over the critical months of gestation, Partula directed parturition, and Lucina brought the child to birth: five deities for the nine months of pre-natal existence alone.

These deities were the counter-images of the slaves in the emperor's household: one looked after his palace garments, another after his city garments, another his military uniforms, another his eating utensils. So hundreds of deities superintended the events of life: the conventional imagination was encumbered with these supernumeraries. No mere imperial edict could put life into such a religion.

Under the influence of the East, however, this hard-headed, practical people, unused to subtle ideas, formalists in ritual, uninventive in philosophy, found themselves grappling with new dreams which denied all the Roman values. The first stirring of this new consciousness was, as we have seen, in the mystery religions; for these were the first religions in the ancient world, at least in the West, to proclaim a universal brotherhood of the initiates, divorced from the gods of the household and the city. These religions addressed themselves to Man, and they emphasized those fears and hopes that men have in common, because of the human condition itself. In the mysteries, the repressed elements of classic society burst forth with volcanic fire: the Divine Lover and the Holy Family took possession of the inner life.

Kybele, the Great Mother, stood for fertility and love and passionate power. When the storms shook the forests, the peasants thought that Kybele was being drawn through the forests by her team of roaring lions, mourning the death of her husband and lover, Attis. Crowds of worshipers trampled through the woods, mingling the wild notes of the flute with that of the wind, chanting the worship of the Great Mother. Phrygian music, Aristotle had written, tends to enthusiasm; and the cult of the Great Mother, settling in Rome in its own Temple, with its Phrygian priests, was a bold departure from Greek frivolity and Latin formalism. The populace could not understand the philosophers when they talked of the one Supreme Being; but the Phrygian goddess was "das ewig Weibliche," without whom life would come to an end: she was the great mistress who commanded the lions, fierce, demanding, passionate; and she was the Great Mother, protective, tender, all-enfolding, who attracted to her the ungrown child and the responsive man, the eager girl and the fulfilled matron.

Here, as in Greece, it was through religion that woman recovered her ground, and found a career more true to her central impulses than mere "emancipation." Consider what happened to the Isis cult, which the Romans took over from the Egyptians. Isis was the goddess of spring and the fruitfulness of nature: like Aphrodite she graced the familiarities of lovers; her votaries included prostitutes and in her temples people made assignations. But in the course of a few centuries in Rome this

Egyptian goddess underwent a puritanic transformation: she became the goddess of chastity and protected virginity: even before Christianity came, her companion God, Serapis, sent the faithful into the cloister. By the second century A.D. Isis had become a counterweight to the flaccid sexuality of Rome: she took the role that the Queen of Heaven was to have in the thirteenth century.

But there was a masculine side to this need for turning once more to the sources of life and seeking once more to purify its muddied stream: around 70 B.C., after the suppression of the Cilician pirates by Pompey, another cult came to Rome, this time from Persia: the cult of Mithras. Mithraism was an offshoot of Zoroastrianism, in something the same fashion that Christianity was later an offshoot of Judaism: this went along with the similar passage from a closed to an open society. But Mithras was not a human person: he was the spirit of light, originally attached to the great deity of light, Ormuzd, the eternal opponent of darkness and evil, incarnated in Ahriman. "Persia," says Cumont, the chief modern interpreter of Mithraism, "introduced dualism as a fundamental principle in religion. It was this that distinguished Mithraism from other sects, and inspired its dogmatic theology and ethics, giving them a rigor and firmness unknown to Roman paganism."

By its mythology and ritual, Mithraism satisfied the need for a common basis upon which the members of this mixed society could meet: people who had left their native land and their native gods were no longer "lost": they were saved and redeemed by being brought within the fold of a larger society. Mithraism had a cult of initiation similar to that which attended induction into the army: the neophyte was compelled to take an oath of loyalty, and an indelible mark was branded on his body with a hot iron. The rite of purification was as solemn as it was terrifying: the member who was to be baptized was lowered into a pit: above him, a bull was sacrificed, and the dropping of the warm blood was supposed to purify and render powerful the receiver of the gift. This sacrifice of the bull, or Taurobolium, originally belonged to the rites of the Great Mother; but in its westward march, Mithraism absorbed the rite and made it its own. Mithraic temples, or Mithraeums, originally dotted the landscape of Europe: they were particularly numerous along the Rhine and the Danube, where the Roman legionaries, who were great devotees, were quartered.

Mithraism shifted the time perspective from the individual life or even the individual community to the eternity of Godhood. The aim of living was not immediate reward but preparation for eternal happiness: not tangible gains but the salvation of the soul. The ceremonies of Mithra dramatized darkness and light, befoulment and purification, sin and repentance; and the theology restored a healthy tension between animal needs and ideal ends.

The sacred grotto, concealed in the solitude of the dark forests, became the outward emblem of the turning inward of the Western eye. While the original Greek or Roman temple was mainly an exterior, it was the inner space in the new domed buildings that became important. In Mithraism the priest ceased to be an officer of the state: for his sovereign belonged to another world, and his community was the united body of initiates and believers, the sacred militia of an invincible God: a veritable Church militant. From the second century A.D., Mithraism became the chief rival of the old gods; by the third century it occupied a dominant place.

But the very forces that aided this spread were responsible for Mithraism's retreat before a rival cult that incorporated much of its mythology and many of its rites. For Mithraism was carried to the ends of the empire by civil servants and soldiers. When the army ceased to conquer, when the outposts were withdrawn, Mithraism contracted, too: the Sacred Bull had lost his power; and the battle between darkness and light was translated into another series of world visions, those of the followers of Christ and Mani.

On the spot where the last Taurobolium took place in the fourth century, in the Phrygianum, the basilica of the Vatican now stands. As late as 393 Isis processions through the streets of Rome were described by an eye-witness: but the Great Mother of Thrace, the Egyptian Virgin, and the Persian Bull made their exit together. Patches of the fabric they had woven were sewed into the many-colored tapestry of Christianity. The new man had appeared: no longer a figment, a mere wraith. Out of conquered Palestine appeared the Galilean, whose words of meekness and resignation denied the power and belittled the destiny of Rome.

CHAPTER II. THE PRIMACY OF THE PERSON

1: The Shadow of Things to Come

The life of Jesus of Nazareth has been both magnified and diminished by the growth of the Christian Church. His message was swallowed up in his myth: his personality was enveloped by the special claims of divinity that were attached to it: his human presence was lost in a miraculous Annunciation and a divine Transfiguration. But the myth was plainly a collective projection of the peoples who formulated it and embellished it; and from what remains in the New Testament of Jesus's unmistakable insights, one must assume that much of his actual doctrine, perhaps part of the kernel, was misunderstood or rejected by his more simple-minded recorders. Too often we see the form of Jesus and hear only the words of Paul. The pale but more visible satellite partly eclipses the sun.

What was the reason for Jesus's unique triumph? The explanation of Christian theology is a simple one: he was the Son of God, and his incarnation, his suffering, and his death were part of a divine plan in which he, by taking man's sins upon himself, began a new dispensation for mankind. Why omnipotence left such an imperfect record of this event, shrouded it in such obscurity, and performed it at such a late point in history are minor problems beside the vaster mystery which faith accepts.

But the historic mystery is increased, rather than diminished, if one regards Jesus solely in his human aspect. On such terms, his power is like that of the tiny grain of mustard seed: an evidence of the absolute weight of the human personality in the face of institutions and material circumstances that would seem destined to overwhelm it and blot it out.

"Come unto me, all ye that labor and are heavy laden; and I will give you rest. Take my yoke upon you and learn of me; for I am meek and lowly in heart; and ye shall find rest unto your souls. . . . Whosoever will be great among you, let him be your minister; and whosoever will be chief among you, let him be your servant."

The classic world had long been waiting to hear those words. Year by year its emptiness had been growing heavier; year by year the chains that bound men to their imperious burdens and their played-out pleasures had become more galling: the calluses deepened on the spirits of the proud and the raw blisters multiplied on the bodies of the lowly. In a few decades, in a few centuries, everyone would be ready for the new dispensation: not only the slaves but the centurions: not alone miserable Lazarus, but the Ethiopian Royal Treasurer.

The prophet who uttered these words was brought up in the land of Galilee, the Boeotia of Palestine, among farmers and fishermen who mingled with the busy, prosperous patricians from Jerusalem. Like Hesiod, whose Works and Days reformulated the Hellenic religious consciousness and established a higher concept of justice, Jesus was alienated by humble birth from the dominant society of his time. Though he argued with the learned rabbis in the synagogue, there is no indication in his teaching that he was burdened by any weight of abstruse learning, or that he even had such acquaintance with the philosophers and poets of Graeco-Judaic civilization as Paul probably had. The carpenter, the shepherd, the fisherman, the husbandman, the worker in the vineyard, were the familiar types he knew: their ancient occupations provided him with homely images of the common life; and he shared some of their distrust for the proud merchants and the sharp moneylenders who made life hard for the poor. At home with his neighbors, he had words for simple men.

Jesus's contemporaries were more than ready for him—indeed for anyone who was certain of his inner light, and set to lift their trouble and confusion. They would read portents in the sky, even as the contemporaries of Augustus read into the approach of a comet the beginning of a new age: they would not be surprised to find the Messiah, one of the House of David, sitting by a well in the middle of their village. In the recurrent poverty of the war-torn countrysides there was an underlying connection, the connection of want and pain and fear, with the proletariat of the cities: so that once the prophet came forth, his doctrine would prosper most swiftly in the crowded, world-weary metropolises of Africa and Asia Minor. John the Baptist had come among the Jews, purifying people by baptism and predicting a new day at hand. When Jesus came to John, the latter promptly recognized his qualities: he declared he was not fit to tie Jesus's shoelaces. That act of recognition and homage started the young prophet on his way.

Presently, Jesus retired to the barren hills, where he fasted and nourished his visions. Alone in the desert, he was tempted by dreams of power: the power to control the physical world, common to magic and to science, the power to rule the political destinies of the masses of men, the vulgar ambition of emperors and tyrants: all these avenues of worldly achievement he put behind him. Jesus's interest was in the redemption of man's very humanity, in the perpetual renewal and re-dedication of the living to the task of self-development: he sought to bring the inner and the outer aspects of the personality into organic balance by throwing off compulsions, constraints, automatisms. No one else has spoken of the moral life with fewer negations or with so many positive expressions of power and joy. His mission was not to govern men but to release them. The new doctrine would round out and fulfill the work of the law and the prophets, not leave it completely behind. This connection with the past did not save Christianity from the perils of mere apocalyptic futurism, but it showed that Jesus rejected the current impulse to break loose entirely.

There was work to do, and Jesus set about it. Inevitably he drew to him a band of disciples, for the most part plain, unlearned men: people incapable of protecting themselves by book-learning from the shock of fresh ideas and from the emotional impact of a great example. What they were capable of assimilating, mankind itself would be ripe for. Unlike the philosophers who taught initiates and students they had brought to a certain intellectual level, Jesus addressed the poor and the ignorant: he thus overcame the class limitations that had narrowed the province of philosophy and limited the political effectiveness of a Socrates, a Plato, a Zeno.

Like a guide to the hill passes, Jesus took shortcuts across the untraversible mountains of class pride, intellectual arrogance, and professional specialization. In his philosophy, the dialectical wisdom of Aristotle might not lead one as close to the core of life as the innocence of a little child. He devaluated the inflated currency of the intellect. Faith in the realities of life and spirit made the great and the humble stand on the same level. This was a shocking assumption to those who had paid dearly for wealth, knowledge, position: Were all their efforts then worthless? Were the poor and the ignorant their equals?

Jesus's most venomous opposition came from conservative groups in the synagogue: not from the indifferent, but from the strict, not from the backsliders, but from those who knew the law and fulfilled it to the letter, proud that they were more virtuous than their neighbors: men who clung to the moral laws and sanitary regulations of Moses, who followed the noble duties of the Pharisees. These opponents of Jesus were proud, justly proud, of their great heritage. Jewish morals, Jewish hygiene, were both close to the order of nature: Judaism had long been uncontaminated by supernaturalism, and until it was infected by the death of neighboring cultures, it harbored few phantoms: its God operated in history, and its invisible world was truly invisible, the kingdom of the ideal, continuous with the domain of nature and inherent in the plan of nature.

Now, in Jesus, a rival to Moses appeared. With a sure instinct for attack, Jesus singled out the strong elements in Jewish culture as a point for his radical departures: he broke the Sabbath openly to stay his hunger: man did not exist for the Sabbath but the Sabbath for man. The periodic day of rest was the very citadel of the Jewish vital economy: perhaps, as Sudhoff, the medical historian, remarks, its greatest contribution to health. When Jesus challenged the sacredness of this good custom, the currents of life were indeed rising: the day of fossilized virtue was over. For Jesus, the Pharisees were "actors": that was the word he used. Such people played a part: their actions were therefore never adapted to life's surprising demands. They treated life as a set piece, and so denied it.

If Moses was the moralist, the hygienist, the organizer, Jesus was the mystic and the psychologist. The first worked on the mind through the body, and on the person through the community. The second reversed this process: the divine in man must be nourished if every other law and duty be pushed aside; and the divine was that which furthered the processes of growth and made it possible for man to slough off his dead selves, as the snake sloughs off its skin. Jesus saw that no wider, stricter observance of law could recover for life the freedom and energy it had lost in the very perfection of human institutions: in his view, goodness could obstruct life no less than wickedness, and without a perpetual challenge would undoubtedly do so. Among modern poets and philosophers, Emerson, Whitman, and Bergson come closest to sharing this philosophy.

What was needed was a radical change in attitude: an assertion of the primacy of the person, and a shift from outer circumstances to inner values. Adultery, therefore, did not consist simply in going to bed with another man's wife: that was only its most obvious form. He that looked on a woman to lust after her had already committed adultery in his heart; and a sensitive judgment would be more concerned with the concealed impulse than the open accomplishment, for it might be more obstructive to growth. Though comfort for the poor and the lowly was an essential part of Jesus's creed, he outraged his disciples by sweetly accepting the perfumed oil that was poured upon his head: oil that was bought with money which, they indignantly urged, might have been spent upon the poor. But Jesus pointed out that the woman who had anointed him had been prompted by love: her impulse was sacred. To obey that impulse was more important than to be concerned with food or clothes—even the food and clothes of the poor. For love was the highest manifestation of life. Why should the poor be fed if love were allowed to disappear from the world?

With Jesus, the possibilities of love were no longer confined to friends and lovers, to members of one's family or one's tribe: the love of God and the love of one's neighbor were equally imperative. To love well was to participate in a life that went beyond one's immediate animal need for self-preservation: for he who lost his self would find it, and he who gave up everything, as passionate lovers do for the beloved or as parents do for their children, would find himself the member of a wider society which would offset his abnegations and renunciations.

The great empires of the ancient world, Babylonia, Persia, Macedonia, Rome, had tried to build a universal state on the basis of power and law alone: Jesus sought to found a wider community on the basis of love and grace. Power meant the capacity to appropriate, to possess, to dominate: love meant the capacity to share, to renounce, to sacrifice. Jesus was indifferent to the need to bring these two efforts together; and he bequeathed the problem to the Christian Church, which failed at the height of its own powers by losing sight of Jesus's example.

2: Doctrine, Life, and Love

There is more than one fashion of interpreting Jesus's doctrine of Eternal Life, which runs through the Gospels. A hopeless society, blocked in every effort at worldly security and satisfaction, would emphasize immortality and eternity as the most important promise of the Christian faith: life *eternal.* But it is equally consistent to interpret Jesus's words in a humanistic and naturalistic sense: *life* eternal: "Thy will be done on *earth.*" In this fashion, Jesus renewed the vision of Isaiah.

The Greek philosophers had praised temperance, courage, prudence, and wisdom: they had sought to discipline the flesh and fortify rational judgment: but even when, in the doctrines of Plato, love sought beauty and perfection, no longer mere physical possession, its province remained limited: it was never strong enough to unite the Greek and the Barbarian even so that the polis itself might be saved, still less was it capable of uniting them for the Barbarian's benefit. Jesus gave love a social mission and a political province. Who was one's neighbor? Anyone who needed one's help. The parable of the Good Samaritan is a condemnation of every form of isolationism.

This was a simple doctrine, backed by simple demonstrations. While the accounts of some of Jesus's miracles are incredible if one judges them by their actual contents, most of them are consistent with his whole vision of life if one judges them by their direction and intention. The restoration of sight to the blind, of speech to the dumb, of the use of their legs to the crippled: the casting out of neurotic "devils" and the return to sanity—always the end of the miracle is normal health, and the ability to go on living. Those whom Jesus converted to his faith did not receive any superhuman powers: they were not endowed with an insight into the future or with a detailed remembrance of the past: the feats of astrology or clairvoyance were not for them. Nor were they gifted with a special knowledge of the physical world which would mock the science of Alexandria: they cannot make the sun stand still or behold the beauty of Helen of Troy. Dr. Faust would have turnèd away from Jesus unsatisfied—to conclude his bargain with Mephistopheles.

The upshot of Jesus's typical miracles is that the patient becomes whole again: *life goes on.* The return to life was not postponed until the Resurrection Day. The very simplicity of Jesus's performances as a whole carries conviction: indeed, it is fairly easy to distinguish miracles that are consistent with his own vision and our own knowledge of psychotherapy from those that plainly reflect the cheap magic understood by Jesus's too credulous followers, who sought to turn a prophet into a mere wonder-working charlatan. Jesus's healing of the sick showed a vital insight into the unconscious: the possessor of those powers did indeed know something about the mystery of the soul that even Socrates' *daimon* never plumbed.

When one turns from Jesus's demonstrations to his words, the transparent meaning of his acts disappears. One is confronted by paradoxical truths, gnomic insights, homely parables that sometimes shock one by their crass acceptance of unjust conventions, figures that lend themselves to either a natural or a supernatural explanation, mysteries that seem like mystifications. But Jesus is hardly responsible for the confused state of the record: the tale of his life was long carried by word of mouth, probably for more than a generation, before the first written record was made. Some of those closest to him, like Paul, deliberately turned away from the image of Jesus, the man, in order to worship with unrestricted abandon the crucified God, a being born of the worshiper's own sick needs and ambivalent desires. In the course of time, much that was precious would disappear, and not a little that was rubbish would be added. But above the confused murmurs of the witnesses, Mark, Matthew, and Luke, rises Jesus's life itself: it reveals a consistent purpose and an inner unity: the mark of a real personality and not, as Mani later asserted, of a wraith.

The very heart of Jesus's faith, Matthew Arnold pointed out, is incommunicable in words: his "secret." To unlock this secret fully, one must have beheld the light in the master's eyes; one must have interpreted the enigmatic smile that surely hovered on his lips; for there is both an agility and a power of penetration in Jesus's sayings that were, one feels, but lamely passed on by his disciples. Is it any wonder that, all too soon, they sought to turn him into a more familiar figure: a magician, a sacrificial scapegoat, an Orphic initiator, a redeemer, a Messiah: that step by step they interpreted his vision of eternal life, life forever self-renewing and self-transcending, as a mere promise of golden glitter in a changeless heaven: that they transformed into a God a prophet who, on their own testimony, said he was not God. ("Why call ye me good? Only God is good.")

Jesus's acts all affirm natural life; and for him the Kingdom of Heaven did not await death and eternity but might open before the awakened soul at any moment. He declared that natural life might rise above its animal foundations: that man indeed must pass beyond his creaturely limitations if he is to enter into *his* natural kingdom. He aimed at simplicity, spontaneity, integrity, freedom: these were the conditions for man's growth and his perpetual rejuvenation, conditions which Goethe was to declare the special property of the man of genius, but which the Son of Man sought to pass on to all the Sons of Men. The civic obligations of Rome, the moral code of Jerusalem, the astronomical lore of the Chaldeans, and the art of the Greeks were all as nothing to him: his mission was to cut under every institution, every habit, every purpose, even those that were avowedly good. Was it not a failure of love that was responsible for man's self-love, out of which grew his indifference to the welfare of the poor and humble, that is, to the mass of humanity? On all minor reforms, he had nothing to say.

"John," Jesus sardonically observed, "came neither eating nor drinking, and they say, He hath a devil. The Son of Man came eating and drinking, and they say, Behold a man gluttonous and a wine-bibber, a friend of publicans and sinners. But wisdom is justified of her children."

Wisdom was indeed justified. Jesus undermined the knowledge of the learned, the pride of the powerful, the morals of the virtuous: he saw that sin and imperfection, with their self-humiliation and self-criticism, were far less dangerous to life than complacency; for sin might pave the way for an inward change which raised life to a higher pitch than unblemished virtue was capable of reaching. This inward change, the grace of the holy spirit as it was to be called, was all important: repentance must precede regeneration. Mere willing, mere rational efforts in themselves, could not bring about such a change: it needed the encouraging example of a living image, and that image was the personality of Jesus himself.

The effect of Jesus's doctrine, boldly set forth in the Sermon on the Mount, was to give strength to the humble and the weak, and to make the principle of yielding stronger than the principle of domination: a complete reversal of values. Man's weakness, for the fifth century Greeks, came from his ignorance. Jesus's position was just the opposite of this; but he did not make the fatal error of dissolving the very idea of virtue, like the Skeptics. In the scribes and the Pharisees Jesus beheld the danger of a premature crystallization: the personality might be handicapped by the very qualities it had sought so painfully to achieve. To know oneself, from his standpoint, was to realize the miserable failure of one's successes and the redeeming success of one's failures. The capacity to recognize one's inevitable shortcomings, to profit by every occasion of disintegration, was the only guarantee of continued self-development. That was a salutary doctrine for the heirs of a disintegrating civilization.

Jesus's transvaluations were a permanent contribution to all moral doctrine. Naturally, this challenge affronted the more respectable members of the community: for the very condition of the proletariat gave them a better chance of entering the Kingdom of Heaven than the rich.

In sum, virtue could not be accumulated: the prudent investor of moral capital might find himself bankrupt overnight and the spendthrift might by a last moment's repentance find himself possessed of riches. This seems a perversion of both psychological experience and natural justice; but there is an aspect of both personality and community for which it has real meaning. Jesus came into a society encrusted with venerable superstitions and slavish usages: afflicted with pieties that had become profanities, with knowledge that stifled curiosity: a society choked by the debris of ancient cultures, threatened by those very processes of accumulation which ordered production and government make possible. The simplification of life was the very essence of salvation in such a society: the first and the last, the poor and the rich, the earlier and the later, the wise and the foolish, the saint and the sinner must all start from scratch: were they not all Sons of Men?

Every word and act of Jesus can be interpreted as an attempt to disinter the corpse of man: to raise the dead. Ceremonies, books, forms, rituals, prayers, duties, administrative regulations, laws, might all seem good in themselves, because goodness had once passed that way; but nothing was good for Jesus unless it furthered life in its perpetual process of self-transcendence and self-liberation. Or as Emerson put it: "Life only avails, not the having lived." So the Child, with its multiple potentialities for growth, is the true symbol of this doctrine. One must throw away one's accumulation of riches and learning and become poor again, poor as a beggar, innocent as a child. Old, indeed, is the belief that the good man must disencumber himself of material possessions; but Jesus, like Lao-tse, applied this injunction equally to immaterial possessions. For him it was necessary to redeem knowledge from limitations no less deadly than stubborn ignorance, and to chastise the law-abiding, no less than the more obvious criminals. The price of life was a willingness to wipe out all one's precious accumulations and begin all over again, whenever they got in the way. The virtue of the pioneer.

3: The Paradox of Personality

When Jesus's followers came to interpret his message in the patristic age, they sought a too-easy shortcut. If one must become as a little child again, was not ignorance itself then a virtue, almost a passport to heaven? If mercy and love stand above political justice, why go through the forms of political justice or bother about whether they are good or bad? And why cultivate mathematical or astronomical knowledge, if it leads to pride of learning and hardness of heart? To hold to such simplism is to mistake the true provenance of Jesus's ideas. His truths were *especially* valid for those who gave themselves to the study of science or the execution of justice: they provided a corrective to institutions Jesus otherwise did not care to challenge. In time, unfortunately, Christian virtue became a cloak for political irresponsibility, for scientific know-nothingness, and for self-righteous indifference to the humane pursuit of literature, philosophy, and art.

Jesus himself cannot perhaps escape some blame for this miscarriage: he left a gap which the Church took many centuries to fill up. What was lacking in his creed was what was lacking in his native environment, the back country, far from the big cities with their art and learning; when Jesus entered Jerusalem he entered it as an enemy, deliberately scorning its ways. He did not say: I was ignorant and ye taught me, or I was cast down in spirit and ye revived me with the sound of the harp and the tabor: the joy of Solomon and the joy of David find no echo in his spirit. The great prophet of the soul left out of his mission the traditional food of the soul. Music, poesy, painting, philosophy, science, counted nought for the salvation of man. It was to life at the humblest level that Jesus appealed; and he cast out of his reckoning the great sin of all class cultures, that they deny the common man the wealth and the leisure needed to partake of man's highest goods. His was a gospel not so much of renunciation as of etherealization. When the spirit was truly alive, it could throw away all canes and crutches, and dance.

The same judgment applies to Jesus's indifference to political improvements. The easy explanation in both cases is that the current apocalyptic conviction of doom was shared by Jesus himself: if the heavens were soon to fall, what difference did it make if the arts prospered or if justice prevailed? On this matter, Renan's criticism is certainly well-taken: "To establish as a principle that we must recognize the legitimacy of power by the inscription on its coins, to proclaim that the perfect man pays tribute with scorn and without question, was to destroy republicanism in the ancient form and to favor all tyranny. Christianity, in this sense, has contributed much to weaken the sense of duty of the citizen, and to deliver the world into the absolute power of existing circumstances."

So much must be said in negation; but there is another side to the matter. The essential originality of Jesus's thought can be better grasped if one realizes that the person is an emergent from society, in the same fashion that the human species is an emergent from the animal world. The function of personality both includes the facts of community and transcends them. While the person is dependent upon the community, in the same fashion that the organism itself is dependent upon the material it absorbs from nature, one cannot fully describe the person merely in terms of its social relationships: a radical qualitative change takes place at each ascending grade in emergence. The very concept of the person was once the exclusive property of the ruler and his intimate circle: in Egypt immortality was first reserved for them alone. The gradual building up of personality and its extension in theory to every member of the community was the great contribution of the prophets and redeemers: a process that reached a new plateau in Christianity. Lloyd Morgan's doctrine of emergent evolution has sociological as well as metaphysical significance.

Jesus's insights apply only to the higher realm. In his new dispensation, for example, "to him that hath shall be given and from him that hath not shall be taken even that which he hath." Applied to political society such a conception would be plainly monstrous: a vicious miscarriage of justice. But it was not meant for society: that should be equally plain. In the realm of personality it reveals a truth in the very order of nature: it is the truth of habit, that every good act makes goodness easier and every bad act makes badness more incorrigible; it is the truth of knowledge, that those who have labored diligently acquire more than they have bargained for, while those who shirk become the victims of their own lack; it is the truth lovers know: that he who gives most receives most, and that he who withholds becomes empty.

Social equity is based on another principle, the principle of even interchange and common advantage: self-interest, not self-abandoned love.

But in the personality this higher law cannot be evaded; and Jesus's special insights are applicable to all persons, even in the most perfect human societies, working under the most exemplary conditions. Hence the difficulty of applying the moral truths of Jesus to a community: so difficult that the wise Mary Boole once suggested that no officer of the State should ever countenance the belief that, as officer, he was or could be a Christian.

Actually, Jesus's truths seek to transcend the inevitable limitations of even the best corporate order: the new dispensation does not deny the need for the old dispensation, but applies to a realm it does not touch, the realm of the person. The failure to understand this fact is the great limitation of Quakerism, otherwise so close to the spirit of Jesus: in their attitude toward the Nazis, for example, many members of the Society of Friends have failed to see that Christian charity is a corrective of justice, not a substitute for it.

The social message of Jesus therefore remains ambiguous; but the personal injunctions are clear. "Do good and lend, hoping for nothing; and your reward shall be great." That sentence of Jesus, which parallels a similar one in the Bhagavad-Gita, placed conduct on a superior level. Its ultimate word was a paradox: he that loseth his life shall find it. When Jesus's transpositions were finished all the negative elements in life were on the positive side of the equation and had changed their sign: death in all its forms, vice, disease, ignorance, paralysis, had been used as a condition for a fuller and richer life. No part of existence was indifferent to spirit or untouched by it. Not merely water but poison was transmuted into wine.

. . . Jesus's life was a brief one, consummated in loneliness, betrayal, and torture. His personality moves across the stage of history in a few swift gleams and flashes, tantalizing in their incompleteness; and his figure is muffled by the opaque bodies that surrounded him. He is fated to be betrayed for a few pieces of silver by Judas and to be denounced by the people he came to save: he sees that fate as his end approaches and the acceptance of it exalts him. The man who is nailed to the cross on the Mount of Calvary is the incarnation of humility, love, and sacrifice: humility proudly worn, love lifted into a kinship with all humanity, death made the willing utterance of life itself: a complete affirmation of man's condition and man's end.

The tragedy of Jesus rises to a swift climax. The epilogue, as told in the Gospels, lacks the austerity, the white illumination, the decisive gesture and the telling word, that mark the more visible acts of this personality. The breath has scarcely left Jesus's body before he becomes enshrouded in myth. Jesus, the man, passes out of the picture: in his place is the God foretold in prophecy and celebrated in a score of pagan cults. Karl Marx once said of himself that he was not a Marxist; and of Jesus one may say, without irreverence, that he was not a Christian. For little men, who guarded Jesus's memory, took him, drained off the precious life blood of his spirit, mummified his body, and wrapped what was left in many foreign wrappings: over these remains they proceeded to erect a gigantic tomb. That tomb was the Christian Church. The figure it holds is both greater and less than the man who walked and talked by the shores of Galilee: more indisputably a traditional god, more doubtfully an illumined man. But which figure points to the more miraculous historic fulfillment? I have no hesitation in saying—the man.

4: The Mission of the Christian Church

How did Christianity survive? How did the figure of Christ supplant the false Messiahs whose coming he had predicted? How did the Christian super-ego impose itself upon a hostile pattern of life?

There have been many modern answers to these questions, from Edward Gibbon to Renan and Engels: for Gibbon it exhibited a sort of Gresham's law in history, while Engels somewhat glibly accounted for it by saying that the universal state of Rome required a universal religion. But the latter hardly explains the actual process; for the rise of the new religion, as the disturbed Romans were quick to point out by the third century, was accompanied by the downhill course of the State. Rome saved Christianity, perhaps; but Christianity did not save Rome.

Now, ideas do not take possession of a society by mere literary dissemination: that is the fallacy of eighteenth century rationalism, or the conceit of modern publicity. To be socially operative, ideas must be incorporated in institutions and laws, enacted through a daily discipline of the individual life, finally embodied in buildings and works of art that create an effective background for the new drama, and transpose its theme from the dream world where it originated to the world of actuality, where it is tested, challenged, modified.

The beginning and the end of this process is the incarnation of the idea in a human person: first in that of a single man or woman, and finally in the everyday members of the community: a whole society. By the process of "mimesis," on which Arnold Toynbee has wisely written, a new pattern of personality and a new plan of life take hold of many individual lives and give them a common task and a single goal. Though the word "incarnation" has been restricted by Christian theology to the appearance of God in human form, it has a far wider application. Incarnation and mimesis are essential to the social process; and for lack of insight into their operation most of our thinking about social institutions has been shallow, because it treated institutions and organizations as if they were self-begotten and self-existent: denying the influence of ideas because it ignored the role of persons. What we can learn here about the development of Christianity will apply equally to the development of capitalism or colonization or the machine.

We have now reached the third act in the drama of Christian renunciation. The essential ideas of Christian theology have long been in existence, and have begun to converge toward a common creed, a genuine syncretism, stimulated by the new insights of Jesus: few ideas will come into Christian theology that were not already latent, indeed sometimes fully formulated, before Jesus appeared. The incarnation has taken place; but Christian man has still to be born; and a long process of infiltration and crystallization must now follow. Primitive Christianity, that is, churchless Christianity, had only a short career. One has a glimpse of Jesus's original followers in Jerusalem, calling upon those around them in the synagogue to receive baptism and enter into fellowship. Those who had wealth sold their possessions and shared their wealth: they practiced primitive communism and lived as a true society of friends: patient castaways, these first Christians, sure that a ship would soon pick them up and bring them to a paradisal port.

The first step toward an organized Church was the break with Israel. Christianity became a mystery religion: one entered it, not by birth or residence, but by being initiated: baptism and the communion of the Lord's Supper were the chief rites. As Christianity passed from group to group, from synagogue to synagogue, it gathered to it many things besides the sayings and deeds of Jesus: the Roman marriage ceremony in almost every detail down to the bridal wreath; the Persian conception of the Eternal war between God and the Devil, light and darkness; the Egyptian notion of the Last Judgment and the resurrection of the body; the neoplatonic metaphysics of the Greeks, already visible in the Gospel of St. John. All these elements of cult and creed had been shaped by the human imagination over many preceding centuries: they helped to create an official personality for Jesus; and the meaning and attributes of that personality became the main theme of a new discourse: theology.

Christianity took doctrinal form in the letters that passed from one group of believers to another, in Jerusalem, Antioch, Ephesus, Athens, Alexandria, Carthage, Ecbatana: letters introducing a brother carrying greetings of fellowship, citing the testimony of eye-witnesses, re-defining principles, answering questions relating to belief and the daily discipline of life. Those who believed in Christ had still to transform their sense of beatitude and salvation into the forms of a Christian life. That process required centuries. Meanwhile the good word spread by direct word of mouth, by messenger, or by post, during that mild Indian summer of order and peace which preceded the dreary, stormy November of Roman civilization. From Paul to Augustine, doctrinal Christianity was essentially the product of an informal revolutionary committee of correspondence. These local groups held the scattered ranks of the saved together until they had strength enough to challenge the Roman state and become the official religion of the late Empire.

Essential to Christianity's survival were its Jewish foundations. The Jews might reject Christ as a God, even as a prophet, but Christianity could not afford to reject Judaism. When dealing with situations on which the new doctrine had nothing to say, it was helpful for the Christians to be able to fall back on Jewish morals and Jewish law. The silversmiths of Ephesus even denounced the Christians as a menace to trade because they spread contempt for graven images, like the Jews. From Israel, moreover, came a most radical theological conception: the belief that the Will of God is worked out in human history: that every historic event is a judgment of God upon man's understanding of the Divine Will and his readiness to co-operate with it. This saved the Church, partly, from a sterile otherworldliness, even as the Jewish conception of family obligations, reluctantly admitted by Paul, saved it from race suicide, despite the open contempt of the Christian fathers for all carnal ties.

Not the smallest contribution of the Jew was a political one: that of the regular meeting of the faithful in the synagogue on the Sabbath. Every synagogue, ecclesia, or assembly tended to be, at first, a miniature democracy. Even rites that would eventually be monopolized by an ordained priesthood first took shape within the congregation: witness confession and absolution. The informality and decentralization of these groups were a great contribution to the Church's strength during the period of persecution: it offered no single critical point whose extermination would paralyze the rest of the body. Rome found it hard to kill such a many-celled organism, each cell self-renewing. Wherever two or three were gathered together in fellowship under Christ, there the Church existed. Like the congregations of the Mithraic Church, the Christian groups returned to the human scale: they combined the intimacy and solidarity of the primary group with a universality that passed beyond the borders of the Roman Empire, to Persia and even to Chinese Turkestan. This double change of scale should be noted: it permitted local concentration and super-national extension. In the Church the lost internal proletariat recovered its sense of identity; and people scattered over a wider area than any existing Empire thought, felt, and acted as one.

Greece made its chief contribution to Christianity through organized thought: most of the important early Fathers, like Clement and Origen, were Alexandrians, schooled in Greek philosophy. The Greek theologians took the obscure statements and the flowery oriental allusions of the founders of Christianity and applied to them the precise logic of the schools: the trickling water of Jesus's thought, true water of life, was thus turned drop by drop into the sharp stalactites and stalagmites of dogma; and what was true in an allusive poetic sense became false, or misleading, by the very act of definition. Opponents, like Celsus, might revile Christianity on the ground that it was only the commonplaces of Greek and Roman philosophy, plus magic; but the Greek mind set itself to the tricky task of reconciling magic with philosophy, and mystery with logic: explaining how God, who was Unity, might be three persons, each co-existent, co-eternal, equally omnipotent: how the Son and the Father might be one, and how the attributes of personality might be expressed in a God that had neither body nor members: how the omnipotence of God was reconcilable with the presence of evil and the tragic sacrifice of a Son for the purpose of redeeming that evil.

The facile dialectic of the Greeks, separated from the experience that had given it an underpinning in the sixth and the fifth centuries B.C., confused words with things and experiences, and erected a pretentious structure of exact knowledge about the hypothetical attributes and powers and functions of God: the "science" of theology. That structure took a thousand years to build: we will examine the final fabric in the thirteenth century as it was finished and given an edifying coat of whitewash, in the manner of the medieval builder, by Thomas Aquinas.

Theology was almost as much a Greek creation as philosophy. And one must not undervalue that contribution; for it kept alive the important tradition of unity, and the sense that all the parts of human experience are attributes of a meaningful whole, through processes that are not fully comprehensible within any human compass of time. Even the errors of theology bore fruit. The error of claiming positive knowledge and an objective existence for experiences that belong to the unconscious, or at least, the subjective world, pointed to the reality of these hidden areas of personality. Words are often the medium in which a new life takes shape in society: they indicate possible avenues of experience long before the pavement for that avenue can be laid. Politically the terms of Christian theology became passwords: they established the possibility of social relations between those who used them in the same fashion. By this means, theology went much further than the bare narrative of the New Testament in differentiating the doctrines of Christ from those of other poets and philosophers. But in creating Christian theology out of neo-Platonism, the Greek fathers undermined a large part of their classic heritage, and they fostered a mystical tradition of contemplative withdrawal which was at odds with the prophetic tradition of passionate struggle and involvement with the evils of earthly existence. Plotinus was not a Christian; but the shadow-world of Plotinus too long dominated the Christian mind.

5: The Apotheosis of Suffering

Two hundred years of intermixture and fusion profoundly altered the shape of Christianity and the super-ego of the Christian man: it created a Church under whose altars many other dead, and not-so-dead, Gods were buried. Organized Christianity proved as a creed to have a power of digestion that Rome, precisely because of its tolerance and skepticism and greedy receptivity, had long lacked. And the difference lay in this: Rome merely accumulated the detached fragments of other cultures and put them side by side in its mental Pantheon, whilst Christianity in the process of its growth, slowly assimilated them and manufactured muscle and bone and organs for its own body. If none of the pagan beliefs could enter Christianity without undergoing a change, none could seem altogether foreign and unfamiliar within the walls of the new Church. In a crumbling society, the very rigidity of the Church's dogmas, the very exclusiveness, indeed the fierce intolerance, of its claims, were as solid land to the queasy, shipwrecked souls who had too long been tossed about on the boundless waters: their own timbers were too shaky to permit them to question the Church's rigidity.

The vision of Jesus was one of health, life, renewal. But the religion that grew up about his person and sought to fulfill his mission fell into the cracks of a disintegrating society; and those who were most attracted to the creed were those who had no health in them, and who found in the afflictions, the ignominies, and the living sacrifice of Jesus a sympathetic image, shared by their very God, of their own tribulations. From the massacre of the innocents to the Crucifixion, the outer details of the Christian story centered on suffering and death. Instead of keeping this part of life in true perspective, the Fathers of the Church, themselves harried, persecuted, martyred, dwelt on these terrible experiences as if they were typical of human life at its best no less than its worst. "We glory in our tribulations also:" said Paul, "knowing that tribulation worketh patience; and patience experience; and experience hope: and hope maketh not ashamed."

In short, the Christian did not wait for death to come to him: he went forth to meet it. By self-deprivation and martyrdom, he deliberately accepted death as a present element in his life, and built his own values out of these very negations. Thus death ceased to be a shocking accident that cut short one's natural joys: it became, like Jesus's own death, a matter of willing choice; and to the extent that it was chosen, accepted, willed, it could no longer undermine the Christian's existence, for those who killed his body could not claim his soul. By this attitude, the Christian recovered the initiative for life: he led the counter-attack.

In their emphasis on life's evils, the Christians compensated, indeed overcompensated, for the dominant effort of the pagan world to drown its sense of despair in aimless sensualities and hollow distractions. But the Christian's own consciousness was infected by the very decay against which it protested. A good part of the ancient world was suffering from an overwhelming and unevadable anxiety: fear of the future, fear of death, fear of loss and alienation, had begun to haunt even apparently healthy souls from top to bottom in this society: the favored classes no less than the slaves—might they not, by a fickle turn of Fortune's wheel, become slaves?

This corrosive fear of life, this constant sense of insecurity, was possibly passed on in subtle ways by the servile classes to their masters: subjective emanations conveyed by glances and gestures could not be concealed or altogether overlooked. A growing sense of guilt on the part of the exploiters would only increase their anxiety as to the future. So corrupted were the pleasures and duties of life that Gregory of Nyssa even held up the normal mischances of parenthood as an argument against having children: for might they not sicken and die and bring unbearable grief?

By giving to suffering a noble role in man's life, the Christian Church confirmed these anxieties and yet comforted the anxious: their trials were not unique, but were rather the universal lot, rationalized by man's original sin and redeemed by the historic sacrifice of the Son of God. By anticipating an eternity of bliss, provided he redirected his energies and transformed his aspirations, the Christian could face the worst. Were not his sufferings indeed a sort of otherworldly life-insurance, payable at death? Could death then come too soon? "There flourishes within us," exclaimed Cyprian in the third century, "the strength of hope and the firmness of faith. Among these very ruins of a decaying world our soul is lifted up and our courage unshaken." The ruins and decay were a confirmation, rather than a denial, of the Christian ideology.

Out of every disability and misfortune, the Christians found a new source of strength: their joyous resolution, revealed in hymns, chants, prayers, convinced and converted many pagans: surely that joy had some foundation? Not merely were the Christians drawn together into more compact bodies by persecution, which lopt off the faint-hearted and the unpersuaded, and encased in iron the souls of the steadfast: not merely did they thus acquire the discipline they needed to show eventually a united front against the pagan world. But in addition the great dogmatic decisions of the Church established a central orthodoxy. A succession of Councils, beginning with that of Nicaea in 325, disposed of a series of heretical doctrines. By their acceptance of these decisions the Christians learned to sacrifice individual preferences to group needs, and to establish a line of continuity in thought and policy which guaranteed their political survival. In a disintegrating world, heresy becomes a political crime; and schism becomes the greatest of sins because it disperses the energy needed for renewal.

If Rome had shown itself capable of any such sacrifices, any such concentrated purpose and direction, a far larger part of the goods of classic civilization could have been carried forward into a new order: perhaps a major renascence of classic civilization would have taken place. But Rome was politely neutral on questions that demanded passionate adhesion or a strong intellectual counter-attack: it was bored or blandly amused by the Christian claims, at a moment when it should have been prompted by them into a ruthless appraisal of its own weaknesses. One may today easily criticize the Christian Church, as the Romans did, because of the superstitions and obscurities that clung like burrs to the cleansed garments of faith. But the Christian had a vital sense of integrity: he knew that cohesion and continuity were needed for survival, as nothing else was. In this weakened society, the fact of agreement was more important than the dogma that might be agreed upon. The vital lies of the Christian's creed were a better answer to the desperate and the disheartened than the numb truths of the pagan philosophers. Faith was needed now: faith in the incredible and the impossible: such a faith as men need on a sinking ship. Nothing less than faith would enable the survivors of this world to go on.

Until Rome's military power came to the aid of the lowly Son of Man, Christianity itself remained a heresy in a world choked with new creeds and claims. Long after Constantine's Edict of Toleration in 313 A.D., long after Christianity had been made the official religion of the Roman Empire, other religions and philosophies remained in open competition: was not Augustine himself a Manichee until he reached the age of thirty? Teaching, example, self-discipline, and local self-government did not alone give the Christian Church an unchallengable place: the final act to ensure its survival was the seizure of the power of the State and the banning of other cults. By utilizing the mechanism of the State, the Church lived through the ruin of the State: lived to tell the tale. That act betrayed the spirit of Jesus and established the reign of Christ—yet without it, the very name of Jesus might today be as dim and meaningless as that of Mani, and no part of his vision might have survived.

As the Church became conscious of itself as an independent organization, an ecclesiastical polity, with a bureaucracy, a central executive, graded ranks, dignitaries, a system of universal taxation, well-defined jurisdictions, powers, privileges, it tended to take over the tyrannical powers of the empire itself: presently, the day of congregationalism was over. On matters of theology alone Rome remained, down to the Council of Trent, relatively humble. Heresy repeatedly carried with it, even before Rome took a commanding position, some assertion of local political freedom, home rule or nationalist self-assertion: the theological departure partly rationalized a political motive, from Priscillian to Luther.

Four centuries were needed for this entire transformation. By the time Augustine appeared, the structure was almost finished: only the temporal scaffolding of secular authority waited to be removed. This happened none too soon. As Augustine lay dying in Hippo, the Vandals were already fighting at the gates of his city; and, as a contemporary observer remarked, the screams of those dying in battle were mingled with the shouts of the undisturbed crowd in the arena. All the disorders that Cyprian had enlarged on in his address to Demetrianus had now become unevadable realities: society was in retreat, and in anticipating the worst long before, the Christians had achieved a power to face the worst when it finally came. Only those capable of renunciation and sacrifice could take a positive attitude toward what the future held. Only undivided men, at one with themselves and their God, could carry such heavy burdens.

6: From Personality to Community

As revealed in the Gospels, Christianity stands for a simplification of life: almost for a complete unraveling of the whole web of social relations. I have tried to show the social need for this radical re-affirmation of the person. When a society is hopelessly corrupt and incapable of reforming its institutions, it is the individual who must first be saved: saved by escaping the meshes of his society and becoming part of a new community in which his life-needs are respected and satisfied.

But the community that is so formed does not exist in a platonic heaven: through the processes of growth and change it becomes subject to the same temptations, the same corruptions, as those against which it revolted. From the standpoint of Jesus's teachings, no small part of the history of the Christian Church was a story of compromise and subterfuge, of misinterpretation and misdirection: a feast for the cynical, in all its impurity. But is pure Christianity possible? Let us have the courage to question the very notion of ideological purity in the development of any human institution.

Only at the moment of formulation is an idea its very self: then it has the clarity of a Platonic form, the property of one illumined mind: a metaphysical and logical whole. But to survive, the idea must adapt itself to an impure medium, the medium of life: otherwise it is doomed to sterility. If it imparts form to new institutions, it will also in turn be deformed by existing institutions which are still strong: so the absolutism of the Czars, the ruthlessness of Ivan the Terrible, the stubborn zeal of Peter the Great, and the tedious obstructionism of a graded imperial bureaucracy all entered into the Soviet revolution and modified the original ideas of Marx and Lenin: modified them, but also enabled them, in a different fashion, to survive. Those who expected to see Utopia in Russia were disappointed; but those who expected to see Czarism and capitalism return were also disappointed.

People who do not understand the nature of this process tend either to despise ideas, because they cannot recognize their presence and their functioning in the institution affected by them, or they despise the mundane world, because in the process of vulgarizing an idea it inevitably warps it. The first was the mistake of Spengler and those who like to call themselves realists in politics: the second is the error of ideologues, who cannot bear to look their idea in the face once it has been toughened and tarnished by contact with the actual world. But the materialist and the idealist are polar figures: they stand at opposite ends of the historic process and are united by it. Ideas do not become formative till they strike root in society: until, as we say in English, they "materialize." That materialization is inevitably both a betrayal and a fulfillment.

Religions are never simply the expression of disembodied ideas: they require the aid of men, who must be sheltered and fed, and they work through human figures, images, symbols, buildings, which require an ever more elaborate material apparatus to express their growing complexity and exhaustiveness. Vital knowledge can never be fully covered in words: to know the doctrine one must live the life, and to live the life one must create a background, with fixtures, furniture, properties, that will enhance every act and meaning. The Christian super-ego was esthetic as well as moral: it affected costume and legal codes as well as moral choices. Through all these agents and processes, the original seed-idea became modified and brought forth unexpected fruit: bitter fruit and sweet fruit, rusted fruit and bright. Who that heard the Sermon on the Mount could have predicted the pious cruelty of the Inquisition—or the glories of the Cathedral of Chartres?

In this whole socializing process there lies a snare. Jesus himself was perhaps the first in the Western World to be fully conscious of it, though again Lao-tse in China anticipated him. To survive in a community an idea must, I have said, rely upon the external supports of new habits, disciplines, laws, buildings: it must take shape in domestic relations and political organizations. The cross reminds the believer of Christ's cosmic agony; the Eucharist recalls a sacred fellowship; the dark interior of the new Syrian or Romanesque Churches gives a spatial expression to the Christian feeling of withdrawnness, unity, inward concentration. Not until all these expressions are achieved, does the Christian community become a reality. But there is a drawback: all these envelopments of the idea tend more and more to conceal the original kernel: the outer form displaces the inner conviction.

Therefore, if the original idea that has been incorporated and embodied in the community's life is itself to remain alive, there must be a perpetual going back to its original sources, and an equal capacity to anticipate and formulate new experiences which will enable further growth to take place. The first step is relatively easier than the second. Hence every attempt to throw off the corruptions of the Christian Church, from Manicheeism to Quakerism, goes back to the New Testament and attempts to re-establish the purity of the original inspiration: to touch Jesus without accepting all the intermediary steps of social organization. In the beginning is the word; and next to it comes the personality that lived the word and demonstrated its total meaning. Without a perpetual recovery of Jesus, in later terms, by a Paul, an Augustine, a Bernard, a Francis, a Loyola, a Calvin, a Fox, a Grundtvig, a Canon Barnett, a van Gogh, the truth of the original incarnation would have been lost. Each of these figures was less than Jesus; yet by his response to new stimuli, new pressures, new challenges, he reformulated the truths of Christianity in a manner that re-opened a path to the future.

Let us sum up this hard truth. Every formative idea, in the act of prolonging its existence, tends to kill the original living spirit that brought it forth. And yet, without undergoing this transformation and extension, the idea would have remained inoperative and self-enclosed. In this perpetual tension between the life-forming impulses within the self, which are the source of creative social developments, and the fulfillment of the idea in life and practice, in the processes of community, lies the very kernel of history. Both processes are necessary, and both harbor danger.

Materialization and etherealization are the inhalation and exhalation of the same breath: when there is social health, both processes are rhythmically at work. All our material activities become significant for life only if they take form in the mind as an independent reality: in that act of taking form, they shrink to the outer senses and expand in the world of meaning: they may even, as Arnold Toynbee points out in his discussion of etherealization, become actually smaller in bulk and more refined in their operation. Similarly, our ideal activities matter because, in their ultimate issue, they touch every process of life and condition even our animal existence, our very health and efficiency.

All this bears on our immediate argument. One cannot criticize the Christian Church because it did not retain the primitive purity of the original brotherhood, any more than one can criticize an adolescent for not retaining the features of a baby: once born into the world an idea has an independent life, apart from the hopes and intentions of the parent. By the same token, one cannot reproach Jesus for not having devised the monastic community or for not having drawn up a detailed code of Christian law. The Church was not a foreign excrescence any more than Jesus himself, in relation to the Church, was a supernumerary. These observations have a wider province than the history of Christianity.

7: What is a Christian?

The naïve answer to the question, What is a Christian? is that he is a person who follows Jesus Christ in the spirit. But it was much easier to follow him in the well-worn rut of the mystery religions; "If thou shalt confess with thy mouth the Lord Jesus," says Paul in his Epistle to the Romans, "and shalt believe in thine heart that God has raised him from the dead, thou shalt be saved." For those incapable of understanding Christ's life, his death offered the simpler, if more superstitious, approach.

Around the beginning of the fourth century the formal answer was worked out, first in the Nicene creed (325) and then in the Athanasian creed, which reconciled the views of Alexandria and Rome. In these terms, a Christian was one who believed in the historic myth of the annunciation, the passion, the resurrection, and the last judgment: one who was received into a body of the faithful by the rite of baptism, and was from time to time confirmed in fellowship by the rite of communion: partaking of bread and wine as the symbol of the body and blood of Christ. Porphyry, a vegetarian, was horrified at this doctrine; but he could hardly know, as modern anthropological studies explain, that it was the survival of more primitive ceremonies in which the representative of the god was actually eaten, in order to partake of his divinity and his strength. Such mysteries, carrying man back to buried parts of his past, have a power perhaps to evoke latent elements that still swim, like blind eyeless fish, in the deepest waters of the unconscious.

But Christianity was not merely a formal belief: it was a rigid way of life, marked by none of the mobile sallies and freedoms that Jesus had shown. To be a Christian was to place before all the positive goods of the classic order a negative sign.

The Christian way of life involved a retreat from the world and a perpetual humiliation of the body. Jesus's organic affirmations were turned by Paul into a dualistic principle of denial, which abased the body and glorified the spirit: and Paul, not Jesus, became the model Christian. First of all, the body must be covered up. The easy indiscriminate nakedness of the public baths was a constant menace to the faithful, according to one Father of the Church after the other. To reduce sexual desire, the avenues of visual excitement must be closed by decent dress and habits of personal privacy. If the Pope still from time to time issues exordiums on the subject of womanly modesty in dress, he is only carrying on one of the most ancient traditions of the Church. Other incitements to lust must also be lessened: women must refrain from rouging, painting, perfuming, coloring blue pouches under their eyes to make it seem that they had enjoyed a passionate night with their lovers. Even in the fifth century the campaign against the feminine coquetry of cosmetics continued.

Fasting was another means of subduing the flesh. While there were pagan philosophers like Seneca and Plotinus who advocated it, fasting became a duty for the Christian. Abstinence in eating and drinking made the path to heaven smoother. The hermits of Alexandria, who lived on pulse and water, only carried to extreme the duty of all devout Christians. Naturally, sexual abstention was considered all-important. Continence became a supreme virtue, and virginity passed for the ideal state; indeed, in the first zeal of his conversion, Tertullian even tried to prove that marriage itself is little better than outright fornication. The married, Paul said, strive to please each other; whereas the solitary individual seeks to serve God; but he grudgingly admitted that it was better to marry than to burn, without perhaps seeing to what a low state he thereby consigned marriage.

Finally, the Christian is one who escapes from the dominion of time: eternity lies before him. If he exhibits a power to endure evil that would drive a pagan to suicide, it is partly because he has already committed suicide in slow degrees by cutting himself off from the world and by focusing all his thoughts on eternity. Long-sufferingness, patience, endurance of evil became the true mark of the Christian; and no one can say that a more fitting psychological adaptation could have been made to the world he confronted. That which cannot be cured must be endured, says an old proverb; and the Christian found the world about him incurable. What would require centuries of strenuous effort to reform in society, could be corrected overnight within the soul of the convert. "Accept," says Cyprian, "what is felt before it is spoken, what has not been accumulated with tardy painstaking during the lapse of years, but has been inhaled by the breath of ripening grace." That change marked the Christian: inner control became a substitute for outer direction.

Within the Church, then, the Christian worked out a new drama: preparation for death as the essential way of life. Socrates had said that this was the task of the philosopher: now it became the practice of all Christian believers. Christ's life became in the new eschatology a symbolic pageant of Death, centering more and more on the Road to Calvary, on the Crucifixion, and on the Resurrection. "Even in peace," Tertullian pointed out, "soldiers inure themselves to war by toils and inconveniences. . . . In like manner, O blessed, count whatever is hard in this life of yours as a discipline of your power of mind and body." So the Christian was most at home by the sickbed and in the prison. "Evil, pain, and death," according to Lactantius, "earn one the reward of immortality."

In this process, the Christian Church itself replaced the promised Kingdom of the Lord. As Troeltsch remarks, "Even in the Apostolic Age, the idea of the Kingdom of God became merged with that of the Church, and the idea of the coming of the Kingdom was replaced by the exaltation of the Church. . . . Otherwise the Kingdom of God was replaced by 'eschatology,' Heaven, Hell, and Purgatory, immortality and the future life, a contrast with the teaching of the gospel, which is of the highest significance. But even the 'final end' was deferred, until at last the Thousand Year Reign of Christ was applied to the Church."

We may now answer our original question. The Christian is a person who rejects the usages of a dying society, and finds a new life for himself in the Church. He overcomes the local forces of dissociation and disintegration by attaching himself to a universal society. He builds his life around the themes of rejection and succorance; and he balances all his temporal difficulties against the hope of a divine justice that will punish his oppressors and give him a share in eternal glories. When Christianity came to be defined in these terms, it should have been apparent that Jesus of Nazareth was the first heretic.

CHAPTER III. THE STRATEGY OF RETREAT

1: Paganism at the Crossroads

Not easily did classic man accept the cleansing baptism of Christianity. If the new creed attracted him by asking him to give up evils he had come to hate, it also demanded that he give up goods he still properly valued. He could not bring himself to strip his life so bare. But it was these very possessions that kept Roman society from renewing itself—or rather, not the possessions as such, but the Roman's inordinate love for them, his reluctance to part with any of them.

Between the second and the sixth century a long debate went on within the Roman soul. The divided man, torn by social and personal conflicts, haunted by doubts and uncertainties, lost the energy that goes with unity. In the process of general disintegration, the various organs of society ceased to support each other and the over-all pattern of life became meaningless. Result: a breakdown in stable forms of behavior, with a defiance of law, an evasion of common morality, rising outbreaks of violence and criminality. Out of all this came a steady loss of communion: the different social groups no longer understood one another or trusted one another: class conflict was no longer held in check by any common underlying purposes. Finally, schism in the soul became manifest: a sick vacillating between alternative beliefs and incompatible lines of conduct.

All these sinister phenomena were the inevitable penalties of Rome's failure of creativeness: a failure that carried back to Hellas itself. In time, even the hand lost its cunning and the tongue its skill: when the Arch of Constantine was built, there were not enough good stone carvers left to carry through the ornamentation, and the Arch of Trajan was pillaged of its figures to build into the "new" work.

The point to note is that the victory of Christianity in the fourth century was not the submission of a minority of die-hard Romans to an overwhelming majority of Christians: it was rather the capitulation of a confused, self-distrustful, greedy, superstitious, defeatist majority to an organized minority that knew its own mind and shrank from no public effort and no private hardship in executing its will. The same spirit the Christians showed in establishing the Church might have enabled the Romans to save the State and renew the social order. But the upholders of classic culture knew only how to fight a delaying action: they were incapable of inventing the strategy for a new campaign.

2: An Autumn Day in Ostia

All the poignant conflicts between the old classic and the new Christian culture are summed up in a dialogue that seems to date from the third century A.D.: the Octavius of Minucius Felix. This is perhaps the most charming work in the whole library of Christian apologetics. The writer describes a long, acrimonious discussion that takes place, one autumn day, as he and his Christian friend, Octavius, and their pagan companion, Caecilius, walk along the Tiber from Rome to the seaport of Ostia. Minucius Felix evokes the atmosphere of that walk with such skill that the centuries fall away: one sees the gently rippling waves "smoothing the outside sands," the hulks of the boats lying about at low tide, and the figures of Roman boys, eagerly gesticulating by the sea-shore, skipping shells over the water. But through the soft autumnal sunlight sounds the rasp of argument: it begins when Octavius denounces Caecilius's salute to the image of Serapis.

For all his literary skill, Minucius is too earnest to keep the conversation on the level of his descriptive prologue or to give it the smooth felicity of one of Lucian's classic dialogues: this conversation is a series of fierce harangues, exhortations, sermons: neither side pulls his punches or seeks merely to parry the other's blows. On the contrary: Caecilius is as didactic as Octavius and as hot in his replies: the Christians have gotten under his skin, and he has the educated Roman's snobbish pain over the fact that "certain persons—and these unskilled in learning, strangers to literature, without knowledge even of sordid arts—should dare to determine on any certainty concerning nature at large, and the majesty, on which so many of the multitudes of sects in all ages have disputed and philosophy itself deliberates still. . . . Things which are uncertain ought to be left as they are."

"Where," demands Caecilius, "is that God who is able to help you when you come to life again, since he cannot help you while you are in this life? Do not the Romans without any help from your God, govern, reign, have the enjoyment of the whole world, and have dominion over you? But you, in the meantime, in suspense and anxiety, are abstaining from respectable enjoyments. You do not visit exhibitions; you have no concern with public plays; you reject the public banquets; and abhor the sacred contests. . . . Thus you stand in dread of the gods whom you deny. You do not wreath your heads with flowers; you do not grace your bodies with odors; you reserve unguents for funeral rites; you even refuse garlands to your sepulchers. . . . Thus, wretched as you are, you neither rise again, nor do you live in the meanwhile. Therefore, if you have any wisdom or modesty, cease from prying into the regions of the sky and the destiny and secrets of the world: it is sufficient to look before your feet, especially for the untaught, uncultivated, boorish, rustic people: they, who have no capacity for understanding civil matters, are much more denied the ability to discuss the divine."

Octavius of course replies in kind: he explores every weakness of the pagan philosophy and exhibits an unyielding confidence, which is almost insolence, and certainly pride, in the Christian certitudes. This dialogue surely sums up the substance of a thousand conversations between husband and wife, between teacher and pupil, between master and slave, between friend and friend during the whole painful period of transition. Finally, Octavius even denounces Socrates as an Athenian buffoon, who confessed that he knew nothing. His contempt for the philosophers is unbounded. Let "all the multitude of Academic philosophers deliberate; let Simonides also forever put off the decision of his opinion. We despise the bent brows of the philosophers, whom we know to be corrupters and adulterers and tyrants, and ever eloquent against their own vices. We who bear wisdom, not in our dress but in our mind, we do not speak great things but we live them; we boast we have attained what they sought with the utmost eagerness and have not been able to find."

By any intellectual criterion, Caecilius has the better of the argument; for if Roman polytheism had reached the last limits of petrified absurdity, Christian apologetics, which argued glibly on matters where Aristotle and Plato had arrived at sounder judgments, was often bumptiously self-confident, and proud of its very limitations. Not until Thomas Aquinas did theology generously acknowledge the wisdom of pre-Christian philosophy or accept its help in ironing out insoluble contradictions and in disposing of superstitious relics. But despite Caecilius's intelligence and dialectic skill, he is finally vanquished: the points at issue could not be decided by reference solely to intellectual values; and in actual life, Octavius holds the moral advantage. Suddenly, Caecilius's boasts begin to ring hollow in his own ears: it is the past he is praising, not the indefensible, unpraiseworthy present. With a suddenness that parallels Paul's conversion, Caecilius's defenses crumble and he becomes a glad convert to Christianity. This is not just a literary happy ending: it symbolizes an actual transformation.

This abrupt flight from reason to faith, from an overladen past to a pinched and threadbare future, took place in every quarter of society. "Saying good-by to Roman pride and Attic pedantry," Tatian defiantly announced, "I laid hold of our barbarian philosophy." Logic and prudence might be against the Christian's argument; but somehow life was on his side. No other creed was humble enough to lay its foundations among the buried hopes, fears, and desires of the masses; no other creed was willing to give the poor and the humble a parity with the rich and the wise and the proud. Christianity tunneled underground to a region where faith, not reason, where hope, not scientific demonstration, were established: in the catacombs of the personality it not only buried the dead but assembled the living. Christian faith prevailed, not because the Christians had better reason than the pagans to hope for a renewed world, but precisely because their unbounded hopes defied reason. As Paul had said, God chose "Things which are not, to bring to nought things that are." Only those who believed in the impossible were prepared to carry on in this dying society. It was the realists who did not understand reality.

3: "Sauve Qui Peut!"

Toward the end of the fourth century A.D. the Roman world lay dying. Death was in the air: never more visible than when the old Roman families painfully pretended to keep alive their ancient ways, as though by rouging the face of a corpse they could bring it back to life. The letters that these families exchanged, their pious excursions into archaeology, their allusions to Cicero and even Plato, had become purely decorative: a senile grimace before a cracked mirror. Death was in the air, though the Column of Trajan still towered upward in the sunlight of the Forum and the crowds in the Hippodrome still roared with pleasure.

The specters people fancied they witnessed with their eyes were only too real: they were the projections of their tortured souls. But those whose souls were dead still saw nothing, and therefore had no premonition of the terrible changes that were in store.

Between Tertullian at the beginning of the third century and Cyprian scarcely more than a generation later, there had come a sharp change in the political climate. Tertullian still boasted of the increase of Rome's population and wealth; Cyprian asserted, on the contrary, that Rome was dying of iniquity and the disorders of old age. Events presently confirmed the darker intuition. After all, a predatory economy cannot last forever. The very success of the *Pax Romana* actually cut down the number of slaves who came to market. Meanwhile the forests around the Mediterranean and the Adriatic had been mined, because wood was used for fuel on a large scale as well as for building: long ago George Perkins Marsh, in The Earth and Man, pointed out the effect of the ensuing soil erosion on classic agriculture. Swamps, no longer drained, formed a breeding ground for the mosquito, carrier of malaria.

Overburdened by their debts, the independent farmers who had once made Rome great turned their bodies over to their creditors, or sought relief by serving as colonni or serfs on the big estates: they bartered freedom for security. Desperate peasants, hopeless of getting a living off the soil, wandered around Gaul in the fourth century, Spain in the fifth century. Roman manorialism, brutal as ever, over-reached itself: Salvianus mentions that many poor peasants preferred to migrate to the domains of a Gothic chief, rather than stay on those of a Roman proprietor: the outlander was more humane.

The predatory economy of Rome no longer had either the self-confidence or the discipline to extend its conquests. Parasitism had continued steadily to eat into the Roman vitals: the blind vulture could neither seize new prey nor remove the maggots that battened on its own body. The very people who profited most from this culture were the first to evade its obligations: the patricians turned over to the conquered peoples the task of guarding the Empire; and their private affairs, particularly their private amusements, engrossed them more than their public duties. In an attempt to maintain some sort of order and public discipline, the late Empire fell back on the hereditary principle: every son must follow the calling of his father: no man might desert his hereditary post. All in vain; the very class that promoted these laws was the worst offender against them.

As early as the third century the new barbarian incursions had produced a marked effect on the character of the towns. In the days of the *Pax Romana* they were built in the open, without the protection of walls, except perhaps in the border districts. Now they were surrounded by ramparts; each town became a fortress, capable of isolated self-defense even if the army failed them. When the population crowded in for protection, space was lacking and overbuilding took place. Up to this time the aristocracy had enjoyed both their urban homes and their rural villas. Now the patricians retreated permanently to the country. When Arcadius, in 396, sought to forbid "the impious exodus to the country" he was talking to the empty air. The exodus had taken place. Eventually the cities began to suffer from depopulation; and one of the first signs of this, on the testimony of Libanius, was the cutting down of the salaries of professors at the municipal universities.

As life worsened, people deserted their posts and slipped out of their remaining duties: every man for himself: *Sauve qui peut!* In the years between 396 and 412, Honorius issued nine edicts on desertion and concealment of deserters from the army, according to Dill. Even the guilds that supplied food to Rome tried to escape their hereditary tasks. Everyone aimed at security: no one accepted responsibility.

Mark the fact that there was at first no lapse in technical facilities. The great engineering works were of a stable nature, with small need for repair and replacement; indeed, there were large-scale expenditures for public works in the fourth century, and the visible show of temples, baths, municipal universities, and monuments was never grander than in the early period of the decline. Even the Roman state postal organization, according to Dopsch, was still operating in the Kingdom of Toulouse as late as the seventh century. What was plainly lacking, long before the barbarian invasions had done their work, long before economic dislocations became serious, was an inner go. Rome's life was now an imitation of life: a mere holding on. Security was the watchword—as if life knew any other stability than through constant change, or any form of security except through a constant willingness to take risks.

In the face of this steady deterioration and regression, the Roman's belief in the "Roman way of life," the optimism of the self-centered upper classes, remained incorrigible. There would always be a Rome and the patricians would always be on top. So they said and so they thought. Rutilius Namatianus, who had witnessed the sack of Rome in 410, observed that the disaster might have been worse; at all events, the Empire would recover. Orosius, a contemporary Christian apologist, was no less sanguine: were not the plundering Goths after all fellow Christians? Indeed, the rumor that the barbarians had spared Christians in Rome accounted for a large-scale conversion of the indifferent to Christianity.

Meanwhile, at short intervals, the old landmarks fell. The blows of the barbarian conquerors only hastened the inner decay. The last Olympic Games—first instituted in 776 B.C.—were held in 394 A.D. Soon after 404 the Flavian amphitheater in Rome was closed to gladiatorial combats. Water ceased to flow in the baths of Caracalla after 537; and the last cartload of wood for heating the water had made its way into the city many years before. Even in the Eastern Empire, where the fossilization of Graeco-Roman culture checked for almost a thousand years the final processes of decay, the School of Athens was closed in 529 and the remaining philosophers were driven to Persia. One by one the old classic lamps went out; one by one the new tapers of the Church were lighted.

Naturally, a pinched, day-to-day existence continued. Patches of the old culture still survived in Gaul or the toe of Italy for many centuries. In the country manors there were even signs that might be taken for a genuine revival: Venantius Fortunatus, describing the smoke of villas arising among the pine woods and the olives, observed that, as in the century before, the great lords were restoring their country estates with new baths, stately porticoes, and fountains.

Four centuries of political tyranny, military negligence, economic rapine and helpless ideological dissolution, had preceded the symbolic Fall of Rome: four centuries more were necessary before its institutions had definitely changed their sign. These were not the dark but the dwindling ages. The scattered fragments of the Western Empire were like a needy genteel family trying to live on its capital. No matter how it scrimps, every year finds it poorer.

In Byzantium, the old life held its own in a fantastic combination with the new Christian forms. One can tell from the sensual melancholy of the faces in the Byzantine mosaics that one is witnessing an exquisite corruption in which extreme sophistication blends with extreme naïveté. But the great Code of Justinian and the Greek Anthology were the monuments of a non-renewing creativity. For the life of man, the continuation of the Eastern Empire proved less rewarding than the disruption of the Western Empire.

In Arabia, the Judaeo-Hellenistic-Syriac culture escaped the perils of retreat and fossilization: indeed in the seventh century it underwent a sudden renascence. The formative ideas of Magian culture, incarnated in Mahomet, made available fresh energies in art, politics, and thought: proof that the actual Christian avenue of escape was not the only exit available from this dying society. At first, the religion of Islam seemed so similar to the Christian that many contemporaries regarded it merely as a new heresy: it was here that the composite world culture of the earlier epoch finally took positive form. If one judged the relative merits of Islamism and Christianity solely by their immediate political and cultural results, it should be plain that Islam proved far more effective in saving and re-invigorating this corrupt society than did Christianity. But in the long run, the Christian idolum covered a larger area of human life.

4: The Mood of Withdrawal

By the fifth century, life had become a swamp; through its oozy bottom a few springs gurgled into the mud. Christianity dammed the outlets and created a lake: the water no longer flowed but it deepened. In time, the reservoir rose sufficiently to create a head at the dam, which could be used for power and irrigation.

Some such figure was not indeed remote from Christian minds. "We often see water," observed Gregory of Nyssa, "contained in a pipe, bursting upwards through this constraining force, which will not let it leak, and this in spite of its natural gravitation: in the same way the mind of man, enclosed in the compact channel of an habitual continence, and not having any side issues, will be raised by virtue of its natural powers of motion to an exalted love." *Not having any side issues:* there lay the secret. In this restraint, in this concentration of purpose, lay the motive power eventually for a new life. We have now to watch the cleansing waters at work, pouring through the Augean stable of classic civilization.

This transformation is most compactly symbolized by the life of Paulinus of Nola, a Roman born to the patriciate, possessing immense wealth, a senator and a cultivated poet, a governor of a province and Consul before he was thirty. Such a man inherited all that the surviving classic world could offer anyone. Suddenly he disappeared, and his friends' anxious letters to him remained unanswered. After four years of silence he at length replied to the entreaties of his old friend, Ausonius, the Bordeaux professor and poet. The letter came from Spain; but the voice it carried rose from the grave. Rome was already dead for Paulinus, as it was presently to become for the world. In his monastic refuge in Spain, Paulinus had found a different light, a higher glory: the light of eternity, the glory of God. Living on scanty fare, serving as parish priest, Paulinus devoted his great fortune to ransoming prisoners. When his fortune was gone, he sold himself into slavery to ransom a widow's son.

In that story, a whole epoch is reduced to a lifetime. There is only one way now to breast the incoming tide of misfortune, and that is to dive into the threatening wave before it breaks. In this mood, patricians became Christians and Christians became hermits and monks. We can witness the general transformation of life in two great Fathers of the Church: Jerome and Augustine: the older man, the translator of the Bible into Latin, the younger one, a diligent and voluminous author, known best for his Confessions and for The City of God. Augustine's personality left an impression on the Christian mind second only to Paul's; and because of the nature of his times and his personal crisis, he left behind a turbid sediment in both dogma and conduct: predestination and puritanism both acquired from Augustine a special impetus.

5: The City of God

Augustine, a son of Numidia, was born in Tagaste: his mother, Monica, a Christian, his father a pagan. Like any other North African boy in the second half of the fourth century, he grew up in a world that was nominally Christian, but in which Christianity was still under a pagan sign, molded by the civilization it despised and opposed, every move on the chessboard determined by its opponent's original gambit. When Augustine came to write his Confessions, he was shocked by the paganism of his boyhood: he recalled his father's easygoing attitude toward the human body and remembered with disapproval the older man's delight that day at the Baths when he first noticed the new growth of hair about the adolescent's genitals. Even in Rome girls married at fourteen at this period; and in the sultry atmosphere of an African town, sexual passion and carnal knowledge had every opportunity. Augustine's body ripened early; and despite his balkiness over learning Greek, his mind quickly followed.

In Augustine's works one still feels the tempered edge of almost a thousand years of Greek dialectic. But classic learning had now ceased to be organic and vivid: all its original perceptions had become dim, embellished with glosses that made it even dimmer. After Augustine became a lecturer and a teacher of rhetoric, he reached the high point in his secular career when he was called upon, in Milan, to deliver a public eulogy of the reigning emperor. Once an honest piece of Latin eloquence, in celebration of the great deeds of great men, the oration had now become as hollow as anything else in the Empire: Augustine's fulsome words sang the praises of a mere boy, a nincompoop, who had done nothing. On reflection, the clever young professor became nauseated over his self-betrayal.

Intellectual curiosity drew Augustine toward Manicheeism: perhaps its flagrant metaphysical dualism made it specially attractive to a young man whose mind flew to the ethereal realms of the neoplatonists while his body still inconveniently hankered after the flesh. Even when he had become a full-fledged Christian, Augustine continued, on his own sad admission, to be haunted in his dreams by unchaste delights. But Augustine was too healthy ever to share bat-eyed Plotinus's contempt for physical needs; and no one could have expressed himself in the hot, vibrant words that Augustine used to address God in his Confessions, who had not known the yearning, the madness, the ecstasy of full-blown sexual love. Augustine's whole theology bears the visible scars of his battles with himself: he was no Paul. And the vein of morbid over-scrupulousness which Augustine reinforced in Christianity had its origin in his own self-chastisement: he never dared relax his grip, nor could he sit at ease in the company of publicans and sinners.

Augustine's conversion to Christianity had devious personal roots: not merely did it answer all his spiritual demands, but it enabled him to regain his mother: by embracing Christianity he became fully restored to her own aching bosom. In turn, he transferred his mother-fixation to the Church. But his conversion, for all that, was an heroic step for a man to take at the height of his sexual and intellectual powers: it called for a double renunciation. His ruthlessness toward his mistress, who was mother of his children, reveals the force demanded by the conquest: this separation was a black episode in his life which reveals both a lack of sympathy for her who had shared his life and a lack of self-understanding. No wonder that the books Augustine wrote in late maturity still throb with his earlier passions: even in translation one cannot help feeling the violence and tumult of his heart, pounding through the strong rhythms and transmuted into majestic rhetoric: the wild eye and the snorting nostril of the stallion in heat, on the other side of the fence that will forever separate him from his mare. Is it altogether an accident that evil, for Augustine, was no positive force, but a deprivation or absence of the good?

As one might uncharitably anticipate in a believer who began his life as a heretic, Augustine became the arch-opponent of heresy: the Donatists, the Pelagians, above all the Manichees, his own original tribe, were to fall before his impetuous attacks. Much of what we know about the doctrines of the Manichees comes from the treatise in which Augustine attacked them. From the end of the third century the Manichees stood forth as formidable rivals to the Christians. Their founder, Mani, accepted Christianity but considered Christ only a phantasm whose mission had been to proclaim the arrival of the real God, Mani himself: a Persian prophet who, daring too much, was finally executed.

Mani carried Persian dualism to its logical conclusion: he separated heaven completely from the world and the soul completely from the body. Everything that belonged to the earth was by that fact evil. Hence, according to Alexander of Nycopolis, "because (they believe) it is the divine will and decree that matter should perish, they abstain from those things which have life and feed on vegetation and everything which is void of sense. They abstain also from marriage and the rites of Venus, and the procreation of children."

At every point, the Manichees outbid the Christians in their contempt for the world, the flesh, and the devil: their standards of purity, at least for the elect, were absolute ones, and their habits of observance seem to have been steadier. What little evidence remains gives us ground for believing that many Manichees actually practiced what the Christians preached. But this is not to justify Augustine's original faith. For the Christians were saved by that part of their doctrine the Manichees most despised, the Old Testament, with its earthiness, dominated by a God whom the Manichees regarded as a devil. There was still enough of the organic Jewish vision left in Christianity for the most ascetic saint to remember that the earth is the Lord's and the fullness thereof. So Christianity remained on the side of natural existence: its Pauline rejection of the world was never complete, because through Jesus it had kept its connection, so to say, with the joyous House of David. When Augustine demonstrated that the sun, the very embodiment of light, was sometimes helpful to man and sometimes baneful, he triumphed over his Manicheean opponents by plain good sense: for he demonstrated that goodness and badness are not contrasting properties of the physical world, like light and dark, sky and earth, but become so by their relation to the human spirit. In itself, the body was not bad; in itself, the soul was not good: indeed, it might be devilish.

Augustine's theology had little of the mild epicene humanitarianism of Origen, who thought that all men would finally be saved: little of the intellectual hospitality of Clement of Alexandria. It was only by a steel bit that Augustine could control his own unbridled spirit; and he fashioned a similar bit to curb the laxer spirits in the Church. Not by accident did Augustine lead the fight against British Pelagius, who had declared it was possible for Christians to live without sin. Augustine had found life otherwise. Doubtless he was right; but only one who had been violently prompted to pride and lust would have recognized it so easily in the "innocent" behavior of an infant who had scarcely left its mother's breast. Augustine's interpretation of childhood was a different one from Jesus's: but Augustine was essentially, when one allows for differences of terminology, a forerunner of Freud—or to put it more correctly, Freud was an unwitting Augustinian.

For Augustine, man was a "rational soul with a mortal and earthly body in its service. Therefore he who loves his neighbor does good partly to the man's body and partly to his soul. What benefits the body is called medicine; what benefits the soul, discipline. Medicine here includes everything that either preserves or restores bodily health. It includes, therefore, not only what belongs to the art of medical men, properly so-called, but also food and drink, clothing and shelter, and every means of covering and protection to guard our bodies against injuries and mishaps from without as well as from within." In this fine passage, Augustine ably translated the classic Greek doctrines into Christian terms. And from this time on medicine was destined to play an increasing part in the ministrations of the Christian Church: hospitals for long remained exclusively under its wing, and the merciful care of the sick, particularly those afflicted with the most loathsome infections, like leprosy, remained one of the special acts of Christian zeal. The last great expansion of Christianity, fourteen hundred years later, came through Christian missionaries carrying medicine, surgery, hygiene into the jungles of Africa and the plague-ridden villages of the East.

Apart from such ministrations, Augustine despised knowledge about the physical world; for, he said, it led its devotees to think only under material images and to have no belief but that which the bodily senses imposed: moreover they were puffed up over their little learning, and failed to acknowledge the fullness of the universe, known only to divine wisdom. The main task of the Christian, therefore, was not to deal with science, politics, the worldly life: his task was to prepare for citizenship in the City of God.

Careless writers sometimes refer to The City of God as if it were a utopia; but in fact, this book is just the opposite: an attempt to establish the proposition that, for the Christian, there is no hope for salvation in the state or in temporal society, because of the inherent character of the human condition. Augustine dwells at length on the histories of Greece and Rome to confirm his renunciation of the polis and his interest in an otherworldly state. What is hurtful, imperfect, unattainable, must be rejected if man is to find happiness; and all earthly things partake of these weaknesses, even the wisdom of the wise, which is lost by their death. Note Augustine's emphasis: it tells much about the actual state of life. "The chief good . . . must be something which cannot be lost against the will. For no one can feel confident regarding a good which he knows can be taken from him, although he wishes to keep it and cherish it. . . . How can he be happy while in such fear of losing it?" (De Moribus Ecclesiae Catholicae.) That which alone can be loved and possessed must be above all earthly corruption: perfect, immutable, all-embracing, in short—God, "absolute being, that which is." To seek God is the only fair goal for an earthly life. Thus Augustine.

By one mode of emphasis, Augustine's doctrines would lead Christianity toward a mysticism that had no need for the Church: a direct communion, a flashing encounter with deity, was possible for the truly chaste and regenerate soul. No intermediary could effect this grace of the Holy Spirit. That emphasis laid the groundwork for Luther.

But if man will never by mere political measures achieve a City of God on earth, there nevertheless remains on earth an institution that claims to transcend the limits of earthly existence through the very condition of its foundation: the Christian Church itself. Not only does the Church's history connect it directly with God, but its sacred offices identify it with God: in the sacrament of the Mass the priest actually makes God manifest in the transubstantiation of the bread and wine; and the representatives of God, the clergy, become the visible hands of the invisible Superior whose instructions they alone can properly interpret and carry out. That emphasis leads to unqualified authoritarianism. It puts the highest officers of the Church beyond human criticism and human judgment.

Pope and priest, bishop and saint, might be creatures liable to sin; but the Church, through its powers of absolution, was above sin: it possessed the keys to heaven. This was a dangerous doctrine to put into the hands of finite and fallible men. It still holds almost unlimited capacities for mischief.

There is one passage in The City of God where Augustine distinguishes between the three possible kinds of life, the active, the contemplative and the mean between. In the spirit of the Greeks, Augustine insists on the mean: "One may not be so given to contemplation that he neglects the good of his neighbor; nor so far in love with action that he forgets divine speculation." But it followed from his doctrine of the highest good that the contemplative life was, after all, the ultimate choice for man: how else could one behold God? Augustine contrasts the lot of Martha and Mary: the first clings to the present, the second to the future: the first to the laborious, the second to the quiet: the first to the troublous, the second to the happy: Martha to the temporal, Mary to the eternal.

The *future*, the *quiet*, the *happy*, the *eternal*—these states had come to represent the highest condition of man. They were the final goals of human existence, for the sake of which people would gladly forfeit every other opening or opportunity. The past was a bucket of ashes; the present was the groan of a woman in travail bringing forth a dead baby. Augustine spoke of peace, repeatedly, as if it were an unconditioned and absolute good. In that error he recorded the exacerbated nerves of his generation and age. They wanted peace as a sick man driven frantic by the sound of a vacuum cleaner wants silence.

In treating peace as an absolute, Augustine went back on his own better judgment. For in a healthier mood, he had described the world's course as "like a fair poem, more gracious by antithetic figures": a dim reflection of Heraclitus's philosophy. But by now strife had become intolerable and world-weariness had become universal. Peace, even at the expense of truth and justice, was the indispensable attribute of salvation and its greatest reward. Augustine sounded the final retreat.

6: The Organization of Retreat

The days of the early Christian martyrs and saints were over. Now the persecuted would become the persecutors: woe to the heretic! woe to the unbeliever! But meanwhile a new type of martyrdom appeared, self-inflicted, chosen so as to make the mood of withdrawal prevail. Already the new life had carved a shape for itself at the edge of the Egyptian desert, beyond Thebes and Alexandria. Once man had demanded an Empire to give scope to his ambitions; now his confidence shrivels, and he is content to hollow a cradle in the sand. From that point in space the perimeter of his vision widens to infinity: from the pattern of those vacant days, he can draw a picture of eternity. Seeking holiness, above all seeking peace, the Christian finally built a self-contained life around the themes of rejection and death.

No longer does the eye focus on the middle distance: one sees either the dirt beneath one's feet, the offal, the worms, the crawling scorpions, or one beholds a heavenly radiance in the sky. All that lies between becomes unreal, or at least delusive. The avenues of the senses must be closed. Even indirect passages to worldly existence must be barred: it is only a little while before Gregory the Great will reproach Desiderius, Bishop of Vienne, because he has expounded grammar to certain friends. "Regard everything as poison," warns Jerome, "which bears within it the seed of sensual pleasure."

Fear and grief have their outlets in flight, withdrawal, cowering. In most animals these emotions lead the creature to take refuge in a hole, a cave, a thicket; frequently to reject food or animal comfort. Darkness and grief go together; for sunlight is a last affliction to those who mourn. One shuts one's eyes, one buries one's head in one's hands, draws curtains, goes abroad only at night, eats little and talks less. By making a purposive discipline of these instinctive reactions, the Christian gave them a social context and meaning. Is it strange that in the modern world those who have rejected strong emotions and fancied that life holds no humanly irreparable evils, have also lost all the primitive gestures of grief and have even thrown off the formal costume of mourning?

In withdrawing to a psychological tomb, the Christian treated himself to a second burial, reproducing a condition like that in the mother's womb, when life was in complete equilibrium and held nought beyond bare animation: silence, protection, and peace all recall that primal state of animal unity. If one is not strong enough to fight, one must be discreet enough to pass unnoticed: to lie still and sham death. Grief filled men's hearts everywhere during the long period of violence that broke out in the third century and reached its height, perhaps, in the ninth: grief at parting, grief at the brevity of life, grief over injuries to one's beloved ones, grief at the most terrible memory that haunts the refugee—the memory of happier days. It was Boëthius, himself a victim of arbitrary barbarian power, who first pronounced this kind of sorrow the worst of all, and later exiled Dante echoed him.

Algasia, a Christian lady living in Gaul, anxiously wrote to Jerome to find out what Christ meant by the terrible predictions reported in the Gospel according to Matthew: "Woe to them that are with child. . . . Pray that your flight be not in winter." She had reason to suspect that the day announced in the scripture was at hand. From the end of the fourth century on the odds against security and peace worsened; therefore security and peace were all that men desired, and they would cheerfully barter all the sweet vanities of the world to ensure the existence of even a patch of normal civil life. That would be heaven. Out of this situation issued monasticism.

Like almost everything else that came to a head then, monasticism had long been under way. What everyone felt in the fifth century the persecuted Jew had already experienced before Christ's coming: witness the Therapeutae, a Jewish sect described by Philo. "They divest themselves of their property, giving it to their relatives; then, laying aside all the cares of life, they abandon the city and take up their abode in the solitary fields and gardens, well-knowing that intercourse with persons of different character is not only unprofitable but injurious." As early as 250 A.D. the Decian persecutions had caused thousands of African Christians to seek refuge in the nearby deserts. The most famous of these early hermits was Anthony, who began to live alone on the outskirts of his village, and who kept moving further and further into the desert in order to remain alone till in 305 he reached the edge of the Red Sea.

With Pachomius, who was born in 297, an ordered routine for these withdrawn people began; and when in 386, Jerome retired to the monastery of Bethlehem, this way of life had already achieved a certain communal form and discipline. The new monastery was a House of Refuge, or, if you will, a prison. Did not Tertullian say: "The prison does the same service for the Christian which the desert did for the prophet"? The terms and the conditions were almost interchangeable: in either case, you not merely "are free from causes of offence, from temptation, from unholy reminiscence, but you are free from persecution, too."

Jerome has left us an excellent description of the primitive organization of the coenobites or monastic communities. They were divided like an army into squads of ten, with one member having authority over the other nine; and ten squads formed a hundred presided over by a single authority. They lived apart in cells, but met "after the ninth hour" to sing psalms and to read the scriptures. Inevitably there entered into this life a strain of selfish preoccupation. Jerome knew well both the outward and the inward difficulties of withdrawal.

"How often," he exclaimed, "when I was living in the desert . . . did I fancy myself among the pleasures of Rome. . . . Now, although in my fear of Hell I had consigned myself to this prison, where I had no companions but scorpions and wild beasts, I often found myself among bevies of girls. My face was pale and my frame chilled from fasting, yet my mind was throbbing with desire and the fires of lust kept bubbling before me when my flesh was as good as dead." The lion that was so often pictured at St. Jerome's side in later paintings and drawings served as a symbol of his passions, seemingly tamed, but ready to spring.

Meanwhile, Jerome gave rational justification to another side of monasticism: its withdrawal from cities. For the new monastery developed as an essentially rural retreat. Once more Western man sought in a bucolic Eden a foundation for a satisfactory life. Jerome's description is admirable.

"Seeing that we have journeyed much of our life through a troubled sea, and that our vessel has been in turn shaken by raging blasts and shattered upon treacherous reefs, let us, as soon as may be, make for the haven of rural quietude. There such country dainties as milk and household bread, and greens watered by our own hands, will supply us with coarse but harmless fare. So living, sleep will not call us away from prayer, nor satiety from reading. In summer, the shade of a tree will afford us privacy. In autumn, the quality of the air and the leaves strewn underfoot will invite us to stop and rest. In the springtime, the fields will be brightened with flowers, and our psalms will sound the sweeter for the twittering of the birds. When winter comes with its frost and snow, I shall not have to buy fuel, and whether I sleep or keep vigil, I shall be warmer than in town. . . . Let Rome keep to itself its noise and bustle, let the cruel shows of the arena go on, let the playgoers revel in the theaters."

Jerome wrote those words of parting in Rome in 385. Already, in anticipation, he had outlined the life of the early Middle Ages; he had painted a series of scenes for a Book of Hours, or a medieval calendar, following the routine of pious life through the seasons. In this little idyll he recalled Theocritus and leaped ahead to anticipate Rousseau. Much must be renounced before this life will be possible: "How can Horace go with the Psalter, Virgil with the Gospels, Cicero with the Apostle?" How, indeed, St. Jerome? But if there is any rational form for living during the next six centuries, it is mainly in the monastery that one will find it. This walled retreat would rise from the landscape, as isolated as a fortified villa or a rock-dominating castle, those symbols and agents of a rising feudalism. Here the shattered armies of civilization nursed their wounds and gathered strength.

Jerome announced Western Europe's spiritual hibernation: a long period of suspended animation, marked by darkness, torpor, and sleep. The peace of the tomb.

7: Poverty, Chastity, Obedience

The new monastic form of living sprang up everywhere, from Egypt to Ireland; but the man who gave it a firm outline was Benedict of Nursia. He had no desire to add to the clerical establishments of the Church or to found a special order for the elect. What he sought to do was to create a new kind of domestic institution *for laymen,* who wished to live as fully as possible the Christian life of renunciation. This but continued a tradition Augustine had already found in existence in Rome almost two centuries earlier: boarding houses where a group of Christian zealots would live together under a deacon.

Instead of giving up the family altogether, Benedict turned the new monastery into a collective family. Excluding all sexual relations, the brothers not merely pledged themselves to live in a common domicile, but likewise to take each other for better or worse and remain together for life. The monastery became a stable family and the abbot a patriarchal father: thus the tendency to both vagabondage and individual self-seeking was overcome, and the fear of insecurity and discontinuity—the worst of fears in a disintegrating society—was nullified.

In addition, Benedict enjoined daily labor in the fields and workshops, no less than in the chapel, the library, the scriptorium. This not merely ensured the house's survival and put the order on a self-sustaining basis, but it eased the tensions of ascetic restraint, giving balance to the whole personality. Benedict's breakdown of the classic contempt for menial labor, his combination of spiritual discipline and manual exercise, was an essential contribution to education; and the slipping away from this salutary union in the Cathedral Schools and the later universities contributed to the recurring sterility of the intellectual caste.

The industry of the Benedictines, at all levels, became proverbial. In time, pious bequests would make these Benedictine Abbeys great ground landlords; and the daily work in the extensive fields, vineyards, orchards, glassworks, and forges might call for more hands than lodged in the monastery itself: secular help would be needed and secular gains would pour in all too freely. John Wesley's later perception that Christian thrift, sobriety, and regularity would inevitably lead to worldly success, and worldly success would endanger the Christian's soul, was verified many centuries before English pietism proved it once more. But the vigor of monasticism showed its value as a social adaptation: the monasteries of

Europe formed, as Coulton pictures them, a chain of blockhouses across Europe, holding down the barbarian lands for Christianity.

Benedict collated and codified the various existing rules and carried them further. The monk who entered this new institution took the Benedictine vow: he bound himself to poverty, chastity, and obedience; and he gave himself over to a life of labor, prayer, humility, and self-denial. Economic greed, concupiscence, and pride were his everlasting enemies; though as to the first temptation and the last, what he renounced as an individual the order would eventually enjoy as a corporate body. Like Benedict himself, the monk gave up his worldly goods on entrance and accepted the communism that went with this dedicated life. He died *to* the world, not *for* the world: died so that he might, in the actual round of daily life, have a glimpse of that ineffable peace which was promised for the after-life by the sight of God.

In the Benedictine monastery, Plato's condition for the founding of an ideal commonwealth was at last met in actual life: a crisis, an able leader, a good constitution, a just division of labor, a communist economic order, and a group of guardians concerned with the eternal verities and reluctant to undertake the task of government. Those who are contemptuous of Plato's uncompromising "idealism" might ask themselves how many power states have lasted as long as the Benedictine order.

To make this death-in-life more acceptable, the monk habituated himself to a premature senility: the bald head of the aged, the grave manner, the confined circuit of movement, as if limited by lameness, characterized his appearance and his habit. Dr. Rosenstock-Huessy has suggested that this adaptation was primarily an effort to redress the lack of actual old people in this society: a lack due to the excessive shortness of human life, which gave a preponderance in numbers to the immature and thoughtless, with their high vitality and their limited experience. About the brevity of the life-span there can hardly be any doubt: famine, murder, plague, war, made their rounds with growing regularity. For this reason, monasticism may have prospered as both a social and a psychological adaptation.

"Dig and sow," said the founder of Clonfert Abbey, "that you may have the wherewithal to eat and drink and be clothed; for where sufficiency is, there is stability, and where stability is, there is religion." Not merely did the monastery provide a fixed and orderly abode: the order in space was accompanied by an equally regular order in time. Here, if nowhere else in the Western World, one could live according to plan and look ahead: here, if nowhere else, was a calculable and imaginable future.

Does this life seem constrained, uneventful, downright monotonous?

There precisely lay its attraction: a supreme attraction to harried souls that had seen too much, had been forced to make too many dreadful decisions, and had been the victims of too many exciting events. Once the novice made the final surrender, he was free from the burden of intolerable accident: once the great choice was made, all the little choices tended to themselves. One day was like another: thanks be to God! In that comforting regularity, the spirit at last became free. No small part of what has survived of the ancient world, apart from buildings and monuments, has been transmitted to us by the slow patient hands of the monastic copyists, who transferred the contents of the fragile papyrus rolls to sturdy parchment. With their animus against paganism, they doubtless winnowed out much that would be precious to us; but much, too, they let slip by—perhaps stupidly, perhaps slyly, perhaps with a calm eye to a better future.

Because of the monks' care for Roman manuscripts, due partly to Cassiodorus, Benedict's contemporary, the Roman methods of agriculture were conserved in the monasteries even after they had disappeared, through lapse of oral tradition and visible example, in the manors. As a result, the monks probably had a better balanced diet than their secular contemporaries, and this perhaps compensated for its sparseness.

The uniformity of monastic existence touched every detail. Monks were the first wearers of uniform costume in modern times: by comparison Michelangelo's uniform for the papal guards was a parvenu. More than that: regularity and order bore fruit in economic practices. In every department of work, order, repetition, standardization are great economizers of labor. These monastic habits, spreading into every part of estate management, brought their natural reward in increased wealth. Not merely is Coulton correct in describing the Benedictines as essentially the founders of capitalism, but it is equally correct to add that the business man, the bureaucrat, and the mechanical worker are all the specialized end-products of monasticism. Some of the life-denying practices of modern capitalism had their origin in the withdrawal and retreat of this early epoch.

Narrow and suffocating would be the monk's solitary cell were it not for the spacious common structure; and bleak would be his poverty were it not for this handsome exhibition of collective wealth: the individual indigence of communism was balanced by its collective magnificence. In the monastery, every activity had its place and form: the whole made an articulated organism. Contrast this with the domestic order of the feudal regime, which existed only for the lord and his lady: a little closet, a solitary private toilet high above the castle moat, plucked out of the drunken huddle and disorder of the feudal household. The monastery, as Paulinus of Nola described it, truly made an end to "all the noisy crowding up of things and whatsoever wars on the divine."

One further fact of later significance must be noted. In monastic life the equality of the sexes was first acknowledged: convents for women, no less than for men, took their place at an early date in the new order. In the convent or nunnery woman fashioned a role for herself for which the secular Church gave her no scope; she even acquired a certain skill in the political arts, in the autonomous government of the nunnery; and a great abbess, like Hroswitha of Gandersheim in the tenth century, might become a significant dramatist.

But if one emphasizes the economic and social consequences of the monk's traditional routine, because of its influence upon the Western personality, one must not forget its contemporary meaning. The main business of the monk was the praise of God, and his special activity, as monk, was beatitudinous contemplation. In their devotion to the service of God, the monks elaborated if they did not invent the mass. By a steady refinement, they created a unified whole out of the procession, the choral chant, the vocal prayers and responses of the entire congregation: all enhanced by the smell of incense, the burning of candles and lamps, the solemn familiar words, the dark high hall. . . . Even in a tawdry church today, cut off for a moment from a dusty street loud with the screech of brakes, the whine of motors, within an interior set with hideous sculptures and paintings turned out by the gross lot, even here the mass has a power of evocation that goes far beyond the beginnings of Christianity: it carries overtones of an unintelligible ritual magic that perhaps existed as early as the dawn of human speech. Long before the modern painters had explored the values of abstract art, the Church had created an abstract and depersonalized art which penetrated the recesses of human feeling far more powerfully than words and gestures better understood.

But weaknesses developed out of this life of praise and worship. In seeking to escape the sins of the world, the monks were nevertheless compelled to create another world in miniature. The walls of the monastery might be high; visitors might be infrequent; but within this sanctuary, small and narrow though it might be, the world would inexorably enter. Gregory of Nyssa believed that he who has exiled himself from human life by abstaining from marriage and treating the world as dung "has no fellowship whatever with the sins of mankind such as avarice, envy, anger, hatred"; but this belief showed an optimism that was not borne out by further experience. The sins came in: the devil's advances caught up with the monk's retreat. In the course of time, the monks even found themselves the victims of a special infirmity of their own creation, acedia, the weary indifference and laziness that spring out of a life too well-regulated, too prudently safeguarded, too nicely adjusted.

In addition, of course, the monastery and convent had to deal with the grosser insurgencies of the body, greed for food and drink, sexual lust, to say nothing of such threats to communal existence as romantic attachment to a single person. Sexual scandals already existed in Italian monasteries and convents, according to Dudden, by the end of the sixth century. We know from Jerome's much earlier admonitions that Christian virgins sometimes took potions to induce barrenness, committed abortion, and lived as professed spiritual sisters with the unmarried clergy, defending themselves against the censorious by saying, "To the pure all things are pure." The same Eve, the same Adam, espoused monastic life.

At a much later period, the time of Louis XIV, the convent was a place where the unmarried daughter was supposed to go, as an alternative to becoming a loose woman, when her chance for marriage was definitely past: by that time it served chiefly as a haven for the sexually rejected. But in the earlier days of monasticism just the opposite of this happened: many mere boys and girls were dedicated to this life by noble families, often for highly sordid reasons, without their having manifested the faintest vocation for it: they were trapped before they could express themselves. If such people remained pure, they defrauded the race; if they lost their chastity, according to the Church's code they defrauded God. But maybe in the long run their cheating served God better than the Church knew. Was it not perhaps through such sins and lapses that some of the worst biological defects of monasticism on European society were to a degree annulled? Monasticism tended to withhold some of the best human strains from reproduction. If everyone had flocked into the monasteries and if the rule had been observed to the last letter, the resulting holy society would have gone under entirely, through depopulation, precisely like the Shaker colonies of the nineteenth century.

The most serious weaknesses of monastic life were of another order. While the slow round, the even tempo, the repeating pattern of the days overcame the memories of anxiety and terror, the security thus produced was itself no final virtue: it created problems no less real than anxiety and terror. The even round, too long repeated, becomes trivial and meaningless; a prayer, said once too often, becomes a curse. The problem of spiritual re-animation was one that concerned a succession of monastic leaders: every century or two brought a new wave of reform, seeking to quicken a life whose very perfection led inevitably to corruption.

The moral insulation of monasticism raised an even more serious problem which had both a personal and a community aspect. There is a great difference between lessening one's temptations in society and removing temptation altogether by cutting oneself off from society. Virtue and vice are social attributes: they presume the existence of the biological and social functions normal to society. Withdrawal from a disintegrating society is a rational and moral step only if it is the first stage toward building up an integrated community.

The real mistake of the monastery was that it turned into a whole lifetime's vocation the normal withdrawal and retirement which should be part of the life-rhythm of every well-planned life. The complete social process, as Toynbee has amply demonstrated, is withdrawal-and-*return*: the retreat is a strategic gathering of inner forces which opens the way for an effective counter-attack. But the cloister perpetually lures men into an inner maze of dreams that become in themselves a substitute for real life: retreat begets isolationism: isolationism indifference, and indifference results in irresponsibility.

"Such being the peaceable and calm disposition of the times," wrote the Venerable Bede in the first quarter of the eighth century, "many . . . as well of the nobility as private persons, laying aside their weapons, rather incline to dedicate themselves and their children to the tonsure and monastic vows, than to study martial discipline." As a desperate cure for a desperate evil, monasticism had a valid reason for existence in the Time of Troubles that extended almost without a break from the fourth century to the eleventh: Charlemagne's great imperium proved but a passing interlude. Once this original pressure was lightened, the failure of the monastery to encompass the whole life of man became flagrant: once terror and anxiety lessened, the conditions that made Benedict's rule so successful gave way to conditions that inevitably undermined it. It remained for the Friars, and still more for the early Protestants, to bring the function of withdrawal back into the normal life of normal men.

8: Centralization of Authority

The Christian Church as a whole had a different role to play than the monasteries. Picking its way among the ruins of the old order, the Church came face to face with the barbarian.

Between the fourth and seventh centuries a succession of invasions poured over Gaul and Italy and over-ran Africa: those invasions continued at intervals until the end of the eleventh century: Saracens from the South and Norsemen from the North executed a sort of pincers movement on what was left of the old order and finally met in Sicily. With these barbarians there was no question of restoring a waning vitality:

"it is one of the advantages of all rude and exposed life," as the wise Nathaniel Shaler once wrote, ". . . that in it the man wins again his natural adjustment to life and death which he is deprived of by his super-civilization."

A crude stomach for life was exactly what the barbarians possessed: they fought for the joy of fighting and when they needed relaxation they ate and drank with gigantic appetites. They needed no circuses to animate their lust for blood; they needed no obscenities to awaken their flagging genitals: they killed and copulated out of a powerful animal desire to work their will upon appropriate human obstacles. They were hunters, pastoral nomads, fighters: their game tasted better to them when they had brought it down themselves with spear or bow, and doubtless their women tasted better when captured and conquered by sheer bodily prowess.

Some of the earlier Gothic tribes had in more than one sense been taken in by Roman civilization: they admired the pomp and beauty of the Roman cities with a sort of primitive veneration that anticipated the three stars and the heavy type of their descendants' Baedekers: the grace and culture of the South drew them away from their docile bovine women and their crude tribal ways. But although their raw animal vitality might be tempered by a pedantic respect for the culture they raped and looted, they needed a far different treatment at the hands of the Church from that of the defeated populations of the big cities. One must treat a parasitic animal to a different discipline from a predatory one: in the first case, the problem is to make him leave his host and become a self-sustaining creature again; in the second, one must reduce his crude animal vitality as a first step toward sublimating it. In order to make the barbarian accept his role in the Christian drama, the Church was forced to resort to a sort of spiritual bleeding; and its course was necessarily a zigzag one: now it threatened, now it cajoled, now it banned superstition and again it took it over bodily and gave it its own special stamp.

Fortunately, the Christian creed had one great power that eventually overcame the barbarian's contempt: it had an answer to his intellectual pessimism, which so queerly accompanied the "optimism of the body." Northern mythology, for example, foresaw a time when even Wotan would be overthrown and the universe consumed. But the Christian God was Eternal and his Heaven was Eternal Light. The new creed from the South had something of the lure of Mediterranean sunshine for the rude men of the North. If it was only a dream, it was still a pleasanter one to sleep through than his own nightmare.

Historians have occasionally talked about the barbarian invasions as if they were responsible for the invigoration and re-building of a decadent Europe by a process of purely biological regeneration. If blood were the true key to cultural change, however, there were enough barbarians within the Empire, long before its downfall, to have effected a wholesale regeneration. Biological changes no doubt continued to take place, and the wholesome effects of hybridization may have worked in the human stock; but it is next to impossible to give any rational, scientific account of them: this realm is the favorite haunt of superstition. Cultural intermixture, on the other hand, did take place through the invasions and migrations: this is a matter of plain record. Such regeneration as actually occurred can be attributed to the fresh mingling of cultures: the surviving institutions of Rome, the growing institutions of the Church, and the traditional institutions of the barbarian camps and villages formed fresh combinations which in the course of five or six centuries finally acquired an organic character.

To maintain the place it had carved out for itself, the Christian Church was forced to struggle for power as well as salvation: in the West this fact ensured the eventual primacy of the Bishop of Rome and so gave to Italy a preponderant part in the development of Western civilization. On the side of the Church were the legions of misery and despair: the oppressed whom it championed and the homeless whom it fed and sheltered. By the sixth century the offices of the Church had enfolded the greater part of life: it actually was fulfilling the mission that had been described by Augustine: "Thou shalt exercise and instruct the child with simplicity, the young strongly, gently the aged, not only according to the age of the body but also of the spirit of each. Thou shalt make women submit to their husbands not for purposes of carnal satisfaction but for the begetting of children and that, through united endeavor, the fortunes of the family may be advanced. Thou shalt place husbands before their wives, not that they may take advantage of the weaker sex, but rule with the laws of true affection. Thou shalt bind children to their parents, as in free servitude, and parents to their children by loving authority. Thou shalt tie brother to brother with the bonds of religion which is stronger even than the bonds of blood. Thou shalt teach servants to be faithful to their masters, not because their condition demands fidelity, but because in the fulfillment of duty they will find happiness. Thou shalt teach masters to be kind to their servants, remembering the Almighty who is Lord of all, and thou shalt unite the citizens of one place with those of another, nation with nation, and in general all men among themselves, and thus not only shape society but also form a fraternal alliance; thou shalt teach kings to cherish their subjects and subjects to obey their kings. Thou shalt diligently point out to whom is due honor, to whom affection, reverence, fear, consolation, admonishment, exhortation, instruction, blame or punishment, showing at the same time that not to all are all things due, but to all is due love and to none injustice."

Here was the program of the Church: the sum of its self-imposed ideals, as they touched practical and political relationships. Under the Church's traditional leadership, the traditional bread and circuses which had debauched the Roman proletariat, gave place to charity and spiritual consolation. So the basilica became the church: Caesar's rule took second place to Christ's. Law became an inward impulse toward conformity with the divine; and what was important was not the degree of the crime but the measure of repentance—not the judge's stern sentence but his merciful pardon.

The man who now lifted the Church up to a plenitude of power and enabled it to perform skillfully its mission of succor and salvage was one of the great political leaders of all time: the theologian known as the Fourth Doctor of the Latin Church, the Pope called by later ages Gregory the Great. His lasting influence on the Church was as great in the realm of politics as was that of Augustine in theology: an influence with which we must still reckon today.

Gregory was born in Rome around 540; he became prefect of the city and governor in 573. But in 574, at the height of his official career, he entered a monastery. "Those who wish to hold the fortress of contemplation must first of all train in the camp of action," Gregory once wrote: a wisdom that sprang out of his own experience. As prefect of Rome, he had had jurisdiction over all civil and criminal matters for the space of a hundred miles around the old capital: he was in charge of grain supplies, doles, the repair of aqueducts and other public works, as well as the police force and the bureaucracy. When the Lombards swarmed around the city, however, he apparently realized that life on the old terms was no longer possible, not even in shadow play. He renounced his great political office and even more decisively his great wealth. With the latter he founded monasteries, and became Abbot of Saint Andrew's in 586. When he came back to high office in Rome in 590 it was as the supreme pontiff of the Church of Rome: the only institution that could hold its own against the barbarian.

Gregory brought to the Church the pride and loyalty of the old Roman aristocrat. Under him, the Church learned to give commands. Up to the time of Augustine, the Church had been essentially a congregation of congregations: it included the whole body of believers; and the ultimate seat of sovereignty rested in the great Councils of the Church, which served as a sort of Supreme Court on matters of dogma. Even as late as Augustine the choice of the Bishop was a wholly local matter: he was the appointee of his congregations. Under Gregory, the people became supernumerary: they ceased to exercise active political functions within the Church. As local life itself became disrupted, the Church assumed what were originally the self-directive functions of the Christian community. Now the mass of Christians in the West were ruled by a self-perpetuating hierarchy, composed of bishops, priests, and minor clergy, all appointed officials bound ultimately to the Pope. The loose federal union of congregations, with shifting seats of power and authority as one great doctor or another waxed and waned, gave place to a centralized government headed by a spiritual Emperor. This was the true Holy Roman Empire, which would in time clash with its more tenuous temporal counterpart.

Not least among the Church's growing powers was the centralized control of finance: not merely did the Church claim its tithe of the annual income of all believers, but it steadily increased its holdings of land as the result of bequests from both the living and the dead, seeking to find favor in this world or in Heaven. Pope Simplicius, says Dopsch, ordained that from 465 on the income of the Church should be divided into four parts—one fourth to the bishop, another to the building of Churches, another to the maintenance of the clergy, and a final fourth to the distribution of alms to strangers and to the poor. As Rome's power dwindled, the visible presence of the Church grew; and as the bankrupt municipalities of the Empire abandoned their provisions for education and for social welfare, the Church took over their functions.

One other result followed from this centralization of power and authority. No longer were the theological leadership and ecclesiastical administration, the spiritual and the temporal functions, bound closely together. The Papacy will govern: it will bring into its ranks notable statesmen and leaders of men; but they will exercise their power mainly by their temporal characteristics, their firmness of decision, their vigilance, their skill in fencing with practical issues: politicians not saints, administrators not mystics, organizers not originators. Thenceforward the Papacy will succeed as an agent of efficient political organization, not as a repository of spiritual enlightenment. Its efficient bureaucracy and its long memory will give it an advantage over every ephemeral rival: an advantage it still possesses. Without doubt, it has proved the most successful form of government in human history; and its political constitution and organization deserve a closer study than political theorists have ever given them.

In one matter the Church had a great political superiority over the Empire it took over: it had discarded the hereditary idea for the recruitment of its officialdom no less than for the election of the Pope. No one was a Christian by birth; and no one became an officer of the Church solely by inherited claim of rank: the peasant's or the cobbler's son might become the highest officer in the Church. Though feudalism fought hard to establish succession in office by birth, Church doctrine rigorously rejected its claims and usurpations. By preserving the democratic principle here, the papacy tempered the evils of absolutism and reduced the dangers of caste and vested privilege—though nepotism might and did creep in under the surface.

Gregory's theology, according to his biographer, Dudden, "bears the legal stamp. It centers in ideas of guilt and merit, satisfaction, and penance; and by means of these it may be wholly construed. Retribution and merit are the conceptions which determine its form. God's dealing with mankind resolved into a series of legal transactions, and Christ, the Saints and angels, and the devil, all have their part in the legal process. In setting forth this scheme, of course, Gregory was but reverting to the standpoint of the old theological jurist, Tertullian, who was the first to graft onto theology the categories of law."

Gregory's final departure from the older democratic conception of the Church showed itself, too, in his transfer of the source of its ultimate sovereignty. Even in the days of the Empire, Roman philosophers and jurists traced political authority back to the people. But Gregory, by pushing sovereignty back to God, placed it out of the reach of the people and put it, in practice, in the lap of the Church, or rather, in the hands of the Pope, as God's representative on earth. The famous act of submission at Canossa centuries later marked the ultimate triumph of Gregory's conception, backed by the terrible power of decreeing exile for Eternity which the Pope wielded through the weapon of excommunication.

Under the influence of Gregory's thought, unfortunately, all governments became sacred, and all sacred duties might claim not only the spiritual authority obtained through persuasion but all the physical force that might be necessary to exact consent or enforce punishment. Even if the existing government were patently irresponsible and wicked, the fact that it came from God made its very evils only a just visitation of punishment upon the sins of the oppressed. Such a doctrine might justify anything, support anybody. And in time it was called upon to justify tyranny and to support the usurpation of popular control: right down to our own time it has been used in this fashion. Mussolini, Hitler, Franco, have all been the beneficiaries of Gregory's doctrine.

I. THE CHRISTIAN OVERWORLD

For almost a thousand years the divine figure of Jesus preoccupies the Christian imagination. From the catacombs to the later Romanesque churches the same solemn austere image presides over Christian worship. Then the medieval sense of humanity reclaims both Jesus and his Mother: the painter depicts his life in warm, human terms: his birth, his baptism, his temptations, his crucifixion.

II. MEDIEVAL LIFE

Medieval life was a pilgrimage and a crusade, a hunt and a feast, a struggle and a tournament. Up to the 13th century, its dominating figures are the priests and monks, representatives of eternal values, and the warrior nobles, who exercise military power and temporal authority. Close to the foundations of this life lie the primitive occupations: picking and gleaning, hunting and fishing. Its feudal chiefs remain primarily hunters and fishermen (Vikings), people used to killing savage boars and stags, to confronting storm and shipwreck, to imposing their wills upon weaker men. Often this life descends to piracy and brigandage; but sometimes it rises to the Truce of God, or to the manly chivalry celebrated in Chevy Chase. Sassetta's Journey of the Magi (*top*) might equally be Chaucer's Canterbury Pilgrims: still in search of at least the relics of divinity. By the 13th century new urban forces modify this life: behind the city's walls the protective guild economy arises, founded on the crafts of woodman and shepherd, carpenter and weaver, with their ordered routine and tranquil ritual. The image of the Holy Family dominates the mind: above all, the Virgin Mother. Charonton's The Triumph of the Virgin consummately brings together all the aspects of medieval life and mind, actual and ideal. The bottom illustration is a fragment from the larger work whose central theme is shown above. Note the figures of the damned beneath the medieval city: Hell was as visible as Heaven. Henry Adams's interpretation of the Virgin cult, both in his Mont St. Michel and Chartres and in his The Education of Henry Adams, showed true insight. The centering of religious feeling on woman and the function of motherhood restored a balance that had been upset by the Church's original defensive response to Rome's sexual dissipation. This mothering impulse found an outlet in the creation of guilds, hospitals, asylums, and other protective institutions.

This Latin "realism" of Gregory's was responsible, not merely for condoning tyranny, but for incorporating superstition. Gregory made many compromises with barbarian habits and beliefs, and opened the way to further corruptions. Harnack points out that Gregory "united the hitherto uncertain thoughts regarding the intercession of the saints and the service of the angels. . . . He legitimized the pagan superstition which had need of demi-gods and graded deities, had recourse to the holy bodies of the martyrs, and joined the service of Christ with that of the saints." Thus, under Gregory, the cult of the saints closed the awful gap between man and God: the saints were friends at court who interceded at the right moment with the judge; they were messengers, go-betweens, who used their influence to swerve justice out of its path, or at least saw to it that the sentence was shortened and an eventual pardon granted. Nothing could be farther from Jesus's secret.

Yet Gregory's establishment of a strong system of Church government and administration, his creation of an authoritative political center, was no small contribution to stability at a time when stability meant survival. This system reached its climax in the eleventh and twelfth centuries when the doctrines and processes of Canon Law put all the officers of the Western Church under an independent ecclesiastical jurisdiction.

Meanwhile, wherever the barbarians upset Roman order a quite opposite process took place: a hundred different legal codes came to compete with each other: tribal codes that had never been subject to rigorous philosophic appraisal, to experimental probation, to the refinement of progressive decisions under skilled lawyers and judges. These new codes multiplied, and in addition, unwritten custom took the place of absent laws on the almost self-sufficient manorial domains. The centralization and unification of spiritual society went hand in hand with the breakdown and increasing subdivision of temporal authority, which achieved its final form in the feudal system.

As men became more illiterate, they relied on use and wont, what they called immemorial custom, to guide them. Arbitrary rules, made in the local manor court, might become such immemorial customs within a generation or two, when the mind of man "runneth not to the contrary." How many people today realize that the British custom of afternoon tea, which now seems as old as Anne, did not actually become prevalent till the eighteen-seventies, or that the New England custom of Thanksgiving Day did not become a national holiday in the United States till about the same time? The collapse of civil standardizations and uniformities took place in every department of life during the Dark Ages: in coinages, weights, measures, market rules, and above all, in languages. The Christian

Church in the West alone preserved the memory of a unity and provided the framework for universal intercourse and a wider common life. Out of a wedding of the universal and the local the Middle Ages were finally born.

9: The Domination of Fantasy

The past was a faded dream: the present a nightmare: the future a golden illusion. In that subjective atmosphere the Christian personality formed itself and spread its way of life over the greater part of Europe.

For at least half a millennium daily life was ruled less by intelligence than by habit. The best one could hope for was that today would be like yesterday and tomorrow like today. To remember the customs of the past was to know the rules for the present. Even irrational practices will wear the appearance of reason if one continues them long enough, and illusions will dominate reality if everyone participates in the same hallucinations at the same time. Yet invention and ordered intelligence were not altogether excluded from this life, even at its lowest level: water mills became more common and the tide-mill was invented, the horse-shoe came into general use, a correct harness for horses, which put the load against the chest, was finally devised, the folding camp-stool was in use as early as the time of Charlemagne, and steam was even used to pump an organ—the invention of Pope Sylvester II. The "rise of chivalry" is only a poetic paraphrase for the "increase of horsepower."

Nevertheless, life was hard, oppressive, difficult: provision for bare physical survival became all-important. When the time for spring plowing comes, even the animals, half starved through the winter, will hardly have enough strength for the task; half a dozen oxen may be necessary to make the plow cleave the shallow topsoil. To make the stock of salt meats, barley, or rye last through the winter required ingenuity; few were rich enough to escape the need for parsimony, for the richer one was, the bigger the number of household dependents. A stunted life: many underfed bodies, many undernourished minds. If anyone lives well outside the monasteries, it is the hunter-warrior who adds to the trophies of the hunt the dues of the peasants he protects.

Animal hardships alternating with a muzzy, dreamful routine: this made up the sentient existence of Romanesque man. All his dominating institutions, monasticism, manorialism, Christian dogma, bore the sign of his period—protection. It was more important that there should be some continuity than that there should be rational criticism of the habits and values continued. Every hour lived in peace was a gain. To widen the span between birth and death, to punctuate the grievous days with repetitious tasks, to live like one's ancestors, obeying one's overlord and the priest, to look no farther than the close horizon, to remember Christ in one's prayers and always to make the sign of the cross against demons and magicians, to stand by one's neighbor in his trouble and to know that trouble is never far away, to keep one's station and be contented with one's lot—here was the essence of this life. Monk, warrior, noble, peasant, nun, lady, and householder lived every moment of their lives surrounded by visible and invisible walls. So much for the outward manifestations. Immobilized in ritual, it is still the essential life of Catholic countries today, molded by a dead past, prudently uncreative; prospering best when society prospers least.

Within, the picture is even more full of pressure and anguish. Western society, as I have pointed out, had been undergoing a long siege of anxiety. Although the triumph of Christianity had converted the natural impulses to shrink and cower and retreat into socially more useful forms, terror and disruption still continued to leave their dreadful imprint on every aspect of the new life. In the new ideology, everything was a little tainted: religion was tainted with superstition, medicine with nostrums, and holiness with pathological masochism. The coarse health of the barbarian chieftains and their swaggering retainers did little to offset these inner weaknesses: it would take centuries before their animal faith was even touched by spirit.

In the historic experience of the Christian community there lay, moreover, the source of an even more terrible reaction which gave psychological depth and substance to the new manic-depressive visions of Christian theology. The long tradition of suffering at the hands of the Roman mob had left a deep mark on the Christian soul, and it affected both doctrine and practice. Close to the core of the Church lay the experience of the martyrs: the cruel, degrading ordeals to which the early Christians had been subjected left a smoldering sense of outrage which flamed into active revenge. Under Jesus's dispensation there was no place for punitive justice; but the wounds and cries of the victims drowned out the Master's plain words. The Christian fathers summoned all eternity to their aid to work out a revenge sufficiently frightful to match the terrors to which the faithful had been subjected.

"When Christians are injured," Cyprian pointed out, "the divine vengeance defends them. . . . For this reason," he added, "it is that none of us, when he is apprehended, makes resistance or avenges himself against unrighteous violence, although our people are numerous and plentiful. Our certainty of vengeance makes us patient." And what was the great reward of those who had suffered for Christ? From Cyprian up to

Thomas Aquinas the doctors of the Church are wholly at one on the answer: part of the Christian's sweetest delight in Heaven, throughout eternity, would consist in beholding the tortures of the damned. This divine consecration of cruelty perhaps accounts for the fact that cruelty was never included among the seven mortal sins.

These facts explain the cardinal points in the new idolum: Heaven and Hell. The dreadful fires of one, the hopeful radiance of the other, were more real to the Romanesque Christian than the flames of a burning city or the delights of a pied meadow in spring: more real, more immediate, indeed, more visible. The hope of Heaven and the fear of Hell presided over his daily actions. Even the sixth century invention of the intermediate realm of purgatory, a sort of quarantine for the soul, did not ease the tension or lessen the force of the terrible alternatives that confronted the sinner. Gloom and delight, despair and irrational joy, mark the up and down movements of the spirit: flagellation alternates with exaltation, and the pious moans of the entombed hermit outside the Cathedral would mingle with the Jubilate that rose within.

With the map of Heaven and Hell as his true guide to the world, the Christian found all other places vague and shadowy, lacking in firm outlines: the monks who copy the old herbals make their plants less and less true to life, more and more formalized, without once recognizing their ability to reclaim the original truth by comparing the drawing with the actual specimens growing in their gardens. In this strongly subjective world, remote and present, near and far, all mingled in one confused picture, in which Alexander and Charlemagne were contemporaries, in which Hercules and King Arthur, Venus and Iseult, belonged to the same society, in which "last year" might mean last month or last century.

For Romanesque man, the subjective and the objective world did not unite into a single vision. As sometimes happens with divergent eyes that do not fuse to form a clear image, the vision of one eye was suppressed—and the eye that was suppressed was that which looked at external nature and actual history. Hence the acceptance of discontinuity in natural events: miracles were daily occurrences; for nothing that could happen in dream seemed impossible in actual life.

All the phenomena of dream, the sudden appearance and disappearance of people, the capacity to understand a strange tongue or to speak glibly in a foreign language, the ability to fly or become invisible, were plausible elements in the imagined experience of this dark epoch. Fantasy and fact changed places: the character of the actual world was defined and its goods evaluated by reference to the conditions laid down in a supernatural dream. This obsession with uncontrollable images, clustering about the central theme of a neurosis, is a commonplace of abnormal psychology: here it left marks on a whole culture. Demons, imps, ghosts, populated this world, side by side with cows, sheep, horses, serfs, warriors, and merchants.

This dominance of the subjective was the outcome of Romanesque man's inheritance: he relived in fantasy the terrible experiences of the generations that had gone before him as well as those he faced from day to day. In Christian theology, Romanesque man found a subjective antidote: against the projection of his helpless infernal fears, he found a new source of comfort: from the same region of his soul he could also project angels, seraphim, saintly protectors who would counterbalance the evil powers. Imagined servants of goodness offset both the real and the fancied evils that pervaded this society. By invoking these angels and ministers of grace his life found some sort of temporary equilibrium.

There is scarcely a single aspect of this culture which does not become clearer when one interprets it as a neurotic dream phenomenon. From the use of the ordeal to establish legal guilt in criminal procedures to the magical use of Holy Water to ward off evils, from the application of physical torture to effect spiritual regeneration to the use of relics of saints to effect medical cures: it is in the dream world that these methods and remedies operate effectively. All these facts form part of a logical whole. But of course the suppression of the natural world was far from complete, and even the concealment and repression of the classic heritage were not final. There were many sane, lucid, waking moments, even gay, joyous moments, as the reader of Helen Waddell's admirable study of The Wandering Scholar will recall.

As a child who goes to sleep will still clutch to its bosom the doll that was part of its waking world, so Romanesque man still grasped a last battered relic of the classic order: Boëthius's The Consolations of Philosophy. Boëthius had a place in the Romanesque culture which lasted deep into the Middle Ages: if this place seems out of proportion to his merits, one must not forget that he came to symbolize the whole classic world. Manuscripts of the Consolations are scattered all over Europe; even today there are some four hundred manuscripts in existence. Mark the title: philosophy, not religion, was what Boëthius stood for: he was the last direct descendant of that ancient line which was founded in Ionia. According to Boëthius, the end of man is to see that there is nothing in the world that is not divine, nothing absurd, nothing unintelligible, nothing merely natural. That was a grand goal: a reminder of a world that was lost, but not altogether lost, so long as Boëthius's work itself remained.

CHAPTER IV. MEDIEVAL SYNTHESIS

1: The Freshets of Spring

As the year 1000 approached many people thought that the millennial reign of Christ would come to an end: the end of the world was at hand. These apocalyptic hopes and fears were by no means universal, but when the year simply came and went there was a widespread feeling of relief among those who still clung to mortal life, making wills and planting orchards for the sake of posterity. Glaber, a contemporary, records that "it seems as though the world shook itself and cast off its hoary age, and clad itself everywhere in a white robe of Churches." Spring was coming to Western Europe: the darkness and cold were almost over. But it did not unwinter suddenly: the first half of the eleventh century was full of tribulation. Only the reddening beech buds against the blue sky announced the change.

Spring, however, symbolizes all the changes that were taking place in the Western community and the Christian personality. Spring is first of all a season of beginnings: seeds long dormant, buds tightly folded, begin to show signs of life. In the new warmth of the sun, the strain and effort that kept one barely alive during winter no longer are needed: one relaxes. In the part of the world where I live, as in most of Western Europe, too, there may be treacherous changes in spring: sudden frosts, beating attacks of sleet; so that it is never safe to count the yield of the orchards by their wealth of blossoms. Similarly, no one can say what fine fruit crops were blighted by the terrible plague of the fourteenth century.

Spring goes with youth and erotic adventure: that also makes it symbolize the resurgence of medieval culture. The flesh is pricked with desire: when young, one must wander through the woods or throw oneself down on the fragrant warm grass, if one cannot rush to the arms of one's beloved. The goodness of the world is no longer a promise in the sky but an actuality on earth: the carols of the mating birds, the perfume of the wild grape blossoms and the locust trees, reinforce one's inner conviction that one need not seek farther for the meaning of life. Spring, in short, is a period of waxing power, rising vitality. The lyric poetry of the Middle Ages not merely records this ecstasy: it hardly knows any other season.

Those who have a different image of the Middle Ages, who think of it in terms of gloom, austerity, abstention, read into it the agony of an earlier disruption or a later decay; or they mistake the institutions of the Romanesque period, now recessive in the emerging society, for the dominant ones. Even Jacob Burckhardt, one of the great interpreters of culture, made this mistake: indeed, he bears no small blame for the popular falsification, for the reason that he attached to the concept "Renascence" every vivid outburst of medieval life, even if it occurred in the thirteenth century.

The fact is that by the eleventh century Western Europe had at last broken through the cracked mold of Roman civilization: for better or worse, it now had its own life to live. This life took form in monastery and castle and newly founded town; and however much its outward gestures might be governed by the habits and compulsions and overmastering images of the past, it was no longer condemned to live a life of helpless renunciation: it had nothing to escape from except itself. If rejection remained the great theme of the Church, and if the Church itself remained the supreme institution of society, a tendency to cut loose from the stabilities and sanctions of a more troubled age nevertheless characterized the new culture. The slow monastic procession, chanting its plainsong, now became a bright-pennoned cavalcade.

Even the Church was deeply affected by this change: perhaps the Church above all; for it was faced with the need to enlarge its own ideology so that it might take in all things human as well as those otherworldly. Defensively, Rome now prohibited the marriage of priests, lest the new flood of erotic energy overwhelm it and undermine its authority; dynamically, it reluctantly sanctioned a womanly redeemer, nearer to the popular heart than the Holy Trinity—the Virgin Mary, for whom some of the greatest of the new Gothic churches were built, Notre Dame in Paris, the Marienkirche in Lübeck.

In an effort to master the social processes that were undermining the very structure of Christian salvation, the new scholastic philosophy created a more rigid framework of doctrinal authority and ideological proof. Though the Church might still talk of sin and redemption, though there was still need to recognize one and effect the other, the existing corruption was no longer that of the muck-pile, many feet deep, which formed classic civilization: it was no more than the night-soil which could be removed the next day. The problem was not how to cut out the rot in a dying culture: the problem was how to prune a burgeoning one.

The medieval economy, as it developed between the eleventh and the fifteenth century, rested on two pillars: a feudalized agriculture and a corporate municipal economy which regulated the greater part of industrial production, including the production of works of art. The feudal mode of existence had been the chief answer to post-Roman disorganization: it wove together the loyalties of the Germanic war-band with the necessities of the expropriated peasant and the runaway slave seeking or submitting to a new master. The hardening of this feudal pattern between the tenth and the fourteenth centuries gave rise to a series of bold reactions: efforts to get around the feudal oath, to break free from slothful security, to establish new centers of loyalty in the free cities, a loyalty based on common economic and social purposes, on common human needs. This brought about a characteristic change from custom to written law, from status to contract, from fixed, all-embracing duties to specified privileges: from servility to civility. Crusade and pilgrimage, town charter and national parliament, all bore the same mark: they were attempts to escape both spatial restrictions and prescriptive duties.

The signs of this change were many. The villein ran away to the new town: if he stayed there a year and a day he was free. Merchants, protected by armed bands, began once more to venture across Europe: they founded great international fairs and built up an international trade in silks and spices, in wines, jewels, works of art. The illusion of isolation and the illusion of self-sufficiency cannot survive in a growing society; and the end of these illusions meant the end of both monastic and feudal autarchy. By the time Luther attempted to revive the principle of autarchy, it was already lost: to put autarchy into effect the new national states had to turn to imperialism, which is the internationalism of brigands.

Colonization and crusades both left their mark on this new society. The opening up of new land in Europe, between 1000 and 1400, provided a fresh outlet for the population. Forests were felled, fens drained, in the thinly occupied parts of Northern Europe: the Cistercian order was active in this land reclamation. Every fresh acre of arable land, every new barn, every new water wheel, increased the working stock of agricultural capital: for the first time since Charlemagne there was energy to spare, and hardly less important, the will to exert it. Still another waste area was opened up: the Mediterranean, long closed to regular commerce by pirates. The Genoese and Venetians, arming their ships, ventured back upon the sea; they reopened a trade and intercourse which still existed at the time Charlemagne founded a library and hospital in Jerusalem.

The Church, threatened by the growing power of the Arabs, did not passively wait for a fresh blow from Mahomet's followers: it took the offensive and led Christendom on a series of Crusades: the First Crusade was proclaimed by Innocent III. Threatened on its flank through the Moors in Spain, the Church opened up a second front. Many motives made the Crusades a popular cause: the desire for land, for trading stations, for booty: the desire to escape famine and to save souls, the desire to obtain merit toward a happier after-life by going on a pilgrimage to the Holy Sepulcher itself. But the underlying psychological drive was plainly a need for release from constraint: such a release as men get only when they go abroad and are out of their neighbors' sight. The great fact about the Crusades, then, is that it was a *movement.*

For the government of men, the Roman Church had found that fear and anxiety no longer sufficed: their restlessness and their pride must now be called into the service of Christian institutions. The Song of Roland, a secular epic, had already contained the suggestion of a Holy War against Islam; indeed, the idea of composing difficulties at home by uniting to attack a remote enemy continued to intrigue Christian minds for many centuries: down to Erasmus, otherwise so prudent and so benign, the suggestion was repeated. But the sheer vitality of the common sensual man must now also be reckoned with: he wanted to go places and see things.

Joinville, the companion of Louis IX, tells in his memoirs how that pious king tried to make him "firmly believe the Christian laws which God has given us." But it is plain that the King's injunctions were about as convincing to him as the Widder's preaching was to Huck Finn. Once the King asked Joinville whether he had rather be a leper or have committed or be about to commit a mortal sin. And how did Joinville reply? Like an honest man, "who would not tell a lie: that I would rather have committed thirty deadly sins than be a leper." With people of Joinville's strong frame and healthy appetites coming into the open, the Christian's traditional concern over his sins was, to say the least, no longer morbid. Since the Church's authority rested on man's dire need for salvation in a world of sorrows and anxieties and disappointments, it was forced to reckon with these changes of temper.

The Church found a form for the growing restlessness of medieval man in the pilgrimage: the pious visit to some great shrine, like the Chalice Well at Glastonbury, where Joseph of Arimathea was supposed to have dropped the Holy Grail, to Rome itself, where one might behold the Pope, or to Jerusalem, where one might walk on soil hallowed by Christ and his apostles. Pilgrims formed bands for mutual protection; and the holy mission leveled all travelers, so that Chaucer did no violence to fact when he put the Knight and the Miller, the vulgar middle class widow and the refined nun, in the same cavalcade.

One must remember, to appreciate the extent of this change, that the custom of making pilgrimages had been disapproved by some of the early fathers of the Church. "The Holy Life," Gregory of Nyssa wrote, "is open to all, men and women alike. Of that contemplative life, the peculiar mark is modesty. But modesty is preserved in societies that live distinct and separate. . . . The necessities of a journey are continually apt to reduce this scrupulousness. . . . Ye who fear the Lord, praise him in the places where ye now are." Under the influence of the Cluniac monasteries, beginning in the tenth century, pilgrimages became increasingly frequent: the wandering knight, seeking adventure, the journeyman, getting wider experience in his trade, the traveling scholar, seeking a famous master, were at one with the wayfaring pilgrim. Life itself was now a pilgrimage: it involved movement, progression, and a goal. One no longer waited for the next blow to fall, but went forth to meet and master one's fate. When, in the fifteenth century, the movements of men sought wider horizons, their plans were still colored by pious memories, pious hopes: the conquest of the New World was Christian Europe's last great crusade.

2: Love Breaks Bounds

As the new tides of life swept over Europe, Venus arose once more from the waves. Love, violently excluded from the super-ego except in the most sublimated form, now came back with doubled intensity, and the service of Venus occupied a growing part of the human imagination.

If avarice and sloth were perhaps the typical sins of the Dark Ages, lust was probably the most formidable sin of the medieval period. With the eleventh century erotic interest began to overflow and spread over every part of life: the lover gained general regard as a superior person, and the call of love upset even the life of the cloister: it tempted the great Abelard from his vocation, prompted knights to risk their lives in war or tournament, and introduced into prayers and devotions the douce womanly face of the Virgin Mary. The Virgin was so close to Venus that, like her pagan prototype, she even had a dark counterpart: the Black Madonna. The more biological Holy Family tended to replace the metaphysical Holy Trinity in the popular mind.

For the Church, virginity was still the ideal state, particularly if dedicated to God. But in actual life, virginity meant little more than biological immaturity. In most classes of society, an early marriage for girls went with a relatively late marriage for men; for the latter had either to gain independence through advancement in their craft, or they had to inherit, or receive by voluntary retirement, their father's land. A girl put aside her dolls to find herself nursing a baby. As late as the fifteenth century, the Paston Letters show us a prospective husband, coaxing his wife-to-be to eat all her food, like a good little girl. Marriage at thirteen, fourteen, or fifteen left a girl no room for either physical or emotional development before marriage. Defrauded of her adolescence, was it any wonder that woman, reaching maturity, restored an adolescent conception of love to the very heart of the erotic life?

Though the Church preached continence, it also emphasized the Old Testament belief in fertility. In country districts, as Homans reminds us, fornication was sometimes an accepted incident in courtship: it was the child that made marriage inevitable, not marriage that made the child possible. But once the family was in being, maturity, with all its responsibilities and prerogatives, was accepted: the family itself had the status of a public institution: it was an integral part of shop or farm or castle; and servants, helpers, retainers, not merely formed part of it but participated in the love and protection first accorded to the child. Education, even for aristocratic youth, was essentially service in a family: the new grammar schools of the merchants in the towns while supplementing this conception with systematic book instruction, hardly replaced it. But the Church's otherworldly ideals had an effect upon the erotic imagination; and there grew up a convention of romantic renunciation which has had an effect upon the Western super-ego ever since: possibly never more so than in the nineteenth century.

Courtly love was the name for this new erotic development. One of the great efforts of the twelfth century troubadours, self-conscious exponents of love, was to lengthen the period of love's probation. They sought to create for sexual passion a psychological distance, which was conspicuously lacking in the domestic and sanitary arrangements of the medieval household. In Provence, the earliest center to revive, the greatest of the troubadours composed their songs and elaborated a new love ritual: here the cult of love was associated with the heresy of Catharism, an offspring of Manicheean religion which had been preserved in the mountains of Bulgaria and reappeared in the South of France to present a bold, confident challenge to Christianity. The Catharists preached an extreme dualism of body and soul: the first was dark and ugly, the second was all purity and beauty. True love was an expression of the soul, a longing for the immaterial union of the lover and his beloved. Its essence was not physical union but fidelity and service. To woo was better than to win.

Plainly there was something adolescent in this conception of love: one can perhaps explain it as an imaginative attempt to enrich the limited and narrow experience of current marital conventions. By defaming the rites of sex, the Church had emptied them of any ideal content: even Thomas More, a sensitive enlightened man, spoke of sexual intercourse as if it were on the same level as urination: mere relief to a distended organ. Medieval sexual relations were abrupt and to the point. To make wooing more of an end in itself, the Court of Love in Provence decreed that the object of love must be already married: hence she was inviolate to her true lover. Yearning supplanted carnal conversation: the chivalrous lover, if he wished to keep his lady, ran away from her.

Romantic love, as preached by the troubadours, as practiced in courts and cities, carried both Catharist and Christian dualism to their perverse conclusions: indeed, one suspects a vein of homosexuality in this doctrine, and one is not surprised to find that inversion was treated by the Catholic Church as a sign of Catharist heresy. Was romantic love perhaps partly due, likewise, to the reactivation of the Oedipus Complex during adolescence: that protection against incest which makes woman seem a superior being, one whose least wish must be obeyed, and not least, one with whom copulation is forbidden, if not unthinkable? In maturer life, at all events, the etherealization of courtly love was an overcompensation for the matter-of-factness of domestic love. But note the result. Romantic love gave to sexual attachment an unconditional quality that organic love never has. Unfulfilled love may feed on its own denial forever: but in real life, lovers do not look into each other's eyes for eternity: they wrestle and become sweaty, they get hungry and want something to eat, or they get tired and fall asleep. In the romantic world of the troubadours love was never forced to accept the responsibilities of parenthood or risk the ups and downs of sharing a household together.

No love is possible between man and wife, according to a decision in the Court of Love held by the Countess of Champagne in 1174; for, pursued the decision, "whereas lovers grant to each other favors freely and from no legal necessity, married people have the duty of obeying each other's wishes and of refusing nothing to each other." In this decision love itself was made to participate in that general change from relations of status to those of free choice: to make sexuality itself an attribute of personality rather than an institutional fixture. But this effort was so contrary to the whole burden of tradition, it so detached erotic feelings from domestic, economic, and religious usages, that it could find no form in society: romantic love appears ultimately as a death wish.

The great legend of Tristan, so realistic in its treatment of the low stratagems that usually attend adultery, is also remorseless in its revelation of the essential sterility and morbidity of isolated romantic love. Neither Tristan nor Iseult wholly give themselves to each other: neither is capable of renunciation for the sake of the other's fulfillment—Tristan's career as an honorable knight, Iseult's life as a loyal wife. Their final fate, in Gottfried of Strassburg's poem, is to go off to the Grotto of Love, with its brass door barred with bolts: there, sitting side by side like two hermits, they tell each other tales of those who had suffered or died for love before them. Is their final mood love or hate?

Medieval love, reacting against a boredom born of mere concern for physical needs, posed one of the deepest problems of sexuality: how shall married lovers remain in love and recapture the possibilities that fresh courtship awakens. But medieval practice left a remedy that could only prolong the original disease. The precious moment of love, so well described in the earlier episodes of Tristan, could not last forever: after three years the love potion wears off: after three years the lovers who cling to the purity of their initial passion simply cannot stand each other. Pure passion, like pure thought, must eventually submit to a common domicile and a corporate life: it must accept growth and change, new interests and new duties, if it is not to wither at the roots.

The actual love of Abelard and Héloise differed from the mythical love of Tristan and Iseult because it brought into a single lifetime almost all the possibilities of human love: lust and friendship, discipleship and parenthood, dedication and renunciation. From this archetypal story, celebrated in popular song almost before the lovers' bed was cold, one may understand what this society had to reckon with when it presented a code of conduct framed for the survivors of a corrupt and dying society to a community bursting with the brave insolence of life.

Abelard and Héloise, the great scholar in his prime, the clever young girl in her first flush of loveliness, were not courtly lovers: their love was no plaintive song of non-fulfillment. Open marriage was impossible to Abelard without a loss of his status in the Church, which meant in effect becoming an intellectual outcast as well: hence they came together, under the very eye of Héloise's guardian, in that magnificent recklessness of delight which is close to the recklessness of despair. When Héloise found herself with child their love, paradoxically, reached a dead end: the terrible castration of Abelard, devised by Héloise's uncle, only turned an impossible hope into a goading defeat.

In the melancholy correspondence into which this passionate tie subsided, the outstanding fact is the unrepentance of Héloise: she declared that she did not take the convent's veil for Christ's sake but for Abelard's sake. "In the whole of my life (God wot!) I have ever feared to offend thee rather than God: I seek to please thee more than Him." Nor does she deceive herself for a moment as to what she has lost, though her words must have cut Abelard's unyielding spirit like a goad. She remembers the incentives of lust and the warm pleasures of the body: those who call her chaste, she says, have not discovered the hypocrite in her. Her body yields, but her mind does not consent to be cut off from her lover. And the years do not quiet her.

Loyal to Abelard, Héloise still feels the call of sex: she baits him with questions about conduct, just to have the occasion to use words that recall vivid sexual feeling. Should an Abbess, she asks him, extend hospitality to men and eat with her guests. "Oh, how easy a step to the destruction of the souls of men and women is their dwelling together in one place. But especially at table, where gluttony prevails and drunkenness, and wine is drunk with enjoyment, wherein is luxury." These are the words of a woman of spirit who knows herself for what she is: clean in heart, fierce in love, proud of her role as mistress and parent, far more proud of her sins than of her life of renunciation, though in that life her love had given proof of its unselfishness: morally superior to Iseult's greedy clutching for the mere shadow of love.

The Catholic Church had no mold for the life that Abelard and Héloise were capable of living and sharing: it had opened too wide a gap between the erotic and the spiritual; and though it could by a rigorous sublimation give to the latter some of the benefit of its erotic energy, it had no formula for the reverse process. These lovers had either to become outcasts or to make their love outcast. Because the assault that made Abelard a eunuch decided that question automatically, the issue was never fought out; though but for his physiological handicap Abelard might have risen to Héloise's brave challenge.

3: The Price of Dualism

For all its new energies, medieval society continued the warfare between soul and body, between the holy life and the earthly life: in that, the troubadour and the priest were one. This dualism was one of the sources of its eventual disintegration. Dante and Petrarch were each in love with a feminine phantasm: not his own wife, not a mistress, but one who was beheld at a distance and worshiped without any solid hope of a nearer approach. The three most important love poets at the close of the high Middle Age, Dante, Cino da Pistoia, and Petrarch, lost their ideal mistresses by death. But death was the only possible terminus for such an idealized relation: the beloved could live on only in the imagination, a Blessed Damozel leaning out from the gold bar of Heaven. The adoration of the Virgin Mary was the collective expression of this animus.

What chance had a wife against such unearthly rivals? She served merely as a receptacle for frustrated passion: at best, her life was in her brood. Who indeed became the model wife in an age that dedicated itself to courtly ladies and heavenly virgins? The writers of the Middle Ages answer with one voice: The Goodman of Paris says the same as the writer of the Decameron. The ideal of married womanhood is the patient Griselda. Griselda's allegiance to her husband is so constant, her attitude is so replete with bovine submission, that she endures the cruelest trials to the human feelings without a murmur, without a doubt as to the decency of her husband's position, without a question as to his authority: "what the old man does is always right." Aquinas rated patience lower even than the secular virtues; but the patient Griselda was what the men of the Middle Ages wanted. When they thought of family love, they thought of a creature who ideally took orders like a servant and accepted her bitter destiny like a slave: who would see nothing and endure everything—the Fair Annie of the ballad.

In medieval love, if the highest ideal was too high, the lowest was too low: the Queen of Heaven and Patient Griselda, Dante's divine mistress, Beatrice, and his real wife, were too far apart to be embodied in a single person. The descent of the erotic impulse itself, as the Church lost its hold on the popular mind, can be followed step by step in literature: one need only trace the path from the sonnets of Petrarch through the Romance of the Rose as completed by Jean de Meun down to the bawdy love poems of Villon to cover the whole distance. In the Romance of the Rose, the apparatus of courtly allegory and veiled reference remains; but the whole theme of the poem concerns the approach, not to a disembodied spirit, but to an earthly woman whose genitals are symbolized by the rose. Nature, according to Jean, is engaged in an eternal struggle against Death: man alone sometimes willfully abets her enemy by refraining from procreation. Love—"willing, waking love"—has now become an ideal goal: it is virginity that has become suspect and chastity that brings no reward.

This naturalism was not an extravagant departure in an age that patiently followed pious maxims; far from it. Without the tedious apparatus of learned allegory, the same attitude was present in The Miller's Tale in Chaucer, with a more healthy comic touch of earthiness. This great challenge to the accepted Christian way of life did not come from avowed heretics; it came rather from those who, still calling themselves Christians, rejected the restrictions and inhibitions the Church had placed on their natural functions. If the bawdiness of the late medieval period was almost as dream-ridden as its chivalrous romanticism, as Huizinga suggests, it nevertheless brought into the very heart of this culture a repressed constellation of interests which now demanded open acknowledgment.

Though one hesitates to call sex itself a sort of heresy to the Christian way of life, it might nevertheless push one into heresy. Listen to the effect of Nicolette on the orthodoxy of Aucassin: those two popular characters of medieval fable and song.

"In Paradise," exclaims Aucassin, "what have I to do? I care not to enter, but only to have Nicolette, my very sweet friend, whom I love so dearly well. For into Paradise go none but such people as I will tell you of. There go those aged priests, and those old cripples, and the maimed who all day long and all night long cough before the altars, and in the crypts beneath the Churches; those who go in worn old mantles and old tattered habits; who are naked and barefoot, and full of sores; who are dying of hunger and thirst, of cold and wretchedness. Such as these enter Paradise and with them I have nought to do. But in Hell I will go. For to Hell go the fair clerks and the fair knights who are slain in the tourney and the great wars, and the stout archer and the loyal man. With them will I go. And there go the fair and courteous ladies, who have friends, two or three, together with their wedded lords. And there pass the gold and the silver, the ermine and all rich furs, harpers and minstrels, and the happy of the world. With these will I go, so only that I have Nicolette, my very sweet friend, by my side."

When such words could be uttered and repeated in public one thing was sure: Heaven and Hell had already become, for a part of the population, chiefly figures of speech: otherworldly promises no longer sufficed to serve as substitutes for present goods. Did not our Nicolette, indeed, cure a pilgrim near to death by appearing before him and raising her gown and smock, so that he might behold all that a girl could offer to recall him to this world? The psychology was excellent: Venus, too, could perform miracles in restoring the dead to life.

Here is a new spirit, a new vitality: under the sweetest forms of courtesy, it appears in the Prologue to the Decameron. Here is the spirit which, in the year 1283, infected the merchants and the craftsmen, and especially their Guelf lords, according to the Chronicler, Villari, in Florence. "A social union was formed, composed of a thousand people who, all clad in white, called themselves the Servants of Love. They arranged a succession of sports, merry-makings, dances with ladies; nobles and bourgeois marched to the sound of trumpets and music, in wild delight to and fro, and held festive banquets at midday and at night. This Court of Love lasted nearly two months, and it was the first and most famous that had ever been in Florence, or in all Tuscany."

In the Middle Ages, then, love ran the full gamut of expression: austere divine love with Bernard of Clairvaux, compassionate human love with Francis of Assisi, courtly love with the troubadours, Platonic love with Petrarch and Dante, carnal love with Jean de Meun and François Villon, irrational passionate love with Gottfried of Strassburg, organically mature love with Héloise and Abelard. In some degree, the ideals and practices of medieval love overcame the crippling paradox of Christian doctrine; for originally that doctrine, founded on love, had, thanks to the influence of Paul and his successors, sternly rooted out those natural occasions that testify to love's ideal capacities and feed it: the love of a man and a woman, the love of parents for children, the love of friends and neighbors: the natural prelude to every sublimation, to every wider sharing, of love. In seeking to purify love, Christianity had actually sterilized it: made it hard, formal, spinsterish, restrictive. Love of God turned into a mere hatred of man's animal impulses; and love, denying its own roots, became strained and pathological, seeking to recover its lost ground surreptitiously by brooding over the Song of Solomon and turning its exultant eroticism into a fable about the Church's union with Christ. Through the cult of the Holy Family, the people of the Middle Ages overcame their tendency toward metaphysical dualism even in sexual relations; and their practice was in fact more ideal than their idealizations. On this point, I would cite the testimony of a contemporary psychiatrist, Dr. Gregory Zilboorg:

"Families were large and parents were able to live their instinctual lives on a fully adult, genital level. They were physiologically as well as psychologically real fathers and real mothers. The cult of an affectionate and obedient attitude toward the actual father and his socialized equivalent was universal. All along the line of psychological father substitutes—from the benevolent authority of the Church through the protective and considerate authority of the master of the guild to that of the real head of the family—there operated the principle of being loved and taught and protected and being grateful and loving and responsive in return for love and protection at the hands of the father. It was an almost ideal psychological constellation of adulthood, from the standpoint of the proper alignment of instinctual drives."

So much for the medieval achievement: a great re-orientation, particularly when one remembers the original Christian need to overcompensate against the self-defeating sexuality of the classic world.

Nevertheless, a series of fissures ran through the medieval conception of love and weakened its integrity. Though it encompassed every phase of erotic activity between unawakened virginity and placid senescence, it tended to fix each phase in a separate station of life and even in a separate social caste. No single life was supposed to encompass love in all its varieties: if holy, one was excluded from family life, if dedicated to motherhood, one was excluded from the platonic excitements and blandishments of courtship. Hence the successive phases of a developing erotic experience were turned into states of premature arrest; and for an organically mature love there was no established life-pattern that reconciled the holiness men desired with desires that too easily became unholy. In re-asserting the claims of love, the Middle Ages identified it all too quickly with unsuppressed carnality: and that way was no less a blind alley than the flushed asceticism of the Catharists.

4: The Brothers of the Open Road

Joachim of Flora, born around 1130, was the herald of a new movement. He announced it in a series of prophetic visions whose palpable heresy did not prevent his getting a patent from the Pope to set up a new monastic order. In a grand conspectus of history, Joachim outlined the three ages of man. The first was the Age of God the Father, lasting from Adam to Christ. Like the Manichees, he regarded this as a carnal period. The Age of the Son, from Jesus to Benedict of Nursia, was an age of grace, partly given to the body, partly to the spirit. The final age, the age of the Holy Spirit, belonged to the monks: it began with Benedict and would reach its first consummation around 1260: an age of liberty and joy: an age when the sacraments would be suspended and the world would be ruled directly by love. Fear, law, a life of labor governed the first period: wisdom and grace and discipline belonged to the second: but the third period was to be one of love and happiness, fulfilled in a life of contemplation.

However shocking to medieval doctrine was this separation of the Holy Trinity, Joachim's philosophy of history seized the imagination of adventurous minds. As late as 1349, Rienzi sought out the Emperor Charles IV at Prague and repeated the gist of Joachim's apocalypse: he even predicted that a universal religion would be established by 1357, and that the Pope, the Emperor, and Rienzi, as Roman Tribune, would form a trinity to represent God on earth. But before that abortive mission took place, Joachim had served as John the Baptist for a greater, if less philosophic, personality: Francis of Assisi.

The life of Francis of Assisi was almost as marked by contrasts as that of Jesus. He was born to the family of a well-to-do merchant, around 1189; and his adolescent years found him one of the gay irresponsibles of his little town; one who liked to play pranks, enjoy pleasures, dress like a lord. A succession of little incidents altered this lightness, or rather, put his divine levity at the service of mankind. While waiting on customers in his father's shop, he turned out a poor beggar who had asked for a few pennies in Christ's name. When the beggar was gone, Francis became horrified over his own callousness, on realizing that if the beggar had mentioned some local magnate, instead of Christ, Francis would immediately have given him the money.

Step by step during the next two years Francis withdrew from his companions; finally, much to his father's anger and disgust, he decided to withdraw from his father's business, which was marked by dishonesty and avarice. Meditating on the character and mission of Christ, Francis sought to imitate it and follow his example. He drew around him a group of men and women who renounced property in every form, and who took to the highways to preach the original words of Christ and to live in his spirit. At the very height of medieval Christianity, in the century that saw its magnificent consummation in architecture and philosophy and poetry, Francis resumed the task of Jesus: the task of dismantling and disembodying human institutions and challenging their mighty triumphs. As the last stone was lifted to close the tomb, where the dead body might repose forever, the person reappeared: transfigured.

The guiding principles of the Franciscans were love and poverty: with love they welcomed poverty, and in poverty their riches lay in love. But instead of withdrawing themselves from the society of other men, to achieve a waxen holiness, they sought it precisely in companionship and service. The troubadour of God, as Francis was well called, incarnated a gay, giving spirit: in his holy innocence, he would cast off every article of dress and preach to a congregation, in order to bring home the fact that the soul was not bound up with its clothes or its buildings, but faced its divine destiny in all nakedness. Though he preached much, his life was his ultimate word.

The contrast between the new friars and the old monks was, by the thirteenth century, an overwhelming one. Despite numerous efforts to reinstate the rigors of an earlier age, the monks had done all too well by themselves: even their good works contradicted their original intentions. Once they had retired to the wilderness to live a life of holy contemplation; but, as Abelard had pointed out, they had multiplied "their dwellings on the pretext of hospitality" and had turned into a city "that solitude which they sought." This life tended to produce self-centeredness and self-complacence.

Francis challenged current religious conventions in two ways. First of all, he denied that Christianity could be segregated or that its prescriptions for a holy life applied to the Church alone and not to the laity. He felt, too, that everyone must be freshly converted to a Christian way of life; and the very fact that he believed this, and applied the doctrine even to the officers of the Church, no less than to the rich man, poor man, merchant, thief, doctor, beggar, and feudal chief, shows how far Christianity had failed in its original task. What Jesus had taught had been forgotten: the Church had disembarrassed itself of the daring peripatetic moralist and centered attention almost exclusively upon the sacrificial god and that god's expositors, Paul, Augustine, Gregory. Francis's great achievement was that he restored, in his proper person, the defaced image of Jesus: at least he made the humanity of Jesus credible again by the humble beauty of his own actions.

With the simplicity of the wise, Francis took Jesus's words literally and did him reverence by attempting to carry them out. If Jesus said one must be poor, then one must in fact give away one's wealth: this doctrine was a guide for daily living, and could not be satisfied by any deathbed bequests to charity. If buildings, by their fixity, keep one from serving where one is needed, and meeting quickly whatever problems life brings forth, then one must do without buildings, not omit service. Here Francis's insight was profound: every fresh movement of the spirit involves a casting off of the old body, the old garments: even the grandest works of art must be treated as reckless trifles, mere improvisations, to be abandoned or destroyed on a moment's notice as soon as they begin to stifle the spirit—abandoned with the faith that while the spirit remains alive it will produce as good or better as soon as needed. One must live, as Augustine had observed, according to the creator, not according to the created thing; and this applied to the human creator no less than to the divine one. It was no accident that Francis sang his Canticle to the Sun under the open sky, and preached his overflowing love for all life to the creatures of the field and the forest. Under the open sky Francis was at home. The squirrels and the foxes, the falcons and the doves, might understand him.

By accepting Jesus as his daily model, Francis for a brief time restored the spontaneous affirmations of Christian faith. Heedless of clothes, untrammeled by property, cast loose from obligations to follow a trade steadily or preserve a condition in society, the Franciscan could at last work in the spirit of love, from which self-love was almost wholly parted.

Women, too, were equals now in a way they had never been under the monastic dispensation: the love of Clare and Francis made possible a woman's order under the same dispensation. At that great meeting of the Franciscans at Portiuncula, in which Dominic participated, one notes with amusement the Spaniard's apparent discomfort over the lack of plan, method, authority: the absence of decent living accommodations, the failure to provide beforehand for the commissary. Yet when Dominic found that the people of the district brought provisions to the several thousand friars that were assembled, in greater quantity than was needed, he was profoundly moved: gospel poverty no longer seemed a literary figment. So Dominic went into retreat and founded a parallel order of preaching friars.

As for Francis himself, he had no wish originally to create an order: still less did he dream of incorporating the principle of mendicancy. What he sought to create was a new attitude toward labor, to infuse all work with the spirit of fellowship, to create a group of people, united by the simple duties of accepting poverty and service in a spirit of glad outgoingness: people who might even remain in their trade or in their household, provided they stripped themselves of material props. The brother or sister of Francis might ask for alms for others, not for himself; his duty was to do whatever work lay at hand that would compensate for the bare bed or meal he received.

This was a popular creed; and the fact that it was popular is evidence of a growing sense of conflict between formal professions and actual practices that many of the new middle classes experienced. So long as agriculture was the mainstay of life, poverty was natural and Christian simplicity required no effort. Now, with trade and urban building, riches and the temptations of riches were always near; and those who respected the tenets of Christian faith could scarcely respect themselves when they so frequently flouted its central doctrines. At the beginning of the thirteenth century the order of *Humiliates,* or people vowed to a humble life, offered Francis a precedent. Even when the Franciscan order was threatened by its very overpopularity, by its worldly success, similar groups like the Waldensians would spread. Under pressure from the Papacy Francis finally institutionalized his order; but he still provided for Friars Minor, people who continued to follow their callings but who received the reward of their labor in kind.

But what happened to Francis's vision? Within his own lifetime, its essential insights were betrayed and its principles undermined. This order, which challenged the unchristian preoccupations of the Church, became a useful instrument of the Papacy: in spite of Francis, the order accepted gifts for itself and built buildings. They worked less and they begged more: their eloquence as preachers filled the churches with listeners but robbed the world of their own more eloquent practice. Apart from the example of Francis himself, the main contribution of his preaching friars was to turn attention from the ritual of the mass to the inspiration of the spoken word. Going on missions in every part of Europe, indeed invading the Saracen world in the person of Francis, the friars spread the words of the gospel, in the language of the common man, as it had not perhaps been spread since the Apostolic Age. Afoot and light-hearted, the Franciscans took to the open road. That movement, from the cloister to the cathedral, from the cathedral to the marketplace and the palace and the town hall, culminated in the Roman Church with the Jesuits.

Francis preached, not Christ crucified, but Christ arisen and at work in the hearts of men: he lived and taught with a tenderness, a compassion, an inner joy, for which the word Franciscan, with all its overtones, is alone adequate. Such lovers as Francis are rare in any age; such sincerity as Francis showed in matching faith and acts keeps alive a sense of mankind's utmost possibilities. But the frustrations and contradictions in Francis's career illustrate the limits of his understanding no less than the difficulties of his task.

Now the first thing to note in appraising Francis's essential failure was that, in turning his back on his father's shop, he was choosing the easiest way of following Christ. Voluntary poverty and beggary both automatically remove one from the temptations that go with wealth; but they both assume without critical reflection the existence of other men and women who continue to live under these temptations, so that they may produce that surplus on which a holy life—or an intellectual life—must depend. Unless human society itself is to disappear, the majority of men must devote themselves to planting, spinning, building, bartering, providing; and in the nature of things, this constant preoccupation with the means of living tends to give instruments the status of ends. The great problem for the growing middle classes in Francis's day was how—in Ruskin's words about his father—one could remain in trade and be an "entirely honest merchant." That was the problem the Flemish weavers had set for themselves in the twelfth century when they founded the order of Beguins. Bergson pointed out that though mysticism evokes asceticism, the charity and love that arise out of the mystic's experience of the whole would not spread if humanity were obsessed by fear and hunger. Man will rise above earthly things only if he has the earth to stand on: "in other words, the mystical summons up the mechanical." Charles Péguy underlined this point by stressing the difference between salutary poverty and sheer destitution. So the problem of life in Francis's period was not to emphasize the renunciations appropriate to a dying culture: the new task was to hold a balance between worldly mastery and the spiritual demands of justice and brotherhood. It was easy to denounce the flesh and flee from the scene: but such virtue was too lightly purchased.

The true path of Christian economics lay through the development of the guild. Here was a fellowship which at first subjected trade to other aims than mere worldly success: honest standards of workmanship and measure: a leisured pace and esthetic sensitiveness in actual work: brotherly relations between worker and worker, filial relations between apprentice and master: sympathy for the departed and relief for the widowed and orphaned—all these developments were of a life-fulfilling nature. In economics, the Christian super-ego that Francis offered was only a negative one. Whereas if the guild had received the intellectual and moral attention that the individual soul received, it might have passed from the stage of protective isolation to that of dynamic unification, from a local monopolistic equilibrium to a co-operative commonwealth. Lacking such impetus, the agents of unification in post-medieval society were on the side of aggression and exploitation.

But Francis was guilty of an even grosser obtuseness and an even more serious self-betrayal. He sought to get rid of all the encumbrances to Christian living; and he completely forgot, or rather, he heartily embraced, the most formidable of all these encumbrances in the thirteenth century, the Roman Church itself. He bade men renounce property—and worked hand in hand with the greatest owner of properties. He renounced worldly wealth—and bowed obsequiously to the institution that commanded the greatest store of wealth. This was a one-sided renunciation: Francis thought himself back into the life of Christ and yet he was too blind to make the final effort that would have put him on the same level as Jesus. By his very docility he demonstrated that there was no real turning back.

Have we not here the source of the betrayal and corruption of Franciscanism even in its own time? Ideal patterns that are inappropriate to their environment are as incapable of surviving as biological maladaptations: there must be an underlying connection between the universal and the local with its special pressures and needs and claims. Every past achievement in culture, no matter how high, is only a reminder of a new way of life that must be sought, not a substitute for it. Francis chose to follow an archaic pattern. Like the courtly love that the troubadours celebrated, the way chosen by God's troubadour pulled further apart practical and spiritual activities that were already separated—and in return the practical dominated his order and brought it down to the common level.

Franciscanism widened the breach between the Christian ideal of holiness and the new capitalism that was in process of formation: in later times, it did nothing to prevent a steady loss of mutual aid and brotherly equality within the guilds and the municipalities. In this it resembled those forms of utopian socialism which remained outside the co-operative and the trades union movements of the nineteenth century. The result of Francis's failure to understand and direct the developing forces of medieval society was pitiful: less than a century after Francis's death, according to Coulton, four of his friars were publicly burned at Marseilles "for adhering with heretical obstinacy to their master's first ideal of poverty."

Francis was in love with life and he lived a life of love: that example was beautiful in itself, but ineffectual for the community. What Francis actually achieved as an organizer of Christian life could have been accomplished by a Dominic: did not Dominic in fact accomplish it? In a little while Francis's friars would join Dominic's in combating heresy. He left the task of intellectual understanding to Thomas Aquinas; he abandoned the will-to-justice to Wycliffe, the Lollards, the Waldensians. Even that love which prompted Francis to wash the sores of lepers was less effective, indeed less kind to afflicted humanity, than the new medieval medical practice of isolation, which, though it might narrow the province of love, also lessened the incidence of this disease and finally wiped it out. The love that Francis preached needed the support of positive knowledge, economic foresight, rational order, so that it might also take firm hold of the university, the guild, the court of justice, the parliament. As an isolated and dissociated love, Francis's divine love, like Tristan's carnal love, was doomed to defeat.

5: Cathedral-Building and Scholasticism

The thirteenth century was an age of high energies and great constructive activities. Its two greatest collective products—the Gothic cathedral and scholastic philosophy—stand in strong opposition. The cathedral was an image of medieval society as a whole and expressed its utmost vitality. Scholastic philosophy was a reflection of the new super-ego. The first risked security for the sake of its own audacious self-fulfillment: the second courted stultification for the sake of finality.

The new type of church building actually flaunted its daring constructional logic: punctuated by thinning walls, made more spectacular by widening windows, the gigantic cathedrals of Notre Dame or Winchester thrust their weight into the upper air: their great towers or spires were lances thrown into the infinite. In the moment of breaking away from the stolid securities of Romanesque architecture, the builders of these cathedrals showed their confidence in the self-sustaining energies of their own community, using thrust and counter-thrust to raise higher the fanning vaults of the nave, sometimes enclosing and leaving untouched portions of the old building they lacked the patience to tear down or the respect to carry through to completion. The whole structure was in a state of dynamic tension. These builders weakened the dogma of the wall in order to lift it higher with the flying buttress of reason.

Sometimes the builder's faith over-reached itself and the whole structure would collapse before it was finished, like a pyramid of acrobats that tumbles to the ground before the last man succeeds in balancing himself on the topmost shoulders. Proverbially, these cathedrals remained unfinished in the generation that conceived them. Unique among architectural forms, the Gothic cathedral allowed for and incorporated the changes wrought by history: successive layers of time and culture were worked into the fabric without destroying the living unity: the towers of Westminster Abbey were raised by Wren only in the seventeenth century and great parts of Cologne and Ulm Cathedrals were not built until the nineteenth century. So the audacity of the medieval builder was mixed with humility: he left something to time, chance, fate.

In conception and in constructional daring, the Cathedral was the crystallization of a new spirit: its symbolism went much further than the formulated dogmas and the conscious reason of its age, for it embodied the conflicts, even the heresies, that were an integral part of the real community. By the fourteenth century the Romanesque catacomb had turned into a brilliant lantern: light poured into it by day through the wine-red and sapphire-blue windows, and every change in the sky, from morning to night, was recorded in altered light and color within. Fantastic shapes that brooded batlike in the upper air competed for the eye with stone sculptures nearer at hand: nestling birds, sprays of hawthorn and twining grape leaves, that seemed like nature trapped unawares in the rock, gave way to the attenuated shapes of noble men and women, saints and kings, symbols of wisdom, piety, or honor, gravely arrayed about the portals. The dream of the Middle Ages now became palpable in stone and glass and wood and iron.

Gargoyle and Virgin, flying buttress and glass wall, utilitarian organ loft and decorated choir stall, earth and sky, were thus wrought into a living unity. The Gothic cathedral was a true epitome of medieval life, inner and outer; for it possessed qualities that went far beyond the greatest rational formulations: above all, in its originality, its gift for improvisation, its readiness to accept tension and to welcome change. The Gothic cathedral came to sudden life in the thirteenth century and already, by the fifteenth, it was singing its swan song. But when one recalls the feeble mechanical energies commanded by medieval Europe, an age of limited manpower and even more limited horsepower, the Cathedral bears witness to a concentration of vitality and power that ranks with the greatest epochs in history.

In sum, the Cathedral was more than the stone Bible of mankind, as Victor Hugo was finally to call it; for it was likewise the Grand Encyclopedia: the sum of medieval knowledge as well as medieval faith. Indeed, this building became the solid core around which the acts and ceremonies of life were wound, as around an iron armature, in order to raise to higher tension the current of daily living. Polyphonic music now translated into sound the complicated visual music of the stones themselves. Each man had his part; each order, each class, had its part; every member of corporate society, from beggar to king, realized his own existence within an audible, visible, rational whole. Here medieval beauty, strength, sanctity, and science found their ultimate embodiment.

Scholastic philosophy was closely tied to cathedral-building; but it presented a direct contrast and sought to formulate a different kind of order: it was an attempt to find a comprehensive resolution of the intellectual conflicts of its day, and to give the unqualified dogmas of the Church the same kind of support that the physician, the lawyer, or the working artisan had in the practice of his profession or trade. This philosophy arose with the university: a guild of masters and students devoted to the orderly acquisition and extension of professional knowledge, in jurisprudence, medicine, theology. Differentiating itself from the Cathedral School, the university perfected its students in the technical arts of formulating ideas and establishing verbal proof. By its command of books and texts, the university established its intellectual authority, but it lost the discipline of active working life that the other forms of the guild retained. Even in medicine, Lanfranc complained, the masters of book knowledge would have nothing to do with operative surgery: a great loss. Nevertheless, the new corporate form of the university proved indispensable to the codification and transmission of the existing body of knowledge, and to its eventual extension.

In scholastic philosophy, the bold constructional logic of the Cathedral builders gave way to a formal logic which aimed above all at certainty and order. The scholastic philosophers quarried their stones from widely separated outcrops, from the Fathers of the Church, from the Arab philosophers, Avicenna and Averroës, from the broken stonepile of Greek philosophy, above all, from the dilapidated Alexandrian museum whose ground plan had been laid out by Aristotle. But in this new philosophy, it was not faith and sheer animal vitality and rational experiment that created the great structure: the active element was predominantly reason, represented by Aristotelian dialectic and logic.

Scholasticism, if one may prolong the architectural figure, was not so much the finished Cathedral as the scantling of wood by means of which the actual work of building is made possible. It created little new knowledge; but it sought to make existing knowledge form an orderly and intelligible whole. Scholasticism soared to no heights of its own, but it endeavored to support those who were capable of soaring: Aquinas made Dante possible. In short, this philosophy was mainly a constructional device: hence its deliberate lack of beauty and outward grace, its harsh utilitarian outlines, its pedestrian pace. Scholasticism was a machine for sifting evidence, for collating authorities, for manufacturing proof. It attempted to make faith reasonable and reason faithful: thus it recorded the moment of conflict within the Christian Church when it was no longer enough to quiet reason by shutting one's eyes, or dispose of doubt by appealing to the very authority that was in fact doubted.

Like the work of the great Cathedral builders, scholastic philosophy was a new style of thought. Though in the ninth century it had an important precursor in John Scotus Erigena, it arose as a body in the twelfth century; and among the first of its great exponents was Abelard, whose faith in the divinity of logic brought him into a head-on collision with Bernard of Clairvaux, who sensed the danger of bringing revelation before the bar of formal proof. Abelard's treatise, Sic et Non, placed side by side the contradictory statements contained in the Bible and the writings of the Church Fathers: if all these statements were revelation, which revelation should be chosen, since in reason they were conflicting and contradictory? Scholasticism was an ingenious attempt to reconcile these Yeses and Noes.

In the shabby boarding houses and garrets where the new university at first flourished, scores of ingenious minds worked to produce a stable synthesis out of these impossible contradictions. Within a century the schoolmen became one of the great props of the Church: the university with its wide international connections and presently even its traveling scholarships, did for the intellectual life what the preaching friars did for the emotional life of the community: it created a framework of belief and dogma in which coherence and intelligibility, founded on arbitrary postulates, temporarily did service for truth. Scholasticism stretched the

Church's dogmas to their extreme limit, to make them do justice to the complexities of life. When the last gaping seam was sewed together, it became apparent that the fabric itself was threadbare and weak. . . .

6: The World of Thomas Aquinas

Among the scholastic philosophers, great doctors arose: Duns Scotus, William of Occam, John of Salisbury, Hugo of Saint Victor, Vincent of Beauvais, Albertus Magnus, "the master of those that know," and his even greater pupil Thomas Aquinas. Logicians, moralists, political philosophers, these men sought to create a formal ideology that would include the reports of revelation, of authority, and of experience.

Let us examine Thomas Aquinas. It would not be true to suggest that scholastic philosophy, with its many divergent minds, realist and nominalist, platonist and aristotelian, could be characterized by the work of this single mind, any more than it would be fair to say that the Gothic cathedral is Salisbury or Bamberg or Rheims or Segovia. But it would be true to say that if one possessed only the works of Thomas Aquinas one would have the soundest and best contribution of scholastic philosophy. While Aristotle was known as The Philosopher in the medieval schools, Aquinas has a better right to the title.

This resolute monk, nicknamed the Dumb Ox because he was slow and heavy, massive in bulk and no less massive in act, was one of the great formal thinkers of all time. But his greatness lies in his accomplishment as a whole, not in any single part of it. Certainly no one else could hold such a title with as little originality as Thomas Aquinas possessed. He was not a discoverer of new paths: not a daring mind that flew from peak to peak: his very value, on the contrary, lies in his resolute pedestrianism, in his refusal to admit any truth that has not been reached in a series of formal logical steps. His faithfulness to logic was like that of a prudent modern scientist to experimental demonstration. The mechanism of his proofs, in the Summa Theologica, was undeviating: First, statement of the negative case: objections, 1, 2, 3; contrary statement, counter argument, answers to objections, 1, 2, 3—and final resolution. No step was omitted; no different apparatus of proof was erected in order to break the monotony.

Thomas Aquinas could have boasted with honesty that he had never ventured to utter a truth not long sanctified by reason, by experience, by the common sense of other men. In no derogatory sense, one may call him a master of platitude, provided one adds that in medieval culture some of the platitudes of Greece and Rome came forth from their ancient graves as breathless discoveries. Aquinas's thought was so impersonally conceived that it might have been a collective product: he was most himself when he was anonymous. His greatest gift was a gift of reasonable discrimination. He took the mixed-up, disordered, unevenly shaped fragments of human experience, and, as methodically as if he were putting together a jig-saw puzzle, he fitted the bits together so neatly that one might have thought he was reproducing the original picture and that he himself was the painter of it.

Aquinas's strength is that he seems to know all the answers, or at least knows where to look for them: his weakness lies in the fact that his questions do not bring under rational scrutiny either the method of his logic or the postulates of Christian theology. He trusts reason entirely, but only so long as reason remains in the natural world. Under his spell, one mistakes a plausible formal coherence for verified truth.

Yet when this great Dominican's work is taken as a whole, one cannot dispute the power of his mind or the sheer aggregate wealth of its operations: no one, except perhaps Aristotle, had ever taken in so much or had ordered his results with such thoroughness. Here is an astounding grasp of both the grand outlines and the minute details of human existence: of life divine and human, eternal and transitory, life domestic and life political, life actual and possible, life as the mystics behold it in rare moments of visionary ecstasy and life as men and women in every walk of life experience it, day by day. Here, perhaps, the secrets of the confessional, never before available to philosophers, were utilized with astonishing skill and unshakable poise: never again to be equaled till the Jesuits in the sixteenth century, or the Freudians in the twentieth, devote themselves to the further cure of souls. Here was a new kind of saint: one who took all knowledge for his province. In this mind, one measures the height of the Church's accomplishment; and in the Summa Theologica one sees that mind at its fullest mastery.

The Summa Theologica is not a book; it is not even an encyclopedia. One cannot treat it as a literary achievement in the degree that one might refer in this fashion to the work of Aristotle, who is a model for academic exposition: the Summa is rather to be considered as a work of engineering, conceived on a cyclopean scale, by one of the ablest technical minds of any age. Roger Bacon, in the thirteenth century, dreamed of motor-driven carriages and airships; but Thomas Aquinas erected a fabric that had nothing to equal it in technical organization until the great textile mills of the nineteenth century were designed and built. Even works of engineering may show imagination and esthetic command; but those are the last qualities to look for in the Summa. An immense textile factory, with a thousand looms, each bringing forth a uniform product—that is the closest image.

In the Summa, one loom is like another: each uses the same warp, the same thread, the same shuttle: it is only the color and the pattern that differ. God, the angels, the principalities, the demons, the Holy Ghost, the saints, the Church, men and women, the secular and the theological virtues, the forms of law and government, the ordering of the economic life—each has a special loom, each loom its product, each bolt unrolls as part of an orderly plan. There are no surprises, once one understands the organization of the factory. An unexpected result would imply a defect in the machinery. Every part of this work is directed toward a single goal: life perfected in the sight of God, consummated in Eternity. This is man's last end; and the best words for it are perhaps to be found in a passage in Aquinas's Summa Contra Gentiles:

"Man's last end is the term of his natural appetite, or that when he has obtained it, he desires nothing more: because if he still has a movement towards something, he has not yet reached an end wherein to be at rest. Now this cannot happen in this life: since the more man understands the more is the desire to understand increased in him,—this being natural to man,—unless perhaps someone there who understands all things, and in this life this never did nor can happen to anyone that was a mere man. . . . Happiness is the last end which man desires naturally. Consequently unless together with happiness he acquires a state of immobility, he is not yet happy, since his natural desire is not yet at rest. . . . Now in this life there is no sure stability. . . . Therefore man's ultimate happiness cannot be in this life."

In Thomism, the Catholic Church found a logical doctrine of evolution from nature to supernature: from the potentialities of this world of flux and change and imperfection to the actualities of complete realization in a state of rest and immobility in another world. This philosophy allowed for the fact of change within the temporal process: it accepted the imperfections and shortcomings of biography and history. But it transferred the ultimate meaning of life to an eternal realm in which the historic process was both consummated and rationally justified in terms that transcended mere human reason. Perhaps the best modern discussion of this essential Christian position is that in Dr. Reinhold Niebuhr's The Nature and Destiny of Man.

Each part of the mechanism of argument and proof in the Summa is devised for supporting the belief that the ultimate meaning of life lies not in any temporal process but in its eternal consummation: the realm where time, history, change, come to an end: where virtue is immobilized in bliss and where sin is finally also immobilized in damnation. Theology supplied the pre-designed end for this proof: Aristotelian logic furnished the method. One follows the argument in a series of articulated steps: if one accepts any particular chain of demonstration, it will be easy to follow with equal conviction all the rest, for they are established in the same fashion.

Only one proof is missing. Unfortunately, it is that on which every other part depends for both its function and its end: the proof of God's existence. Life is too short, Thomas observes, to make that possible. Lacking this ultimate authority, the philosopher contents himself with limited authorities, backed by divine revelation—a logical error since the truth of revelation remains that which is to be proved. This is a serious weakness in one who trusts logic itself so unreservedly. All Thomas Aquinas's care is devoted to the superstructure, and that, accordingly, is solid and tight: it is the foundations that remain shaky. When reason must appeal to authority, authority should remain open to reason. By accepting its special revelation as final, Christian dogma provided no means for revising its postulates and replacing its crumbled underpinnings.

Nevertheless, the weaving itself is a prodigious achievement: however monotonous the process of thought in this doctrinal textile mill, however dull the surface texture of the goods, the fabric itself, when it comes within the province of actual human experience, could hardly be sounder. What rests upon observation and common sense is truly seen and wisely pondered. For Thomas Aquinas had a supremely healthy mind; nothing daunted it; nothing surprised it; nothing could shake it from faith; nothing could upset its superb equilibrium.

Let us try out Thomas Aquinas at the point where the Church's original doctrines had been most opposite to man's common needs and his biological destiny: marriage in all its aspects. And to begin with, the status of the body. "Happiness," Thomas said properly, "does not consist in bodily good as its object, but bodily good can add a certain charm and perfection to happiness." That is not an isolated expression: Thomas's supernaturalism was based on an acceptance of nature itself and of man's place in the realm of nature, even as his acceptance of revelation was based on the use of reason wherever it did not contradict revelation. His understanding of nature made him quietly oppose the holy doctrine of denial. "Now just as in respect of his corporeal nature man naturally desires the pleasures of food and sex, so in respect of his soul, he desires to know something." Both desires, in Thomas Aquinas's eyes, are rational as long as they do not actively impede the practice of a holy life: being natural, frivolity and relaxation, in due measure, at the right time, can also be justified.

Berthold of Regensburg might condemn women's preoccupation with finery and their growing love of pleasure, but the Neapolitan philosopher uttered no unconditional reproof. "If a married woman adorn herself in order to please her husband, she can do this without sin" since this may be a way of keeping him from falling into adultery. Or again: "Whatever is contrary to the natural order is vicious. Now nature has introduced pleasure into the operations that are necessary for man's life. Wherefore the natural order requires that man should make use of these pleasures, in so far as they are necessary to man's well-being, as regards the preservation of either the individual or the species. Accordingly, if anyone were to reject pleasure to the extent of omitting things that are necessary for nature's preservation he would sin, as acting contrary to the order of nature. And this applies to the vice of insensibility."

Take a critical question in Christian marriage: "Whether it is a mortal sin for a man to have knowledge of his wife, with the intention not of a marriage good but merely of pleasure." In contrast to the present opinion of Rome, Thomas Aquinas boldly replies: "On the contrary . . . carnal intercourse of this kind is one of the daily sins for which we say Our Father. Now these are not mortal sins. Therefore, etc. . . . Further, it is no mortal sin to take food for mere pleasure. Therefore in like manner it is not a mortal sin for a man to use his wife merely to satisfy his desire." By the same token, what is called in Thomas's quaint terminology the payment of the marital debt, that is, sexual intercourse, he treats as a remedy against "the wife's concupiscence. Now a physician who has the care of a sick person is bound to remedy the disease without being asked. Therefore the husband is bound to pay the debt to his wife although she ask not for it"—provided she give unmistakable indications of her desire. The analogy, like so many analogies that seemed plausible to the medieval mind, is plainly specious; but the common sense is excellent.

In Thomas Aquinas's very abundance of common sense, in his cool, straightforward logic, in his naturalistic open-mindedness, the Church plainly came to terms with the vitality it had once so severely opposed and thwarted: it no longer sought to dam up life altogether, but was content to direct it and to do so was willing to carve a wider channel for it. There lay a profound wisdom, which has enabled the Catholic Church to keep its benign grip on a vast body of believers down to our own time. But in that change, plainly, one fact stood out: the period of rejection was over and a period of dangerous consummations was at hand.

It would be a pleasure to watch Aquinas's great mind confront a thousand other problems and difficulties. While his feet trudged painfully over every foot of the ground, his eye never lost sight of the horizon and his path never deviated. Such a combination of powers is too rare to miss: his inclusiveness, his balance, his strong sense of justice, his wide variety of genuine interests, are to the last degree admirable.

As for his central vision of life, I cannot withhold here a passage that sums it up. "Now if we wish to assign an end to any whole, and to the parts of that whole, we shall find, firstly, that each and every part exists for the sake of its proper act, as the eye for the act of seeing; secondly, that less honorable parts exist for the more honorable, as the senses for the intellect, the lungs for the heart; and thirdly, that all parts are for the perfection of the whole, as the matter for the form, for the parts are, as it were, the matter of the whole. Furthermore, the whole man is on account of an extrinsic end, that end being the function of God. So, therefore, in the parts of the universe also every creature exists for its own proper act and perfection, and the less noble for the nobler, as those creatures that are less noble than man exist for the sake of man, whilst each and every creature exists for the perfection of the entire universe. Furthermore, the entire universe, with all its parts, is ordained toward God as the end, inasmuch as it imitates, as it were, and shadows forth the divine goodness, to the glory of God. Reasonable creatures, however, have in some special and higher manner God as their end, since they can attain to him by their own operations of knowing and loving him. Thus it is plain that the Divine Goodness is the end of all corporeal things." That philosophy wrought every part of life into a meaningful whole: an etherealized image of feudal gradations and papal unity.

Accordingly, it is the logician, not the man, who disappoints one: it is his theory of knowledge, his theory of meaning, his theory of the relation of symbols to experiences that are gravely at fault. His logical and grammatical order are very partial contributions to objective proof. Granted that postulates must be finally tested, not by any immediate self-verification, but by their adequacy in providing a basis for experimental and empirical proofs, there is such a thing as an economy of faith as well as an economy of hypotheses: if faith is incontinent, it will spawn figments and chimeras—and reason will then be impotent. Without faith in his senses and his symbolisms man cannot create a reasonable world: but one must not tax faith with camels when gnats are easier to swallow.

Thomas Aquinas sought to unite naturalistic observation with a supernatural cosmos that was on the point of disintegration. Hence it was not reason, but false prudence, that caused him to assert that "it is unlawful to hold that any false assertion is contained in the Gospel or in any canonical scripture." Could the truth itself be unlawful? Must revelation protect itself by the aid of the Father of Lies? Actually, a great part of Thomas Aquinas's work consisted in adroitly getting around the falsehoods and errors in canonical scriptures that were in contradiction to experience and reason. Therein lay many of his most substantial contributions: for he repaired the mischief wrought by Paul and rehabilitated the very philosophers to whom Christianity would indeed have been a stumbling block. To refuse to challenge the authority of Holy Writ because faith would be deprived of its absolute certitude was to pitch faith at the level of obstinate irrationality and to dishonor all true authority.

Faced with the need for choosing between experimental evidence and rational demonstration on one hand, and arbitrary authority on the other, Aquinas chose authority for purely pragmatic reasons: it greatly simplified his task and guaranteed his orthodoxy. He still needed the protecting walls of the Church, and in contrast to the Cathedral builders, he was unwilling to weaken the piers of dogma. Had he been altogether easy in this decision he might have spared himself much of his pains; but his uneasiness led to an elaborate comparison and selection of authorities. By intelligent acts of discrimination, by testing the Bible against Plato, the Church Fathers against Aristotle, the philosopher lessened the dangers of clinging to a single text and giving that finality. Unlike Augustine, he was far enough away from the Greek philosophers no longer to feel that they might pollute his faith. Aquinas's fresh contribution to Christian doctrine came through this deliberate introduction of rejected sources: above all, Aristotle. He thus escaped the error of later Protestants who again narrowed their intellectual heritage. Within its self-imposed limits, the Summa Theologica was an effective synthesis of rational knowledge.

But note one curious neglect: the words of Jesus himself were relatively seldom invoked as authority. It is almost as if the Angelic Doctor understood that Jesus's doctrine of life as the manifestation and exaltation of love was the grain of radium that might disintegrate this complex scholastic structure. Perhaps his understanding of Jesus's simplifications came to him in the very course of writing his great Summa, for he left it unfinished. According to legend, Thomas had had a vision, and from that time forth he wrote no more. Did he suddenly understand Jesus's secret? Did he remember that the only words Jesus wrote were written in the sand?

One final weakness. Like most other philosophers, Aquinas understood everything except the limits of philosophy: deeply though he accepted Christian faith, he did not realize that knowledge is not enough. What can be reasoned about, what can be ordered or fabricated, was here: what must be dumbly felt, passively experienced, intuitively revealed, what must be told in hints and parables, the truths that Plato himself would not commit to writing despite his command of language, truths that escape through the finest logical filter and are deformed if caught in the gauziest of philosophic nets—all that is left outside the Summas. That itself only deepens the parallels with the textile mill: there are some Dacca cottons so fine that they must be spun by hand on the human knee and woven on the most primitive of handlooms. . . . Only Dante's vision can add the colors of life to Thomas Aquinas's severe fabric.

Wherever one may put the Summa, its doctrines belong to the World as well as to Heaven. As such, it was an organic expression of medieval society, not merely as it meant to be but as it actually was. But this philosophy belongs to the world in its highest sense: it is an endeavor to re-think and rationalize all human experience, omitting nothing that is important for man's development, stressing everything that worked toward ultimate human happiness and human perfection. Who better than Aquinas had a firm sense of the structure of the community: who but he dared place justice and fortitude above temperance, for the reason that the good of man is more godlike than the good of the individual, wherefore the more a virtue regards the good of man, the better it is? (That was a long way from the concern for purely individual salvation, the *sauve qui peut* mood, of early Christianity.)

Aquinas was a realist in both the medieval and the modern sense of the word. In him, the urban-minded friars espoused the cause of corporate order and human solidarity against the individualism of the more rural monks. But if Thomas Aquinas set the social virtues high, he inevitably put prudence and the theological virtues, faith, hope, and charity, even higher. The entire structure mounts logically upward to God: at the topmost point, matter reaches into the immaterial, the natural world into the supernatural, and man's mastery into God's mystery.

At some critical points, I have already noted, the fabric of Aquinas's philosophy is composed of whole cloth, like the garment woven by the clever tailors in Hans Andersen's fairy story: the proof of the existence of angels can satisfy one no better than the proof that the body, when resurrected, will be thirty years old, because that is the most perfect stage in human life. But despite the gaps that are now so plainly visible in the cloth, the very will-to-unity was life-sustaining. By sheer technical ability, Aquinas accomplished a task that his nearest equals, Aristotle before him, Leibnitz, Kant, and Spencer after him, could not surpass. With good reason, Pope Leo XIII proclaimed it in 1879 the official philosophy of the Roman Catholic Church.

So closely, however, was Aquinas's synthesis an expression of his culture that, unlike the Cathedral, it did not point beyond itself or allow for further passages of time, thought, and experience. It was a closed synthesis: if it opened avenues to the past, it made the future a dead end. No further intellectual or spiritual development was possible within this tightly mortared structure. Medieval man was thus caught between a conceptual world that remained fixed, that seemed completed for eternity, and a practical world that was continually expanding the field of action and challenging the integrity of the synthesis by which he chose to live. His idolum had originally been fabricated to give him protection in a time of decay: it was now called upon to perform the contradictory task of providing a rational basis for action in a time of constructive change. The stout piles that had been used as a breakwater against the winter storms were of no use to those bent on building ships and traversing new seas.

7: The Dawn of Naturalism

The rationality of Thomas Aquinas's structure must be gauged in terms of what he excluded; for he admitted of the undemonstrable only so much as was needed, on his premises, to create a logical whole. Beyond that point he was rigorous. The popular world picture, on the other hand, covered life with a crazy-quilt of subjective fantasies: arbitrary connections, irrelevant numerical relationships, mythical attributes, supernatural visions, formed the medium of everyday experience.

The stars that interested medieval man, for example, were not nature's stars, but the stars of astrological lore: stars that guided the Magi to Bethlehem or foretold one's luck in love or war. The four points of the compass were not just geographical directions: they pointed, as Honorius d'Autun made clear in De Imagine Mundi, to a mystical arithmetic: there was a mysterious connection with the four elements, air, earth, water, and fire; with the four rivers of paradise; with the four winds; with the four humors of the body; with the four cardinal virtues of the soul. The four sciences of the Quadrivium, plus the three sciences of the Trivium, produced seven: both three and four, magical in themselves, had magical consequences: the seven planets, the seven virtues, the seven deadly sins, the seven tones of the Gregorian chant all exhibited this secret correspondence between thoughts and things. Even Thomas Aquinas pointed out at length the exquisite fitness of the seven sacraments, which corresponded to the seven ages of man.

Every factual observation, every actual experience, had at least a double meaning: its mundane and its super-rational meaning: sometimes layer upon layer of devious meanings. Life was an allegory, a mystery, a miracle.

In medieval culture, the dream-ridden Don Quixote, not Sancho Panza, leads the way, even when they travel together. In that figure Cervantes captured, not just the belated romanticism of sixteenth century Spain, but the deeper dream world of medieval Europe. Dreams governed: for it is only in dreams that people are roasted in Hell for eternity without being consumed: it is only in dreams that the physical body, long dissolved, is resurrected at the Judgment Day and becomes flesh without continuing any of its specific biological characteristics: it is in dreams that the sins and errors committed on earth justify an eternity of misery, and that even perfect virtue, without the rite of baptism, has no claim to heavenly felicity. Dreams these were: childish dreams. No mature life could be founded on such fantasies.

Fortunately, the medieval personality made a resolute effort to achieve maturity; and from the twelfth century on, if not before, the symbols of fantasy had a rival: the symbols of nature and reason. If the first covered and colored every aspect of life, the second quietly made headway in one department after another, not denying fantasy or revelation, but paying ever more attention to nature: the topography of Heaven shrank as that of the earth itself was depicted in greater detail. Naturalism grew out of the daily occupations and the working life of the craftsman: in his struggle with obdurate materials, melting glass, hammering iron, hewing stone, beating copper, he learned to respect the nature of the materials and the objective conditions for successful operation. Prayer would work only if one added to its efficacy by intelligently manipulating the environment. That was the daily lesson of craftsmanship. Results might be fanciful; but the process of achieving them was matter-of-fact.

Naturalism in the Middle Ages came like the returning consciousness of a man awakened from an absorbing dream. Heavily, he hears the stir of people in the neighboring room; he sees the sunlight coming through the curtains; he even smells the bacon frying in the kitchen: gradually all his senses become alive and he realizes what o'clock it is; yet the ragged ends of dream images, with their residue of emotional disturbance, may hang over and blot out the clarity of the waking moment: reminiscent flickers of dream may remain with him all through the day. So with the medieval personality. The eye first awakened, not only to color but to light: the outlines of shapes became clearer. Knowledge now presented itself under the figure of the speculum or mirror: an accurate reflection of the outer world. Vincent of Beauvais, who died in 1264, compiled the Speculum Naturale, Morale, Doctrinale, et Historicale. The belief in the unseen and the incredible now had a rival doctrine to face: "seeing was believing."

This new attitude was well put by Roger Bacon, the Franciscan scientist, in the part of the Opus Majus that concerned itself with experimental science. "He therefore who wishes to rejoice without doubt in regard to the truths underlying phenomena must know how to devote himself to experiment. For authors write many statements and people believe them through reasoning which they formulate without experience. Their reasoning is wholly false. For it is generally believed that the diamond cannot be broken except by goat's blood, and philosophers and theologians misuse this idea. But a fracture by means of blood of this kind has never been verified, although the effort has been made; and without that blood it can be broken easily. For I have seen this work with my own eyes." Note the phrase: *with my own eyes*. Human sight began to displace supernatural visions: the two can still be seen, side by side, on the façade of almost any thirteenth or fourteenth century cathedral.

Though Bacon's work brought him into rank disfavor with his ecclesiastical superiors he was not alone. Albertus Magnus produced a treatise on plants that, according to Singer, is perhaps the best work on Natural History in the Middle Ages. For the first time the illustrators, instead of copying the drawings of previous writers and gradually deforming them, went out into the woods, like the stone carver, and copied the living plant. While chemical and physical investigations went on more slowly, they were not altogether absent; for the founders of alchemy, the Arabs, had paved the way, and the results of their work were now filtering into Europe.

All this knowledge depended upon the first-hand investigation of the properties of matter. The hand and the eye together, aided by glass lenses and glassless telescopes, began to reveal aspects of the external world hitherto unfamiliar. Nor were these efforts entirely at random. In the desire to relieve pain, for example, the medieval physician, if he did not follow up the uses of ether, nevertheless employed a variety of plant products, including opium, for soporific sponges. Nicholas of Salerno describes these sponges in his Antidotarium. In an age that knew no limit to the use of torture for punishment, either on earth or in the after-life, such a growing sensibility to the body's feelings was significant.

The body itself was both an object of naturalist observation and an instrument for its further advance. If saints still despised the body, that rejection no longer held for the burghers and the knights. The public bath, whose passing was almost a symbol of the fall of Rome, came back again in every town. In The Decameron, a lady waiting for her lover prepares a bath for him, and when he fails to appear, takes it herself: a measure of economy, an act of hygiene, perhaps a display of physiological insight and moral prudence. From the twelfth century on the interest in health and hygiene and sanitation steadily grew. The center of this movement was the great medical school at Salerno. Along with Montpellier, this school was one of the chief transmitters of Arabic and Jewish medical science; so that there is more truth than fancy in the legend that it was founded in the seventh century A.D. by a Jew, a Greek, a Saracen, and a Latin. There is no doubt, furthermore, that it numbered occasional women students among the men: as late as the fifteenth century a certain Costenzella Calenda received a degree.

From Salerno, above all, came the famous treatise on health and personal hygiene: the Regimen Sanitatis Salernitem. This book was first addressed to the upper classes, professedly to England's king; but in interminable translations and paraphrases it made its way throughout Europe; and its precepts became the main source of modern hygiene. Here one finds a regimen for both the day and the whole span of life: advice to keep the head free from care and the heart from wrath: to be moderate in eating and drinking: to avoid postponement in moving one's bowels: to rise early in the morning, wash hands and eyes, comb the hair and rub the teeth. Wine, women, and baths do good or harm, according as they are used or abused. Lodge in clean light quarters, away from stagnant water or excrement; eat according to the season; wash your hands frequently; do not suddenly break your habits of diet, and observe that a good diet is "a perfect way of curing." Bodily temperaments do not by themselves breed virtue or vice, yet they give them inclinations one way or another, and since they are dependent upon physiological states, they may be altered. As for medical care, the best physicians are Dr. Quiet, Dr. Merry-Man, and Dr. Diet. This whole treatise was, in fact, the epitome of medical common sense, and its influence was deservedly enduring. We are all in its debt.

Not merely did the notion of contagious diseases become current in the thirteenth century, but thirteen diseases were identified as such: including phthisis, anthrax, trachoma, and erysipelas. Leprosy, the worst of scourges, was wiped out in the course of a few centuries by absolute quarantine: a triumph of preventive medicine. The quarantine itself, forty days in a house of isolation outside the city's gates, was a definite medieval device to curb collective infection: its only weakness was that it erred in giving a longer time for the incubation period than any disease is now supposed to require. But it was more adequate on all counts than the "advanced" medicine of the early nineteenth century, which looked upon both contagion and the quarantine as relics of medieval superstition.

This increase in positive knowledge of the body in health and disease was a salutary challenge to medieval supernaturalism: it rubbed against the grain of irrational belief. But faith in verbal magic and disdain for the body and its works still acted as a brake. That fact was recorded in the ban against a priest's becoming a surgeon, because he would thereby shed blood: it also showed itself in imputing a higher status to book knowledge and the unimplemented workings of "reason" than to observation, manipulation, and manual skil. Allbutt notes that the faculty of the University of Paris, in the twelfth century, expelled those who worked with their hands. Students of medicine could not let blood, bandage wounds, pull teeth, or perform any operations. From this time on, surgery and dentistry were both in disrepute; and their historic separation from internal medicine, so called, has done mischief which still exacts a toll today: the glorified garage mechanic, the pompous faith healer, and the mental dissectionist who treats diseases, not human beings—all these are still witnesses to the ancient quarrel between the unhandy minds and the unminded hands of the thirteenth century.

In all, however, a growing faith in the order of nature acted as a counterweight to unverified revelation or parroted authority. One has a notion of how commonplace this attitude became when one sees how it seeped through to those who were unschooled directly in either science or philosophy. How does the Goodman of Paris, that pious burgher of the fourteenth century, commend the Christian virtue of loving faithfulness in marriage to his young wife? He is not content to quote the Church's precepts and warnings alone; by now that is no longer the final word. He calls all nature to witness. . . . "Even the birds and the shy wild beasts, nay the savage beasts, have the sense and practice of this, for the female birds do ever follow and keep close to their mates and to none other and follow them and fly after them." There is no doubt about the Goodman's feeling of kinship: a remote prelude to Darwin's observations on the emotions in animals. For the merchant tells story after story that shows how men had come, despite Christian supernaturalism, to accept man's life as part of the general order of nature.

Yet the concepts of theology had a pragmatic value for science: they kept open the doors of the imagination, gave confidence in the essential order and rationality of the universe, that is, in the reign of law; and schooled the mind in the use of operative terms which have no physical counterpart. The conception of a disembodied angel is unverifiable by the senses: so is the concept of a mathematical point or a line, an atom or an electron: the difference is that the latter concepts bring order and clarity into the behavior of physical bodies, while a guardian angel, when invoked to explain human conduct, adds an ultimate mystery to an immediate one. So the Arabic-Hindu conception of zero, the notion that no-thing is a kind of thing, could hardly have occurred except in a culture that had originally concentrated on the annihilation of the senses. Zero and infinity are essentially theological conceptions: neither belongs to the phenomenal world, except by symbolic representation.

Is this perhaps why the most creative minds in physical science have often been at home in the realms of orthodox theology? One need only mention the names of Newton, Pascal, Leibnitz, Faraday, Clerk-Maxwell. After one has dealt faithfully with the incorrigible muddle of medieval symbolism, one must still pay tribute to the vitality of its imagination and its faith. The very development of naturalism would have been disordered and unprofitable without the abstract sense of order that theology itself had created. Astronomy and geometry and arithmetic and music were essential subjects in the medieval curriculum: no educated mind could escape their discipline. Time-keeping, spatial measurement, and numerical calculation at length transformed the study of nature. The medieval Church, with its concern for Eternity, lengthened the time-perspective and helped to translate mechanical order into time and time into mechanical order: the great clock in the Cathedral at Lübeck, which dated from 1405, was equipped with a calendar which reached forward to the year 2000. Even astrology, which professed to correlate earthly events with planetary movements, popularized the art of exact observation and exact calculation; it caused people to record promptly the hour of birth, if only to make the horoscope more accurate. The dramatic regularity of the heavens gave man a sense of an external order that guaranteed and fulfilled his own inner will-to-order. The very fruitfulness of naturalism as developed during the Middle Ages was bound up with its confidence in an all-pervasive determinism: the predestined will of God. That logic, that order, would eventually declare itself to man by way of science.

8: Earthly Tragedy: Divine Comedy

The Middle Ages reached a unique culmination. At the height of its achievement, all that it was and hoped to be, all that it had created and all that it failed at, its orthodoxy and its heresies, its conflicts and its resolutions, found their way into a single work of art, The Divine Comedy.

Fully to understand Dante Alighieri's poem, one must understand the experience that led up to it and made it what it was. The two magistral volumes that Karl Vossler devoted to this task are a minimum preparation for that understanding. But when one has fully encompassed the poem itself, one has almost exhausted the period: what remains over is little more than a few notes scribbled on the margin. In Dante, the whole Middle Ages found a voice; and in the poem itself that voice came from the other side of the grave. Writing to Can Grande, Dante said that the true subject of The Divine Comedy was the state of the soul after death: "the whole work was undertaken, not for a speculative but for a practical end," and its purpose was to anticipate the Judgment Day, in effect, by removing "those who are living in this life from the state of wretchedness and to lead them to the state of blessedness."

The writing of such a poem was a solemn and audacious ambition: an attempt to circumvent the slow processes of history and make the poetic imagination anticipate the ultimate revelation of the divine order: an heretical effort for an orthodox end. Since the state of the soul after death depended upon man's earthly actions and his eventual achievement of grace and salvation, it included everything, in the order of significance chosen by medieval man. Yet it was in the deepest spirit of his culture that Dante utilized his poetic insight in order to make the unimaginableness of eternity concrete—as concrete as the work of a peasant breaking clods with a mattock, as minutely particular as the decisions of a court of law, as subject to logical order, as clear and demonstrable, as a geometer's proof. Classifications, boundaries, limits, protective walls were essential to this culture: the vague and the shadowy and the unformed had no part even in pure fantasy: the most grotesque gargoyle on the highest pinnacle stood out in clear silhouette, done with as fine detail as a hand or a face that would be seen almost at eye-level. It is only when Dante reaches the very center of Divine Being that he finally confesses his task as impossible as the mathematician's squaring of the circle: for the final revelation words fail him.

Dante concluded the medieval pilgrimage and anticipated its final Day of Judgment. That is why today Dante seems at first blush the most distant of poets. Homer's world, with its fights, quests, brazen deities, capricious doxies, and strong vain men is so near that it could be dished up, a decade or so ago, as a popular novel. Hamlet in modern dress might be any wealthy young man who has temporarily escaped the care of his psychoanalyst. Horace furnishes themes for newspaper columnists. The things that separate us from Horace's Rome or Shakespeare's London are largely decorative and topographical: with one short leap of the imagination we are over the wall. But Dante is not so easily approached; for he belongs to a quite different spiritual organism. His world still had a dimension which even the Orthodox Christian can now keep before himself only by a rigorous effort: it had the dimension of eternity, not as an occasional but as a constant accompaniment of living. The proud turbulence of medieval life was dwarfed and darkened by the solar shadow of another world.

For Dante, as for every other true member of this culture, life was at its best still a dying, and death, even for the damned, was the beginning of man's essential career. The credulous market women of Verona, who believed that Dante could descend at will into Hell, pointed to his smoky complexion for proof. But they scarcely exaggerated the closeness of the supernatural, even in the crowning years of medieval culture. The realm toward which Dante's vision was directed in The Divine Comedy had been described with the same sort of authority that now convinces the common man of the existence of electrons and vitamins: to believe thus was a test of sanity. Only a few people suspected that the body of dogma on which this certainty was founded could be successfully assaulted, or even—and that was more serious—could simply be laid aside and ignored. Life existed for Dante within the walls of a great Necropolis: the universal city of the dead. To penetrate the Hereafter and to understand it was an immediate, an objective task. More: it was the very condition of Dante's triumphing over the evils of life and tasting the final fruits of ideal love.

The Divine Comedy follows the journey of the poet through Hell, Purgatory, and Heaven. At the beginning of his journey he is accompanied by the noble shade of Virgil, his spiritual master and guide—given his special place for the same reason that Christ, Dante thought, chose the Roman Empire itself as the state in which he was born. At the end, Dante is guided through Heaven by the fragile girl he worshiped and loved with an otherworldly love, and finds himself completed by discovering his place in the divine whole.

At every stage of this journey, Dante was his own all-too-human self: full of veneration for his classic master, viewing the damned both with hatred and pity, revenging himself on his enemies, giving way to fear before the monsters who presided over the various places of punishment, displaying his friendship in Purgatory and his theological scholarship in Paradise, remembering his mission as a poet, seeking for intellectual clarity and ideological certitude: always a Florentine, though bitterly conscious of his exile from his city, and always a proud man, ambitious for fame, and sure that his ambition would be fulfilled.

In short, Dante was a man of great virtues and grave sins: instead of discreetly leaving himself out of the poem, as a minor poet might have been tempted to, he suppressed nothing and spared no one, not even himself. Contemptuously, he placed those who had lived blameless lives in the meanest part of Hell, mixed with the caitiff choir of angels who were not rebellious nor were faithful to God, but were for themselves: even the downright wicked would have some glory over such people. In this honest revelation of his own weaknesses, as he passes from one circle of the afterworld to another, Dante formulated the Christian conception of the good life, not as one free from error and sin, but one that, by baptism and repentance, may overcome its inevitable failures and earn a final place in Heaven.

The essence of The Divine Comedy is that this is a moral world and that sin and virtue not merely have a practical issue but an eternal significance: they not only matter, but they matter infinitely, they matter eternally. The stoic's insensibility to suffering was no guarantee of happiness: the later utilitarian notion, enunciated by Bentham, that the aim of life is to increase pleasures and lessen pains was equally at fault. According to Dante's deeper science, "the more a thing is perfect, the more it feels pleasure and likewise pain." It is this very capacity for perfection, this will to experience intense feeling, this need to embrace pain as well as pleasure, that explains Dante's strange journey: pain and evil now have a positive value, and he who cannot face them cannot understand life or participate fully in its rewards. That salutary capacity to embrace all the dimensions of human experience gives Dante's vision its organic completeness. Never was there a more deliberate effort to purge the soul through pity and terror, through horror and disgust and unbearable anguish, than in the Inferno, where some of the damned are turned into trees, wracked by the careless twisting off of a twig; and others are "dipped in excrement that seemed as it had flowed from human privies" and others gnaw at their own flesh. Symbols of horror for spiritual states that are no less horrible. Following these encounters, the song and light that suffuse Heaven at the end are hardly enough to remove the turbid residue of this nightmare. Dante earned his final state of joy.

The Divine Comedy is a true synthesis precisely because it touches life on every side and makes use of discord and conflict, of irrationality no less than reason, of wordless existences and essences no less than logical formulations: hence, to speak boldly, it is both the Summa Theologica and the Cathedral wrought into a single whole. The poem has the concreteness of art and the abstract clarity of metaphysics: an imagination that is all-embracing resolves experience into an order that is absolute. The very structure of The Divine Comedy is, naturally, an integral part of its meaning. In this supernatural landscape with figures, the entire design reveals a predestined plan and purpose: nothing is left to accident or to fitful inspiration. The stanzas of three lines, the three divisions of the hereafter, the thirty-three cantos in each division, the completion of each part by the final symbol of spiritual illumination: the star—all this reflects the cosmic harmony.

The main subjects of Dante's poem, the fall and redemption of mankind, the contrasting states of the soul after death, would have lost their power to hold us today had Dante merely given expression to the limitations of medieval theology. It is because Dante included all the varieties of human expression and experience, the natural and the cultivated, the concrete, the transcendental, that this poem still enriches the human spirit. Every part of Dante's personal life contributed to this impersonal result: Dante the municipal official, Dante the technician, familiar with the construction of public works if not the designer of them, Dante the amateur artist and the friend of Giotto, Dante the diplomat and political theorist, the author of De Monarchia, were as necessary to this poem as the youthful follower of the Provençal poets or the student of Thomas Aquinas.

In Dante's supernaturalism there was a place for all nature. This indicates the task that confronts the philosopher and the poet in our own time: for in one sense, our natural order is but Dante's world in reverse; and our task is to bring a sense of the eternal and the infinite back into common daily life: to recast our narrow frame of reference so that it will encompass all that remains humanly valid in the medieval conception of the supernatural: not by claiming false knowledge about the unknowable, but by understanding that our life, too, is an allegory, because what man makes of it in the soul is ultimately as important as what is given in the senses. In our naturalism there must be a place for the unresolved mysteries of the world, and life, and time: for every extension of our knowledge and mastery only deepens our ultimate problems as to the nature and meaning of life. In short, it was not simply the supernaturalism of the medieval dream, but its smug humanness, that betrayed its essential flaw. In so confidently revealing God's purposes Dante only disclosed the narrow human limits of his own.

But in this one respect Dante still rings true: since life *is* an allegory, the life that man re-lives in the mind is his true heaven and hell. Human existence is a twice-told tale, and only through that part of it which is translated into meaningful symbols and valuable patterns of conduct does man truly come into possession of his kingdom. The great task of human life is to remain fully alive both on the plane of organic existence and on the plane of symbolic participation. The movement of life into the ideal realm in which all existence has meaning, form, and value, and the passage of these ideas back again into life is the essential systole and diastole of the human heart. All the extra dimensions added by man's symbols provide both a deeper fulfillment and a further continuation of his biological existence: to reproduce and develop himself he must equally reproduce and develop his immaterial heritage. Man's earthly life, in short, involves the existence of another transcendental world: a world of durable meanings and values that in time detach themselves from the flux of history, and loose their narrow ties to time and place. Only a small part of human existence actually goes into this other world; and a still smaller fraction is passed on from generation to generation, from culture to culture, from epoch to epoch. But that little is infinitely precious; and its accumulation is what constitutes human progress.

Religion, art, ethics, philosophy, poetry, science—these are the ultimate agents in man's self-transformation. All man's other acts, deeds, acquisitions, discoveries, masteries, are significant only to the extent that they finally find expression in these realms. This is an old conception; it could hardly be otherwise. With good reason Dante was grateful to his old teacher, Brunetto Latini, whom he encountered in Hell, because he "taught me how man makes himself eternal." There are many ways of interpreting this task, and man has often childishly misconceived the means of bringing it about: but it remains the supreme task of every community and every personality. That is why the supernatural theology of the Middle Ages was closer to reality than the crass materialism of an age which fancies that the achievement of an "economy of abundance" will automatically ensure a maximum of human felicity.

Because Dante's poem was eternal in the manner I have just defined the word it gives a sense of reality in all its dimensions that enables the work of art to live beyond the limits of the society for which it seemed an ultimate revelation. What one calls the medieval synthesis was no fixed and final thing: indeed, the very appearance of such a comprehensive philosophy as that of Aquinas's and such a comprehensive vision as that of Dante's is almost a signal for further changes and transformations. Every synthesis, however full and all-embracing, is the expression of a particular cultural moment: the more complete the structure seems, the more surely must it be shattered if it is to hold future experience. To aim at unity is the prime condition of life: to hold on to this unity, to immobilize it, is the prelude to death. The very forces that make for unity must in time break it down through further growth.

There was a dramatic finality in the fact that, when Dante himself died in 1321, at the age of fifty-six, this culture was on the verge of the abyss. Though Dante's verse continued to enchant and discourage the poets of

Italy, his vision of life disappeared with the finality of a meteor whose very speed and heat, as it drives through the atmosphere, causes it to leave no mark in the earth where it buries itself. In Dante, the medieval personality had completed its pilgrimage.

9: The Moment of Integration

By the end of the twelfth century the Church of Rome had reached the highest point of internal unity and external influence. This was a period of consolidation. Now the looseness and uncertainty of Christian practice, vaguenesses in dogma and solecisms of thought, had become intolerable. In this century the codification of Canon Law took place: the Church from now on administered justice to its own numerous officers under a unified system of jurisprudence. Now, too, the seven sacraments of the Church were finally established: baptism, confirmation, ordination, marriage, absolution, holy communion, and extreme unction. In 1170 the Holy See reserved for itself the right of canonizing saints; in 1215 the great Lateran Council made confession obligatory once a year. Finally, in the twelfth century, the systematic persecution of heresy began, under forms that restored the Roman practice of torture—a practice that had practically disappeared during the so-called Dark Ages. The mechanization of torture was not the least achievement of medieval technics.

This process of unification and incorporation hastened the final embodiment of the Christian way of life, in cities and buildings, in statues, book illuminations, and paintings: the Invisible Kingdom now became the Church Visible, Visible and Beautiful, administering its offices every hour of the day, dominating every horizon with walled abbeys and towering churches, filling the ear with chant and prayer and song, giving the final grace of art and ritual to every moment of life.

During the twelfth and thirteenth centuries the Christian lived in what was mainly a Christian World, not the world of Jesus of Nazareth, but the world that his historic mission had finally brought into being. Dante so exulted in this world that he thought it justified the Roman Empire itself: not merely did he give Virgil the task of conducting him through Hell, but he held that Paul and Aeneas, the founders of the Roman Empire, were the only creatures who had had this privilege before him. One could not perform an act in this world without being openly or silently reminded of the presence of the Church: the very house of prostitution had Mary Magdalen for its patron saint.

Hatred, strife, injustice, all the sins of the decalogue and many unmentioned there all remained in this civilization: the Church acknowledged that fact and took it as the inevitable result of man's original sin, which only belief in the Holy Trinity and reliance upon the Church itself could lift. But the super-ego the Church had formed subdued the fierce vitality of the barbarian and turned no small part of the human energy available into social channels. Emerson greeted the export of pianos to the American frontier with the observation: "The more piano the less wolf." That held in the Middle Ages: where art was omnipresent, man could not be altogether vile. In his esthetic consciousness, the medieval craftsman, even the dumb peasant, lived on a higher level than his modern counterpart: his feelings were more fully developed if his intellect was less sharp; and though his domestic life was coarse his public functions were often magnificent, for he daily had the experience of a sacred art which as yet did nothing to sacrifice its austerity or its depth in order to meet a degraded popular demand—though it had a place for vulgar humor, which added a counterpoise to its solemnity, in the same fashion that the passage with the porter in Macbeth intensifies the tragic moment that follows.

At a time when actual living was still often brutal, harsh, foolish, and cruel, the Church embodied rationality and ideal purpose: it gave collective dignity to human life at large as no other institution had ever done for so large a part of the Western World before. The medieval Christian was no follower of the intuitions of Jesus: nor was he, like the Romanesque Christian, one who turned away from the corruptions of a dying society: he was rather a person living according to the usages of the Christian Church, accepting its moral precepts, its laws, its ritual, its art, its language of symbols, its cosmology as the medium of his own personal existence. Never, not even in Greece, had any previous Western society been more completely dominated by respect for the spirit and respect for the authority of those who represented the spirit.

The Christian Church now presided over birth and death and all the momentous crises between. For each of these occasions it had a form and a ceremony; to each of them it gave a rational meaning within the larger pattern of being. The Church fed the hungry traveler; it nursed the ill and the wounded; it solaced the tired and the defeated. It baptized the new-born infant and it crowned the last moments of the dying with awful dignity. At no moment of his life was even the worst sinner outside the circle of fellowship, unless he had drawn upon himself the Church's most bitter punishment, excommunication: a living death. Repentance was always possible, redemption was always near. Note the many sudden conversions Boccaccio exhibits in The Decameron: a miser is reproved and becomes a liberal man; a king who has suffered indignities himself is appealed to by a wronged woman, and thereafter becomes an efficient prince. Medieval people lived in this daily expectation of a miracle; and to make that miracle credible, the Church held up the cosmic miracle of Christ's death and resurrection, for the salvation of Man.

Once a week at least, but usually more often, every member of the community had a glimpse of the highest life possible: lord and peasant, master and journeyman, lady and wench, worshiped together in the same buildings, watched and took part in the same processions, heard the same chants, beheld the same icons, listened to the same sermons, followed the same mass: all equal in the sight and presence of God. On earth their lots were unequal: plainly the proud and sinful often had the better of it. But in Heaven, worldly advantages and disadvantages were nullified; and the Church itself, by its very ministrations, stood in the relationship of that Earthly Paradise which was the last stage in Purgatory on the way to Heaven. At no moment in the Church's corruption did it altogether lose its sympathetic relation with the poor: if it took their pennies it paid them back in more than full measure with its unceasing offices: always most prompt in those hours of trial or bereavement when the worldly light-heartedly turn aside and go their own way. Fellowship and beauty were the Church's great gifts: fellowship and beauty followed medieval man into the marketplace, the guildhall, the workshop. . . .

What caused the medieval synthesis to break up, the medieval synergy to slacken? What caused the medieval Christian personality to be disrupted? There were both internal reasons and external causes for this change: if we follow their complex interworking, we shall add a further clue to that disclosed by the classic disintegration: a clue that will finally deepen our understanding of the present condition of man.

CHAPTER V. CAPITALISM, ABSOLUTISM, PROTESTANTISM

1: The Break in Continuity

Seven hundred years separate us from the height of the Middle Ages: many different layers of experience, many rival super-egos and idola have come between us and medieval man. But the passage from thirteenth century Unity to twentieth century Multiplicity, as Henry Adams described it, reads one way if one looks for continuity and another if one looks for discontinuity.

The literary and archaeological discoveries of the humanists have often been held up as outright challenges to the medieval order: attempts to restore man to his natural sphere and in particular to give sanction to his natural appetites. But what is the truth? Archaeological piety began in the time of Petrarch: John of Salisbury was as enthusiastic about Plato in the twelfth century as Italian Platonists were in the sixteenth, and his Polycraticus refers continually not merely to academic philosophers but to Ovid, Juvenal, Martial, Terence. The very weakness of the Renascence, its too slavish concern for classic precedent, was visible in Dante himself, not as a poet but as a political thinker. What was this but a continuation of the medieval habit of being more aware of its heritage than of its own fresh discoveries? People remembered too much and saw too little: hence the theoretic grasp of medieval politics and corporate life awaited the analysis of Maitland, Gierke, and Ashley in the nineteenth century.

From one standpoint, the Renascence and the Reformation only carry out the leading ideas of the Middle Ages, as the discoveries of Vasco da Gama and Columbus only push further the daring of Leif Ericsson and the travels of the Polo family. From another standpoint, however, all the great movements that followed the thirteenth century bear witness to the disintegration of medieval culture, and to the unseating of medieval man.

The transformation of a culture is unlike either a change in the seasons or a breakdown in the body's organs and functions. But there are parallels to both processes. As with the seasons, a certain orderly succession of changes can be observed and even predicted. As with the body, the institutions of society cease to maintain a dynamic equilibrium: morbid conditions undermine normal reactions; and the whole culture no longer forms a unified whole, into which the individual part blends like the theme of an instrument in the orchestra. Once the over all pattern of meaning dissolves, the breakdown becomes inevitable. But precisely because the parts of the culture are no longer united, separate activities, no longer restrained and moderated by their union, may exhibit a bounding vitality. Hence this paradox: the downfall of the culture as a whole may lead to rapid advances in this or that part of it. This social fact is fairly close to what follows when an ecological balance in nature is upset. The excessive prosperity of the intruding species is a sign of imbalance. So the death of an old institution or the appearance of a new one may equally upset the balance of a culture.

The notion of a discontinuity between the Middle Ages and the Renascence does not, however, rest solely upon the misconceptions of nineteenth century historians: there was an actual physical shock that partly accounts for the social collapse. For in the fourteenth century the whole Western World was shaken to its foundations by the worst plague on record since that which occurred in the Eastern Empire in the sixth century: the bubonic plague, known as the Black Death. This disease appeared in Western Europe in 1347; in a short course of years it had stricken down and killed between a third and a half of the population. The most conservative estimates do not place the number at less than a third; and since this applies to Europe as a whole, there is no reason to cast doubt on contemporary local authorities who recorded the wiping out of fifty per cent or more of the inhabitants. The incidence of the plague was doubtless higher in the cities than in the rural areas: precisely where the damage to the higher culture would be greatest.

Coming suddenly, defying medical remedy, spreading swiftly and inexorably from town to town, the Black Death struck terror to every heart. Boccaccio has left us an extremely idyllic picture, in the prologue to The Decameron, of the ladies and gentlemen of Florence whiling their time away in the country while the plague raged in the city. But there is a different tale from the cities themselves: husbands deserted wives, mothers deserted their children: corpses were piled high without anyone's daring to carry them away even to lessen the dangers from putrefaction. Out of terror and desperation people almost forgot what it was to be human. The effects of this plague were far worse than the most ruthless and murderous war. Take a modern comparison. Add to the eight million killed in the

First World War the seven and a half million who died throughout the world in the influenza plague of 1918: a grievous loss of life from which our civilization will long suffer. But our own actual loss is insignificant compared to that of the fourteenth century. To make it comparable our sixteen million dead would have to be raised to at least six hundred million.

Now this visitation occurred in a society that felt secure, that had acquired a certain easy pleasure in the "good things of life." Suddenly everything vanished: security, hope, friends, neighbors, fortune, life itself: vanished almost overnight, in foul disorder and hideous misery. The Black Plague had the effect of a prolonged Blitz. The breach thus opened marks a line between two ages: on one side, unity and on the other disintegration.

Such a shaking up of European society was the occasion for pious hopes no less than for terror: in this, too, the First World War resembled it. A contemporary Florentine chronicler, Matteo Villani, observed: "those few discreet folk who remained alive expected many things, most of which, by reason of the corruptions of sin, failed among mankind, whose minds followed marvelously in the contrary direction. They believed that those whom God's grace had saved from death, having beheld the destruction of their neighbors and having heard the same tidings from all the nations of the world, would become better conditioned, virtuous, and Catholic . . . and would be full of love and charity towards another. But no sooner had the plague ceased than we saw the contrary; for since men were few, and since, by hereditary succession they abounded in earthly goods, they forgot the past as though it had never been and gave themselves to a more shameful and disordered life than they had lived before."

These words recall a similar experience that took place in America after the Civil War, and in both America and Europe after the wholesale devastation of the First World War: a tendency to seek relief from remembered horror in unbridled drinking and fornicating, and to swing from a harsh facing of reality into an over-indulgent escapism. Even minor events may cause such a breakdown of the super-ego. But in the Middle Ages the general letdown was of the same dimensions as the catastrophe; for not merely was the super-ego deflated but an actual loss of continuity between the generations took place.

Even historians forget too easily that the largest part of every culture is transmitted, not through a few institutions and a handful of texts, but by a million daily acts and observances and imitations. Remove even a third of the population, and with it will go a multitude of skills, a vast heritage of living knowledge, an abundance of sensitive discriminations, passed from parent to child, from master to apprentice, from neighbor to neighbor. There is no mechanical substitute for a living tradition.

In short, the Black Death produced a break in social continuity, an emptying out of the social heritage, between the thirteenth and the fifteenth century: this amnesia exaggerated the actual physical discontinuity. When the people of the fifteenth century in Italy again resumed the heritage of Greece and Rome, they had the illusion that they were departing from their benighted "Gothic" ancestors whereas in fact they were only taking up once more the interests that had lapsed as a result of plague and social upheavals. According to Burdach, the term Middle Ages, "media tempestas," first appeared in 1469; "media aetas" appeared in 1518. To a community that had lost its living tie with the past, it seemed easier to begin on fresh foundations than to resume old connections.

But though the Black Death was catastrophic, one must not give to it a too decisive influence in the changes that followed it. Without doubt it loosened connections with the immediate past, unbound ancient feudal ties, checked the course of medieval development, and hastened the demise of the whole medieval order. But a crippling illness in middle life, which may cut short a great career, should not obscure the fact that death was bound to happen in any event: so the Black Plague itself only hastened a series of changes that were already visible and already under way—changes brought about by the inherent weaknesses in the medieval synthesis.

One can see this fact in the architectural transformation. Even thirteenth century Gothic had lost too much of the clean, sturdy rationalism of the twelfth century Romanesque: it already presaged the stony filigree of the Flamboyant style and showed a lack of spinal conviction by an over-elaboration of external ornament. Huizinga, in his classic work, The Waning of the Middle Ages, has fully documented the morbid processes in late medieval society. Indeed, the return to Roman methods of construction was not due merely to the rediscovery of Vitruvius: it was more fundamentally an attempt to escape the progressive corruption of medieval form and to cleanse the imagination more completely of meaningless fantasy. This cleansing process took place in every department of life. Nowhere was the process of dissociation more rapid, nowhere did a fresh mutation show more vigorous life, than in the domain of economics.

2: The Role of the Musical Banks

As Europe grew more prosperous and more populated, the Church automatically increased its financial power: its tithes guaranteed that. This in itself proved a serious temptation to forget its heavenly tasks; but the very offices of the Church served further to undermine its spiritual authority. Economically speaking, the Catholic Church had become a machine for manufacturing salvation. Its churches, its shrines, its art, above all its relics, were so much capital goods devoted to the production of its peculiar form of immaterial wealth. As the institution grew in power, this whole apparatus of production rested more and more upon an elaborate system of credits and debits, cleared through its "musical banks."

The internal finances of this system lent themselves, unfortunately, to inflation. Every priest, by a twelfth century doctrine, solidly established by Hugh of St. Victor and Thomas Aquinas, had an unlimited right to issue credit: by the act of absolution he could wipe out an unfavorable moral balance, while by special prayers, gifts, candles, masses, the purchaser of salvation could indefinitely increase his assets; so that if he died under the proper forms of the Church, all his speculative certificates would be redeemed at par in Heaven.

I have deliberately used an irreverent figure to describe this system; for when one examines its workings nothing could be more obvious, nothing could be more shocking, than its gross materialism. In the satire of Erewhon, Samuel Butler used the conceit of the Musical Banks to describe the unrealizable assets and the otherworldly accountancy of the Christian Churches; and that was a doubly felicitous stroke, in that it touched the specious theology of money no less than the specious economics of redemption. If economic historians were as versed in theology as in economics, they would have realized long ago that credit finance has a close affiliation with the system of ecclesiastical accountancy for sins and good works that preceded its establishment. By the twelfth century the Church had been transformed from a body of believers, such as it was in the apostolic age, into a highly mechanized instrument of salvation. Salvation was protected by exclusive monopoly patents: the Christian dogmas. Out of its holy offices and rites the Church had created at long last an organization which was committed largely, not to spreading the gifts of the spirit, but to offering spurious magical substitutes for these gifts to those capable of making cash payments.

This abuse did not come into existence without awaking strenuous internal protest. The best spirits within the Church, from Petrus Cantor to Thomas Aquinas, campaigned against its growing venality: they were shocked by the practical consequences of some of their own doctrines and resisted the steady weakening of the divine power which their Church wielded. These honest men denounced the abuses of buying offices, appointing rich magnates to ecclesiastical posts, extorting gifts from terrified or repentant sinners of wealth, and in general, using Christian doctrine as a means of buttressing the Church's worldly position. If one wishes to understand why a man of the stature of Dante could be on the side of the Emperor rather than the Pope, in the grand contest between the two powers, one must realize that the greatest actual abuses of power were visible within the Church: the Emperor could seem an ideal figure because he possessed no such opportunities.

The mechanization of salvation was abetted by the very growth of wealth and economic activity in the community at large. All the opportunities for constructive activity, for travel, for the enjoyment of varied foods and beautiful clothes and perfumes and jewels only added to the general sense of guilt: in a moment of crisis, an illness or a bereavement, the sinner would feel the need for removing this burden. Even Boccaccio, after the plague, repented of his lusty, worldly stories and took to theology. The words of the Church still held men; the doctrines of the Church had become automatisms, accepted without question: the super-ego, coupled with so many functions and needs that served the ego in a positive way, still kept its hold on the whole personality. Believing the doctrines of the Church, it was evident to most people that a good part of their life was lived in mortal sin, and that they were therefore certain to meet an eternity of torture.

So an uneasy sense of guilt grew more general, and the need to avoid blame grew with it. Dr. Henry A. Murray and his associates have listed the need for "blame-avoidance" as one of the universal human needs; and the Church, deepening the sense of guilt, self-reproach, and anxiety by its heavy demands on the conscience, now brought into existence an elaborate mechanism for removing this very guilt and ensuring a future state of bliss. In the eighth century the Church had instituted the practice of private confession: a potent psychological release. But now the confession was definitely put into the hands of the priest as a means of increasing the Church's police surveillance over the community; and along with it, came the device of priestly absolution. This was a new weapon of power. Nought was secret from the priesthood: the sinner could not take refuge in indifference and silence. If he sought to jump out of the frying pan of the confessional he might find himself in the fire of the Inquisition.

Other means of lifting guilt multiplied, besides the holy pilgrimages and the confessional. Self-imposed torture, originally practiced chiefly by those dedicated to a holy life, became common. The sect of Flagellants arose in the thirteenth century, first in Bohemia, then Italy: processions of them appeared on the road, armed with scourges, their heads covered but their bodies bare to the waist: they whipped each other to ease their guilt. Peter Damian got involved in the mathematics of penance: three thousand blows equaled a year of penance. But Dominicus Loricatus used a rod in *each* hand, and doubled the number of blows: according to Damian he boasted he was capable of doing a hundred years' penance in six days. Record breaking and credit finance: both these were signs of spiritual bankruptcy.

In short, the so-called "age of faith" left a long record of naïve blasphemies and sophisticated self-betrayals. Medieval Christianity, in the act of holding the super-ego at an impossible height, had helped to create this dualism, this ambivalence, this intolerable tension. Thus the split between profession and practice widened; and the attitude of most Christians became double-faced: they wanted to make the best of both worlds. In terms of their everyday lives, few men could remain Christians and keep their self-respect: they failed too often. But in meeting the common need for blame-avoidance by a contrivance that poured wealth into the treasury of the Church, the officers of the Church threw open the doors to doubt, cynicism, and heresy. The cure for a bad conscience brought on a worse one.

All these contradictions gave rise to doctrinal doubt. Alain of Lille was forced to combat people who thought that the soul disappeared with death and could not be resurrected: Amalric of Benes, who died at the beginning of the thirteenth century, was a pantheist; and Frederick II of Sicily, who became one of the persecutors of heresy, was himself a savage, unprincipled heretic, who called Moses, Christ, and Mohammed the three impostors. Joinville cites a truly pious man who nevertheless disbelieved in the Eucharist; and in the midst of a sermon, Berthold of Regensburg was taunted by a voice from the congregation which said: "Brother Berthold, thou speakest oft and oft of these devils and all their sleights, yet we never hear or see or touch or feel a single devil."

Doubt was in the air: the reign of the Two Popes was a political symbol of a far deeper schism in Christendom: those who date this change from the Reformation simply ignore the abundant evidence that springs from the twelfth, thirteenth, and fourteenth centuries. The elaborate apparatus that the Church erected in every part of Europe for the extirpation of heresy is sufficient proof that the old unanimity was gone. Doubt entered, not chiefly as an expression of materialism, but as a challenge on the part of the more intelligent and the more virtuous against the Church's unscrupulous use of magical remedies and its enjoyment of financial rewards.

Not merely did the spectacle of ecclesiastical corruption cause doubt to enter: even piety became self-critical of its anomalous results. Lea cites the admirable wisdom of the early members of the Priory of Grammont, who all-too-well knew from what quarter the foul wind came. When the relics of its founder, St. Stephen of Thiern, commenced to show his sanctity by curing a paralytic knight and restoring sight to a blind man, the brothers became alarmed. Stephen's successor, Peter of Limoges, thus addressed the departed saint: "Oh, Servant of God, thou hast shown us the path of poverty and hast earnestly striven to teach us to walk therein. Now thou wishest to lead us from the straight and narrow way of salvation to the broad road of eternal death. Thou hast preached solitude, and now thou seekest to convert the solitude into a marketplace and a fair. We already believe sufficiently in thy saintliness. Then work no more miracles to prove it, and at the same time to destroy our humility. . . . If thou doest otherwise, we declare, by the obedience we have vowed to thee, that we will dig up thy bones and cast them into the river."

The attitude of these sensitive monks was as rare as the evil they sought to avert was omnipresent. Christianity paid a heavy price for that supernaturalism which over-rode common sense and science and reason, and which gave to a merely human institution, open to corruption, the airs and constant attributes of divinity. The cult of salvation, over-reaching itself, became progressively more materialistic: its gifts had less than nothing to do with the spirit. Outward penances became substitutes for inner repentance. By the time Evelyn visited the Cathedral at Saint Denis in the seventeenth century he found the following "holy" relics: "a nail from our Saviour's Cross in a box of gold full of precious stones, a crucifix of the true wood of the Cross, carved by Pope Clement III . . . a box in which is some of the Virgin's hair; some of the linen in which our blessed Saviour was wrapped at his nativity"—and so on. Those were the tangible assets of the Musical Banks.

3: The Heresy of Capitalism

Max Weber's thesis, that Protestantism played a prime part in the conception and development of capitalism, has become current during the last generation. In view of the patent facts of history, this belief is as strange as it is indefensible: for it assumes that modern capitalism did not take form until the sixteenth century; whereas it existed as a mutation at least three centuries earlier and by the fourteenth century it pervaded Italy: a country where Protestantism has never been able to gain a hold.

Capitalism was, in fact, the great heresy of the Middle Ages: the chief challenge to the ideal claims of Christianity. And if medieval theology failed to expunge this heresy, the cause of its failure should be plain: the heresy had been nourished in the very bosom of the Church, and almost from the first had the protection of the Papacy. It was not Calvin in the sixteenth century, but Vincent of Beauvais in the thirteenth who first admonished people to work, not just for a living, but for the sake of accumulation, which would lead to the further production of wealth.

The prudent side of capitalism, its thrift and regularity and mechanical order, developed in the Benedictine monasteries: this counterbalanced an adventurous side which went to the establishment of trading posts and the staking out of new territories for commerce and colonization. Here, too, the Church had a part to play. Just as trade in the nineteenth century followed the flag, from the thirteenth century on it followed the Cross. The traders themselves could hope to acquire spiritual merit in the act of filling their purses in heathendom. The shift from religion to finance was so subtle, the inter-actions so complicated, that it is sometimes hard to say which came first, and which motive was uppermost.

There is no doubt, however, that theological capitalism made its appearance far in advance of any protestant doctrine in either religion or economics. It was the schoolmen who invented the decisive theory of the "Treasury of Salvation." According to this theory, Lea points out, the Church had accumulated a great treasure through the merits of the Crucifixion and the martyrdom of the saints. The Pope, as Vicar of God, had the unlimited dispensation of this treasure, by issuing pardons, either plenary or partial. What was this but a theory of capital accumulation and investment for profit? The cardinal who went to Augsburg to examine Luther pointed out to him how this doctrine had been established by the Bull Unigenitus issued by Clement VI in 1343.

The very fact that the Church arrived at such a doctrine when it did, is a proof that its original ideology had become tainted. Because of the vast amount of property and income it commanded, the Church inevitably got tangled in finance; and though it might buzz its spiritual wings, like a fly that has been caught on a ribbon of flypaper, its feet were nevertheless firmly glued to the institutions of property. The official Church could not oppose capitalism without threatening itself with a loss of practical power and a loss of human influence, as a bank for the issue of spiritual merits and for the writing off of spiritual debts, in return for cash payments and certain other good and valuable considerations. The change to cash payments in commutation of sins went along with the change to cash payments in meeting feudal dues.

For a while, Christians attempted to combat the evils of unrestricted trade by transferring their more sinful economic actions to a scapegoat.

The Jews were conveniently at hand to serve in this role. Ever since the Dispersion the Jewish traders had plied their trade wherever the faintest protection was offered, from China to England: in a community whose wealth was immobilized in land and whose economic horizon was limited, the Jews specialized in the fluid medium of money and their international connections furthered wider interchange. If they lent their money at usurious rates, the risks were appalling, even in the safest channels of commerce: on personal as well as commercial loans the interest might be as high as forty per cent. At worst, the usurer existed in the medieval community like the hangman: he performed a necessary function that still, in terms of Christian doctrine, was so repulsive that it placed him outside the pale of ordinary living.

As money accumulated and the opportunities for investment grew, the Church made various compliances with the need for commercial loans. Though one could not exact interest for a loan, one was permitted to exact an indemnity for non-payment: so usury was given and received by making short term loans, with an indemnity to cover the intentional non-payment and the consequent extension of the loan. (This exactly parallels the usurious exactions on second mortgage renewals, long current in the United States in the face of anti-usury laws.) The displacement of Jews by Lombards and Tuscans neither furthered Christian practice nor lessened the opportunities for usury: on the contrary, the desire for riches and the opportunities for getting rich increased by leaps and bounds. The change from a goods economy to a cash economy came swiftly: so early that the essential difference could be described by Thomas Aquinas.

"Wealth is twofold, as the Philosopher says . . . *viz.* natural and artificial. Natural wealth is that which serves man as a remedy for his natural wants: such as food, drink, clothing, carts, dwellings, and such like. While artificial wealth is that which is not a direct help to nature, as money; but this is invented by the art of man, for the convenience of exchange, and as a measure of things salable. . . . The desire for riches is not infinite: because they suffice for nature in a certain measure. But the desire for artificial wealth is infinite, for it is the servant of disordered concupiscence, which is not curbed." It was disordered concupiscence that became a driving force in the fourteenth century. Even two centuries before, Alain of Lille, in the Complaint of Nature, had said: "Not Caesar now, but money, is all."

Capitalism as a method of business and a habit of life undermined medieval institutions at many points. But the greatest challenge of all was that to its ethical standards and its notions of a holy and seemly life. The capitalist personality, directed to self-help and gain, was the antithesis to the Christian who sought to love his neighbor as himself: indeed, to the medieval moralist, the capitalist was little better than a criminal. "Alas! how many folk there are who strive for filthy lucre and gain filthy lucre!" exclaims Berthold of Regensburg. "Such are deceivers in their trade and handiwork; such are men thieves and women thieves, within the house and without; usurers, pawnbrokers, money-lenders, and forestallers that they may buy cheaper." Berthold would not have been shocked at Proudhon's dictum that property was theft: indeed, in Dante's time, as Vossler points out, a common saying in Italy was that a rich man had either committed injustice or was the heir of one who was unjust.

Between the thirteenth and the nineteenth century one may sum up the change in the moral climate by saying that the seven deadly sins became the seven cardinal virtues. All the practices of the worldly life, which had been hitherto banned by the Church, were now either tacitly sanctioned or actively stimulated. Avarice ceased to be a sin: the minute attention to the care of worldly goods, the hoarding of pennies, the unwillingness to spend one's surplus on others—all these habits were useful for capital saving. Greed, gluttony, avarice, envy, and luxury were constant incentives to industry: without envy, the potential enterpriser might be content with his lot in life instead of trying to climb out of it. Riches now acquired sanctity: they opened the gates of the Kingdom, they furnished the power, they created the glory. The Catholic Church itself put no bridle on its own wants: it rather succumbed faster than any other institution to the pomps and vanities of this wicked world. One must not forget that it was partly to pay Raphael and Michelangelo that simony and indulgences flourished in Rome.

In short, the Church, in the interests of its own survival, flouted Christian faith, which is not in the least concerned with mortal survival.

The whole moral change that took place under capitalism can be summed up in the fact that human purposes, human needs, and human limits no longer exercised a directive and restraining influence upon industry: people worked, not to maintain life, but to increase money and power and to minister to the ego that found satisfaction in vast accumulations of money and power. In replying to the Diet of Nürnberg's inquiry on monopoly in the sixteenth century, the financiers of Augsburg said: "It is impossible to limit the size of companies, for that would limit business and hurt the common welfare; the bigger and more numerous they are, the better for everybody. . . . If a merchant cannot do business above a certain amount, what is he to do with his surplus money? . . . Some people talk of limiting the earning capacity of investments. This would be unbearable and would work great injustice and harm by taking away the livelihood of widows, orphans, and other sufferers, noble and non-noble, who derive their income from investments in companies." All the articles of the capitalist faith are implied in that classic statement: even the precious widows and orphans are there.

Now, up to the emergence of capitalism, economic life had had a strong moral foundation. It was rooted in the notion that every act of life was under the Judgment of God: the trade of market stall no less than the judgments of the market court. Hence the conception of the just price: a price determined by the intrinsic value of the commodity and its actual cost of production, divorced from the accidents of individual preference or material scarcity. The guilds set themselves to establish standards of workmanship and to maintain price levels: an active war went on against those who debased commodities, who tried to corner them, or who sought to avoid selling them in the open market at the standard price, first come, first served. Against the Roman legal motto, Let the buyer beware, the medieval economist held rather, Let buyer and seller both fear God. Medieval production, down to the sixteenth century, centered on security, regularity, equity: social justice was more important than private advantage.

But the capitalist transvaluation of human values went on steadily; and its supreme success was in making pride and luxury the central virtues. Though the Church, in its real wisdom, regarded pride as the worst of sins, it now became the very pillar of the economic and political order. It was pride in wealth that made the great wholesale guilds draw away from the petty handicraft guilds. It was pride that promoted the luxury trades and that increased the visible gap between the high and the low, the fat people and the lean people. Now the doctrines of meekness and humility served not to dethrone the mighty but to bind in chains a growing proletariat.

Yet at first, before capitalism had cut loose entirely from the medieval community and formed a new social complex of its own, the very fluid nature of this institution made it a welcome release from the fixed usages of feudal society. Apart from the great textile industries of the thirteenth century and the mining enterprises of the fifteenth, the chief form of capital investment was in ships and cargoes: a medium of social circulation no less than of transport. Money was both an instrument for wider trade and a symbol of freedom: freedom from feudal status and feudal dues: freedom of economic choice, in contrast to the narrow opportunities of local barter. Urban industrial centers used money to purchase their political freedom. Even to the common man, therefore, the growing power of finance might seem at first a happy advance over ancient feudal compulsions. And there is no doubt that, in breaking through the cake of irrational custom, in undertaking fresh enterprises, in encouraging the processes of rational agreement, in accustoming men once more to the idea of taking risks in other fields than war, capitalism was often in its early phases a healthy, liberating influence.

Five centuries must pass before the pure Economic Man will appear: a shipwrecked middle class individualist, living by his wits on a desert island: Robinson Crusoe. But the willingness to take risks on the part of the new merchant adventurers, emphasized a new boldness and hopefulness about worldly existence. To make profits and to take losses, to balance up accounts on earth instead of expecting nothing but losses on earth and waiting for Heaven to even up accounts—this was a profound change for both the community and the person. It turned covert practices into overt ones, and it removed the perpetual bad conscience of the Christian by dropping his super-ego onto a much lower plane. Capitalism emphasized self-reliance and trusted the human will. One could take risks and remain solvent. One could lose all, and still survive, to try again. If gains were not permanent, losses were not irreparable. Bankruptcy cleaned the slate and one might start again. All this had a moral overtone. A new sense of self-confidence spread from the individual trader to society at large.

4: Outlines of the Economic Man

From the beginning, the new economy, with its stress on thrift, was faced with a rival motive that grew out of the very nature of capitalist ambition: the desire to raise the quantity of goods consumed and in particular, to turn luxuries into daily necessities. This double pull resulted at first in a seemingly simple division of labor: the aristocracy remained the spenders and the merchant classes became the savers: meanwhile, a growing proletariat, deprived of land no less than the individual tools of production, remained outside the new order, or rather, was shoved down beneath it. Power and wealth, in fact, were achieved at the expense of the poor and the powerless.

Part of the success of capitalism came through its taking over for its own purposes Christian doctrines and Christian habits: for example, the postponement of present pleasures for the sake of much greater future rewards, which is the core of the doctrine of heavenly salvation. Capital saving was based on this pious formula: the justification of interest and profits was connected with the original act of abnegation and deferment: present self-denial promoted future self-aggrandizement. "In our times," observed Machiavelli, "we have seen nothing great done except by those who have been esteemed niggardly; the others have all been ruined."

Between 1278 and 1340 Genoa, according to Lucas, began to keep its municipal accounts by double entry; and in Venice, as early as 1494, Luca Pacial published a treatise on book-keeping by this method. These facts are landmarks in the new development; for in commercial book-keeping the day of judgment is always at hand. No matter what one's hopes, ambitions, schemes, the figures themselves provide a check upon the unbridled human imagination.

This methodical use of numbers, furthered by the Arabic notation, was a profound contribution to the human economy: systematic quantitative thinking in the modern world began at this point. By means of reading, writing, and arithmetic, the merchant systematically recorded his transactions in the marketplace, kept track of the stock on hand, noted the coming and going of ships, followed the reports and letters of far-flung agents, calculated the risks on future investments, and eventually in insurance reduced to predictable regularity the chances of death, fire, and physical accidents. The actual transactions of business might still be devious and intuitive and therefore somewhat chaotic; but the notation in the account books was systematic and clear.

Numbers thus came to exert an independent hold over the imagination: quantitative thinking and cash values displaced qualitative discrimination and esthetic and moral values. It was not by accident that Marco Polo was derisively nicknamed Marco Millions. Like any other merchant, he was impressed by figures; and millions were more important to him than thousands. Size in itself became a value. Bigger was better: more expensive was more important. Even in the age of Cathedral-building that spirit had taken root.

Along with this arithmetical regularity went a regular habit of life: the introduction of town clocks in the thirteenth and fourteenth centuries is but one symptom of the fact that business was no longer regulated by the sun and the powers of the human frame: the clock tells the hour, reminds one that the day is short and that time is money. The methodical expenditure of hours matched the methodical accountancy of money: indeed, the growth of the large-scale textile factory in the late Middle Ages was prompted, possibly, by a desire to enforce diligence on the worker through an overseership that could not be exercised so easily in the loose routine of the small shop. By a rigorous economizing of the worker's time, a loom in a big factory would turn out more ells of cloth per day than in the small workshop where a worker might stop to gossip or stretch his legs. This is perhaps the one case where Karl Marx's theory of surplus value, as derived from the extra hour of work appropriated for himself by the capitalist, is anything but a metaphysical phantom.

Firm steps toward a regulated, sober life were already taken by the fourteenth century: the praise of this new mode of existence was sung by the Venetian merchant and public servant, Louis Cornaro, in the next century. He wrote a veritable hymn to orderly living; and he held up the regular and temperate life he had lived from middle age onward as the chief cause of his practical success. "It is through order," he exclaimed, "that the sciences are more easily mastered; it is order that gives victory to armies; and finally, it is due to order that the stability of families, of cities, and even of governments, is maintained. Therefore I conclude that orderly living is the most positive law and foundation of a long and healthy life." Benjamin Franklin, with the account book in which he entered his virtues and his sins, could add nothing to this prescription.

These new habits had direct moral consequences. Work ceased to be merely the curse of Adam: it gave dignity to man, and St. Antonino of Padua therefore reviled nobles "who are unwilling to work and yet who directly seek by lending their money to merchants to secure an annual interest besides the eventual return of an undiminished capital." The regularity of the merchant, his respect for objective truth, his habit of quantitative reckoning, gave him a position above those who credited their hopes and fancies too easily: the merchant was a man who could be trusted. When John Colet, Dean of St. Paul's, refounded the grammar school of that Cathedral, Erasmus tells us that "after he had finished all, he left the perpetual care and oversight of the state and government of it, not to the clergy, not to the Bishop, not to the Chapter, not to any great minister at Court, but among married laymen, to the Company of Mercers, men of probity and reputation. And when he was asked the reason of so committing this trust, he answered to this effect: 'that there is no absolute certainty in human affairs; but for his part, he found less corruption in such a body of citizens than in any other order or degree of mankind.' "

That was high testimony; and one will not grasp the commanding position that the capitalist personality finally assumed, as an ideal type, unless one realizes that the confidence was once, in no small part, earned. The very mechanism of exchange through notes and drafts, issued by correspondents in remote places beyond the reach of law, presumed a degree of honor and truth and equity that far outweighed the occasional abuses that followed. A certain kind of moral soundness, not without a tinge of self-righteousness, went into the new bourgeois character: a firm will, a sober regard for consequences, an unflagging zeal that evened out the ups and downs of temperament. The ultimate praise for a merchant went beyond fidelity to a written contract: "His word is as good as gold."

But the two moralities, one associated with the protective economy of the Middle Ages, the other with the expanding economy of the new period, remained in conflict down to the eighteenth century, when the guilds themselves, long petrified, were finally buried. It was in the spirit of the earlier culture that the Goodman of Paris, around 1393, observed to his wife: "The Devil giveth six commandments to the avaricious man: the first, that he take good care of his own; the second, that he lend not without gain, and do not good before his death; the third, that he eat all alone and do not courtesy nor alms-giving; the fourth, that he restrain his household from eating and drinking; the fifth, that he give away neither crumb nor remnant; the sixth, that he seek diligently to pile up for his heirs." If he followed these sinful commandments, his descendants might live like lords.

In line with this, the capitalist morality was one founded on pride and aggression: it was directed toward the overthrow of Holy Poverty; toward the substitution of individual possessions for the communism of the monasteries and for the brotherly plenitude of the guilds; toward the detachment of the acquisitive enterpriser from the personal interests and distributive generosity of the family group. The new capitalist personality stood progressively outside the municipality, the guild, the family, and rejected their restraining ties and their humane preoccupations.

Those who fancy that this capitalist morality is a spontaneous and altogether natural one, founded on man's "real" nature, do not understand the amount of positive indoctrination and effortful conversion that its eventual success demanded: the mere instinct of possessiveness, which a dog displays in the guarding of a bone or an infant in claiming a doll, had little to do with the unceasing preoccupation with arithmetical gains and the masterful acquisitiveness that motivated the capitalist.

Property has natural limits: limits of use, beyond which more property is a burden. But capital has no limits whatever. No glutton can eat a hundred pheasants; no drunkard can drink a hundred bottles of wine at a sitting; and if anyone schemed to have so much food and wine brought to his table daily, he would be mad. Once, however, he could exchange the potential pheasants and Burgundy for marks or thalers, he could direct the labor of his neighbors, and achieve the place of an aristocrat without being to the manor born. Economic activity ceased to deal with the tangible realities of the medieval world—land and corn and houses and universities and cities. It was transformed into the pursuit of an abstraction—money. Business credit supplanted religious belief: solvency took the place of salvation.

The important point to grasp here is that the capitalist super-ego was as much in conflict with man's diversified biological and social needs as that of the Christian Church: it was based on an equally wholesale system of denials and negations; and that fact is no less true, because capitalism denied another area of the human personality than that which the Church endeavored to subdue. Nothing could make this clearer than the history of the House of Fugger, the great Augsburg bankers. Why did this great firm of international bankers and enterprisers come to such an early end? Because even in that day, the traditional anti-capitalist morality and the traditional way of life had a greater appeal to Anton Fugger's nephews. His eldest nephew, Hans Jacob, refused to take over the direction of the business "on the ground that the business of the city and his own affairs" gave him too much to do. Hans Jacob's brother, George, said that he had rather live in peace: a third nephew, Christopher, was equally obdurate. None of these sensible fellows had sufficient desire to add to the Fugger millions.

Decades and centuries must pass before the capitalist personality became supreme, before an entire civilization was ordered by its regular habits, stung by its acquisitiveness, lured by its promised comforts and luxuries, and debilitated by its automatisms. Before that state could be reached, the economic pattern of aggression needed reinforcement from the agents of government: their combined efforts were required to create the debased super-ego of the utilitarian man.

5: The Arts of Power

In the Middle Ages, government was dispersed but moral authority was concentrated. Legal codes varied: the moral code for Europe was uniform. From the fourteenth century on these conditions were reversed.

Financial concentration and political despotism went together; and while M. V. Clarke is correct in pointing out that the democratic processes of government held on longest in cities like Florence and Venice, which were the most advanced examples of the new money economy, the relation between economic monopoly and political monopoly is nevertheless a close one. Like Athens, Florence kept the forms of democracy as long as it united all its classes in the tasks of imperialist aggrandizement: when Florence had absorbed the surrounding municipalities and the countryside, the Medicis vaulted into power. Once the reins of government were in his hands, the appointed war leader could maintain his tyranny only by replacing citizen armies with paid armies: this gave power to the big financial magnates, like Bardi in Rome, Medici in Florence, Sforza in Milan, Pepoli in Bologna, Vignate in Lodi. Where concentration of power took a more national form, as in England, Spain, France, political government courted the co-operation of the great bankers and business men, and repaid them handsomely in titles, lands, and commercial monopolies.

The post-medieval period was a period of wide enclosures and large-scale consolidations. Within the definite boundary lines of the new territorial state, unified areas of administration were established. Burckhardt has been reproached as a mere dilettante in political thought because he characterized the state established by the Italian tyrants as a deliberate work of art; but his insight here was better than that of his critics. In politics, as in painting after the invention of the easel picture, the new life was held together in a rigid frame: the unity imposed by despotism had an esthetic as well as a practical object; and that esthetic end, as I demonstrated in The Culture of Cities, was embodied in the layout and in the architectural development of the Baroque city. In the Middle Ages the historic patchwork of feudal and municipal privileges, duties, and rights, based upon dedications, pre-emptions, conquests, charters, marriages, could only be *remembered:* outside the Church there was no continuous field of government. But the new territorial state, on the contrary, could be *seen* or at least visualized: it was a visible whole, and each country that was politically unified became, so to say, a self-contained picture. This visualization of power became possible only when territorial continuity became an attribute of the sovereign state. Where geographical boundaries aided such visualization, as in England, the national state had its earliest and its longest continued growth.

Even deeper however went the likeness between politics and painting. In contrast to medieval graphic design, in which the eye shifts easily from one part of the picture to another, taking in details, without presuming the existence of a fixed spectator with a fixed point of view, everything that happens in the new style of painting that took form in Italy results from the artist's own rigid intention: the details are related to a central observer. So in politics. The king and his bureaucracy no longer moved around to hold court and dispense judgments: in the fourteenth century they began to settle down in the new political capitals. Control no longer required personal presence: it could now be operated at a distance from the center, by means of a bureaucratic and military mechanism. Just as all the sight lines in renascence perspective converge on the artist, so all the lines of political force in the new state converge on the central magnet: the Prince. The whole effort of absolutism is to build up in the capital city a ritual that will be so attractive, a presence that will be so commanding, that no one will voluntarily cut himself off from the throne or attempt to challenge its claims. Here or nowhere was "real life": here or nowhere one counted *in the picture*. The incarnation and embodiment of power became, accordingly, the great preoccupation of courtly politics.

The first of these despotic states was that which the Emperor Frederick II erected in Sicily: here in the germ one may behold all the vices of tyrannical government from Napoleon to Hitler. It was perhaps no accident that Thomas Aquinas, a subject of Frederick's, wrote a justification of tyrannicide. Typically, Frederick broke down the power of the feudal lords, centralized the administration of justice by providing for appeal from the feudal courts, did away with popular elections of all kinds, and wiped out the integrated corporate life that had hitherto prevailed. In general, citizens were reduced to subjects, and the new state became their universal prison. Under Frederick, people were forbidden even to marry out of their country without special permission: they were forbidden any leeway in religious belief; and they were not allowed to study abroad: in short every detail of totalitarian tyranny was present.

Herewith began the cult of uniformity: uniform laws, uniform taxes, uniform obligations. Various technical devices, including the revival of the Corpus Juris Civilis of Justinian abetted this uniformity: late Roman law emphasized the rights of property and the despotic power of the Prince, and it encouraged the revival of torture as a shortcut in obtaining evidence and manufacturing power. With the backing of despotism this code made its way far beyond the Latin countries: into Germany, Scotland, Scandinavia. This wiping out of meaningless irregularities and functionless diversities was, up to a point, a real boon: it was a help to the merchant to have the constant protection of the sovereign on the King's Highway: it was an aid to national trade to have a common system of weights and measures and coinages in every part of the kingdom—though this came tardily. In the Middle Ages even the Calendar had not been uniform: the year began at Christmas in some places, in March in other places; and it was not till the sixteenth century that January first became the acknowledged date for beginning the year. On all such matters, the acts of centralized authority tended to promote a wider community.

Unfortunately, power battens on its own success and its appetite grows with every morsel it swallows: that is one of the surest lessons of history. Dante was not deceived by this new phenomenon when it appeared, though he was innocent enough to believe that a universal emperor might remedy it. He was not deceived even though tyranny was embellished from the first by an increased patronage of art. "What mean their trumpets and bells, their horses and their flutes," he exclaimed, "but 'Come hangman—come vulture!' "

The hangman was ready, and the vulture pounced on its prey. As in the twentieth century, despotism was fortified by a deliberate cult of violence. Those who raised their voices against oppression were quickly put out of the way: poison, the stiletto, the dungeon, the stake were all at hand for those who opposed the Prince's pretensions to unlimited power. Cannon and muskets placed power in the hands of those who could pay for these expensive weapons and feed the ruffians who were commanded to use them. This terrorism within the state produced subjects who closed their mouths, minded their own business, and ceased to have a part in public affairs or even to be interested in them. Much of the so-called growth of individuality during the renascence was in fact a growth of social irresponsibility: divorced from their normal social obligations in the guild, the municipality, the Church, people became self-centered and self-absorbed. As for him who made the law, he believed himself above the law: hence the fiction of unlimited sovereignty. But in fact every despot was the victim of his servants: he prospered to the extent that he fed their vanity and satisfied their appetite. Not even a Colbert or a Turgot could ultimately stand up against the contrary opinion of the Court.

The tyrant had certain technical advantages over the municipal administrators he supplanted. He governed for a lifetime instead of being elected to office for a few months or at most a year: he concentrated responsibility instead of being forced to divide it with a jealous committee of rival fellow-guildsmen: he could forecast his expenditures in an annual budget—a device that even the most progressive cities long lacked. In short, the Prince extended and unified the affairs of state in time no less than in space: an indubitable advantage. But, as Castiglione pointed out, "licentious liberty" grows out of despotic rule and therefore despots never understand the truth of anything: "their mind is so corrupted through seeing themselves always obeyed and (as it were) worshiped" that they will take no counsel or advice from others. Self-infatuation and self-aggrandizement: the pathology of power: suspicion and isolation.

Once Christian doctrines and Christian insights were reduced to mere rote, the pathology of power ceased to be understood; and then the sin of pride knew no bounds. Louis XIV's inflated ego could not bear the appearance of anything that seemed to curb his absolutism: the Sun King must not be put in the shade. So he deliberately avoided Paris, because it was not inhabited by people who shared sufficiently in the illusions his courtiers kept up for him. The dream of absolutism was like a leaky tire that needed continually to be re-inflated: a continued pressure toward expansion was the price of its survival.

6: The Cult of Corruption

If Petrarch gave an idealized picture of the Prince, Machiavelli sought to unmask the ideal and draw closer to the iron face of actuality. Ideals, according to Machiavelli, have no office in the real world except to serve as a disguise for the actions that contradict and betray them. The Prince must always seem on the side of virtue only in order to work more effectively in the cause of power; for within the state, power alone is virtue, and like virtue, is its own reward. In the breakup of medieval society, the divorce between ethics and politics had now become complete: Machiavelli sought only to give this divorce the authority of a written decree.

But note: Machiavelli, in his little handbook for despots, The Prince, still found a justification for his nurture of baseness in one of the dogmas of the Christian religion: original sin. According to him, men are innately bad and no one would do good unless he were obliged to. This has always been the standard excuse for absolutism. In Christian doctrine, however, original sin does not stand alone: it is bound up with the possibility of grace, redemption, perfection. Machiavelli conveniently turned a half-truth into a brazen lie; on this assumption there were only three weapons of effective government: force, terrorism, and corruption. Plainly, evil can be simple-minded as well as virtue. There was something essentially callow in Machiavelli's admiration for a treacherous, murderous villain like Cesare Borgia. Such adolescent fixations should confine themselves to the world of pure fantasy and not pretend to deal with the affairs of men.

The doctrines of Christianity assumed that man was something more than a mere animal; but the philosophers of despotism were forced to assume that he was something less.

Machiavelli held, for example, that a man would always be more aggrieved because his property was taken away than because his father was killed: that looks as if he had discovered a political use for the Oedipus complex. But his understanding of human nature was too limited, for he held that men in general were "ungrateful, voluble, dissemblers, anxious to avoid danger, covetous of gain." All of this was true, provided one did not forget to look on the opposite side of the scales: for there is equal historic evidence to show that men are also loyal, honest, ready to face danger, indifferent to personal gain when principles are at stake or loyalties are awakened. If Machiavelli had even remembered the history of the Inquisition, that remorseless agent of power, he would not have overlooked hundreds of heretics, from the time of the Albigensian massacres on, who suffered horrible tortures and accepted death rather than make a verbal retraction which would satisfy the demands of the Church they despised.

It is this capacity for both badness and goodness, for conduct that would disgrace a healthy animal and for conduct that would honor an angel, that gives human character its range, its variety, its unexpected debacles and upsurges. Man's very loyalty to symbols, to "mere" words, and "mere" personal feelings, confounds every purely materialist code of conduct. Machiavelli did not say a word too much when he pictured the devices of corruption whereby men may become the willing accomplices of those who wield power: all surrender to tyranny begins with self-corruption, that is, in the unwillingness to attend to public duties and in the readiness to give up precious political rights in return for a life of undisturbed self-indulgence. But unfortunately for Machiavelli's ability to deal with reality, he was forced to treat virtue itself as a mere variant of corruption: a more subtle disguise for the same evil propensities. His political philosophy accounted for an Alexander, a Caligula, a Frederick II, a Cesare Borgia; but it had no key to the character of a Demosthenes, a Thomas More, a Garibaldi, or an Abraham Lincoln.

If human beings were always as base as Machiavelli pictured them, despotism would be the only available system of government, and men would deserve nothing better: then the dream of Dostoyevsky's Grand Inquisitor would come true. But to make despotism work, one must first eviscerate humanity of its animal virtues: tenderness for the young and helpless of the species: the fierce adhesive loyalty of the herd: even the caged rat's cunning desire for freedom. Over short periods of time, this operation can be successfully done: we in the twentieth century have seen it take place before our own eyes—and we have also lived to see its natural terminus: the resurgence of man's elemental humanity. Sometimes nature takes a hand in the despot's downfall, as when Cesare Borgia, close upon his father's death, found himself unexpectedly dying; so, too, Napoleon may have met his Waterloo in cancer of the stomach long before the battle itself occurred. But what is more important, the extirpated human tissues reappear again in the organism, like tonsils that have been only partly removed by a clumsy surgeon: the whole man reasserts himself.

What has become of the great princes whose ruthless force and persistent fraud Machiavelli admired? What permanent work did they establish? It is not in politics that the answer to this question can be found, but only in art; they were lavish patrons, and the only commands they gave with any lasting success were to the artists who painted them or set them monumentally on bronze chargers. Since they had no similar success in politics, Machiavelli's whole theory falls to the ground. The one absolute system of government that has proved successful, the Catholic Church of Rome, has always weakened itself by actually relying upon armies, police, and prisons: indeed, the Papacy has never been endangered politically except during the periods when it has followed Machiavelli's methods.

Where have the permanent gains in political government been achieved? They have arisen in states that respected the will and intelligence of their citizens: that slowly perfected the practices of corporate consultation and action: that learned to substitute law and orderly procedure for untutored tyrannical whim: that supplanted the arbitrary commands of hereditary or self-chosen leaders by a periodic canvass and a formal consent, expressed through the ballot and through parliament.

During the very period when absolutism gained ground most rapidly, democracy and representative government, though often driven underground, did not entirely accept defeat. The problem of federated power and unified government was solved by the citizens of Switzerland: an example destined to spread ever further through the world. And meanwhile, in a hundred different clubs and societies, drinking clubs, burial societies, singing societies, friendly associations, religious sodalities, insurance associations, in scientific societies and trade unions, the methods of rational government, by co-operation and consent, were firmly outlined. Consider this new process itself: the written charter or constitution, the regular election of officers, the debate, the committee; the open meeting, the quorum, and the regular order of procedure. All these were political devices of the highest importance: evolved by democratic communities in the course of a long, anonymous evolution, by men of narrow interests and low estate who nevertheless imposed laws and regulations upon themselves that were to have powerful consequences upon political society at large.

Now these advances took place without the outward flourishes of leadership: so steadily did they take hold, so quietly, that they now seem to their present day inheritors as inevitable acts of associated life. But in truth, these devices of democracy were the hard-won inventions of individuals and groups: once their original secret is forgotten, once they continue by mere automatism instead of being re-thought and revised each generation, their doom is near.

But here I would emphasize the political feebleness of despotism, except in such technical devices as I have mentioned—the budget and the lengthened term of office. Whereas despotism threw ingenious bureaucratic shackles around industry and commerce, democracy created an order which made each individual or group a starting point for fresh initiatives. Despotism, in other words, was not a method for subjecting political power to rational control, but for making irrational claims powerful. Though it attempted to make the state a finished work of art, it sacrificed the variety and exuberance of life for a formal unity that turned all too easily into blank mechanical uniformity.

Political society is like a cable composed of many strands: the twisting together of these different strands not merely increases its strength but its flexibility. There are strands of economic interests, strands of national and family feeling, strands of religious belief, strands of different grades of experience and education. The cable itself is complex by nature; and the political knots that cry for untying make it more so: but one condition must be preserved in sound politics—Alexander's example, of using the naked sword to cleave the Gordian knot, must not be resorted to. Any fool can solve the problems of political power by martial law: but only a fool would mistake that process for government.

This was a fact that Machiavelli and his successors never understood. In a crisis, political power may have to be concentrated: the Fathers of the American Constitution understood this no less clearly than Machiavelli. But despotism is forever driven to prolong its crisis in order to preserve its power: hence it is doomed to live in a state of improvised emergencies, in order to keep political power from flowing back to the limbs and organs that would normally utilize it.

Machiavelli was hypnotized too easily by the theatrical successes of absolutism: he mistook a brilliant stage performance for a slice of real life. And he never understood how much actual political power does not reach the surface: how much is exercised by the whole community in daily evaluations, actions, and judgments. He saw the weakness of the little man and the power of the great: that lay on the surface. But he did not understand the weakness and dependence of the great nor yet the mole-like power of the little man, whose silence may be mistaken for consent, and whose patience may even be confused with applause. In other words, Machiavelli, long given credit as a "realist" because he despised mankind, was in fact a wistful, worshipful romantic, a schoolboy capable of traipsing after a gaudy uniform: a thinker whose scorn for humanity's baseness kept him from understanding all the facts that qualify that baseness. Men are governed not only by the tyrants they fear but by the institutions they love: and in the long run love, not fear, will prevail.

7: Automatons as Subjects

What was the ultimate tendency of despotic government? This was finally revealed by Thomas Hobbes in The Leviathan. The true destination of such government is automatism, and its real province is in the world of machines. Despotism can succeed, in other words, only to the extent that it can turn men into automatons.

Society for Hobbes was a battleground of brute power: life begins in a state of war, every man against every man; and each demand for power fosters a claim for more power in order to protect that which is already possessed. For what, according to Hobbes, *is* life? He answers straightforwardly: it is simply "a motion of the limbs," and just as automatons, like watches, moved by springs and wheels, may be said to have artificial life, so may man be treated as just the opposite of this: a natural automaton, a self-operating machine. To make men mechanical was merely to reverse the process of making machines human.

Historians have hardly noted with enough emphasis the effect of the advancing technics of this period upon the concepts of political rule; although Professor Geroid Tanquary Robinson has applied this insight to the contemporary rise of totalitarianism. The ideology of mechanical invention and the ideology of despotic government have been treated as if they were in watertight compartments; but in fact they were closely interrelated at every step of the way. Hobbes and Descartes both, in their separate ways, carried Machiavelli's theories a step further because, coming later, they accepted more fully the lesson of machinery. For Machiavelli, man was still more corrupt than mechanical: he accepted the more pessimistic half of the Christian dogma about man's nature. But for Hobbes man was already more mechanical than corrupt: all the claims of despotism could be justified on the ground that man was a machine to begin with, and therefore had need for no more humane system of government. If men fell short of the despot's ideal, the remedy was more mechanization.

The systematic application of force through mechanical drill was reintroduced into armies at the end of the sixteenth century: it turned the army into a human machine. The soldier thereby became a coglike unit without any will of his own: clad in a newly fashioned uniform, itself a product of mass production and standardization, he became the uniform replaceable part of the ideal modern machine. Once thoroughly drilled, his conduct could be predicted with mathematical certainty: princes and soldiers, Goethe observed to Eckermann, have a fondness for mathematical figures. Such mechanical responses saved the ruler time and energy:

choice, discretion, freedom, could exist only at the top, theoretically in the person of the Prince.

The uniformed automaton became the very image of despotic regimentation; for the underlying aim of despotism was to make every rank, every class, every set of dispositions equally responsive to simple signals. The nation in uniform was the ultimate political goal of this idea; but by a paradox worthy of a great ironist, this goal was first achieved by universal conscription in the armies that defended France during its great revolution against despotism. Before that, however, the iron-willed industrialist Arkwright had organized the new factories on the same despotic principle, and wherever the factory system went, a rigorous centralization of power and a ruthless dehumanization of the worker *as* a working unit went with it: so that the ballot-box democracy which was achieved in the nineteenth century was nullified on every working day by the routine of the factory itself—the factory where human responses were at last reduced to that "motion of the limbs" described by Hobbes, and where the right to hire and fire gave to the industrial despot a power of life and death over his subjects which even emperors had hitherto trembled to exercise.

The cult of centralized irresponsible power fed mightily on the increasing stores of non-human power that became available: horses, gunpowder, coal, steam, windmills, water-wheels; and it is no accident that a reckless love of speed for its own sake flourished among the aristocracy in France long before it altered the actual tempo of production: driving at breakneck pace between Paris and Versailles was the height of aristocratic elegance, and the coaches of the nobility drove over people in fact as well as in spirit. The insolence of horsepower had its origin here: the power in the animal or the machine inflated the human ego and removed a just sense of its limitations. The biggest prime mover of the seventeenth century ministered to the vanity of Louis XIV by providing energy to work the fountains at Versailles.

If the aim of the inventor was to make machines take the place of men, by analyzing, simplifying, reproducing, and magnifying the motions of the human frame, the aim of despotism was to make men fit more subserviently into the pattern of a larger machine: the state or the factory or the bureau. By diminishing the intensity of human responses, by narrowing the range of human actions, by reducing human sensibilities, by exterminating every tendency to autonomous (read "unauthorized") action, the despot sought to make men responsive to simple words of command. In no department was the success immediate and complete: it took centuries of tyrannous indoctrination and mechanical habituation before men could be reduced to a state in which the assembly line could be looked upon as a *normal* process in production. But by the seventeenth century the ideological framework was at least built; and by the eighteenth century La Mettrie in Man the Machine could treat man as a purely mechanical phenomenon: a mere product of matter and motion.

Such a doctrine could not at once be pronounced unscientific, for the reason that science itself had been formed in the same milieu of mammonism, mechanism, and despotism and had carried into its own department the same narrow preoccupations. By successive abstractions, man was dissociated from his personal self, his social self, his biological self, until finally all that was left was a bare skeleton, worked ingeniously by wires: a contraption of pumps, levers, retorts, tools: ultimately, if one crushed the skeleton and carried the analysis far enough, a mere sack of chemicals: carbon, oxygen, hydrogen, nitrogen, and minor quantities of elements that could be found in any chemist's shop. That process reduced the mechanical picture of man to absurdity: at all events, when one puts Hobbes' notion alongside the conception of the personality and the community set forth by Plato, Aristotle, Cicero, Augustine, or Thomas Aquinas, one can only marvel at its crudeness. The clarity of the mechanical explanation of conduct veiled its essential obscurantism: it was indifferent to human realities.

The insufficiency of the mechanical theory of man was in fact proved by the very activities of despotic governments. They pushed mechanization, drill, and military repression as far as they dared to: but at the same time they made their task easier and their position securer by providing a safety valve which recognized another side of man's nature and took advantage of it. They counterbalanced regimentation by encouraging a primitive violence of the passions, by giving play to an untempered eroticism, by turning the external environment into a fairyland of sensuous delight. In short, despotism needed both the Prison and the Carnival. Since only a limited part of the population can, at any one time, be thrown into prison, Carnival proved the more useful device: it erected around the whole community a more subtle prison house of the senses.

"Youth and maids, enjoy today: naught ye know about tomorrow." Thus sang one of Lorenzo de Medici's choruses in a pageant. Hitler used the same prescription in its most brutal and debased form to undermine the conquered peoples of Europe: pornography. By expensive shows, by elaborate dances and games, above all, by gorgeous masques and public celebrations in which the great artists of the period were employed, the despot both enhanced his own self-esteem and acquired the good will of the people whom he mulcted and governed. In this department, the interplay of the mechanical and the sensuous was constant: its synthesis was the final achievement of baroque art in the seventeenth century.

Vasari documents this process for us in his biography of Il Cecca. The need to exhibit power and riches "originally produced buildings, then their ornamentation, and finally the dispositions; statues, gardens, baths, and all those sumptuous accessories which everyone desires but few possess, so that emulation not only produced buildings, but has rendered them luxurious. In this way artists have been compelled to display their industry in methods of traction, in machines of war, in hydraulic apparatus, and in all those employments by which engineers and architects render the world beautiful and luxurious."

The breaking down of the citizen's self-respect was an essential device of despotic government; and the baroque carnival was one of the chief means of substituting an empty sensory excitement, accompanied by a suspense of public duties and by sexual promiscuity, for the ordered emotional life of the home and the guild.

Now, the love of luxury is an even more insidious kind of corruption than the love of money, because it draws more directly on a variety of entirely normal human needs. Luxury prolongs pleasures beyond their natural physiological span and in time deforms the personality by making pleasure alone take the place of the full circle of interests, tasks, duties, sacrifices, joys, and fulfillments that constitute man's life. The enchantment of Circe is deadly for the reason that all human life, even the highest, must begin at the animal level and is subject to arrest at that level. Wines, songs, dances, wooing, visual delights are all organic parts of a fuller life; but when they dominate life and become its sole object they lead to psychological disintegration.

Even in the fourteenth century Petrarch described the growing emptiness of life, which made people ready to do anything to kill time and fill the idle moments. But with the advance of despotism and the decay of the ideology of salvation, the emptiness became more appalling—and more demoralizing: once the Prince had absorbed the normal political duties of men no small part of their existence was devaluated. Protestantism may be partly interpreted, particularly in the seventeenth century phase, as an attempt to recover the individual's self-respect: it had its counterpart in emotional reactions like Savonarola's earlier Bonfire of Vanities in Florence, at the end of the fifteenth century: a prelude to the Counter-Reformation, which began with the Council of Trent.

Public luxury, then, counterbalanced mechanical regimentation: both processes simplified the art of despotic government. And as corruption and brutality gained the upper hand, an overladen estheticism sought to take the place of morality.

Classic culture served a special purpose in this new economy: it was the secret language of the upper classes. Burckhardt points out that in the time of Dante, the best old manuscripts belonged originally to the artisans, and it was for their higher democratic culture that Brunetto Latini, Dante's teacher, published his popular encyclopedia: but as despotism flourished, humanism became the handmaid of the new rulers. To know the gods and the graces, to be able to distinguish between the Five Orders in architecture, to appreciate the exquisiteness of a broken torso exhumed from a Roman villa, to glow over the find of a new manuscript—all this became the badge of upper-class culture: the common acquirement of parvenus. Mars and Venus made love on the sly: Vulcan was a cuckold and Mercury was a thief: plainly all these wraiths of a forgotten world were more genial to the habits and desires of the new élite than the examples of the martyrs and the saints. Dreaming of an ideal Rome, which existed only in their imaginations, these merchants and scholars and rulers sought to embellish their own world with reconstructions and adaptations of the classic past. Pomponius Laetus, at the end of the fifteenth century, would stand entranced before Roman ruins and burst into tears. For people who were attempting to escape the supernaturalism of the Middle Ages, it was easier to retreat into an embalmed culture than to venture out into a new world. The pathos of time particularly affected people who had lost their faith in eternity.

But the affectations of classic humanism served another purpose: they helped to debase and degrade popular art. The great efflorescence of the thirteenth century had produced a vernacular literature and a vernacular art: Dante, with a true instinct for the living, chose to write his Divine Comedy in Tuscan, rather than in the scholarly Latin of the Church or the aristocratic language of Provence: a deliberate choice. The cult of the Virgin was a popular cult; and the guildsman not merely took part in public processions and enacted characters in religious plays: but he helped to choose the architect and to criticize the workmanship and the decoration of great buildings: the function of criticism was as universal as the opportunities for esthetic creation. All the sources of creativeness lay in the common life.

To make the new order of capitalism and absolutism succeed, it was necessary to cast this popular culture into disrepute: to belittle and besmirch everything it had created: to defy its morality and to ridicule its esthetics: to characterize as crude or barbarous all its highest achievements: to pretend that the Romans were better architects than the people who had built Chartres and that a third-rate comedy by Terence or Plautus was infinitely superior to the indigenous mystery play or the commedia dell' arte. This denigration went along with the transfer of authority from the workers themselves to an esthetic despot: the man of taste, he who had read the classic treatises and memorized the classic rules. Classic taste meant obedience to stereotyped formulae: now the worker, as Ruskin well pointed out, must conform to a higher authority and utilize his skill in mechanical imitation of dead forms: the machine system of production re-enters architecture with the repetitive standardized ornamentation that went with the classic orders.

In good part, these claims of excellence were mere upper-class superstitions: in the act of esthetically exploiting the past the new connoisseur smoothed the way for those who were commercially exploiting the present. Even the mystery play and the commedia, though they were not on the level of the Cathedral, were the embryonic form of a much more original and noble art than Rome had ever known: Shakespeare, Racine, and Molière touched heights that had been reached only by the Greeks in their greatest period.

The worship of the classics deliberately sought to raise culture above the popular level: by definition, a shoemaker, a stonecutter, or a weaver could not be a humanist. The acquisition of culture now became a by-product of the acquisitive impulse itself: it rested on a boundless capacity to collect and pile up physical treasures. In one's home, the sign of culture was to be surrounded by fragments, reproductions, or ornamental simulacra of the antique world: in conversation one would trot out quotations from one's favorite classic authors, in the original language, to prove that one had spent one's time almost exclusively in their company: even Montaigne often becomes tedious by his parade of ancient citations, not because his own thought needs them, but merely for the decorative effect. Thus a despotism of the spirit, such as only blind conformity to the dead can produce, matched a despotism of political and economic deed. But the repression was, of course, never complete: in the very violence of baroque sculpture and architecture in the seventeenth century one witnesses a covert resurgence of gothic vitality.

If Protestantism was, as I shall show, an uprising against the corruptions of medieval culture, an attempt to recover simplicity and sanctity, classicism was a snobbish counter-revolution to the vulgar naturalism and the buoyant creative imagination of the Middle Ages. The upper classes fenced off pagan culture for themselves: whatever was not within the fence was not, for them, culture. Did not Leonardo da Vinci complain that artists like himself were dismissed by his more learned and more literary contemporaries as mere mechanics?

8: Protestantism's Challenge to Capitalism

Protestantism in religion came into being, not as an ally of capitalism, but as its chief enemy: not as an effort to swell the energies of the *id* but to curb them before they had become too powerful. This fact has been too lightly passed over by those too innocent historians who date the rise of Protestantism from the sixteenth century; and I would therefore underline it. Instead of Protestantism's being the new creed of the rising bourgeoisie, Protestantism when it appeared in the twelfth century was an attempt to prevent the rise of the bourgeoisie. For the most stubborn challenge to the Roman Church came from those who were sickened by the spectacle of its open alliance with capitalism: it came from those who wished to do away with the venal elements that were making a mockery of its sacred professions. The Waldensians, the Fraticelli, the Lollards, the original Protestants, were all in opposition to the overheated desire for worldly gain Alain of Lille described.

At its source, Protestantism was an attempt to check the commercial spirit and prevent it from getting hold of the Church: that is why the early Protestants had many allies within the institution itself and had no desire for separation: that is why, too, the early movement was in good part an agrarian one. But the Catholic Church by the thirteenth century was definitely on the side of property: in 1344, when Brother Francesco d'Ascoli was accused of heresy, he cleared himself by recanting the belief that Christ and his apostles held no property. This came after almost two centuries of protest. Is it an accident that the first organized movement, that of the Waldensians, was an act of repentance and revolt started by a merchant, Peter Waldo of Lyons, where the great international fair was held?

One Sunday, according to tradition, Waldo turned aside to join the crowd listening to a sermon; and he was so touched by the preacher's words that he sold his property and founded the Order of the Poor Men of Lyons. Waldo caused the Bible and the saints to be translated into the vernacular, so that laymen could understand the Scriptures; and he himself began preaching, with the Pope's permission, in 1179, only to have the movement condemned by the Vatican in 1184. The Waldensians were joined in time by other sects; one and all, these Protestants attempted to bring poverty back to Christianity and to give Christianity its original humble foundation in daily life. Their efforts were more successful than Francis's, because they shunned the Papacy; and they continued far

III. MEDIEVAL DISSOLUTION

Pieter Brueghel superbly exemplifies the spirit of medieval democracy and, like Bosch, he records the disintegration of its idolum. Faith in the Church, recorded in the print at the bottom, was still the foundation stone of his personality. But in the Low Countries, home of the great weaving guilds, the first challengers of feudalism, that faith was coupled with a robust belief in nature, a solid confidence in the works of man, and a joyous interest in all the manifestations of man's social life, from the pastimes of children to the feasting and dancing of holiday times, from the legends of the Church to the sayings of the folk. In Brueghel's landscapes one is conscious, too, of season, climate, weather: the bleakness of a hunt in the snow, the shimmering opalescence of plowing time, the drowsy heat of harvest.

In Brueghel's compositions the idea of democracy becomes fully embodied: not alone in the importance he gives to the common man but in the equal value he assigns to every figure. (Even in his great painting of The Carrying of the Cross, Jesus, though placed in the exact center, is lost in the middle distance mid the crowd.) Brueghel's folk-humor is close to Eulenspiegel's, but he has a grimmer side, shown here in the contrast between the Lean People and the Fat People: a contrast that, from the 15th century on, became ever more acute as the reciprocal obligations of feudalism and the brotherly co-operation of the earlier guilds gave place to a one-sided capitalist exploitation of the weak by the powerful and the privileged. In Brueghel the health, sanity, and moral earnestness of medieval protestantism took positive form. Like Chaucer he heartily affirmed life; but like the author of Piers Plowman and Calvin he showed grave concern over contemporary social disorders. Brueghel's fantasy was at the service of his moral convictions; yet even his healthy mind was haunted by obscene figures of disruption: no longer do the gargoyles share the sky with the saints and angels. The deformed shapes and transposed organs of Brueghel's demons link them to the nocturnal underworld of the unconscious. The top print, representing the sin of Luxury, is one of a series of surrealist studies which link his imagination to that of Goya. Here the disintegration of the Middle Ages becomes as plain as that of modern culture in the paintings of Picasso or Dali: see Plates XIII or XIV.

IV. UPSURGE OF VITALITY

The man on horseback—Prince or Centaur—dominated the post-medieval world: a period of rising appetites and over-reaching powers. Piero di Cosimo's Battle of the Centaurs expresses both the joy of violence and the violence of sensual joy. But this unleashing of appetites had firmly established biological roots: Titian's amatory canvases swarm with naked children, and these little figures of Eros, worshiping Venus, are still regarded as the natural attendants and inevitable consequences of her rites. The birth records of the ruling families remain objective testimony of this fact.

longer. They even made an impression upon their official persecutors, for one of these reported, according to Lea: "Heretics are recognizable by their customs and speech, for they are modest and well-regulated. They take no pride in their garments, which are neither costly nor vile. They do not engage in trade, to avoid lies and oaths and frauds, but live by their labor as mechanics. They do not accumulate wealth, but are content with necessaries."

With Waldo the revolt within the Church concerned itself chiefly with a return to Christian economics. But Wycliffe, in England, during the fourteenth century, was even more in revolt against the ecclesiastical assumption of unique office: against sacerdotalism itself. For him all Christians were equal in the sight of God: therefore to assume that the priest alone had the power of converting the bread and wine of the communion into the body and blood of Christ was to exalt him above all other Christians. The only cure for this was to return to the rule of the Gospel. The common people of England pushed that doctrine much further, and in the revolt headed by John Ball—as reported by Froissart—one has a clear indication of both their criticism and their intentions. Says John Ball:

"My good people,—Things cannot go well in England, nor ever will, until all goods are held in common, and until there will be neither serfs nor gentlemen, and we shall all be equal. For what reason have they, whom we call lords, got the best of us? How did they deserve it? Why do they keep us in bondage? If we are descended from one father and one mother, Adam and Eve, how can they assert or prove they are more masters than ourselves? Except perhaps that they make us work and produce for them to spend. They are clothed in velvets and in coats garnished with ermine and fur, while we wear coarse linen. They have wine, spices, and good bread, while we get rye-bread, offal, straw, and water. They have residences, handsome manors, and we the trouble and the work, and must brave the rain and the wind in the fields. And it is from us and our labor that they get the means to support their pomp."

This Christian communism did not die out under persecution and political oppression: the English peasants' revolt of 1381 and the German peasants' uprising in 1525 did not finish the story: the protest against both feudal and capitalist exploitation was still alive in the Digger Movement in Cromwell's time, and it returned again in various communistic settlements, like those of the Shakers and the original Mormons in the New World.

Nor was this all. Protestantism was essentially a layman's rebellion. The will to apply Christian standards to economic life finally laid the foundations for the great consumers' co-operative movement which was started by the Rochdale weavers in the middle of the nineteenth century. In less than half a century these pious British nonconformists built up a great organization for distribution and manufacture, rivaling the biggest capitalist organizations in technical skill and managerial economy. The chief figure in building up this great enterprise, J. T. W. Mitchell, never received more than £150 a year for his services: a proof that other incentives were available besides the gross rewards capitalism offered. That co-operative movement was perhaps the last embodiment of medieval Protestantism, with its demand for a truly Christian economic order: its further spread in our day awaits a moral and spiritual regeneration at least as deep, as engrossing, as that which created the protestant personality. Without such a moral change, co-operation is open to the attritions, diversions, and dissipations resulting from the impulses it seeks to supplant: acquisitiveness and worldly self-seeking. . . .

By the sixteenth century, capitalism and Protestantism had drawn closer together; but their opposition remained; and Protestantism, so far from riding smoothly to success on this "wave of the future" sought to form breakwaters sufficiently strong to maintain the Christian way of life. In both economics and politics, the protestant super-ego served in the narrow Freudian sense, as a brake and a block to the aggressive energies that were transforming daily life. If the eventual result of Luther's theology was to buttress the absolute state, and that of Calvin's theology was to fortify with self-righteousness the capitalist enterpriser, both results were far from their patent intention.

9: Luther and Nationalism

Martin Luther was the son of a peasant who had turned miner. He lived within the cultural milieu formed by what was socially the most backward and technically the most advanced industry of sixteenth century Germany. Not merely was he a contemporary of Dr. Georg Bauer (Agricola), the great authority on mining, metallurgy, and technics: they were even born in the same town of Eisleben in Saxony.

As a monk in the Augustinian order and a professor of theology, Luther was awakened to the dangers of pious good works by examining at first hand the apparatus of spiritual finance that Rome fostered: this, and the general indulgence of harlotry in that holy city, which he visited, awakened a deep feeling of repulsion. "The way things go now," he wrote in his Treatise on Usury, "they apply the high title of 'alms' or 'giving for God's sake,' to giving for churches, monasteries, chapels, altars, bells, organs, paintings, statues, silver and gold ornaments and vestments, and for masses, singing, reading, testamentary endowments, sodalities, and the like." In his conflict with his ecclesiastical superiors in Rome, he fell back upon Augustine's position: that without faith and divine grace nothing availed. No outward acts could bring the soul nearer salvation.

Luther's father flogged him mercilessly when he was a boy. In young manhood he was deeply shocked by the death of a dear companion: this roused thoughts of his own untimely end; and the terror evoked by a gut-quivering thunderstorm, which caused him to fall flat on the ground, had led him to the monastery. Safety and freedom were to be found only in the inner world: not that of the monastery, where authority also threatened, but within the citadel of the private self, outside the range of tyrannical fathers and tongued lightning. At this point the contrast between capitalism and Protestantism becomes dramatically incarnated in two personalities: for at about the same time Jacob Fugger II, who was to become the paragon of modern financiers, left the monastery where he had already taken orders so that he might carry on the Fugger enterprises.

In pitting himself against the materialist vices of the Church, Luther continued the spirit of medieval protestantism. Like his English forerunner, Wycliffe, he held that all Christians, not merely the clergy, belonged to the "spiritual estate," and that there is no difference at all between priest and laity but that of the office. "Gospel and Faith make us a 'spiritual' and a Christian people." In all this, by a certain bullheaded manly courage, Luther helped wipe away centuries of double-dealing and hypocrisy, and came out with the essential truth of religion, namely, that it is a relation between the self and the divine purpose, between microcosm and macrocosm—a relation forever endangered by the visible symbols and allegorical references man creates in order to further his own understanding of this mystery. The healthy straightforwardness of Luther on such matters can still invigorate the reader of his Table Talk. Who could improve on his observation that "mere lust is felt even by fleas and lice; love begins when we wish to serve others"?

But unfortunately Luther's servile fear of external authority undermined the clean position he had taken in opposition to Rome. Casting off the Pope's control, Luther submitted, alas! only the more readily to powers nearer home. At first, this theological revolt was interpreted by the discontented peasants as evidence of his human sympathy and his understanding of their case. They saw in Luther a legitimate successor to their earlier leader, Hans Boheim, later called the Little Piper, a cowherd who used to pipe and drum at festivities. This Hans, in 1476, had a vision in which the Mother of God told him to burn his pipe and drum and go forth to preach: he performed this mission, urging people to lay aside ornaments, become brothers, share all things, withhold their taxes and dues, dethrone pope, emperor, and prince. The German knights captured Hans and burned him; but they did not quickly halt the movement he started.

From Augsburg in 1476 came a pamphlet called The Reformation of Emperor Sigismund: this was widely circulated between 1520 and 1525. There were eight major proposals in this remarkable pamphlet: they included the restriction of taxation to the upkeep of roads and bridges, their original purpose; the abolition of guilds, because of their insolence, exclusiveness, and corruption; the doing away with dishonesty and extortion and monopolies by the merchants; the regulation of prices and wages by municipal commissions, the abolition of serfdom; and even—notable in such an agrarian program—the establishment of public physicians in every city to treat everyone without charge.

When Luther saw that his revolt was being taken seriously by the peasants of Germany and was being connected with their own hopes and plans, he violently repudiated them. He even rejected the plea for the abolition of serfdom on the ground that this would "change the spiritual Kingdom of Christ into an external worldly one. . . . An earthly kingdom can not exist without inequality of persons." Is it strange that the peasants should have believed, as Luther complained to Dr. Brueck in his Table Talk, "that religion has been invented by us and is not divine"? So far indeed from combining his own religious rebellion against ecclesiastical authority with the gathering social revolt against secular authority, Luther expressly said: "Changing and bettering conditions are as far apart as heaven and earth." Man could change; only God could *better*. But somehow Luther failed to explain why God worked so exclusively on the side of the ruling classes.

In short, if Luther weakened the foundations of the Church, he reinforced the gates of the Castle: indeed, he ultimately rendered exclusively to the soldier and the state functionary the authority that had once been divided between them and the Church. Luther's headstrong, arrogant spirit, his vituperative contempt for those who opposed him, his insistence upon giving homage to those who had military power, his reluctance to oppose the exploiting groups,—all this denied his best doctrines. Having given in so subserviently to the ruling classes, Luther's many efforts to establish Christian principles in economic affairs naturally came to nothing: if Christian politics were not practicable in this world, why should anyone fancy that Christian economics were more feasible? Luther might preach against usury; he might seek to break down monopoly and abolish the unchristian and inhuman conduct of buying cheap and selling dear; but he left his words hanging cloudily in the air, and never dared the act that would have made them rain down on the proud and the powerful.

Theoretically, however, Luther's attempt to establish Christian justice helped lay the foundations for a no less formidable heresy than capitalism itself: the heresy of nationalism. Luther's great translation of the Bible into German did for Germany what Dante had done for Italy: it gave the Germans a common language, one of great vigor. But though the standardization of regional speech through a national language was a natural consequence of the invention of printing, and a highly beneficent result, in that it widened the range of the common life, it was accompanied throughout the Western World by an effort to achieve cultural self-sufficiency: a perverse rebound from the Universal Church. Protestantism, for example, had spread from Wycliffe's England to Bohemia through the very internationalism of scholarship, which brought Bohemian scholars to Oxford. But the followers of John Huss overthrew the internationalism that made their own movement possible: King Wenzel's decree giving Bohemians three votes to one over the other nations in the conduct of the University of Prague caused a wholesale withdrawal of German scholars to Vienna, Leipzig, and Cologne. Luther carried this mischief further: he associated internationalism with corruption and isolationism with purity: this applied in economics no less than in theology.

Luther's own words were authority for the doctrine of "autarchy" or the walled national frontier. He advocated the cutting off of all possible commercial relations with people beyond Germany, so as not to "let the 'foreigners' take out German gold." Though he sanctioned trade in local commodities as "gifts of God, which He bestows out of the earth and distributes among men," he drew the line at articles that came from "Calicut, India, and such places." Luther's belief in the gifts of divine providence stopped short at the German frontiers. This nationalist economics, somewhat misleadingly called mercantile economics, worked hand in glove with absolutism: it prepared the ground for both political nationalism and for its inevitable offspring, imperialism. Martin Luther was the early Bismarck of this nationalist religion, as Bismarck was the belated Luther of nationalist politics: today Hitler, their joint heir, has brought the whole movement to its demonic consummation. Hitler's religion of power, with himself for God, was an effort to overthrow what was left of the universal and the human: an effort to turn the world as a whole into the German fatherland. One has only to listen to Luther's denunciations of the peasants to hear the same shrieks of vituperation that rose in Hitler's mouth against democrats, communists, liberals, and Jews. The justification of both absolutism and isolationism has its spiritual foundations in Luther.

The overbearing subjectivism of Luther's thought, later unsuccessfully sublimated in the metaphysics of Immanuel Kant, left a deep imprint on the minds of his countrymen. For Luther's doctrine of faith lent itself to exploitation by far darker powers than those this doctrine opposed: the very fact that the private world of the believer became sacred for him, prevented him from acknowledging the criterion of sanity—the congruence of private conviction with the historic experience and the common sense of other men.

That seed reached its final monstrous growth in Hitler: its deep theological origins only made more easy its common acceptance and its swift success among Luther's descendants. By the beginning of the nineteenth century, Fichte and Hegel talked as if the Prussian State was the divine event toward which all creation moves. An inevitable debasement. For the gospel of self-sufficiency and self-determination is no innocent one: the self that has escaped oppression is as open to the corruption of pride as the greater authority from which it has escaped. Morally speaking, the cant and conceit of a village may be as vile as the claims of an empire.

10: Calvin: The Responsible Community

Jean Calvin was a man of entirely different cut from Martin Luther—straitlaced where Luther was genial; tight and passionate, where Luther was coarsely argumentative; methodical, systematic, rigorous, where Luther was empirical and contradictory. In short, Calvin was the classic Frenchman: a Cartesian before Descartes, a Robespierre whose God of Reason was better grounded in human realities than the Goddess whom the revolution sought to crown. The great French theologian who fortified the Augustinian doctrine of predestination, and enlarged the precincts of Hell to receive the multitude, must however be remembered for another and better reason: he laid the foundations for civil liberty and self-government: the City of Man. Plainly it is absurd to treat as a single movement a cause that harbored characters and doctrines as profoundly opposed, in their ultimate consequences, as those of a Luther, a Calvin, a Milton, a Penn, a Wesley.

Jean came of a family of bargemen on the Oise; but his father had escaped from that low trade and become an apostolic notary and a member of the rising middle class. Calvin's education was that of a humanist, and, like Luther, he had prepared himself for law. Calvin never lost his respect for this discipline: since the civil magistracy was for him a holy and legitimate calling, "far the most sacred and honorable in human life," it was no small praise for him to call law a silent magistrate and the magistrate himself a speaking law. His creed became a code. Calvin's task was to legalize moral conduct and to give it an active function in the community, not treating it merely as a preparatory step toward the City of God. This was the very opposite of Luther's endeavor.

In pure theology Calvin, younger than Luther, did not materially differ from him or from other protestant reformers like Zwingli and Melanchthon. Like them, he was acutely conscious of the prevailing abuses in the Roman Church, and he sought to correct them by recalling men to apostolic forms and experiences. When Calvin accepted a post at Geneva, he saw an opportunity to combat the laxity and indifference that was creeping into every corner of this society and that widened the theoretic gap between sacred and secular offices whilst it practically united them in a common worldly aim. Though Calvin's first experiment led to a revolt among the Genevese that resulted in his exile, he eventually returned to Geneva with more power than ever: a power he used to make outward conduct conform to ministerial conviction and admonition.

Calvin's effort was audacious for two reasons. In the first place, he brought together in a single institution the temporal and the spiritual powers: they were now coeval and they had the same boundaries of jurisdiction. He thus ended an impossible dualism of functions, symbolized in the opposing figures of Pope and Emperor: a dualism which tended to make the temporal power brutal and the spiritual power irresponsible. Unfortunately, though Calvin properly recognized the disintegrating results of having these two aspects of the personality separated into social castes, he did not provide for maintaining their natural polar tension within the personality and the community. When the civil order devoted itself to the systematic establishment of the moral order, heresy became in effect treason and moral delinquencies, hitherto treated only by reproof and absolution, were now prosecuted as civil and criminal offenses. A sin was a crime against the State: a crime was a sin against the Church. A girl who sang vulgar songs was sent into exile; a couple whose adultery was uncovered could be publicly disgraced and punished. Originally, this placed too much power in the hands of civil authority. At no moment of the day was the citizen free from the inquisition of public guardians. To make such a system work, spies and informers were needed; and a grosser evil was sometimes introduced in order to chastise a lesser one.

Thus Calvin's Church claimed for itself a more constant supervision over every detail of human life than Rome had claimed. So long as the sinner did not cut himself off from God by heresy, the Catholic Church was lenient to him. But Calvin's government practiced no such indulgence: its aim was to reduce temptation and to root out sin: even little errors in conduct required correction. That endeavor exacted from the ordinary man and woman a standard of conduct that had never been rigorously achieved even by any great body of the clergy: in effect, it turned every man and woman into a monk and a nun, living a dedicated life, watching each moment, consecrating every part of it to the service of God. Forgiveness for sins depended upon an act of grace: that rested with God alone. But civil conformity required both an inner searching and an outer inquisition: this was a matter for the individual sinner in his private closet and for the civil council in its public administration.

The pursuit of moral perfection, in and through one's trade and one's domestic circle, became the sign of Calvinism: no indulgence, no absolution, no penance could lessen the inner tension that created the upright, God-fearing man. Such a doctrine was calculated to restore the conscientious man's self-respect: self-examination, self-help, self-improvement were now the marks of religious insight.

For Luther, the world was a hopeless place for virtue: no effort by the Church or the State could make human affairs better. One must therefore resign oneself to superior force and sedulously permit those in authority to exercise their special calling in their own selfish interests, no matter what abuses and oppressions might arise. Though pure Lutheranism did not believe in the State, it was incapable of challenging it or modifying it: just the opposite, it washed its hands of responsibility for the ruling classes' immoral acts and patiently submitted to them.

Luther's essential anarchism in theory swung easily toward its opposite pole: the practical acceptance of despotism. Calvin understood the dangers of this double negation. "At present," he said in the Institutes of Christianity, "we only wish it to be understood, that to entertain a thought of its [government's] extermination is inhuman barbarism; it is equally necessary to mankind as bread and water, light and air; and far more excellent. For it not only tends to secure the accommodations arising from all these things, that men may breathe, eat, drink, and be sustained in life; though it comprehends all these things while it causes them to live together, yet I say this is not its only tendency: its objects also are that idolatry, sacrileges against the name of God, blasphemies against His truth, and other offenses against religion, may not openly appear to be disseminated among the people; that the public tranquillity may not be disturbed; that every person may enjoy his property without molestation; that men may transact their business together without fraud or injustice; that integrity and modesty may be cultivated between them; in short, that there may be a public form of religion among Christians, and that humanity may be obtained among men."

Calvinism, on the basis of the same general dogmas in theology as Lutheranism, sought rather to institute the reign of God on earth: it emphasized the political will and it applied this will to the moral life: it educated the citizen for his immediate public duties and left salvation or damnation to the inscrutable Election of God. If the concern for the individual ego was thus sharpened, private life, strictly speaking, disappeared: one's conduct must be an open book to one's neighbors and the correction and castigation of sin was the natural office of the elders of the Church. Inevitably, hypocrisy became the special Calvinist vice: hiding the real facts from one's neighbors.

In origin, Calvinism was far from being the creed of individualists: the needs of corporate life steadily concerned the author of the Institutes of Christianity, as the key word of the title indicates. Calvin's system, rather, was one in which ecclesiastical institutions were brought into conformity with the existing methods of guild control. The Church, under Calvin, was the supreme guild, establishing common standards of living, where the guild had exacted mainly standards of workmanship and brotherly help for other members of a particular craft. Every member of the new Church was compelled not merely to pass through a difficult family apprenticeship, under the eye of the house-father, but to subject his own life at any moment to the inspection of the Guild Masters, so to say, in order to prove that there was no fraud or shoddiness in its execution.

Hence in Calvinism the congregation had a collective function it never exercised in the older Christian Church since the patristic age; for in Calvinism the congregation was the true seat of economic and political and moral authority, and the Protestant Church, except where it was nationalized, was a political federation of autonomous congregations. The capacity of the Huguenots to survive in exile, the tough resistance of the Scotch Covenanters, the strong collective life of the New England townships, so medieval in their fundamental pattern, may all be explained by the corporate foundations of Calvinism: the Church was a religious guild. If Calvin allowed for greater freedom of economic enterprise than the early medieval Church had done, it was because he expected the new Church to exercise a vigilant supervision of law and morals at every hour of the day. In no department were "good works" an excuse for bad work.

Theologically speaking, Calvinism was a true consummation of the medieval order: it was a belated carrying over into the province of the Church of all the great organs of civil life: a radical incorporation of Christianity into the institutes of civil society, at which the Fathers of the Church, from Paul to Augustine, at which Jesus himself indeed, had always boggled. Calvinism was a real attempt to render unto God the things which are Caesar's: a return to that classic republicanism in which civic virtue counted high in the human scale: a return to Christian principles in realms from which it had been progressively banished: a re-union of eternal doctrine and daily deed. Politically, therefore, Calvinism was the first systematic expression of the new democratic order, which made citizens equal on earth as their souls were supposed to be in Heaven. In Calvinism's emphasis on political *will*, in its acceptance of individual responsibility, in its utilization of positive law as an instrument for moral and social change, it announced the hope for a wider democratic revolution: so that it is no accident that the chief revolutionary writer of the eighteenth century, Jean-Jacques Rousseau, was a citizen of Geneva: proud of his title and his republican inheritance. Though free compulsory education had been provided in Geneva by Farel in May 1536, before Calvin's arrival, the Calvinists' emphasis upon the citizen's intelligent participation in the affairs of the Church and the City made such a system an inevitable aid to faith and morals.

In all, the political and educational practice of Calvinism was its enduring contribution: far more so than its somber theology. It boldly challenged the immoral claims of absolutism and it created citizens who were capable of taking over the affairs of state and handling them with a skill that equaled that of the best tyrants, and with a probity that surpassed any earlier political society, even Athens. Calvinism was Christianity reinvigorated by the morality of the Jewish prophets and the political and educational traditions of the Jewish synagogue.

Calvin's distrust of pure democracy, his wise words in favor of a mixed form of government, which combined monarchic and aristocratic leadership with democratic participation, was not merely exemplified in Geneva: it was incorporated, with even greater skill, in the Constitution of the United States of America. Even the salutary doctrine of checks and balances, as Dr. Reinhold Niebuhr has observed, owes something to the Calvinist distrust of the claims of centralized authority and its pessimistic insight into the inevitable corruptions of human pride. Though Luther failed miserably in curbing capitalism and in his very failure formulated the more sinister doctrine of autarchy, Calvinism succeeded brilliantly in preparing the downfall of absolutism.

Unfortunately, the rationality and good sense of Calvinism suffered from an imperfect incarnation. Whereas St. Francis's personality was far greater than his words, Calvin's words were more admirable than his personality, though it was the personality that his followers too often imitated.

One would hardly think from the sect he founded that Calvin, as writer, was no blue-nose and no joy-killer: that he spoke excellently on the obligations to cheerfulness, fellowship, and understanding in the giving of charity: that he relaxed the conditions for marital divorce and made it possible on grounds of desertion: that he benignly reduced to absurdity an ascetic worriment over the morality of using table linens, eating delicate foods, or drinking good wines. But the Institutes of Christianity form a large tome, not easily read or mastered: Calvin's actual character, undermined by gastric disorders, was more easy to follow than the sounder maxims in his book: a morose and petulant and acerbic strain of personal conduct flows from Calvin, as from a vat of vinegar. He was capable of writing great lines, like that sentence in a letter to Melanchthon in 1555: "You know that our duties do not depend upon the hope of success, but in the most desperate cases we must do precisely what God requires us." But in practice he was capable of conniving with his enemies to persecute the Spaniard, Michael Servetus, that free-thinking physician and theologian whom Geneva itself finally burned to death. In short, Calvin was a self-righteous moral curmudgeon and he begot a race of stiff-necked Chillingworths: chilling worth indeed.

Though Calvinism contributed more to both the theory and practice of responsible political government than any other body of doctrine—*pace* the advocates of Bellarmine!—it had weaknesses that were closely allied to its positive virtues. The chief of these was a blindness to every aspect of life which did not directly concern conduct. Preaching, moral admonition, law, administration, government—these are Calvinism's main fields. But that men are deeply united through art, that they may learn the lessons of faith through systematic doubt, that they may be corrupted by a pharisaic virtue and saved to humanity by their very sins, that the love of God may be expressed in a Franciscan gaiety and that relaxation has its place in maintaining high moral tension—all these things Calvin knew but imperfectly, and most of his followers knew not at all.

Unlike Aquinas, the Protestants saw no essential parity between goodness and beauty: beauty, which the Roman Church had claimed for its own, was essentially a delusion and a snare. Not merely did the Calvinists strip the venerable decorations and images off the Cathedral in the Old Town of Geneva, leaving its interior bleak and empty: not merely did they make men and women forfeit all the playful lures of dress which enhance their sexuality: not merely did an inflexible note of mechanical discipline begin to invade every portion of protestant life. All these were temporary reactions: they might be forgiven and forgotten if they had served merely to make possible a fresh start on the right road.

But Calvinism did not stop with the mere dethronement and demolition of worldly vanities; or rather, it removed the golden serpent only to replace it with a more formidable monster, less tempting to the eye, whose very ugliness and inhumanity the Calvinist misinterpreted as a mark of moral value. That monster was the machine: here and only here does Max Weber's theory of the interplay of Protestantism and capitalism at last receive the corroboration of historic facts. It is no accident that the theorists and practical inventors of the machine, in its initial stages, came so often from protestant and particularly Calvinist circles. Did not Geneva become the chief center for making watches: the last word in precision, regulation, mechanical order? With Calvinism, the Noes had it: not for love, not for enjoyment, not for delight, not for curiosity or wonder, were all the Calvinist virtues. The machine was the true symbol for the Calvinist's unrelenting God and his predestined order: its very austerities and abnegations and self-denials, the driving discipline of the factory, with no time for idleness and therefore no opportunity for sin—all this gave the machine a foundation in protestant culture that it long lacked in countries like Spain and Italy which remained under the laxer and more human forms of the medieval Church and of medieval craftsmanship.

The machine became thus a double-headed symbol: it stood for both despotic authority and for the power that challenged that authority: it stood for them and it united them. The bourgeoisie became the new Elect; and the proletariat, even down to the mere infant hardly out of the cradle, were obviously those predestined to damnation. Thus the Calvinist concentration on the will, delivering into the world generation after generation of moral athletes, with bunchy spiritual muscles and proud chests, nevertheless throttled the full human personality; and the City of Man was once more undermined by the very engines of power that the Calvinists themselves so ingeniously, so inventively, helped to install in its catacombs.

11: Protestantism as Fission

Though Lutheranism and Calvinism were both expressed in authoritative forms, their very authority was established by a doctrine that in time undermined Protestantism and contributed further to ideological disunity: the right of private judgment. If one might tear oneself loose from the parent church, because one did not accept the authority of the Pope, why should one bind oneself to accept indefinitely the authority of a Luther, a Calvin, a Zwingli? Each man could read the Bible for himself, once printing had multiplied the text: each could interpret the Bible in his own way, live his own life, perfect his own doctrine.

The right of private judgment went to people's heads: precisely those who knew least about the history of the Christian Church and its doctrines felt themselves able, with the sanction of the Bible, to speak in a new voice of certainty. From Spain to Sweden merchants, weavers, miners, peasants, became intoxicated with a new sense of intellectual power which sprang out of their naïve contact with the historic truths in the Old and the New Testaments. They took the Bible figuratively and they took it literally; and each man found what he wanted in it—a staff to lean on, a whip to scourge his enemies, a missile to hurl at the devil, a shield and buckler for domestic battle.

Now, the right of private judgment is a necessary corrective to the principle of authority. It limits the power of dogmas that have ceased to be examined and of truths that have ceased to be open to further experimental verification or disproof. The heretic and the unqualified amateur—a Hahnemann in medicine, a Mayer in physics, a Mesmer in psychology, a Samuel Butler in biology—unearth buried possibilities to which the orthodox, whether in science or theology, are either smugly indifferent or downright hostile. Without continuous appeal to private judgment, open-mindedness would disappear; and the world would be locked in a circle of consistent, self-enclosed errors it mistook for eternal truths.

But in all matters of truth, private judgment has no standing except as a starting point for a fresh revision of public judgment. One cannot entertain a private judgment about the sum of the angles of a triangle except as the foundation for a new system of geometry in which a different series of postulates will be laid down and accepted in time by all competent mathematical authority. Only a minute span of experience is really open to private verification and adequate experimental proof: the rest must be taken on faith in the integrity of authority, in science no less than in theology.

As a healthy safeguard against superstition, science and reason must keep open the right of private investigation and private judgment: but only so that ultimately these efforts may be collectively verified and sealed with the proof of other men's repeated experiments and collated interpretations. This verification of truth by a collective historic process is what knits men together in a universal society that overpasses the boundaries of space and time, and eventually removes, not merely the Baconian idola, but also errors due merely to one's position in space or time. This process begins, not with each new investigator, but with the historic heritage that makes his existence possible, his language comprehensible, and his work rational.

Protestantism, unfortunately, never properly understood the collective process in which private judgment must play its part. For the Protestant, the message of the Bible was founded, not on reason but on revelation: he rejected the efforts of the scholastic philosophers to weld reason and revelation, experience and authority, together. Reason for the Protestant was already visible in the actual text of the Bible: was not the Bible an open book?

What was the outcome of this doctrine of private judgment? Exactly what might have been expected: perpetual schism, perpetual splitting off of one sect from another. Richard Baxter remarked that during the seventeenth century Abraham Scultetus, like many other Protestants in Europe, expected a golden age of Protestantism: the princes of France, Bohemia, England, and many other countries were all favorable to its doctrines or at least tolerant of their spread; but "within one year either death or the ruins of war or backslidings had exposed all their expectations to scorn and had laid them lower than before."

Because of this inherent tendency toward fission, the protestant sects were almost as inimical to each other, as fiercely intolerant of their own divergences, as they had been toward the Roman Church. Each sect dreamed of a private golden age. The Anabaptists of Münster, for example, engineered a brief social revolution that aimed at eliminating serfdom and establishing a community of property: they extended the doctrine that the Elect could not sin to a point that enabled them to cohabit freely outside the bonds of marriage, even sanctimoniously urging women to lose their chastity because Christ had said that harlots and publicans would enter the Kingdom of Heaven before the righteous. This was a radical symptom of a difficulty that became chronic in protestant thought. The Silent Brothers among the Anabaptists held that preaching no longer was necessary: George Fox and the Quakers held that a clergy was superfluous: the Socinians dismantled the Trinity.

Some of these protestant doctrines were not, perhaps, without merit; but one and all they lacked the merit of intellectual and political cohesion: they were therefore hard put to it to hold their own in a hostile society.

Thus individualism turned into mere atomism. And the final flower of protestant teaching was a willful denial of the need for unity: each man lived in a private world, described by a system of private science, edified by a private religion, governed by a private code, subject to no law but his own conscience, obedient to no impulse but that of his own private will. That was indeed the Utopia of the irresponsible bourgeoisie: it erected specious moral foundations for the utmost caprice. Seeking personal freedom to avoid the vices of an arbitrary ecclesiastical authority, the Protestant finally became an advocate of freedom in order to establish an equally arbitrary authority of his own. If he lacked the outward power of a despot, he tended toward negative despotism: nonconformity—ultimately nihilism.

The internal tendency toward schism finally undermined the protestant super-ego even more than did the later growth of rationalism and humanitarianism. One can follow that story best in New England, where the protestant scheme was established on a fresh foundation, where for long it had no serious rivals, and where it created, perhaps, the highest culture of which Protestantism was capable. Congregationalism, Presbyterianism, Unitarianism, Baptism, Methodism, were all variants of the original stock. But in time new Messiahs appeared with more romantic claims to divine authority: the Swedenborgians, the Shakers, the Mormons, the Christian Scientists, continued to spring up like mushrooms from the same compost. There was no principle within Protestantism whereby it could combat its fatal tendency to fission: each generation, as the Vermont farmer said, grew wiser and weaker. The process might go on indefinitely until every man had his own Church and served as his own Messiah. A society of one is the ultimate denial of human unity: the very negation of the true person, who seeks to be at one with all humanity.

Thus once the medieval search for unity was abandoned, Protestantism lost the power to prevail: Matthew Arnold's none-too-gentle reproof for its parochialisms and solecisms was well-merited, for they undermined the very truths that Protestantism had in fact nobly expressed. When religion ceased to be a political force, politics became a substitute religion. We shall witness the results of this change in the nineteenth century.

12: The Protestant Character

By the seventeenth century Protestantism had created an ideal ego: that which comes down to us in the image of the Puritan. The dominant traits of this character were austerity and perseverance: a narrowing of the circle of human interests and an immense concentration of the will.

The Protestant shut himself off from the sensual expansion and the erotic dilation of the baroque order: all the avenues of sense were now carefully guarded, sometimes completely shut. Not only did images and figures disappear from his architecture, but even figured patterns, which the silk manufacturers of the period had learned to manufacture in their sumptuous brocades, disappeared from personal adornment. Grave attire and somber colors became the distinguishing marks of the Reformation. Among extremists, such as the followers of George Fox, the break was cleanest: ribbonless dresses, simple undecorated costumes were as much a mark of the Quakers as the habit of using simple affirmatives; and the color-blindness of Dalton, so far from being a handicap, was affirmed as a virtue and copied. The Protestant was dressed for business, not for show: his clothes revealed the same dropping off of decorative and ceremonious forms as his speech, with its simple Yes and No, and its refusal to use ceremonial titles and courtly forms of address. In a word, the Protestant personality was businesslike even when there was no business in hand.

Not merely were the images of the Catholic Church rejected: all images became suspect as superstitious idols, too easily worshiped for their own sake: the Puritan heeded the Old Testament. But to this rule he made one exception, with a gesture of naïve self-betrayal: that exception was his own image. The Protestant admitted art in the form of the portrait: his alter-ego in oil would watch severely all the inmates of his home, even when he was absent. But to dance, to attend theaters, to witness public spectacles, to participate in carnivals, and above all to gamble at dice or at cards all lay outside the pale of his daily practice: when he was not actively engaged in business he turned to the sermon, the tract, the newspaper: the world of black and white.

The new Protestant was intent on his individual salvation, and the vehicle of that salvation was the Bible. Literacy, even among those debarred from school by poverty and neglect, became common: so great was the passion for salvation that unlearned craftsmen became masters of noble speech, through their close reading and memorizing of the Bible in the great vernacular versions of Luther and King James's scholars: Pilgrim's Progress, a spring of pure English, was written by a tinker.

Today, with almost universal literacy, the popular mind sinks to the lowest possible level of entertainment and instruction, for sheer lack of spiritual ambition: the vulgar tabloid newspaper and the illustrated weekly set a level of frothy dullness which is only one step away from a drugged sleep. But under the protestant passion for individual salvation, the common man lifted himself up by heroic mental efforts: he read and mastered the history, the laws, the ethics, and the poetry of one of the greatest cultures the world has known: that of the Jews. For daily companionship he not merely had the words of Solomon and Isaiah and Paul, but the texts of ministers who knew those words in Hebrew and Greek and were capable of spinning theological subtleties over which the congregation might mull for the rest of the week. The things of the spirit were not debased to meet the level of the common man: the common man was encouraged to reach the highest levels of the spirit. Was not the metaphysical Jonathan Edwards a preacher in a frontier town?

Spurred by his vision of realizable virtue, the Protestant had before him at each great crisis of life the image of a noble patriarchal or a tribal personality: an Abraham, a Joseph, a David, a Job, a Daniel: he felt in himself and in his community a fresh responsibility for making the will of God prevail. No priesthood, no organization, could carry that burden for him. If his image-breaking might turn into a callous contempt for all art, if his Bible-reading too easily turned into a fanatical bibliolatry, nevertheless it was true that these efforts were the perversions of a sound aim: the attempt to re-build religion on the basis of the highest personal integrity. The straitlaced Protestant was an upstanding personality. He would not bow to dead forms any more than he would take off his hat to a living king.

Thus precisely at a time when the expansion of bureaucratic methods in business and government, and the expansion of large-scale manufacture were making the whole routine of practical activity an ever deadlier grind, Protestantism developed a special faculty for getting pleasure out of that grind. This was Protestantism's special contribution to the development of capitalism and mechanism: not to initiate them but to make them tolerable and to pour into them all the energies of the moral life. Drudgery served the Protestant as a valuable mortification of the flesh: valuable in a worldly as well as a spiritual sense, for unlike the hair shirts and self-whippings of the medieval saint, his unflagging concentration on dull work brought tangible profits.

For the Protestant business became holy, not least because it tended to grow more and more odious in its performance. The Catholic holidays were abandoned; the guild pageants and processions and mysteries were rapidly disappearing; the feastings of the guild brothers were reduced to annual banquets and were unknown in the new unorganized industries: all the playful and esthetic accompaniments which sweetened the day's toil were now pushed to one side: business was business: profits and dividends were its sole embellishments. To save money by paring the costs of production, to sacrifice present goods for future rewards, to drive one's self for the good of one's soul, and to drive others quite as mercilessly for the good of *their* souls: all this was the very essence of the new protestant morality. Thrift, foresight, parsimony, order, punctuality, perseverance, sacrifice: out of these austere protestant virtues a new kind of economy was created, and within it, a new kind of personality proceeded to function. At one end of classic capitalism stands Jacob Fugger II: at the other end, John D. Rockefeller I.

Believing that the main duty of man was moral instruction, the Protestant too often mistook profit for pedagogy. Intolerant to all who opposed his will he treated as a grievous moral sin every form of life except that which he had worked out for himself. He would manufacture textiles and inculcate the virtues of the handkerchief and the Mother Hubbard gown to his primitive customers: he would sell rum to the Indian and interpret the subsequent debauchery as a sign of the native's awful nature: he would oppose the slow lazy ways of the Negro and sell him into slavery with the proud consciousness that he was bringing him redemption by word and by act. Melville's Captain Bildad was a caricature; but behind that caricature was an even starker reality.

By a habit of dissent and nonconformity the Protestant contracted the whole horizon of social life, and by his unremitting attention to business he gave to instrumental goods a value that would be justified only by the highest kind of consummation. Yet when the protestant sense of duty was wedded to a rational collective aim, the result was the creation of a new kind of martyr and hero: Cromwell at the head of the Parliamentary armies, Milton sacrificing his ambitions as a poet to perform the office of political secretary; Livingstone bringing the Gospel to the remotest tribes of the African jungle; John Brown leading the revolt of the slaves at Harpers Ferry; Abraham Lincoln rising to saintly tenderness and charity in his high-principled conduct of a stern war. Better than these, what creed can show?

CHAPTER VI. UPRISING OF THE LIBIDO

1: Lust of Life

The Protestant sought to curb the capitalist spirit and in the end he deepened its channels: he challenged the political rule of the despot and brought into business enterprise the ruthless ego that had hitherto dominated only the machinery of state. The spread of capitalist enterprise meant the extension of absolutism in the economic field: each business office, each factory, though it might be organized on the principle of the divided risk (joint stock holdings), was also conceived on the principle of undivided responsibility in direction and management.

But although mammonism and mechanism were the two great molders of human character between the sixteenth and the twentieth centuries, they were attached to a negative super-ego, that which had been created by the Christian Church. In the communities where they ruled, the new tyrants in government and industry required nothing further than docile conformity to all the tenets of Christian faith: witness the physical multiplication of churches and the increase of pious endowments. Not until the nineteenth century did these life-denying forces gain the upper hand; for in the meanwhile, the dissolution of the medieval synthesis had given rise to a counter-movement: an uprush of the libido, an intensification of the senses, an introduction of the mind to its own labyrinths, an expansion of every activity that promoted animation, joy, bodily exuberance. With this went a desire for free movement, for exploration, for understanding and commanding all the processes of natural life. Against the growing repressions of the machine, a series of positive expressions now manifested themselves in the fields that lay outside the mechanical ideology. In horticulture and colonization, in exploration and pioneering, in art and in love the libido came forth; Tintoretto and Michelangelo, Rabelais and Shakespeare, Montaigne and Rubens, are the noble names that stand for this great insurgence of life: a floodtide of vitality that spread into every cove and channel of the spirit.

At the very moment the iron frame of the machine was being bolted together, the organic and the human reasserted themselves with redoubled energy. For a moment, these two aspects of man's existence were held together in the forceful patterns and rhythmic undulations of baroque art: the spiral column of baroque architecture, in which the classic *stasis* becomes a sinuous whorl, is the emblem of this union. Meanwhile the negative forces redouble their profound assault against nature and man under the pretext of conquering the first and liberating the second.

This movement and counter-movement came within the same cultural milieu: from the first there was an interplay between the impulses of power and love: the machine fed the libido and the libido counterbalanced the machine. Physical energy and money provided the material wherewithal for the artful luxuries whose enjoyment became the principal end of upper-class existence: just as the increased yields in agriculture, coupled with new food crops brought in from the New World, enriched the dietary of Europe and perhaps even increased the rate of conception: certainly made possible a continued expansion of the population after the seventeenth century. Wheaten bread and sugar, increased quantities of fats, due to better winter fodder for the cattle and the hunting of the whale, finally the potato—renewed the lust of life at its sources. The eye dilated: the belly grew big: the genitals swelled. An insuppressible vital energy manifested itself in the life of the upper classes, as in the art they produced and patronized.

Unfortunately, this energy never found for itself a satisfactory outlet in the community as a whole: for it rested upon gold and upon the power that gold symbolized. All this high vitality rose to its natural peak in the royal and aristocratic courts of Europe, from Mantua to Hampton Court: part of its energy was due to the fact that it mercilessly drained off the life of its conquered peoples and its depressed internal proletariat. The cult of luxury has many of the attributes of a religion but it lacks its essential attribute: universality. To enjoy this life you must do more than believe in it: you must be ready to pay for it.

Yet no manifestation of the released libido has made a profounder impression on humanity than the art and science and exploration that took place between the sixteenth and the nineteenth centuries: for perhaps never before did so much sheer animal vitality fructify the higher products of the spirit and become translated into such a wealth of esthetic and practical forms. By contrast, other periods seem pale, famished, attenuated: too ethereal to survive in a gross world. One cannot say that of Michelangelo's figures in the Sistine Chapel: alongside them, it is the great athlete who seems anemic and the great prince who seems impotent.

The new libido left its mark upon the human personality: it created a commanding presence and a fearless self-reliance: the great conquistador was capable of burning his ships behind him, when he marched toward the territory he sought to conquer.. The pride that was thus exalted defied reason and in the end fed on its own flesh: witness the ignominious fate of Napoleon. But before this movement had run its course it created two ideal types: the gentleman and the artist.

2: The Birth of the Gentleman

From the scholar, the feudal knight, the humanist, the Christian and the classic pagan, a new type of character emerged in the sixteenth century: the gentleman. J. E. Spingarn once proposed to write a treatise on The Birth and Death of the Gentleman; and his failure to write it is our loss. For lack of such a comprehensive study, one of the principal personalities of post-medieval culture has not been fully characterized or understood, and one must turn to the novelists, to the creators of a Colonel Newcome, a Sir Willoughby Patterne, or a Swann for individualized variants of the type.

In contrast to the great vocational patterns of the Middle Ages, the gentleman was above all an amateur: he was the non-specialized, non-professionalized man, in whom manliness itself became incarnate: like his Athenian prototype he became the exemplar of beautiful conduct. In him, a dying morality was graced by art, and an emerging art was tempered by moral considerations.

The forming of the gentleman was the very essence of post-medieval higher education down to the nineteenth century. The new ideal rested on cultivation, discipline, a balanced interplay of all the impulses natural to man, except those that had to do with menial labor. By good nurture, as Castiglione pointed out, men were to be turned from wildness. In the gentleman, what cannot be cultivated must be rooted out: no matter how succulent or how nourishing the moral root, it is in the flower of manners that the gentleman's nurture was justified. Like the knight, he must know the use of weapons, must ride and hunt: that went without saying. But he must also swim well, leap, run, vault, play tennis: his body must be agile, ready for every test of endurance, so that he may be confident in action and courageous in pain.

For the gentleman the knowledge of the classics was more than a decorative acquisition: Horace taught him wit, Cicero eloquence, and Plutarch morality and public service. In the exact mastery of grammar and a foreign vocabulary, from childhood on, the gentleman learned every day a fresh lesson in patience and method: in the composition of Latin verses, he enlarged his mastery. The classics furnished him with a ready-made outfit of thoughts and feelings, far more neatly cut to his own requirements than the clumsy garments of so much popular medieval literature: he would respect most those contemporary writers who cut their costumes to the same outline, or at least utilized a similar quality of cloth. To know something of everything; to know nothing too thoroughly; always to preserve the golden mean, this was the essence of the gentleman. Instead of showing the intense passion of the artist, he showed the willing receptivity, the appreciative omnivorousness, of the connoisseur. Self-effacing self-assertion: high-spirited humility: a personality that commands everything so completely that to all appearances it claims nothing: there lies the glittering paradox of the gentleman. His most precious possession was his self-possession.

This new ideal was no mere natural outgrowth of feudalism: it contrasts with the master of the old manorhouse or castle, as described by Pace in De Fructu. He tells how "one of those whom we call gentlemen who always carry some horn hanging at their backs, as though they would hunt during dinner, said: 'I swear by God's body I would rather that my son should hang than study letters.'" Quite the contrary, the gentleman lost his unqualified fondness for brutal sports: indeed, compassion and sympathy entered his relations with horses, dogs, menials: from the summit of the gentleman's position, no one was too low to be unworthy of his consideration and courtesy. Even Louis XIV took off his hat, with all grace, to a serving maid when he met her, out of a gentleman's respect for a woman. For in the gentleman's training, manners attain the status of morals: even if his conscience is not touched, his taste becomes a guide, sensitive, exacting, unyielding. Within the limits of his code, which allowed a certain latitude to adultery and self-indulgence, conduct unworthy of a gentleman is a condition for ostracism—one had almost said excommunication.

If the hygiene of the present world derives largely from the Regimen of Salerno, almost all that is left of good manners derives from the gentleman; and Baldassare Castiglione, in The Courtier, was his prophet. In the sixteenth century Giovanni della Casa, too, wrote a treatise called Galateo; or Concerning Manners, in which the essentials of gentlemanly conduct were prescribed: his code was to stand for three centuries. The great mark of the gentleman, as della Casa put it, was his self-control. "In company, and most especially at table, you should not bully or beat any servants, nor must you express anger, whatever may occur to excite it; nor talk of any distressful matters—wounds, illnesses, deaths, or pestilence." The aim of agreeable manners, for della Casa, was to afford delight, "or at least . . . not produce any vexation to the feelings, appetite, or imagination of those with whom we have to do. A man should not be content with doing what is right, but should also study to do it with grace. And grace is as it were a light which shines from the fittingness of things that are well-composed and well-sorted the one with the other and all of them together; without which measure even the good is not beautiful and beauty is not pleasurable. Therefore well-bred persons should have regard to this measure, alike in walking, standing, and sitting, in gesture, demeanor, and clothing, in work and in silence, and in rest and action."

Composure and measure: both these attributes of the gentleman continued to owe no little, of course, to the active discipline of the Christian Church. When the Duc de Saint-Simon found himself intolerably provoked by one of his rivals, he retired to a Trappist monastery for a week in order to get over his anger. Hence came the feeling that true nobility was not something derived from blood and soil, but was a thing of the spirit, having no connection with lineage and escutcheon: the doctrine of the troubadours about love here resumed its sway. In 1525 John Rastell, a brother-in-law of Thomas More, even wrote an Interlude of Gentleness and Nobility, which he described as a "dialogue between the Merchant, the Knight, and the Ploughman, disputing who is a very gentleman and who is a nobleman and how man should come to authority." The plowman, anticipating his Burns by almost three centuries, gets the best of the argument. He points out that gentle conditions make a gentleman, and these are "meekness, patience, charity, liberality, abstinence, honest business, and chastity," and he claims that in respect of these he is superior to the other two.

Gentle conditions and good surroundings became the essential requirement of the new education. Vittorino da Feltre, the humanist educator, sought to isolate youth in the open country during the critical period of growth: he was revolted by the debauchery and drunkenness of the students at Padua. Vittorino founded his school under the patronage of Francesco Gonzaga of Mantua. Not merely did the school have a rural setting: Vittorino surrounded it on three sides by a large enclosed meadow, which was used as a playing field. From Plutarch, Vittorino learned to be concerned with health, diet, games: from now on these became a systematic part of the gentleman's nurture. This cultivated rural background must be stressed. In his concern with the countryside, in his understanding of the processes of life and growth, in his resourceful study of horticulture, gardening, and landscape architecture, the gentleman, by the seventeenth century, had created an environment that embraced in equal measure the vital and the esthetic; and as a many-sided life disappeared in the city with the decay of the guilds and the growing preoccupation with mechanism and finance, the gentleman created a fresh environment for a rounded culture in the new Country House, with its library, its art gallery, its portrait gallery, its curio cabinet, its ballroom, its concert hall, and its garden. That environment is worth a closer examination: it became, by default, the chief positive ideal of the industrial age.

War, politics, and agriculture were the great provinces of the baroque gentleman; and they remained his typical fields in the period that followed: the first required courage, the second administrative skill and personal presence, and the third a certain capacity for both esthetic and economic organization. From the standpoint of his own fulfillment and satisfaction, the gentleman led a balanced life. But how could he live this balanced life in an unbalanced society? How could it be lived, with a good conscience, at the expense of the poor, the exploited, the oppressed? For this difficulty, the gentleman had only an esthetic solution: he put the facts of this life out of sight, and ignored them on the ground that they were distressing. In the country, an elaborate plantation or a wall would separate the stables, the dungheap, the vegetable garden from the less utilitarian parts of the estate: in the city, poverty and squalor were also tactfully removed to the East End.

Complete detachment from economic responsibility, and therefore ultimately from human feeling, was the final mark of the gentleman: that in itself disclosed the ideal as the other side, the smiling esthetic mask of baroque insolence and exploitation. Ideally, the gentleman was rich, or at least economically secure, but he was bound to act as if money did not matter, and he had only contempt for those who took it seriously—though his own world would have vanished without it. Tolstoy shows this ambivalent relation clearly in War and Peace. Yet these riches provided leisure; and the obligation to use his leisure, not solely for his own amusement, but for the help and comfort of his family, his relatives, his dependents, his retainers, his neighbors went along with the cult of the gentleman: a direct inheritance from feudalism. Thanks to this tradition, the gentleman at times achieved a high career as a selfless public servant, which those who needed to court popularity seldom equaled: witness the two great country gentlemen who established the English and the American revolutions: Oliver Cromwell and George Washington.

3: The Esthetic Synthesis

As the new courtier may be considered a feudal knight whose business has turned into play, so the artist of the baroque period may be understood as the medieval craftsman turned gentleman: released from the rules of his guild only to come under the more servile conditions of his aristocratic patron's caprice.

The change from the all-round craftsman, with his productive workshop, ready to turn out a candlestick or an altar piece, a chair or a triptych at an honest price, takes place almost before one's eyes in the person of a Pollaiuolo or an Andrea del Castagno. Their greater pupils have all their craftsmanlike virtuosity; but now one element in their discipline predominates—the skill of the painter. While the artist of the Middle Ages was primarily an artisan, the artist of the renascence is primarily a designer: the drawing takes precedence over the slower manual processes of production: the original conception governs the final execution instead of being constantly modified by the nature of the materials and the character of the fabricator, learning as he goes along, taking advantage of unsuspected qualities in the materials, or submitting to a fresher inspiration under the hypnosis of his own esthetic concentration. More and more the artist's drawing governs the paintbrush, the chisel, the mallet, the saw: time and experience play a lesser part in the final product. No matter how long it takes to build, every part of a baroque building must look as if it were conceived and produced in one instant: unified and complete. In the painter's studio the ambitions of the absolute Prince found their ideal fulfillment.

The baroque artist, from the sixteenth century on, was primarily a visual investigator and an exponent of the esthetic synthesis: a magnified eye, scrutinizing the outside world, analyzing it, dissecting it, imaginatively putting it together in compositions that have lost their original cultural significance: in taking the orthodox symbols of religion and mythology he re-states them in a fashion that conveys only esthetic meaning. A Holy Family by Leonardo is a study in light and shade, a treatise on geology, almost anything except a religious icon. An Adam and Eve by Michelangelo is essentially an exciting anatomy lesson: a demonstration of idealized vitality. Now the superficial symbol and the latent meaning of the picture are two entirely different matters. Witness Leonardo's John the Baptist and his Bacchus: they are the same persons, drawn in the same fashion, and what does this mean, except that Leonardo is interested in neither theology nor mythology, but in the human form, and considers—to use his own words—that "man does not vary from the animals except in what is accidental."

The visual revolution that took place in the late fifteenth century happens to coincide with the dominance of the humanist movement in Italy and its rise elsewhere: hence the interpreters of this change have sometimes attributed to the revival of the classics a progress due largely to the enfranchised experiments of the artist. For the most part, the humanists were contemptuous of both science and modern art, all the more because the artist, apprenticed to a jeweler or a goldsmith at the age of ten or twelve, usually knew little Latin and less Greek.

Even in the Middle Ages the artist had often been a close observer of nature, as the notebooks of that great master mason, Villars de Honnecourt, plainly show. But now the artist was both an observer and an experimenter: he not merely saw everything but made a record of it: and not content to look at the surface alone, he took the object apart: a flower, a formation of rocks, the human body, a machine were all equally worthy of his attention. This broad inquisitorial interest was not confined to Leonardo da Vinci: he differed from the artists around him not so much by the extent of his interests as in the extraordinary mind he brought to bear upon them. From Uccello on, the painter's art demanded a growing knowledge of chemistry, anatomy, optics, mathematics, botany, geology, and even engineering—for he might be called upon to improvise the defenses of a city, design a public building, or provide the scenery and realistic properties for a stage.

The many-sidedness of the painter's education and discipline made him the ideal handyman in a period of colorful improvisation: not bound to the rules of his guild, to the established conventions of his art, he was capable of moving forward in new directions. By his emphasis on technique, without regard for the ethical or ideological content of his paintings, the artist became the destined interpreter of the technicians of politics and finance who arose in the same period. Just as there was nothing the Prince might not do, so there was nothing that the painter might not see or paint; his curiosity and his inventiveness flowed over into every department of human activity, not least into technics itself, from Leonardo to Fulton and Morse. More than a century before the baroque stage was invented, the painter had developed its chief convention—that of presenting a three-sided room with one wall removed. Long before Descartes conceived of his cartesian co-ordinates, the painter devised a similar form which enabled him to correlate size and distance. It was only in painting that there were order and comprehensive understanding of the nature of life and an indication of its ideal possibilities. And it was by *visual* aids, by telescopes, microscopes, magnifying glasses, that a new world was brought concretely into modern man's consciousness: the world of the infinite and the infinitesimal: cosmic space and molecular space.

The artist shared with the gentleman the discipline of an all-round development. But in one respect he was greatly the gentleman's superior:

he was not bound by caste limitations to deny himself the use of his hands: his real virtue lay rather in the fact that he could turn his hand to anything. The artist was an amateur, but a passionate amateur, with a driving zeal that compared with the financier's or the Puritan's: Michelangelo underwent greater risks and endured greater fatigue than any of his helpers in the painting of the Sistine Chapel; and even a rogue like Benvenuto Cellini, a little later, became momentarily transformed in the hot process of work: he rose from a sickbed to give orders for the casting of the Perseus when the process had been muffed in his absence, and he triumphantly surmounted every obstacle. By swift thinking, dogged industry, luminous periods of creation, the artist of the baroque order contrived to give a show of order and harmony to a life that was becoming disordered and chaotic for lack of an inner coherence between acts and facts, dreams and deeds.

For lack of moral and social solidity, this visual synthesis was as thin as a piece of stage scenery: its beauty and order were completed in the picture: they did not pass over into the community. Under the new despotism of the machine, the universal qualities of the painter were a handicap: those who survived best were fragmentary men, applying a shriveled part of their personality to achieve the utmost efficiency in a little job. In the new rationale of science, as laid down by Galileo, the painter's world of figure and color had become irrelevant: in the new processes of industry, beauty and use were progressively separated, and mere quantitative production became the goal of mechanical improvement. In this change, the artist, who was the most courted figure of the fifteenth century, became ultimately the chronic unemployable of the nineteenth century.

Yet the extraordinary achievement of the artist between the fifteenth and the eighteenth century in the Low Countries, Germany, France, Italy and Spain, left a clue to the scope and method of education that the educators themselves long failed to interpret or apply. In the artist's training, sensory discrimination and manual exercise, comprehensive design and detailed execution, were the daily lessons of the workshop: all these elements played a part in the development of full-bodied minds, capable of ordering every dimension of experience: if this visual synthesis was not the end of education it was at least a fruitful beginning, for lack of which the inner and the outer worlds must inevitably remain apart and unevenly developed. Early in the nineteenth century Froebel picked up one essential part of the painter's education in the Kindergarten. He laid the foundations for a radical change: a basic universalization of the artist-craftsman's personality. Unfortunately, all the maturer perceptions in Froebel's The Education of Man were overlooked by his followers: they seized upon the obvious and at first introduced their innovations only into those years that the conventional school did not attempt to discipline. When the lesson of art and play was finally brought into the progressive schools of England and America, the nineteenth century conception of the artist as a licensed Bohemian, an irresponsible eccentric, doing what he pleases, passed into education, with an over-stressing of the spontaneous element in creative activity—namely, that very moment in the creative act over which the master or the teacher can exercise no control.

But the real lesson of the baroque artist was quite a different one: not that of play alone, but play disciplined by severe intellectual effort, and delight brought to a higher pitch by masterly design: in short, it was the lesson of symmetrical development, the equal cultivation of hand and eye, of feeling and manual skill, of emotion and intelligence: so that every part of experience might be ordered into a symbolic whole. Here was the baroque artist's permanent contribution to education: one as worthy of imitation as the Benedictine sense of regularity and order.

4: The Disrobed Divinity

The courtier and the gentleman had their counterparts in the other sex: the courtesan and the lady. The transformation of woman from a working partner into a sexual free-lance and from a distantly worshiped ideal into a more tangible divinity, disrobed and ready for play, came about through the increase of idleness and luxury; so it is a story that belongs mainly to the upper classes. But the change was not without democratic significance by reason of what has followed. For a profound modification of sex, love, and parenthood took place between the sixteenth and the nineteenth century.

The great theme of art, during the post-medieval period, was the celebration and enjoyment of woman. The courtesan not merely became the principal luxury of the market: she was the very reason for that vast process of spoliation and conquest which ultimately brought into her boudoir carved mirrors, sparkling jewels, heady perfumes, cosmetics, silks, brocades, and the gold wherewith more could be bought. I have dealt with the psychological role of luxury in relation to militarism and the machine in Technics and Civilization. Here it is important to realize that woman performed a special function in baroque life: she herself became the very symbol of expensive sensuous refinement and glowing vitality.

The artists of the sixteenth century had no small part in creating the new image of woman. In medieval art there might be occasional nude figures, and nakedness itself was doubtless as common a fact of nature in the medieval household as in the medieval baths. But the body was taken matter-of-factly. Indeed, the limited amount of water available for bodily cleanliness gave the sexual act an association with dirtiness. Erotic interest was concentrated almost wholly on the genitals: in cold rooms, or in the open, hampered by clothes, the secondary attributes of sex made but small claims upon the lover's attention. Now the painters created a new image of feminine loveliness: they disrobed woman and in the very act of revealing the charms of nature they further idealized the possibilities of erotic experience. Tactile values supplemented the visual delights of rhythmic outlines; and both played a larger part in actual life.

In the fifteenth century one of the first manifestations of the growth of luxury was the private bedroom: a room devoted exclusively to love-making and sleep, without the constant threat of interruptions and intrusions. In Carpaccio's painting of Saint Ursula's Vision, the furniture and bed-covering of the room are already very close to present-day requirements. While the ordinary arrangement of putting a bed or a couch in a room used by day for other purposes never entirely disappeared, the new bedroom had a highly specialized office: it was a room built about a bed. Such an arrangement not only permitted privacy at night: it removed the need for haste in love-making and permitted it to take place at any time of the day.

Do not underestimate the contribution of the painter: he remodeled the sexual super-ego. Stimulated no doubt by the images of antiquity, the painter began to draw from the living model. Alone with her in the studio, he looks upon her for hours at a time, catches the sheen of her hair, the satiny surface of her skin, observes the swell of her breasts and the curve of her belly. By enlarging the intermediate function of the eye the painter prolonged and enriched every response. With his flair for life, the artist never forgets its sexual sources: from Raphael to Renoir, he not merely reminds other men, preoccupied with machines or books, of what is most desirable: he teaches them how to desire it and sets before them a high standard of fulfillment. The painter's worshipful admiration of woman added a fresh force to the erotic act itself and at the same time guarded it against that boredom which follows early satiety. Now the eye temporarily halts the sexual attack and heightens the tension. In front view and profile, standing or sitting or lying down, woman reveals as for the first time the charms men had demanded too peremptorily and captured too swiftly in the intimacies of action.

And what happens to woman? In her coy disrobing, in her frank exposure of herself, woman in turn feels her power: her power to withhold and to give. By the grace of postponement she becomes more fully roused, and when the erotic mood at last brings her lover close, she becomes more deeply fulfilled. In the alternation of visual excitement and sensory fulfillment the painter helps to heighten erotic ecstasy: now the "marital debt" is repaid with interest: with psychological and esthetic interest. What the cold mirror could not reveal to woman, the painting of a Titian or a Giorgione easily disclosed: how desirable she could be. The very milk of her breasts, that bovine attribute of peasant motherhood, now became, in Tintoretto's The Origin of the Milky Way, a source of erotic titillation. No small part of the erotica of this period has been destroyed; not a little went up in smoke on Savonarola's bonfires; but there is enough left in "respectable" painting to supply every gap in our knowledge. Nathaniel Hawthorne and Mark Twain were both deeply shocked by the paintings of the renascence. This was perhaps a sign of their naïve puritanism; but it was also a sign of their excellent understanding of the painters' intentions. These beautiful nudes were not abstract essays in design: like a Congo fetish, they served to intensify the faith of the believer.

For medieval woman, her proper life as a woman began with motherhood. With baroque woman, her life was rather halted by motherhood: she was closer to the courtesan than to the virgin, and she had less authority as a wife because she had a larger place as a mistress. Sacred and Profane Love: Faithful and Unfaithful Love—what are these but the images of the same woman, clothed and unclothed, the older woman of duty and the newer woman of pleasure? The courtesan will set the style for her hair, will dictate the fashion in clothes, will command the services and attentions of men. So great was her reputation that as late as the eighteenth century Rousseau, in Venice, felt it almost a duty to make the acquaintance of one of the popular courtesans, though his diffidence won only her contempt and displeasure.

This heightening of desire and this widening of the channels of the erotic life were possibly a by-product of the richer dietary that prevailed from the sixteenth century on throughout Europe: at least this laid solid physiological foundations. The more frequent use of wines and the growing habit of drinking cordials among the upper classes likewise must have contributed to the general dilation of the senses, and to the urgency and persistence of sexual desire. Compare Rubens' voluptuous figures with the pallid, undernourished men and women who appear so frequently in the paintings and tapestries of an earlier day: compare the sexually reserved costumes of the thirteenth century with the male exhibitionism of the sixteenth. Music and the visual arts completed what food and drink began: they concentrated on sex and opened all the avenues of delight. Pride and luxury flourished together: *in* sex and *through* sex. The id, released from the medieval super-ego, gushed upward in the sexual life, a newly tapped pool of oil, set afire by the imagination. "A woman not possessed of a light and rare grace can no more abstain from a man than from eating, drinking, sleeping, or other natural function. Likewise a man cannot abstain from a woman." That sentence does not come from Aretino or Cellini: the man who uttered it was Martin Luther.

Unfortunately, the enlargement of woman's sexual role, while it restored the depleted vitalities of post-medieval society, failed to curb the aggressive and destructive tendencies of this culture. For the cultivation of sexual life was embarrassed by the fact that syphilis, possibly long latent in Western Europe, took on a more virulent form. A relatively mild type of this disease, which was diagnosed and even treated by mercury in the middle of the fifteenth century, gave place to a more violent type in the decade when the New World was discovered. In this more fatal form it traveled from country to country, bearing with it a national stigma: the French called it the Spanish disease and the Germans called it the French disease. The classical name it received, in the poem that celebrated its existence, was speciously decorative; for it actually had a devastating effect upon health, hygiene, and morals. Now every occasion for sexual intercourse became tainted with fear, so difficult was it for the untrained to recognize its symptoms in the first stage.

For the timid, syphilis justified a puritanic abstention. But it also had another effect: it resulted in the invention of the first sure contraceptive, the linen sheath (1564): a device prescribed by the physician Fallopius, as a means of preventing syphilitic infection through intercourse. Meanwhile, the deepened interest in sex, and the desire to dissociate sexual enjoyment from parental responsibility, had stimulated investigation into other contraceptives, at least among the upper classes; and the ancient pessary was either revived or re-discovered.

Note the unfortunate association of ideas that now clustered around the acknowledgment of sexuality. Sex becomes not merely the road to sin but the road to physical corruption. The readiness to enjoy sex opens the body to disease and in that process the innocent may suffer as well as the sophisticated, for the infection may spread without sexual contact. The chaste wife may receive this dreadful disease in marriage, transmit it to her children, become disfigured by it, finally lose control of the limbs, suffer acute mental deterioration, and die. Prostitution ceases to be a device for stabilizing bachelorhood at a time when long apprenticeships demanded a deferment of marriage: the prostitute becomes the center of infection: her favors have become deadly, or rather, doubly deadly, now that syphilis adds to the old menace of gonorrhea. As early as 1469 Salicieto described syphilis as a disease due to coitus with a prostitute: so she is now a menace to both health and morals. But who escapes the disease? Those who use Fallopius's invention: the habitual libertines, skilled in the arts of sex—a second unfortunate association. The trade in sheaths and abortifacients fell into the hands of brothel-keepers and procuresses, bawds and barbers. Right down to our own day, in England, the contraceptive shop has often been an annex of the barber's.

In other words, contraception was originally associated, not with marriage, but with the violation of marriage: not with the spacing of child-births, for the better breeding and nurture of children, but with the prevention of offspring for the sake of pleasure. The most revolutionary invention of modern times, even more significant to humanity than the printing press, made headway, not as a beneficent aid to family life, not as a contribution to erotic culture, but as a safeguard against disease and a device for making possible an irresponsible sterility. Ignorance and disreputability surrounded contraception: hence it remained until the nineteenth century very largely one of the privileges of the upper classes.

Though the sexual practices of post-medieval culture were strongly affected by the widened province of the courtesan, one must utter a word of warning against the misinterpretation of this fact. Ideals are rarely translated bodily into life: their mission is rather to deflect, to hasten or retard, to diminish or magnify, needs that already exist independent of the ideal, and to re-arrange these needs in new constellations. Thus in the most lax periods of sexual morals, faithful marriages of course continue to exist. The effect of a more copious demand for sexual enjoyment would be felt within such marriages: in seeking to meet outside competition the loyal wife might attempt to fill a sexual demand that a less voluptuous age would hardly be conscious of: similarly the wider provenance of sexual images and symbols would deepen the unconscious suggestions of sex. This happened in the baroque period: witness not merely the decorative use of the spiral and the scalloped shell and the cornucopia, but even the one fresh element in building, the staircase. The formal staircase may have been in origin what it now is in dream—a symbol of the sexual act, projected into space and formally embodied in the setting of the palace; for the grand stairs led from the public rooms on the lower stories, where the charms of sex were exhibited, to the bedrooms in the upper stories where they were fulfilled.

But besides the gain in erotic expression, a social gain must be noted.

V. THE COURTLY HEAVEN

No one better expresses the propulsive energies and vitalities of the post-medieval period than Tintoretto. Note how thickly these new paintings are populated: thronged with people who surge and sway and float and climb to the very throne of Heaven. Here energy, as Blake said, is eternal delight; and most of the artists are like Milton: they belong to the Devil's party without knowing it. Now the Christian theme remains as a literary tag: who would guess in The Marriage at Cana, that Jesus was the principal figure? Tintoretto was plainly more interested in the palatial banqueting hall and the charming guests: the spirit is that of Castiglione. Rubens' crowning of Marie de Médici presents the courtly counterpart of Heaven: an attempt to translate to earth the blessings of the afterlife. The Court even had its own seven holy sacraments: Inheritance, legitimation, coming out, reception at court, honors, promotion, and pension. In masques and spectacles, the Court outdid itself. "In 1618," observes Allardyce Nicoll, "James, by no means the most financially reckless of monarchs, devoted £4000, a sum to be valued now at £40,000, on a single production." . . . Once again the expensive, the emptily spectacular, become substitutes for the good life in which all men have a share. Privilege-holders and profit-seekers now have a common purpose: to pre-empt for themselves the values that belong to the community and to enjoy privately what were once public functions and possessions. Music well symbolizes this new concentration of private power: the unanimity of Romanesque plain chant, the complex social inter-relationship of Gothic polyphony, give way to baroque solo singing: an age of prima donnas in politics, business, overseas exploration. And the less natural cohesion between social groups prevails, the greater becomes the need for a uniformity imposed by force from without.

Meanwhile, insolent self-confident men were exploring the four quarters of the globe; and though that fact was rarely embodied in formal paintings, Rubens symbolized it in the figures shown at the bottom.

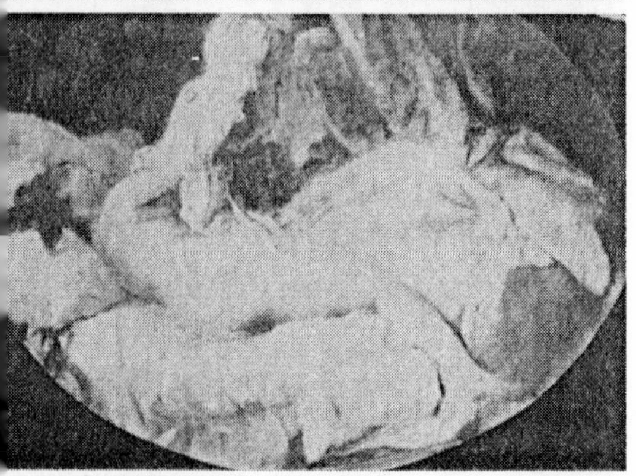

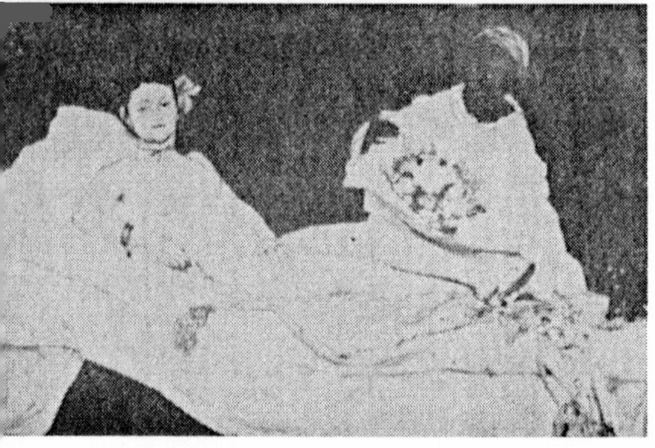

VI. EROTIC TRANSFORMATION

Woman became the symbol of the whole erotic ritual. From the 16th to the end of the 19th century her figure dominated the imagination of the painter. In Cranach's many nudes she still has a virginal austerity: his Caritas here shows her giving suck to a child and surrounded by children. Titian, painter of courtesans, reveals her more voluptuously; but if her breasts are still immature her pelvis and belly show her ripe for motherhood: in spite of improvements in contraception, she is still close to the crisis of pregnancy and the miracle of birth. By the 18th century woman has lost some of her vitality and has perhaps, as in Fragonard's charming disrobement, become too copiously self-indulgent: sex now threatens to become a diversion rather than a central fact in human relations. But the romantic generation which restores the edge to the erotic act shrinks from overt symbolism: not until Renoir and Rodin does the mingling of tenderness and sexual vitality become fully embodied. Meanwhile, Manet's Olympia shows the boylike courtesan, new style, whose contrast with the rich vitality of women by Titian or Rubens is blatant. She remains a symbol of defeminized love-play: prelude to a decadence that Proust, Mann, and others will interpret. In our day the New Woman, the "career woman," is once more giving way to a more enduring ideal, founded on the desire for family life, for motherhood, for the deeper erotic fulfillment that more permanent ties—and tensions—make possible: a life-course that may include a working career, but keeps a balance between biological and social and personal fulfillment. Woman's freedom now has the positive task of recapturing the central themes of life: the elaboration of erotic art and ritual, the selective improvement of mating, the application of maturer psychological insight to child care and family relations; in short, the widening and deepening of the province of love.

The life for woman that Héloise had dared to dream in the twelfth century had now become an actual possibility: having found herself once more in sex, woman achieved a mature self in spheres outside sex, and her influence counted for more in political and intellectual spheres. If woman by the seventeenth century had eroticized the intellectual life of Western Europe, she had also had the opposite effect: she had intellectualized and partly sublimated her own erotic existence. "Who knoweth not," exclaims the Lord Cesar in The Courtier, "that women rid our hearts of all vile and dastardly imaginations, vexations, miseries, and the troublesome heaviness that so often accompanieth them? And in case we will consider the truth, we know moreover, as touching the understanding of great matters, that they do not stay our wits, but rather quicken them."

At the very moment, then, when sexual relations were treated as something more than a brief interlude in practical activity, the woman of the upper classes began to achieve a life, a dignity, an office, that was partly independent of her service to man. And she had this, without renouncing her sexual career, as she had been forced to do in the medieval nunnery. Montaigne wrote his admirable essay on education for a woman; and the treatise on astronomy that Fontenelle wrote for the edification of another woman was something of a landmark in the altered relations of the sexes. Perhaps it is to this growing regard for woman as a person that we must attribute some of the improvement in the physical care of children that went on in middle-class households.

For meanwhile the care of children indeed underwent a transformation. The chief symptom of this change was the invention of apparatus designed to soothe or train the little child. The rocking cradle was one of the first of these devices: perhaps not altogether accidentally associated with an age that had taken so hardily to the sea and that had experienced the lulling motion of a vessel in an even sea. But in the well-to-do burgher's household another piece of apparatus appeared in the sixteenth century: the toddler, a device on wheels to enable the child who could not walk to master the art without falling and so move freely around the room. The multiplication of toys, for amusement and edification, went on at the same time: children benefited from the essentially childlike amusements, the costumes and masquerades and shows, the music boxes and the puppet shows of their elders: they inherited these devices in time as they inherited their elders' books: La Fontaine's fables and Swift's Gulliver's Travels.

5: The Culture of the Country House

Though the power motive achieved its main embodiment in the absolute courts, it was in the new Country Houses, the private courts of feudalism and mercantilism, that this new mode of life achieved its most successful setting. The Country House spread over Europe, from the gardens of the Medici to the polders of the Low Countries, from the palaces on the Loire to the great houses in the Cotswolds, and finally from Europe to America, in the stately tide-water mansions of Virginia.

Here was the ideal environment for the Gentleman and the Lady: here leisure was ennobled with art and art itself was extended into a landscape equally ideal, equally responsive to the human spirit. Here, too, leisure created a school of manners and a routine of life which compared in beauty, if not in intellectual productivity, with the best Greece had created. Even today a good part of our culture consists in an attempt to subsist on the pickings and leavings of the Country House. On the side of consumption, at least, our department stores are but enlarged wardrobe rooms, our games and shows but professional specializations, of the masques, revels, dances, routs that once were "made to order" in the Country House. What is Suburbia but an attempt to universalize the setting of the Country House: to do with limited means and economical gestures what the rich families of Europe once did with almost unlimited means? Our whole routine of expenditure, indeed, still rests on the systematic vulgarization of Country House ideals. The mechanical democratization of luxury became one of the earliest—as it remains one of the most persistent—motives for mass production: from brummagem jewelry to silk stockings.

The idolum of the Country House coalesced in the sixteenth century. One can best picture the animus behind it by examining its literary prototype: the setting that Rabelais imagines for the Abbey of Thelema, the new type of institution Gargantua proposes to build. This abbey was in every respect what the ideal medieval abbey was not. And first: the symbol of protection was razed: the new Country House, unlike the castle, is to lie in the midst of open country, and unlike the monastery, it is to have no walls. For the baroque man the horizon line is the only bounding wall: a wall that moves with his own movement, ever luring him on.

In these new quarters all the habits of the monastery are turned upside down. Whereas it was the custom, in some monasteries, to wash and clean the room in which a woman had by accident passed through, in this new abbey the process of disinfection was reserved for one who had entered the religious orders. In the Abbey of Thelema both men and women were admitted, and were at liberty to depart at any time. But the women must be fair, well-featured, and of sweet disposition; while the men must be comely and well-conditioned. Instead of practicing poverty, chastity, and obedience, the new requirements are that the inmates may be honorably married, may be rich, and may live at liberty. So far from rising at the sound of the bell and going through the canonical hours, the inhabitants of Thelema lie in bed as long as they wish, rise when they think good, and eat, drink, and labor when they have a mind to. The only rule of this order is written over the entrance gate: *Do what you please.*

This ideal of life takes form in the new monastery, which is really a city in miniature. It consists in a series of buildings, arranged hexagonally, and bounded on the north by the river Loire. Every member is furnished with a generous apartment, consisting of a principal room, a withdrawing room, a handsome closet (private chamber), a wardrobe (dressing room), and an oratory; and the house itself is to contain not merely libraries in every language, but fair and spacious galleries of paintings. Besides these lodgings there is a tilt-yard, a riding court, a theater or public playhouse, and a natatory or a place to swim. By the river there is to be a Garden of Pleasure, and between two of the six towers there are courts for tennis and other games. Add to this orchards full of fruit trees, parks abounding in venison, and archery ranges; fill all the halls and chambers with rich tapestries, cover all the pavements and floors with green carpets, endow the Abbey with a vast annual rent, keep a corps of goldsmiths, lapidaries, jewelers, embroiderers, tailors, busy manufacturing costumes and accessories—and the physical setting of the Abbey of Thelema is complete.

This is not simply a Rabelaisian dream. On the contrary: Rabelais's picture is so close to the reality of the Country House, as it developed between the sixteenth and the twentieth century, that to fit any particular house one would have only to alter details. You will not find the goldsmiths and the tailors in the neighboring village; but you will find them in Bond Street and the Rue de la Paix and the Ringstrasse. All the inmates will not live permanently in the Country House; but on weekends the wings will be filled with guests and the hospitality will equal the dream in its abundance and its variety. Special ships will not go to the Cannibal Islands to come back laden with gold, raw silk, pearls, and precious stones: but whole empires will spread out from Spain, France, England, the Low Countries, that will seize hold of trading posts in India, China, and America and subject immense continents to a constant drain of goods for the building of country houses and for the decoration and delectation of their inhabitants. Fleets will ply back and forth in that service: arms will clash, blood will flow, to secure that luxury.

The loot from distant lands will fill the curio cabinet and the trophy room: the memory of exotic adventures will form the substance of the stories told at the dinner table or recounted in memoirs: prowess in conquest will give to the younger sons of the family their share in domestic glory. Hunting, fighting and traveling are the missions of the men-folk in the morning of their lives: to return to the Country House, laden with honors, quickened by adventure, to found families by mating with other Country House families, is the mission of their maturity: to this end their ladies patiently await them. Ancestral portraits will remind them of sires and dams, and foreshadow their own progenitive duties. Respect for blood turns attention to new strains of horses, oxen, sheep, chickens, pigeons; and the culture of new strains, the continuance of pure strains, contributes to a flourishing interest in biology. (In a little country house near Down, Charles Darwin finally gave this existence its intellectual consummation: The Origin of Species, The Descent of Man.)

The inhabitants of the Country House, with their seasonal migrations between town and country, with their intense self-sufficiency at home and their zest for exploration abroad, understand and master the world they live in better than any other class: for they touch it at every level—that of the stud-farm and the field as well as the court and the counting house. In short, they have both biological vigor and intellectual command: both moral discipline and skill in action. In the special environment they create for themselves and their retainers, the gentleman and the lady, the artist and the scientist, the citizen and the courtier, are all finally united. For those at the top, the Country House was perhaps the most admirable environment the race has yet produced; and the best all-round routine of living.

Is it any wonder that in an attenuated and vulgarized form, counterfeited, caricatured, defiled, the ideals of Country House existence are still the only positive ideals of life that compete either with the Christian Heaven, or the pragmatic Heaven of the industrial age, wherein machines beget better machines in order that machines, not men, may flourish? This appreciation is a necessary prelude to rational criticism.

The Country House ideal had severe limitations; and to begin with, the Country House was not concerned with the happiness of the whole community but with the felicity of its governors. The conditions which underlie this limited, partial good life are political power and economic wealth; and in order for that life to develop well, both of these must obtain in almost limitless quantities. Honest labor cannot achieve such wealth or command such leisure: it is possible only through privileged exploitation of the resources and labor of an entire country, for the benefit of a minority. The ease, the grace, the dignity, the spacious days of this society are therefore purchased at the price of the toil, the constriction, the ceaseless economic anxiety of the mass of the population: not only at home but in the exploited territories abroad. Under all its patent refinements goes a ruthless monopoly of land and political power. Force and fraud, either remote or recent, are the twin foundations of Country House existence. The motto, "Do what you please," means in fact: "Help yourself, the world is yours."

Possession and passive enjoyment were the keys to this existence. In order to keep laborers and artisans at work, at depressed wages that would enable luxury to be enjoyed on the widest scale by the rich, it was necessary to prevent the common man from having access to the land on his own account: the usufruct must go to the landowner, not the worker. Guild standards of living must be broken down and privileged commercial monopolies set up in opposition to the guilds themselves. This emphasis upon the rewards of passive ownership, upon the building up of an irresponsible class of absentee owners or rentiers, points to a more general fact: that there was little practical intercourse between the Country House governors and their environment. Even improvements in local agriculture, like the abolition of the three field system and the creation of large walled or fenced fields, increased the efficiency of centralized management at a sacrifice of precious common rights which even the poorest serf once possessed. Such activities as remained in the Country House after the sixteenth century—the pursuit of game for example—were damaging to agriculture and could not have been maintained had the latter been wholly dedicated to alimentation.

In general, the pattern of Country House existence called for imitating in play that which once had had a serious social function: hunting game for the sake of shooting rather than eating, riding horseback for the sake of exercise rather than locomotion. This led in time to the conception that an ideal existence is primarily a functionless and irresponsible one: the idle filling of an empty day. Marcel Proust notes in his final inquisition on a decadent aristocracy how the empty custom of paying formal visits, leaving cards, was the last ephemeral imitation of more serious social duties. Real life in the Country House was performed by functionaries: the people for whom the work was done drifted into the class of supernumeraries and spectators: at best, they gave commands. Only in play, only by way of amusement, did the gentleman and the lady have the opportunity for a more active existence, closer to the core of real life. To invent risks, to simulate dangers, to transform play itself into an exacting species of work, became the chief occupation of the upper landed gentry: hence mountain climbing, tiger hunts, horse races, and fatiguing ceremonial, all of which sought in some degree to recover the taste of reality.

This Country House life did not remain completely vacuous: here literature and the fine arts both undoubtedly flourished; and even the arts of gardening and landscape design were often energetically pursued. But on the whole, the arts flourished as objects of appreciation rather than as active, creative elements in a community's life: they served to inflate the ego of a class and to give it unmistakable symbols of its supremacy. A gourmandizing habit of mind, the habit of craving sensations and diversions, came to prevail: so that instead of the artist's becoming the center of the creative act, the connoisseur took that place for himself. To meet his tastes, to flatter his prejudices, to respond to his interests, became the secret of esthetic success.

Now the patron has a new claim to infallibility: the claim of money. Does he not pay for the work of art? By a slow process of replacement, money values take the place of real values: rarity and distance become the fashionable criteria of art. Age, fragility, exoticism, novelty become standards of achievement. Imported wares come successively into fashion: Persian carpets, Chinese porcelain, Indian silks and cottons, Turkish turbans; and with them enter exotic habits in eating, drinking, and ceremonial: ices from the Orient, coffee from Arabia, tea from China, tobacco from North America, wines from special districts, bottled in special years. All these habits were first given the stamp of respectability at the Court and the Country House before they began to spread, in the seventeenth century, to inns, coffee houses, bourgeois households.

The ladies and gentlemen of the Country House did not see that enjoyment rests on active achievement and is indeed inseparable from achievement. Do what you like is a good motto only if one accepts the obligation to do as one must. In every just conception of free will there necessarily enters an element of necessity, for otherwise to be free is to be the slave of caprice. Politics and war afforded this element of necessity in the heyday of Country House culture; but as the ideal itself spread, only the irresponsible and the relaxing elements tended to remain. Here we have the social conditions for the largely acquisitive spiritual culture of the nineteenth century. In the travels of a patient connoisseur like Aeneas Sylvius Piccolomini or John Evelyn, we have the early pattern of the effortful tourism and sightseeing, the museum-collecting and museum-visiting habits, of a later age.

In the long run, Country House existence was an aimless existence: one could increase its possessions and widen its hospitalities; but one could not make it fit the needs of a society based on justice. The ultimate fate of such an institution is to become irrelevant and finally to disappear with the economic dissipation of the class that created it. The Abbey of

Thelema ends up its career as Heartbreak House and is chopped to the ground with the Cherry Orchard. The Country House was the ideal expression of an oligarchic economy: a world within a world, self-centered, self-contained, self-seeking. In the culture of that life, in the balance between social and biological development, something of permanent value was achieved: but it could not be translated into a general program for a democratic community without completely altering every term.

What a mechanistic and acquisitive age would make of this culture was only an instrument of more universal debasement; it would spread its vices without inculcating its disciplines. The luxuries of the "successful" today are the last orts of that baroque masque and banquet.

6: The Gentleman as Saint

The warring impulses of baroque man found their ultimate resolution in religion: they were incarnated in a personality who could have taken form only in this epoch: a man who was a soldier, a courtier, and a saint. On the path from military service to Holy Orders, Ignatius Loyola conceived the possibility of creating within the Roman Church itself a power capable of ruling and governing the world. Within one formidable organism he united the medieval idea of unity with the baroque idea of uniformity.

This dream of Ignatius Loyola was an ambitious one; but so far from being a fragile theatrical creation in staff and gilt, imitating marble and gold, it came close to solid fulfillment: even down to our own day it continues to play a part in the political calculations of the Vatican and partly accounts for the various shifts and stratagems Rome employed to make smooth the path of totalitarian conquest during the last generation. Perhaps only one thing kept Loyola's disciples from ultimately wielding absolute power both within and without the Church: the fact that power became their goal. If they used the resources of baroque culture, its command of machines and its love of theater, they also shared its critical weakness.

The transformation of the Spanish caballero, Ignatius Loyola, into a soldier of Christ took place when he was recovering from a wound received on the battlefield of Pampeluna. On asking for a knightly romance, Amadis of Gaul, to while away his time, he was given a Bible. The reading of that book, by this unlettered and undereducated young soldier, had such a profound effect that he withdrew from the army and his family, to meditate in a cave in the mountains. There he began a process of reorientation and self-education that led to the writing of his Spiritual Exercises. Still feeling inadequate to the task he set before himself, Loyola went as a full-grown man to the University of Paris. At Paris he gathered together a few fellow students by whose help he founded a new order, the Society of Jesus: an order almost as different from that of the Carthusians or the Dominicans as was Rabelais's jocose institution. He sought to save the medieval Christian synthesis by giving it the tools and weapons of the modern mind: the discipline of the new scientist, the imagination of the new artist, the psychological penetration of the new dramatist.

To understand the boldness and greatness of Loyola's conception one must realize that he was a profound Christian, and in the act of establishing his faith, an austere one. Like his contemporary, Calvin, he had a sense of his own unworthiness and regarded this as the very beginning of Christian faith: "to behold myself as an ulcer and an abscess whence have issued so many sins and iniquities and such vile poison" is almost the starting point of his Spiritual Exercises. But to regenerate the personality, Christianity now required a more subtle method than it had used at a time when hardship and violence had lessened the seductiveness of worldly life: it was necessary to re-dramatize Christ's mission by the very latest contrivances of art.

Instead of attempting an artificial separation of the Christian soul from society, Loyola boldly employed the new mechanisms, the new symbols, the new forms of thought and feeling that were the special expressions of his own age. If the Jesuits did not indeed conceive baroque architecture, they made it their own, just as they turned to their own account the new mechanical discipline of the army. There was nothing archaic or backward-looking in his conception of the Christian mission: he took his faith at the point where he found it and went on from there. For Loyola, as for Shakespeare, all the world was a stage; and he saw that the drama could not be effectively produced unless the time and the setting were taken into account. By putting at the service of the Church the new gifts of dramatic visualization, as in painting, and the art of visual dramatization, as in the theater, Loyola took Christian theology out of the Schoolman's shell.

In the Spiritual Exercises Loyola showed himself a true man of his time, in his insight into the theater and in his virtuosity in playing upon the human soul: Shakespeare is possibly his only rival in both departments. It is not for their contents but for their novel technique that these Exercises have remained a powerful instrument of renovation among Catholics. At every point in these Exercises, the first requirement is to recall the history: to place the drama in time. And the second procedure also belongs to the theater: to *see the place.* The third step is to behold and consider what the actors are doing: to understand the drama itself.

Instead of emptying the mind of its normal imagery in an effort to achieve purity of purpose, Loyola rather directs these images. Step by step, the practitioner of the Spiritual Exercises contemplates his relation to Adam, to Christ, to the Last Judgment. Hour by hour, day by day, his contemplation and his prayers are carefully fixed on Christ's journey; and on the seventh day the person in retreat contemplates the whole passion at once.

One may look upon the Exercises as a series of stage directions for a private drama, in which a sacred historic theme displaces a secular interest. Like a good director, Loyola did not attempt to overburden the actor with a part beyond his capacity: by experiment he learned to mitigate some of the rigors he at first thought necessary, and to vary the duration and intensity of the exercises so that they might do the most good to the persons following them. In the Constitution of the Order of Jesus itself Loyola made equally radical changes in method and attitude. He got permission from the Pope to dispense with the monastic costume and the monastic tonsure, no less than with the celebration of the canonical hours. A Jesuit brother might go everywhere, and in pursuit of his mission might even adopt a disguise. The Jesuits had in this, too, the instincts of actors: a sense that the costume changes the ego. Like actors, they doubtless sometimes overplayed their parts.

In this manner, the new order became a secret society; and the terror and hatred the Jesuits long excited among their opponents were probably founded on their gift for secrecy and the art of disguise: these servants of the Papacy were everywhere and nowhere. Just as in the new Churches the Jesuits took over the luxurious fantasies of the palace and created churches as gay as ballrooms, as sensuously conceived as the setting for a carnival, a palpable heaven in plaster and gold, so in the use of disguises Jesuit theatricality sometimes over-reached itself.

Yet the very frailties that in time disclosed themselves in Loyola's order derived partly from the real solidity of his own social understanding. Probably better than any other spiritual leader of modern times, he understood the period he lived in, valued precisely those elements that were fresh and original, and grasped what was necessary in the development of the Church itself if it were to remain an active spiritual force in this society, instead of hanging on as a mummified survivor of an outworn culture. Loyola saw that something more than a negative movement was necessary: no mere tightening up of discipline, no mere return to old practices, could make the Christian Church become once more a universal institution. If the Church did not expand its mission the expansion of the world would inevitably contract the importance of Christianity.

Loyola came to the conclusion, accordingly, that the Church must fully utilize the existing organs of education, of discipline, even of entertainment: it must turn pomp and worldliness themselves to its own uses. On these matters, Loyola was far more revolutionary than Calvin and Luther; for whereas they recoiled from the New World that had opened before them, Loyola both figuratively and actually sought to embrace it. The Jesuits did not confuse holiness with poverty, or even with pain and renunciation. The problem for the Society of Jesus, in the sixteenth century, was to recover the essence of Christianity even under forms that seemed to contradict it. In a letter to G. P. Caraffa, possibly as early as 1536, Loyola defended the practice of letting those who had wealth and noble position retain these advantages after joining the society: "for it is right to yield to the needs and circumstances of the moment, and not merely consider what is absolutely the most perfect thing."

Though their opportunism often led to the undoing of the Jesuits, it derived partly from Loyola's remarkable psychological tact: a trait that perhaps owes something to his Spanish culture, but even more to his native grace and understanding. In an age of great intuitive psychologists, when people were turning from an acceptance of the outer badge to a probing of the inner man, Loyola stood on the same high level as Cervantes and Shakespeare, his nearest rivals. Despite all outward differences in career and fame, an inner similarity binds these three exquisitely self-conscious gentlemen: they probed the baseness of human nature with the swift delicate touch of the surgeon, and if they prescribed no harsh purgations, if they sometimes preferred to leave the bullet in the wound rather than risk its extraction, it was because they understood better than anyone else what a difficult business it is to interfere with the personality's balance even for the sake of improving it.

Loyola's good sense was impregnable. In the matter of diet, for example, he advised not severe abstinence but vigilant moderation in eating and drinking, so that neither the body nor the spirit would be undermined; and in order to make moderation more effective, he advised the practice of imagining how Christ looked and talked when he ate with his disciples. He was so aware of the nice inter-relationship of mind and body that when Lent came he used to summon a doctor and have him examine every member of the community before he gave permission for fasting. So with vigils, so with all the other instruments of holiness: like any other tool they needed to be carefully inspected and their indiscriminate use restrained. To serve God was the end; but the means to this end were more various for Loyola than the Church had been wont to allow. The main thing was constantly to order and re-order one's life, to achieve a mobile equilibrium of virtue, to ward off emptiness, doubt, and defeat—

the mood of desolation. His dictum—never to make an important decision in a period of desolation—has indeed been rediscovered by modern psychoanalysts.

Is it too much to claim for this superb psychologist that he reunited the disciplines of medicine and theology, and that his methods of treatment were closer to the needs of the total personality than those which are even now current? Theology itself Loyola exhibited with medical vigilance: he warned that Christians must be very careful in their manner of speaking and treating of predestination, faith, and grace. Hence Loyola's general avoidance of doctrinal change; his whole emphasis was upon method, upon the *technique* of Christian living. His imitation of Christ was not a saint's soliloquy, as with Thomas à Kempis, but a dramatic and gymnastic exercise.

The chief doctrinal emphasis of the Jesuits, indeed, was on free will; and this position was something of a paradox; for it was combined with an insistence upon an obedience perhaps more absolute than that undergone by any other monastic order. The Jesuits formed a military hierarchy. Under the supreme commander of the order were the various provincial generals; and a readiness to follow the orders of his superior, as unconditional as that of a soldier on the battlefield, was exacted of each member. This paradox runs all through the order. No Jesuit may exercise the right of private judgment, even on the smallest matters that fall within the province of his superior. Yet, in relation to the growing power of the absolute state, Jesuit writers like Bellarmine were on the side of republican government.

As early as 1562 Lainez, the second General of the Jesuits, held the view that the laws of the Church were from God; but that society had the right to choose the government itself. Divine right, accordingly, was not a possession of individuals but of society as a whole: monarchies, so far from existing by divine right, were no more sacrosanct than any other man-invented institution, and the people therefore have the right to change the forms of their government.

Unfortunately, as de Sanctis points out, the Jesuits sought to have the argument both ways. If power in the secular state rested with the citizens, why did not power in the Church rest with the whole body of Christians, or with the Council of the Church, rather than with the Pope? Why could not the faithful, indeed, depose the Pope or punish him like any other servant when he commits crimes and misuses his power? The early doctrines and practices of the Church had certainly not been on the side of ecclesiastical absolutism: that was a typical corruption that sprang from the orientalized Roman Empire.

At this point, the inconsistency of Jesuit doctrine came out. They refused to acknowledge either the logic or the historic authority of the democratic position for a simple reason: they sought to establish themselves as the political bodyguard of the Papacy; and as the power behind the Papal throne, they might hope to exercise an even greater absolutism—both prompting the Pope's commands and executing his orders. The justification for Papal absolutism could only be a pragmatic one: it provides continuity. But to match the Jesuits' psychological and sociological adaptations of ancient dogma to current circumstance, they should have carried through a political transformation, too: so that continuity should no longer impede the process of self-reform. Halting here, their transformation remained abortive, and their acts of liberation only forged heavier fetters.

Into an age of extreme contrasts, violent fanaticisms, exorbitant claims, Loyola himself nevertheless brought a moderating influence. He put before sinful men and women an ideal of life that was within their possible limits of achievement: not so high as to promote a despair that easily led to cynicism and then to outright denial. Intuitively, Loyola recognized the place of quantitative measure in the moral life. Goodness and badness were not just a matter of kind but a matter of degree. Moral judgment was a matter of gauging, at every moment of life, the size and intensity of the sin itself in relation to the occasion and the general end in view.

With this conception before him, the Jesuit confessor became no mere inquisitor: he became a subtile assessor of sins whose nature afforded a genuine play to intellectual discernment and psychological tact. Under these circumstances casuistry flourished. Instead of seven deadly sins there were now seven hundred, depending upon the time, the place, the circumstance, the intention. Moreover, to understand the true inwardness of sin no less than its coarse outward manifestations, the confessor might well follow Francis Bacon's observations: "It is not possible to join serpentine wisdom with columbine innocency, except men know exactly all the conditions of the serpent. . . . Nay, an honest man can do no good upon those that are wicked to reclaim them, without the help of the knowledge of evil." To their honor as physicians of the soul—but also of course to their peril—the Jesuits sought to make use of that knowledge: they even guarded mechanically against the intimacies of the confessional by inventing the Confessional Box. Only the Talmud rivals the Jesuit books of casuistry in knowledge of the circumstances of sin: in particular, the active temptations and deviltries of baroque society. And not until psychoanalysis renewed the endeavor, were the complexities of personal conduct so patiently, so thoroughly, so sympathetically explored.

To those who sought to live a pious life, Loyola advised the same kind of moderation and forbearance that served in elevating the sinner. Here Ignatius' self-analysis must have given him a key to the dangers of fanatical devotion. Loyola's letters to Sister Theresa Rejadilla were exemplary in pointing out the temptations and dangers of unrestrained virtue. "In two things," he wrote on June 18, 1536, "the enemy makes you err. . . . The first is that he sets before you, and persuades you, into a false humility. The second is that he suggests extreme fear of God, on which you dwell too much, and to which you pay too much attention. . . . We must then be very careful; and if the enemy lifts us up, we must lower ourselves, counting our sins and miseries; and if he lowers and depresses us, we must lift ourselves up in true faith and hope in the Lord."

One may sum up Loyola's creed by saying that he took both man and society as he found them. Upon neither did he impose a wholly ideal standard, or a principle of living derived exclusively from another epoch and another moment of culture. If men were to adapt themselves to Christianity, the Christian Church, as its vehicle, must adapt itself to men, to the time, the place, the action demanded by contemporary culture: that was the Jesuit method and doctrine. The Jesuits sought in a more than Pauline fashion to be all things to all men. In order to win others over to the Lord, Loyola counseled Fathers Broet and Salmeron to "follow the same course that the enemy follows with regard to the good soul."

Pursuing this method, Father Ricci in China, at the court of the emperor in Peking, used his knowledge of science to excite the curiosity of the ruler: the Jesuits even made clockwork automatons for the emperor's amusement, so that Christian teaching might more easily gain his favor. With consummate good sense, again, the Jesuits adapted the Gospel itself to the Chinese: instead of damning the great sages and religious leaders of the Chinese past, they sought rather to show where the universal truths of Christianity had been incorporated in the Analects of Confucius. In the eighteenth century Father Noël even translated Les Livres Classiques de la Chine: the thought of China thus made its way into Europe, along with wallpaper, porcelain, and tea. By introducing maps, astronomical calculations, clocks, mirrors, reading glasses, oil paintings, as well as the Bible and Christian doctrine, the Jesuits succeeded in identifying their religious and metaphysical beliefs with practical ingenuities the Chinese valued more highly: an astute use of the conditioned response.

This method of spreading the faith incensed the rival orders: it seemed to them an indefensible laxity, a defiance of every otherworldly claim. But was it not a generous catholicizing of Christianity? Had it been carried further, it might have paved the way for a genuine syncretism, comparable to that out of which the doctrines of Christianity itself had grown. For lack of willingness to meet other religions on common ground, the Christian churches showed a pride that could only awaken a pride equally stubborn in those they sought to convert: they brought down on themselves an odium derived from Western man's crass belief in his own inevitable rightness, superiority, and uniqueness: his lack of perspective on his own and the world's development. The Jesuits showed a more apt humility in dealing with the ancient cultures of the East: they were careful not to antagonize their possible converts. Unlike the Franciscans, they courted no martyrdom, but sought to avoid it. In this sense, the Society of Jesus was, perhaps, closer to the spirit of Jesus than the more severely orthodox missionaries. What was such doctrinal courtesy and chivalry but an imaginative interpretation of the Christian injunction to walk two miles when one is asked to go one mile?

In short, the Jesuits exemplified the meekness of the proud and the courtesy of the powerful. Yet at times that courtesy might seem complaisance; that complaisance might be mistaken for indifference; that indifference might lead to active collaboration; that collaboration might turn into active corruption. For there is a real danger when one fights fire with fire: the direction of the wind may change and the fire escape one's neatly laid plans for control. Nevertheless the good side of Jesuit "laxity" must not be forgotten: perhaps its greatest triumph came among the Indians of Paraguay, that beautiful communist despotism the Jesuits erected there and almost maintained in the teeth of official Spanish jealousy and opposition. In economic provisions and social arrangements the Jesuits succeeded better than any other group, possibly, up to the early Mormons in Utah. As with the Mormons, part of the opposition to the Jesuits sprang out of their indubitable virtues.

As an order their numbers were never great. Preserved Smith gives their membership as some 8975 in 1620, and in 1750, according to the Jesuit authority, Campbell, there were only 22,589 members, "of whom about half were priests." But their influence in both the educational and the political worlds was immense.

From the first, however, the Jesuits provoked hostility, even within the Church itself: an hostility not exclusively confined to the ill-disposed. The contrast that they offer with the Franciscans will bear reflection. The Franciscans, thanks to their founder, have a name for purity, the Jesuits for corruption. Francis's ideal intentions are treated by the world as if they were fulfilled facts; whereas Ignatius's well-fulfilled missions have been treated almost as a certification of his bad intentions. Yet two centuries after Loyola's death much that he had planned for had already come into existence: the principles he had established had created an institution with a martial discipline that maintained its unity and caused it to prosper.

More than once, during those two hundred years, power seemed within their grasp: a power that might have enabled them to wield ultimate authority over Christendom and perhaps over the world. But the more they plotted and planned for power, the more it eluded their grasp, for here precisely was the point at which Loyola's psychological insight came to nothing. The soldier in him kept a blind spot for the soldier's defects. By binding the order unconditionally to the Papacy, without effecting a political revolution within the Church that would have decentralized its power and opened it up to co-operative and democratic processes, the Jesuits themselves ultimately became the victims of the creature they sought to control. As Christianity weakened in the eighteenth century, the Jesuits became, not the agents of its regeneration, but a further justification for its downfall, so that finally, in order to save itself, the Papacy was forced to ban the order in 1773 and command its dismemberment.

This temporary banishment was ironical but inevitable. No one could trust the Catholic Church in the eighteenth century because it might be in the control of the Jesuits: no one could trust the Jesuits because their most innocent proposal might have as its ultimate purpose only the wider domination of the Church. The Jesuits sought power and power corrupted them: adopting the enemy's methods to advance the cause of God, they readily became identified with the devil himself.

"Altogether," Loyola had said, "I must not desire to belong to myself, but to my Creator and His representative. I must let myself be led and moved as a lump of wax lets itself be kneaded, must order myself as a dead man without will or judgment." The mischief of this admonition lay not in submission to the will of God but in the equal power accorded to His representative. No human being can be safely entrusted with such powers over another: here the Jesuit inclination to diminish the theological importance of original sin, their main point of contention with the Jansenists of Port Royal, closed their eyes to an inherent source of corruption. Human power can be used safely only when it is open to division, conflict, challenge, rational opposition. By the absolutism of its constitution, the Society of Jesus, like the Papacy itself, shared in the major sin of this period: the belief in unqualified power. Without both inner and outer curbs, those who exercise power become unprincipled, or rather, they hold to only one principle: to keep what power they have and to acquire more of it. Right and justice become what suits the convenience of the governing class and enables them to maintain themselves in office.

We have seen this corruption overtake a group in our own day that bears many resemblances to the Jesuit order: the Communist Party. Here, too, discipline was absolute: here, too, the noble purpose of the founders, to remove human exploitation, served in time as a cloak for unscrupulous deeds, selfish personal ambitions, shameless ideological transformations, and brazen political perversions. Here, again, experts in the technique of revolution used the wicked devices of the enemy and became the victims of their own adopted wickedness: here, finally, the fear of opposition, the fear of submitting to criticism and of dividing with others their dearly bought position and power, led to a ruthlessness that deformed the personalities of those who wielded it, even more than it did those who were forced to submit to it. With this came the betrayal of the fundamental idea that communism had formulated and partly incorporated in Russia's economic order.

Ends and means limit and modify each other. If unrealizable ends are empty and futile, unqualified means, whose very nature cuts them off from their legitimate human goals, are no less empty. Neither the Jesuits nor the Communists were sufficiently on guard against the perversities of self-exploitation by both individual and group, rationalized as the greater glory of God. Obedient corpses, galvanically summoned to action by their superiors, are not effective or desirable substitutes for living men. Nor is *rigor mortis* an equivalent for unity of spirit.

Loyola's doctrines might have enabled a company of saints to govern, or at least mightily to influence, the new world. In order to have fulfilled this mission, however, each member would have had to be as indifferent to power as the ideal guardians of Plato's Republic—and Christian theology was at hand to remind them that this condition could not be fulfilled. Fortunately, the world was spared from the too-limited providence of the Jesuits by their own faults of character: thanks to their corruption, virtue again was saved.

No limited order, no class of privileged men, consecrated to absolute obedience, aiming at absolute power, could perform Loyola's mission: there lay his mistake. The readiness to meet evil with understanding, the readiness to widen the scope of the experimental method in dealing with human conduct were admirable; but they can work to human advantage only when every person in the community is a candidate, an adept, a practitioner, a critic, and a stern judge. The Society of Jesus, unfortunately, was conceived under the sign of the Despot. What was valid in its intentions could be executed only under the sanative forms of democracy: the co-operative thought of science and the co-operative government of a community of equals, aiming at the best life possible.

CHAPTER VII. THE NEW HEMISPHERES

1: Belief in a New World

The dissolution of medieval culture, so far from weakening the grip on life, had actually strengthened it: precisely those elements that had been violently repressed or shamefacedly hidden became the nucleus for a new life: the impulses to dominate the earth, to expand the senses, to nourish and exercise all the organs of the body. Even destructive processes have a positive value when they are the prelude to a new period of constructive activity: at that moment, the wrecking crew becomes an essential arm of building. It was not the re-birth of Rome or Greece that counted, but the fresh awakening to the animate world. Now that world was seen as if for the first time, as Miranda beheld Ferdinand in that play whose far-fetched symbols recapture more of Shakespeare's society than realistic observation could hold.

O wonder!
How many goodly creatures are there here!
How beauteous mankind is! O brave new world,
That has such people in't!

From the fifteenth century on, the dominant spirit in Western Europe was that of expansion. People were no longer content to remain within their walls: walls of class, walls of occupation, walls of fixed duties and obligations, walls of cities and territories. They had a sense that a new world lay outside their self-imposed boundaries: space summoned them to movement and movement devoured space. The spirit of adventure, long before loosed by the Crusades, was now re-instated, and gathered further headway with each new report that came back from Africa or India.

The New World of which people began to speak from the early sixteenth century on was both a practical discovery and an ideological construction: both a place and an idolum. The concentration upon exploring and settling this world undoubtedly hastened the disintegration of medieval culture; but at the same time it quickened the processes of recovery, for it gave Western man a new task to fulfill and a new drama to enact. People turned from their inner life, which was disordered and confused, an inner life in which old traditions and faiths were daily being challenged by new discoveries in astronomy and physics: they centered their attention upon the outer world and turned impulses that might have been suicidal into acts of aggression and mastery, perpetrated against nature and nature's children. In other cultures men had practiced withdrawal: in this new world economy migration became the new form of retreat. Now the wilderness served as cloister, and for the extravert hermits of the age, the ocean itself was an Egyptian desert: nowhere was this impulse better symbolized than in Herman Melville's Moby-Dick: a classic which deliberately drew upon three centuries of recorded experiences.

In many respects, this new drama of expansion and conquest was superficial; its plot was over-simplified and its action gory: but the scenery it employed was distractingly magnificent. Indeed, the very defects of this drama helped release the energies of men, for it gave them a solid confidence in being themselves able to exercise a godlike providence over the vast domains of nature and its countless creatures: in a few centuries man altered biotic relations on every part of the planet, upset the balance of nature, and transformed the biological possibilities of existence, not merely for himself but for countless species of animals and plants. Out of man's mythic sense of his own self-importance, fostered by his very acts of exploration and conquest, Western man forced himself to feats of courage and derring-do which would have been inconceivable in people who had a more judicious sense of their own limitations or a more critical understanding of their own unworthiness.

The earliest modern explorations of the planet by sea extended the European world to Iceland and reached over to touch the shores of the New World: ventures comparable only to the epic canoe voyages of the Polynesians. In the fourteenth century the Portuguese pushed out to the Canary Islands and traced the outline of the African coast, till they finally joined up on the east coast with Arab sailors who had pushed down from India. By degrees, Western man lost his respect for boundaries: the unknown, the untried, the unbounded began to tempt his imagination and release his inhibitions. The compass, the three-masted sailing ship, the astrolabe gave him confidence to set his course and get his bearings and find his way back to port.

So Western man unfurled his sails to the wind and set forth to conquer, league by league, the unexplored seas and lands of the world. Skill in navigation, ability to chart a course through strange seas, under strange stars, with a few planks separating him from a watery grave meant command over space. All this promoted confidence: the fear of the unknown was thus transposed into the lure of the unknown: the negative sign became positive. The sea, that symbol of the unknowable and the infinite, became an open book: its boundlessness was encompassed and its mightiest monster, the whale, became for the first time the desired prey of the sailor-hunter. Canst thou hook Leviathan? The answer was Yes.

Each success made European man more daring, and each act of daring increased his success. The explorer brought back captives and slaves; he brought back silver, gold, ivory, incense: best of all, he brought back himself, and with him a belief in his own ability "to strive, to seek, to find, and not to yield" in the face of the most savage obstacles thrown up by nature. Stay-at-homes participated imaginatively in these adventures and were spiritually enriched by them.

The first break in the self-contained medieval world had come chiefly from the infiltration of Moslem thought through Spain into the universities, and of Arab technics into the arts of steel-tempering, distillation, and the like: algebra and alchemy were its decisive contributions here. But in the fifteenth century the belief in a new world became a possibility of action as well as thought: penned up in a Europe they could not wholly master either through war or religion, people dared to dream of altering this drama by a quick change of scene.

Within a century, current concepts of time and space underwent profound modifications. The systematic exploration of space, astronomical space and terrestrial space, presently microcosmic space, became the goal of both practical and scientific effort: the natural philosopher and the sailor, the free-thinking scientist and the free-booting soldier were engaged on the same job. To explore space, to conquer space, to put the vagueness of undefined space within a definite frame, the frame of latitude and longitude, became a necessity for thought no less than practice. And the expansion of living space by means of trading posts and colonies altered both the biological and political conditions of life. The discovery of America, showing the greatness of the world, increased Western man's sense of his own greatness. Like Jack Horner, he stuck in his thumb and he pulled out a plum, and said what a good boy am I! By extending his domain he erroneously thought he had increased his own stature. This, unfortunately, was far from true.

The New World of the fifteenth century included both India and the lands of the Western Hemisphere: Vasco da Gama reached the first a year later than Columbus landed in the Bahamas. But whereas China and India were cultures, far more ancient, far more deeply saturated with tradition than Europe itself, the lands toward which Columbus set sail were under-peopled, and the European desire to dominate and conquer and explore and ransack had here an almost unobstructed field. A handful of men, at once brutal and fanatic, detestable and sublime took possession of the Western hemisphere: by guile and gunpowder and treasons and stratagems, by inflamed cupidity and desperate courage, the Spanish and Portuguese conquistadors first claimed these lands for their monarchs and for the Roman Church.

Most of the detailed acts of this conquest degraded the conquerors and cast a blight over the population they reduced to servile misery; and yet the act itself was one by which mankind, for the first time, established contact as a common unit, the *humanitas* dreamed of by the Stoic philosophers. Before this, what had been called the human race was only a European figure of speech: people had left most of the race out of their calculations. No longer was the world a disorderly patchwork of landscapes and cities, ending abruptly a few miles out of sight of land: it had the geometrical unity of the spheroid it was now discovered actually to be: the globe itself was the very symbol of unity and completeness and continuous movement.

The finding of the New World laid every part of the earth open to discovery: it even threw the familiar regions into a new set of relationships: Italy, which faced eastward in its voyagings, lost out to Spain and England, which faced westward. Exploration and expansion increased, almost automatically, the area of human potentialities: not only potential wealth, potential power, potential food, but potential knowledge and potential political freedom. In short, the era of discovery had a moral and personal outcome: it helped bring into existence a new ideal of the human personality, one whose wishes, no longer locked up in dreams and returning circuitously in subjective emanations, now worked upon the outer world as pure will. The outer man conquered: the inner man abdicated. And the fear of the inner life, the fear of metaphysical depth, the fear of man's very self, went along with his conquest of fear in every other department of life.

The wider meaning of the New World was at once clear: it did not wait for the twentieth century to be interpreted. Poliziano, the great humanist, from the court at Florence addressed an epistle to the King of Portugal complimenting him upon opening up new lands, new seas, new worlds, even new constellations: those were his words. He politely suggested that this story should be written up by himself while it was still fresh: no modern journalist could have had a prompter eye for the great news of the day. The narratives of adventurous open voyages were speedily set down and eagerly devoured by intelligent men all over Europe: Hakluyt and

Purchas were but the forerunners of many other writers and editors. The basis for these narratives was the ship's log, which combined the methodical record of the merchant with the adventurous tale of the traveler—dry entries sometimes embellished with lovingly executed illustrations.

"We are living in a New World today, and things are being done differently," wrote Luther. That spirit was everywhere: things were being done differently. For the first time it became possible to think of making a fresh start, scrapping all the existing dogmas, prescriptions, and customs: attempting on the basis of untrammeled observation and rational experiment to lay down the foundations for a better social order. Every question became an open question, no longer to be peremptorily settled by tradition and revelation; and the new world was an open world: one might revise its outlines every year as the mapmaker revised his charts and maps, on the basis of more systematic soundings.

In short, the discovery of the geographic New World resulted in a similar upheaval in the mind; and one of the first lands that was thus brought to the surface was none other than the lost continent of Atlantis, which Plato had reported in his Critias: the seat of a more perfect society.

Within a generation Plato's ideal commonwealth was reborn in a great critical and constructive work, the Utopia of Thomas More. The New World did not long remain a purely geographic concept: it meant a new technics, a new science, a new education, a new social order, a new hemisphere of the mind. But it began first with the bold conception of the possibilities of constructing a better commonwealth: a series of utopias accompanied the practical movement for colonization. If the immediate effects of More, Campanella, Andreae, and Vayrasse were fitful and insignificant, they nevertheless paved the way for more comprehensive efforts many centuries later. At the moment of its germination, the idea of utopia was an integral part of the conception of a New World.

2: Utopia as New World Symbol

Thomas More's Utopia was finished by that busy statesman in 1516. Far more decisively than in many later works, with More's Utopia a new current of air came into the stuffy medieval chamber. More was palpably shocked by his own audacity in conceiving a world so different in social outline and customs from that of the England of Henry VIII: so shocked that he hid his serious purpose behind a façade of facetious names; for Utopia is nowhere, the sun-burned sailor who tells about the commonwealth is called Raphael Hythlodaye, and his last name means "skilled in nonsense."

More's debt to Plato's Republic is plain: the fuller knowledge of Plato was once more having its seminal influence upon European thought. But there is still another possibility about both the actual origin of the work and the general conception of a communistic society that More set forth; and that is, that some rumor of the Empire of the Incas may have already been blown over the Andes and so passed, with numerous changes, into Antwerp. Rumors travel faster than documents. Such a possibility would make a little less strangely clairvoyant the political parallels between the actual Peru found by Pizarro and More's imaginary Utopia.

The challenge of the New World was quite boldly put by Hythlodaye himself in More's masterly introduction: an unsparing piece of social criticism to appear under the very eyes of a despotic and quasi-absolute monarch. Hythlodaye points out that the counselors of kings often reject suggestions for improvement on one pretext or another; and when driven into a corner they say: "These things were good enough for our ancestors, and we only wish we were as wise as they were."—"As if," drily remarks Hythlodaye, "it were a dangerous thing for anyone to be found wiser than his ancestors."

By the sixteenth century the appeal to hallowed custom and prevailing authority was no longer sufficient. Men's eyes were beginning to open to the possibility of a more rational order and a better life than their ancestors had known. The revolting peasants of Germany were at one with the revolting imagination of More; and the communism of the Anabaptists was no less defiant of the privileges of the rich than the communism of the Utopians. More's conscious official self was that of a lawyer and statesman, participating in his daily life in that "nobility, magnificence, splendor, and majesty" which the "community of life and goods without any money dealings" would utterly overthrow. His religious views were those of a faithful Catholic: so he imposed harsh sentences upon heretics without apparent compunction. In the end, his Church called him Blessed, and finally gave him the title of Saint. There can be no doubt as to his conscious orthodoxy, his honest loyalty to Church and State.

But the New World had already taken possession of More's unconscious: once he turned his imagination loose, it stopped at nothing that might improve the lot of men in society. His humor, his persiflage, his apparently irresponsible fantasy were only mechanisms whereby his deeper self could make its appearance in public. Every part of his Utopia shows the effect of a new world consciousness. Witness the application of mechanical invention to work, as in the creation of the chicken incubator, the universal participation in manual labor, the acceptance of woman as co-partner on a full basis of equality—and finally, the institution of adult education. Consider the main political innovations of Utopia. The common ownership of property, the closer union of town and country, the stabilization of the population, the provision of economic security, the transformation of a money economy into a planned economic order, with a six hour day and a share in all the work and full provision for the care of the aged—here were suggestions that were not merely critical and sly, but positive and beneficial. In More's Utopia there was no need for lawyers and no place for litigation: he bowed out his own class and guild. The love of gold was mocked by using that metal deliberately for the manufacture of chamberpots.

But the most significant fact about Utopia is the positive breath of freedom that sweeps through it. Freedom of action was deliberately encouraged; and alternatives were permitted even to such good customs as the nightly dining together in commons in the neighborhood community. Everywhere More introduced a shattering innovation: the principle of deliberate choice. Nowhere was this more conspicuous than in the Utopian provisions for religion: the commonwealth's original ruler believed that "if it should be the case that one religion is true and all the rest false . . . if the matter were dealt with reasonably and moderately, truth by its own natural force would come out and be clearly seen; but if there were contention and armed violence were employed, seeing that the worst men are always the most obstinate, the best and holiest religion would be overwhelmed. . . . So he left it all an open matter and made it free to each to choose what he should believe, save that . . . no one should fall so far below the dignity of human nature as to believe that the soul perishes with the body, or that the world is the mere sport of chance and not governed by divine providence."

This new sense of freedom rested on the possibility of economic equality: More goes back again and again to this point, in terms that leave no doubt as to where he stood. Not merely was the Christian religion favored in Utopia "when they heard that Christ approved the common way of living": but More boldly denounces the system whereby the idle classes live in grandeur and luxury, "doing nothing at all, or only that which is superfluous," while "in the meantime the day laborer, the carter, the smith, the husbandman by continuous toil . . . get such a poor living and live such a miserable life that the condition of beasts of burden might seem far preferable." What is this state, says More, except "a conspiracy of the rich who are aiming at their own advantage under the name and title of the commonwealth"?

The justification of economic equality, originally uttered by medieval protestantism in the form of denial, here came forth on positive grounds:

the duty of universal service and the right to an equal share in all the goods produced.

In short, this New World offered alternatives to the tyrannous customs and the customary tyrannies that governed so much of the Old World. On the other side of the globe men had managed things better, and by colonizing those distant lands the fettered European might find the freedom and the equality of which the common man began increasingly to dream. More's prophetic vision picked out all the principal objects on that distant horizon: even if their future shapes were vague, he placed them accurately. No small part of what he formulated in the sixteenth century became the working program of the democratic and socialist movements that took shape in the nineteenth century.

From More's time on, a growing body of people came to feel that Europe no longer mattered. They paid lip-service to its venerable institutions, they went through the motions of fealty; but their hearts were in the New World, and their actions falsified their open professions. At first dozens of men, then hundreds and thousands, no longer were content to sit at home and enjoy the delights of a relatively safe but limited existence, surrounded by the sanctities of home and Church. They would risk their lives, endure hideous suffering, cut themselves off from their kind for years at a time, in order to break loose from the parent body. Europeans ceased to be parts of a stable organism, anchored to its own past: they became active, motile, free-living, picking up their cultural good where they could find it, sampling everything, driven by a hunger that was partly curiosity, and by a curiosity that was partly a need for action. No longer were they content to stay in the old theater, with its fixed cast, its stock pieces, its too-well-remembered lines: they sought to improvise a new drama, and the first step toward that end was to change the scene. Scene-shifting was indeed the very symbol for this New World adventure: with an ocean voyage the past melted into air: the cloud-capped towers, the gorgeous palaces, the solemn temples dissolved: history could begin anew.

The scene changes. This device of the baroque theater now had its counterpart in life. What were exploring and pioneering and colonization but an attempt to consign the past itself to the lumber-room, and to solve man's social problems, not by disciplining and refining his whole nature but by changing his background alone?

In the medieval culture, Heaven was "given": it came as the ultimate reward for a life of renunciation or a moment of true repentance; but one's only prospective part in it was that of passive enjoyment: the bliss of immobility: peace. Now Heaven lay on the other side of the globe; it could be discovered by man, or at least the materials for it were lying there, waiting for man to shape them. The European saw in the relatively open and unoccupied lands of the New World a chance to slough off his past and make a fresh start. If the walled town was the symbol of the early medieval period, the sailing ship was the symbol of post-medieval adventure: for it gave large bodies of men a freedom of movement they had never known before—and a new field of action. Those who took their lives in their hands and went on long voyages across the seas, to New Spain or New England, to the Cape of Good Hope or the Malabar Coast, had a moral advantage over those they left behind.

Detached and disaffected men now appeared in every part of Europe: people who were unwilling to stand the gaff any longer, now that they knew there was an alternative. These people found the life of their parish dull and meaningless: impiously, they used the New World as a means of escape from control, from responsibility, from self-discipline. "Better to reign in Hell than to serve in Heaven," exclaimed Lucifer in Milton's Paradise Lost; and that was the temper in which countless people faced the prospect of finding a place in the New World. Once the daily network of human associations had become valueless, one place was as good as another, and the less its past was visible the more its future could be idealized. The hatches that kept the id in confinement were unbattened: before the ship was a day out of port the super-ego was bound, trussed, and tossed overboard. The spirit that animated this conquest was well summed up by the Abbé Raynal in the eighteenth century, in his classic treatise on colonization:

"Since the bold attempts of Columbus and of Gama, a spirit of fanaticism, till then unknown, hath been established in our countries; which is that of making discoveries. We have traversed, and still continue to traverse, all the climates from one pole to another, in order to discover some continent to invade, some islands to ravage, and some people to spoil, to subdue, and to massacre. Would not the person who should put an end to this frenzy deserve to be reckoned among the benefactors of mankind?"

In fact, the New World performed a two-faced service to the disintegrating medieval culture: it both hastened its end and made that end more tolerable by throwing open an alternative life, even to the poor craftsman, the shopkeeper, the peasant. In addition, it sent back to the Old World a host of sustaining foods and raw materials, to cushion its old age. In itself, the New World was both Utopia—the good place—and Penal Colony: both a haven of refuge and a place of bitter exile. To the farthest ends of the earth went the outcasts of Europe: those who sought salvation outside the established Churches; those who wished to throw off the irksome restraints of authority and who fled from their fathers instead of slaying them; or those who wished simply to better their condition in other lands where, as Adam Smith later observed, rent and profit did not eat up wages, and so the two superior classes were less tempted to oppress the large inferior one. Explorers and conquistadors, missionaries, traders, administrators, agricultural colonists—people who sought gold and loot, people who sought freedom, people who sought to solve the conflicts of society by living too far from their neighbors to quarrel with them—all these took possession of the New World and seized the fringes of Africa and Asia: forerunners of the tidal migrations of the nineteenth century.

The sense of the New World perhaps remained more alive in the imagination of Europe than in the practices of those who first took possession of it from the sixteenth to the eighteenth centuries. Once the breach was made, old memories welled up: weary and homesick, the new settler would reproduce in the New World the little Spanish or Dutch or English town from whence he had come. Generations, sometimes centuries, were needed before he felt at home enough to explore to the full the possibilities of the new life: two centuries separate Cotton Mather and Henry Thoreau.

With few exceptions, the new colonists established themselves by fraud and by main force: they came to exploit and dominate these new lands, rather than to fathom their true possibilities for human existence and charitably share their own blessings with those of the original inhabitants. Contempt and guilt mingled with this whole process of exploitation: once Western man admitted the contributions of the "inferior" races he could scarcely bear to look his own ugly conduct in the face. Hence he was more conscious of the precious gifts he gave to the native peoples than he was of the equally precious gifts he received from them: right down to our own day, the immense debt of Western culture in general, and especially of Western technics—Western man's particular pride—to the more primitive peoples has rarely been acknowledged, or even recognized. His ignorance and insolence served as hypnotics to Western man, and doubtless temporarily lessened his sense of guilt and self-reproach.

But the facts themselves should at least be noted. The New World was no mere treasure house of gold and silver and furs. It is from the Amerindian culture of the New World that over half the world's agricultural wealth is derived: from this source came the potato, which in the nineteenth century for the first time supplied Europe with a sufficient quantity of Vitamin D in winter, to say nothing of increasing the amount of daily energy; from Peru came the quinine which proved one of the few true specifics in the medicine chest up to the invention of the sulphur compounds. This is only a small part of the debt: Asia, Polynesia, Africa had likewise rich contributions to make. Too easily did the appropriators of these goods pose as their creators: too lightly did the discoverer claim the title of inventor.

Yet to forget the variety of material goods and the multiplicity of technical facilities which the age of exploration opened up, would be to forget one of the most important ingredients of the New World picture. Alternative stuffs, alternative methods, alternative finished products gave the common man opportunities that only a handful of rulers had hitherto possessed. The mind as well as the market was glutted with new goods. In seizing these goods, however, Western man made the fatal mistake of neglecting the cultures that had produced them: worse than that, he actively destroyed or lamed these cultures. He was still too sure of his Christian ideology, or he was already too preoccupied with his new capitalist and mercantilist accountancy, to make any reckoning of mankind's cultural losses from his conquest: nor did he have any appreciation of the permanent values of the primitive civilizations he despoiled.

The interest in the New World cultures as cultures, their due consideration as living communities that had given rise to values, meanings, forms, sometimes worthy to be put alongside the best that Palestine, Greece, or Rome could show, did not appear till most of the damage was done: till Western man had ravaged, defaced, or corrupted the people to whom he brought "civilization." By his very pride Western man contributed to his own impoverishment.

3: The Half-World of Science

The search for the fountain of youth and the riches of the Indies did not merely lure men to Florida with De Soto or to the Pacific Ocean with Magellan: it promoted the study of anatomy; it led to the testing of new chemical compounds; it kept the alchemist performing random experiments in his furnaces and retorts, in the hope that some lucky combination of magic words and chemical compounds would turn a pellet of lead into gold, or a tincture of alcohol into a powerful elixir, capable of renovating the human frame.

Paracelsus, in the sixteenth century, did not find gold; but he found something more precious, mercury, which happened to be a fairly helpful, if also pernicious, specific for the new disease, syphilis. What radium is to cancer today, mercury was originally to syphilis: its timeliness atoned for its therapeutic limitations. Leonardo da Vinci did not learn the secret of flight; but his observations of birds and his researches into anatomy put him on the trail which the inventors of the late nineteenth century were to follow to its appointed destination: the conquest of the air. Yet Leonardo's preoccupations with mechanical problems were only typical of a more general effort on the part of craftsmen, painters, and military engineers to exert a wider mastery over the new external forces that were at their command.

When one lays out all of Leonardo's brilliant inventions and anticipations, side by side with the speculative technics of later thinkers like Porta, Besson, Bacon, and Glanvill, one has a conspectus of a new world: the world of the machine. The belief that automatons would ultimately displace human labor was common to the new Utopias: Campanella, the Calabrian monk, was as sure of this in the seventeenth century as Bulwer-Lytton, the author of The Coming Race, was in the nineteenth century. The world that all these artists and technicians dreamed of and peopled in great detail was that in which twentieth century man actually lives. And like the microscopic fissures that can already be detected in an embryonic tooth, the weaknesses of our present mechanical order, the painful cavities that are now visible in the social structure that only a little while ago seemed so sound, were already in evidence by the seventeenth century. The worship of the machine went hand in hand with the displacement of the human.

The appetite for knowing the nature of the physical world by the methods of dissection and analysis must not be confused with medieval naturalism. Both efforts, indeed, centered on the external world; and in both cases there was an effort to break through a shimmering web of fantasies and obscure symbolisms and turbid desires in order to come closer to the actual nature of things. Accurate observation, keen sensory discrimination, systematic description, careful measurement, prompt notation, piecemeal analysis and piecemeal results, characterized this new search; but whereas medieval naturalism sprang largely from the study of medicine, the physical sciences owed a greater debt to the merchant with his systematic accountancy of money and to the metallurgist and the miner, with their systematic assault upon the natural environment.

These new quests of technics and physical science were prompted, in no small degree, by Western man's growing disregard for the human soul and for its ultimate fate in eternity. The new inventors sought to simulate life by mechanical motion, and to prolong life by transferring its attributes to machines. They dreamed of automatons that were "as good as alive": and Descartes, by a reverse process, demonstrated that all the attributes of living organisms could be explained in terms of mechanism —the human soul alone being politely left out of the reckoning, in deference to Christian theology. The machine, not man, became the measure of all things.

One may, however, measure the extent of this change by comparing Petrarch's Reflections in his "Solitude" with Francis Bacon's in The Advancement of Learning three centuries later. If practical inventors, Petrarch grudgingly admits, are entitled to honor, "provided it be human and reasonable . . . what glory shall be showered upon the inventors of literature and the noble arts, who have provided us not with a plow to make furrow nor woven garments for our bodies nor tinkling lures for our ears nor oil and wine for our gullet . . . but have furnished us with nobler instruments wherewith to procure nourishment, raiment, instruction, and healing for the mind?" There spoke a man who still put the things of the spirit at the summit of his grade of values.

Bacon turned these values upside down. The people who are honored as benefactors of the race in his fragmentary utopia, The New Atlantis, are all scientists or inventors of the practical arts. For Bacon the "seal and legitimate goal of the sciences is the endowment of human life with new inventions and riches." Feelings, emotions, states of mind, were becoming unreal to him and his scientifically minded contemporaries: they faced the perils of subjective hallucination by closing up that side of the personality and declaring it utterly bankrupt. All that had been freely expressed in medieval culture was now either completely segregated from the working mind, or it was repressed and driven underground.

Mark this change: it was to have important consequences. One of the chief marks of the ideological New World of science was the progressive abandonment of the inner and the subjective in every form: the irreal world of wish and fantasy became for the scientist an entirely unreal sphere: by definition it lay outside his province and by an ever-deepening prejudice, not effectively broken down until the emergence of psychoanalysis, it became "untouchable." Religion and the general care of the soul had a more or less honorific place in Bacon's scheme, a sort of clothing necessary for decency. But it had become expedient, indeed imperative, to separate the new book of God's works, which was natural philosophy, from the old book of God's word, which was revealed religion; and one must not unwisely let them mingle or confound their learnings together.

Thomas Aquinas's world presented man as shut up in himself—surrounded by self-conditioned ideas or divine revelations. Science opened up the external world and bade it welcome; but it shut out the self; it enlarged the horizon but contracted the center.

Here lay the beginning of a deeper split in the Western personality.

The separation of positive science from normative science, of instruments from ends, of causal knowledge from final knowledge tended to encourage the pursuit of the first and to belittle and devitalize the concern for the second. The very increase of scientific knowledge, however, only increased the need for moral discipline. To encourage a mature technique for controlling the external world and enlarging all of man's physical powers, whilst permitting man himself to remain at an infantile level, was to place dynamite in the hands of children. Leonardo deliberately suppressed his invention of the submarine, because he felt it was too devilish a contraption to be placed in the hands of wicked men: but that sound inhibition was not generally followed; nor would a merely negative action have been sufficient.

What was needed was a positive cultivation of humanistic knowledge, as rigorous, as extensive, as energetic, as that of science. Unfortunately the economic motive was lacking: the fuller development of the human personality did not promise large installments of riches. Hence the most important problem of all was left out of the new world-picture of science: who is to control the controller of nature? This weakness disguised itself as scientific purity, and this moral irresponsibility paraded itself as a godlike concern for truth alone: but in actual practice both qualities played sedulously into the hands of unscrupulous men and groups that were seeking for riches and power and that accepted no moral limits to the unqualified satisfaction of their egos. The very indifference of the scientist to the consequences of his thought—though it could be justified in an economy that gave full play to the whole personality—sanctioned a general indifference to the actual consequence of a new invention or a new industry upon the lives of the workers concerned and the social state of the whole community. The civilization so created, we have now learned to our bitter discouragement, utilizes its full energies only in war: its positive achievements all magnify the possibilities of destruction. . . .

Bacon had little conception of the *method* of science: on this matter a few pages of Galileo are worth the entire works of the Elizabethan courtier. In so far as Bacon conceived of a division of labor in science, he looked forward to a sort of graded officialdom in which each worker would attend to but a fragment of the process of discovery, in a sort of straight-line assembly of knowledge. But Bacon had, better than many of his more able technical and scientific contemporaries, a keen sense of science's immediate social goals and the part the sciences would play in creating a New World. With a far wider sweep of the imagination than the astronomers, physicists, or anatomists of his time, Bacon outlined the possible objectives of this new type of research—from hormone rejuvenation to the preservation of food by refrigeration. The mechanical arts, founded on nature, operated by scientific knowledge, were to him the social prime movers: he asserted plainly that printing, gunpowder, and the compass had "changed the experience and state of the whole world."

In the first edition of the New Atlantis there is a list of the gains that Bacon anticipated from scientific discovery. I shall set down only those that have been accomplished. "The prolongation of life: the restitution of youth in some degree: the retardation of age: the curing of diseases counted incurable: the mitigation of pain: more easy and less loathsome purgings: versions of bodies into other bodies: making of new species; instruments of destruction, as of war and poison: force of the imagination either upon another body or upon the body itself [autosuggestion and hypnotism]; acceleration of time in maturations: acceleration of germination: making rich composts for the earth: drawing new foods out of substance not now in use: making new threads for apparel, and new stuffs such as paper, glass, etc.: artificial minerals and cements." Note the importance of retardation and acceleration in this list: the conquest of time accompanied the conquest of space.

Moreover, Bacon saw that the universities of Europe, dedicated to the established professions, had no place for the arts and sciences not already attached to law, medicine, or theology. In a "device" or masque presented at the Christmas revels he appealed to the mock sovereign of the revels for the establishment of a large general library, a botanical garden, a museum of science and industry, and a laboratory fully equipped with "mills, instruments, furnaces, and vessels." "Miracles and wonders shall cease," Bacon boldly announced, "by reason that you shall discover their natural causes."

In recent years Bacon has been unfairly written down because he showed little comprehension of the important work being done by his contemporaries, Gilbert and Galileo, and because he had little immediate influence on the development of science through any experimental advances of his own. Even here his detractors have gone too far: for there is no doubt that his project for Salomon's House in the New Atlantis was directly responsible for the constitution of the Royal Society in London some half a century later—even though his project may have been occasioned by the actual founding of the earlier Academia Secretorum Naturae at Naples in 1560.

So, too, despite Bacon's palpable failings as both a scientist and a human being, he had a prophetic vision of the world to come: if it was less well-grounded than that of a Leonardo da Vinci, it was no less striking. Bacon looked forward to the "enlarging of the bounds of human empire," not merely for the improvement of man's estate but "to the effecting of all things possible." In his own philosophy, Bacon was concerned, not only for the promotion of biological and medical research no less than mechanical or physical investigation, but for a fuller study of mind-body relations: he looked forward to a development of the experimental method even in realms where mathematical knowledge was lacking or inapplicable.

But Bacon reckoned without his social milieu: a period of regimentation dominated by the twin gods, Mars and Mammon. The tendency of this culture was to narrow the scope of knowledge to the mechanical arts: might not more extensive investigations trespass on the established interests of the Church and the State? Little though the Roman Church might relish the upshot of Copernicus's investigations, in that they moved the center of gravity, so to say, from the earth to the sun, there was nothing of a heretical nature in the physical sciences themselves: quite the contrary. The pursuit of mechanics and hydrostatics infringed as little upon the holy dogmas as the invention of pumps and fountains: indeed, it took the inquiring mind off more dangerous subjects, like the scholarly investigations of history which established the fact that the Donations of Constantine, on which the Roman Church had rested its claim to temporal power, as directly taken over from the Roman state, was in fact a later forgery. This partition of interests, in turn, well suited the new practitioners of science, many of whom were merchants daily engrossed in the pursuit of pecuniary gain. Hence the founders of the Royal Society, according to John Wallis, barred "all discourses of Divinity, of State Affairs, and of News."

In other words, the sciences cut loose from the major provinces of human life at the very moment when physical discoveries and technological improvements were about to revolutionize both the material and the social basis of Western civilization. That proved a twofold misfortune: not merely were these departments left without the benefits of the scientific rationale, but the sciences themselves in perfecting the analytic method of dismemberment and dissociation, lost the sense of the whole and failed to develop a method of dealing with wholes.

The New World, as conceived through the mechanical sciences, was a world of isolates, presided over by isolatoes. The depersonalized scientist was at his best in a world from which the personality itself had been removed: his own first of all.

The immediate results of the new mechanical philosophy were plainly salutary, and the gains in knowledge were swift: the elliptical path of the planets, the speed of a falling body, the relationships between the pres-

VII. NATURE UNVEILED

Progressively, the natural world dominated the mind. In the 15th century the great landscape that spreads behind Hercules and Nessus already is more important than the mythical rape. In Brueghel's The Fall of Icarus all that remains of classical allusion is the famous inventor's leg—which Brueghel is pulling. The true subject of this landscape is Soil and Sea, Home and Adventure. Finally, in Ruysdael's landscapes, attention centers on earth and sky and sea, everywhere, beheld with eyes newly opened to their beauties, their uses, their significances.

VIII. ABSTRACTION OF THE OBJECT

Interest in the external world was not confined to the scientist. What the physicist observed in terms of matter and motion, the painter described in terms of light and shape, color and texture, seeking verisimilitude and life-likeness, independent of the more hieratic traditions of his art. The search for the object began early; but, as in the detail from Tintoretto's Last Supper (*top*) the object remained a subordinate part of a painting whose meaning lay elsewhere. In Vermeer's The Cook interest is divided between the figure and the utensils, both treated with almost photographic realism. But in the painting below the maid's face is hidden: she herself has become part of the "still-life." Finally, in Chardin's characteristic study (*bottom*) the object becomes completely detached from other human interests, and is significant in its own right: the breadishness of the bread, the copperiness of the copper, have become values. Nothing was quite real for primitive man until he subjectified it and personalized it: now the test of reality becomes objectification and depersonalization. The last step in this process is the invention of the camera, which transfers the very process of record to the machine. But nowhere is the elimination of the human complete: behind the most automatic machine still stands man, who designs, operates, utilizes it. Science itself now moves toward the recovery of the subjective: part of the renewal of interest in the organic and the human. Having by strenuous self-elimination achieved objectivity with respect to the external world, man must now by an equally rigorous discipline achieve a complementary subjectivity, by a renewed command of the inner world. Instead of freezing out feelings, emotions, internal states, he must utilize them more intensively and rationally: only so can he do full justice to all the dimensions of human experience. This healing of the split personality of modern man is today one of the critical tasks of education.

sure, temperature, and volume of a gas, the gravitation formula which gave a common denominator to the pull of the moon on the tides and the dropping of an apple to the earth—all these physical facts could now be described and summarized in accurate terms: the repeatable gave rise to the predictable, and what could be predicted could be circumvented or controlled. Mass, velocity, time, temperature, pressure, were all categories that fitted into the new mechanical picture, and what is more important, prepared men to deal more competently with the machines that human ingenuity was now creating. Crucial experiments and swift generalizations took the place of tedious extensive observations. History, as the cumulative enregistration of experience, could be discarded for practical purpose. Mechanical time was non-cumulative: it accompanied only changes of motion, changes of position, both open to external observation. This excluded the very stuff of the humanities: likewise the essential method. Participation and imitation, sympathy and empathy, which are the chief means of verifying subjective experience, remained outside the domain of science.

Now, every new quantum of accurate knowledge was precious: that fact must be emphasized before one proceeds to criticize science's self-imposed limitations. Accurate, repeatable, verifiable knowledge, based on a standardized technique and capable of creating universally valid results, was no longer confined to the ideal world of the mathematical sciences, but brought order and clarity to one whole aspect of reality—whatever could be conceived as a physical system and temporarily treated as such. The sciences that were so created were masterly symbolic fabrications: unfortunately, the symbols of science were treated as if they represented a higher order of reality, when they actually represented only a higher order of abstraction. Human experience itself remained, necessarily, multi-dimensional: one axis extended horizontally through the world open to external observation, the so-called objective world, and the other axis, at right angles, passed through the depths and heights of the subjective world.

Treating his own abstractions as primary elements, the new scientist discarded the complex data of actual experience: whatever was unmeasurable was not, for him, intelligible. In other words, the physical sciences tended to identify the quantitative with the real, the qualitative with the unreal. David Hume, who ably translated the practices and unconscious assumptions of science into metaphysical terms, put the scientific attitude in a nutshell. "When we run over libraries, persuaded of these principles, what havoc must we make? If we take in our hand any volume of divinity or school metaphysics, for instance, let us ask: *Does it contain any abstract reasoning concerning quantity or number?* No. *Does it contain any experimental reasoning concerning matter of fact and existence?* No. *Commit it then to the flames; for it can contain nothing but sophistry and illusion.*" In that dismissal Hume failed to take account of his own illusion: his identification of successful symbolization with the whole nature of reality.

The naïve metaphysical bias of seventeenth century science had an important effect upon the conceptual New World; and it ultimately had an effect upon the whole New World idolum. The impersonality of science was associated with many practical achievements that had a direct human value: it created a positive bias against feeling and emotion, as being inimical to cold reason and effective practice. A certain frigidity, a certain capacity for inhumanity, began to be a sign of the progressive mind. In an effort to avoid the perversion of truth through emotional distortion, the scientist was rightly on guard against an attitude which had undermined man's grasp of the external world; but as soon as he approached areas of human reality in which emotion and feeling must play a part in objective judgment, he leaned over backwards, and created a new kind of emotional distortion by the deliberate evisceration of feeling. He wisely learned to beware of the ways, "sometimes imperceptible, in which the affections color and infect the understanding," but he did not take account of the ways in which the understanding might repress and pervert the affections—and thus undermine the very impersonality the scientist sought to achieve.

Kepler had no sense of this danger, but he stated the bias of science very clearly in Volume I of his *Opera:* "As the ear is made to perceive sound and the eye to perceive color, so the mind of man has been formed to understand not all sorts of things but quantities. It perceives any given thing more clearly in proportion as that thing is close to bare quantities as to its origin, but the further a thing recedes from quantities the more darkness and error inheres in it." This divorce of the scientific mind from the rest of the body, even the eye and the ear in their qualitative capacities, was an attempt to secure accuracy even at the expense of truth. In both ways, the results were highly successful—but by that very fact the human personality became further disintegrated: a mind that is divorced from all the natural organs of personality is incapable of facing reality or of dealing with more than a fragment of human experience. Regimentation and fragmentation were the necessary outcomes of this pragmatic ego: an increasing mechanical subdivision of the productive processes not merely in science and in industry, but in education and government.

The extraordinary advances of the physical and mathematical sciences in the seventeenth century made this one of the great world epochs of thought: that is beyond dispute. The very limitations of the scientific method turned it into a marvelous labor-saving device: for by stressing uniformities and forgetting the complexities of history, the scientist was able to explore the physical world methodically: when one has abolished organisms a relatively small quantum of matter, which can be weighed, crushed, dissolved, or otherwise subjected to experimental examination may stand for a much vaster quantity and a larger number of instances. So rich and stimulating was this period that its great philosophers still loom high above the horizon: in particular, Pascal and Leibnitz show an understanding that transcends even the limitations of the mechanical world picture itself. One is not surprised to find in Leibnitz's conception of the monad a logical exposition of a non-materialist interpretation of "matter," in which mind and body are unified at the very starting point, and the classic atom is dropped in favor of an energy quantum that has no dimensions.

But popular interest in these thinkers was strong precisely where their thoughts were most closely in harmony with the new conception of the world itself as a machine, and of man as a special kind of contrivance, a self-regulating automaton: a view best represented by another scientific philosopher, Descartes. Utilizing only a part of man's faculties, the scientist sought to explain a part of his actions in terms of a part of the world. Unfortunately, this fractional milieu was described as the real universe, and the mechanical Caliban who inhabited it became the paragon of the New Man. This new world had no place for either the divine or the fully human: both Ariel and Prospero were banished.

4: The Moral Authority of Science

So much for the limitations of the mechanical idolum. Nevertheless the systematic exploration of every part of the physical universe had a similar effect to the exploration of the globe itself: it was a powerful agent of release, and it opened up new horizons for human effort. The natural sciences carried into the life of the mind a little of that democratic respect for human handiwork which the artist and the craftsman of the Middle Ages had held; but which the universities had never properly appreciated. For the older type of scholar, the mind was supposed to operate by its own motive power alone, on its own subject matter: by the strict ordering of concepts, axioms, and propositions, the eye and the hand were rendered inoperative or, at least, insignificant. The alchemist and the natural philosophers, in their new laboratories and observatories, had a different notion: Bacon cited the alchemists as calling upon men to sell their books and to build furnaces: "quitting and forsaking Minerva and the Muses as barren virgins and relying upon Vulcan." Paracelsus, he whose loud claims gave the word bombast to the world, was humble enough to learn from the miners of the Harz Mountains, and Agricola, too, was taught by the miners and metal workers of Saxony. The sailor, seeking to plot his course more accurately and swiftly, made new demands upon the astronomer, the mathematician, and the inventor: the sextant, the chronometer, and logarithm tables were all direct answers to this demand. Bernard Palissy, who himself began life as a potter, proceeded from an interest in his potter's clays and glazes to his brilliant studies in geology.

For the schoolmen, knowledge came either through divine revelation or through the skillful manipulations of signs and symbols: they were not interested in creating new truths, but were rather content to refine and refurbish truths that were already, to all appearances, solidly established. For the scientist, on the other hand, fresh discoveries were more important than certainty: as long as he made progress, he preferred to leap from hummock to hummock in the swamp of his ignorance, rather than to stay in one spot and attempt to sound bottom: did he not indeed suspect that what lay beneath the mat of accumulated experience was bottomless? The scientist therefore sought truth through a systematic exploration and manipulation of the environment: hence manual skill, skill in lens grinding, in making balances, in blowing glass and baking porcelain, now became useful for the pursuit of knowledge: the basic processes of science, as Dr. Charles Singer well points out, were originally the work of artists—Leeuwenhoek discovered micro-organisms because he had the patience and zeal to grind his own minute lenses, just as Galileo privately invented the telescope. If the conceptual frame of science had no place for the full human personality, in its actual operations it partly made good this lack: man the worker became companion to man the knower.

From now on no one was excluded from the circle of scientific workers, provided he added a grain of verifiable knowledge to the countless sands of empiric fact. Common workmen, amateurs, outsiders had a part in making this New World, though only the creators and manipulators of its symbols could enlarge its boundaries and fully exploit its resources. For this reason, Leibnitz was anxious that German should supplant Latin as the medium of instruction in his own country, so that new knowledge might be open to the whole nation.

Not less important than this extension of thought by operative and manual exercises was the discovery of a method for establishing agreement. Here the most radical transformation took place. Scholastic philosophy rested its hope for agreement upon authority: every chain in logical reasoning must ultimately lead back to an indisputable source, a passage in an accepted treatise: finally to the revealed word of God. If this final rock should crumble, the structure established on it must inevitably fall down; and this, in fact, was what went on happening as men applied the methods of common sense and reason to an examination of Biblical and saintly revelation.

Scientific reasoning, on the other hand, rested on a floating foundation. Observation, manipulation, and measurement furnished the basis of interpretation; and a process of going forward, from hypothesis to observation, from observation to experiment, from experiment to prediction, from prediction to verification, now served instead of a retrospective appeal to the old, the established, the venerable. By making additions to knowledge in small, carefully tested increments, instead of large, sweeping statements whose acceptance would transform every part of the structure, the scientist made it possible to correct error or approximate more closely to truth without having to begin all over again. The very method was self-corrective: nor was it necessary to prop up an original error because it had become so deeply embedded in the resulting structure that its removal might cause even the sound parts to collapse. Even fundamental over-all changes in science, from Newtonian to post-Newtonian physics, from creationism to transformism in biology, still leave the constituent increments of verified truth intact: they serve like permanent officials who carry on no matter how radically the government itself may change. This was a precious contribution: a great advance over dogmatic religion.

Science did not overthrow either intuition or authority: it placed them within an organization that subjected them to constant scrutiny and open correction. The sciences relied, not on a single authority, but on the multiplied evidence of countless men, endowed with the same faculties, ballasted by the same education, modified by differences in temperament and outlook and capacity. Individual scientists could and would continue to err; but the sciences themselves would become more accurate. The underlying postulates might change; individual parts might be revised; but the whole structure nevertheless remained intact.

This was such a radical change in the procedure for arriving at truth that scientists themselves for long failed to understand the implications of their method. Great as Sir Isaac Newton was as a mathematical physicist, he showed a testy dislike of all criticism, and stood on his authority with as much insolence as an absolute prince. But science was essentially an open synthesis: open at both ends, at the top for each accretion of fresh knowledge, and at the bottom for each necessary modification of its own metaphysical and logical substratum.

I have dwelt at length on this transformation, because it gave science, from the seventeenth century on, a moral authority that had once been pre-empted by the Church. Not merely was all our verifiable knowledge about the cosmos in the hands of men detached from the Church, but the divine attributes of disinterestedness and impersonality now went with science, rather than with theology. If the outlook of the scientist was restricted to external phenomena, his method was nevertheless exemplary in every department of thought. In a time of deepening schisms it created solid common ground. Humanistic scholarship progressively recorded that change: turning from the external authority of Aristotle it re-acquired and extended his method.

Christian discipline had, however, been carried over into science, as monastic regularity had been carried over into capitalism. Whitehead points out how substantially the scholastic view of a rational order in nature contributed to the common use of the experimental method, giving science a faith that its separate findings would eventually fit together and make sense. So, too, the Calvinist doctrine of predestination lent itself to the conception of scientific necessity. Halley's successful forecast of the appearance of his comet in the seventeenth century did much to transfer the sense of the miraculous from the unpredictable to the predictable event.

Finally, the ascetic element in Christianity was carried over into the scientific laboratory: not what one wishes to find, but what one actually finds without respect to one's wishes or hopes, became the hallmark of science. Self-restraint and self-abnegation were carried to a high point. There is no little suggestion of Christian asceticism in science's willingness to deal with disagreeable facts, to encounter repulsive sights: once the attributes of sainthood. In the Middle Ages a saint might wash a leper's sores: in the seventeenth century Athanasius Kircher will dare to look at the blood of a plague victim and discover, in the crawling white worms that are visible under the microscope, the first evidence of the germ theory of disease. This willingness on the part of the scientist to face facts and to venture into the unknown, heightens the likeness between the new terrestrial exploration and the new intellectual explorations.

In sum, the same underlying animus prompted the explorer and the scientist, the pioneer and the inventor. They opened up new fields for rapid colonization and exploration: they fostered an immense expansion of human powers. But the New World that they revealed was but a half-world; and in their impatience to exploit it swiftly and profitably they overlooked no small part of the real world's essential characteristics and its permanent values.

5: Social Atomization and Uniformity

The opening up of the New World, then, had a profound effect upon the human personality: it gave scope and power to the dissociated man, the man who could readily divorce himself from his birthplace, his traditions, his community, his family ties. The traveler, the explorer, the colonist were people who dissociated themselves easily in space: the archaeologist, the classic humanist, the collector of antiques were those who dissociated themselves in time. One way or another, the living connection with Europe's historic culture, in which the personality of Western man had originally been formed, was broken: and those who were spiritually prepared to make the break found the New World more easily and lived there more happily.

Now, from the standpoint of personality, this period of expansion must be looked upon as one of disintegration: the outer man flourished but the inner man shrank, and the strains produced by this process opened up serious cracks which weakened the whole structure. Opposed to this interpretation is the more common notion that this process was beneficial to the personality and indeed created a new type, that of modern man himself, whose very dissociation and fragmentation were an indication of his freedom. This idea was sedulously advanced by the great cultural historian, Burckhardt, in the middle of the nineteenth century: he asserted that while in the Middle Ages "man was conscious of himself only as member of a race, people, party, family, or corporation" in the renascence "man became a spiritual individual."

This interpretation rests on a false conception of personality: a conception which in fact accepts the medieval belief in a permanent soul that is unaffected by the accidents of historical development, and which encourages the mistaken belief that one can find out the true nature of man without reference to what he sees, does, eats, handles, feels, believes, loves, hates, attaches himself to. This so-called spiritual individual is a romantic ghost. When one strips man of all his functions as a "member of a race, people, party, family, or corporation" one reduces the very province of personality; for personality emerges, not by a rejection of social ties, but by their more complete assimilation and incarnation. The unfettered individual was less of a man than the man of the Middle Ages: the proof of this is that he was presently forced, like the despot, to take to himself privately all the functions of society in order to be truly alive.

The wholeness of the individual depends upon his association within a whole community. Those who escaped the claims and duties of life in a community did not achieve freedom. They either floated in a void of self-indulgent fantasy or they sank down to the level of animal existence; and they proved this by their capacity for violence, brutality, deviltry.

In point of fact, social detachment is death. At every minute the detached individual is kept alive by the labors of other men, by knowledge he has acquired in society, by hopes and dreams that recall his social affiliations: the very words he uses to deny the claims of society are themselves the oldest artifacts of human society. "I think, therefore I am" proves nothing about the existence of a thinking individual, contrary to Descartes; but it does point to the indubitable existence of human society: the words as such indicate the existence of *other* selves and imply the entire history of the human race. To lose hold of this social tissue is to court madness and even risk physical death: that is why the stranded explorer and the lost aviator wisely keep themselves alive by making records for those who may find their dead body or by holding on in their own minds to the images of their families and friends. Thus they reinforce, by psycho-social devices, the mere animal will-to-live. At its best, the act of detachment is only a preliminary step to joining another society, actual or imagined. We saw this take place before in the passage from the Classic to the Christian order.

Burckhardt indeed was on the trail of the essential truth about the new "individual" when he observed that the private man, indifferent to politics, "seems to have been first fully formed in the despotisms of the fourteenth century." That points to a more correct interpretation. What was called freedom was freedom to do without society: freedom to withdraw from public life and give up active associations with one's neighbors and fellow-guildsmen: the "individualism" of isolation. But no community can long exist when it fosters this dissociation and disconnection: artificial elements of cohesion must be found if the natural alliances and sympathies are withdrawn. So it is no accident that an age which boasted its freedom, its individualism, its contempt for historic ties and traditional civic duties, should also have succumbed to absolutism and have widened the province of the uniform. An impulse toward unbounded individual self-assertion was checked by an equal impulse to servile conformity. One might defy the moral laws of God and man, provided one did not ignore the latest fashion in wigs or ruffs. Abandoning the search for spiritual unity, the atomic individual accepted mechanical uniformity.

6: The Book and Book-learning

As the ideological New World took form, it became plain that some special preparation must be made for entering it. Left to themselves, the greater part of the community would cling sluggishly to the established forms of religion, thought, and technics: they would dig and mine and build as their ancestors had done before them, following the well-marked ruts in the road. What, then, was the essential instrument that overcame this inertia? Nothing less than the printed word. The invention of printing from uniform movable type, which had spread with incredible rapidity from Korea to Europe in the fifteenth century, was the new carrier of the common life. Those who would read the printed word became part of a new community, the literate: instead of resting content with the little they could see, hear, or feel in their immediate neighborhood, they became part of an ever-enlarging group for whom secondhand experiences, simulated feelings, and verbal understandings of matters hitherto out of sight and out of mind occupied a larger share of their daily life. The book became the prime agent of community; and the process of embodiment no longer demanded the co-operation of all the other arts, as it had in the days of the Cathedral. Paper became the chief medium of embodiment: to become real was to exist on printed paper.

Before the fifteenth century, the higher culture of a civilization was confined to a minority in every community for a very simple reason: that part of it which was transmitted other than by word of mouth rested on the existence of hand-copied books: at the height of Roman civilization, despite a great corps of slaves, perhaps a few thousand copies was the very highest circulation any single book could achieve: right down through the Middle Ages, a few hundred manuscripts for each title, sometimes only a few dozen, served to perpetuate and to spread the science, literature, philosophy, and religion of the ancient world. So narrow was the margin, that an act of deliberate persecution, such as the burning of the books in China, or the persecution of the Albigensians in Provence, could wipe out a whole literature, without the possibility of a single book's escaping intact.

By reason of the invention of printing, the personal power of the writer whose works might be printed and reprinted in age after age was increased potentially many millionfold: so that for the first time it was possible to think of a writer addressing mankind, without meaning by mankind solely the chosen few who exercised political and economic power. Printing broke the class monopoly of culture. Though for a while this monopoly was maintained in some degree by the high capital cost of establishing a press, and by various restrictive privileges that were handed down by the State to control the production and distribution of books, in the long run the printing press was a great agent of cultural diffusion and equalization. No treasury in Mexico or Cuzco was equal in value to the immaterial heritage that now, for the first time in history, became open to the race.

As long as books had been few and precious, their function was necessarily restricted; and young and old were forced to rely heavily upon their own immediate experiences and their own fantasies for both knowledge and entertainment. The printed word changed this: it fostered a purely verbal and dialectic approach to life, and gave to the writer a higher authority than the painter, the sculptor, or the musician could exercise. This change worked great gains and great losses: the first have usually been magnified and the second overlooked. Because of the authority of the printed word, every member of the community now became a schoolman, or at least a candidate for the school, no matter what his future profession. Whereas the grammar schools of the Middle Ages had taught the rudiments of calculation and writing and reading to the sons of the rising bourgeoisie, from the sixteenth century on there was a growing demand for schools that should teach every class and that should instruct children, by book, in all that seemed worth knowing.

In short, the mass production of books, which the invention of printing made possible, was followed immediately by a demand for the mass production of suitable standardized minds: indeed, one was dependent upon the other, and they were tied together by a common belief in the reproductive process itself.

Note that the belief in wholesale systematic education took shape in the sixteenth century; but at first the spread of book knowledge was looked upon merely as supplementary to the more usual practices of acquiring and enlarging experience. Thus Luther said that "my idea is to let boys go to . . . school for one or two hours daily and spend the remainder of the time working at home, learning a trade, or doing whatever their parents desired; so that both study and work might go hand in hand while they were young and able to do both. They spend at least ten times as much time with their pea shooters or playing ball or racing and tussling." In his Preface to an Ordinance of a Common Chest, Luther suggested that the expropriated monasteries should be turned into schools for boys and girls; and he appealed "To the Councilmen of all Cities in Germany that they establish and maintain Christian Schools," so that children might acquire "languages, the other arts, and history." The training that is undertaken at home, Luther went on to observe, "attempts to make us wise through our own experience," and that seemed to him a task for which life itself was too short. Education, that is book-learning, was supposed to abbreviate the slow necessities of life: a typical New World concept; a veritable Baconian "acceleration" of mental germination.

Provisions for founding schools were common to all the reformers: Calvin founded academies and schools in Geneva, and when his theology was transported to Scotland with John Knox, a school as well as a church was planted in every parish: indeed, it was in the congregational communities of New England that free compulsory primary education was introduced in 1647, by order of the General Court of Massachusetts. The man who first unified the whole process of education and associated it with the nation itself was the great Moravian teacher, John Amos Komensky, whose humanist name was Comenius. He associated each stage of intellectual growth with an appropriate institution: the mother's knee, the vernacular school, the Latin School or Gymnasium, and finally, the University and Travel. His treatise on education, The Great Didactic, was perhaps the first to seize the revolutionary implications of systematic universal education; and it was the first to propose a thorough union of head, heart, and hand; for pictorial illustrations and manual exercises were placed on a par with verbal discipline.

Comenius was the paragon of modern schoolmasters; but he endeared himself to later generations less by his pedagogical insight than by his errors. He was completely under the spell of the mechanical world picture: note his description of the "movements of the soul." "The most important wheel is the will; while the weights are the desires and affections which incline the will this way or that. The escapement is the reason, which measures and determines what, where, and how far anything should be sought after or avoided." With that ideological basis, it is not surprising that Comenius's whole conception of education was based on the requirements for mass production. In his endeavor to make education cheap enough to include the poor, he sought to effect economies by the skillful arrangement of time. Long before Lancaster and Bell in England, Comenius invented the monitorial system of teaching, as a means of reducing costs. "I maintain," he said, "that it is not only possible for one teacher to teach several hundred scholars at once, but that it is also essential." On no account, Comenius specifically warns, was the teacher to give individual instruction.

"As soon as we have succeeded in finding the proper method," Comenius elsewhere explains, "it will be no harder to teach schoolboys, in any number desired, than with the help of the printing press to cover a thousand sheets daily with the neatest writing." Close upon this follows a revealing sentence: "It will be as pleasant to see education carried out on my plan as to look at an automatic machine, and the process will be as free from failure as these mechanical contrivances when skillfully made." Precisely; and what Comenius formulated in the seventeenth century, Gradgrind and M'Choakumchild will carry out in the nineteenth.

Comenius invented modern pedagogy and helped ruin modern education. He sought to make the school a self-sufficient environment; and by a rigorous control of the process of teaching he tried to ensure the production of a uniform human type: the mass citizen, so to say, of the modern State. For Comenius, as for his fellow-encyclopedist, J. H. Alsted, and as later for John Locke, the mind of the pupil was a blank sheet of paper. The task of education was to leave on this sheet the desired imprint. Again the image of the printing press. Again an unconscious tendency to rely upon the formal processes of despotic authority. The new schoolmaster mistook printed symbols for knowledge and verbal instruction for discipline: like the inventor and the physical scientist, he achieved a partial mechanical order—and eliminated life. From the beginning, the humanitarian ideal of a systematic education for all was combined with a mechanical pedagogy that invalidated it; and this weakness was the very point upon which the most vehement reformers were agreed. Witness Pestalozzi in How Gertrude Teaches Her Children, published in 1801. "I believe that we must not dream of making progress in the instruction of the people as long as we have not found the forms of instruction which make of the teacher . . . the simple mechanical instrument of a method which owes its results to the nature of its processes, and not to the ability of the one who uses it." In that spirit the teacher, whose greatest gift is the capacity to inspire the love of his pupils and make use of that love for their own self-development, has been sedulously transformed into the pedagogical technician: the exponent and the victim of a method. Only with difficulty have real teachers survived that discipline.

The mechanization of education, if conceived as early as the sixteenth century, did not finally take hold on a large scale before the nineteenth century. Its ultimate perversion, as elaborated in the credit accountancy practiced in American schools and colleges, in which knowledge itself is reduced to that which can be automatically regurgitated in examinations and evaluated by mechanical devices, has become fully apparent only in our own day. But the essentially complementary nature of the various means that were invented for mechanizing the mind must be understood. Because of the ingrained anti-communal, anti-personal bias of the New

World ideology, all the great devices of liberation—not least of course the machine itself—tended to work in precisely the opposite direction. The axioms of this new education were well laid down by Alsted: they indicate how far the dissociation from the historic, the communal, the organic, the personal, had gone. Alsted addresses schooolmasters in these words:

"Men are by nature a *tabula rasa,* on which nothing is written, and on which anything you please may be inscribed. . . . Man is by nature like a white line which can be given any colour . . . Men when first born into the light of day are like stones out of which you may fashion any sort of figure." From this time on every ruler of men will implicitly hold these words in mind when he seeks to maintain his power; every reformer will seek to make his will prevail by the same method: Condorcet will petition for national schools and Napoleon will establish them. The reasons will be lofty: education will speak for piety and the vocation of man, for reason and the Will of God, for the banishment of servile ignorance and the establishment of a more perfect society. But all these purposes will be betrayed by the intellectual method and the actual social context. The underlying aim of New World education will be the fabrication of Mechanical Man: one who will accept the mechanical world picture, who will submit himself to mechanical discipline, who in thought and act will enlarge the empire of the machine.

Was this aim only imperfectly accomplished? Naturally enough; and that came about for an unshakable reason: the real world continued to exist, and men were forced from time to time to confront it even when their symbols led them astray. Large tracts of life never fitted, despite the most strenuous efforts, into the new ideology. Dickens was right: the circus manager, Sleary, knew more about life than the utilitarian educator, Gradgrind. The new mechanical dream remained a dream no less than the old Christian dream of angels, sprites, demons.

7: The Mechanical Idolum

So it came about that the discovery of the New World, on all its levels, was a process which both extended and narrowed human experience. It covered vast territory, hitherto untraversed by the human mind, and it measured that territory accurately. There was no part of life, in fact, where instruments of measurement might not penetrate, to do away with uncertainty and guesswork: Torricelli used a column of mercury to measure the pressure of air, and Sanctorius, with the aid of another tube of mercury, the thermometer, measured the heat of the human body. These measurements brought real gains in predicting the turn of the weather or the reaction of the body in fever. Detail by detail, by a simple logical process, new knowledge was created; one conclusion—as Descartes pointed out—led inevitably to another, provided that one accustomed oneself to taking short steps, and did not attempt like the metaphysicians to cover the whole distance in a single jump. This continence, this patience, this restraint, were all admirable qualities. So far good.

The new skeleton of knowledge was beautifully articulated: the bones were scraped and scoured with loving care: but the organs and the flesh had been removed, and the breath of life was gone. The interests of physical science were indeed well symbolized by the figure that now became popular in art: the human skeleton. It appears in the earliest known printed woodcut, The Dance of Death; it then is repeated in pictures, on tombstones, on the frontispiece of books. Here was the irreducible geometrical form of the human body: all that was organic, therefore delicate, transitory, precarious, subtile, now was reduced to something solid, definite, clear. Clarity at the expense of life. But what clarity! Read Galileo, Descartes, Spinoza, Newton, Locke: it is like taking a bath in crystal-clear water. Their universe is clean, neat, orderly, without smells, without flavors, without the rank odors of growth, impregnation, or decomposition: above all, without the complications of real life. Their maps show the bare physical contours of the landscape: if one remains in the air they are adequate. But this new world picture gives no hint of the soil, the bacteria, the mat of vegetation, the animal life: it retreats from the dense atmosphere of actual experience to the stratosphere of its own rarefied abstractions. All the forms and processes of reality, to which other ages had given a full, if muddied, expression by means of fable, superstition, myth, allegory, now dropped off in the fresh water bath of science, as the barnacles that impede a ship drop off when it casts anchor in the channel of a mountain stream.

No doubt the ship sailed faster: but what was it that dropped off? Precisely that which involves the community and the personality: organic experience, memory, feeling, the unconscious: the non-uniform and the non-repeatable: those very elements which cannot be acquired in a single sitting or repeated in a modest experiment: in short, human history, the results of *life*time, and the accumulation of lifetimes. René Descartes gave expression to the New World distrust of history in a significant passage in his Discourse on Method. "I fancied that those nations which, starting from a semi-barbarous state and advancing to civilization by slow degrees, have had their laws necessarily determined, as it were, forced upon them simply by the experience of the hurtfulness of particular crimes and disputes, would by this process come to be possessed of less perfect institutions than those which, from the commencement of their association as communities, have followed the appointments of some wise legislator." This false simplicity, this deceptive neatness, were purchased at a price.

For if the new mechanical order was strict and geometrical it allowed fitful, unexpected, speculative elements to gain the upper hand outside its narrow realm. And as anarchy forever lurks beneath the outward forms of tyranny, so chaos lurked beneath the uniformities of physical science. Once present time becomes more important than life's manifold connections between past and future, the mere contemporaneity of events gives them a special value. Whatever is, is important, once origins and consequences are left out of account. Now, no small part of the merchant's success between the sixteenth and the nineteenth centuries often rested on his advance knowledge of accidental, unpredictable events: the breaking out of a war might close a trade route, or a shortage of wheat in England might give an opportunity to corner the wheat market in Rostock. To get such information, big merchants and financiers had their agents posted in every part of Europe: the news furnished by such agents contributed in no small measure to the huge financial profits of the great Augsburg banking house, that of the Fuggers. These valuable private communications presently were gathered together to form a new institution, the newspaper: the first on record was the *Avisa, Relation, oder Zeitung,* which began weekly publication in Augsburg in 1609.

The newspaper was primarily a record of political and financial items: the price of corn, the sailing of ships, rumors of war, reports of negotiations and treaties, announcements of new business enterprise. Dealing with the facts of human association, the newspaper's contents was a litter of disconnected events. To have a place in a newspaper an event must have taken place in actual life; it must be reported by an eye-witness or indirectly obtained from one; above all, it must not be a product of rational thought or poetic imagination. The more singular an event, the more important it was for a newspaper. This disorderly collection of the contemporaneous events was, in a sense, a massive counterpoise to baroque uniformity. What now? What next? are the questions that arise before the reader of the newspaper. To become acquainted with disconnected happenings, day by day, week by week, imported new excitements into an otherwise increasingly regular and uniform existence. The newspaper bound together the scattered fragments of life by the simple mechanical device of putting them all under the same dateline.

As with many other inventions, the social function preceded the mechanical instrument. Just as photography appeared in the realism of the

Low Country painters centuries before Daguerre's great invention, so love of news preceded the newspaper. In 1550 Robert Crowley said:

Some men do delight
strange news to invent
Of this man's doing
and that man's intent;
What is done in France
and in the emperor's land;
And what thing the Scots
do now take in hand;
What the king and his council
do intend to do;
Though for the most part
it be nothing so.

As time went on, the tempo of news increased: by the beginning of the eighteenth century a daily paper, *The Daily Courant,* appeared in London. Decade by decade the local news included more varied items and the foreign news more distant items; and decade by decade the news was presented more quickly and the number of editions multiplied, till finally by the twentieth century, the reader of newspapers expected fresh news from hour to hour, and the trivial became important as long as it could be served up as news. This combination of rigorous periodicity and mechanical proficiency with social fragmentation and disorganization makes the newspaper a true symbol of the new world picture. With all its mechanical triumphs, with all its uniformities, this new order remained pseudo-rational: indeed, it was a systematic devaluation of rational order. In the newspaper and the encyclopedia the external order of the calendar and the alphabet concealed the conflicts and irrationalities of actual existence: the absence of true organic relationships in either life or mind.

In such a dispersed and scattered world, a world of random events, inarticulate "news," it would seem absurd to look for any comprehensive synthesis. If this feat is conceivable, it will be only within the limited world of mechanics: certainly Newton's Laws of Gravitation came close to such an achievement. Not that the attempt will remain unmade: so great is the need for unity in every period that partial syntheses, pro-syntheses, now make their appearance in greater number than ever: for the culmination of the baroque effort is a series of philosophical systems, each one of which attempts to encompass, on the basis of a purely personal vision, every part of the universe.

The great mark of these systems is their solid contempt for their successors and their contemporaries: there is no attempt to fit, to articulate, to inter-relate, to build: that effort was ended with Thomas Aquinas. No: now each philosopher is a despot in his own right: he has his private system, his own code of laws, his own way of looking at things: you shall see every part of the world through his eyes, no more, no less: if by chance he takes as his starting point another philosophic system, it is only for the sake of pushing it farther away from him when he leaps.

Spinoza sought to build the certainties of God and political freedom and ethical order on a few well-chosen postulates and theorems about life: Descartes combined geometry with experiments in physics and mechanics to arrive at certainty: Leibnitz, with a profounder logic and an amazing wealth of curiosity and scholarly skill, came perhaps nearer than any other to open the way to a true synthesis; his only serious rival before Kant was Vico. But all these efforts were partial, incomplete: in their tidiness they disregarded the complexities of existence, and in their attempt to establish exact truth they forgot, until Vico reminded them, that truth may lie outside the bounds of mathematical inventory. The very agreement on method that made scientific advance possible lessened the likelihood of synthesis: for that agreement left out of account the whole nature of man and nullified his subjective creations.

8: The Emergence of "Modern Man"

These, then, were the ideological foundations of "Modern Man." The concept of Modern Man must be taken as an historical term which covers a type of existence, a mode of thought and social life, an ego and a super-ego, which first took shape around the fifteenth century. The word modern was used to distinguish the contemporary beliefs of this period from those which were held by the ancients: later it became a term of special eulogy, as the moderns became more proud of their achievements and more confident of their position. Nothing that twentieth century man sang in self-praise could surpass that which Voltaire bestowed on the seventeenth century. And by now the triumph of Modern Man has resulted in a profound irony: he himself is dated—as dated as the "advanced" men and women in Bernard Shaw's early plays.

The very word modern comes from a Latin word which means "just now." To be modern means, accordingly, to be in the mode: that is, fashionable—which means to discard the past as one would discard last year's garment, and to wear the same uniform as one's contemporaries. In the sixteenth century the term "new-fangled" was still a constant epithet of reproach: Philip of Spain later classes "innovators" with insolvents, malcontents, and lawless men. But presently the newness of a custom ceased to weigh against it: to smoke a pipe, to ride in a stagecoach, to eat potatoes, to drink tea, to prefer Descartes to Aristotle or Swift to Juvenal ceased to be a daring solecism. Change, innovation, progress, became the order of the day. With this a new faith dawned: the latest and newest is the best. So let us act "that each tomorrow finds us *farther* than today." The calendar simplified the whole problem of values: to be outdated was to be emptied of value. That was too simple.

In brief, Modern Man was an ideological scarecrow: a creature formed during the period of expansion, and destined to live only as long as the conditions and needs that gave rise to him continued in existence. Being the product of an age of expansion, he believed whole-heartedly, fervidly, in movement and locomotion: no small part of his existence was devoted to accelerating the speed of the sailing ship, the railroad train, or the airplane. The abstractions of time, energy, and money are more real to him than any other system of abstractions, and from them he deduces a quantitative ideal of life: more energy, more speed, more motion, more money, more time. By crowding his sensations and multiplying the eventfulness of his days, he hoped to achieve a fuller life: the speedup, so far from being a recent device to get more work out of the factory operative, is a universal conception. Modern Man believes in the mechanical world picture, not as a useful instrument of order—which it is—but as a final revelation of truth. Whatever does not fit into this idolum ceases to be real. Objective uniformity: subjective chaos.

Modern Man fashioned himself for the conquest of the external world: he had faith in machines and that faith was justified by works. He projected the infantile dream of limitless power upon adult society and looked forward to a time when a push button would command food as easily as the infant's cry brings the bottle or the breast. But after four centuries of strenuous effort his mythic powers are still illusory. Despite his machines he starves in the midst of plenty: despite his knowledge of distant stars and intra-atomic worlds, the civilization he has created has given rise to a barbarism that now has swept across the planet. In a series of world wars and world revolutions Modern Man has in fact been painfully committing suicide.

CHAPTER VIII. THE INSURGENCE OF ROMANTICISM

1: Faith in Progress

"Energetic faith in the possibilities of social progress has been first reached through the philosophy of sensation and experience." Those words of John Morley referred to the working beliefs of Locke and Newton; but the more one ponders this generalization the more it wears an air of paradox. Christianity had at least believed in Heaven as a goal, but the new mechanist philosophy, banishing Heaven, removed values even from the earth. What hopes, what guarantees, could that philosophy give for a better future?

Progress, however, may be considered in two ways: getting closer to a goal or getting farther away from a starting point. The exponents of progress, taking their own superiority for granted, emphasized the second meaning. What Hume, Voltaire, or d'Holbach meant by progress was the casting loose from a past crippled by negative values: brutality, superstition, ignorance, misery.

The belief in social improvement rested upon a new confidence in man's native impulses and his power to master his own destiny: its very optimism released the actions that justified it and delivered the emancipated minds of the eighteenth and nineteenth century from that tired worldly wisdom, that despair which excused lethargy, that pessimism which condoned injustice, into which Christianity had finally settled. But intelligent observers had premonitions of disaster even at the very peak of achievement. Thus as early as the sixteenth century Louis le Roy had observed that "it is to be feared that, having reached so great excellence, power, wisdom, books, industries will decline, as has happened in the past, and disappear." And at the beginning of the eighteenth century the Duc de Saint-Simon describes the forebodings of his eminent contemporary, Marshal Catinat, as follows: "He deplored the errors of the time, which he saw follow each other in endless succession: the deliberate discouragement of zeal, the spread of luxury . . . Looking at the signs of the times, he thought he discovered every element of the impending destruction of the State, and used to say that the kingdom would never be replaced on a sound foundation till there had been a very dangerous outburst of disorder."

What was a foreboding to Marshal Catinat became, to the *philosophes* of the eighteenth century, a promise. They measured progress by the number of obsolete institutions that mankind could discard and leave behind; and unlike le Roy, they could not conceive that the direction of history might change. Progress thus became an automatic denial of the past. "Reverse the usual practice," said Rousseau, "and you will almost always do right." The reformers looked upon the institutions of society, not as organic expressions of its life, but as artificial and largely malicious instruments for frustrating its natural activities and keeping mankind in chains. By natural they meant "institutionless," and by free they meant historically unconditioned. In this sense, even those who despised Rousseau believed in a return to nature: non-historic nature, as conceived by the mechanists.

"Where can the perfectibility of man stop," demanded Mercier in his eighteenth century utopia, The Year 2440, "armed with geometry and the mechanical arts and chemistry?" This was one of the first of the futurist utopias, and it is significant that it coupled the salvation of man with the improvement of the machine: that was the fresh article of faith.

From now on, a new division discloses itself in society: it cuts across many of the class divisions, for it splits society up into those who wish to go forward and those who wish to stay behind: the party of progress and the party of order, as Comte was to call them: the radical and the conservative. The first was optimistic about the nature of man and poured contempt on the doctrine of original sin; this party believed in the beneficence of invention, particularly mechanical invention; in politics it favored republicanism, or at least sought to do away with ancient privileges, and it was so bitterly against the past that it would abolish even those privileges, like the rights of commons, which kept the poor peasant from being completely excluded from the land; in economics, it long favored free trade and free enterprise. The conservative party not merely resisted all the changes the radicals proposed: it clung to the existing institutions of the State, the Army, and the Church, and attributed the evils that had grown up around them either to man's original sin or the just punishment visited by God upon a world of sinners: it was reluctant to accept new inventions, except when the possibilities of profit muffled the fear of change; and clinging to the old, merely because it was old, the party of order cast disrepute even on those areas of the past which were truly alive, or truly worthy of rehabilitation.

This split was a new phenomenon. It contrasted with the great radical movements of the Middle Ages which were based on a return to an earlier, apostolic conception of Christianity and sought to better the future by restoring the past. Now the conservatives claimed the past for themselves: it was they who nourished the sentiments attached to love of soil, to tradition, to ancient customs and arts: rural life was their special province. And the radicals, in turn, claimed an exclusive patent on the future: they were sure it would belong solely to them; and in their haste to stake out this territory, they underestimated the tenacity of tradition and were overconfident of their capacity to transform society by edict, law, commerce, or education. Because of this split between the party of the past and the party of the future, radicalism deprived itself of roots and conservatism of fresh shoots: both cut themselves off from life.

But note the effect of the doctrine of progress, in the shallow form it took during the eighteenth century: its gains were not cumulative but transitory. Now novelty became a merit and change of any sort a source of hope. For the fashionable exponent of progress, the architecture of the Gothic cathedrals was incredibly ugly; the regulations of the guilds were uniformly mischievous; the rituals and ceremonies of the Christian Churches were hopeless manifestations of human imbecility. One can hardly doubt that Denis Diderot's growing dislike for his friend, Rousseau, rested on his conviction that the solitary hermit, beloved by the medieval church, was downright wicked—and therefore anyone who forwent society, guarded his own soul, and lived on simple fare, like a hermit, was equally wicked. Beneath the radical's very love for change there lay an implicit finality: the notion that his own philosophy rested on foundations that could not slip. He knew that the past held a Genghis Khan; he did not for a moment anticipate that the future might contain a Hitler.

2: The Irrationality of "Reason"

Though the eighteenth century is often called the Age of Reason, that epithet belongs more to the century that preceded it. The mind of the eighteenth century was in fact riven by a series of deep-seated conflicts that reason was unable to remove: the conflicts between rival social classes, between rival political orders, between rival ideologies. Indeed, many of the best minds of the eighteenth century ceased to look upon reason as an influence on human conduct or as a shaper of institutions. Montesquieu attributed the differences in human institutions chiefly to the external influence of physiography and climate; Edmund Burke saw the very essence of society in tradition and custom, mute feelings and dumb allegiances; while Rousseau, who sought to supply political institutions with a rational sanction, was himself the great leader in the revolt against reason. Reason—by which I mean the attempt to include all the facts of life within a comprehensive and intelligible order—was never more in contempt than in the Age of Reason. But a pliant reasonableness, based upon polite conformity and well-controlled emotion, was perhaps never more widely in evidence.

Unconsciously, the eighteenth century continued to live on the scraps and dregs of medieval culture: in particular, it retained a naïve belief in divine providence. At a time when the kernel of institutional Christianity had almost dried up, the husk gave forth a faint aroma that pervaded society. The belief in providence might be stated cynically, as in Mandeville's The Fable of the Bees, where the author established to his own satisfaction that the grossest private vices might, through their influence on trade and invention, become public benefits. Or it might be stated pragmatically, in the belief of Turgot and the physiocrats that by removing restraints on trade a multitude of individual efforts would, even through competition and cross purposes, create a larger quantity of wealth than any effort at mercantilist regulation. When examined these beliefs, like the belief in progress, turned out to rest on a pure act of faith.

What many of the thinkers of the eighteenth century looked upon as reason was rather its deliberate renunciation: a willingness to overlook the irrational, the mysterious, the immediately unintelligible, and a willingness to treat as real only those parts of experience that were open to the external observer and could be readily made plain. The very clarity of the best prose of the eighteenth century, at least among the English and French writers, is perhaps a sign that its leading thinkers never bit off more than they could chew. Only if one accepts the fact that the representatives of "reason" made no serious demands for an over-all rationality can one explain the contradictions in their policy and their conduct: the great libertarian philosophers, like Voltaire and Diderot, court the favors of despots—in the name of freedom! The great theorist of democracy and education according to nature placed his model pupil in the hands of a private tutor and showed how he would educate a young prince, not a citizen. Reason would demand that the philosopher should be aware of these contradictions even if he were incapable of reconciling them.

If we wish to discover the profoundest tendencies of a culture, we must often seek them in their most abstract manifestations, in philosophy and art. This is perhaps especially true during this period of social upheaval and revolution, when the visible institutions are no longer representative. It was not in the bloody operations of the guillotine in 1793 that the forces of revolution and disintegration showed themselves most clearly; for behind the Reign of Terror were centuries of human anguish, the sense of old wrongs and new promises; impulses that took shape in a demand for justice as well as in a demand for revenge: indeed, even the punishment rested upon social premises, however brutally these showed themselves. No: it is in the apparently innocent lucubrations of David Hume that the real Reign of Terror began: the beginnings of a nihilism that has reached its full development only in our own times. In his Enquiry on Human Understanding the assault upon historic filiations and human reason reached a pitch of cool destructiveness. Hume used the technical processes of reason to sap its very foundations. He was far more radical in his attack than Rousseau, far more devastating than d'Holbach or La Mettrie.

Hume's essential doctrine was the autonomy of raw human impulse and the absolutism of raw sensation. In analyzing cause and effect, he broke down the rational connection between human events to a bald sequence of abstract sensations in time. That, however, was a mere refinement of Locke's analysis of sensations as the building-stones of "ideas," and in terms of isolated sense experience Hume's description was the most accurate report possible of the operation of one agent upon another. But Hume went much further. A passion, for him, was an original existence: it did not derive from any sense impression or copy any other existence: impulses were primordial in a fashion that was not true for any response to the outer world. "When I am angry," Hume wrote, "I am actually possessed with passion, and in that emotion have no more reference to any other object than when I am thirsty or sick, or more than five feet high. It is impossible, therefore, that this passion can be opposed by, or be contradictory to truth or reason."

According to this principle, Hume went on to show, there are only two ways in which any affection can be called unreasonable: first, when a passion is founded on the belief in the existence of objects which do not really exist, as when fear in the dark is based upon the supposition of a non-existing brute lying in wait in the bushes, or when, in carrying out a passion, we choose means insufficient for the end. "Where a passion is neither founded on false suppositions nor chooses means insufficient for the end, the understanding can neither justify it nor condemn it. It is not contrary to reason to prefer the destruction of the whole world to the scratching of my finger."

One could not caricature this doctrine if one wanted to. In the last sentence Hume has done so beyond further challenge: it stands self-condemned. But if one pursues the implications of this philosophy, one sees that this imperturbable philosopher has arrived at a position of absolute nihilism: Turgeniev's Bazarov, in Fathers and Sons, is a mere amateur in moral devastation by comparison. For Hume not merely confirms the absolutism of sensations—and completely overlooks the mediation of sensations through symbols—but he completes this work with an absolutism of brute impulse: he unites a despotism of the outer world with a despotism of the ego, or rather, of the id. Life as he pictured it was life in the raw—with a rawness the most primitive savage never exhibited. In his own plain words, the passions that possess man are above reason and beyond reason.

Hume's philosophy rejects the social background; it refuses to admit the social interpretation of events or the social (symbolic) nature of their analysis; it turns its back upon social responsibilities; it shows human beings as living in a moment-to-moment continuum in which the appetites alone have an unqualified claim to existence, and in which no impulses can be called good or bad, rational or irrational, since every impulse that is founded on the existence of real objects and is pursued with appropriate means is *ipso facto* reasonable. Raskolnikov's murder of the old woman for her money, like Hitler's wiping out of the center of Rotterdam, are both in Hume's creed entirely reasonable affairs—though Hitler's invasion of Russia would be unreasonable because it chose means that were insufficient to its end.

This erroneous conclusion necessarily overtakes every theory that excludes values from the fundamental substratum of all human experience: Hume's office was to make the error so openly that it becomes a classic clarification. Since value is integral to all human experience, a theory that eliminates value as a primary ingredient inevitably smuggles it back again by making sensations or impulses, as such, the seat of value; whereas value comes into existence through man's primordial need to distinguish between life-maintaining and life-destroying processes, and to distribute his interests and his energies accordingly. Here lies the main function of reason: that of relating and apportioning the facts of experience into an intelligible and livable whole. Reason inter-connects events that Hume analytically tears apart: for the purest sensation, the most immediate passion, takes place in a world of values, logical order, social duties, by which sensation and impulse are modified, into which they are integrated. Reason is as fundamental a part of the human equipment as bones, skin, viscera, nerves: by a constant process of relation and apportionment, by suppressing this impulse and by encouraging that, it maintains man's self and his community in a state of psychic wholeness.

Reasonable conduct is conduct that holds together in history and that endures under the strain of conflict and challenge: it tends toward continuity, intelligibility, and harmony. Not merely must an impulse compose its claims with other impulses: it must be modified, in turn, within a larger social context, with respect to the needs and claims of other men, present and distant. So far from having the purely supernumerary role that reason has in Hume's analysis, impotent to affect sensation or impulse, reason performs a constant, active function in the human economy. In pursuing the Life of Reason man grasps the reason of life. Even the most barefaced processes of rationalization are attempts to give an appearance of harmony to irrational or self-limiting conduct.

Order, continuity, intelligibility, symbolic expression, in a word, design—all these are basic in human behavior: no less basic than sensation, impulse, irrational desire. To conceive life at the level of the id is to forget that the id is organically bound to the ego and the super-ego, and that when interplay between these portions of the personality ceases, a profound disorientation of the whole personality, tending toward destructive aggression or toward suicide, must follow. Within the narrow historic compass of this book we have already seen this take place in three widely separated periods—and we are now living through a fourth. This, incidentally, explains why pleasure and pain, which are the body's mechanical regulators of behavior, are entirely insufficient to provide a basis for rational conduct or vital expression. If pleasure were in any sense the ultimate end of life, suicide by an inhalation of nitrous oxide, followed by a last insensible whiff of carbon monoxide, might be the last word in human bliss.

Giovanni Battista Vico, the Neapolitan, saw the implications of this nihilistic movement in both life and philosophy even before Hume had brought them to a final formulation: for Vico remarked, according to Flint, that the new philosophy tended to "dissociate men, to lose sight of humanity, nations, and families, in the contemplation of isolated individuals. This individualism or atomism in philosophy was viewed by him with a persistent aversion."

Hume's mission was simply to carry the current atomism to its logical conclusion: the world became a dissociated flux of sensations and the self became a magma of impulses that might occasionally erupt into life without following any orderly channels in descent. No society could manifestly exist on such ultra-nominalist premises. If Hume's ideological disintegration was far more complete than the social disintegration, that was partly because it was easier to explain away reason than to live for a day without having some recourse to it. After all, the very society that nurtured Hume could also raise the magnificent hulk of Dr. Samuel Johnson, who in his piety and orthodoxy would keep hold of a truth Hume denied and his contemporaries sought to confound. "Whatever withdraws us from the power of our senses; whatever makes the past, the distant, or the future predominate over the present, advances us in the dignity of thinking human beings. Far from me or from my friends be such frigid philosophy as may conduct us, indifferent and unmoved, over any ground that has been dignified by wisdom, bravery, or virtue." (Journal of a Trip to the Hebrides.) If those beliefs had been dominant in the New World philosophy, one might better have called this period the Age of Reason.

In practice, one must add, Hume recoiled from his own strict analysis. Having used his logic to dissolve all the connections of cause and effect, to remove value from sensation, to dissociate impulse from intelligence, Hume cast doubt upon the very instruments he had used to accomplish this astonishing result—and so recoiled into the world of history and social convention. No one would have been more distressed than Hume if anyone had taken his metaphysics seriously; actually nothing alarmed him more than raw impulse. One remembers with a smile his discomfort over Rousseau's tearful demonstration of gratitude for being rescued from his persecutors by Hume: "My dear sir! my dear sir!"

3: Rousseau and the Natural Man

Rousseau's role was a quite different one from that of the corrosive Hume. In breaking with the existing habits and conventions of society, he even broke with its typical product, the sensationist philosophy itself. Though Rousseau was at one with Hume in giving a fresh sanction to impulse, he sought to bestow even on his most singular beliefs the force of a social prescription. This radical belief in man sprang out of Rousseau's capacity for love, and it is what made his influence so much more fecund, so much more rejuvenating, than that of his great rival Voltaire.

Voltaire, the petted Lucifer of the salons, satirized, criticized, and condemned the more obvious abuses of his society, in particular those associated with the Christian Churches: he did this on one condition, namely, that their correction should not deplete his income or reform his habits of life. The most unsparing of critics, the one institution Voltaire regarded as sacrosanct was himself. Voltaire laughed at Leibnitz, whom he was incapable of understanding, because he had said that this was the best of all possible worlds, in that it provided the maximum amount of order compatible with the maximum amount of variety. But Voltaire demanded that for himself this should, in fact, be the best world possible, and he scrupled at no dodge that would make it so.

Rousseau was far more conservative than either Hume or Voltaire: what he rejected lay on the surface; what he valued and clung to were the humble things that a sophisticated age either took lightly or altogether despised: the wisdom of Jesus, the wealth of the lowly. Rousseau knew that the outer structure of society was rotten and was about to collapse. "The crisis is approaching," he proclaimed in Emile, "and we are on the edge of a revolution. Who can answer for your fate? What man has made, man may destroy. . . . This farmer of the taxes, who can live only on gold, what will he do in poverty? This haughty fool who cannot use his own hands, who prides himself on what is not really his, what will he do when he is stripped of all? But he who loses his crown and lives without it, is more than a king; from the rank of a king, which may be held by a coward, a villain, or a madman, he rises to the rank of a man, a position few can fill."

Rousseau, with all his frailties and minor vanities, was a much larger figure than any of his contemporaries: he was the Lao-tse of an age that gave its homage to a Machiavellian Confucius. To Voltaire Rousseau once wrote: "You enjoy, but I hope; and hope embellishes all." Rousseau's only true rival was the less famous Vico, a perhaps sounder but no less imaginative thinker. In Rousseau the revolt against despotism, regimentation, exploitation, slavery, polite conformity, callous mechanization, stifling luxury, life-denying custom, received both its formulation and its incarnation. His words rang all over Europe and America, and his visible presence reinforced them. He not merely threw the ornate rococo costume off the figure of contemporary man: he demolished the elegant automaton he found beneath it.

At the very height of the Augustan age, Virgil wrote his Eclogues. In the most refined and polished country in Europe, at the moment when life as a whole had become an elaborate artifice, Jean-Jacques Rousseau wrote his famous essay for the Academy at Dijon, affirming that progress in the arts and sciences had depraved morals. The grounds of the argument were specious, but the impulse was salutary. Like a sick dog, Rousseau had gone out to eat grass.

Rousseau was sufficiently dependent upon polished society to hate it, and sufficiently outside it coolly to understand its workings. The young house-boy who had become Madame de Warens's lover knew the cold sexual curiosity of the stylish woman as well as the maternal warmth which, in his special case, had redeemed it. The young lackey who had blamed a fellow servant for a theft committed by himself would know something about human conduct that could not be explained away on purely mechanical or utilitarian principles: the sense of guilt, the desire for self-expiation and reparation would follow the sinner almost to his grave. Unlike the philosophes, he would not turn his back on a religion that recognized man's deep need for forgiveness. The habit of masturbation would increase Rousseau's shyness; an inflamed urethra would make him a diffident, if not an incompetent, lover; he would even rationalize his sexual weaknesses as chastity. But for these flaws he might have subsided to the plane of animal heartiness upon which his early friend, Diderot, conducted his sentimental life. But Rousseau's sins served him well. His handicaps saved the young dandy who came to Paris wearing a sword and boasting a couple of dozen fine linen shirts. The essay that brought him fame at the age of thirty-eight eventually caused him to live according to his inner convictions.

Rousseau's attempt to live a more simple, integrated life than current society offered was an entirely salutary one; but his rejection of the foolish conventions of his own culture was based upon two profound errors. One was that man in the state of nature was a solitary who stood above human conventions and human restrictions. The other followed from this: that man in society is less in a state of nature than if he existed purely on the level of his original animal needs. Rousseau opposed to man as we find him in history, associated in space and time with his fellows, rarely out of sight, never out of mind—he opposed to historic man a "natural" man who remained outside history. Did not development for Rousseau mean complications, compulsions, corruptions? Beholding the society around him in a state of palpable disintegration, Rousseau argued in favor of a primitive state of non-development. Out of his knowledge of good and evil, Rousseau led a retreat back to mankind's abandoned Eden, and beat in vain upon its gates.

Though Rousseau's noble savage existed chiefly in his own mind, he nevertheless was on the trail of an important notion: the notion, shared by Vico, that if one could behold the human race in its embryonic state one would know something significant about its adult form. The search for the primitive involves the idea of growth and development. His admiration for the crude, the indigenous, the barbarous, for the first time brought home the full importance of the explorations Western man was making in America, Africa, Polynesia: he crystallized as a theory, indeed as a dogma, convictions that many people had expressed more loosely in the previous two centuries: witness the pamphlet of Walter Hamond, published in London in 1640, "proving that the inhabitants of the Isle called Madagascar . . . are the happiest people in the World."

And if the real savage had little to teach about man's future, except by marking an earlier starting point, he had much to tell about the possibilities of fixation and arrest. Civilization itself had been a formidable invention: as costly, as dangerous, as the original Promethean gift of fire. Civilization was founded on the astronomical calendar, on written language, on the higher division of labor, and on the translation of habits and institutions into permanent buildings, monuments, cities: it marked a bold departure from the fossilization of tribal societies: a gain in freedom, an intensification of life, which might be paid for in a disintegration against which the primitives rigorously protected themselves. Static, tribal societies were closer to the heartwood, further from the cambium layer where growth takes place.

But primitive peoples are as deeply enmeshed in social obligations as their more cultivated brothers: there lies Rousseau's main error. If man is everywhere in chains, as Rousseau said, this is particularly true of savage society, as it is of the peasant communities that Rousseau likewise respected. The savage's chains were not forged by his subservience to nature; they were rather due to his submission to his own past selves. Fear kept primitive man close to his ancestral patterns: fear kept him chained to accidental successes to which he gave the force of law and sacred prescription. Rigidity, not spontaneity, is the mark of tribal societies: repetition, not continued growth. The resistance to change is what gives a timeless quality, among savage peoples, to even the most trivial custom. Much of this rigidity, indeed, still left its mark on earlier civilizations like those of Babylonia and Egypt; and it has persisted in the best-preserved cultures, like those of the Chinese, the Jews, and the Hindus. Change, mobility, self-development, free adaptation of means to needs—all this demands the complex forms of civilization, and brings with it an unstable social order, whose depths of corruption are commensurate with its possible heights.

Rousseau's fanciful portrait of man in a state of nature, his glorification of primitive simplicity, was essentially false: but he was not wrong in thinking that primitive life had values which no civilization can afford permanently to forfeit. What made his philosophy suddenly carry weight was the fact that Western man found himself face to face with nature in his colonization of the New World and in those audacious explorations which Bougainville and Cook were conducting during the eighteenth century. The cult of nature was itself an old one. Petrarch had spurned the arts of the city and said: "Let the soft and luxurious men of wealth be far removed from our neighborhood. Let them enjoy their hot baths and brothels, great halls and dining places, while we delight in woods, mountains, meadows, and streams." Erasmus, in his Praise of Folly, had observed that those are the most happy "that have least commerce with Science and follow the guidance of Nature." Piero di Cosimo, as Vasari describes him, would not allow his rooms to be swept, ate when he felt hungry, and would never suffer the fruit trees of his garden to be pruned or trained, leaving the vines to grow and trail along the ground, "for he loved to see everything wild, saying that nature ought to be allowed to look after itself. He would often go to see animals, herbs, or any freak of nature, and his contentment and satisfaction he enjoyed by himself." In short, Rousseau had forerunners and anticipators.

But there is a difference between idealizing the noble savage and believing in a natural order. The latter belief is a salutary corrective to human willfulness and misunderstanding; but it was easy, almost inevitable, that in the eighteenth century the two should be confused. Thus William Penn, one of the wisest of Quakers, advocated studying nature: "Let us begin where she begins and end where she ends, and we cannot miss being good naturalists." Not equally sound, however, was his praise of the Indians' life, on the ground that "they are not disquieted with bills of lading and exchange, nor perplexed with Chancery suits and Exchequer reckonings. We sweat and toil to live; their pleasure feeds them; I mean their hunting, fishing, and fowling." Penn here overlooked the main point: that if hunting was a happier artifice than a bill of lading, the life of the Indians, sufficient unto itself, left a smaller residue of truths and values for mankind.

Here Shakespeare was much wiser than the admirers of the primitive; indeed, it is hardly too much to say that in The Tempest he not only anticipated Rousseau but wisely answered him. If Caliban is more foul and brutal than the worst savage, it is only because Shakespeare conceived him as a more primordial form, while the real primitive is subject to restraints, conventions, values which the idealizers of primitive life mistakenly pictured as absent. Brute power, brute impulse, brute intelligence, nurtured outside society, would produce only a race of Calibans. But Shakespeare's island has other inhabitants who personify wisdom, love, spirit: these are representations of man in his true state of nature—a state as proper to him as that in which the bison or the tiger find themselves. The theme of natural life cannot be divorced from man's dream of transcending the limitations of his own nature: the impulse toward the divine. Man dominates the other creatures of the planet because he has never been content with himself. He is indeed such stuff as dreams are made on:

the dream, the wish, the ideal are organically bound to his very animal existence.

What was man, then, apart from what his institutions had made or mis-made him? This question plagued many of Rousseau's contemporaries. It was prompted by various spectacular events: by the discovery of a Wild Boy in England and a Wild Girl in France: by face-to-face contact with the unhappy Eskimo whom Cartwright brought back to London from Labrador, or with the Polynesian, Oomai, whom Captain Fourneaux brought back to Europe in 1774. All these figures sharpened the problem of man's development. How did man come to be human? What turned the guttural throat noises of the wild creature into human language? Vico, too, had earlier labored to interpret this miracle of miracles, the achievement of articulate speech and significant communication; he imagined the existence of an *Ursprache*. And he, too, felt that barbarism might prove a necessary means of rejuvenation.

This fascination with the primitive was not just a literary speculation; common men shared it. Sailors going ashore in the Pacific would jump ship, with small prospect of being picked up again, lured by the spectacle of sensuous ease and wild felicity: coconuts, breadfruit, dazzling tropical landscapes, and amorous dalliance with brown maidens who were easier than coconuts to pluck. In the American woods the frontiersman, dressed in deerskin coat and "leatherstocking," with a hunting knife always in his belt, learned to live by his unbridled wits and animal courage, like his near neighbors, the Indians themselves. The oceans and the prairies were beginning to be peopled by Ishmaels such as Cooper was to describe in The Prairie and Melville in Moby Dick. On the level of sensation, appetite, and impulse, on the level described metaphysically by Hume, primitive life seemed to have the better of civilized existence. Those who were in revolt against the injustices of society found an outlet for themselves on the frontier. There, subject to nature, they could have life on their own terms.

Rousseau's idealizations of natural man did not, plainly, rest on any extensive anthropological inquiry: it was not a judgment about facts, but a device of criticism, a program of reform. Rousseau himself—becoming "crude, rough, impolite out of principle"—was one of the chief models for the natural man. He properly sought to make his criticism more effective by living up to his own precepts; in that respect his thought had an organic quality not shared by many other thinkers and reformers. But Rousseau did this as a man of his own time and culture, by marrying an illiterate and uncouth girl, because she was good to him, by living in a cottage and earning a pittance copying music by hand, by steadfastly reducing his physical wants. His natural man was in fact closer to the peasant than the noble savage: his spartanism came direct from Plutarch's Sparta, not from the Five Nations.

To live in the country and enjoy its solitude; to be free from minor obligations of attendance and courtesy; to be in harmony with the peasant and artisan, capable of sitting down at their table and enjoying their crude food; to use the empty hours for lonely rambles through the countryside; to gather plants for a herbarium and take pleasure in watching the processes of growth—these were the new elements in life as Rousseau conceived it and lived it. What he meant by living according to nature was this retreat into a rural environment, this pursuit of simplicity and integrity, this sympathy with the poor and the humble. The prescription, given the time and the place, was a sane and liberating one: instead of a hard veneer of manners, feeling and spontaneous affection: instead of a mechanical ceremonial, a human response appropriate to the moment: instead of a complicated ecclesiastical scheme of salvation, based on original sin and fed by the love of power it condemned, the simple morality of the Savoyard Vicar, with its direct appeal to the goodness of human nature and the universal nature of goodness.

Here was the basis for a new manner of living and a new education. Thousands would read Rousseau's books and imitate his example: millions who had never heard of his books would finally be affected. From the headwaters of Rousseau, a dozen mighty streams branch out through the nineteenth century: Chateaubriand and Hugo and George Sand, Cooper and Thoreau and Whitman and Melville, even a Goethe, a Kant, a Tolstoi, an Emerson, will bring into their conception of the personality a new sense of man's relation to nature and nature's relation to man: a sanative belief in the vital and the organic which will in large degree transcend Rousseau's errors and atone for his self-deceptions.

Without this upsurge of romanticism the forces of life might have been routed. Without its many positive contributions the processes of renewal that are now imminent might have been even longer delayed.

4: The Cult of Nature

There are a dozen meanings for the word Nature; but that which the romantic movement recognized best was the sky and the earth and all its inhabitants, untouched by the hand of man. By a simple extension, nature came to mean all the processes of life, change, movement, even within man, in so far as they are independent of his own actions. To live according to nature was to accept the earth and its organic life, and to treat man's existence as having value through participation in this life. In the

IX. RISE OF THE COMMON MAN

The bourgeois personality took classic shape in the towns of the Low Countries: Holland in the 17th century was its ideal environment. Rembrandt's group portrait still continued the collective guild tradition. But already the costume had become businesslike and relatively severe, in the absence of color and frippery. Now private life began to flourish. The bourgeoisie continued and enriched the cult of the family, here jovially symbolized by Jan Steen. To please middle-class children new types of toys were invented, dolls' houses were built, folk tales and fairy stories that the old peasants knew so well were collected in books, and new tales, from Robinson Crusoe to Treasure Island, were written. Christian Weisse wrote Songs for Children and Haydn even wrote a Children's Symphony. But the values of peasant life did not wait for 18th century romanticism to be revealed: Brueghel, Frans Hals, the Brothers Le Nain, brought the unkempt boor right into the bourgeois parlor—at least vicariously, by pictorial representation. The school of Le Nain graphically anticipated Rousseau's doctrines: even to the encouragement of the nursing mother. Here was no idealization of poverty, but a recognition of the peasant's serious claims to be considered as a human being. Neither Millet nor van Gogh can say more. Now the Christian Church's ideal equality in heaven seeks an earthly outlet: even-handed justice to all under a government of laws, equal opportunity for education, equal share in the responsibilities of public service in peace and war: equal part in all collective decisions through the ballot. These ideals, though nowhere completely fulfilled, made steady progress from the 16th to the 20th century. But social equality rests on economic foundations: hence the needed effort to widen participation in the economic processes in accordance with the ideals of co-operation and freedom, and to establish a basic standard of life in terms of regional and universal needs. This involves a making over of both capitalist methods and capitalist goals.

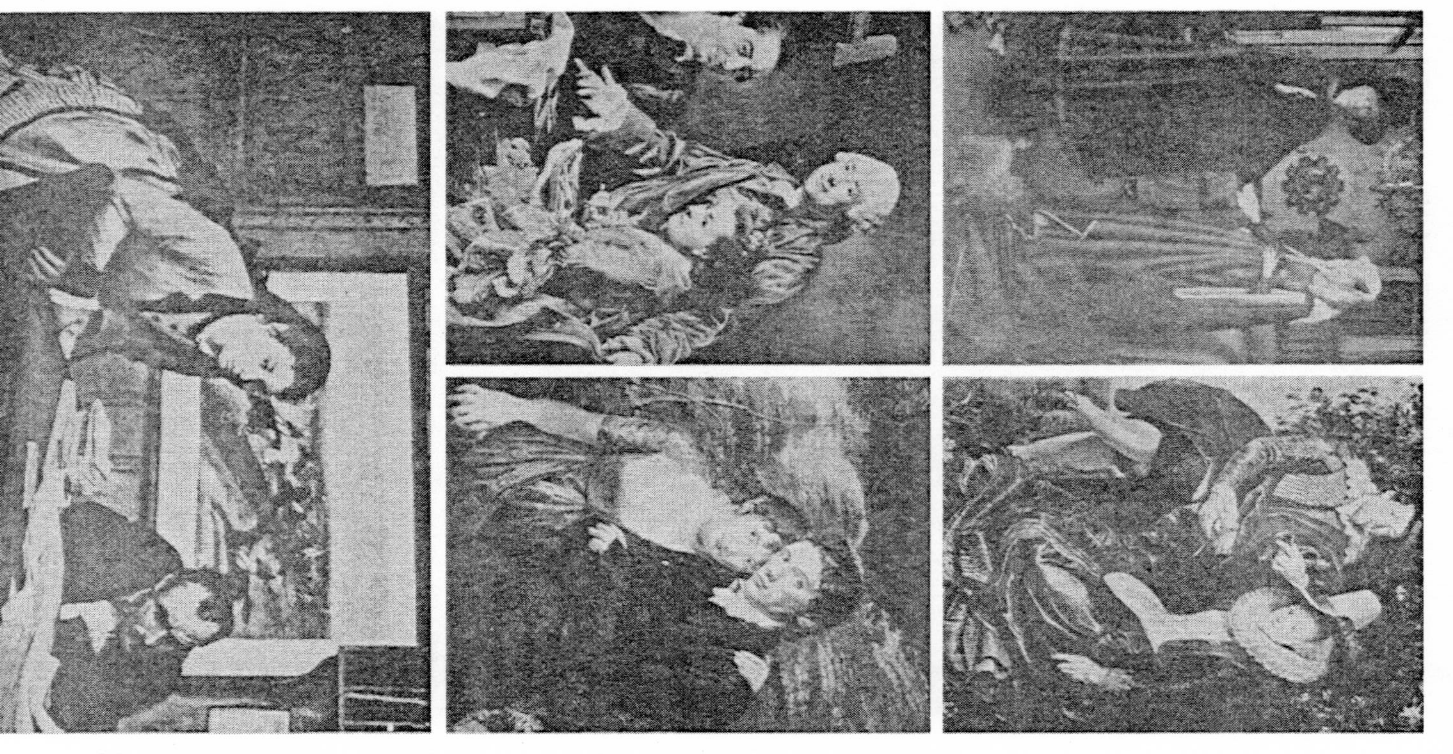

X. MARRIED LOVE: 15TH-19TH CENTURY

common distrust for any tinkering with the life processes, even the elegant and worldly Chesterfield was a believer in nature. "At your age," he wrote his son in 1748, "nature takes sufficient care of the body provided she is left to herself, and that intemperance on one hand or medicines on the other do not break in upon her."

Baroque man attempted to force nature. This fact is as plain in his bleedings and purgings of the human body as it is in the clipped trees and geometrically ordered paths of his parks and gardens. Romantic man, on the contrary, submitted gladly to nature: with Wordsworth he faced nature in a mood of "wise passiveness." Just as the new landscape parks respected every contour of the ground, its paths twisting and turning in order to conform to the topography, its designer so valuing spontaneity that his very plantations attempted to counterfeit the random order of nature, so it was in the treatment of human character. Everything that savored of discipline, purposive order, sharp outlines, was tabu: the methodical moral accountancy of the Protestant, the methodical practical accountancy of the business man, were both foreign to "nature." Ignoring nature's massive repetitive patterns, a forest of trees, a meadow of grass, the lover of nature glorified singularity and caprice, the accidental and the undesigned.

In a social group, romantic man yielded to his impulses and despised the manners and the code of the company: alone in nature, he yielded to the scene outside him, and became a mirror on which the outer world left its spontaneous but fleeting impressions. The positive feeling toward nature reinforced the negative feeling toward society. Thus romantic man exaggerated his own sense of uniqueness: Rousseau opened the story of his life by proudly proclaiming his unlikeness to other men, unconscious of the fact that he had not a sin to confess that had not already been broached at a million confessionals.

For all his appearance of yielding to nature, romantic man did not avoid the need for choice: his only change was to introduce a new principle of selection. It was nature untamed, nature terrible and menacing, to which the romantics returned: but in that very choice they only disclosed their underlying connections with the society they imagined they had left behind them. What was this new love of stormy skies and ancient ruins, of powerful waterfalls and blasted trees, but a literary and pictorial symbol of the new violences of energy that were being unchained in the social movements of the eighteenth century—violences that would uproot the old institutions as a tree is rooted up in a tornado.

In his positive liking for the "sublime," as such elemental manifestations of form and energy were called, romantic man was, accordingly, not as withdrawn from the currents of life in cities, courts, harbors, factories, as he affected to believe. Even Diderot, that solid urban bourgeois, had a passion for being abroad in high winds: those winds, which began to blow in Ruysdael's landscapes, were still blowing at almost hurricane violence in the paintings of Géricault and Delacroix. For it was not in the cultivated landscape, on sunny days, that the new man felt himself at home: he left such insipid moments to the departing figures of the baroque stage, the ladies and gentlemen of the court, who played at being milkmaid in the English village at Versailles, or who reclined at ease in a sunny glade in the open woods. "It is already understood," Rousseau observed in his Confessions, "what I mean by a fine country. Never can a flat one, though ever so beautiful, appear such in my eyes; I must have torrents, fir trees, black woods, mountains to climb or descend, and rugged rocks with precipices on either side to alarm me."

For the first time, perhaps, the more cultivated minds of the West actively began to incite fear and mystery within themselves, not by conjuring up ghosts, witches, demons, invisible powers, but by pitting themselves against the elements: going abroad in thunderstorms, with the lightning streaking across their path, climbing high mountains even above the snowline, exploring caves: in short, doing for an esthetic reason the same undaunted actions that the sailor, the peasant, the woodsman, or the miner were wont to do in the course of their works and days. It was in the presence of the primitive and the violent that romantic man found himself, and, thinking to escape society, disclosed in his unconscious symbolism the very conditions he must face when he returned home. The forces that Dante had depicted in the Inferno as utterly paralyzing to the human spirit, fit only for the punishment of rebellious souls, now became the very food on which rebellion was deliberately nourished—and to be in the midst of these forces was to be in the romantic's paradise.

This cult of nature was, plainly, a compensation for a society that was fast becoming too cultivated to remain healthy, too neatly ordered to leave any play to the free imagination, too fully rationalized to use the full force of the id. The growing belief in a curtailed mechanized existence, marked by the organization of factories, the improvement of chimneys and water-closets, the concentration upon the empty symbols of power, wealth, civility, at the expense of their real contents—all this fostered the romantic reaction and defined its major goals. But if the cult of nature provided the main line of reaction there were many sidelines: the retreat into the national past, with its resurrection of the Middle Ages (Scott), the interest in folkways and folk-poetry and fairy stories (the Brothers Grimm), the effort to find talent, if not genius, in "natural man," in poems produced by washerwomen or peasants (Burns)—all these offshoots of romanticism diversified its attack on existing society.

Romanticism completely reversed the mechanical world picture. As opposed to the physical sciences, the romantic now associated nature with his own subjective states, while he associated the objective with people, conventions, society, man-made things. Even here the romantic failed to recognize how much of his historically conditioned self he imported into nature: the principle of *laissez faire*, for example, as set forth by the physiocrats of Paris, served the business man in throwing off the shackles of the state no less than the artist in his opposition to society's "interference with nature." And the romantic's hatred of plan and design, his glorification of disorder, in turn justified the nineteenth century industrialist's callous disregard of all decency and all humane purpose in his exploitation of the environment for profit.

Despite these confusions, two main types of personality clearly defined themselves toward the end of the eighteenth century: the romantic and the utilitarian. Their earliest visible prototypes, expressed with anything like completeness, were Shakespeare and Bacon. Both of these types emerged from the contradictions and fragmentations of the post-medieval order and challenged the continued dominance of older social forms and older expressions of personality. Though these archetypal figures were necessarily at war, it is interesting to find them united in a common ancestor: the image that came to life in the mind of Daniel Defoe—Robinson Crusoe.

The long career of Robinson Crusoe is instructive; for it is due to something more than the beautiful cadences of Defoe's prose: it is due, I believe, to the fact that he put into a single situation the two great themes of the epoch that followed. Defoe's hero was a philistine of the philistines, a man "born to the middle station of life," who as a castaway on a desert island became the ideal inventor and organizer of his own private civilization. His patience, his method, his perseverance, made him the very pattern of utilitarian man. But he was also a hero of pure romance: for he was man alone, man in a state of nature, surviving a storm, mastering the rough earth, communing in solitude with the ocean and the stars: an Ishmael by accident, yet not without a romantic delight in his situation. Even his companion Friday only completes the symbolism: for he was primitive man himself, the dark unconscious self of modern man.

Everyone fell under the spell of this book: Adam Smith as much as Rousseau. Indeed, the classical theory of economics was worked out on a series of academic assumptions based on the supposed behavior of a castaway on a desert island—as if this were anything but an exercise in casuistry. But Robinson Crusoe was the first book Rousseau would give Emile: he considered it "the best treatise on education according to nature." Whichever path a child might take, toward romantic rebellion or utilitarian prudence, he would still find in Robinson Crusoe the images and feelings that would support him: the black sheep of art and the lone wolf of capitalism could both treat it as a useful guidebook: it might lead a Gauguin to Tahiti and an Andrew Carnegie to the steel mill.

And here, too, is a fountainhead of modern man's dilemma. He wants both the primitive and the civilized, both adventure and regularity, both romance and comfort; but alas! neither Defoe nor Rousseau gave him any prescription for incorporating these elements into a single life, once Robinson left his desert island to return to civilization.

5: Return to Childhood

Perhaps Rousseau's greatest contribution was to understand the savage in the midst of his own society: the child, that perpetual primitive of the race. He found the child neglected: pushed around as ruthlessly as Christianity had pushed around man's elemental nature: curbed, punished, reproved, indecently polished, turned with all possible haste into a little manikin or a little ladykin—or, if one of the poor, turned with even greater haste and ruthlessness into a docile cog in the new industrial machine. Do not think that the latter process waited for the paleotechnic factory system. Evelyn, commenting upon the public charities of Amsterdam in 1641, noted with admiration that "there is hardly a child of four or five years old, but they find some employment for it."

Rousseau challenged all this. He demonstrated that the main business of childhood was growth. He centered attention on the long life-process of education, rather than on the quickly finished product whose thin veneer would soon crack.

Not that education in the formal sense was neglected by Rousseau's contemporaries. The common school, contrary to popular belief, is no belated product of nineteenth century democracy: I have pointed out that it played a necessary part in the absolutist-mechanical formula. Friedrich Wilhelm I of Prussia, following Luther's precept, made primary education compulsory in his realm in 1717, and founded 1700 schools to meet the needs of the poor. Two ordinances of Louis XIV, in 1694 and 1698, and one of Louis XV in 1724, required regular attendance at school. Even England, a straggler in such matters, had hundreds of private charity schools, some of them founded by the Society for Promoting Christian Knowledge, which had been incorporated in 1699. Vergerius, one of the earliest of renascence schoolmasters, had thought education an essential function of the State; and centralized authority was now belatedly taking up the work that had been neglected with the wiping out of municipal freedom in the greater part of Europe.

Education, however, was still largely identified with training in letters and numbers: drill in the tools of learning alone. "The welfare of society," observed La Chalotais in his report on education in the midst of the Enlightenment, "requires that the education of the common people should not go beyond its occupations." Because of his respect for those occupations Rousseau might have agreed with La Chalotais; but as a thinker, he was always climbing above his own prejudices and pushing beyond his own limitations: so in the Discourse on Political Economy, written in 1758, Rousseau came out for public education "under regulations prescribed by the government" as one of the fundamental supports of republican government. "If children are brought up in common in the bosom of equality; if they are imbued with the laws of the State and the precepts of the General Will . . . we cannot doubt that they will cherish one another mutually as brothers . . . to become in time defenders and fathers of the country of which they will have been so long the children." Education as a necessary function of citizenship was the great contribution of Rousseau, the political philosopher: a permanently valid contribution.

But the romantic, individualistic Rousseau was quite another creature from the sober, realistic Citizen of Geneva: he perhaps made a fatal mistake when he retired to the Hermitage Mme. Epinay had prepared for him, instead of going back to his native city. In solitude, beguiled by his own fantasies, Rousseau had another contribution to make; and he made it in Emile, or Education According to Nature. This is the most original and the most paradoxical of Rousseau's works: brilliant but self-contradictory, pregnant but potentially harmful. Rousseau himself coolly uttered the final word about it in a letter to a father who had boasted he was bringing up his own son in accordance with Rousseau's precepts: Rousseau said he truly pitied the boy. By dedicating the entire life of the tutor to rearing Emile, Rousseau showed plainly that, unlike Comenius, he here had no concern for public education; and while he provided all manner of natural conditions, he neglected one essential natural condition: the existence of human society. Unlike Mary Wollstonecraft a little later, who boldly advocated mixing boys and girls in school, Rousseau kept Emile entirely apart from the society of girls, in particular, from Sophie, whom he was to marry: here he showed an almost oriental solicitude.

But there is one main perception in Emile that redeems its sentimentalities and absurd artifices; and this is Rousseau's understanding that education is concerned with the promotion of human growth. He saw that "education comes to us from nature, from men, or from things. The inner growth of our organs and faculties is the education of nature, the use we learn to make of this growth is the education of men, what we gain by our experience of our surroundings is the education of things." According to his experience "those of us who can best endure the good and the evil of life have the best education." And again he said: "Teach him to live rather than to avoid death, and life is not breath but action, the use of our senses, our mind, our faculties, every part of ourselves which makes us conscious of our being. Life consists less in length of days than in the keen sense of living." That was brave doctrine; and it gives a measure of the greatness of the man.

For Rousseau, then, education was not the fitting of an organism into a fixed mold: he rejected the corsets of convention and knew that the well-trained body had its own shapeliness. Education was the direction of the process of organic growth, and it involved every part of the personality. He was in favor of exercising and hardening the body, of avoiding medicine and regulating diet; and he advocated not merely bright clothes to please the child's senses, but loose clothing that would permit movement. Other educators before him had introduced the use of weapons for martial exercises: Rousseau introduced tools and advocated active manual labor in a trade. Thus he challenged an exclusive preoccupation with letters as the only concern of education: he purposed to give his most favored individual just as good training of muscle, eyesight, and practical judgment as a peasant's child. Perhaps he was the first educator, if one excepts Plato, to recognize how much useful education goes on outside the school, without the aid of pedagogy—and to incorporate these spontaneous, self-directed activities in his very plan of education.

Before Rousseau, even tender parents would take pleasure in their child's premature acquisition of knowledge and piety: they were capable of filling a child of five with Latin grammar, classical history, theological conceits of sin and retribution; and would rejoice in its sad, earnest knowingness. But Rousseau pointed out that each stage of growth had its appropriate environment and its appropriate material: he accepted the values of childhood for what they meant to the child, instead of disparaging them or attempting to skip quickly over them, in the interest of the ultimate adult.

This great lesson in growth outweighs Rousseau's perversities and falsities—and Emile abounds in falsities. It was necessary to bring back to an over-mechanized concept of education the notion that feelings and sensations are important: it was erroneous to base this on the dogma that "to exist is to feel." It was good to insist upon the pupil's need for activity and spontaneous expression: it was unwise to say "Do not constrain him in anything, the better to see him as he really is," because one cannot see a human being as he really is unless one also sees him under constraint; and apart from this, to see the child "as he really is" is only a first step toward helping him become what he really should be, a process in which the teacher must exercise the social function of the super-ego, and cannot abandon that function without weakening the student's personality and betraying the community. Finally, it was absurd for Rousseau to fancy that he could educate his pupil "free from prejudices and free from habits," for what would this mean but that he was to be freed from association with the past and deprived of the very possibility of continuity in his own life?

One must not attempt to minimize these weaknesses: for the followers of a great mind are likely to seize upon the solecisms that seem original and to despise those ancient truths whose reinterpretation by the master is infinitely more precious. In our day, many of Rousseau's prescriptions have been belatedly fulfilled in "progressive education": the shallow doctrines as well as the basic doctrines, the weak sentimentalism as well as the shrewd wisdom. Thanks to the inevitable cultural time-lag between formulation and embodiment, the doctrines of willful *laissez-faire* in education were systematically disseminated at a moment when the problems of authority were being raised once more in society, and when the need for common plans and common purpose, a common language and a common background, made Rousseau's negative concept of freedom an obstacle to effective education. Today the need for rational order and rational self-discipline toward a common end has become paramount. To take Emile without the modifications of The Social Contract and The Discourse on Political Economy is to make a lemonade with sugar and water, without adding the lemon juice. John Dewey's wise warning against the confusion of spontaneity with irresponsibility, and the discipline of interest with an indifference to any form of discipline repeated the lesson of Rousseau's own life and thought. Feeling, emotion, spontaneity, autonomy, all had a part to play in human growth: but by themselves they were not enough.

By placing education in a new context and by giving it a new aim, human growth, Rousseau aroused a fresh hope. The meaning of this hope was well put by Thomas Jefferson in his Report to the Legislature of Virginia on Education. "We should be far, too, from the discouraging persuasion that man is fixed, by the law of his nature, at a given point, that his improvement is a chimera, and the hope delusive of rendering ourselves wiser, happier, or better than our forefathers were. As well might it be urged that the wild and uncultivated tree, hitherto yielding sour and bitter fruit only, can never be made to yield better; yet we know that the grafting art implants a new tree on the savage stock, producing what is most estimable both in kind and degree. Education, in like manner, ingrafts a new man on the native stock, and improves what in his nature was vicious and perverse into qualities of virtue and social worth. . . . And it cannot be but that each generation, succeeding to the knowledge acquired by all those who preceded it, adding to it their own acquisitions and discoveries and handing the mass down for successive and constant accumulation, must advance the knowledge and well-being of mankind, not *infinitely*, as some have said, but *indefinitely*, and to a term which no one can fix and foresee."

Jefferson's vivid figure of engrafting is perhaps not altogether a happy one, though it recalls the Pauline distinction between the old man, born of Adam, and the new man, re-born of Christ; but his distinction between "infinitely" and "indefinitely" is a master-stroke. Very possibly Jefferson himself did not read Rousseau. Nevertheless it was with some such sense of grace and liberation that Rousseau's doctrine of growth, as the essential process of life in nature, took hold of his contemporaries, and continued to influence, not only succeeding generations of educators, but people in every walk of life: not least, it stimulated the sciences of biology themselves, by making men at home in nature and encouraging its systematic study in the field. Yet Rousseau's theory of education and his theory of government never came fully together; he never resolved his own conflicting intuitions and hopes; and the problem he bequeathed to his followers still waits for an adequate solution: one which psychologically accepts compulsion and routine no less than spontaneity and interest, and which fully utilizes each man's special talents and capacities without allowing him to neglect his common background with his fellows or evade his common duties.

6: The Erotic of Sentiment

If romanticism's influence upon the child was, in time, profound, its effect upon woman was not less; and in this department, again, the effects of Rousseau's peculiar life and character were significant. The sentimental friendship was almost his private invention, and in his recoil from his own baseness as a parent, he popularized the arts of domesticity.

Apart from the upper circles of the financial and political world domestic life had in fact been flourishing long before Rousseau's appearance. The sentiment of the home seems to have increased with the gradual separation of the dwelling place from the workshop: what the family lost in daily contact with outsiders it gained in private intimacy and warm feeling. Released from more practical duties in the shop, middle-class women had more time left for specialization on their marital and maternal duties. But the disintegrating patterns of upper-class domesticity influenced, in widening ripples, every circle of eighteenth century society. The strictest prescriptions of politeness went along with an increasing latitude in sexual relations, at least among the married. To believe in marriage for love had been a commonplace with the creator of Romeo and Juliet, Antonio and Portia, Ferdinand and Miranda; but by the end of the seventeenth century the belief in such ideality was almost a Quaker heresy.

Among the upper classes marriage had become a sort of license to enjoy society. "I married," Mme. d'Houdetot said to Diderot, "that I might live and go to the Ball, the Opera, the Promenade, and the Play." Not the least privilege of marriage was the license to take a lover. In the eighteenth century convention of love, there was room for the most part for neither passion nor tender absorption: a lover was a trophy which one wore as conspicuously as possible: he was someone who would dance attendance like a footman, be present at a woman's toilet, like her maid, and even on occasion lace her stays. Sexual titillation was too easily satisfied ever to become very importunate. Love was largely a cerebral matter: a licentious curiosity to find out "how it would be with the next one," and in the very ease with which connections were made and broken sexual passion rarely had the opportunity to manifest its two greatest qualities—its capacity for reaching the deeper levels of personality and its gift for endurance, for waxing and waning, for changing on the instant from polar ice to equatorial heat.

Instead of the tight rein with which one drives a spirited horse, love knew only the loose rein one gives to a tired nag who knows the way home. If speed is wanted, it will be furnished by the whip of a new driver or by a bounding away from some unfamiliar obstacle—could it be a husband?—on the road. Benjamin Franklin's defense of the physically unattractive older woman who knows her sexual business, on the ground that experience is worth more than youth or beauty, is not less repulsive for being partly true.

When one couples the psychological facts, for which there is plenty of evidence in letters, memoirs, diaries, with the physical environment of the eighteenth century, the results are even more curious; or rather, the quite tepid nature of this all-too-copious fountain of sexual passion becomes indisputable. The taste of this love-making is like that of Turkish paste, soft and yielding and without any definable savor; it is love in a setting of silken pillows, on couches as voluminous and soft as clouds, with women whose full breasts and large buttocks have been too softened by idleness to be valuable for erotic exercise, even if the very structure of the bed did not tend to smother movement. Is it too much to suggest that the frequent change of lovers was probably due to an unconscious pursuit of the elusive orgasm that only a relatively few, specially sensitive women could have experienced? Did desire seem to bulk so big in daily life because it was really empty of fulfillment?

Confined to the boudoir by her need for contraceptive precautions no less than by her lack of athletic stamina, the eighteenth century woman of the upper classes never, as the Goncourts point out, associated sky, storm, or sunlight with her love: at best, she knew the scent of honeysuckle in the green recesses of the summer house. No wonder ennui prevailed; no wonder that the peasants who encountered each other at a hearty dance under the trees by the village inn, who retired behind a hedge or sank into a hollow beside the road when their feelings became too high, were a better model for an active erotic life than Mlle. de l'Espinasse. Yet despite their softness, the men and women of the eighteenth century had a platonic vision of love in the state of nature: even the upper classes. Fragonard and Boucher depicted their dream; but even more they found what they wanted—above all, they found nature's justification for their own heartless naturalness—in the erotic practices Bougainville and Cook discovered in the South Seas.

The playful eroticism of the Polynesians—"without quarrels, rivalries, jealousies, vengeance"—seemed to Diderot and his fellows eminently rational: untainted by moral strains and theological inhibitions. Tahiti might be Paris! Diderot's prescription for a good life sexually was one of unlimited copulation, without the conventions of marriage: such a life as Casanova carved out for himself by making a vocation of his liaisons. Casanova was the real Don Juan of the century: his first error, that of preserving the chastity of a young serving maid, he repented at once and never repeated. As a result, he knew everything about the physical moment of love-making: he brought to it the ardor of the technician, which went beyond mere convenience or desire; and his passionate enjoyment of sex, springing out of a copious vitality, had perhaps something to teach his jaded contemporaries: the necessity for at least being a good animal. But unless Casanova was a liar as well as a boaster, he sometimes had the misfortune to awaken love. That was an aspect of sex which neither he nor his contemporaries could willingly recognize or easily embrace. At this point, Rousseau made his appearance. It was his mission to make lovers remember that they were men and women—"a position few can fill"—to make men and women proud that they could be parents and to unite love and parenthood with the graces of friendship.

In the name of feeling, Rousseau helped restore the edge to dull sexuality; and because he believed in life according to nature, he made men and women take the responsibilities of parenthood seriously. The poor, of course, had never been able to escape such responsibilities; poor mothers either nursed their own children or lost them. But Rousseau shamed the well-to-do mothers of his time into breast feeding, and because he was equally horrified at the physiological damage wrought by corsets, he was one of the first reformers to induce women to loosen their stays: so that pregnancy, no less than lactation, probably gained from Rousseau's widely followed advice. Here again, however, the consummation of his teaching did not come till the twentieth century. Rousseau's influence on clothes reached its high point considerably earlier: the classic women of the Directoire period, with their proud bosoms, their shapely figures, often naked beneath a single shift, were his true children. In this plea for a healthy and eager maternity Rousseau was expiating the terrible guilt of his own life: his leaving his own children at the steps of a foundling asylum right after their birth.

Out of another defect, his incapacity for easy sexual union, Rousseau helped to infuse the relations of men and women with a new tenderness, a new sense of delicacy and consideration. Voluptuous, shy, exquisitely passionate, he made a kiss on the hand leave a deeper impression than going to bed would ordinarily have done. From Rousseau's first encounter with two young girls on a picnic to his platonic courtship of Mme. d'Houdetot, he created a new intensity of feeling, through giving his love a freer range over the whole personality and a less specific goal. His sensitiveness to nature, his warmth of feeling, his musical responsiveness to moods, his faculty for confession-provoking intimacy, introduced a note that had been lacking in the commonplace sexuality of the time. Though he still kept the ancient belief in woman's inferiority to man, and said so openly, he acknowledged her worthy of the best attention man could give her. And he was rewarded. "You are the tenderest lover I have ever known," exclaimed Mme. d'Houdetot. "No, never did man love like you!" With Rousseau, love preserved the distances of friendship, and friendship, becoming more whole-souled and more all-enveloping, began to achieve the intimacies of love. That example was widely followed.

The novel that popularized Rousseau's sense of love and friendship, Julie; or the New Héloise, became unreadable within a century after its publication; but its influence was immense. To the matter of fact philistinism of the Encyclopedists and their followers, Rousseau opposed the values of sentiment: to the Voltairean grin, he answered with a flood of sighs and tears; to bald desire he opposed an infinite expectation of somewhat diffused if not completely nebulous bliss. But above all, he gave to love a sense of privacy; the boudoir ceased to be almost as open as the salon. The sentimental friendship was consummated now in solitude by the writing of letters: lovers lived through the day for the moment when they could make an account of their secret thoughts to their best friend. Alone, one communed with the other aloneness: alone, one kept one's romantic secret against the whole world, locking it in a diary: a monogamy of sentiment replaced a monogamy of mere habit.

But loneliness has its dangers: that love for the other self might without being aware of the change become only self-love: the egotism for two all too quickly would devour the opposite number. In the erotic life, this kind of intimacy is perilously close to narcissism: hence the reintroduction of incest, as the final possibility of love, both in actual life and in romantic fantasies from Byron to Melville. To be in love with one's sister or one's brother was to be in love with one's biological no less than one's spiritual other self.

Deprived of society, the ego loses any confining sense of its own proper dimensions: it swings between insignificance and infinity, between self-annihilation and world-conquest; between the hidden Sorrows of Werther and the visible triumphs of Napoleon; between the desperation of suicide and the arrogance of godhead. This nebulous reaching for illimitable goals was the result, in Rousseau himself, of his erotic limitations: that seems fairly plain. But the tendency passed over into other departments he touched. Isolation goes with such romantic self-absorption; and isolation in turn helps to create an inflated, suspicious ego, over-touchy to whatever approaches it from the outside, treating every claim of the real world as a conspiracy against the inner self. By tending to cultivate feeling beyond reason, Rousseau lost the benefits of those sanative habits and automatisms which keep the social process in operation when feeling is dead and impulse has vanished: the duties of the parent and the citizen which extend the empire of love beyond the egos of the lovers.

No real society could meet the demands of the exorbitant romantic ego for either isolation or irresponsibility: its perfect society was ultimately a society of one, since in the end the beloved would have his or her moment of detachment, of independent interest, of social duties performed for the sake of others. The romantic wanted to see himself everywhere, above all in the eyes of his beloved: he wanted each outward image to correspond perfectly with the face in the mirror, in a series of retreating pictures, as in a room where the walls are covered with mirrors. Such self-assertion led inevitably to self-extinction: even when the romantic ego took the course of confronting and dominating the outer world, as in the case of Napoleon, the result was fatal. From Werther to Pierre the romantic heroes are all driven to suicide: the final cutting loose from the bonds of community.

Let me sum up. Romantic love began by fostering a new sense of intimacy and tender understanding between the sexes: it ended by fostering self-love; for no other human being could fully meet the demands of the solitary, highly inflamed ego. Rousseau began this vicious circle; Fichte completed it. As a German, responding to the political needs of his day, Fichte gave the doctrine of egoism a peculiarly nationalistic and collective reading. His worship of national history, the national character, the national language, his claiming for all things German a superiority above all similar creations, was a translation of this individual self-love to the national group. Here Irving Babbitt's castigation of romanticism was truly justified. Ultimately, the cult of the inviolable ego, whose impulses are sacred because they are unique, and unique because they rise out of a socially unrestricted self—the cult of this ego led to imperialist expansiveness: to guarantee its own privacy, to nourish sufficiently its own greedy self-love, the ego must dominate everywhere. Since it cannot do this alone, it must do this through the national state. That pathology justified itself in Fichte's doctrines of autarchy and reached its climax in the manic cult of German national socialism: the grossest delusion in a world where every other nation shared similar illusions. By complex but nevertheless traceable connections there is a tie between the private confessions of Jean-Jacques Rousseau and the public confessions—with their paranoid mixture of suspicion and self-adulation—of Adolf Hitler.

7: The Original Goodness of Man

One of the inner contradictions of the eighteenth century is that the doctrine of the unfettered individual should have been coupled with a new belief in the goodness of man and with a new expression of love for humanity. Machiavelli did not make that mistake: he based the cult of the unrestrained individual, the tyrant, upon his belief in human baseness.

In disengaging itself from the Established Churches, Protestant and Catholic, whose ruling clergy were so often corrupt, venal, self-indulgent, the spirit of Christianity took on new life: there was ecstasy in the ranks of the Methodists and fellow-love among the humanitarians. Philanthropy and brotherhood were now to be found chiefly among atheists, dissenters, sectarians, those who sometimes denied the name of God but honored the divine by their actions. Rationalistic thinkers, not being sure of immortality, felt bound by a special obligation to their short span of life, and not believing in an inscrutable divine providence, they sought to substitute a providence of their own. People became acutely conscious of the poor and lowly, of the mute unhonored Miltons still outside the country churchyard, of the criminals rotting away in vile jails where every sentence of imprisonment was doubled in duration by cruelty and viciousness.

The tender conscience of this period found its voice and expression chiefly in laymen. The Englishman, Howard, spent twenty years visiting the prisons of Europe and reporting on their dreadful state, using up a large fortune in that enterprise, even allowing himself to be confined in order to make a more truthful report. The Italian, Beccaria, turned his zeal to the reformation of the penal code. Others began to inquire into the care of the sick and the insane: the Society of Friends built a model asylum at York, and the Friends led the campaign against human slavery. So with the condition of the deaf, the dumb, the blind: Diderot, concerned to relieve their lot, laid down the principles upon which language was ultimately to be taught to them: a noble bequest to his fellowmen. Pity visited even the fool: the last Court Fool, according to Balet, died in 1763. Though the jails and asylums were not at once reformed, and though the process of keeping them clean and humane can never end, these initial efforts honored their generation: the first consciousness of the *need* for reform, of the *possibility* of reform, had at least appeared. The widening of these improvements during the nineteenth century contributed to the belief in progress. Here or nowhere was the spirit of Christianity.

John Wesley, contemporary with Rousseau, was no less an advocate of the simple life and the return to nature. Did Wesley not begin his preaching in 1739 in the midst of the open fields, as the only way in which to capture the industrial workers, who were ill at ease within the formal walls of the churches, pre-empted by their masters? The parallel does not end at this point. Like Rousseau, Wesley warned his followers not to affect the gentleman. "You have no more to do with this character, than with that of the dancing master." Is it any wonder that the Duchess of Buckingham wrote the Countess of Huntingdon, one of Wesley's upper-class supporters: "I thank your Ladyship for the information concerning the methodist preaching; these doctrines are most repulsive and strongly tinctured with impertinence and disrespect toward their superiors in perpetually endeavoring to level all ranks and do away with all distinctions, as it is monstrous to be told that you have a heart as sinful as *the common wretches that crawl on the earth.* . . . I cannot but wonder that your

Ladyship should relish any sentiments so much at variance with high rank and good breeding."

Did Wesley, too, believe in the original goodness of mankind? Otherwise it is impossible to explain the naïvete of his injunction to the pious tradesmen and manufacturers he counted among his followers: "Earn all you can; save all you can; give all you can." In the first precept "all" plainly means *all;* in the last, it means what is left when cupidity has wrestled with charity, when ambition has contended against love; in short, when man's tendency to make his too-partial self the final measure of his obligations to the world has had a full opportunity to exert pressure. Rousseau, on the other hand, solved this problem of the source of evil by holding that "Man is naturally good and . . . our social institutions alone have rendered him evil." The solution was a specious one; for social institutions are but the products of natural man himself, and in so far as they hamper goodness, they derive their capacity to do so either from man's own wayward tendencies, or from that inertia that keeps him from perpetually renewing his achieved goods.

Yet Rousseau himself was aware of the inability of the dogma of natural goodness to account for the disorders of society and for the difficulties that stand in the way of remedying them. In a striking passage in Emile, he puts his finger on the exact spot where an exclusively optimistic interpretation of man's nature and destiny goes astray. "Self-preservation, therefore, requires that we shall love ourselves; we must love ourselves above everything, and it follows from this that we love what contributes to our preservation." This was not a chance observation. In an earlier passage in the same book he even carried it further and in more concrete form: "We are now in the world of morals, and the door to vice is open. Deceit and falsehood are born along with conventions and duties. As soon as we can do what we ought not to do, we try to hide what we ought not to have done. As soon as self-interest makes us give a promise, a greater interest may make us break it. . . . We naturally take refuge in concealment and falsehood." Naturally? Then what becomes of the belief that man is naturally good? Naturally? Very well: that is the theological dogma of original sin, and here it is derived, not from a mythical revelation, but from common experience.

But let Rousseau himself answer this question; for he does so quite candidly in a letter to Cramer, October 13, 1764. Emile, he explains, "is a quite philosophical work on the principle advanced by the author in other writings, *that man is naturally good.* To reconcile this principle with the other truth, no less certain, that men are bad, it would be necessary to show in the history of the human heart the origin of all the vices."

Not in social institutions but in the human heart: note that. Self-preservation, self-interest, self-love: here indeed are the clues to those social injustices and inequalities that Rousseau had sought originally to assign to the development of the arts and sciences, to the acceptance of the complications of social life, to the crystallization in outward forms and conventions of fluid impulses and spontaneous feelings. By setting up an arbitrary opposition between the private self, as the unqualified source of what is good, and the traditional social order, as the equally unqualified source of what is bad, Rousseau avoided as a young man the sad necessity for really knowing himself. For in the customs and uses of society he would have discovered his *own* vanity, his *own* baseness, his *own* pride and inhumanity, his *own* partiality. The doctrine of natural goodness favored, first of all, its enunciator: he did not have to examine a virtue he could take so pleasantly for granted or expiate sins his theory did not permit him to recognize.

And here, too, was the weakness of the whole humanitarian movement, which continued the positive impulses of Christianity and yet kept aloof from the self-knowledge that the Christian doctrine of evil had always carried with it. Rousseau had made compassion the very base and bottom for a regenerated morality: fellow-feeling, emotional identification with the sufferer, was the clue to his relief. One cannot doubt the sincerity of the new charities and philanthropies that came into existence: the attempts to do away with the enslavement of the Negro, to provide soup-kitchens and shelters for the starved, the homeless, to educate the ignorant. All these efforts were generated, sometimes to a truly sublime degree, by the essential Christian impulse of love; but they failed to retain the co-ordinate doctrine of sacrifice. It was easy for the pious English manufacturer who followed Fox or Wesley to prohibit the use of slaves in the West Indies; for he himself had no need for them. But he overlooked the need for an equivalent renunciation in his own life: the abolition of child labor. It was easy for the Abbé de Saint-Pierre to argue for a perpetual Concert of Powers in his plans for universal peace; but he failed to provide for a concert of classes within each nation, which would carry the principles of justice down to the very base of political society. Tolstoy's simple prescription to the rich—that they should get off the backs of the poor—was not included among the humanitarian remedies.

In other words, the doctrine of the natural goodness of man gave a deceptive appearance of ease to the whole process of social reform: it centered attention on institutions and overlooked the painful and difficult process of transforming the self: it asked natural man to "give all he could"—only to be hurt and surprised to find out how little that was. The belief in natural goodness was mainly responsible for the impatience to usher in revolutionary changes almost overnight by purely external processes; and it was therefore responsible for the resentful bewilderment or the cynical self-contempt that followed a whole series of collective disappointments. If all men were naturally good, a show of hands should have been sufficient to vote in the millennium. Was not that indeed the covert hope of the advocates of universal suffrage, beginning with the Chartists? William Lovett said as much. Why the delay?

As in so many other places, the best criticism of the humanitarian doctrine came from the man who had first given it classic expression. "Society at large," Rousseau wrote in a letter to Usteri in 1763, "human society in general is founded on humanity, on universal benevolence; and I say, and I always have said, that Christianity is favorable to that society. But particular societies, political and civil societies, have an entirely different principle. They are purely human institutions from which Christianity consequently detaches us as it does from all that is merely of this earth: only the vices of men make these institutions necessary, and only human passions preserve them. Take from your Christians all the vices and they will have no further need of magistrates and laws; take from them all human passions, and instantly the bond loses all its strength; no more competition, no more glory, no more desire for preference, and private interest is destroyed, and in default of a suitable support, the political state falls into decay." One may translate this passage into a single sentence: abolish humanity and you will succeed as a humanitarian.

The danger of humanitarianism, then, is that its fellow-feeling may become a mere extension of self-love and a vehicle for self-gratification: all the more dangerous when limited motives give themselves the special sanction of an apparently disinterested attitude. Its altruism may be only egoism on collective parade. One must not merely feel for the suffering of other men but, like a physician, know what is good for them, even if that knowledge leads to a remedy so drastic that it involves the physician no less than the patient. One must not be prepared merely to alter institutions for the good of other men: one must be prepared to alter the form and contents and purposes of one's own life. Lacking this kind of self-knowledge, unprepared for this kind of sacrifice, the humanitarian movements too often went astray, and the bolder collective efforts at reform and revolution came to grief for substantially the same reasons.

Humanitarianism not merely carried the main burden of Christian practice but tended to displace the original ideology: from the second half of the nineteenth century on, social service replaced communion with

God. This meant that the moral center of gravity shifted away from the Churches, and particularly from the priesthood: it was Voltaire who led the campaign against capital penalties for minor offenses against pious custom; it was Owen who sought to do away with the iniquities of the factory system; it was John Brown who first gave up his life in the final fight against slavery in the United States. Clerical leaders no doubt took part in all these movements: indeed Protestant preachers turned more and more to practical humanitarianism as the visible justification for their religion. But it was mainly outside the Churches that fresh efforts started.

In the Christian Churches the spiritual power had become largely second-hand: though both clergy and laity might in every generation produce many active Christian souls, as true to their vocation as the best examples in the past, doctrinally Christianity confined itself to mending old fences rather than staking out new fields. At a moment when both the Catholic and the Protestant Churches had lost sight of their universal truths in an effort to preserve the particularities of their dogmas, Rousseau sought to find a basis for natural religion in the human heart. And it was there that many of the most deeply religious minds of the nineteenth century, Emerson, Tolstoy, van Gogh, even Kierkegaard, found it.

If one looks for a saint, a philosopher, or a hero after the seventeenth century it will be a surprise to find him within the Church; for the true Church had become disembodied, while the visible and corporate Church had little to do with the formulation of vital truths and the fresh perception of values. What was called the decay of religion during the nineteenth century was not the absence of active religious sentiment, but the failure to create and unify the organs necessary for its expression. But note: an idea that remains disembodied has no command over the community. If the spirit of religion was more widely diffused at the top of the social pyramid, in the work of the scientist, the poet, the revolutionist, in a Clerk-Maxwell, a Whitman, a Kropotkin, the discipline of religion, that discipline which binds the common man to a more universal super-ego, failed to keep its hold on the masses at the base.

8: The Utopia of Romanticism

The humanitarian improvements started in the eighteenth century were designed to correct glaring social abuses; and many corrections were made. But in the bosom of the romantics there was a picture of life, an image of their heart's desire, that was based on a false scheme of values. This picture explains why so many of their corrections remained ineffectual and why so many of the hopes awakened came to grief. They dreamed of universal peace, and in our time their deficient sense of evil and danger ushered in more calamitous wars: they dreamed of universal brotherhood and their dream ended in a humanitarian acquiescence in fascist slavery.

We shall not find this utopian picture of life in Morelly's Basiliade or in Mercier's pragmatic description of the year 2440: we shall find it, in full detail, in the pages of Emile. It is the utopia of the picnic.

Behind the dream of the picnic there is indeed a long story. The idealization of simple life began for the people of the West with Theocritus's Idylls and Virgil's Bucolics, so different from the tart realities of peasant life in Hesiod's Works and Days. As with the Taoist sages of China who retired with their jug of wine to the Bamboo Grove, this impulse appeared at a moment when the organization of the State and the material perfection of existence had reached a high level. The spirit of the picnic takes form more vividly in the pages of Petrarch and Boccaccio, though the ladies and gentlemen of The Decameron preserved the decorum of their order and station; and if they told frivolous tales to keep their minds off the specter of Black Death, they were not deceived by the belief that they had found, in this countryside excursion, the secret of ultimate human happiness. It was all very fine; but they knew these gay moments would end.

But in the eighteenth century the fête champêtre became another name for heaven. In Emile, Rousseau pictures for himself a country cottage and an estate, both quite similar to the place he himself had escaped to, during the most fruitful years of his life. "There," he says, "I would gather round me a company, select rather than numerous, a band of friends who know what pleasure is, women who can leave their armchairs and betake themselves to outdoor sports, women who can exchange the shuttle or the cards for the fishing line or the bird-trap, the gleaner's rake, or the grape-gatherer's basket. There all the pretensions of the town will be forgotten, and we shall be villagers in a village. . . . Our meals will be served without regard to order or elegance; we shall make our dining room anywhere, in the garden, on a boat beneath a tree, sometimes at a distance from the house or on the banks of a running stream, in the fresh green grass, among the clumps of willow and hazel; a long procession of guests will carry the material for the feast with laughter and singing, the turf will be our chairs and table, the banks of the stream our sideboard, and our dessert is hanging on the trees; the dishes will be served in any order, appetite needs no ceremony; each one of us, openly putting himself first, would gladly see everyone else do the same. . . . No tedious flunkies to listen to our words, to whisper criticisms of our behavior. . . . We will be our own servants in order to be our own masters."

In this passage, the reader will hear echoes, or rather see after-images: images of St. Jerome picturing the bucolic felicities of the monastic life, of Rabelais turning the routine of the monastery into the amiable enjoyments of the Country House: powerful images, evocative of new patterns of life. Rousseau's dream, fed from memories of his own youth with Mme. de Warens, was even more successful. If men now sought power in the factory, the bank, the army, they sought happiness in the sort of life Rousseau here accredited and celebrated: every Sunday, in growing numbers, they would leave their towns, in boats and carriages, on foot and finally in railroad trains, to taste the simple sweetness of this gypsy life: in twos and in twenties, they would seek to forget themselves in Arcadia. The lure of the picnic would bring them to woodsy solitudes where, freed from prying eyes, the young men and the young women would exchange confidences and mingle their kisses with the perfume of ripened field strawberries or wild carrots: after a day in the open they would come back to town with a sunburn on their faces and the sting of kisses still perhaps on their lips. If this was bliss today, why not forever?

Every year, too, the dream of a spontaneous life, free from sordid cares and stiff conventions, close to the countryside, would drive thousands of people to seek a little home in the suburbs, with a green lawn, a few trees, a bed of flowers, or a nearby woodland; an environment in which the whole household might sink its daily cares and find a touch of the picnic in its routine, if only in a walk through the twilight in the fields beyond the last stretch of pavement. Every suburb had its "Retreats": every suburb *was* a retreat. The rambling, the botanizing, the geologizing, the sketching and painting, the flower-picking and shell-gathering, the swimming and boating, hours spent in feasting around the picnic hamper or sitting lazily around an almost primeval campfire, Sundays at Fontainebleau or Epping Forest, vacations in the Tyrol climbing from Alpenhütte to Alpenhütte, or deep among the rocky walls of the Yosemite—all these delightful days were formulated by Rousseau and encouraged by his active example, to say nothing of the cadences of his colorful prose. If one reckoned up all these activities, including the excursion to the beer garden and the road house, one would account for a good part of the daylight leisure of the Western World since the time of Rousseau: leisure for the most part pleasantly, innocently, healthfully spent. Indeed, the more mechanized and routinized that practical life became, the more necessary were these forms of spontaneous, or almost spontaneous, relaxation.

The picnic fulfilled all the conditions for romantic satisfaction. It brought people close to nature, it permitted them to act on impulse, it gratified their senses, their appetites, and their emotions; it sought to "damn braces, bless relaxes"; it gave cooped-up townspeople the exercise they needed to restore their hunger, for, as Rousseau remarked, "there are no such cooks in the world as mirth, rural pursuits, and merry games." In short, the picnic gave form to the romantic quest for happiness quite as much as the tournament gave form to the chivalrous quest of honor.

But the influence of the picnic went beyond these concrete achievements. Not merely did it make the country excursion a welcome alternative to attendance at Church on Sundays and holidays; but it set its own special picture of earthly felicity against the vision of Heaven and Hell that had been presented by religion. The ideal of the picnic was even more potent than its example. There sprang into being the notion that real life must more and more take on the character and quality of the picnic, and that the sum of human felicity could be reached only in moments of free relaxation. This notion made slow headway during the nineteenth century; but it counterbalanced the ideal of mechanical organization at the very moment it secretly subverted it: in the end the ideal of the picnic allied itself to the mechanist's faith that the perfection of the machine would enable men to dispense with painful self-improvement. Hence the image of perfect fulfillment ceased to be within achievement itself: it was confined to moments of relaxation, irresponsibility, letdown which followed achievement. *A nous, à nous, la liberté!*

Now, the conception of life as a picnic has certain serious defects. First of all, it is an infantile aim, bound close to the pleasure principle, chiefly concerned with ego-satisfactions connected directly with the stomach and the genitals; but even worse than this, though closely tied to it, is that the picnic is an affair only for sunny days: when bad weather threatens it must beat a hasty retreat. Finally, this is a conception of life in which one has it all one's own way: a life in which there are no oppositions, no routines, no polar tensions: in other words, life divorced from those very difficulties which give the picnic itself its sanative value. Relaxation is a movement away from convention and constriction: to find continued relaxation, if one begins in a state of relaxation, one must swing back again to an effortful existence. There is no final state that betokens felicity: man knows no security that is not precarious and no bliss that may not be blasted by its own very continuance. Laugh too long and you will cry; prolong pleasure too long and it becomes pain; eat too many good things and food will revolt you; change too often your place of residence and change ceases to be a stimulus.

The picnic, then, is desirable as a relief from routine: it becomes the most tedious of duties, the most tedious and the most empty, when it turns into routine: always the life of untempered pleasure palls, whether one seeks it in a picnic grove or at Palm Beach, in the South Seas, or in a night club. Perhaps the worst sin of the romantic philosophy, to which Rousseau contributed in no little measure, was the fact that it gave its disciples such a sterile dream: the hope of a perfect life free from opposition, free from convention, free from compulsion, free from internal conflict. All the utopian hopes of the nineteenth century rested on the assumption that there was some final state in which life would be free from danger and from struggle: from its essential character of maintaining a finely guarded balance between stability and change, between growth and decay, between renewal and death.

The point is a very simple one. Even a game requires boundaries, rules, restrictions, penalties, losses: that is to say, even a game requires conditions similar to those which give the full dimensions of reality to human life itself. This truth was lost sight of by the revolutionary optimists and the optimistic revolutionaries of the last two centuries: in their weaker moments, they conceived of life as a game at which one might always win, as a picnic for which there was neither a laborious preparation nor an incongruous aftermath.

CHAPTER IX. THE PROGRESS OF PROMETHEUS

1: Utilitarian Ideology

One theme bound the leaders of the nineteenth century together: the conquest of nature and the liberation of mankind by mechanical invention. Even those who did not accept the theme achieved their main energy by recoil from it; for whoever pretended that the advance of the machine was unimportant reduced himself to triviality. Emily Dickinson, safe beyond the hedge that surrounded her Amherst garden, nevertheless composed a poem on the locomotive. William Morris, escaping to the heroic world of the sagas, took as his point of departure the smoke-hung industrial cities in which he worked.

Herewith came a new cleavage in the human personality: for perhaps the first period since the introduction of Christianity, the extraverts now had an idolum *and* a social pattern that responded wholly to their personal needs; and the very possibility of throwing one's whole life into the systematic exploitation of nature widened the gap between the extraverts and the introverts: it contributed to the melancholy, to the brooding impotence, to the mixture of fear and contempt, with which the representatives of the inner world, the artists and poets, greeted the new race of philistines, who were so gloriously at home in the counting-house and the factory.

The romantic and the utilitarian impulses doubtless represent constant elements in human nature. And though they had their origin in different aspects of the personality and sought different outlets, they were nevertheless historically united. It was the pursuit of mechanical efficiency that provided ultimately for the leisure, the privacy, the solitude that the middle-class romantic enjoyed; and it was the cult of the irresponsible individual, glorying in his uniqueness and his unlikeness to other men, that provided a mental escape, if no more, for those who found it impossible to accept the grinding discipline of the new factory or the sordor of the new environment. But the utilitarian aspect was the dominant, the romantic was the recessive, in this new society. To labor unflaggingly from morning to night, to multiply the powers and widen the services of the machine, to produce more cottons and hardware, in order to beget more people who would produce more cottons and hardware, were the goals of the utilitarian effort.

The exuberance of the artist was now attached to machines and utilities. To the ancient categories of the good, the true, the beautiful, a fourth was added—the useful. This was a valuable addition; but the utilitarians managed to spoil their contribution by treating it as a total replacement. Truth was what worked: that was the pragmatism of science, practiced long before William James's belated formulation. Beauty was what raised the price of finished goods, transforming them from comforts to luxuries. Goodness, human goodness, was essentially the capacity to do more work. All the repressed emotional life of the extravert poured into the machine: feelings once evoked by images of feminine beauty now were drawn forth by the sleek cylinders and pistons of machines.

Prometheus, he who stole fire from the gods, became the new deity, and work was the new gospel of salvation. Goethe's Faust, as depicted in his romantic youth, was tempted by Mephistopheles through the traditional desire for knowledge and for woman's beauty; but the Faust of Part II is a different man who solves the great enigmas of life, not by pursuing them further, but by submerging himself in work: reclaiming land from the sea, building canals. Note the conclusion of Faust: "The man who ever toilsome strives, him only can we save." This is the religion of the utilitarian era: it is the connecting link between the capitalist and the worker, between Samuel Smiles and Karl Marx, between Thomas Carlyle and Andrew Carnegie. Work served psychologically in a double capacity, as stimulant and as anesthetic. If it did not bring riches, it brought relief from other worries and disappointments—from poor health, an unsatisfactory marriage, stunted affections. Absorbed in work, life held for the utilitarian mind no tangle of conflicting impulses, no ultimate enigmas, no insoluble problems, and alas! no ideal vistas.

Now, one cannot appraise the futility of this new gospel unless one likewise understands its robust creative qualities. It released people from time-worn occupations that had ceased to have dignity and meaning: the gentlemen of the court and the camp, with their privileges, their vanities, their mincing purposes, were now rapidly displaced by men who organized railroad systems with a ruthlessness that equaled Napoleon at his military best, who bound together continents by cable and telegraph, who funneled wheat into ships that threaded the seven seas, with an eye to actual human needs which was sharpened by their own desire for power and money. And mark this: the appeal of the utilitarian conquest was universal. "Despatch," observed Lord Chesterfield to his son, "is the soul of business . . . Fix one certain hour and day in the week for your accounts, and keep them together in proper order; by which means they will require little time. . . . Business whets the appetite, and gives a taste to pleasure, as exercise does to food; and business can never be done without method; it raises the spirits for pleasure; and a spectacle, a ball, an assembly will much more sensibly affect a man who has employ than a man who has lost the preceding part of the day."

In short, utilitarian habits and interests gave life as a whole a fresh savor; they introduced one to the real world in all its variety and applied the unfettered imaginations of men to tasks they had hitherto performed grudgingly, resentfully, stupidly, like slaves who would not give themselves to their work lest their masters should benefit by it. Business, invention, enterprise excited enthusiasm: to have a job as merchant, sailor, weaver, factor, even as financial speculator, was to have a part in the new drama of Prometheus, not just stealing fire from Heaven, but building a new Heaven on earth, a Heaven with messengers who were swifter than the angels, with principalities and powers who were more audacious than Lucifer. Mechanism, absolutism, and capitalism, all formulated by the fifteenth century, had now reached the state of complete incorporation and embodiment: in the new environment they crowded out every other impulse. A canal, a railroad, a steamship, a factory, a bridge were witness to man's new powers: a thousand factories, a thousand bridges, a thousand steamships altered the very possibilities of life.

Up to this time, practical duties were looked upon as mean compulsions: people had treated work as a curse, not as a means of humanizing man, and similarly leisure was looked upon as a blessing, even if it proved also to be a bore. Now a new possibility opened up: work ceased to be a secret, a mystery, locked up in traditional routine and condemned to exist forever without benefit of spirit: every aspect of it might summon up the intelligence, stimulate the imagination, even occupy the affections. This glorification of work doubtless went too far: but it was but a natural overcompensation for the contempt and disparagement that had—if one excepts the great example of Benedict—been traditional among those who could escape it.

The new utilitarian spirit was recorded in the eighteenth century, not merely by the great paleotechnic inventions that followed Watt's improvement of the steam engine, but in Diderot's Great Encyclopedia. This is one of the main sourcebooks on modern technics: its excellence in this department is due to the gusto with which Diderot applied himself to the task of getting information, summoning workmen from the provinces to describe to him the paper works of Montargis or the silk and velvet works of Lyons. Each new material that utilitarian man brought into use, each new invention he made, each new product he put on the market gave him a greater confidence in his power to make over the world by steady piecemeal reclamation. And no group was excluded from this practical adventure: a printer like Franklin would improve stoves, a clergyman like Cartwright would invent the power-loom, an artist like Fulton would perfect the steamboat.

As a humanizing influence the new interests and the new processes of production were extremely fruitful and they were to have a healthful effect upon the development of the personality. But this is more than one can say without qualification of the goods themselves or of the goals the utilitarians set before the community. This distinction is important. The philosophers of industrialism, from Bacon to Bentham, from Smith to Marx, insisted that the improvement of man's condition was the highest requirement of morality. But in what did that improvement consist? The answer seemed so obvious to them that they did not bother to justify it: the expansion and fulfillment of the material wants of man, and the spread of these benefits, from the few who had once pre-empted them to the many who had so long lived on the scraps Dives had thrown into the gutter. The great dogma of this religion is the dogma of increasing wants. To multiply the powers of production one must likewise multiply the capacities of consumption.

What, then, was man's true life? The utilitarian had a ready answer: it consisted in having more wants that could be supplied by the machine, and inventing more ways in which these wants could be varied and expanded. Whereas the traditional religions had sought to curb appetite, this new religion openly stimulated it: forgetting its hungry Olivers, who could with pathetic justice ask for more, it licensed its Bounderbys to unlimited consumption and surfeit. In the name of economy, a thousand wasteful devices would be invented; and in the name of efficiency, new forms of mechanical time-wasting would be devised: both processes gained speed through the nineteenth century and have come close to the limit of extravagant futility in our own time. But labor-saving devices could only achieve their end—that of freeing mankind for higher functions—if the standard of living remained stable. The dogma of increasing wants nullified every real economy and set the community in a collective squirrel cage.

Thus the universal use of the telephone has caused the abandonment of the far more economic written memorandum or postcard for brief intercommunication: the invention of the radio has caused the time-consuming human voice to displace the swift human eye even in the consumption of daily news: the cheapened cost of printing has added to the amount of needless wordage and unusable stimuli that assail modern man in newspaper, magazine, pamphlet, prospectus, folder, advertisement.

On the basis of its quantitative success, this untrammeled productivity and activity should result in boundless satisfaction: but its massive actual result is confusion, frustration, impotence. The mechanical expansion of human appetites, the appetite for goods, the appetite for power, the appetite for sensation, has no relation whatever to the ordering of the means of existence for the satisfaction of human needs. The latter process requires a humane scale of values and a priority schedule for their fulfillment which puts first things first. No such scale existed in the utilitarian ideology. Without critical inquiry it assumed that the new was better than the old, that the mechanical was better than the vital, that the active was better than the passive, that the financially profitable was a sufficient indication of the humanly valuable. All those unqualified assumptions were demonstrably false.

The utilitarian ideology sought to interpret every aspect of life in terms of the practical: hence truth, goodness, and beauty were either badly warped or crassly neglected in the new environment of industrialism. There is a comical passage in a review of Tennyson's early poetry by J. S. Mill, in the *Westminster Review* for January 1831, which shows the limitations of the new ideology: it may be matched by Herbert Spencer's analysis of the progress of painting. "It would be a pity," observed Mill, "that poetry should be an exception to the great law of progress that attains in human affairs; and it is not. The machinery of a poem is not less susceptible of improvement than the machinery of a cotton mill; nor is there any better reason why the one should retrograde from the days of Milton than the other from those of Arkwright."

In the Golden Day I cited Mark Twain's great howler on the same general theme; perhaps it is worth repeating for the benefit of those who might still accept it as common sense. For Walt Whitman's seventieth birthday, Mark Twain wrote him a letter on behalf of a committee of American men of letters; this is what he said: "You have lived just the seventy years which are greatest in the world's history and richest in benefit and advancement to its peoples. These seventy years have done much more to widen the interval between man and the other animals than was accomplished by any of the five centuries which preceded them. What great births you have witnessed! The steam press, the steamship, the steel ship, the railroad, the perfect cotton gin, the telegraph, the phonograph, photogravure, the electrotype, the gaslight, the electric light, the sewing machine, and the amazing, infinitely varied and innumerable products of coal tar, those latest and strangest marvels of a marvelous age. And you have seen even greater births than these; for you have seen the application of anesthesia to surgery-practice, whereby the ancient dominion of pain, which began with the first created life, came to an end on this earth forever. . . . Yes, you have indeed seen much—but tarry for a while, for the greatest is yet to come. Wait thirty years, and *then* look out over the earth! You shall see marvels upon marvels added to those whose nativity you have witnessed; and conspicuous about them you shall see their formidable Result—man at almost his full stature at last! —and still growing, visibly growing while you look. . . . Wait till you see that great figure appear, and catch the far glint of the sun upon his banner; then you may depart satisfied, as knowing you have seen him for whom the earth was made, and that he will proclaim that human wheat is more than human tares, and proceed to organize human values on that basis. (Signed) Mark Twain."

The thirty years duly passed: the marvels came—airplanes and dirigibles that assailed helpless cities; flame throwers and poison gases that suggested newer and more ingenious forms of torture than rack, wheel, or faggot; explosives and deadlier gases that threatened to exterminate not merely active combatants but every vestige of organic life in the region subjected to them. Towards the end of those thirty beautiful years men applied, in a black rage of warfare, more satanic ingenuities than Mark Twain himself had dreamed when he rigged up the defense which the Connecticut Yankee made against the feudal hordes in the last chapter, and killed ten thousand men by a bolt of electric current. Man almost at his full stature at last! Fifty years after Mark Twain's letter, the irony grew only deeper: for by that time a leader had appeared who proclaimed that tares were more important than wheat and who proceeded to reorganize human values on the basis of giving primacy to the savage, the bestial, the anti-human.

Needless to say, in the admirable list of inventions over which Mark Twain exulted there was reason to exult—provided reason had governed their exploitation and had made them the servants of man's own higher development. In thinking of the nineteenth century as the century exclusively of mechanical improvement Mark Twain had bowed every other type of invention and creation out of the picture: he forgot that this was the century of Goethe, Emerson, Tolstoy, Hugo, of Beethoven, Schubert, Brahms, of Delacroix, Goya, Courbet, Renoir, Rodin, and not least of Whitman himself: men who had sought to re-enthrone the human personality and redress the balance between the inner and the outer world.

But one can hardly wonder at Mark Twain's limitations when one remembers that Goethe himself had, in his old age, duly succumbed to them. Why, according to Eckermann, did aging Goethe think it would be worth the trouble to live fifty years more? To see England build the Suez Canal, the United States build the Panama Canal, and to see the Rhine and the Danube connected.

That spirit was finally interpreted by the brilliant Winwood Reade in a typical Victorian tract called The Martyrdom of Man. At the climax of that work he predicted three inventions: a fuel substitute for coal, aerial locomotion, and the synthetic composition of food. What further triumph was then left for man? The extinction of disease and the achievement of immortality. And then? Having reached the topmost peak of utilitarian fantasy, Reade could go no further: man's final task consisted in a cosmic return to the old theme of colonization: he would migrate into space and would finally, by becoming the architect of systems and the manufacturer of worlds, achieve the ultimate power and perfection of deity itself. The elaboration of that fantasy, with variations, was left to Mr. H. G. Wells: but its emptiness should be plain—it created a religious myth out of matter and motion and reduced the condition of man to that of an enlightened locomotive engineer.

One does not disparage the real utilitarian virtues when one points out that the utilitarians took too much pride in their limitations, and buried too many ultimate problems in the mere routine of busy work. The fact is that they lacked any real perspective on life and death, on the irrational elements in man's psyche, or on the mysteries he confronts in the universe: their answer to all of life's enigmas was to work a little harder and to forget about it. This means that their final remedy was the cultivation of insensibility. They cultivated an esthetic insensibility, so that they would not be too keenly aware, like Ruskin and Morris, of the hideous squalor and disorder and ugliness their careless pragmatism visited upon landscapes and cities: they cultivated a moral insensibility, so that they would not, like Thomas Hood, hear the Song of the Shirt or have anything but self-righteous indignation at the bottomless misery of the people they exploited. They cultivated a biological insensibility, so that they would not be aware of the very animal joy that was missing from the drab routine they imposed on themselves. But they rationalized this insensibility, when they came to think of it, in terms of a philosophy that demanded the greatest happiness for the greatest number, and that made happiness consist in the increase of pleasure and the decrease of pain: so it should be clear that in addition to their other kinds of insensibility they cultivated the vice of intellectual insensibility: for the life they enacted was a tissue of shams and contradictions and self-deceptions.

Unfortunately, the vice of insensibility could not be confined to the factory: tied up with the mechanical ideology itself, it finally spread into every department of life, as a distrust of the emotions and a derogation of feeling. In arriving at intellectual judgments the utilitarian, or the pragmatic liberal as I have called him elsewhere, did his best to eviscerate his feelings, under the hallucination that the judgment of a half-man is more objective than that of a whole man. The result might have been predicted: emotions and feelings came out only in surreptitious, coarse, and degraded popular forms. Either that, or emotions were attached to unsuitable objects: witness the religious veneration that went into the building of the American skyscraper, the highest object on the skyline of the commercial city: otherworldly even to the point of sacrificing profit itself in the fanatic pursuit of altitude: witness the pious esthetic slush that surrounds the marketing of a new brand of perfume or a new kind of electric toaster. The systematic perversion of emotion has gone so far in every aspect of modern life that genuinely gallant Navy captains have to explain the grisly realities of battle in terms of football games, and radio announcers must work hard to make the urgent duties of war seem as real, as warmly compelling, as they have already made the choice of a soap or a cigarette.

Insensibility breeds misplaced sensibility: having banished the full gamut of the emotions all that the utilitarian leaves of them is a wide smeary smile. And in this final act, the utilitarian undermines his own faith: the gospel of work no longer even delivers the goods.

If the romantic never understood the strength and the attraction of the utilitarian dream, the revolutionist never penetrated its weakness or even understood that it was, in fact, a dynamic figment of the human imagination. But if the cause of political liberty did not achieve the good results that the earlier reformers expected, it was partly because people now sought to be rich as well as free, and in shaking off the chains of despotic government they willingly thrust freedom into mechanical handcuffs, so fascinated by the mechanism itself that they did not perceive, until too late, that they were caught by it. For the unrestricted pursuit of riches and power led once more to disparities, inequalities, legalized injustices. No one thought seriously of applying the principles of political democracy to the organization of factories, not even Robert Owen: these organs of man's mechanical liberation were run on absolutist principles, and the automatism of the workers was taken for granted: obedience was enforced as strictly as in the army—without the army's compensating care.

This was an automatic carryover from military to industrial regimentation.

Now to bring men together to work as a corporate body, without undue friction and without any individual purpose except the contribution to the work-process itself, is one of the great tasks of every society: slavery, mechanization, guild-organization, factory discipline are all empirical attempts to solve the same problem, and except in small groups, close to the original family unit, it has never been successfully solved on humane lines. The mere increase in the size or scale of the operation increases the number of human units employed and ultimately tends toward their mechanization: a debasing and inhuman process. This problem is the great problem of political society: never more so than in the age that removed the mechanical obstacles to large-scale organization.

In attempting to ignore this political problem within the mill and the mine, the organizers of the factory system assumed the uncontested right of the capitalist alone to rule in the domain of production. Hence coercion and mechanical organization went hand in hand as if by divine prearrangement. What was the result? It was expressed in classic terms by Pope Pius XI in Quadragesimo Anno: "Bodily labor . . . has everywhere been changed into an instrument of strange perversion; for dead matter leaves the factory ennobled and transformed, where men are corrupted and degraded." The head of the Church of Rome thus showed he had a far more realistic understanding of the penalties of mechanical progress than the effusive Mark Twain: the latter was so beglamored by the surfaces of machines that he failed to look into the recesses of men or even at their worn, sullen faces.

2: Political Reform

At the beginning, romantic man was a non-political animal. Both the commercial and the esthetic egoist dreamed of a private world and wished to be "let alone" to enjoy it. The political attributes of romanticism, its cult of medieval life and national lore, did not appear in any fullness till the nineteenth century, though Percy collected the "reliques" of British balladry and the fatuous Boswell sported the costume of a Corsican mountaineer. Political reform was at first essentially the product of reason in the narrow sense of that word: a belief in the critical intellect, rational contrivance, deliberate effort.

The notion that society was entirely a product of artifice and could therefore be remodeled at will was not in origin a democratic belief: it rose rather with the spread of despotic and absolute forms of government, which attributed to the edicts of the Prince—when backed by a monopoly force—a sanctity of authority and a power of creative evocation which often passed beyond any practicable objectives. Governments tended to arrogate to themselves, as Thomas Paine mordantly pointed out, virtues which belonged to the actions of society as a whole, just as a little boy who jiggles the window-catch in a railroad train sometimes fancies his efforts make the train go faster. Under this self-flattering belief, law became not merely a shortcut to persuasion but a means of peremptorily redisposing the forces of society and re-patterning it. And one cannot deny a certain brief power to such fiats: their potentialities for mischief at least were great: witness the expulsion of the Jews from Spain, the revocation of the edict of Nantes.

In a centralized state, statute law served as a means of universalizing conformities and disciplines that had hitherto been controlled by more local bodies like the municipality, the guild, and the Church.

Now, the believers in political reform had two objects in view during the seventeenth and eighteenth centuries: one was to liquidate the burdensome heritage of abuses, and the other was to provide conditions in which the natural man, released from arbitrary constraints, could flourish. The first object was not incompatible with the existence of despotism. Not merely did a succession of hopeful "men of good will" submit memorials on improving the state of the realm to their absolute monarchs—Vauban's memorandum to Louis XIV and Turgot's plans for Louis XVI are well-known—but even more radical innovators, like Voltaire and Diderot, were happy to woo the absolute monarchs and to rest their hopes for human improvement on their power and wisdom. Because of their identification of themselves with the ruling and exploiting classes, these reformers, in doing away with obsolete privileges, only made it easier for new privileges to establish themselves under the wing of the state.

What was called freedom among the new economists of *laissez-faire* was in fact a negative principle: freedom to escape from the obligations, traditions, and constraints of communal life. Instead of removing the foreign growths that impaired the functions of the old corporations, the reformers took the anti-historic course of wiping out the corporations themselves. Turgot, for example, sought to abolish the guilds altogether, not to remove their anti-social restrictions upon membership, upon new inventions, upon productivity. The French revolution, a little later, went much farther; for it not merely abolished the guilds in 1791, but it abolished religious bodies in 1790 and 1792, did away with literary societies and academies in 1793, and even wiped out financial associations in 1794. In all this, the new political state was merely carrying to its final

XI. REVOLUTION

In all its forms, the spirit of revolution was an immense uprising against meaningless habits and moribund customs. Nature's own violence now encouraged man's efforts to unshackle himself: the fires of the revolution were stoked by the romantic movement. Witness Turner's Calais Pier, "the English packet boat arriving, French fishermen preparing for the sea." Here the insurgent vitalities of the period are as plainly expressed as in Delacroix's noble painting of Liberty Leading the People. Both themes were translated into literature by Victor Hugo: Toilers of the Sea and Les Misérables. Revolution burned the weeds and turned over the soil, preparing for fresh growths; but in the paucity of more positive ideals than rebellion itself the revolution not merely devoured its children but dug its own grave. Violence begot violence: terror begot terror: revenge begot reprisals. The ruthlessness of the threatened classes is here symbolized in Goya's painting—though the firing squad was perhaps the most kindly form of butchery practiced. In the fascist cult of cold violence one marks the final putrefaction of the revolutionary idea: revolution *by* repression. The true alternative to revolution is not the preservation of the status quo: the alternative is perpetual challenge and continued renewal: persistent day-by-day changes harnessed to large, comprehensive, and clearly defined human purposes, working toward justice and brotherhood within a universal society. The deliberate process of renewal is essential to the continued growth of the personality and the community. This insight partly underlay Jefferson's conception of the need for recurrent revolutions: challenges to the encrustations of habit, the insolence of uncontested authority, and the complacent idolization of a dead self. Thus both crisis—often brought on by failure to meet new challenges—and renewal itself are normal events: means of resuming the path of growth. Hence deep revolutions require centuries, not decades, for their fulfillment: witness Christianity and Capitalism.

XII. HELL, PURGATORY, AND HEAVEN (19TH CENTURY STYLE)

William Cobbett was perhaps the first to speak of "starvation in the midst of plenty": the final bitter anomaly of a society that sacrifices life to profit. Van Gogh's The Potato Eaters was done at Nuenen: the work of an artist who knew these peasants as he knew the miners at La Borinage.

"As well as the greatest optimist," he wrote, "I see the lark soaring in the spring air, but also I see a young girl about twenty, who might have been in good health, a victim to consumption, and who will perhaps drown herself before she dies of an illness. If one is always in respectable company among rather well-to-do bourgeois one does not notice this much, perhaps, but if one has dined for years on *la vache enragée*, as I did, one cannot deny that great misery is a fact that weighs down the scale."

Progress was the watchword of this society and movement its chief solution for otherwise insoluble difficulties. Daumier's Third Class Carriage stands for the companionship of the poor and the middle classes in a new form of purgatory: the daily shuttling between factory and dormitory, office and suburb. Salvation by locomotion. Renoir's lunch by the riverside is the opposite pole from van Gogh's Potato Eaters, even as its warm, sunbathed colors are the other extreme from van Gogh's dark blues and blacks. Good food and wine, beautiful women and athletic men, open air and sunshine—all this pointed to renewed health and sanity provided men did not treat it as a permanent resting place or a final goal. Van Gogh's Christian insight into evil complements Renoir's celebration of life's natural goods.

Charles Péguy, who knew the sufferings of the poor through personal experience as painful as van Gogh's, drew a sharp line between a demoralizing poverty in irretrievable misery and that noble poverty chosen by the saint, the artist, the soldier for the sake of intenser dedication to his tasks. The latter poverty promises a life more abundant—as the peoples who rose to their hour of trial were to find during the cataclysmic wars that brought this epoch to its close. An economy of abundance that has no place for this corrective insight will be undermined by its very surfeits.

conclusion the aim of despotic policy: to make the state take the place of all rival corporations, associations, groups, communities.

What was left? On one side an all-powerful organization whose chief end was power: the police, the military, the tax collector give the sovereign state the ultimate decision over the lives and fortunes of its component members: in the society of nations the egoism of states, inflated by the reckless pretensions and paranoid suspicions of the absolute monarchs, takes legal form in the malignant concept of unqualified sovereignty, which places the state above morality and above law. Sharing in that paranoid illusion, the masses of men, daily becoming more impotent in their active economic relations, transfer their own will-to-power to the supreme collective unit, and during the nineteenth century willingly participate in the bellicose assertions, the marauding enterprises, the imperialistic exactions, and the shameless land-stealing, which once were attributes of national monarchies. Refusing to create and to submit to a common law and a common government, the new states, whether democratic or tyrannous in their internal affairs, multiply both the means and the occasions for war.

And what is left on the other side? The atomic individual, divorced from all the associations that give body and texture to his personality, and that lend to him their collective support. An atom or a million atoms: it makes no difference, for against the power of the organized state, they remain zeros, and as the triumphs of fascism have proved, seventy million zeros are still nothing. This atomic individual has a single motive-power, self-interest, and a single aim, self-preservation: in his atomic existence he is under the governance, as Jeremy Bentham said, of "two sovereign masters, pleasure and pain. It is for them alone to point out what we ought to do as well as to determine what we shall do." But this self-interest has only one way of identifying itself and asserting itself, and that is through class interest: this is what unites the otherwise detached individual to the state; and the great battle for power that began in the nineteenth century was for the sake of determining one question: What class shall seize, what class shall control, the state? Atomic individuals, stripped of the powers that adhere by nature to life in groups, naturally fancy that power is all-important: money power, military power, political power.

So inherent to human society, however, is the need to form associations that the progressive abolition of corporate freedom applied chiefly to the older forms of corporate life. At the very moment when the agitation for dissociation was at its highest, in the country where such agitation went farthest, namely in France, new associations and communities, agricultural associations, financial companies, life insurance companies, were actually coming into existence. In short, the theoretic war between the individual and the state was abated in practice by the universal growth of new corporate organizations which covered every aspect of life.

By an even greater irony, the agitation for the abolition of corporate privileges was itself partly the work of a new association, the Order of Free-Masons, which was sedulously patterned after the ancient guilds, and which even professed to trace its history in more or less unbroken line back to the workmen originally engaged on Solomon's Temple. In 1717 the first Lodge of Masons appeared in London: Paris followed in 1725, Philadelphia in 1727, St. Petersburg in 1731. In one aspect, masonry may be regarded as a rationalist attempt to counter Jesuitism; but its other mission was to provide a bond between the members of the middle classes at a time when all other bonds were being loosened by immigration across the political frontiers of nations and the social frontiers of classes.

Masonry was romantic, indeed neo-gothic, in its ceremonial: its initiation ritual was an earlier return to a fantastic Middle Ages than "The Castle of Otranto" and Walpole's domicile on Strawberry Hill. But at the same time Masonry was an expression of the humanitarianism, the rationalism, the cosmopolitanism of the Age of Enlightenment. It used secret methods and promoted public aims: it revived moribund rituals and spread progressive ideas: it appealed to sentimental tradition and the past, but worked for innovations, hoping for nothing but good in the future. Lessing saw in the Masonic movement an organization capable of transcending local differences between states, classes, nations, churches; but though its membership grew steadily, it would seem, until the twentieth century, and though it fostered many imitators, it did not succeed in the self-imposed task of creating an artificial religion of humanity.

Mid the flux of migration and revolution, the Masons established an organization of comradeship and mutual aid. To keep their fellowship from being too nebulous, the secret orders attached themselves to the modern practice of life insurance: on the lowest terms they promised their members a decent burial and a friendly helping hand for the survivors of the departed. The spread of these orders went along with the spread of life insurance, foreign travel, and international salesmanship: the Rotary International was perhaps the last large effort to sustain the original impulse of Masonry, with more public forms and more vaguely innocuous objectives. For a time, Masonry became a rival to that other universal institution, the Roman Catholic Church: in France and even in Italy a formidable rival. But secular forms of fellowship, through trade unions, Chambers of Commerce, and many other forms of association sapped the importance of the mystical fellowship of the Masons themselves: so that it was their secrecy, even more than their actual power, which caused the totalitarian governments in our day to single them out promptly for a killing blow.

But unfortunately Masonry had the weaknesses of a detached rationalist ideology: it was not quite a religion, not quite an appropriate form of international union, not quite a full-fledged life insurance association, not quite an effective political instrument—and therefore it never developed into the social agency some of its founders in the eighteenth century fervently hoped it would become. It was, from the beginning, a sort of post-ecclesiastical museum piece: a hybrid of romanticism and revolution which, like the mule, remained sterile. . . .

The common belief in salvation by political reform was not due alone to the pretensions of the absolute state: it was partly the result of the fact that the reformers, with disarming simplicity, traced all the evils of life to the corruptions of political government. This was a natural reaction to tyranny. Those who live under bad laws and irrational procedures are inclined to exaggerate the beneficent powers of good laws: they are like a lame man with an excruciating toothache, who should fancy that if his tooth were treated he would also find himself endowed with new powers of locomotion. After a century or more of unscrupulous industrial exploitation the Working Men's Association, in their petition to the newly crowned Queen Victoria, attributed the evils of their lot to "the *corruptions* of government, and *the defective education of mankind.*"

Even the Marquis de Mirabeau, politically a fairly sober man, simplified both the source of abuse and the ease of correction when he said: "The more I ponder over the abuses of society and the remedies suggested, the more convinced I am that it needs only that twelve principles expressed in twelve lines should be firmly fixed in the head of the Prince or his minister and carried out in detail to set everything right and to renew the age of Solomon." Some of that simplicity, some of that headlong hope, lay at the bottom of the whole revolutionary movement, both in politics and in industry: it has become part of the weak utopian heritage of our own time. The Chartist, William Lovett, after tracing most of the social grievances of the industrial worker to class legislation, could still hope that a mere rational demonstration of the truth and justice of the workers' cause would effect a change without "the violence of passion, the bitterness of party spirit," or "the arms of aggressive warfare." He did not understand that power belongs, not to naked ideas, but to the organs of corporate life, backed by the energies and vitalities, as well as the moralities, of those who exercise corporate functions.

On this matter, the despots knew better than their more sanguine subjects. Ségur reports Catherine the Great as saying that Diderot's proposals would make fine books but bad politics. He only wrote on paper, which submits to everything and opposes no obstacle to the imagination; but "I, poor Empress that I am, work on the human skin, which is irritable and ticklish to a very different degree."

3: The Basis of the Democratic State

Under despotism, political government had been irresponsible, capricious, costly, and corrupt. As D'Alembert remarked, at the top of the structure one found either eagles or reptiles—and even the noble eagle is a bird of prey. The mercantile politics of the absolute state, with its control over manufacture and trade by minutely detailed regulations and imposts, had expanded the army of bureaucrats, whose salaries were sometimes modest, but whose perquisites usually were large. Despite the example of the Chinese examination system, the bureaucracies were filled with younger sons, hangers-on, and chartered incompetents, hardly even caricatured by Dickens' picture of Sir Tite Barnacle and the Circumlocution Office.

Goethe knew their ways well and, as he told Eckermann, evolved his own strategy of "direct action" to cut through bureaucratic barriers. Result: the more powerful the state seemed at its borders, the more corrupt and rotten it tended to become at the heart: witness France and Russia. For the latter, Alexander Herzen has left us a memorable picture in his Memoirs—a classic document.

Only two courses were possible to make the state serviceable. One was to reform the state by a ruthless military regimentation, which would organize the country as a whole into a single unit, with each class selected, graded, standardized, trained to obedience. This was the course pursued in Prussia, from Frederick the Great to Stein, from Stein to Bismarck, from Bismarck to Hitler. Organization and discipline, without any provision for freedom and development. On the contrary, to make such a state work smoothly, as Fichte boldly pointed out, freedom of the will must be eradicated, and the young so educated that no alternative to the good of the state would be possible.

The other course was to restore political power once more to its source: to make that power legitimate, responsible, and beneficial. The first course led to totalitarian tyranny: achieved and completed in our own generation in the two countries where unrestrained absolutism continued longest:

Germany and Russia. The second course led to a path of development that will never be completed: that of democracy, with its continual re-alignment of forces and redefinition of aims, with its need, like that of the person, for sloughing off its dead selves and transcending the very limitations imposed by successful achievement.

Rousseau set himself the second task. As a result, his Social Contract became the fundamental book of the political revolution: it established a rational foundation for the liberties gained in the past and it sought to guard advances in the future. Taken with his Reflections on the Constitution of Poland and with many political dictums scattered through his letters, it is the most mature piece of political wisdom that the modern world has produced. If it is not as thoroughly seasoned as the Federalist papers or de Tocqueville's Democracy in America, there is a good reason: it came before them. The strength of the argument does not in the least depend upon the fictitious conception of the social contract itself: the historic non-existence of such a contract is no refutation of Rousseau's doctrine of the importance of intelligence and morals, no less than power, in political life. In making the pursuit of power the sole principle of action, Machiavelli and his followers had been forced to disparage the will of the people and to belittle the intelligence of all who did not aspire to active leadership. Rousseau did not make the contrary mistake: he did not underestimate the importance of power in the political state. His object was to make it legitimate, and to make the community itself secure against its abuse.

The Social Contract is not an argument for natural society or for purely organic relations based on the slow accretion of precedents, some deliberate, some accidental, some sound, some frivolous: that narrower effort was left to Edmund Burke. The Social Contract defines the natural state only to reject it: "What man loses by the social contract is his natural liberty and an unlimited right to everything he tries to get and succeeds in getting; what he gains is civil liberty and the proprietorship of all he possesses." In other words, civil government falls midway in Rousseau's scheme between natural life, in which all action originates in impulse and triumphs by force, and supernatural life, in which, according to Christian doctrine, the ambitions and vanities of sinful men are rejected, and life, uncoupled from the engines of power, is consummated by love. Rousseau personally pined for both extremes; but he saw that either would be fatal to security, to continuity, to civil freedom. As a citizen-philosopher, he rejected the weaknesses of both the Christian and the romantic idealizations of society: instead, he took "men as they are and institutions as they might be."

The central doctrine of The Social Contract is that the well-being of all citizens is the prime object of civil government; and that this well-being is more ultimate than special ends like the preservation of property. This is the doctrine that was written, a generation later, into the general welfare clause of the Constitution of the United States, despite the strong bias in favor of the narrow rights of the propertied classes, held by most of the framers of the Constitution: the belief that their private welfare as a class was superior to the general welfare of the "mob" or the "rabble." But in what does the greatest good of all consist, granting that this should be the end of every system of legislation?

We shall find it reduced, Rousseau answers plainly, "to two main objects, liberty and equality—liberty, because all particular dependence means so much force taken from the body of the state, and equality, because liberty cannot exist without it. By equality we should understand, not that the degree of power and riches are to be absolutely identical for everybody; but that power shall never be great enough for violence, and shall always be exercised by virtue of rank and law; and that in respect of riches, no citizen shall ever be wealthy enough to buy another, and none poor enough to be forced to sell himself; which implies, on the part of the great, moderation in goods and position, and on the side of the common sort, moderation in avarice and covetousness. . . . It is precisely because the force of circumstances tends continually to destroy equality that the force of legislation should always tend to its maintenance."

These words were the very core of Rousseau's political wisdom: a core that remains sound today. Had the brief chapter that contains them been conned by heart and followed with zeal by the peoples who experimented with the democratic method of government, the disrepute into which free government cast itself, by weighting liberty in favor of those who already had power and riches, would not have so easily followed. But the existence of class antagonisms at even the lowest levels of the proletariat, between skilled and unskilled worker, between peasant and artisan, curbed the removal of grosser class divisions.

The contrast between Rousseau's actual observations and the beliefs imputed to him by his detractors is so wide that one must pause for a moment to underline Rousseau's position. So far from carrying the doctrine of impulse into political government, Rousseau said just the opposite: "The mere impulse of appetite is slavery, while obedience to a law which we prescribe to ourselves is liberty." And again, he was no less convinced of the clumsiness of direct democratic government, once one passed the boundaries of neighborhood, than were the writers of The Federalist. "It is the best and most natural arrangement," he observed, "that the wisest should govern the many, when it is assured they will govern for its profit, and not for their own. There is no need to multiply instruments or get twenty-thousand men to do what a hundred picked men can do even better." There spoke the wisdom of Calvin. This justification of representative government, however, was coupled in Rousseau's doctrine with its corrective: namely, "as soon as public service ceases to be the chief business of the citizens, and they would rather serve with their money than with their persons, the state is not far away from its fall."

The book that contains these wise generalizations became, with Thomas Paine's The Rights of Man, the Bible of the popular political revolutions of the eighteenth century. It helped modify political life even more decisively than Emile touched education; and fully as much as The New Héloise transformed the personal relations in love and friendship. Such an influence comes, of course, only when formal exposition develops into clearer images the ideas that are more or less latent in public mind and practice; so while it would be foolish to minimize the power of Rousseau's imagination and his pithy style, which is here a model of precision, it would be false to give it the role of prime mover. Rousseau's thought threw a sharp cone of light on a goal already defined in the English revolutions of the seventeenth century, and it accelerated a political force already in motion in some degree even in the most backward state.

4: Demonstrations of Freedom

The circumstances that produced the acts of the American War of Independence also provided the first occasion for testing the truth of Rousseau's prescriptions for a free government. Indeed, it even afforded an instance, which Rousseau's critics have usually overlooked, of the actual existence of a social contract; for such a deliberate compact, involving a surrender of powers to the state for the good of the whole, was the very foundation of the constitution that emerged from this particular revolution.

The American effort became a precedent, and likewise a touchstone, for every other popular movement. Though the American states had a solider foundation in the experience of liberty and local political initiative than the various national states of Europe, handicapped by many more feudal survivals, the transformation that took place in France, with the revolution of 1789, at first seemed even more fundamental, in that it shifted the whole balance of economic power by overthrowing the feudal system and by temporarily effacing all the institutions connected with it. Yet the American revolution proved more durable in its ultimate effects. The causes and reasons for this are worth an examination.

"It has been frequently remarked," said the authors of the Federalist papers, at a critical moment before the adoption of the Constitution of the United States, "that it seems to have been reserved to the people of this country, by their conduct and example, to decide the important question, whether societies of men are really capable or not of establishing government from reflection and choice, or whether they are forever destined to depend for their political constitutions on accident and force."

The success and stability of the new American system of government settled this question decisively. But the terms of its success showed that more than rational intelligence and political good will was needful. First: it involved originally the existence of a large quantity of unoccupied free land, rich in natural resources, not yet individually parceled out. For almost a century this land, increased by the central authority and held in trusteeship by the government, automatically preserved that equality which was essential to liberty. Second: it needed a common set of religious and moral principles, resting upon a common body of literature and the politically autonomous Protestant Churches. Finally, it called for long habituation in the general parliamentary procedure of electing officers, taking counsel, and making decisions, not alone in national political affairs, but in the organization of all voluntary associations. Here the historic experience of the English-speaking peoples gave them a long lead over every other nation except the Swiss. The democratic practice of self-government was the political key to self-development, communal and personal.

The first condition was originally threatened by the extension of slave territory; and that threat nearly sufficed to destroy the Union. But in addition the government, bribed by the desire to open up its internal territory swiftly, with the least effort, the least intelligent supervision, progressively alienated its title to the vast domain: it granted vast tracts to the new railroads and turned over the rest, without permanent restrictions against monopoly, to a host of clamant individuals, whose immediate economic appetites were appeased by the Homestead Act, at the ultimate expense of both liberty and equality. Here the automatic operation of the law of rent justified the predictions made by Macaulay and W. H. Riehl: it brought back those drastic inequalities which had divided the economic classes of Europe into exploiters and exploited.

But the second and third conditions were precarious, too. In the matter of a moral consensus, the doctrine of toleration, on which the American separation of Church and State was effected, requires something more than an agreement on the part of the state not to exercise authority over religious groups or establish an official religion. It also requires that the

Churches, in return for this autonomy, should not attempt to exercise an influence as *unified, corporate bodies* over the state. As soon as a single religious institution, like the Roman Catholic Church, lays down a political policy of its own and seeks to give it the effect of legislation and administrative order, it violates the essential compact which guarantees religious liberty. The reason should be plain. Once the Catholic Church by acting as a bloc can wield enough political power to sway the decisions of the state or to exercise a veto power over its actions, the separation of powers established in the Constitution of the United States is destroyed, and with it, a beneficent state of tension. Under cover, this minority becomes the Established Church.

One must note the important difference between an underlying common moral basis and a prevailing religious doctrine. Thanks partly to its Calvinist heritage, the American Constitution rests upon a division of powers, not merely between the branches of the government, but between the spiritual and temporal authorities within the community. That is a guarantee which not only protects religion from political tyranny but politics from religious tyranny. The entire system of law and government in the United States presupposes the acceptance of the universal principles of morality: public belief in truth, justice, liberty gains in strength because they represent the common denominator in the higher religions and philosophies of the West, rather than the special dogmas of a single Church. Without maintaining this humanist tradition, the Constitution would probably have been unworkable: without renewing it, the system of government will lapse, either through popular indifference or brazen usurpation. That is why the central government had reason to challenge the Mormon Church, as a state religion, in Utah; and that is why those who would maintain our system of government have reason to challenge the efforts of the Roman Catholic hierarchy to work as a compact, authoritarian political unit. When it does that, the Roman Church is in a position to dictate national policy, behind the scenes, if not openly. Indeed, it has already done so.

The adoption of a common instrument of government in the free American colonies did more than abstractly vindicate the principles of democracy and representative government. It solved two of the most vexing problems of political life: how to bring together in co-operation a large extent of territory and a large number of separate, often conflicting interests, without the constant display of force; and how to provide for the common good without exercising detailed authority over every local act. These solutions were of universal importance: not less, certainly, because they were worked out by men who had analyzed the failures of political association in the Amphictyonic Council and the Achaean League, and who knew the causes for despotism and centralization in the petty dissensions and class antagonisms of the Italian cities.

In the American Constitution the wisdom of Rousseau and Burke united, as it were, to create a basis for political life that was rational in structure and organic in content: it was based on current customs, habits, and interests, qualified by historic experience, meeting by masterly compromises discrepancies in size and authority between the founding states, and providing for a continued expansion of the Federal Union itself, and for a continued re-interpretation, through the Supreme Court, of its basic laws. Thus the Constitution combined a respect for going needs with an opening into future possibilities. This, as Price correctly remarked, in his Observations on the Nature of Civil Liberty, was an example to the rest of the world toward building the structure for an enduring peace.

In his essay on the nature of peace Immanuel Kant underlined that perception: at the very moment that the United States, in its first isolationist misgivings, was withdrawing from the universal mission of democracy, Kant pointed toward its ideal goal—an ever more inclusive Federal Union that would subordinate power to law, and make political vitality conform to conscience. There is no rational stopping place, once the logic of democracy is accepted, short of the United States of the World.

The melodrama of the French revolution overshadowed the American example. But the startling nature of its changes, its very "originality," points to a weakness which robbed the French people of a good part of the fruit of their effort, and lent itself to despotism and bureaucratic centralization, rather than to the practice of self-government: the revolution was betrayed at the start by a lion like Napoleon and at the end by a worm like Pétain.

The French revolution, to begin with, wiped out the original divisions of France, based more or less on real feudal and regional unities: for these it substituted with cartesian rigor a system of mechanically defined "departments" without respect for the original geographic substratum, for the actual historic heritage, or for claims of cultural affiliation and self-government. Here the loss canceled out the advantage. Again, the revolution liberated the Jew from the odious restrictions of the medieval ghetto and wiped out the last traces of human slavery; but it deprived the enfranchised serf of the land his ancestors had once held and worked in common, and turned this communal possession over to individual landlords, drawn usually from classes above them. So, too, the revolution swept away effete corporations and privileged monopolies; but it also undermined the very right to voluntary association which is one of the chief guarantees against political absolutism, as well as one of the most precious positive freedoms afforded by society. The French revolution even attempted to institute a new calendar and rename the days and weeks and months; but its only permanent success was a scientific one: the establishment of the metric system on the basis of a definite geodetic measurement.

Final paradox: the most radical innovation in political government that the French revolution made was also the most destructive to human security: the institution of the popular army by conscription: a mass compulsion that went beyond the most ruthless and unscrupulous practices of despotic governments. The latter were wont to commandeer or shanghai a small minority of able-bodied men for their military service, or like the petty rulers of Germany, they enslaved for the army those already enslaved by serfdom. But under Carnot, the revolutionary government introduced the principle of universal compulsory service, so that the whole nation, and in particular all males of military age, became part of the armed forces. Volunteers had won the American revolution, ragged in discipline and unreliable, but free: conscripts saved the French revolution: saved it and betrayed it to a military conqueror, Napoleon Bonaparte. More had advocated conscription in his Utopia, an extension of the medieval levy; but now it became an agent of political mass-production which gave to war the equivocal benefits of factory organization.

This example, spreading to almost every other nation, at last even to those domains of freedom, Great Britain and the United States, multiplied the possibilities of military destructiveness and increased the financial burdens of war. Totalitarianism thus appeared first in democratic war: it inculcated military habits of mind, and caused a further reliance upon compulsion, automatism, drill, in departments of life where they had hitherto been foreign. This extension increased the difficulties of liquidating war as an institution; for national wars became temporary diversions from the class wars that now threatened the internal stability of the nations. Napoleon erected this condition into a strategy for extending power.

In general, the French revolution established no new rights that were not already guaranteed and established by the example of the American revolution. The makers of the later revolution were conscious of this fact: in the report read by the Archbishop of Bordeaux to the Constituent Assembly on July 28, 1789, one reads: "Our soil should by right be the first to which this grandiose idea [The Rights of Man and of Citizens] conceived in another hemisphere, should be transplanted. We co-operated in the events which gave North America her liberty, and now she shows us on what principles we ought to base the presentation of our own. Formerly we carried the fetters into the New World; now it teaches us to protect ourselves from the misfortunes of being obliged to wear them."

In so far as these revolutions succeeded, they became symbols of hope to the oppressed masses throughout the world. Beneath surface ups-and-downs, De Tocqueville was not wrong in saying that the history of the past seven hundred years had been a history of the progressive extension of equality, and the French revolution was a consummation of this long-established tendency. For more than a century, the very word revolution became a beacon, whose light queerly transformed the bloody facts of civil war into a noble idyll of poetic revenge. But the boldness of the act was tempered by the superficiality of the outlook: much that needed amendment was untouched by the revolution, particularly much that looked bright, new, modern, and therefore was sacrosanct. By putting the whole emphasis upon the transformation of institutions instead of giving equal attention to the re-education of men, the revolutionary leaders of the next century and a half turned their promised land into a mirage that perpetually retreated before them. Though they sought to cut society loose from its evil heritage, they forgot that they themselves, they and their guiding ideas, were a product of that heritage: so they evaded the most critical questions: Who is to guard the guardian? What is to revolutionize the revolutionists? The evils they tossed out the window nevertheless remained in the house: remained in the very person who had so valiantly appeared to remove them.

In the myth of revolution, a fresh beginning was taken as the guarantee of a happy ending. What does that mean? It means that when we seek to define the contents of the revolutionary myth, we shall find that it rested on a devout faith in the "New World" of science, capitalism, mechanization, and colonial expansion. So that it was not by accident that Thomas Paine spent his spare time inventing an iron bridge; that the Saint-Simonians projected the Suez and the Panama Canals, and that the greatest triumph of the French revolution was the extension of its benefits, as succinctly incorporated in a legal code, to the peoples subdued by the last of the great conquistadors, Napoleon I. Under this New World impulse, a get-rich-quick economics distracted people from the tasks of democracy: even Enfantin, one of Saint-Simon's most revolutionary followers, ended up as a prosperous railroad engineer.

In rejecting a twofold change, inner and outer, the parties of reform and revolution overlooked the organic connection between personality and community, between the individual and the collective form. They sought to transform the institutions of society through self-interest, and create a high order of social existence without bothering to develop and discipline a higher type of self. But self-interest thereby continued to have its say: it prevented the change from taking place. The scorn and contempt of the revolutionary philosophers during the nineteenth century, when speaking of religion, was due partly to the fact that the Church centered its attentions so exclusively upon the redemption and elevation of the individual soul. But the party of revolution made the opposite error: they regarded all obstacles to social improvement as extraneous: hence, they could be mechanically removed by law; if class opposition had grown too firm, they could be demolished by an overwhelming display of physical force in a popular uprising (the spirit of 1848) or by a ruthless "dictatorship of the proletariat" (the spirit of 1917).

Plainly both groups were the victims of a faulty analysis of society. Personality and community are much more intimately related than either would admit. But religion's knowledge of human nature and its encouragement of man's best qualities in the end showed a superior realism: did not the only open corporate resistance to Hitler in Germany come from the Christian churches?

5: Revolutionary Utopias

The political revolutions that took place throughout the Western World from the seventeenth to the twentieth centuries were important events in the life of Western man. At their worst, they were surgical operations that removed large parts of a tumor: operations performed, it is true, by clumsy hands that, in their haste, hacked into sound tissue and permitted portions of the fibrous growth itself to remain. But the names of Cromwell, Washington, Paine, San Martin, Bolivar, and Garibaldi rank high, not alone for their achievement, but for a promise still unfulfilled: they awakened in the common man everywhere a sense of his own personality, a new self-respect. They gave him the hope of overcoming his disabilities by uniting with his fellows and putting his social relations on a rational basis. They promised him liberty, and as long as he prized liberty, guarded it vigilantly, everything else might be added to it. Above all, they promised him a fully human life. Those hopes and promises still remain operative. And they have still to find fulfillment.

The spirit of revolution challenged irrational customs and invalid privileges; it broke down the barriers between classes, and gave the poorest boy the hope that he might achieve a place in society commensurate with his abilities. A plowboy like Burns might become the voice of his nation: a barber like Arkwright might become an industrialist: a poor printer's son like Michelet might become a great historian; a rail-splitting frontiersman might become a President. Even Napoleon would boast that a private in his army might carry a field marshal's baton in his knapsack. Both the political and the economic revolutions rejected the notion of a permanent stratification of classes: they elevated talents hitherto smothered in obscurity, doomed once to follow the inherited path. In the name of equality the revolution respected the inequalities of intelligence and professional ability, and drew upon the whole community for its leaders instead of confining itself to the established ruling classes. Goethe's grandfather was first a tailor, then an innkeeper. Instead of remaining at this level, Goethe's father went to Leipzig to study law; and Goethe himself attained a position above that of mere official rank. That, too, was part of the revolution: it opened up occupations and professions, as the discovery of the New World had opened up territory. William Cobbett, once an ignorant plowboy and soldier, never ceased to marvel over the miracle of his own self-transformation.

Naturally, the revolutionary ideology powerfully affected the condition of woman, whose economic status had deteriorated since the Middle Ages. Now she found her spokesmen for the right to be a complete, self-directing personality: Condorcet proposed to give her the ballot, and Mary Wollstonecraft raised once more the demand for an equal education: in the New World, around the middle of the nineteenth century, Mt. Holyoke, Vassar, and Oberlin led the way. Among the planks of the utopian platform laid down by Enfantin, the coming of a female Messiah was not the least; and, comically enough, his hopes were both fulfilled and derided by the belated appearance of Mary Baker Eddy.

Though the revolution had been conceived as a means of transforming human society by political action, the revolutionary temper operated in every quarter: it affected dress, manners, business, daily habits. One must beware of attributing to politics alone all the good and bad changes that revolution brought about. The readiness to place oneself in new situations, to participate in new experiences, to welcome new ideas, to adopt new manners, was a mark of the revolutionary personality. Once the barriers had been let down in politics, the spirit of change manifested itself in every department of experience: indeed, change itself came to be accepted as a value, irrespective of what it brought with it. With the blind faith of religious conviction, every break with the past was looked upon as a move toward a happier future.

This rejection of the past was arbitrary; but it had one great quality that distinguished it from the Christian rejection of paganism: it rested on an unbounded confidence in human powers; and by its very overcompensation here it raised the level of human energy. The symbol of that energy was Napoleon Bonaparte. Nothing now seemed impossible; and therefore many operations that had hitherto been impossible, from the spanning of rivers to instantaneous communication, were boldly achieved. The reactionary Joseph de Maistre wryly characterized this spirit when he observed that "the eighteenth century, which distrusted itself in nothing, as a matter of course, hesitated at nothing; and I do not believe that it has produced a single tyro of any talent who has not made three things on leaving college—a system of education for youth, a constitution, and a world." The dreams that were fabricated during this period of liberation continued to excite, to inspire, and to seduce men for more than a century. Only one thing could deflate these dreams: their translation into reality. Then the insufficiency of the revolutionary ideology became plain. Did it demand too much of the future? Not at all; but it had thrown aside too much of the past, and instead of serving and nurturing the whole man, the whole community, it was too easily content with fragments of both.

During the nineteenth century a series of revolutionary utopias were written; in them, the final hopes and aspirations of the revolution were imaginatively embodied. These ideal landmarks tell us almost as much about the condition of man in the nineteenth century as any factual history: furthermore, the utopias of Fourier, Owen, Cabet, Buckingham, and Bellamy all left their imprint upon actual society, above all the first two. Though Friedrich Engels criticized the spirit in which they had been conceived, contrasting it with the "scientific" system conceived by himself and Marx, the fact is that whenever the socialist movement passed from the stage of agitation to that of actual construction, it was forced to fall back upon the imaginative fantasies of the utopians: for if they were wishful idealists as to means, they were keen realists as to ends, so keen that they even defrauded their ideal expectations.

The man who first penetrated the weaknesses of capitalist production, who first devised, out of a fertile imagination, an alternative to the paleotechnic regime, was Charles François Marie Fourier: a genius whose social fantasies pushed common sense to the border of lunacy; or, if you will, a lunatic whose lucid imagination more than compensates for moments of unbridled fantasy. Fourier presents an unusual mixture of fanaticism and shrewdness, of wishful sleight-of-hand and penetrating observation, of daft hopes and rational proposals. He was the last nineteenth century economist, I believe, to begin his work with a series of propositions about the nature of God; he was likewise the first reformer to take full account of the existence of evil, and to propose, in a positive way, to make use of negative and hostile elements in order to generate a better society. One must think of this extraordinary man, a commercial traveler by occupation, as a sort of Balzac of sociology, capable of swift passages from absurd melodrama to robust observation and statesmanlike insight.

Fourier confronted the new conditions produced by paleotechnic industry: conditions for which the political revolutionists had provided neither a diagnosis nor a cure. Industrialism, for Fourier, was one of the latest of scientific chimeras, which produced goods in confusion without any proportional compensation, without any guarantee to the producer or wage-earner that he would participate in the increase of wealth, without any attempt to rectify the social or the personal results of lopsided mechanical toil. Fourier opposed to the mechanical atomism of this society his theory of combinations and groups; and he divided these groups according to the needs or "passions" of men: one of the earliest essays in dynamic psychology. Indeed, Fourier's brilliant intuitive improvisations in psychology and sociology were, in the main, sounder than much of what passed for science in these fields during the nineteenth century.

Fourier takes human passions as given; his utopia is not designed to "effect any change in our passions . . . their direction will be changed without changing their nature"; and the means that he proposed for doing this is to unite a sufficient number of people in an organized community, or phalanstery, whose varied occupations and interests, whose varied landholdings and industries, whose generous civic equipment, will give scope to every variety of human temperament. A good community, for Fourier, was one that would bring these passions into play, in their complex actions and interactions, toward the achievement of an ultimate harmony: for man has a threefold destiny, "an industrial destiny, to harmonize the material world; a social destiny, to harmonize the passional or moral world; and an intellectual destiny, to discover the laws of universal order and harmony." What was at fault in modern civilized societies was that they were incomplete: being incomplete, they thwarted men and created social dissonance: the merchant throve on scarcity, the doctor on disease, the soldier on war.

While Fourier accepted the minutest division of labor, he sought to nullify its evils by frequent change of occupation throughout the day, and by suiting the occupation itself to the temperament of the worker. He proposed to further interest by making every worker a copartner in the enterprise; and he enunciated the principle of social security, in the guarantee of a minimum of goods sufficient to remove all anxiety about the future from the worker and his family. Further, Fourier, with a critical eye for what was happening throughout the countryside, pointed out the current evils of deforestation and laid down a firm policy of conservation: almost a century before William James he proposed to create industrial armies of youths and maidens who "instead of devastating thirty provinces in a campaign . . . will have spanned thirty rivers with bridges, re-wooded thirty barren mountains, dug thirty trenches for irrigation, and drained thirty marshes." It is for lack of such armies, says Fourier, that civilization is unable to provide anything great.

For all his extravagances, Fourier was the first of the revolutionists to project a series of radical institutional changes in terms of the whole man, and to relate the wholeness of the individual to that of the community: here he was not merely the first but remained the last. If he attracted many generous souls in the nineteenth century, not least the ineffectual idealists of the Brook Farm experiment, he remained without influence precisely because of his desire for wholeness: even the utopias that followed were born of an impoverished sense of the human personality.

Fourier's contemporary, Robert Owen, if not less a zealot than Fourier, had the authority of a successful career as a hard-headed mill-manager and owner. When he spoke of the evils of the new industrialism, he spoke as an insider who had worked his way up through the ranks, and when he advocated improvements in the regime, he frequently sought only to widen the scope of his own experiments. Though Owen's career as a philanthropist met with far less immediate success than his career as an industrialist, its ultimate effects were profound. From Owen one may trace direct results in the trades union movement, in the co-operative movement, in the social security program, and in the design of garden cities.

Unfortunately, Owen's simplemindedness handicapped all his efforts and left a sad bequest to his followers. His doctrine of improvement was founded on the conception of the human personality as completely plastic and passive: by artful conditioning and systematic education he proposed to wipe out false ideas, and to replace them with correct ideas about man and his powers. Need I define "correct ideas"? Naturally, they were Owen's. If his doctrine were indeed true, it would be a better tool for despotism than for democracy: indeed, to the extent that it is true, despotism employs it.

Since Owen was exceedingly optimistic about natural man, his illusions about the rich were fantastic: he imagined that they would not oppose the workers' demands for amelioration if they were convinced that their own "comfortable and respectable enjoyment of life would not be affected"; and like many of the New Deal economists in our day, he was naïve enough to believe that the workers' condition could be radically improved without altering the fundamental values of capitalism, and without reducing the wealth or the prerogatives of those on top. Owen's original proposition, that caring for the human machinery was as profitable as oiling and repairing the physical machinery, was sound: but when it made him believe that reform would therefore prove more practicable he deceived himself. He forgot that capitalists must pay for new machinery; whereas, during the nineteenth century, they were provided with such a surplus of human machinery, gratis, that it scarcely profited them to repair what they could so easily replace, now that human skill no longer played so great a part in production.

Neither Fourier nor Owen had any great influence on society in their own day; but it would be a mistake to believe that their thought was without far-reaching practical effects: what they formulated as a complete scheme, the industrial order was to incorporate and embody by degrees: in this utopian ideas were no stronger or weaker than other ideas. Engels in his Socialism, Utopian and Scientific, poured scorn upon the long succession of thinkers who conjured up ideal societies and proposed detailed plans of action, without having the faintest regard for the way in which ideas became historically effective; but in terms of actual results, it is the utopians, not the scientific socialists, who have helped define the ends of socialized production: many of the most important social inventions of the last century and a half can be traced back to them. The imaginative intuitions of Condorcet, Saint-Simon, Enfantin, Fourier, Owen, Buckingham, Wakefield, Bellamy, Wells, once in circulation, undoubtedly acted as a stimulus to thousands of other minds and thus prepared the way for fresh action. When socialists had any concrete problems to face, they could get little guidance from Marx or Engels once the initial phase of seizing power was over: they were forced to return secretly to the very thinkers they had despised. Even the notion of "socialist competition," introduced in communist Russia as an incentive to production, goes back directly to Fourier. Marx's curses and tabus must not be allowed to hide this simple fact.

In one respect, all the utopians from Plato and More onward have implicitly warned mankind as to the price they must pay for mechanical perfection, little though that warning might be heeded: almost without exception they agree that the price of this perfection is loss of freedom, initiative, self-government. Utopia and Icaria are dictatorships: even Bellamy's Looking Backward rests political power in the hands of the superannuated workers, who elect the authoritative heads of the great labor armies. That warning too long remained unheeded: to those who were tired of the strain of free living it might even seem like a promise. But in addition, the utopian revolutionists were guilty of an even graver weakness—not the fact that they dreamed so copiously, but the fact that their dreams were so mediocre. Try as they would, the most optimistic minds of the nineteenth century were all obsessed by the utilitarian ideology: Bellamy no less than Marx, Engels no less than Spencer, could conceive of a better future only in terms of the widening triumphs of industrialism. For all these thinkers, the command of materials and natural forces might be only a preliminary step: but their goals were indefinable except in terms of this step—and beyond that their notions of a developing human life were nebulous. It is important to understand this obsession: the most extreme idealists shared it with the most sordid practical men. It explains the sense of fear that "progressive" and "liberal" minds still experience at the very possibility of a more human orientation. Their vision of perfection too rarely rises above the level of the machine. They do not suspect that when Prometheus stole the fire from Heaven he left even more valuable gifts behind.

6: The Dialectic of Revolution

The utilitarian ideology had above all one serious defect: the society that committed itself to these ideals produced many ugly and evil results that were not specified in the blueprints.

The rigorous order of the machine was opposed by the sprawling chaos of the new industrial towns; the wealth of the manufacturers was denied by the poverty of the workers; the peaks of prosperity for all classes were followed by commercial crises that often bankrupted even the more fortunate groups. On the facts of the case all the leading critics of the new industrial regime were agreed: the communist Marx, the tory Disraeli, the anarchist Bakunin, the bourgeois individualist, Henry George. Even Malthus and Ricardo were agreed as to the facts though they believed that the iron law of population and the iron law of wages were in substance unalterable. Progress *and* poverty marked the new industrial order.

By the middle of the nineteenth century the miscarriage of industrialism had become more conspicuous than its promises. Science and invention and organization, so far from contributing to the relief of man's estate, seemed to have widened his collective capacity for misery. Even those who, like Herbert Spencer, were originally sure that society was automatically following the inevitable path of progress, so that militarism would give way to industrialism, war to peace, and poverty to plenty, would discover before another generation was over that their beliefs stood in need of revision; for the very remedies brought forward to relieve the evils of industrialism seemed to Spencer to bring mankind nearer "The Coming Slavery."

The man who sought to master this situation, who planned to convert the utilitarian hell into a proletarian heaven, was Karl Marx, a German born of a Jewish family in the Rhineland, where industry had had a foothold even in Roman times. If anyone was capable of describing and resolving the contradictions of capitalist production it would be Karl Marx, whose life was a series of contradictions. A son of the bourgeoisie, married to a woman of noble family, Marx devoted his whole life to the emancipation of the working classes. But in his person, Marx never achieved the status of a manual worker, nor had he any first-hand contact with the routine of the factory. Despite his efforts as a newspaper correspondent, he and his family were parasitic on the earnings of his friend Friedrich Engels, who supported the communist movement out of a salary earned in a Manchester cotton firm. Marx migrated out of his class and his country: yet his ideology never overcame the militarist and absolutist bias of his native land, and he scarcely bothered to conceal his contempt for Russia, the country in which his writings were most widely appreciated. Finally, he who thundered against the moral airs of the bourgeoisie was too squeamish to admit Engel's beloved Irish mistress, a girl of the working classes, into his family circle.

The inner contradictions of Marx's background had their equivalent in his thought. He concealed the apocalyptic vision of a Jewish prophet behind an elaborate façade of scholarly investigation; and he called his particular scheme of thought "science" in order to hide even from himself its deep emotional urge and its essentially religious attitude toward human destiny—two qualities that gave it power to gain support among masses of depressed and desperate men. And while Marx despised wealth in the form of possessions and made his whole family live a life of bitter heroic poverty, he worshiped power as much as he hated greed: he had an inner need to dominate every group he became part of, and would unhesitatingly wreck it when it threatened to escape his control.

In the Communist Manifesto he and Engels sang a paean of praise to the bourgeoisie, exclaiming that "it had been the first to show what man's activity can bring about. It has accomplished wonders far surpassing the Egyptian pyramids, Roman aqueducts, and Gothic Cathedrals; it has conducted expeditions that put in the shade all former exoduses of nations and crusades." At one moment Marx hailed the new order because it had swept away all fixed, fast, frozen relations and caused man to face with his sober senses the real conditions of life: at the next moment he condemned the bourgeoisie for performing its mission so brutally, though he himself did not hesitate to urge the workers to take equally brutal revenge when their day came.

One need hardly list all the contradictions and ambivalences of Marx's attitude toward the world around him; for he organized them into a watertight system, a dialectic of history. His first master, Hegel, had taught him that the world as a whole was in a constant process of becoming; this was no aimless ebb and flow, but a purposeful current: it was the result of a struggle between opposites, in which a positive "thesis" begot its negation or "antithesis," and in the course of the struggle created a higher unity or "synthesis." For Hegel, "ideas" generated the material forms and institutions of actual life. Marx accepted the dialectic process as a complete description and turned it upside down: material forms, in particular, the instruments of production and exchange, brought into existence appropriate ideas in art, religion, philosophy, morals: these were mere shadows of the "real" world, the world of economic activity, which was governed by the necessity to eat, drink, have shelter and clothes, and to produce ever-more-elaborate means of securing physical livelihood. Like his seventeenth century precursor, Charles Blount, Marx regarded the forms of piety, justice, or art essentially as "grace before meat."

If Marx had perceived that his version of history actually complemented Hegel, instead of supplanting him, he would have created a sociological synthesis of the first order, in so far as history can be comprehended in the exclusive terms of the dialectic process. But in recasting Hegel's thought in materialist categories he rejected its valid aspects; and in holding that "material relations are the basis of all relations" he proceeded to confuse "basis" with "cause" and "reason." In Engel's farewell eulogy on the dead man, he claimed that "Marx discovered the law of evolution in human history: the simple fact, previously hidden under ideological growths, that human beings must first of all eat, drink, shelter, and clothe themselves before they can turn their attention to politics, science, art, and religion."

That claim gives away the weakness of the Marxian interpretation; for in actual history the developments of language, art, and politics are as early as the technological developments that secure man's physical existence: in society, these aspects of life are organically related and neither precedes the other. Marx was correct in saying that all of man's ideal creations have a material *basis:* he was wrong in confusing "basis" with "cause," and he was doubly wrong in not realizing that all of man's material achievements have, likewise, an ideal *basis*. Hence Marx assumes that economic institutions are self-begotten and all social changes are the by-products of that automatic technological development.

Marx's final mistake was to assume, with Hegel, that all change was of a dialectical nature: he and Engels understood best those changes in which opposition and struggle manifested themselves. They were highly conscious of the drama of life: especially the bloody drama. That made them welcome Darwinism and identify Marxism with that interpretation of nature. But they had no insight into other modes of development and growth: hence they overlooked the role of co-operation and mutual aid, which Peter Kropotkin was to emphasize. Historic observation shows that there are many modes of change, other than dialectic opposition: maturation, mimesis, mutual aid are all as effective as the struggle between opposing classes. In failing to take in the diverse modes of change, Marx compelled himself to overlook a good part of human history.

While the dialectic of history dominated Marx's thought and his plans, his larger significance comes from the fact that he brought together the three dominant streams of historic experience: the British tradition of empirical science and invention, as the basis for a new social order; the French tradition of political revolution, with its image of a complete regeneration of mankind by means of an uprising and a ruthless reign of terror; finally, the German Hegelian tradition of change as an essential attribute of both the order of nature and the order of society, so that each stage of history must be regarded, not as a closed achievement, but as in process of transcending itself by means of the very contradictions and struggles it generates. Marx transformed all three notions in the conception that the "history of all hitherto existing society is the history of class struggles," which ended "either in a revolutionary reconstitution of society at large, or in the common ruin of the contending classes."

Inflated by the yeasty optimism of his period, Marx never took seriously the second possibility. From the funeral pyre of capitalism he expected the phoenix of communism surely to rise. He was certain that the workers would be victorious; he did not admit that they might be more completely enslaved, nor did he entertain for a moment the thought that precisely for lack of class understanding and class collaboration, society itself might be thrown back into barbarism. Yet the very revolution he admired so ardently, that of 1789, provided a refutation of his main tenet. The voluntary renunciation of their feudal rights by the French aristocracy, in a sudden wave of moral enthusiasm and self-abnegation, had done more to wipe the slate clean in the French revolution than the savage guillotine had done. Compared to that single act of class collaboration all that had followed by way of coercion accomplished relatively little of permanent value. Though reason alone is impotent to effect such changes, humane intentions may at the right moment produce a powerful effect: the voluntary abolition of serfdom in Russia, prompted by the bad conscience of the ruling classes, was quite as effective as the forceful emancipation of American slaves achieved in the bloody Civil War.

By his dogmatic unwillingness to admit these facts, Marx made the path of revolution harder; for, by underlining the necessity for the class struggle and the dictatorship of the proletariat, by mingling his confident prophecies with loud threats of violence and revenge, the disciples of Marx roused the determined opposition of the ruling classes: fear urged the latter to anticipate the day of reckoning and to take matters into their own hands. Thus Marx conjured up an equally ruthless tactic of defense, an attitude which the moral and humanitarian scruples of the law-abiding nations had been slowly pushing into the background. When actual revolution finally broke out at the end of World War I, both sides showed a capacity for large-scale brutality which even Czarist Russia had hardly dared to equal during the nineteenth century.

If Marx treated the dialectic process as the revelation of destiny, his detailed interpretation of events proclaimed him a philosopher of history worthy to stand beside Vico and Comte. He realized that the French revolution had divided society artificially into two spheres, the political, in which man functioned as a tolerant, liberal, egalitarian citizen, and the economic, in which he was either a grasping capitalist or an exploited worker. Marx knew that a communistic system of production, such as the factory system by its very technical constitution actually is, could not be run for the benefit of a minority of exploiting individuals without, through its sheer productivity, wrecking this class-limited basis of existence.

But Marx believed that material conditions and technical inventions were self-created entities, existing in and by themselves: prime movers, original sources of social power. If they were otherwise, if they were the products of plan, effort, imagination, choice, they would then be subject to evaluation, rejection, improvement, change by means of the human will, as the utopians believed. This Marx could not admit as possible: hence he accepted the machine process as an absolute, imagined that the proletariat would simply take up capitalist production at the point that capitalism left off, and in 1869 denounced his friend Beesly as a reactionary because he had drawn up a program for the future.

Because of his self-imposed limitations, Marx never carried his social analysis of the machine to its conclusion: he had no plan for the deliberate projection of democratic methods into industry or of communistic processes and ideals into the art and science and morals of this society. From his standpoint, both efforts would have been self-defeating. But in rejecting such efforts, he guarded an even more colossal utopian hope which he never recognized as such: after proving that the industrial worker was brutalized, stupefied, and impoverished by capitalist production, he called upon this degraded creature to take the initiative in establishing a new order: the dictatorship of the proletariat was the key to salvation. That was worse than a paradox: it was a sentimental falsehood. In practice, the dictatorship was seized by a small group, an inner circle of ardent revolutionaries, partly drawn from the bourgeoisie and even the petty bourgeoisie, so heartily despised by the true revolutionist: Lenin was the son of a minor official. Unlike the Christian, who renounced society and therefore had no need of its arts and sciences, the Marxian worker was called upon to control a highly complex and powerful machine, and he was supposed to acquire the skill and insight and moral discipline needed on the spur of the moment.

By merely turning Hegel upside down, the materialist interpretation of history proved to be as limited as the idealist interpretation; and Marx's morbid fear of utopianism actually harnessed him to a past moment in history, that of the French revolutionary uprising. His doctrine of increasing misery, which would drive the proletariat into an armed revolt, gave to a climactic external crisis a role that a more timely sense of grievance and a more alert intelligence would have played without being driven to the last stages of desperation. Since Marx's imagination was chained to the French revolution he had no use for a superior wisdom that might have averted it: he was like a surgeon who rejects a cure done by means of diet because his own training demands the final use of the knife. Both Marx and Engels worked for civil war: indeed, Engels was preoccupied by war in every phase. Without war they could not envision change: "it is precisely the wicked passions of man—greed and lust for power—which, since the emergence of class antagonisms, serve as the levers of historical development." Thus Engels in his attack on Feuerbach. This is a sort of proletarian version of The Fable of the Bees.

As a fierce humanitarian prophet, as a student of the relation of technics to production, as a leader in the attempt to focus the energies of the working classes on their own emancipation, as well as their material improvement, Marx was a mighty figure, great because the moral fervor and humane vision of countless smaller men supported his purposes and gave direction and power to his abstract ideas. Marx is usually at his best when he makes least claim to being scientific, as in the speech in 1856 in which he said: "In our days everything seems pregnant with its contrary. Machinery, gifted with the wonderful power of shortening and fructifying human labor, we behold starving and overworking it. . . . The victories of art seem bought by the loss of character. At the same pace that mankind masters nature, man seems to become enslaved to other men or to his own infamy. . . . All our conventions and progress seem to result in endowing material forces with intellectual life and in stultifying human life into a material force." Who could have stated the case better? Carlyle, Ruskin, Tolstoy have little to add to Marx the critic.

Though the immediate program originally set forth by Marx and Engels in the Communist Manifesto has not been completely fulfilled, much of it has become the common property of every country, even one like the United States, in which the glib defenders of the status quo rationalize their monopolistic privileges as "rugged individualism." A heavy graduated income tax, abolition of all right of inheritance, centralization of credit in the hands of the state by means of a national bank, centralization of the means of communication and transport, extension of factories owned by the state, and the improvement of the soil in accordance with a common plan, equal obligation of all to work, with the establishment of industrial armies, especially for agriculture—all these youthfully utopian proposals of Marx and Engels have actually been achieved, or are accepted as common sense measures that are near to achievement in many countries.

Yet these changes have taken place, not by a revolutionary dictatorship, but, as it were, by a geologic process of leaching and displacement. Under pressure of war in present-day Britain most of the early Marxian program has been achieved without precipitating any struggle between the minority whose income derives from capital and the majority whose income derives from labor: in short, revolutionary changes may come about without bringing with them a titanic and ruinous struggle. On the other hand, the further developments of capitalist institutions have placed serious brakes on change: Marx could not anticipate that the enormous growth of insurance would throw an economic bridge between the classes, nor could he anticipate the extent to which all groups, and above all the capitalists themselves, would seek security, even at the expense of further development.

Apart from the utopian indiscretions of the Communist Manifesto, it is only in scattered passages in Marx—in his letters as well as in his main work, Capital—that the positive side of his vision appears. Then it is plain to see that he revolted against the industrial division of labor and believed the communist state would restore the wholeness of the human personality. He praised the possibilities of life on the American frontier, where the worker was not confined to a single occupation, and he looked forward to a time when a man might practice every occupation, as a man, without becoming identified with his work.

Marx's sense of the whole man, as being the necessary goal of a fully humane system of production, has far more value for us today than Marx's tortuous rationalizations of economic theory, in his attempt to make the facts contribute the necessary incentives to revolution. Though Marx was keenly aware of the difference between the biological and social constants in human life and the cultural variables brought into existence by the historical process, he himself never attempted to describe the constants in the economic process. The evils of Victorian industrialism exercised a serpentine fascination over him, and Capital was an attempt to give a systematic account of the transitory relations of capital, labor, and exchange in nineteenth century society: all that belonged in technics to this phase of capitalism he regarded as beyond modification.

But if one thing should be obvious here, it is that the concept of the whole man must rest upon a theory of production which itself takes into consideration the underlying needs of the human personality. When Marx said that current capitalism was bad, he meant plainly that it was bad for man as a human being. Hence any critique of mechanized production must take into account not only the worker's need for material sustenance, but the need for variety, for fellowship, for work-interest; not merely the need for security but the need for esthetic stimulus; not merely his demand for a just share of the rewards after the work is done, but for an equal share of reward in the work itself. The tenth item of the Communist Manifesto wisely advocated not merely free education for children but the eventual combination of education with industrial production. But who needs such a combination more than the mature industrial worker himself? Too easily did Marx and his followers accept the machine as an absolute: too subserviently did they believe that the replacement of craftsmanship by automatism was an inescapable if not always a benign process.

Here William Morris's salutary contrast to Karl Marx must be emphasized. For Morris was no mere reactionary medievalist: he was too fully immersed in practical activities to linger in his pre-Raphaelite rebellion: on the contrary, he remarked to Patrick Geddes that the iron steamships that were a-building in Glasgow were the Cathedrals of the industrial age, and he exulted not only in their craftsmanship but in the working unison they brought about. Unlike the bourgeois friend of the proletariat, Marx, Morris was a manual worker in his own right. Art, for Morris, was not a precious gift for the few but the daily bread of life, or at least the salt, without which life would lose its savor and the life-blood itself would be depleted.

Morris saw that the machine had devitalized men, and that in the current struggle for money and power the worker was slavishly accepting the ideals of his masters. What the worker needed was not just shorter hours but better hours; not more money but a richer life. Morris's picture of a renovated England in News from Nowhere disclosed a new order in architecture, town planning, and regional development: an idyllic picture that now turns out to be closer to a desirable reality than the vitrified cities and the sterilized personalities that once paraded as the paradise of mechanized and socialized man. Even in industry Morris stood for the primacy of the person. "Simplicity of life, even the barest," he pointed out, "is not misery but the very foundation of refinement." Hence the true reward of labor was in life-wages: self-education, self-expression, self-government: mastery and satisfaction *in* the job, not comforts and luxuries as a relief *from* the job.

Marx closed his mind to the possibility of humanizing the machine from within: he dismissed the values of craftsmanship as ruthlessly as he dismissed the values of rural life—praising capitalism because it had "rescued a considerable part of the population from the idiocy of rural life," though that rescue consisted in throwing them into the foulest slums and the most inhuman factories the world had ever seen. Here we approach the final paradox of Marx's philosophy: it rested on the conception of the continued expansion of the machine, a pushing forward of all those processes that had regimented and enslaved mankind, and yet out of this he expected not only a liberation from the existing dilemmas of society but a final cessation of the struggle. Fichte had suggested that the ultimate aim of government was to make government superfluous; but he was realist enough to put this goal myriads of years away. Marx, on the other hand, believed that as soon as the proletariat had abolished all other classes the state would wither away: with that, the millennial motive-force of history would disappear. Marx spewed out all the utopian minnows only to swallow an ideological whale.

Despite all Marx's rich historical knowledge, his theory ends in non-history: the proletariat, once it has thrown off its shackles, lives happily ever afterward. So he shared the Victorian love for the happy ending, though his theory of history had grasped the fact that processes, not things, are the essence of reality, and that every ending is a fresh beginning—or, as Whitman said, "it is provided in the essence of things that from any fruition of success, no matter what, shall come forth something to make a greater struggle necessary." At the very moment that mankind as a whole is clothed, fed, sheltered adequately, relieved from want and anxiety, there will arise new conditions, calling equally for struggle, internal if not external conditions, derived precisely from the goods that have been achieved.

Marx boldly recognized—it was an essential part of his Hegelianism—that the evils in capitalism might engender goods; but he was not realist enough to anticipate that the goods in socialism might in time engender evils: in short, that no historic achievement is perfect, none final.

Like every futurist utopia, Marxism denies the values that lie in the process of achievement: in plans and struggles and hopes, no less than in the ultimate goal. This is the commonest mistake of a detached idealism: it attributes to some final moment the value which lies in the whole process that the ideal has helped to set in motion: this overestimate of the moment of fruition forgets the fact that it is not the climactic moment, but the whole act itself that is irradiated by the ideal. This applies to social life as a whole no less surely than to some particular phase of it like love and marriage. For the last three centuries the revolutionary movement has abounded in examples of moral fervor, heroism, and self-sacrifice: it has its long role of martyrs from John Milton to Eugene Debs, men who renounced easy careers, who accepted long imprisonment, who showed superb contempt for death, who labored for the unseen and the unattainable without faltering or turning back. All these characteristics gave the revolution the impetus of a great moral act, containing within itself the values it sought to establish: many of those who lived for socialism in the nineteenth century indeed achieved a greater measure of brotherhood and selfless love than those who, in the twentieth century, established a socialist state.

But how different were these real goods from the image of the perfect society that the futurists possessed: that society where, as Eleanor Marx wrote to Beatrice Potter, "people would live for this world and insist on having what made it pleasant for them." Compared to the reality of the revolutionary struggle, that bourgeois idyll in disguise could only be called insipid. Real life, even under capitalism, real life with struggle, pain, disappointment, fellowship, hope, love, is better than utopia. And utopia, to become real, must accept as an incentive to thought and act the dialectic role of evil. Good conditions provide for steady growth, for maturation: hence they must more widely prevail. But negative conditions cannot be glibly exorcized: the problem of evil is to reduce it to amounts that can be assimilated; for evil is like arsenic: a tonic in grains and a poison in ounces.

The paradoxes of Marx's personal life were continued and magnified in the movement he founded. Marxians, by their anti-religious bias, could have no belief in either the religious or the sociological concept of incarnation. Yet Marx's personality continued to form the leaders who took up his work: his arrogance, his contempt, his capacity for vilifying his enemies and his incapacity to learn from anyone—except perhaps Engels—his belief that his personal dogmas were the impersonal deliverances of history, all this tended to create socialist leaders who were more capable of plotting for absolute power than of welding people with different backgrounds, ideas, and purposes into a unified group. The one-party state and the one-man government were the almost inevitable fruit of Marx's character.

In short, socialism suffered from an abortive incarnation. For Marx did not live the life of a socialist: his self-hatred and his self-contempt, which grew out of his sad situation, were magnified by repression and then projected upon every institution and every person that made him conscious of his internal conflict. The poison of Marx's hate contaminated the pure, humane streams of socialist doctrine.

In Engel's life there were more generous strains than in Marx's; indeed, he largely sacrificed his own career as a thinker in order to forward that of the beloved "Moor," as he called Marx. But he, too, hated Feuerbach's philosophy because it preached love and implied reconciliation: he denied his own organic conception of history by assigning the positive virtues to a stage beyond capitalism—as if they did not exist at least in the germ in every society. Here Kropotkin's analysis was far more sound.

Yet a day came when Engels was cut to the quick by Marx's unfeeling comments upon the death of the girl Engels had loved and lived with: a day when he marveled over the sympathy and understanding of some of his commercial friends. That day was almost for Engels an awakening; almost but not quite: the doctrinaire prevailed. And in the great successful personalities of the communist movement, above all in Lenin, Trotsky, and Stalin, Marx's aggressive and domineering impulses played a disproportionate part and rippled on through their followers. Abraham Lincoln in his charity, his humility, and his self-criticism, was a far better incarnation of the spirit of socialism.

One might say of the Marxists what Macaulay said of the Puritans and bear-baiting: that they sought to do away with exploitation not so much because of love of the exploited as out of hatred for the exploiter. Cut loose from the humanizing ideas of the English, the American, and the French revolutions, it was small wonder that Marxism in Germany lent itself so easily to the exploitation of the National Socialists: even the Jew-baiting of the Nazis was a sinister game that Marx himself actually began. The Russian deification of Marx, Lenin, and Stalin marked the downward passage of socialism into its opposite: authoritarian communism, tempered by conspiracy and stabilized by purges: the negation of the democratic and egalitarian ideal.

Before 1914 the ultimate triumph of socialism was often taken for granted. Year by year it claimed more adherents, returned more members to parliament, spread its doctrines more widely: its questions of dogma were debated and resolved with a logic worthy of the early Christian fathers. But the chief problems about which opinions were radically divided were matters of tactics and tempo—not what, but how soon, and by what method. By accepting capitalism as an inevitable stage on the road to socialism, the socialists not merely validated the goals of contemporary society but made them their own. To raise the existing standard of living, to widen the benefits of machine production, were ends upon which the utilitarian ideologists of the right and the left were both agreed.

This is not to belittle the positive moral elevation which a change from capitalist production to socialist production promised. Not merely did socialism stand for a higher morality, in which the creative and co-operative impulses would dominate the acquisitive ones. More than that: the very success of the Russian Soviet revolution in dethroning the conventions of capitalism and in establishing other incentives to work and action than those of profit-making and conspicuous waste, successfully shattered the conceit that the only alternative to capitalism was a return to a more primitive peasant economy.

In this respect, the Russian revolution, no matter what its chequered aftermath, would serve both as an example of achievement and a symbol of even greater hope: no less decisive than the French revolution had been for the movement toward political democracy. For the Russian revolution showed that capitalist methods, capitalist rewards, capitalist ideals were all man-made provisions, not laws of nature as the apologists for capitalism had proclaimed. Other means and other goals were equally possible: communism demonstrated this more dramatically than the co-operative movement had already done. People would even submit for a time to no little regimentation and arbitrary compulsion provided the humane goals of socialism, a true sharing of the goods produced by society, were kept in view by the new rulers.

Yet at the very moment of triumph, when the bolshevists seized power in Soviet Russia, a recoil took place; for the humanitarian face of socialism, its dream of material abundance and democratic fellowship, now hid behind the iron mask of war and authoritarian government. The war was forced upon the Bolsheviks: they were surrounded by hostile states that plotted their destruction. But the authoritarian aspect of socialism was a direct bequest of Marx: in his faithful translation of Marxian theory into practice, Nicolai Lenin progressively wiped out the groups and associations that would have shared and diffused the power of the state: what was not wiped out was incorporated within the state. Espionage, punishment without open trial, secret imprisonment in remote concentration camps or equally secret death, forced labor, the suppression of free speech and rational political alternatives, the creation of an official ruling class almost as remote from the masses as the capitalists and bureaucrats they supplanted, the complete centralization of economic power—all these new attributes of communism helped betray its original aims. Finally, the majority of those who had engineered this revolution were denounced as rascals and punished as traitors: as they had treated the Social Revolutionaries and Democrats who had differed from them, so they were treated in turn by their old comrades. If their accusers were right, this fact cast an ugly shadow over the origin of the revolution: if the accused were innocent, it cast a no less sinister reflection upon the state that had resulted from their efforts.

These were the historical causes for the deflation of communism at the moment when it should theoretically have been in a position to widen its power, as both a religion and a political movement, throughout the world. Wherever official communism penetrated, its tactics had only one aim: to seize power and hold it; and no lies, brutalities, frauds, defamations, or self-contradictions stood in the way of this aim: hence it demoralized its temporary allies even more than it did their common enemy. The final result of this immoral policy was the security pact between Hitler and Stalin: the pact that gave Hitler the green light for launching his attack upon the world. In the end Russia paid a stupendous price for this self-betrayal: paid in unqualified heroism and noble self-sacrifice; but the world paid, too.

When any further seizures of power were accomplished after the rise of the Bolsheviks, it was by nationalist groups which aimed to suppress the working class, to nullify all the international ties and organizations they had created during the past century, and to rule, in imitation of the Communist Party, by means of a single party machine: totalitarian absolutism, or Fascism. In short, the full harvest of practical Marxism was reaped first by the renegade socialist, Mussolini, who rejected all that was sound, humane, and generous in socialist doctrine.

Under the immediate causes of this deflation, however, were more profound ones that had grown out of the larger situation: the fact that socialism had been framed as a working-class counterpart of the utilitarian ideology; for Marx's mission was not merely to turn Hegel but also

Ricardo upside down. This ideology had been founded on the assumption that the means of production would continue to expand, and that the population, even under a planned economy, need never reach any limits. Karl Kautsky indeed reproached More for providing for a stable population in his Utopia. But the New World that had been conjured up in the sixteenth century was now approaching its natural end: the elements that had been left out of the New World picture were now coming back with redoubled force, frequently in regressive and atavistic forms. Emotions and feelings that the philosophers of the machine had neglected or despised, were now reasserting themselves: above all, the trunk of the past, which had been cut down, was now sending up numerous suckers, suckers infested with grubs and covered by fungus almost before they had left the ground. In their baser manifestations, these new forces would curb socialism: in their humane aspects, they would add to its mechanical futurism certain vital human elements it had always lacked.

CHAPTER X. BARBARISM AND DISSOLUTION

1: Compensatory Vitality

The period of exploration and colonization gave the primitive impulses of Western man a fresh outlet at the very moment that the machine threatened to curb them completely. From the fifteenth to the twentieth century those who revolted against the methodical discipline of daily life, who despised its comforts and conveniences, who loathed its efficiency as much as its inhumanity, could with a little resolution carve out a new kind of life for themselves at the edge of the wilderness. There the fundamental primitive types, long sublimated in the city, the hunter, the fisherman, the miner, the quarryman, the herdsman and the peasant, once more were dominant. Melville's sailor, who saw no good in "snivelization" because all it did was to make people snivel, could bury his contempt and assert his manhood reefing sail on a yard-arm in a storm.

As long as these openings existed, the machine could not completely subdue or depress the human spirit: there was a way out. Rather, the effect of the machine was just the opposite: it pushed men into adventure and even provided the few mechanical accessories, guns, compasses, that made it possible to face obstacles as terrifying as the Strait of Magellan or the high passes of the Rocky Mountains.

The throwing open of vast tracts of arable land throughout the planet had both a direct and an indirect effect upon human vitality. By the first half of the nineteenth century it enabled Western man to rival, in sheer numbers, the millions who, at starvation levels, populated the East. From this time on, famines became a sign, not of nature's niggardliness, but of man's economic and political mismanagement. The new foods alone did more than merely enrich the meager diet of the European: the quantitative increase in wheat, corn, and animal products was so huge that the population of Europe, despite enormous mass migrations to the Western hemisphere, was able to double in a century; and countries like England, with its command of both the seas and the overseas colonies, succeeded in quadrupling their population within the same span. Whether the actual birthrate went up during this period is perhaps questionable, though the changes in diet were probably favorable to fertility; but the survival rate increased enormously. For a sudden leap in gross physical vitality, no other period in history compares with the nineteenth century: the nearest comparable advance must have been that which accompanied, probably over a much longer span of time, the original domestication of plants and animals.

This gigantic biological revolution was both a quantitative and a qualitative one. It multiplied the number of people on the planet, and it enabled Western man, with his command of transport and firearms, to occupy the sparsely settled continents he had discovered. Never was the ecological balance of nature so violently upset as during the last two centuries: whole species of animals like the bison and the wild pigeon were practically exterminated in their native areas, while the introduction of the horse and the ox to the grasslands of the New World increased both the available horsepower and the quantity of domestic cattle that could be fed and sent to market. At the same time these farflung adventures upset man's own ecological balance: the intermingling of racial stocks and cultures occurred on a far vaster scale than any historic record bears witness to: the transplantation of the Negro from the continent to which he had so completely adapted himself, was only the first of a series of audacious displacements in which the profit and convenience of the exploiting classes outstripped both biological knowledge and social prudence.

Whereas in China and India a dense population was inevitably accompanied by insecurity, by economic anxiety, by starvation, the same conditions were met in Europe and the Americas with a confidence that approached recklessness. Life was cheap and the means of life seemed all-abundant: the factories of Manchester, Lille, Philadelphia, and Essen consumed men as heedlessly as they consumed coal. As for the natural resources that were thrown open in the new countries, the fertile prairies, the virgin forests, the wells of natural gas, the seams of coal—they were treated as if they were inexhaustible. If the land got poor, the farmer did not bother with fertilizer: he moved on. Everywhere, Western man sold his primitive birthright for a mess of sour pottage. In rebounding from the constraints of the machine, he achieved a negative freedom: the freedom to burn, to waste, to destroy.

Those who had faith in industry, in progress, regarded this temporary condition as a permanent and universal one. This accounts, perhaps, for the fact that the actual state of the working classes, though it dropped during the nineteenth century to levels of foulness and barbarism that recalled the worst degradations of Rome, did not have a discouraging effect even upon the masses that suffered. They still could hope: if not for themselves, at least for their children: if not at home, at least in some land beyond the seas. If they were not released *by* the machine they would be released *from* the machine. In that sense even a penal colony might be Utopia.

2: The Myth of Natural Selection

Western man's aggressive attitude toward nature and toward primitive peoples was, in a certain sense, a diversion from the assaults he had long carried on against his immediate neighbors. It had the advantage of being definitely more one-sided: therefore it provided easier and larger rewards. But man's attitude toward the primitive was ambivalent: one side of him was ashamed of his own greed and hard ambition: it led him to turn with loving interest to the very object he attacked. And just as the development of the machine was promoted by a dispassionate interest in the behavior of matter, so the exploration of the earth was followed by a new sense of awe and wonder over all the forms of life.

In Europe, the works of man are so constant, so spectacular, so stimulating that thought remained predominantly urban till the eighteenth century. But in other parts of the world nature composed cathedrals, arranged triumphal arches, erected the spires of distant mountain peaks, dwarfed to pettiness man's most pretentious handiwork; and the strangeness of the new flora and fauna helped lift all living organisms out of their conventional settings. Horticulturists, cattle-breeders, bird-fanciers, were stimulated by the strange species of plants and animals explorers brought back from the wilderness: as man wandered farther away from his ancestral habitats he found a new kinship with the other migratory species, the cuckoo and the stork, the duck and the swan, the eel and the salmon; and as he turned with new zeal to the improvement of the domesticated animals and plants, he began to reflect intensely on the origin of life itself. By a score of different channels the interest in nature widened: the discovery of the reproductive system of plants enabled amateur botanists of both sexes to talk as freely about sex as the Freudian theory of the libido did a century or so later: Darwin, while studying for the Church, was the member of an eating club that sampled unusual foods: in field and wood and mountain thousands of insatiable Plinys were observing the world of life, day by day, as it had never been observed hitherto, for in the wilderness such knowledge often had survival value. This interest flowed back into the laboratory and the study.

Buffon, Erasmus Darwin, Lamarck, Goethe, were all interested, not merely in the vast variety of living organisms with which man's own life is intertwined, but in their nature and development and transformation. Man began to recognize himself as the topmost shoot of a towering family tree, rather than as an upstart who had been given a divine patent of nobility some five thousand years before. The greatest lesson in the new natural history was a lesson in history itself: a lesson in life's growing dominion over the non-living, as one proceeded from the most ancient strata of rocks to those in which the most primitive worms and crustaceans left behind the evidence of their structure, and from thence through reptile and bird into the age of the mammals: finally the dominance of man and the re-ordering of the entire balance of life on this planet. Here indeed the great chain of being became visible: the interaction of the non-living and the living, the continuity of living organisms, their variety and plasticity, their unsuppressible energy in meeting the hardest challenges and their capacity for planning, beyond mere survival, toward an ever-more-purposive and self-sustaining development. On one hand, stability, dynamic equilibrium: on the other, growth, development, transformation. Geology, paleontology, phylogeny all extended man's time perspective: hence man began to see his own development as part of an historic process in which his fellow creatures, the earth itself, finally the planetary system and the universe were all involved.

This new time perspective was in such contrast to the millennial earthly periods of Biblical history and the blank eternities with which Christian theology had been concerned, that even the most daring thinkers of the early nineteenth century could hardly entertain it. Thus Hegel, who is often given credit for evolutionary views, held that change was an attribute of the spirit alone and that the world of nature was only a perpetually self-repeating cycle, so that the "multiform play of its phenomena so far induces a feeling of *ennui*." But now freedom, novelty and purposive adaptation could be detected within the entire world of life: stability maintained itself within an unending spiral of development. Above all, time itself had a new meaning, for it could be correlated with phases of organic growth, both in the history of the individual and that of the species. The apparent fixity of organic forms was reduced to an optical illusion: life was a process of change, of development: above all for man. Carrying his dead ancestral selves in his germ plasm, he nevertheless sought through his developing cortex and his more fully integrated nervous system to pass beyond himself and establish conditions that supplemented, partly supplanted, nature's.

Give nature sufficient time, exclaimed the evolutionists after von Baer and Schwann, and nature will transform a primordial cell into a band of apes or an Academy of Platonists. The exploration of time became for the nineteenth and twentieth centuries what the exploration of space had been for the sixteenth and seventeenth. Biological time: evolution. Social time: pre-historic archaeology and history.

The discovery of man's own biological roots was the culmination of a long intermittent process of observation and thought that had entered the available written record with Aristotle. Organic evolution became one of the most important themes of human life during the nineteenth century: the recognition of man's animal origin even obscured for a time his divine destination, and led to a cynical disparagement of his ideal achievements. But fresh though this new biological stirring was, the dominant mode of the period remained a mechanical one; and even in the mind man's redoubtable achievements in observing and understanding nature were perverted by his naïve faith in the utilitarian ideology. One could multiply the instances of this miscarriage of thought; but I will confine myself to the largest, that which overtook the doctrine of organic evolution itself. Here, as in the cult of nationalism, the very reaction against the machine was transformed into its opposite.

No one was more at home in the world of life than Charles Darwin. Rebelling against a career as a doctor or a clergyman, he joined the *Beagle* on a five-year cruise as a naturalist: in that ship, he wandered over the face of the earth, observing the natural landscape and the forms of life. Chronic seasickness did not deter him from his task; and though he collected specimens of every kind, his own most systematic work as a naturalist consisted in a two-volume description of the barnacle: all that lived was grist to his mill. Like a good romantic he loved the most naturalist of romantics, Wordsworth: Darwin read and re-read The Excursion. As husband and father Darwin participated in the collective insurgence of life: he became the father of ten children, nine of whom survived.

Now, Charles Darwin, the naturalist, was a model for his kind: he mingled acute habits of observation with a sympathetic insight into the impulses and needs of all organic life: when he sought to observe the behavior of babies, he was a good enough naturalist to place the baby in its natural environment, the arms of a young woman. Darwin's study of the ecological relations of the earthworm gave a formative impulse to the new science of ecology: the study of groups, associations, food-chains, in all their organic complexities, gradually took the place of the isolated analysis of dead organisms and deformed structures. Darwin's investigation of the expression of emotions in animals laid the foundation for the new science of animal psychology, so fruitful in its suggestions of the primordial contents of higher human behavior. Wherever Darwin touched life at first hand his influence was a fertilizing one. If he never had a gift for systematic experiment in the fashion of Claude Bernard or Louis Pasteur, he had the prospector's gift for opening up new veins of research. In paying tribute to Darwin the great naturalist one only humbly echoes the considered judgment of most biologists.

But Darwin was lifted to fame by his contemporaries through something other than his narrative of the *Beagle* voyage or his observations of living nature. He became known as the central exponent of the theory of biological evolution. The doctrine that all existing forms of life had developed from earlier and simpler forms, all of which could be traced back to a central stock, was familiar to the Greeks and had been restated in verse by Darwin's grandfather, Erasmus Darwin: Herbert Spencer's vast philosophic synthesis of evolution had already begun publication before the Origin of Species appeared. But in the Origin of Species the doctrine of evolution was given by Darwin a peculiar twist: his leading idea, the idea he fancied was original to him, was the notion that the population of all species tends under natural conditions to outstrip the food supply, that this brings about a struggle for existence between the members of the same species, and that as a result, the weaker members are driven to the wall, while those who survive reproduce their kind and hand on to their descendants precisely those more favorable variations that enabled them to survive. Extermination became the key to development.

This theory, developed amid a wealth of naturalist observations, put together many widely drawn facts on modifications, fluctuations, and variations which took place within species: Darwin established the prime difference between bodily modifications that took place in the lifetime of the individual and the more radical kinds that were enregistered in the germ plasm and transmitted to the offspring. He linked up observations of the succession of the species, established by paleontology, with evidences of an organic succession found by comparative embryology. Many live fish were caught in this evolutionary net: but the main fish was a fake that had been unconsciously placed there by Darwin himself—the notion that natural selection accounted for organic development. Darwin sought to draw forth a purposive result from the facts of accidental variation: the mechanism of this purpose was the struggle for existence and the survival of the fittest.

On this central thesis, Darwin's contribution remained confused and contradictory. Indeed one has only to state it clearly to see that it is a negative principle, which explains survival, if it indeed explains anything, but does not give an account of the actual processes of variation and transformation themselves: on the latter point Darwin, when pushed to a conclusion, alternated between Lamarckian striving and mechanical changes in the germ-plasm. As for natural selection itself, Hans Driesch properly characterized Darwin's hypothesis of a gradual accumulation of *accidental* variations as one that would equally well create the structure of a house by the method of throwing bricks at random on the site. What, then, was Darwin's contribution? What made the Origin of Species a turning point of thought in the nineteenth century?

Darwin's "original" contribution had been anticipated by Alfred Russell Wallace; and the imminence of Wallace's publication not merely gave him acute pain but made him hasten to finish his own work. Now the answer to this question does not lie in biology. The very theory of natural selection had been partly stated by Diderot in the eighteenth century: "I maintain," he said ". . . that the monsters annihilated one another in succession, that all faulty combinations of matter disappeared, and that only those survived whose mechanism implied no important misadaptation, and who had the power of supporting and perpetuating themselves." What did Darwin and Wallace add to this notion beyond the support of a vast volume of observations? Nothing more nor less than the Reverend T. S. Malthus's theory of population: the belief that population increases in geometrical ratio while the food supply increases in arithmetical ratio; so that poverty, vice, crime, and war are the only alternatives to either Christian abstinence or a voluntary decimation.

This theory of Malthus's performed a special social duty: it explained why the poor must remain poor, and why the upper classes, by getting all they have, are by a supreme law of nature entitled to have all that they can get. In its application to society, it was false; though it immediately suggested to the acute mind of Francis Place the "neo-Malthusian" expedient of introducing contraception to the poor, as a mechanical alternative to such dire extremes of vice and virtue. What Darwin did was to read back into nature the current struggle for economic success: both he and Wallace took Malthus uncritically without asking for proof of his neat generalizations. Thus Darwin came to confuse the fact of survival, which rests on many other circumstances besides individual ability and capacity, with the fact of biological development: he confused fitness with betterment, and adaptation with physical prowess. In short, he justified man's contemporary inhumanity to man by pinning the whole process on nature.

Here lay the secret of Darwin's great popular influence: his theory of natural selection sanctified the brutality of industrialism and gave a fresh impulse to the imperialism that succeeded it. No matter that the over-emphasis of the struggle for existence forgot the factor of mutual aid: no matter that it overlooked the fact that within the species co-operation rather than struggle is one of the mainstays of life: no matter that commensalism is as primordial as a predatory mode of life. Darwinism, if not the gentle Darwin himself, would deliberately interpret the facts of love in terms of economic prowess. Hence it was not as a biologist but as a mythologist that Darwin triumphed: he lent to the brutal assertions of class, nation, and race the support of a holy "scientific" dogma. The industrial world was flattered to find its own reflections in this mythical black tarn of nature: it found the shabby tricks of the factory and the counting-house justified in the stratagems of field and forest: luck, force, ruthlessness, greed were what the ruling classes took to be the secret of survival. No one can dispute, of course, the existence of struggle and bloody aggression in the world of nature: what Darwin's theory did was to magnify these factors and to make them an all-sufficient explanation of the course of life.

Though Darwin got his lead from Malthus, he in turn gave support to Marx. The latter not merely presented Darwin with a volume of Das Kapital when it appeared, but he and Engels hailed Darwinism as a scientific confirmation of their theory of the class struggle. The answer to both Darwin and Marx came from many sources; and it has been steadily increasing in volume with the advance of ecological studies. One of the earliest and best answers came from the geographer and philosophic anarchist, Kropotkin, who pointed out how completely the Darwinists had overlooked the factor of mutual aid in evolution, while another came from Samuel Butler, in Evolution, Old and New, and in Luck or Cunning? who pointed out the strange contradictions between Darwin the naturalist and Darwin the evolutionary philosopher. But for two generations the Malthus-Darwin myth had its way, for it made every act of raw egoism an assertion of nature's fundamental law—and must not nature be respected and obeyed?

Observe the final result. Precisely at the moment when the mechanical means of communication and transport were making the world one, a subversive ideology, on the basis of a partial, falsified view of nature, sanctioned non-co-operation and erected the struggle for existence into a dogma. Men who had guns and who used them ruthlessly—the Americans robbing the Indians, the Belgians in the Congo, the Germans in Southwest Africa, the Boers and British in Transvaal, the united Western powers in Peking—were obviously destined to survive: their brutality placed the seal of virtue on their fitness. To exterminate their rivals was to improve themselves—or so the gunmen thought.

In its popularized forms, Darwinism not merely expelled value and purpose from the processes of life: it relieved humanity of its collective super-ego. The earlier utilitarians had always unconsciously assumed the existence of values: their very faith in machines, which are products of human contrivance, placed them above those who would reduce life itself to a meaningless brawl. Herbert Spencer, George Henry Lewes, James Hinton, Samuel Butler, each of whom had a more humane philosophy, lacked ultimate influence if not immediate homage. What the militant leaders of this society took from biology were not its truths but its errors.

Thus the spreading interest in life-processes fostered barbarism and played into the hands of the unscrupulous. In reacting against the dehumanization of the machine, people identified the natural with the savage, the organic with the primitive, the life-creating with the death-serving. Let us examine more carefully the destructive effects of these perversions within the realm of politics.

3: The National Struggle for Existence

The biological myth of ruthless struggle, coupled with a recognition of the interlocking role of organisms, had its political equivalent in another doctrine whose bellicose falsities undermined its partial truth: the doctrine of nationalism. Both beliefs were protests against the anti-vital rationalism of the "New World" idolum; and it is important to distinguish what was healthy in these protests from what was morbid, for they contained both elements. The common element that unites nationalism and naturalism was a recognition of the organic: the understanding that man lives, not solely by ideas, but by energies and vitalities that underlie his conscious, institutional life and that connect him with the world of nature.

This recognition of the organic was a corrective to the shallow rationalism of the mechanists: their order had been achieved by the process of excluding a great part of life. Naturalism acclimated man to the real world, established the roots of his higher impulses in the very depths of organic existence, related his experiments in social living to the far more ancient experiment of the social insects, connected his home-making with the nesting of birds and even the cruder provisions certain fish make for their domicile, showed how he shared the institution of marriage with many other creatures and even his attempts at monogamy with many species of birds. In short naturalism gave order and continuity and perspective to all manner of human institutions, and made understandable those residual impulses, welling out of a blinder, starker past, to which theology had affixed the name of "original sin." But for the growing worship of life, man's cult of the machine might have proved even more destructive.

In the development of nationalism, the new sense of the organic disclosed itself in both a biological and a social form: it came as a heightened consciousness of racial affiliations, as a cult of rural life and a fondness for special regional backgrounds, as a deliberate appraisal—often invidious—of those differences of face and physique, of language and customs, of memories and habits, which set one regional group apart from another. This sense of identity with a small, earthbound "in-group" is extremely ancient: the sentiment of nationality long antedates any conscious belief in nationalism; but in the eighteenth century both the primitive and the cultivated belief in the nation were in disrepute: the rationalists looked with scorn on the nation as the enemy of "humanity." Christian Gluck boasted of the fact that his music, appealing to all nations, would bring out the laughable weakness of national music: Lessing, in an introduction to Gleim's Grenadier Songs in 1758, rejected the praise of such patriots as would make him forget the fact that he was a world-citizen: Chesterfield said that while a Frenchman would venture his life with alacrity for the honor of the king, he would probably run away if you suggested that he die for the good of his country.

Despite the lift that both the American and the French revolutions had given to national self-consciousness, despite the effect of Napoleon's conquests in encouraging nationalism, by way of reaction, upon the conquered peoples of Europe, nationalism in the larger, securer states seemed doomed. "National differences and antagonisms between peoples," wrote Marx and Engels in the Communist Manifesto, "are steadily vanishing. . . . The supremacy of the proletariat will cause them to vanish still faster." But just the opposite happened: from the middle of the nineteenth century on there came a great resurgence of nationalism: so far from being absorbed in the new mechanical pattern of life, long-submerged nations, the Italians, the Czechs, the Provençals, had a fierce reawakening.

The ground for this national revival had been prepared by the romantic poets, painters, and philosophers: the headwater of these romantic streams was not Rousseau but Shakespeare. In a whole cycle of historic plays Shakespeare had tied the self-regarding sentiment of a people to a landscape and a way of life: "this happy breed of men, this little world, this precious stone set in the silver sea, which serves it in the office of a wall. . . ." The discovery of Shakespeare had awakened German romanticism with Goethe and Schiller and, somewhat later, had aroused the genius of Victor Hugo: the historical dramas of Shakespeare in turn begot the historic novels of Walter Scott, the author of Waverley, and with this came a new cycle of national self-consciousness, promoted by pious antiquarians who identified and restored old buildings, who rummaged among ancient manuscripts or rescued, from living lips, the precious ballads and songs and fairy stories of the folk. Even the archaic elements in nationalism, with their emphasis upon legendary achievements and legendary virtues, only did justice to archaic elements in the human consciousness that rationalism had either disguised or repressed. William Blake's poetry is perhaps the best symbol of this patriotic romanticism, with its summons to build Jerusalem in England's green and pleasant land.

Rousseau understood the part that imagination played in building up the national personality. In his Considerations on the Government of Poland (1772) he sought to show the Poles how they could prevent Russia from swallowing them; and he advised them to revive their national customs, to hold national games, to present national plays and observe holidays that should "breathe patriotism": but more important than all these devices, he advised a national system of education, to give people "a national form." Under this influence, the past and the local, repressed by the utilitarian ideology and banished from the New World, came surging back in life-evoking images: in that new movement, even the humblest peasant who could remember the snatch of an old song, even the most illiterate artisan who could recall the steps of a sword dance, could contribute to the heritage of his nation: under nationalism the repatriation of the folk took place. Utilitarianism was a philosophy; but nationalism was a religion.

Western civilization knows only one religion, indeed, that compares in scope and vitality with the main body of the traditional religions. Even more than the Church, nationalism gave to the inhabitants of every country and region a common faith: belief in an ideal past, hope for a common future. To the suppressed nationalities, the Jews, the Catalans, the Italians, the Poles, it even offered a dream of Resurrection and Redemption. Very few people were persecuted for their belief in Christianity during the past century before the advent of the fascist barbarians; the cause of nationalism has produced a legion of martyrs and saints: men who have lived selflessly for their nation and have died, like Padraic Pearse and his comrades in the first Irish Revolution, in order that their nation might live.

Nationalism is often treated as a political phenomenon of the same order as socialism. But the fact is that its roots are deeper; and the sources that feed it are those remote and subtle elements in the soul that bring together in a curious kinship those who laugh at the same kind of joke or pronounce with the same inflection and modulation the words of their language. Nationalism may be defined as the bond of common purpose that unites those who have the same language, the same background of nature, the same rituals of life: one or more of these is necessary, but the patch of earth is all but indispensable, if only to serve as common ground in the imagination—and a common speech, a dialect if not a language, is part of it. Clusters of emotion form about such ways and objects; and nationalism overcompensated for the general neglect of emotion by giving it full sway.

Now the individuality of groups of men is as genuine a fact as personality itself. Of old the inhabitants of Boeotia were slow and the Athenians quick; the Italians were subtle and polished and the Germans uncouth; the French volatile and the English steady. As with all living personalities, groups, too, change their characters: the blood-thirsty Norsemen who spread terror throughout Europe in the ninth century are today the peaceful Scandinavians who dismantled their armies and offered Peace Prizes. But the sense of group identity, preserved and fortified through historic memories, is the very essence of nationality. This was true before nationalism had taken on a political role; it will remain true, though the apparatus of democratic political life be shattered. He who uproots nationality kills personality.

The nation has had two opposing forces to contend with during the past century. One was the development of those pragmatic habits of mind and those impersonal mechanical organizations which ruthlessly pushed the personal life itself to one side. In that attack, the nation suffered no less than the individual. But by the very rigors of repression, the nation developed the capacity to resist and to hit back; so that the very century that saw the spread of all the unifying mechanisms, railroads, cables, telephones, also saw the unprecedented re-birth of national languages and national literatures. A new sense of national self-respect led to creative efforts in all the arts. Standish O'Grady in Ireland restored the heroes of the Red Branch and Deirdre of the Sorrows: Emerson, with eyes turned to the future, hailed The American Scholar: Herzl renewed the ancient dreams of Zion.

The progressive minds of the past generation treated these national revivals as largely reactionary phenomena. If they had any political significance, according to these views, it was merely as a disguise to the naked search for power in new states that sought to be unified and politically strong. But reaction itself is a question-begging word, like revolution: the point always is what one is reacting from, or what one is throwing off. Nationalism was a reassertion of group personality, in the face of the organized suppression of personality. In this sense, it was not an alternative to rationalist cosmopolitanism: it was rather a corrective. Both forces were necessary, a universalizing process and a localizing, regionalizing, nationalizing process. The machine tended to spread modern culture on the horizontal plane: nationalism assimilated and absorbed modern culture, taking what it could use, modifying it, mixing it with the old, acclimating it to the local scene.

The other inimical element lay within nationalism itself. This was the tendency to identify the national and the local with the interests of the state and its ruling classes. In the case of England that state contained nations as conscious of their identity as the Scotch, the Irish, and the Welsh; in the case of a country like America, it led to an attempt to identify as American a particular set of political institutions which spread over a continent of great diversity: here "national interests" tended to blot out real regional diversities and the geometrical uniformities of sectional land subdivision increased this tendency. Love of one's land, love of one's folk, are both very deep elements in the human psyche; but they were thinned out in order to provide motive-power for political and economic combinations that occupied the rulers of the modern state. Local industries might be suppressed in order to increase the profits of distant shareholders, seeking a national market.

One further result followed. By treating national boundaries as military walls, each national government came to assert an attitude of jealous belligerency toward other national governments. The wall itself engendered a non-co-operative spirit in those behind the wall. If political nationals had much in common, they had it mainly in opposition to other sovereign nationalities. National self-respect was turned into belligerent self-assertion: national unity promoted international disunity. And so the innocent emotions and feelings which bind men to their village, with its familiar landmarks and familiar faces, were canalized into fuel tanks of emotional suspicion and hatred directed against other nations.

In this new mythology, the nation became god; and the state assumed the position claimed by the Catholic Church, as God's representative on earth. But the new god was a tribal god, a jealous god; a god who grew strong on the strife that existed between nations, a god of war, not peace. This paranoid nationalism, with its absurd claim to the uniqueness and greatness of its own chosen people, with its intense fear and hatred of all rival nationalities, was but the pathological overstimulation of feelings and perceptions and sentiments that were, in origin, mainly sound— if always dangerously limited and stultifying until mingled with more universal interests. Such an animus prepared for war and throve on the very idea of war. By the same token it denied value to all the unifying instruments and institutions that promised to make men at home wherever they walked or traveled on earth: brothers in the common life, neighbors in a common world, co-operators—as G. A. Borgese says—in the common cause.

In its evil aspect, nationalism begins with a sense of exclusion and it ends with a desire for domination: the very Carbonari of the nineteenth century, who sought to widen the ideals of cosmopolitan freedom on the French revolutionary model, became the agents of the new French nationalism rather than apostles of humanity. Nationalist isolation induced delusions of grandeur accompanied by an equally neurotic claustrophobia—a sense of being hemmed in and suffocated. In order to feel secure it turned to conquest and expansion: witness the ugly landgrabbing of the United States from Mexico, the conquests of Napoleon, the steady encroachments of the German states upon their neighbors, from Frederick the Great to Hitler the Near-Great.

To establish a political form for the national group, Garibaldi marched, Fichte preached, Bolivar fought, Herzl planned, Pearse plotted, Masaryk organized. If a religion consists of the beliefs and hopes for which men, when challenged, will sacrifice their lives and fortunes in the assurance of participating in a greater life, then nationalism was the vital religion of the nineteenth century. For every Livingstone in Africa who was ready to die for Christ, there were a thousand humble men who would die for their country, and call their death good. There were depth and nobility in this new religion: it seized men, for a century or more, with a fanatical passion similar to that which Christianity had once stirred. Even at its shallowest, nationalism tended to restore many elements in the human personality that had been repressed by the machine. But one element was lacking that was needed to counterbalance it and humanize it: the element of universality. It offered to a tribal god that devotion which only a more universal divinity should claim.

The neurotic manifestations of nationalism come to a final state of disintegration in fascism. As hatred mounts and power grows and self-love increases, the ruling nation, no longer confined to its native soil, no longer content with self-cultivation, seeks to blot out every other nation, or to make it over in its own image. At that moment of frenzied self-worship no sacrifice seems too great for the leader to demand of his followers, no humiliation too base for them to inflict on their victims. The regressive impulse of imperialism, recoiling on itself, begets totalitarianism: nothing outside the state, nothing above the state, nothing beyond the state.

Joseph Mazzini did his best to rescue nationalism from this horrible self-destruction. In the middle of the nineteenth century he attempted to give the sentiment of nationality a broader basis: he emphasized duties instead of rights, and he returned to the vision and practice of Dante, though he did not make Dante's mistake of putting his faith in an absolute Emperor. Mazzini saw that the nations of the world are no more self-sufficient, no more independent, no more isolated than the individual personality. They are the focus of energies and ideas that lie outside their national boundaries both in space and in time. In serving themselves, they must also serve all other groups: whereas by imagining themselves self-sufficient, by clinging to the myth of isolation, they actually encompass their own doom. Hence the recognition of nationality, the overthrow of foreign rulers, the redrawing of national boundaries, the unification of national states, were for Mazzini but preliminary to the larger political and cultural synthesis toward which mankind moved: the unity of the human race.

Why did Mazzini's great dream fail of immediate realization? We may trace the causes back, I think, to the initial split between the romantic and the utilitarian super-egos. In its historical aspects romanticism tended to foster the archaic even when it held to the organic: whereas the utilitarian, prompted by a vision of security, comfort, ingenious mechanical superfluities, conjured up a future that had no roots in the past and no secure hold on the deeper levels of the human personality: its antiseptic, colorless, neutral world was hostile to the blind, self-preservative impulses of life. Regarding nationalism as a musty costume play, the utilitarian made the mistake of overlooking the need for emotional support for his new mechanical structure: he held that the cash nexus or class interest, if not self-interest, was sufficient to displace all other loyalties and create a life wholly favorable to his main preoccupations. The First World War showed the weakness of both philosophies and the fatality of their split.

Nothing could be done to make nations and cultures perform their universal mission without modifying the methods and the objectives of the machine economy. Until that was done, nationalism could be only a disguise for corporate egoism and unsuppressed economic rapacity: national interests meant national economic interests, the right of unlimited exploitation of economically backward peoples—the external or the internal proletariat. Beginning as a reaction against the machine, nationalism was presently captured by its enemy, precisely as the evolutionist's interest in organic life had been captured. This phenomenon puzzled many sober rationalists. Not merely Herbert Spencer, but even as late as 1914 the historian, Cunningham, in an appendix to his Christianity and Economic Science, observed: "Twenty-one years ago I noted the revival of national life and national sentiments in many quarters, but I regarded it as an anachronism. . . . This disparagement of nationality as a factor in economic life now seems to me premature."

Premature it was. Instead of nationality's attaching itself to a more general sentiment of humanity, just the opposite happened: the universal instruments of mechanization attached themselves to the nation. By taking advantage of nationalism the aggressive capitalism of the second half of the nineteenth century, bent on capturing world markets, utilized the pride and egotism, the vainglory and the self-worship of nationhood to promote its own lust for power and gain. Millions of men who were not a penny the richer talked about the land "they" had captured, the economic concessions "they" had demanded, the markets "they" had won, and they lived on the almost wholly vicarious enjoyment of the wealth that had been seized in their name. Economic rivalry led to fresh military rivalry, and military rivalry to childish assertions of cultural eminence, attempts to establish exclusive claims to supremacy for Russian music as opposed to Italian music, for French medical science as opposed to German medical science, for American invention as opposed to British invention. These efforts at cultural autarchy all denied the outstanding triumph of the past two centuries: the fact that all the great achievements in culture had been the results of a worldwide interchange of ideas and a worldwide collaboration of peoples.

Yet for a while the irrational forces of nationalism were in balance over against the more rational forces of industrialism: prior to the First World War collective reason seemed even to have the upper hand. People migrated freely across national frontiers, without regard to occupation and status and without using passports, which were needed only in the surviving despotisms of Russia and Turkey. Freedom of the person existed as it had never existed before, and even the humblest profited by this: when oppression grew unbearable the common man could migrate. International capital had investments in every country and colony: a single fire insurance policy might divide the risks between a company in London, one in Paris, and one in Moscow or Vienna. If tariffs still halted the flow of goods at many frontiers, they did not put an end to an interchange of surpluses and specialties. A common sense of law and order prevailed over large parts of the planet, to a now-astonishing degree: peace, security, continuity reigned as under the Antonines. So deep had become respect for the personality, so sure was the sense of individual freedom, that when a single lame cobbler was attacked by a German officer in Zabern, because the humble man had not yielded the sidewalk to him, a cry of outrage rose throughout the world—not least in Germany, where the Reichstag censured the government by a vote of 293 to 54.

In this atmosphere, a true internationalism offset the swollen claims of imperialism and in no little degree atoned for its evils. International congresses of science, art, and religion might disclose great cleavages in ideology: nevertheless, like the succession of World's Fairs that followed the Crystal Palace Exhibition of 1851, they registered the underlying desire for a wider sharing of goods, values, ideas. Nationalism, imperialism, and scientific rationalism were engaged in a three-cornered contest; and for a time it seemed that the last would ultimately displace the other two. The rationalist's heaven seemed near.

A whole generation, thirty years, separates us from the outbreak of the First World War; and by now we know that the impression of inevitable scientific and humanitarian progress was an illusion: for the new utilitarian ideologies had never mastered the realities of life or understood the conditions for their own further development. The barbarism into which we have sunk during the last thirty years can be measured by one further incident: the fate of the historian Henri Pirenne during the First World War. This Belgian was torn away from his home and his university by the invading Germans: his rights of immunity as a noncombatant and a scholar were violated and he was sent to a concentration camp.

That single act of violence was enough to awaken protest throughout the world: Scandinavian scholars, in the shadow of German might, protested as valiantly as Americans; and finally, in response to a combined appeal from the Pope and the President of the United States, Pirenne was given decent conditions of lodging by himself, in a German village, and an opportunity to work on a book. Respect for human liberty was still strong enough at that moment to command the actions of an autocratic enemy government.

Would I had space to enlarge on the contrast between the fate of Pirenne and the fate of thousands of noble scholars and scientists who have suffered under the totalitarian tyrannies. The story should be underlined, repeated, pondered. The world has regressed so far toward political barbarism that it is scarcely conscious of the depth of its present degradation. As for the fate of the Jews—to say nothing of the Spanish republicans, the Abyssinians, and the Chinese—this is a far darker blot against our whole civilization. For the more flagrant crimes of Nazidom have been amplified by the sinful indifference, by the heartless passivity, of the non-fascist peoples. Are not the present sufferings of the latter but the prompt historic retribution for their collective guilt? Rarely has justice worked more swiftly or more terribly.

4: The Dilation of Sex

If man's discovery of his biological affiliations had both a liberating and a morbid effect, the same was true of the re-awakening of sexual interest that went along with it. The scientific re-investigation of sex began with the discovery of the precise nature of the ovum and the spermatozoön and it culminated toward the beginning of the twentieth century in Freud's sexual interpretation of the dream and his enlargement of the role played by sex in the development of both child and adult.

If life had been ruled out of the mechanical idolum, sex was even more completely taboo: for the Christian super-ego reinforced the preoccupations of the utilitarian, for whom sex was a disturbing influence, as upsetting to methodical calculations of the system as Richard Feverel's running away with Lucy. The first serious investigations of the rites of marriage were those of the American pioneer in birth control, Charles Knowlton: his book on sexual relations, along with Robert Dale Owen's, was an attempt to justify a deeper interest in sex than that which sufficed to beget babies. Even Balzac, in a country famed for its lovers, found it worth while to write The Physiology of Marriage.

Love was attended by polite inhibitions and affectionate acquiescence for lack of any full understanding of man's sexual capacities or any care for their cultivation. Those who attributed any value to sexual life, apart from benign domesticity, were the specialists in sex, the gay, the voluptuous, the irresponsible. Sex was the province of the outcasts of utilitarian society: the artists, the sportsmen, the actors, and rovers; whilst specialized houses of prostitution served almost as much as social centers, as vehicles for relaxed companionship, as they did for a sexuality that remained thwarted or unsatisfied at more respectable levels.

Fourier in theory, John Humphrey Noyes in practice, led the way toward social experiments in sex that gave the subject a public hearing: Noyes's Oneida Community not merely tested the possibilities of group marriage but instituted a physiological discipline for men which openly acknowledged the woman's need for sexual satisfaction as a lover, no less than as a mother. Burton's Arabian Nights, to say nothing of his private inquiries into the sexual habits of the people his wide travels threw him amongst, gave to European man a firsthand knowledge of the more complex, more highly developed eroticism of the East: the Arabs, the Hindus, the Chinese all had something to teach Western man, who was not so much restrained, as callow and unimaginative about sex: a subject to which he dared not give the benefit of his waking fantasies without incurring a sense of guilt.

Much of the renewed sexual interest of the nineteenth century sought only verbal channels or legal forms of expression: the defiance of convention went no farther than the praise of the prostitute, with Swinburne, or the living together without binding legal ties, as with George Eliot. The right to have a child without a responsible father was the theme of Grant Allen's The Woman Who Did: this became the symbol of woman's emancipation—a purely legal change of status which, whether good or bad, might be coupled with prudery, frigidity, and sexual ineptitude. If the conventional language of sex, particularly in Protestant countries, took long to recover the forthrightness of the seventeenth century, a steady outflow of erotic interest characterized, with increasing intensity, the art of the nineteenth century: it reached its highest point, perhaps, in Rodin, whose supple nudes float, ripple, undulate in the visual blur that intense passion itself produces. Every medium left a record of this passional flood: Whitman sought to enshrine sex in a sort of poetic physiology, while Alfred Stieglitz, more faithful to love and more close to love's object, transfixed the equivalent of every erotic moment in a series of noble photographs.

This dilation of sex at length found a philosophic exponent in Havelock Ellis, whose work began in the eighteen-eighties. In a series of monographs on the nature of sex, in all its aspects, he brought together not merely a vast amount of specialist investigation but a great many private biographies, for lack of which even the medical knowledge of sex had been unduly restricted. For him, sex was one of the major movements in the dance of life: he celebrated sex in all its aspects, with conviction if not with passion: he peered where no one had dared to look: he spoke where no one in public had dared to speak: like Whitman, he ventured to challenge the very idea of obscenity, and turned the tables on the puritan by convicting him of inverted prurience. That part of Ellis's work was sanative. More than any other modern thinker, perhaps, Ellis gave people the courage to embrace their sexuality: on the side of erotic expression he expanded and completed the lesson of Rousseau. That gift was precious.

Yet Ellis's own work, many-sided, all-embracing as it seems, reveals how completely sex had departed from its normal place in consciousness and practice. Ellis's description of the sexual act becomes a study of the "mechanism of detumescence"; and in all his studies, although he wrote on marriage, he never follows the sexual embrace as far as the child or allies his fresh insights on sex to the nature of the family and the psychological re-conditioning of sex that springs out of permanent parental relations. This prophet of sex celebrated the flower and forgot the seed. This self-absorbed bachelor, whose marriage was a denial of marriage, whose own low-keyed sexual life was as slow as Napoleon's pulse, alas! exemplified the sterility and the impotence that the *civilisee*—as Fourier called the type—carried along with his mechanical advances.

Far more original in its insights, and far more profound in its effects, was the work of Dr. Sigmund Freud, who was brought to the study of sex by his work as a psychiatrist on neuroses, following the pioneer efforts of Charcot. Freud not merely revealed again the primal energy of sex: he not merely identified the undifferentiated manifestations of sex in infancy and traced their topographical fixation, their conversion, their reawakening and further maturation at adolescence: he not merely established the role of sexual shock, injury, and repression on the development of the whole psychic structure: Freud further showed the protean disguises of sexuality in the dream and in all those concrete modifications of dream and waking consciousness and rational intelligence that manifest themselves as art.

By recognizing the role of sexuality and by charting the dark, repressed side of life, that to which he first gave the label of the unconscious, Freud made it possible to describe and evaluate the whole personality: to understand its characteristic drives, desires, wishes, lusts, both in their infantile nakedness and in the elaborate garb that maturity devises for society. In the delicacy, the subtlety, the skillful unraveling of Freud's analysis he was without rival among psychologists: psychoanalysis, by a feat of imaginative insight and scientific dexterity, at length recovered for objective research that vast subjective domain to which science had denied both its name and its method in the seventeenth century. This was a major revolution—as well as a revelation. The irreal, the world of dreams, became a starting point of that self-realization through which man passes from the pleasurable illusions of infancy to the mastered realities—in which pleasures and pains are accepted but not sought—of maturity. And the very motive force of self-realization is love: love of the ego, love of the alter-ego, love beyond the ego, whose ultimate nature springs out of the primal urge toward reproduction.

Once Freud had supplied the original clues, the swift unfoldment of psychological and sexual insight was like the unfoldment of buds in the spring sun: the need for a vital revaluation of sex and for a sexual revaluation of life was never greater, perhaps, than at the moment when Freud and his followers appeared. Sex now became an open subject: the very theory of the censor lifted the long-maintained censorship. Not merely did the psychoanalyst liberate the neurotic from his obsessions, his morbid compulsions, his impulses toward self-destruction: he gave to those whose development had been more fortunate a license, as it were, to expand the contracted sphere of their sexuality. If repression were the cause of illness, might not unlimited expression be an adequate preventive? That insight, that tacit permission, coincided with a great period of anxiety, constraint, and emotional depletion, beginning with the First World War: sexual facility, sexual relaxation, became an imaginary panacea for the ills of life, while all the by-products and sublimations of sex—devotion, loyalty, sympathy, esthetic transfiguration—became subject to a systematic denigration as futile escapes from life. From the romantic over-valuation of the object of love, the new lovers turned to a matter-of-fact over-valuation of the instrument. Jealousy was taboo: who could be jealous of a sexual organ? Only envy was permissible.

The great truths that Freud discovered cannot be reproached with the manner of their exploitation, any more than scientific biology can be reproached with Spengler's perverse interpretation of man as a carnivore. But just as Darwin's misuse of Malthus started a whole train of derivative falsifications, so Freud's essential pessimism, coupled with an active resentment against the historical role of culture, played a part in deflating the modern super-ego and in favoring an insurrection against it.

Freud's flashing originality as a psychologist was balanced by an uncritical mediocrity as a philosopher: he took over the atomic materialism of the scientific philosophy current in his youth and, apart from his biological inheritance, he regarded the individual as a self-contained unit, upon whose assertive will society acted as a check, a curb, a censor. Society, apart from man, imposes standards of conduct and creates repressions: for Freud the super-ego has the role of the hostile patriarchal father, denying the sexual activities of his rivals, his sons, forbidding, threatening, punishing: it never assumes the mother role of nurturing and liberating the positive expressions of life. He even said that the object of psychoanalysis is "to strengthen the ego, to make it more independent of the super-ego." Aware of the need for reclaiming neglected portions of the id, he passed over the coeval task of replenishing the exhausted super-ego of the contemporary personality.

In attempting to harmonize man's warring impulses, Freud therefore had no interest in bringing into existence a more life-enhancing super-ego, the product of a maturer art, philosophy, and religion: his object was rather to lessen the weight of man's traditional super-ego, at least to cushion its pressure. For him art was a mere mechanism of escape, philosophy a rationalization, and religion an outright fraud. Despite the scope Freud gave theoretically to man's deepest subjective impulses he looked to science alone to effect man's improvement. Unconsciously, he accepted as a final revelation of truth the ideology that was formulated in the eighteenth century: that of Locke, Hume, Voltaire, Diderot. . . . A certain philosophic innocence thus robbed him of the fruits of his scientific sophistication. One who had disclosed the significance of even "accidental" behavior in everyday life should not have been so ready to treat religion as a gigantic vermiform appendix: a meaningless vestigial organ that might poison the personality but had never had a positive function.

Freud's theory of the dream, in its essence, shows the human mind, the very simplest and commonest, as a fountain of creative activity: active and fecund, with cunning powers of transposition and symbolization comparable to those of a Shakespeare. This should have given back to his contemporaries some of their self-confidence, long shaken by the dominance of the machine and by the displacement of wish and dream and imagination by the neutral techniques of science. But in Freud's own hands, his discovery had just the opposite effect. Having discovered the function of the dream through his analysis of the neurotic, he tended to preserve this original association. In this narrow context the dream became a device for evading reality or circumventing the restrictions of the super-ego: a concealed refuge from a hard world, not an adventurous flight to a better one.

Freud understood and popularized the defensive reaction of the dream: this enabled him to probe motives and impulses that had hitherto never been effectively interpreted. But he did not have an equal interest in the positive role of the dream, that which by day and night transforms the experience of life into more enduring and more endurable patterns: the function of art. When Freud spoke of art he referred, pathetically, only to weak art: he did not understand that dynamic quality of great art which brings the mind closer to, not farther away from, reality. Freud's theory reasserted the creative functions of the human mind as a whole: but Freud's metaphysical doctrine confined respect and authority, not to the creative function itself, but to the method that had discovered it. At this point, the "heresies" of C. G. Jung and Otto Rank opened the way for a more vital application of this knowledge.

Freud's habit of regarding human culture as superimposed on man, rather than as an integral part of his biological makeup, led him into the realm of sheer fantasy, on a par with the religious myths he despised: in the slaying of the primal father by his sons, Freud re-created man's original sin and even accepted the notion that a single symbolic act might hang like the Ancient Mariner's albatross round the neck of every succeeding generation. He thus evolved a private religion which introduced a universal guilt without providing for any more universal method of redemption than a prolonged analysis of the sufferer by a competent psychoanalyst: a new priesthood whose very scientific scruples must condemn their method of salvation to remain the boon of an even smaller body of elect than Calvin thought merited salvation.

But this was the least of Freud's ambivalent gifts to mankind. The most sinister conclusion to be drawn from his teachings was that the needs of the id were more important than the curbs of the super-ego: if the super-ego dammed the currents of life, maintaining a perpetual tension within the personality, accompanied by distressing feelings of anxiety and guilt, why should that dam not be removed? Freud did not draw that conclusion; but the generation into whose minds Freud's ideas filtered sought a shortcut to psychoanalysis by a general relaxation of tensions: why should one not start by rejecting all the ideal claims that culture makes upon the personality? This task was not confined to the fascists, who indeed restored an infantile "innocence" in their lying, torturing, and murdering: it had a far wider provenance in the belief that "history is bunk," and that good and bad, true and false, ugly and beautiful, were mere words that served nothing but the ego's appetites. Once the needs of the individual are separated from the claims of society, no criterion for their selection and expression remains. Social claims must balance personal needs as duties balance rights: otherwise the self becomes de-socialized, if not actively anti-social. Unlimited self-assertion leads to the destruction of personality.

Life without tension. What does that mean but life without direction, without purpose, without the ability to shake loose from the automatism of habit or the familiar local environment of the ego: life without any headwaters of energy, spilling aimlessly in every direction, undammed, uncanalized, therefore incapable of creating power or light? Once one rejects the creative role of the super-ego only two other courses are open: the course I have just described, and the fascist's effort to create a positive super-ego out of the raw elements of the id: blood and carnage and booty and copulation, *as ideals.*

5: The Ideology of Barbarism

"The mind, after traversing its course of progress, after rising from sensation successively to the imaginative and the rational universal and from violence to equity, is bound in conformity with its eternal nature to relapse into violence and sensation. . . . Civilization comes to an end in the 'barbarism of reflection,' which is worse than the primitive barbarism of sensation; for while the latter was not without a wild nobility, the former is contemptible, untrustworthy, and treacherous."

These thoughts of Vico, expressed before Rousseau, have the fault of erecting an incomplete observation into a law; but they contain a fragment of truth for which self-confident rationalism has no explanation. Pure intelligence ceases to be a useful guide to life as soon as it attempts the role of absolute ruler; or to put it in psychological terms, a rational super-ego, exclusively preoccupied with its own order, denies the function of the id and cuts itself off from the vitality that should serve it. Carried far enough that repression must lead to the destruction of the personality, or to an explosive discharge of the id elements. Instead of sublimating barbarism civilization then produces a more terrible variety of barbarism, for to the animal energies in which all men share it adds those powerful technical and social facilities which civilization has itself created.

Even at the height of Victorian optimism this view was not unfamiliar to the sounder interpreters of human history. Comte, for example, pointed out that though intelligence must always exert a powerful influence on human affairs, "such supremacy of intellect in political government as the Greek philosopher desired can never be more than a dream." Burckhardt went even farther: he predicted a reversal of progress and a descent into barbarism.

This threatened reversal of the course of Western civilization, this return to the level of brute sensation, this renewed admiration of barbarism became visible shortly after the middle of the nineteenth century: the racial theories of Gobineau, the cult of violence expressed by the nihilists, the glorification of brutality in Carlyle's defense of Governor Eyre, the repressor of the Jamaica insurrection, had common roots. Wagner's music sounded the *leit-motiv* of his conscious resurrection of barbarism: his written political testament left an estate to future Ludendorffs and Hitlers. In the lion's den of Wagner's youthful disciple, Nietzsche, with his cult of the superman, the stinking hyenas of Nazism already lurked. Nor was the Western hemisphere immune to these dark forces. In the United States, the South's attempt to revive and extend the long-moribund institution of slavery brought with it all the characteristic phenomena of fascism: racism, militarism, caste, theological perversions and scientific lies.

The nihilism of brute impulse, theoretically established by Hume, now became as it were the last refuge of vitality. To rape, to torture, to hate, to kill became a method of redemption: in fantasy if not in fact.

Every profound change records itself on sensitive minds as on a seismograph, long before any actual upheaval becomes generally visible in society. So the new ideology of barbarism was described and remarkably interpreted by Dostoyevsky in a succession of characters, Raskolnikov, Stavrogin, the wild Karamazov, above all, in the revolutionary thinker, Shigalov, whose philosophy he described in The Possessed.

Shigalov begins as a humanitarian revolutionist, bent on creating a world organization and moving into action; but he is perplexed by his own data, and his conclusion is a direct contradiction of the original idea with which he starts. "Starting from unlimited freedom, I arrive at unlimited despotism." One of Shigalov's admirers, Verhovensky, goes into details. "He's written a good thing in that manuscript. . . . He suggests a system of spying. Every member of the society spies on the others, and it's his duty to inform against them. Everyone belongs to all and all to everyone. All are slaves and equal in their slavery. In extreme cases he advocates slander and murder, but the great thing about it is equality. To begin with, the level of education, science, and talents is lowered. A high level in education and science is only possible for great intellects, and they are not wanted. . . . They will be banished or put to death. . . . Slaves are bound to be equal. There has never been either freedom or equality without despotism, but in the herd there is bound to be equality, and that's Shigalovism. . . . The one thing wanting in the world is discipline. The thirst for culture is an aristocratic thirst. The moment you have family ties or love, you get the desire for property. We will destroy that desire; we'll make use of incredible corruption; we'll stifle every genius in its infancy. . . ."

When Dostoyevsky wrote The Possessed that seemed a mad passage; and Shigalovism was only a madman's program. Few could dream that Dostoyevsky had embodied in a few paragraphs the essence of a whole book, composed by a connoisseur of human weakness, treachery, and corruption, who was to arise in the twentieth century: Adolf Hitler. Fewer still could guess that the ugliest fantasies of Shigalov would be surpassed by the systematic tortures practiced by the Nazi government upon its legion of victims. Had not Germany long led the world in philosophy, in music, in scholarship, in the sciences? So convinced, indeed, was a large part of mankind of the soundness of this civilization that it refused to heed the malignity of the fascists' intentions or the hideous results that flowed from them. When the heroine of Ibsen's play committed suicide, the philistine Judge Brack exclaimed: "People don't do such things." When millions of Germans, Italians, Spaniards, and their imitators in other countries openly espoused barbarism those who still clung to the New World idolum said: People don't do such things. Faced with the need for revising their faith in the smooth curve of progress, which automatically gave to the latest institution the title of being the best, the apostles of progress blandly closed their eyes to the facts that contradicted their faith. And the progressive's retreat hastened the barbarian's advance.

Shigalovism contained the core of fascism: it is not beyond possibility that Dostoyevsky even planted the seed of self-consciousness in more than one fascist mind. War, sadism, and corruption were the methods of the new creed: totalitarian despotism was its end. Even the most extravagant suggestion of Shigalov, that the world might be turned over to the Pope, through an agreement between Shigalov's corrupt International and its Christian predecessor, no longer was beyond possibility. When fascism came into power in the nineteen-twenties, the Papacy met it half-way: the older authoritarian system welcoming the younger as an ally. When the fascist campaign against civilization was at its height, the Papacy could find no words to denounce it by name or to point out the moral abyss that separated it from the peoples and governments it had attacked.

The present generation has seen the next to the last stage in the fascist revolt against human traditions and human values: a concrete synthesis of evils. The name chosen by Hitler unites in degradation two good things: nationality and socialism. False nationalism, false socialism: a nationalism dedicated to an attack upon the human, and a socialism whose common efforts and common sacrifices are devoted to war and plunder, not to the building up of a peaceful commonwealth in which all good men may participate. Only a universal hardening of heart, combined with an ebbing of spiritual courage and conviction, with a complete deflation of the super-ego among those who counted themselves civilized, enabled these fascist regimes to gain a foothold in Europe, to begin their war upon humanity. Spurred by cupidity, the powers that the fascists had openly threatened long in advance, equipped their fascist enemies with the machines and the raw materials they needed to accomplish the destruction of democracy: many American "free enterprisers" hoping to make a deal with the new conquerors, even slavered adulation upon them, praising the power of their new arms and the punctuality of their trains.

Thus the active barbarians in our society were aided by the passive barbarians, who had lost their hold on central human values and who saw no reason to risk pain or death in behalf of human ideals—for ideals that had become empty words. Disguising itself too often as Christian pacifism, as humanitarianism, as scientific dispassionateness, passive barbarism opened the gates to active barbarism. This moral cowardice, this inner corruption, this unwillingness to recognize fascism's brutal ways as evil or to accept evil itself as real—all this was not unexpected. The leaders of fascism had predicted it and counted upon it. Hitler had prophetically poured contempt on the democratic escapists in Mein Kampf.

But one need not look to fiction or philosophy alone for a prophecy of the corruption of nationalism and socialism into a twofold slavery: history had already foretold that in the covert partnership between Bismarck and Lasalle—that vain, brilliant, treacherous leader of the socialist party in Germany whom Marx, with such good reason, hated.

In a letter Lasalle wrote Bismarck, dated June 8, 1863, on sending him the statutes of the recently formed Workers' Association, he wrote: "But this miniature picture [the statutes] will clearly convince you how true it is that the [German] working class feels an instinctive inclination toward a dictatorship, if it can first be rightly persuaded that the dictatorship will be exercised in its interests; and how much, despite all republican views—or rather, precisely because of them—it would therefore be inclined . . . to look upon the Crown, in opposition to the egoism of bourgeois society, as the natural representative of the social dictatorship."

6: Dithyramb to Doom

Barbarism had many prophets during the last century, from Houston Stewart Chamberlain to Georges Sorel, from Nietzsche to Pareto; but the man whose work most fully displays the sinister lure of barbarism was Oswald Spengler, the author of The Downfall of the Western World, timidly translated into English as The Decline of the West. Spengler had a free mind and a servile emotional attitude: he presented a formidable upright figure, with a domed bald head and a keen eye, but in the presence of authority, particularly military authority, his backbone crumbled. Representing the intellect he yet abased the function of intellect before the power of "blood"; elaborating the concept of the organic in history he used it to justify the acceptance of the machine.

Conceived before the First World War, published first in Vienna in 1918, before the war had ended, Spengler's treatise was something more than a philosophy of history. To begin with it was, from the German standpoint, a work of consolation. It was written to rationalize the state in which the new German found himself: he had acquired great wealth and high physical organization by repressing most of his vital impulses except those that directly or deviously served his will-to-power. But in his heart, he was not at home in this new environment. Measured by humane standards, the relatively feeble, industrially backward, politically divided country of the Enlightenment had been a better place for the spirit: Kant in Koenigsberg, Goethe and Schiller in Weimar, Mozart and Beethoven in Vienna, had put the Germans on a higher cultural level than centralized Berlin had achieved.

If Germany was defeated in her attempt to achieve military and economic control of Europe, all was lost; but if Germany won, how much was gained? Nothing was left except to go on with the empty conquests of the past forty years, building railroads to Bagdad, throwing steamship lines across new trade routes, manufacturing genuine Scotch marmalade in Hamburg, and above all, giving larger scope to Junker arrogance and prowess: the too easy sack of Peking had but whetted army appetites. Thought itself had become technicized, indeed partly militarized: it tended toward adding-machine accuracy, but the values algebraically represented in this process came to so many zeros. Those who still felt a sentimental pull toward the older and deeper German culture were appalled by the battlefront bleakness of the intellectual landscape. Spengler himself was appalled: in this he was more keenly alive than that army of American scholars who had imitated German methods with clever facility without realizing how little they had gained or how much they were to lose.

Drawing upon world history for consoling comparisons and precedents, Spengler found them in his theory of historic development. According to him, there are two kinds of peoples in the world: those who merely live and those who enact history. The first, if they exist before the cultural cycle begins, are mere vegetables: their life is directionless: they endure on a timeless level of pure being. If they come at the end of the cycle they also tumble into a Spenglerian limbo: they are "fellaheen," without ambition, without creative capacity, different from the true peasant because they clothe themselves in the tattered garments of an old civilization, continuing its forms even though they progressively lose all its meanings.

Opposed to this dull village chorus are the actors, the creators: the latter experience "Destiny"; they are drawn by a dominating idea from a state of culture, in which life is bound up with a common soil and a deep intuitive sense of the importance of blood and race and caste, to a state of civilization, in which their waking consciousness progressively transcends their more instinctive earlier life, and in which the external conquest of nature takes the place of the harmonious cultivation of life. In this second state, they cease to be fettered to a particular region and become, instead, cosmopolitan, highly urbanized, increasingly indifferent to all the vital processes that meant so much to both townsman and peasant during the earlier period, deeply hostile to those unconscious or unformulated forces that cannot be glibly translated into word-symbols or money-symbols. Rationalism and humanitarianism devitalize their will-to-power. Pacificism gives rise to passivism. Optimistic and cowardly to the end, the denizens of this civilization are ripe for butchery.

In the phase of culture, life germinates and flourishes; in the state of civilization, the sap sinks to the roots, the stem and leaves become brittle, and the whole structure of the organism becomes incapable of further growth. The promise of culture's springtime ends in the dormant period of civilization's winter. From the organic to the inorganic, from the living to the mechanical, from the subjectively conditioned to the objectively conditioned—this, said Spengler, is the line of development for all societies.

By making the rise and fall of cultures an immanent, automatic process, Spengler got caught in the net of his organic metaphor: he was thus forced to treat each culture as a unified body, dominated by a specific idea, which in turn would be symbolized by its architecture, its mathematics, its painting, its statecraft, its technics. Not merely is a culture incapable of receiving the ideas or contributions of other cultures; it cannot even understand them. All intercourse with outside cultures is an illusion: all carryovers from the past are, in Spengler's system, a myth. The processes of self-repair, self-renewal, self-transcendence, which are as observable in cultures as in persons, were completely overlooked by Spengler. His many vital perceptions of the historic process served only one purpose which he kept steadfastly in view: as apology for barbarism.

Applying his theory to "Faustian" culture, that of the last thousand years, Spengler pointed out that the Western European was about to enter the frigid state of winter. Poetry, art, philosophy were no longer open possibilities; civilization meant the deliberate abdication of the organic and vital elements: the unqualified reign of the mechanical, the desiccated, the devitalized. The region was shriveling to a point: the world city or megalopolis. (The original Megalopolis in fourth century Greece had emptied out a whole countryside in order to create a single large center.) The earth itself was now being plated with stone and steel and asphalt: man dreamed of growing crops in tanks, taking food in capsules, transplanting foetuses to protoplasmic incubators, conquering the air in stratoliners by means of oxygen tanks, and burrowing into underground cities in order to have security against his wonderful conquest of the more rarefied medium. In that process, the individual shrank once more into a mechanical atom in a formless mass of humanity: the sourest satire of Aldous Huxley's Brave New World or Zamiatin's We scarcely did justice to the regimentation that was actually under way. To succeed in terms of such a civilization, one must be hard. What remained of life, if one could call it life, belonged to the engineer, the business man, the soldier; in short, to pure technicians, devoid of any concern for life or the values of life, except in so far as they served the machine. Was there no way for life, then, to reassert itself? Spengler answered Yes: by brutality, by brutality and conquest. The sole outlet open to the victims of civilization was to replenish their barbarism and consummate their will-to-destruction. In politics the hour of Caesarism was at hand.

This invocation to barbarism fascinated many of Spengler's more literate contemporaries. Hence it is important to realize, not so much the illegitimacy of the poetic figure Spengler used, as the even deeper unsoundness of the grand division Spengler made between culture and civilization, by putting them at opposite ends of a cycle. These two terms represent the spiritual and the material aspects of every society; and the fact is that one is never found without the other. The overdevelopment of fortifications and castles in the fourteenth century, for example, was as much a mechanical fact, an example of sheer externalization, as the overdevelopment of subways in the modern megalopolis, though the first belonged to a vernal feudalism of blood and caste, while the other belongs to finance capitalism. So, again, the building of new towns on rectangular plans was as much a characteristic of the springtide of Faustian culture as it was of the autumnal period of the nineteenth century. Spengler's theory of cultural isolationism—unfortunately a typical example of Germanic egoism—prevented him from correctly interpreting the organic inter-relations his theory pretends to demonstrate. At every point his organicism gives place to dualism: for without that dualism he could not sanction barbarism.

To follow the real drift of the Downfall one must read the pamphlets which were all that Spengler published in the following years: here the hidden aim was unveiled. In Man and Technics, and in The Hour of Decision, Spengler divested himself completely of the forms of scholarly judgment: he beat a frenzied tattoo on the tribal drum, attempting to summon together the forces of reaction. For Spengler was no Aristotle: he was the revived Fichte of the barbarian revolution whose name was fascism in Italy, Nazism in Germany, and totalitarianism everywhere. In its very characteristics as a work of art, a poem of devilish hate and darkening fate, Spengler's Downfall was an image of the fascist states that were to be erected during the next two decades: their irrationalities, their phobias, their humorless limitations, their colossal brutalities, their perverse animus against all life, except at the blindest levels of the id, were prophetically mirrored in his work. He who understood the significance of Spengler's act of prophecy had little to learn from the further course of Europe's history.

Spengler's historical thesis took possession of a defeated and war-weary world. Men had everywhere dreamed of justice, democracy, peace. But the fruits of war were shabby efforts to achieve "normalcy," that is, forgetfulness. Instead of peace, there was a continuation of military efforts on other fronts, and a solemn determination on the part of the governing classes to stave off the deep economic changes—as urgent then as today—that threatened their power. In order to avoid the harrowing possibility of further struggle, men sought peace by paring down armaments instead of establishing more firmly the organs for political justice, and by retreating into dreams of tortoiselike isolation, with schemes for Imperial Preferences, Maginot Lines, Autarchy, and Hemispheric Solidarity.

The title of Spengler's book had an even more immediate appeal than its contents, which were difficult for even the educated to understand. For the title whispered the soothing words, *downfall, doom, death.* The post-war challenge to effective, purposive action, action in the light of human ideals, action in behalf of a better life, was dissipated by Spengler's very doctrine of "pure" action—that is, action without rational motive or ideal content: the work of expansion and aggrandizement as practiced by the masters of the machine.

The war machine, the finance machine, the industrial machine, the education machine—all these agents redoubled their interest in technique for its own sake: the *l'art pour l'art* of practice. Witness the manner in which American bankers foisted loans on German industries and municipalities without even a touch of the banker's traditional prudence about the ultimate recovery of the capital they so glibly manipulated. Capitalism, re-invigorated by war-profits, entertained itself with prospectuses of limitless expansion. Artful dodgers in financial technique, sheer fantasts and forgers like Ivar Kreuger, were hailed as industrial statesmen. Advertisement writers, masters of propaganda and publicity, exponents of polished insincerity, desecrated truth and beauty in the interest of their commercial clients—and thus made even genuine truth suspect and even actual beauty seem meretricious and purchasable. Such truth, bent on profitable seduction, became more degrading than a brazen lie.

So far from urging men to depart from these vicious forms of action, Spengler proclaimed that no other course was possible: history only urged the strong to gird themselves for greater depredations and the weak to prepare for greater disasters.

Because Spengler respected only physical force, the pure act, he prophesied with accuracy the nature of the post-war world and he diagnosed its typical disease—the paralysis of will, on the part of humane men and women, which followed by sheer exhaustion the over-keyed energies of the war itself. Reacting against the intensified emotions of war, men avoided all emotions: shrinking from the horrors and harshness of war, they evaded all occasions for physical struggle or hardship: too feeble, too disoriented, to achieve at once the noble ideals for which millions on the Allied side had given their lives, the post-war generation debunked all ideals: that avoided the necessity for further struggle or responsibility. Even if they did not read Spengler they were his disciples in practice.

For all his breadth of vision, Spengler succeeded only in reading back into world history the limitations of his own country, his own generation. In his scheme of living he had no place for the very class he represented: the priest, the artist, the intellectual, the scientist, the maker and conserver of ideas and ideal patterns were not operative agents: he not merely asserted that no fact has ever altered a faith, but he even said that no idea had ever modified an act. If that were true, he need not have spent so much time attempting to shout down the ideas of those who opposed the acts he favored.

Every society consists of organizers, energizers, creators, and followers: in each group and association within society a similar social division of labor can be detected; and all social action is the result of their combined efforts. For Spengler, the organizers, the men of blood and will, were supreme. The work of the creators, strange to say, he associated with death: the fixed, the immobilized, the no-saying seemed to him their only attributes; and he hated the activities of the men of religion and the men of thought because it curbed the raw outbreaks of animal passion and physical prowess that his drill sergeant's mind gloried in.

The truth is that Spengler feared the deep humanness of humanity, as he feared those domestic sentiments, truly native to man, that work against the rule of his mythical "carnivore." Spengler recoiled from the fact, so obvious in history, that dehumanized power in the long run is as pitifully weak, as impotent and sterile, as a merely wishful humanitarianism. He hated the independent power of the mind, creating values, erecting standards, subduing ferine passions, laying the basis for a more universal society, precisely because he knew in his heart of hearts, for all his loud contempt, that this *was* a power: a power men obeyed, a power even the humblest could feel within himself, at least in milliamperes, as in a radio receiving set, recording the same feelings, the same hopes and dreams, that had left the original transmitting station at full strength.

What makes Spengler so significant was that he expressed in so many words the premises upon which Western society as a whole acted: the man

XIII. DREAM AND NIGHTMARE

The inner world, discarded by the scientist and left threadbare by the failure of organized religion to renew its experiences and its symbols, reappeared in benign form in the paintings and drawings of Blake: a seer who admonished his fellow-artists to see through, not with, the eye. Redon, like Blake and Ryder, carried on this exploration of dream consciousness and subjective symbolism. In psychology, Dr. Sigmund Freud and his followers reinstated the dream as a key to man's unconscious urges: for pathology at least the inner world again became meaningful. Encouraged by the psychoanalyst, the artist reclaimed subjective impulses. So nightmares became visible again, pointing ahead to deeper psychal and social disintegration. Note the emptiness of di Chirico's ominous urban perspectives: precursor of the fascist revolution. External rigor and internal emptiness. Later surrealists, from Grosz and Ernst to Dali, portray even more malignant forms of evil: prophetically representing in symbol those utmost horrors which the Nazis and the Japanese have consummated in fact.

XIV. DRAMA OF DISINTEGRATION

Pablo Picasso is perhaps the outstanding painter of our time. More completely than any other artist, he represents both our achievements and our disfigurements. His entire work is a series of shocks; and with each shock part of the structure of our civilization symbolically is revealed—and collapses. His maturity begins with haunting pictures of poverty and misery: the deep humanity of his blue period. Haggard columbines and famished harlequins connect him with the surviving playworld of baroque society. Then comes the primitivism of Negroid idols and masques: an effort to reassert our waning vitality by a return to primitive sources: almost synchronous with the rise of jazz. After that cubism, neo-classicism, and such empty technical virtuosity as the Figure in a Red Chair, here shown. Finally a real emotion overpowers Picasso: the actual horror of the fascist uprising in Spain grips him and tortures him: hence the powerful symbolization of woman's utmost misery in this study for the Guernica mural. Disintegration can go no farther this side sanity. In every phase, Picasso's paintings have given a truer image of the world we live in than the so-called documentary realists, who show only what the most superficial eye sees.

of fact, who despised values, was the product of the New World idolum, native to that habitat, flourishing there almost without competitors like the jack-rabbit in Australia. With the rest of Western society in decay, the anti-vital tendencies of the mechanical ideology now could exercise themselves unrestrained. Nothing that Spengler advocated for the coming dictatorships was outside current practice: the gangsterism he preached on a large scale had already been achieved in the one-man rule of the American political boss, petty but sometimes not so petty: his contempt for the poet and the painter, his devaluation of all ideal activity, were but the working principles of the successful philistine in every land: his glorification of technique at the expense of rational content was the very principle by which men currently advanced themselves in medicine or in education, in law or business: did not advertising condition the masses to this philosophy?

Unlike his liberal and democratic opponents, Oswald Spengler drew the inevitable conclusion from this situation. If values are unreal and if humane purposes are chimerical, then even scientific technique must ultimately become subservient to brute force: the need for rational restraint and self-discipline of any kind disappears. Thus technicism leads directly to irrationality—and the cult of barbarian power salvages the technician's otherwise growing sense of frustration and futility. It is no accident that Germany produced both the most mechanized type of personality in its robot-like soldiers and civilians, and the most unrestrained reaction against humane discipline, in the form of an exultant sub-animality.

Spengler ignored all the creative tendencies in modern life, except those associated with the machine: little though he relished the thought, his essential creed favored Russia and the United States even more than it did the fascist countries. Spengler accepted as "real" only those elements which emphasized modern man's automatism, his deflation of values, his subservience to mechanical organization, and the savage irrationality which takes the place of reason in other parts of the personality. And because these forces cannot be confined within their original frontiers, Spengler predicted, far more accurately than hopeful philosophers, the disastrous downward course that modern civilization is still following, at a steadily accelerating pace. Through its emotional impact, Spengler's work as a whole constitutes a morbid Saga of Barbarism. It began as a poem of defeat; it finally became an epic justification of the fascist attack on the very humanity of man—an attack that has already gone so far that even democratic peoples have torpidly swallowed as their own, without retching, the fascist doctrine of totalitarian air warfare: one of the deepest degradations of our age.

Spengler's day is not yet over. These are ominous times and Spengler is like a black crow, hoarsely cawing, whose prophetic wings cast a shadow over our whole landscape. The democratic peoples cannot conquer their fascist enemies until they have conquered in their own hearts and minds the underlying barbarism that unites them with their foes. In the passive barbarism that the United States now boasts under the cover of technical progress, there is no promise whatever of victory or even bare survival. Without a deep regeneration and renewal, the external triumph of American machinery and arms will but hasten the downfall of the Western World. Only those who are ready for that renewal, with all its rigors, its sacrifices, its hard adventures, are entitled to celebrate even our temporary victories.

7: The Lure of Decay

The actual force of barbarism can easily be over-rated: any positive minority of equal energy, even one as weak as Christianity in the second century A.D., would possibly have enough élan to take over Western Society. For we are living through a time of decay. The oldest and most obvious form of decay is that of Christianity, with its millions who go numbly through the motions of a faith that every waking hour of their day contradicts. Even the Sabbath is no longer a day of spiritual change: no longer a day dedicated to inner communion and contemplation.

With all the talk of reunion between the Churches and sects, which has occupied the leaders of Christianity during the last half century, there are few real signs of the deeper spiritual effort required for Christianity's renewal—its admission of the local and relative nature of its original mission and its willingness to merge, for the sake of the universal values all men should share, with the faiths of other races and peoples which Western man too long spurned. An unchristian pride, disguising itself as a unique revelation of a truth not granted to other peoples, still blocks that essential sacrifice. A Hindu sage, like Ramakrishna, could understand Christianity by espousing it, disciplining himself to it, thinking and willing himself into its very marrow: but the Christian Churches sought to conquer the rest of the world on easier terms, with the aid of Andrew Undershaft's devices, money and gunpowder. The fruits of Christianity's decay have ripened to rottenness in our own generation: the Quaker pacifism that would not resist fascism, the Buchmanism that flattered fascism, the Roman Catholicism whose hierarchy, with a few noble and memorable exceptions, openly co-operated with fascism.

The decay of secular ideals has been equally conspicuous; but until the present generation they were not so visible, not so distressing: those who were aware of them, like Thoreau and Melville and Tolstoy and Ruskin in the nineteenth century, like Albert Schweitzer or Reinhold Niebuhr in our own time, were looked upon as spoil-sports and eccentrics—though in fact it was society itself that was eccentric.

Moreover, as long as the machine itself was still in a formative state, its limitations were less significant than its emancipations; and man's pride in his new discoveries in physics and chemistry, in biology and physiology, was a wholly legitimate one: positive knowledge replaced mere opinion, as rational opinion had once replaced authority. In a whole and integrated community, none of these advances would have been inimical to the personality: on the contrary, they would have nourished man as, under the favorable conditions that prevailed from 1830 to 1860 in New England, they nourished the mind and personality of Ralph Waldo Emerson: his journals are proof of that.

In our time, the forces that counter cultural decay have been weakened: weakened by death and desertion, by psychological depression and economic depression. What positive values does a disintegrated society possess for those who have lost their inner go, who are no longer a dynamic part of a visible or imaginable whole? Outside the values of raw barbarism, the only values that remain are those derived from decay itself: the black opalescent film on putrid flesh which obsesses the imagination of a Hemingway. Here again art is prophetic: some of our best modern works of art are those in which the dissolution of our world is pictured with masterly fidelity: Proust's Remembrance of Things Past, Joyce's Ulysses, Eliot's Wasteland. Were these not the most eloquent witnesses of the generation whose disillusion and dissolution touched bottom at the end of the First World War, and sank deeper into the mud for the next two decades? Each of these works stands high as literature: each is proof that some of the best energies of this society were the energies of decomposition.

After 1918 those with a gift for action became gangsters, fascist hoodlums, organizing terrorism and corruption on an ever-widening scale: now drawing tribute (in America) from chicken-hearted citizens, themselves willing to break the laws themselves had made, or again seizing possession of whole states, as in Italy, Germany, Spain, Hungary, Poland, in order to work out larger schemes of blackmail and plunder. Those who had no taste for action could only carry the processes of decay further by a passive acquiescence and an inner corruption, seeking nourishment from the spiritual products of decomposition. The incoherent language of

Da-da and the irrational forms of surrealism made their entry at the same moment: further symptoms of an emptiness and a debasement that was not uncoupled with technical ingenuity, even esthetic mastership. These artists had a twofold audience: the connoisseurs of illness and the connoisseurs of violence; and a positive antipathy to beauty, wholeness, or health was a qualification for discipleship.

Under the circumstances, it would seem futile to look for evidences of integration; but out of the surviving energies of this society more than one such work of art appeared. Perhaps the most satisfactory esthetic symbol of this period was Thomas Mann's The Magic Mountain.

The Magic Mountain portrays an ailing world: symbolized in a tuberculosis sanatorium, the Berghof, situated on a high mountain in Switzerland. Everyone who inhabits this world is ill or deeply involved in illness, from Hofrat Behrens, the chief physician, to life's delicate child, Hans Castorp, who is the hero of this romance of hypochondria, this Odyssey of disease. Yet the illness of the inmates is an essential part of their life: the source of their drama and the plot of their days. A plentiful supply of food, continuous medical attention, the luxuries of perfect service and studious care, endless sports, diversions, amusements, not a care in the world except the disease itself make this house of disease that very paradise of the heart toward which the New World had concentrated its energies. Is it not to universalize the "happiness" or at least the euphoria of the Berghof that the modern world has come into existence—that self-consuming happiness which has, as the only corrective to the pleasure principle, the perfect routine of science, the lofty zeal of medicine and surgery, with the x-ray, the radiograph, the surgical resection of the ribs, the deflation of the diseased lung, a thousand little ingenuities for arresting or diverting the forces of disintegration?

As in Melville's Moby-Dick all the races of the world compose the crew that has gathered to pursue the White Whale, so in The Magic Mountain, all the nationalities of Europe, even Mynheer Peeperkorn from the East Indies, and all classes of society, the penniless intellectual, the vulgar bourgeois widow, the business man, the soldier, have a place in this sick institution. No matter how healthy they may seem when they arrive, they belong there, and despite their efforts do not easily escape the Rhadamanthus who presides over its destinies. Only the members of the working class seem to escape the luxury of the disease, though they are present as waitresses and porters.

Mann's characters are ill, and they form part of an ailing world, a world he had depicted in his numerous stories of a decadent Germany, from Buddenbrooks to Tristan and Death in Venice. It is not the vulgar strength of modern man, but his tendency toward perversity, self-defeat, and suicide that Mann shows best in these imaginative works. All these elements come together in The Magic Mountain. Perhaps consciously, perhaps by a more hidden process, Mann causes every personality to caricature and betray his function in society: not one of these people is genuinely what he professes to be. Hofrat Behrens, the purveyor of health, is himself a hypochondriac, perhaps tubercular: worse than that, his very sanatorium, famous for its pure mountain air, is surrounded for a good part of the year by clouds and fogs that are never acknowledged to be such: atmospheric conditions which the people of the flatlands fancy they have escaped. Even worse, one suspects that some of the patients, beginning with the hero, acquire the disease in the very act of taking precautions against it: in them is a will-to-illness, first stage of the will-to-dissolution. Hans Castorp, the engineer, dreamy and reflective, is fit for anything but engineering: his cousin Joachim Ziemssen, the soldier, dies before he establishes himself in his profession: Peeperkorn, the incarnation of inarticulate vitality, commits suicide: Naphta, the jesuitical advocate of violence, cannot even fire a gun to kill his enemy, Settembrini: instead he shoots himself.

All this elaborate care of the diseased has produced a counterfeit life; but out of the situations Castorp encounters he discovers truths he would never have had time to reflect upon had he remained healthy enough to take his place among "normal" people in the shipyards of Hamburg. Two men wrestle for Castorp's soul, the Italian humanist, Settembrini, a liberal but a windbag, the disciple of reason, convinced that even madmen can be brought to their senses by merely commanding them to become rational, and the Jewish convert to Catholicism, Naphta, who speaks for all the dark forces, for superstition, terrorism, violence, and death—who in fact rejects the too bland heaven of republican humanism for the "anointed Terror of which the time has need," thus linking a totalitarian state to an authoritarian church.

The true climax of the book occurs in the chapter called Snow. Lost in a snowstorm, after he has wandered far out of bounds on skis, prey to hallucination and dream, utterly alone, close to death, Castorp rejects the teaching of both men: he has a vision of both a dark underground cruelty close to life's roots and a redeeming light that transfigures the mind and the world. But Castorp is still ill: his new vision of life quickly fades from him and his actions are unaffected: at the end of seven years he is drawn away from the sanatorium, not by any inner growth of character, not by any will of his own, but by the call to war. He has grown, he has veritably matured: yet he remains unconnected with life, except through war and death. The disease that afflicts this ailing world has realized itself at the expense of life, which has become, not reality, but the form of illusion.

The moral of this novel does not have to be underscored: it is present on every page and is amplified by the scene that greets the eye when one looks away from the pages of the book. Disease has counterfeited life: disease has reorganized science, technics, art, love for its own purposes; and death has now become the main goal of our living, lovingly circumvented, profitably elaborated, but no less inexorably perverting every hour of life. War alone can bring awakening: can renew the sense of self-direction and responsibility that a healthy personality always carries with it.

Here, then, is the modern world, with its over-charges of empty stimuli, its perpetual miscarriage of technique, its materialistic repletion, its costly ritual of conspicuous waste, its highly organized purposelessness: here is a veritable clinical picture of the cultural disease from which that world suffers. The x-ray photograph, the bacteriological analysis of the sputum, the auscultation, the temperature chart, all add up to a prognosis of the final result, death. The patient is in the midst of a mortal illness, and his feverish efforts to remain alive are themselves a disguised mechanism of the death wish. Syphilis, tuberculosis, cancer, hypertension—they come to the same end. The power of choice has gone: paralysis seizes every limb. When the President of the most powerful industrial nation on the earth boasts that no act of choice, such as Woodrow Wilson had been brave enough to make, brought his people into the war against fascism, few challenge that avowal or question its morality. Invalids do not choose.

Now we see the perfection of Thomas Mann's central symbol: the sanatorium. In terms of current ideals, what life could be more perfect than that of the sanatorium? What life more secure, more carefree, more capable of realizing to the full all the modern world can offer, not least by way of medical and psychological knowledge—even psychoanalysis, that last refinement in medical care? If life is a matter of multiplying pleasures and skillfully fending off death, what better use can be made of it than these sick people make? The essential sickness of the modern world, with its defective understanding of the personality and its needs, is that its ideal existence is really an invalid's existence, even as the repetitive motions that it inflicts upon its busy, hard-driven workers transform into a collective ritual the elements of a compulsion neurosis: the mechanical repetition of a limited set of motions. With illness and hypochondria and neurosis as the *norms* of civilization, is it any wonder that life itself reappeared in savage, pre-civilized guise as the will to violate, the will to kill, the will to destroy?

Once the death wish has become so prevalent one conclusion is inevitable: the present condition of man admits no easy relief. No minor remedies, no small, timid measures of reform, will bring life and health back to such a society: only the most dire catastrophe can now summon up the energies necessary for the reassertion of life and the values of life. Anesthetics may temporarily blot out the terrors of this state: chloral and whiskey, sexual dilation and speed, may ease the tensions; but in the end they add to the enfeeblement. Barbarism and war: these were the re-awakeners. And the catastrophe came. For that reason, perhaps, we may sardonically hail Hitler as the friend and redeemer of modern man.

8: Alternative to Dissolution

During the past century, then, the forces of life have turned against themselves. The interest in living organisms promoted a biological mythology, in which Kali, the destroyer, had a more positive role than Brahma the life-breather. The interest in living societies, nations, selfishly broke down those processes of international collaboration which justified and completed the life of the individual group. So, too, the interest in sex permitted the mechanics of sterility to undermine the very basis of Western man's existence. Everywhere there was a positive reactivation of life: yet everywhere this reactivation took destructive forms which led to extermination and suicide. As in cancer, the uncontrolled expression of life only hastened the breakdown of the healthy tissue that remained.

For a long time the vital reactions I have described were topographically separated: the vital, the national, the sexual, were contemporaneous but not interacting; they occurred spontaneously at different points in modern society and they failed to alter the dominant pattern of life. If the forces of life were finally to dominate the machine, if man's whole personality was to displace the disruptive activity of its separate organs, it was necessary that these forces should meet in a single mind and be fused in a living experience. A dynamic syncretism of doctrines and creeds and philosophies was needed, if the idolum of the machine was to unite under a new sign with the idolum of the organism.

That union, that syncretism, was attempted in many different minds; but the fusion long remained incomplete, partly because those who were on the side of life did not understand that the machine itself, properly utilized, was also an instrument of life: thus men like John Ruskin were too deeply influenced by Gothic architecture and Reformation pietism to break through these archaic molds, which denied them access to the living forces of their own time. Both Ruskin and his follower Morris, a much more robust person, were unwise enough to pour their new wine into old bottles. Tolstoy labored under the same handicap: his return to Gospel Christianity remained unhealthy because it sought a mere return to the primitive: he mistook an old starting place for the end of the journey.

Those who were closest to formulating a positive synthesis were Emerson and his successors in America: Thoreau, Whitman, and Melville: Walden, Moby-Dick, Leaves of Grass, and Democratic Vistas were both positive affirmations of life and steps toward a fresh expression of the super-ego. Each was an attempt to bring together the New World idolum and the Old World: each was an attempt to find a new Passage to India. The insights of these writers will be as significant for a new period of integration as the work of Plato and Aristotle was in the formulation of the new truths of Christianity. Perhaps no work could be closer to our present purposes than Whitman's Democratic Vistas.

Now, in the new world-picture that will replace that of the machine, the submerged or recessive forces of the last century—democracy, vitalism, co-operation—will become the dominants in our emerging society: elements in a new syncretism which will nourish once more the spirit of man. Their period of formulation is nearly over: their incorporation and embodiment remain to take place in a world theater.

Happily there is one figure whose life-interests fully represent the forces I have been describing: one whose conscious philosophy reached a fuller stage of formulation than either Emerson or Whitman: one whose actual life, coming later, faced more fully the corruptions and devitalizations of the present scene. Obscure in his own lifetime, hardly better known today, a dozen years after his death, he incarnated the organic and made an orderly constellation of its vitalities. Patrick Geddes was his name. What he was, what he stood for, what he pointed toward will become increasingly important as the world grows to understand both his philosophy and his example. Lincoln, observing Whitman striding past a White House window, is reported to have said: There is a *man.* So one who followed the darting glance and eager footsteps of Geddes, rambling through a city, or wandering with an armful of plants along a country road, might have said: There goes one enriched and energized and sensitized by the life-force he has studied so fervently: his is the touch that will make the dry wand burgeon. Such a man has worshiped the burning bush and beheld from afar the Promised Land.

Geddes was born in Scotland, the main home of the paleotechnic revolution, in the decade that saw the publication of Spencer's First Principles and Darwin's Origin of Species. He passed from his boyish experiments in chemistry to the study of biology under Huxley and Haeckel. From the beginning, he was filled with Darwin's wonder of life and never lost his appetite for all its varied phenomena or his esthetic love for its forms: life's sheer variety and luxuriance, its progressive mastery of the non-living, were constant incitements to increase his own vitality. No man in our time has shown a higher degree of intensity: an intellectual energy that matched Leonardo's all-devouring curiosity, a practical grasp that organized masques and planned cities, a sexual vitality, continent but volcanic, that recalls the pan-like figures of Victor Hugo or Auguste Rodin. Geddes's work in biology not merely made him a natural heir of Lamarck and Darwin: it brought him to the life-long study of sex in all its manifestations. His survey of The Evolution of Sex, written with his pupil and colleague, J. Arthur Thomson, remained for more than a generation a unique summary of the subject.

But this naturalist was also open to the positive currents of life that sprang from the folk: not for nothing was he born in the land of Robert Burns and Walter Scott. As a student, he had watched the resurgence of the French nation after 1870, when it rose from its humiliation to rebuild the country: an interest in Provence, the birthplace of Comte, made him aware of the kindred movement toward regionalism and political decentralization which Frédéric Mistral had started. From Geddes's Outlook Tower at Edinburgh on the summit of Castle Hill, came the first publications of the Gaelic Renascence in the early nineties. But Geddes's nationalism encompassed all that Mazzini taught and went even farther: from the first, he treated the nation, not merely as a political and a cultural entity, but as a social and economic unit within a worldwide community. As a mere biological group, a product of "blood and soil," maintaining and perpetuating a primitive element in the social heritage, the nation was as important to human culture as the primitive occupations of miner and woodman were to the technology of the machine. At the same time the nation was a conflux of energies, a focusing of light-rays, that came from every part of the social cosmos: blood and soil were the foundations of man's larger humanity, not a substitute for it.

Geddes's Scotland embraced Europe and his Europe embraced the world. Dundee jute came from India, as did Paisley shawls. In his correspondence with Margaret Noble, who had become a Hindu sister, Geddes said of the cultures of the East and West: "Each in turn for thousands of years has stimulated the other; each in isolation has suffered—we were hardening into external growths within which life shrivels: you concentrating yourselves in this inner life, till the external is depressed or forgotten. The strength of our youth is ever sallying forth resolved to gain the whole world, sure it will profit him: the silent depth of yours retires, to seek the saving—the finding—of his own soul, which profits him much: yet may let the other's die. Has not each now in turn to share the conquest of the other's kingdom, each in turn to help save the other from his supreme danger—himself!" The great Odyssey of Geddes's old age, a decade of teaching and town-planning in India from 1914 on, was not merely a repayment of Scotland's debt to India: it served a higher purpose and involved the acceptance of a fuller obligation. Geddes learned from the Hindus even deeper habits of withdrawal and contemplation than those he had long practiced: he more fully united Eastern passivism and Western activism in his own life. His biography of Jagadis Chandra Bose was not merely a tribute to a great experimental physicist but a tribute to the Hindu intuition of the unity of all being that had made Bose's researches possible. He thus carried forward the earlier initiatives of Thoreau and Emerson. That example is a starting point for our future world culture.

Geddes coupled thought to action, and action to life, and life itself to all the highest manifestations of sense, feeling, and experience: organic life did not merely culminate in man's superior cunning but in man's superior ideals. Man's existence did not stay at the biological level of organism, function, and environment, nor even at the tribal or folk level of folk, work, and place: man perpetually renewed himself and transcended himself by means of that heritage of ideal values, of self-surpassing purposes, which are covered by the terms polity, culture, and art, as these terms were used by Geddes's earlier contemporary, Burckhardt. For Geddes life had more than its animal destiny of reproduction and physical survival: it had a high destiny, that of revamping out of nature's original materials, with the help of nature's original patterns, a more perfectly harmonized, a more finely attuned, a more complexly balanced expression of both personality and community. Olympus and Parnassus were as real for Geddes as the primeval slime out of which the protozoa had emerged. In the gods on Olympus, indeed, he discovered the ideal embodiment of the Seven Ages of Man.

The depletion of vitality, the arrest of growth, the domination of the living by the non-living, the persistence of fixity and habit over flexibility and purposive change—against all these forms of disintegration Geddes endlessly battled. Geddes was on the side of life, wherever it was threatened or besieged. Into the piled-up tenement districts of Edinburgh he brought gardens; into the plague-ridden streets of Indian cities, he brought cleanliness; into the cram-schools of "verbalistic empaperment" he brought the regional survey, which sent the student out into the city and the countryside, seeing with his own eyes the realities behind his academic abstractions; into the movement for sexual development, with which he sympathized, he brought the sense of the family, the need for children, the acceptance of mature responsibilities. With the wand of life, he tapped the rock and made water flow forth. He challenged every success that was bought at the expense of further growth, further self-renewal.

Geddes published little but he propagated much. From his thought came about the revitalization of history and geography by first-hand exploration and regional studies: likewise a more vital kind of nature observation which encouraged the sense of beauty as well as that of curiosity, which stimulated the feelings no less than the understanding: Geddes's own joy in the presence of nature's marvels and delights was infectious. From nature study arose a more comprehensive kind of social diagnosis: that of the civic and the regional survey, which became as fundamental to social action as the physician's record of the patient's history and his systematic observation of his body. Geddes thus laid the foundations for a movement for city and regional development that had more vital aims than the multiplication of sewers or the facilitation of traffic: into all these activities, educational, civic, practical, he carried his sense of the organic, displacing the mechanisms and automatisms that had hitherto been central.

In Geddes's philosophy of life, mechanism had a constant place as the servant of life, but never as its master: life paid the piper and must call the tune. As a scientific interpreter of Ruskin, he knew the essential truth of Ruskin's great saying: "You do not educate a man by telling him what he knew not, but by making him what he was not." In Ruskin's fundamental economic treatise, Munera Pulveris, he saw that the new doctrines of energetics had been applied to all economic phenomena: a more vital contribution than any of the economists, even Marx, had made. He perceived, too, that Ruskin's definition of value—that which avails for life—displaces all spurious values based on convention and fashion and pecuniary manipulation. From this standpoint, production must be educational as well as technical: "first, the production of a thing essentially useful; then the production of the capacity to use it." And the highest type of work, accordingly, is not complete automatism, but just the opposite—the activity of the artist. All work serves for life in that it produces art and gives men the liberated vitality of artists. If we have only trash and trivialities to sell, we must produce trashy and trivial personalities to serve as consumers. Our apparatus of education, advertisement, and propaganda, as developed under capitalism, exists to produce such monsters.

In his own person, Geddes exemplified the radical changes that are imperative if the limitations of the New World idolum are to be overcome. Paralleling the great example of the distinguished American physicist, Joseph Henry, Geddes devoted himself to citizenship, even at the cost of retarding his own fruition as a scientist: to make a full life possible his own work in science remained incomplete. Never indeed did he turn aside completely from his original interests as a biologist: indeed, the year before he died he published a monumental two-volume survey of Life: Outlines of Biology, in collaboration with his old pupil, Thomson. But Geddes was too deeply concerned with what was going on outside his laboratory and his study to be content with a personal success made possible by civic indifference. Instead, he brought to civic and political affairs the same habits of systematic observation, accurate report, patient diagnosis, that biology passes on to the physician. In 1911, he not merely predicted the outbreak of the World War, not later than 1915, but laid plans for a series of books on The Making of the Future, to speed the transition from wardom to peacedom.

Geddes the biologist mastered Comte, Spencer, Le Play, Durkheim, Veblen, and systematically reinterpreted his biological data in terms of human society: he thus laid the foundations for a sociology capable of including all the divergent schools. Similarly, as sociologist he turned to philosophy and had vivid intercourse with Bergson, James, Dewey, Lloyd Morgan. His was not eclecticism but synthesis: not a midden-heap of ideas but a closely articulated central structure, from which radiated wings that were intentionally left unfinished. Geddes had respect for all specialized knowledge, wherever he found it. "Every man knows more about his own business than I do: even the street-sweeper. If I want to teach him I must first learn from him." But Geddes had no respect for those walls of habit and class pride that make intercourse between specialists impossible: like Aristotle and Leibnitz he took all knowledge for his province, not merely in order to add to his own power and wisdom, but to make possible a continuous interchange between the isolated provinces of thought: isolated and sterilized by their failure to begin and end with that unity which is life.

The reclamation of science by citizenship was practiced by Geddes long before the over-development of the physical sciences had led to a demand for a long holiday from all scientific research. Geddes did not make the false answer that more science would automatically cure the evils produced by science: his answer was rather to accept social responsibility in his life and work, to inter-relate scientific investigation with social need. Once that responsibility is accepted, there must come a slackening of the feverish tempo of research, often over-stimulated by those who have sought high position or money rewards, often mis-directed by those who are looking for exploitable territory rather than socially useful channels of research. Within the field of knowledge itself, an organic approach to a particular problem—in contrast to the method of isolation and detached analysis—must inevitably produce a slowing down of the tempo. Partial solutions put speed before completeness: organic solutions demand completeness without promising quick returns.

Whatever the ultimate fate of the notation of ideas which Geddes labored so long and so arduously to perfect, it vastly furthered his own powers of assimilation and understanding: the art of co-ordinated thinking was one that he carried to a new height of discipline and organization. He did not however rely upon thought alone to effect the change needed: action must accompany it. As citizens, conserving and fostering life in their own community and their own region, co-operating with other citizens throughout the world, Geddes believed that the specialists would rise to common views, common purposes, common plans.

Vivendo discimus was Geddes's motto: We learn by living. Or, as he said in his pamphlet on Co-operation in 1888, "it is only by thinking things out as one lives them, and living things out as one thinks them, that a man or a society can really be said to think or even live at all." That interaction of thought and action, of ideal and deed, was as important for man as a worker or man as a citizen as it was for the intellectual: without this constant weaving back and forth between the inner life and the outer life, between thought and action, between images and plans, life itself was arrested.

The basic change exemplified by Geddes was the unification of all the processes of life, the subjective and the objective, and the equal cultivation of the sciences, the arts, and the humanities. As a scientist, Geddes, like Freud, had been trained to look upon religion as but a muddled precursor of science, whose residue was now mainly superstition. But as a surveyor and planner of cities, Geddes discovered the permanent function of the cloister and the cathedral: the first grew out of the need for withdrawal, for quiet brooding, for a deeper plumbing of memory and a stimulus to the imagination that comes only through detachment. Thus the cell, the tower, the grove, the woodland path, the high mountain, were all forms of the cloister that had been used at one time or another by religious, philosophic, and scientific minds: the laboratory was only its latest phase. Similarly, the Cathedral was a generic name for that embodiment of common purposes and common ideals which unites men in feeling and action, no less than thought, in dumb animal faith as well as rational expression: the Acropolis in one age, the Temple in another, the symphony concert or the museum in a third. Geddes indeed anticipated that the art museum and the natural history museum would make no small contribution to a living religion for our time: it was only a spurious religion that sought to attach itself to an outmoded science or an archaic form of art.

For Geddes, the taboos and superstitions of religion of course deserved to wither: not its essential core. From Christian, Jew, Mohammedan, from Parsee, Hindu, Buddhist, from agnostic and atheist, Geddes sought to extract the essence of a more catholic creed and a deeper understanding of man's drama and destiny. In Siva he found the doctrine of natural selection, in Brahma the *élan vital,* in Judaism the oneness of cosmic and biological and historic destiny, in the Muses of Greece the nine essential notes in man's higher emotional and intellectual development. To him all the phenomena of a rich subjective life, myth, poesy, painting, music, were as real and significant as the earthiest conditions that underlie man's life: love and sacrifice were as proper to life as lust, physical prowess, animal survival.

Nothing in life was foreign to Geddes; and no expression of life in history was altogether without meaning and value: even a broken shell was witness to the fact that life had once been present and had molded it. Implicitly, he believed in the Chinese principles of Yin and Yang: the alternation of the passive and the active, the internal and the external, the introvert and the extravert moods was for him the very rhythm of life itself: the key, not alone to sexual differentiation, but to all activities. To block that process was to thwart life: to participate in it was to be one with life's drift and meaning.

Far from rejecting the primitive elements in our civilization, Patrick Geddes insisted that they were an integral part of man's inheritance: he knew that the roots of life lay deep. But instead of giving these vitalities a barbarous outlet, he proposed to attach them to man's higher culture. He would cultivate the region, not alone for the sake of the local life but for the sake of the world's life, too: he helped to revive national traditions, not to inflame a "sacred egoism" but to contribute to the wealth of humanity. So, too, he counseled youth to go out with the fishing fleet, to accompany the shepherd on his rounds, to stalk game with the hunter, for the sake of the human insight and self-respect that the discipline of these primitive occupations brings with it. For Geddes the truly educated man was one who was capable of mastering the work and life of any part of the valley section.

Geddes's doctrine that every part of the environment, every part of the social heritage, must be unlocked for the common man is today the basic theory of American army education. And its extraordinary success in transforming the timid, the slack-willed, the over-specialized, the self-defeated into alert and highly activated soldiers, capable of finding their way over strange terrain, of handling complicated weapons, of inflicting their wills on hostile men, suggests similar activations, similar masteries, for a militant peace: a peace based upon a race re-educated for co-operative and creative tasks. If the Army can bring Geddesian methods—including many characteristic Geddesian shortcuts—so successfully into the business of inflicting death, is it not time that this philosophy were applied with similar intensity to the preservation and intensification of life?

In Geddes's life and mind, the sundered fragments of the modern world were restored to unity, not by returning to their original simplicity, but by going forward to a more highly developed synthesis and to a more inclusive pattern of action: a synthesis that was always open to the test of fresh action, to the challenge of fresh experience, to the incursion of fresh ideas and ideals.

For such a view of life no early success was possible in our time. Viewed in its immediate effects, his life was a succession of failures and its final acts, the building of his Collège des Ecossais at Montpellier and the foundation of an International Trust for its maintenance, were the worst failures of all. Nor did any success with the written word redeem these failures: indeed, by the very fact that he too long avoided publication his thought and insight were never adequately passed on to others except by way of example and oral communication: as with Socrates, his ultimate act of synthesis, the final justification for his boundless activity and tireless thought, was himself.

But today the insurgent mind of Patrick Geddes is more alive than it has ever been: he is both the precursor and the initiator, the formulator and the incarnation, of a way of life that shall be directed once more to life's highest purposes. With Goethe, Geddes used to say: "Animals are always attempting the impossible and achieving it." That, he would add, is the essential condition of man.

Through his life-work, Geddes is the Bacon and the Leonardo, perhaps the Galileo, of an idolum that will replace the half-world of the period of expansion. In his personality a new mutation took place, and by his example and practice the path of redevelopment and renewal for modern man becomes clearer. He would have been the first to disclaim such a role as the gift of any single man: and I would be the last to make such an exclusive claim for him. I have used him as a symbol of a change that has been going on for more than a century and that now approaches the moment when it can take the initiative and openly challenge the forces that stand in its way. This movement has been taking place in many parts of the world and in many different kinds of activity, under many different circumstances. From Goethe to Louis Sullivan, from Claude Bernard to Osler, from Emerson to Whitehead, from Ebenezer Howard to Henry Wright, from Whitman to Stieglitz this new sense of the organic has made its way steadily into every sphere of creative activity: nowhere completely triumphant, yet everywhere gathering fresh energies, staking out fresh territory, projecting fresh objectives. There are many people in obscure places whose true life will be realized, not alone in the community they immediately serve, but in that which they are helping to bring into existence: these people and hundreds like them exemplify the Geddesian doctrine of life: many-sided participators in its growth, reproduction, renewal, and insurgence. What they feel and think and do today, millions may do and feel and think a generation hence.

The challenge of war and the threat of death has given many men and women throughout the world a new courage in facing life and a new confidence in their abilities to outwit the men and mechanisms that would enslave them. *Vivendo discimus.* Only those who are already dead and defeated need accept defeat and death as their final destiny. Our civilization has not said its last word. Man is at length ready to depart on new missions.

CHAPTER XI. THE BASIS OF RENEWAL

1: The External Crisis

Henry Adams was right: the last thirty years have been witnessing the active disintegration of Western civilization. In a disintegrating society, decay is its form of life; and all the dynamic forces that are available have worked either to corrupt the human fiber or to multiply the agents of physical destruction. If we go further along the same route we shall fare worse. On our courage in facing this fact and on our promptness in meeting it, all plans for the renewal of personality and community depend. "Bombs educate vigorously," Adams observed, "and even wireless telegraphy or airships might require the reconstruction of society."

Has the destruction yet gone far enough to promote a genuine renewal —or has it already gone so far that it will prevent it? No one can yet answer this question. But only the ability to put the question to ourselves will provide an effectual answer in life and action.

The makers of the New World idolum confidently expected that the older part of the human heritage would disappear: science and technics seemed thoroughly able not merely to reconstruct man's institutions and his personality, but to displace any older forms of art, thought, or practice. If anything, the utilitarians would have been surprised at the persistence of institutions that were manifestly at odds with the utilitarian way of life. But they forgot that the moral and intellectual traditions of Judaea, Greece, and Rome were essential to the development of the New World ideology itself: so that, with the ebbing away of this older tide of culture, the insufficiency of their own creed as a guide to life would become plain. A science that disclaimed all interest in human values, except the satisfaction of curiosity and the increase of manipulative skill, cannot be useful even in its own limited sphere when the general dissolution of values leads to a contempt for science and a deliberate perversion of its results.

Modern civilization has been arrested in mid-flight: its technical advances in saving labor, perfecting automatism, mechanizing the daily processes of life, multiplying the arts of destruction, and dehumanizing the personality have been responsible for this arrest. The rise of the machine and the fall of man are two parts of the same process: never before have machines been so perfect, and never before have men sunk so low, for the sub-human conduct that the Nazis have exhibited in the torture and extermination of their victims drops below any level of merely animal brutality. That degradation is shared by those who passively condone this sub-human conduct, by belittling its horror and denying its terrible significance.

This catastrophe and this debasement have no parallels in earlier history; for now, for the first time, the entire world is involved. All consolations that are based on past recoveries are meaningless. What happened to Greece, Rome, China, or India has no parallel in the world today: when those civilizations collapsed, they were surrounded by neighbors that had reached nearly equal levels of culture, whereas if Western civilization should continue its downward course it will spread ruin to every part of the planet; and its going will consume the very forces and ideas within its own tradition that might have given a start to its successor.

The present crisis has long been visible. Jacob Burckhardt observed its early stages in the middle of the nineteenth century: in the series of brilliant essays, now published in English under the title, Force and Freedom, he not merely diagnosed the malady but accurately predicted its outward manifestations. In a letter written to Henry Osborn Taylor in 1905, Henry Adams remarked: "At the present rate of progression since 1600, it will not need another century or half century to tip thought upside down. Law, in that case, would disappear as theory or *a priori* principle and give place to force. Morality would become police. Explosives would reach cosmic violence. Disintegration would overcome integration." Henry Adams did not live to observe fascism: he anticipated it. He knew that the detonators of violence and destruction were present in every part of the social structure of Western society.

Like the die-hards of fourth century Rome, most of our contemporaries are still unaware of the dimensions of the present catastrophe. They were so completely self-hypnotized by pride in man's control over nature that they overlooked all the palpable evidence of the fact that this control did not extend to his own self and his own very life: they were unprepared to believe that a fiendish barbarism could arise in the midst of an advanced scientific country like Germany; and they were unable to analyze in their own reactions to this the characteristic symptoms of decay: a moral inertia, a flight from reality, an unwillingness to face danger or hardship on behalf of an ideal cause. The democratic peoples, inheritors of a universal culture that had actually spread throughout the globe, were willing to barter all their advances for the sake of "peace." When they finally found that the choice was not in their hands, they made ready to fight—but skeptically, reluctantly, stupidly, as men answer an alarm clock when still thick with sleep. This feeble response to the challenge of barbarism was as much a sign of disintegration as the barbarism itself.

The war itself has shocked people into facing the grimmest of realities; but it is not in itself sufficient to promote an understanding of the forces that have brought on this world catastrophe. In its later phases, the war has caused people to accept unthinkable sacrifices: but they have yet to accept the hardest sacrifice of all, and that is, to give up their illusions about this civilization. Modern man is the victim of the very instruments he values most. Every gain in power, every mastery of natural forces, every scientific addition to knowledge, has proved potentially dangerous because it has not been accompanied by equal gains in self-understanding and self-discipline. We have sought to achieve perfection by eliminating the human element. Believing that power and knowledge were by nature beneficent or that man himself was inherently good when freed from external obligations to goodness, we have conjured up a genius capable of destroying our civilization. The disproportionate development of the sciences themselves only hastens this malign end.

The physical victory over the barbarian in war is no answer to the problem that the barbarian's existence has conjured up: it merely clears the way for an answer. Even if valor and skill in war give the democratic peoples a temporary military ascendancy, that in itself will not be sufficient either to secure a lasting peace or to raise up this battered civilization. For the disease that threatens us is an organic one: it is no localized infection that can be lanced, cleaned, bandaged; on the contrary, it requires a reorientation of our whole life, a change in occupation, a change in regimen, a change in personal relationships, not least, a change in attitude and conscious direction: fundamentally, a change in religion, our total sense of the world and life and time. If we seek salvation more cheaply, we shall not be ready to undertake the heroic feats and sacrifices, the spiritual and practical efforts that will be necessary to create a life-sustaining community and a life-directed personality. To make use of our vitalities and energies—and potentially these were never greater—we must reassert once more the primacy of the person.

The obstacle to renewal does not merely lie in the fact that in so many parts of society the agents of destruction have gained the upper hand, and the organization of destruction has been forced upon us by the barbarian's attempt at world enslavement. Worse than that: organization has become in itself destructive of human values: everywhere the machine holds the center and the personality has been pushed to the periphery: a process which remains sinister even when the intention is benign—as it undoubtedly is, for example, in our overorganized institutions for teaching the young or for healing disease. The only way to renew the forces of life is to begin once again with the repressed and displaced elements: to dismantle a large part of the physical structure, to loosen up the automatisms of habit, to challenge even successful forms of routine, to give time, thought, attention, to all those changes which do not, in their first stages, require the collaboration and support of existing institutions. Our society is now at the stage where conversion—an inner change and redirection—must precede every outer change or transformation.

Here is the benign moment of disintegration: the moment when the old life is sufficiently shattered and broken to make a new life conceivable. When this moment of germination comes, the individual's experience of renewal, or at least his radical readiness for renewal, widens into a collective act. Such a change took place in classic civilization during the fourth century: it occurred again on a similar scale throughout the Western world in the eighteenth century: in both cases responses to disintegration. That inner change, under the pressure of a powerful experience, universally shared, is the prelude to every significant outer change. If rational demonstration cannot bring such a change about, it can nevertheless hasten it and clarify its goals once the personality has made itself ready and the conditions favoring it have come into being.

2: The Inertia of "Progress"

The Chinese symbol for crisis is composed of two elements: one signifies danger and the other opportunity. If the dangers that the world faces today are greater than the majority yet fully realize, the opportunities are equally great. But these opportunities are of a different order than those of the past. Talk of goods and benefits to be shared among mankind after the war too often has been in the familiar utilitarian terms, and those who have been most confident of technical progress show themselves pitifully incapable of understanding either current dangers or future promises. Such people are the bemused victims of the very values they question least.

In anticipations of the post-war tasks, perhaps the most important thing to remember is that our mission is not the simple one of re-building demolished houses and ruined cities, converting war industries to peacetime manufactures, repairing the broken bodies of the wounded or the broken souls of those who have borne witness to more violence, terror, and misery than the human spirit can endure. All these tasks are essential; but they are only first aid. If the material shell of our society alone needed repair, if only the more obvious human wreckage needed to be restored to the human estate, our designs might follow familiar patterns. But the fact is our task is a far heavier one. In every department of our culture, we must lay the foundations for a new set of purposes, a new drama, a radically different mode of life. The "New World" of the fifteenth century is now the *Old* World: our dawning new world must take in far larger tracts of both the earth and the human personality. The bulk of our institutions no longer corresponds to the needs and possibilities of human life; and this is true, not merely of traditional structures, but of many that boast their unqualified modernity: some of the last, indeed, are already the seediest, the most completely disserviceable, in terms of valid human purposes.

In short, the crisis we are now in the midst of does not admit of a return to our original condition, in the fashion that a crisis in pneumonia, once passed, enables the patient to recover his original health. The fact is that before the war there was spiritually little health in us. Our elaborate mechanical organization of life had resulted in an increasingly purposeless society, in which some of the parts were neatly articulated and ordered, while the whole made little sense in terms of life-satisfactions and life-fulfillments. In its very mechanical elaboration, our civilization had become emptier, because it had not originally been shaped in conformity to the basic needs of human life. Only after the human voice had been transmitted around the world with the speed of light did it become plain that the words so widely disseminated might still be the same words one could hear from the village gossip or the village idiot or the village clown or the village hoodlum.

Man himself did not mirror the perfection of his instruments. Behind this empty technical fabric was an emptier ideology: one which multiplied quantities and forgot qualities: one which centered on the means of life and forgot its consummations.

Western man has exhausted the dream of mechanical power which so long dominated his imagination. If he is to preserve the instruments he has so cunningly created, if he is to continue to refine and perfect the whole apparatus of life, he can no longer let himself remain spellbound in that dream: he must attach himself to more humane purposes than those he has given to the machine. We can no longer live, with the illusions of success, in a world given over to devitalized mechanisms, desocialized organisms, and depersonalized societies: a world that had lost its sense of the ultimate dignity of the person almost as completely as the Roman

Empire did at the height of its military greatness and technical facility. All that the Nazis have done has been to bring to a more rapid climax a process that was more slowly, more insidiously, undermining our whole civilization.

But another symptomatic weakness should by now be equally plain: even those who cling to the old drama of expansion and conquest, of mechanical organization and material exploitation, no longer wholly believe in the plot. Georges Sorel observed this fact early in the twentieth century: he compared the new capitalists disparagingly with the American robber barons of the mid-nineteenth century, and he was afraid that the revolutionary élan would disappear in a society whose business men and industrialists had lost their original ruthlessness if not their original greed. The signs of this inner exhaustion multiplied steadily during the last thirty years; one of the most critical of them is the widespread unwillingness to play the game if the player happens to be losing. When people are really interested in a life-theme, they cling to it even under the most adverse conditions; indeed, the pressure of difficulty only intensifies their interest. When the Christian theme was in the making, persecutions welded the faithful together and finally resulted in a unified Church. When the interests of capitalism were dominant, adventurous enterprisers accepted losses and bankruptcies without wincing and began all over again: the Christian did not cease to believe in his religion because it brought personal grief, nor the capitalist in capitalism because it might result in personal ruin.

Now, we have seen just the opposite of these qualities in our time. Capitalists accepted the closing down of the world market for the same reason that democratic peoples accepted without even a timid countermovement the cancerous spread of fascism. And why? For the sake of peace: for the reason that a counter-movement implied risk and sacrifice; and risk and sacrifice were not accepted, since the faith that would have made them self-justifying had evaporated.

Had the old plot become too complicated to follow? Had the old rewards proved disappointing? Had new motives appeared which cast into disrepute the accepted themes of the old drama? In varying ways all these things had indeed happened; but the main fact to be noted is that the old game no longer thrilled the players: until the war actually was forced upon the anti-fascist powers, neither nationalism nor capitalism had the pride, the self-confidence, the initiative to summon together energies that were still visible as late as 1914. In the course of fighting the war, nationalism and capitalism have both received a powerful stimulant: the nationalist shows a truculent egoism toward allies in victory that might have staved off the war altogether had it been originally present in the face of fascist bluff and bullying; while capitalism, like an old man who has miraculously begotten a baby, actually fancies it has recovered the potencies of youth. Both responses, however, are automatic ones: mere by-products of the war. Examine the motives that are still dominant and they turn out to end up in dreams of escape, escape via the golf-links, the motor highway, the night club, the helicopter, a life of expensive automatism and automatic expense: the tag ends of baroque luxury and baroque futility in a setting of slick machines.

Unlike the rapacious industrialists of the nineteenth century, the leaders today no longer treat the industrial system as an end in itself. Western man demands a special price for further mechanization: bread and shows, physical security, and semi-mental distractions. He must be bribed and coaxed to perform acts his forefathers performed gladly, wholeheartedly, with an almost religious conviction. This applies to both owners and workers, leaders and led. The very economies the machine makes possible bring with them a train of dissipations.

In general, one may say that in the present crisis nothing was real enough to fight for at the beginning because nothing was significant enough to live for at the end.

If technics is the sole key to success, the American cartels that connived with the Nazis to suppress patents essential to democracy's preparation for war might write off their treason to the account of profit. If technics alone constitutes man's desirable future, then the Nazis, who have applied cold technics to the state-controlled copulation of future mothers or to the bestial murder of Jews, were indeed the "wave of the future." But what a future! The danger to human society today does not come solely from the active barbarians: it comes even more perhaps from those who have in their hearts assented to the barbarian's purposes. This lapse was part of a decay of faith in the primacy of the person that people of the most widely assorted convictions succumbed to: the very Churches that had originally sprung from this faith were among its most sinister betrayers.

Unfortunately, the war itself has reawakened a confidence in the future on the basis of a simple restoration of the motives and methods of the past—that very past which has terminated in the present catastrophe. Above all, the capitalist dog has returned to his old vomit. The investor, the organizer, the industrial worker, even the farmer, have once again had a glimpse of that hitherto unattainable heaven which the innocent regard as a practical equivalent of the good life: the heaven of full productivity based on unlimited demand and leading to the hope of unlimited profits. That heaven, it is true, will remain real only until the day of reckoning comes: the day when each country adds up the costs and starts to balance the books. Indeed, no better evidence exists of the mental disorder that is rife in present-day society than the capitalist's confidence in his ability to resume this game on his own terms—when *on his own terms,* that is, on the terms of redeeming the existing debt at par value, and paying to boot the interest charges he has already lost.

Mazzini long ago remarked when he was promoting the national independence of Italy that people were much more willing to sacrifice their lives to the good cause than their pennies. When the time comes to shift from war production to peace production, we shall find that the utopia of full production is a capitalist mirage, as long as the old capitalist super-ego remains in control. Capitalism by nature and principle subordinates public need to private profit. On capitalist terms, there is no satisfactory "moral equivalent of war." That was the illusion of the new capitalism: an illusion that should have been buried forever by the calamitous depression that started in 1929.

But there is far more impressive evidence of the vanity of all these great expectations than I have yet shown. The fact is that most of the current plans for remolding our civilization ignore the vast secular change that has crept up on Western Civilization during the past century, almost unawares. That change is nothing less than the end of the Era of Expansion, and the collapse of the major premises, metaphysical, moral, social, economic, on which it was based.

3: The End of Expansion

The world crisis that has existed for the lifetime of a whole generation indicates that a radical shift in the direction of social movement has taken place: this shift began during the last quarter of the nineteenth century and now, directly and indirectly, has affected almost every institution. The crisis has two aspects: an external and an internal one. Here I shall deal mainly with the causes of the external crisis. The external change may be summed up in a brief sentence: an age of expansion is giving place to an age of equilibrium. The achievement of this equilibrium is the task of the next few centuries.

So far this change has been a blind and blundering one. Not merely have the underlying causes themselves been ignored, but the interests and attitudes that were formed by the tradition of expansion have kept every community from meeting by rational means the new conditions of life that open up. Those that have accepted the premises of stabilization have attached the movement itself to regressive purposes and have cut it off from its creative mission. Those who have resisted stabilization have striven to perpetuate a past that is beyond recall: a past that would not be worth recalling even if that were possible. Both the tempo and the direction of our life are about to undergo a profound change: this will prove a change for the better provided we can throw off the fatal temptation to worship our dead selves and perpetuate our past mistakes.

The present period is a painful transition between two eras. The first I have traced in some detail since the fourteenth century: it is associated with the rise of capitalism, militarism, scientism, and mechanization: likewise with the counter-movements of protestantism, romanticism, and democracy. All of these institutions made positive contributions to human culture: even militarism. The total effect of the era of expansion, however, was to increase man's power over nature, and in particular Western man's power over the more amiable or more feebly armed peoples that inhabited the rest of the planet; but the civilization that resulted has been rent by internal conflicts and contradictions which have nullified many of its real triumphs.

The outlines of the period of humanization that approaches are not so easy to describe: many of the characters have still to be invented and their lines have still to be written: at best, some of their costumes and a few odd parcels of scenery indicate what the play is to be about. But by way of broad contrast one may characterize the approaching period as one of dynamic equilibrium, such an equilibrium as the human body maintains at every stage in its growth. The theme for the new period will be neither arms and the man nor machines and the man: its theme will be the resurgence of life, the displacement of the mechanical by the organic, and the re-establishment of the person as the ultimate term of all human effort. Cultivation, humanization, co-operation, symbiosis: these are the watchwords of the new world-enveloping culture.

Many of the miscarriages of the present period are due to the fact that our statesmen, our industrial leaders, our administrators are still trying to apply the ideology of the age of expansion to a social organization that has an entirely different set of requirements: an organization in which the careful timing and spacing of activities, in which the proper diversification of opportunities and the balancing and interlocking of functions must take the place of those spectacular one-sided advances, colossal but incoherent, which were characteristic of the period of expansion. Every department of life will record this change: it will affect the task of education and the procedures of science no less than the organization of industrial enterprises, the planning of cities, the development of regions, the interchange of world resources.

The facts of the present stabilization are familiar to students of history and sociology; but the interpretation of these facts has proved tardy. Yet strangely enough, our present state was accurately forecast by at least one early observer, John Stuart Mill: witness what has become, by force of events, a great chapter in the second volume of his Principles of Political Economy. That chapter is devoted to a theoretical discussion of what Mill misleadingly called the "stationary state." By this he meant an economic order in which the area for new capital investments had dwindled by a natural process of self-limitation, in which, through birth control, the population had become stable, and in which the rates of profit and interest tended, as a result of this twofold curb, to fall toward zero.

This is the chapter that most people know by only a single sentence, one in which Mill doubted whether labor-saving machinery had yet lightened the day's burdens of a single worker. But it was here he made a far more significant observation: namely, that a state of dynamic equilibrium, though it might be dreaded by the profiteer, was precisely the condition required for translating mechanical improvements into social welfare. In re-stating Mill's observations as history I only accentuate their merit as prophecy.

The era of Western expansion had three overlapping and interacting phases: land expansion, population expansion, and industrial expansion. All three phases have usually been treated as if they were constant phenomena in any healthy society; whereas they were extremely unusual and highly localized changes that had a definite beginning and an inevitable terminus. In our time the whole process has come to an end, or very nearly approaches an end. Other peoples who a hundred years ago existed on a primitive level have fast become masters of Western machines and weapons, producers in their own right. Such people will no longer consent to being treated as packbearers and servants: they properly claim their place as partners, and they reinforce their claim with the Christian doctrine of the infinite worth of the individual, and the democratic doctrine of the freedom and equality of all men as men. We cannot disown either doctrine without betraying our own precious heritage. World trade, world production, world intercourse must now be based upon equivalent advantages for all the regions concerned: it must now be a two-way process: consciously and deliberately so. Meanwhile, equally radical changes are under way in the other departments where expansion has prevailed. I propose to examine these changes and to point out their consequences.

4: Close of the World Frontier

Land expansion was the prime source of the industrialization that took place, with accelerating speed, after the seventeenth century. This process had both a material and a psychological result: it gave Western man boundless confidence in his destiny and in his own drives, and it gave him a wider theater of action than he had ever had before. Westward the land was always bright, and every landfall might turn out to be a windfall.

By 1893 an American historian, Frederick Jackson Turner, pointed out that the United States had reached the limits of its last important frontier: the entire continental area had been staked out, if not fully occupied; and the habits that were appropriate to a pioneer period were no longer in harmony with the new facts of existence. As a country, we could no longer evade the necessity for settling down and making the most of our resources: it was impossible to overcome the evils of gutting out the forests, mining the soils, annihilating the wild life, merely by pulling up stakes and moving on to a virgin area. Conservation became the price of survival.

What is true of the land settlement of the United States has, within the last generation, become true for the world at large. Little remains for the explorer except barren mountain tops or polar wastes. What new areas remain for settlement are negligible: regions of difficulty like the high Andes, Manchuria, Siberia, or Alaska are almost the last important frontiers.

In other words, the grand cycle of exploration and conquest and random appropriation is over. Western civilization, now that it has girdled the planet, can go no farther: the airplane completes the conquest by multiplying the ties and shrinking space further, not by opening up more desirable territory hitherto unknown. Our problem is not to add to the existing land areas but to make better use of them. We must systematically apply our new-found geologic, climatic, ecologic, and social knowledge to the better ordering of man's estate; and to make this knowledge more valuable, we must acquire a deeper insight into the biologic and historic nature of man. Our hope of increasing these resources must be based on more thorough knowledge and more intensive cultivation—not on a broader reach and a more prehensile system of exploitation.

Without this deliberate effort at humanization, further land expansion would only take the regressive, savage pattern that German land expansion assumed in Europe: the enslavement and expropriation of neighbors. Plainly, then, the old period of land expansion has come to an end. The hopes once derived from it, those that were once substantial and those that were always delusive, are no longer capable of sustaining fresh efforts.

Do not deduce from this condition the conclusion that the possibilities of new population movements are over or that the face of the earth will show no further changes by occupation or withdrawal. There are areas now sparsely occupied, like the Tennessee Valley and the Columbia River Basin, that will benefit by added population; there are others, like the blighted areas of our great metropolises, which are due to be turned into park land, even in some instances into market gardens, as the rundown farms of the Adirondacks have been turned back into forest. Arid regions from Arizona to Australia, waiting to be harnessed to the sun by means of sun batteries and sun motors, will become the Egypts of a new cycle of civilization in which the desert, collectively reclaimed, will bring human life to a higher pitch of cultivation. But this new population movement, this new resettlement, cannot proceed from the same motives that governed the past: the will to power and the will to profit. Co-operation must replace conquest, and systematic cultivation must take the place of heedless and often destructive extraction. Man wants no new Egypts for the purpose of building even more gigantic and enigmatic Sphinxes.

The closing of the world frontier has been accompanied by a reversal of the whole process of emigration and colonization: in particular by the closing down of national frontiers. Barriers to human travel and immigration were raised, two decades before the open war of 1939, that would have seemed incredible in the nineteenth century. The United States immigration laws of 1924 were symptomatic of the wider process. Instead of proceeding from the anarchy of nineteenth century land-seizure and emigration to a policy of co-operative colonization and cultivation, just the opposite course was taken by the cowardly and short-sighted statesmanship that followed the First World War: this led to irresponsible isolationism and economic autarchy, an irrational course that was followed even in countries like Great Britain and the United States, which had profited most by the planetary movements of the nineteenth century. The ugly isolationism of a Luther, a Fichte, a Father Jahn, a Hitler, had its polite counterparts in countries whose liberal traditions had once been their glory.

Compared to the sullen folly of the isolationists, the working beliefs of the imperialist and the international financier had actual moral superiority: for at their brutal worst, the latter had at least been interested enough in their remote brothers to wish to exploit them. This low, negative sense of human solidarity was more defensible than the notion that a country could at will cut itself off from the rest of the human race, to its own profit and pride, as the national isolationists, the continental isolationists, and the hemispheric isolationists advocated. All these regressive tendencies aggravated the conditions they affected to help. That way lay chaos: chaos and war. Under the mask of self-sufficiency the fascists disclosed the ultimate tendencies of such a process and their own real purposes: one-sided world domination.

While the process of land expansion postponed the period of regional and worldwide stabilization until the limits were finally reached, the fact that these limits have now been attained must be accepted as a governing condition. Utopia can no longer be an unknown land on the other side of the globe: it is rather the region one knows and loves best, re-apportioned, re-shaped, and re-cultivated for permanent human occupation. This conclusion makes imperative what was still only an ideal project at the end of the nineteenth century: Ebenezer Howard's plan, first outlined in Garden Cities of Tomorrow, for the internal recolonization of every country. There lies a bigger task for peace armies than Fourier ever dreamed.

As for the migration and intermingling of peoples which marked the past age of land expansion, this must now take place on markedly different terms: the physical interchange of goods and travelers is not nearly so important as the process of cultural understanding and harmonization. Those naïve souls who conceive world co-operation in terms of vast armadas of airplanes plying back and forth across the continents and seas, are secretly thinking of making the standards of Paris and Hollywood, New York and Moscow, prevail throughout the planet: a bad dream, but only a dream, for if such a limited understanding prevails, its chief result will be further wars of extermination for the purpose of ensuring "an American century," or its British or Russian equivalent. Such mechanical intercourse would merely continue the irrational and irregional expansion of the past: a blind automatism that must result in a final destruction of the civilization that thus seeks to perpetuate a moribund self.

Cultural intercourse demands a slow tempo of interchange and assimilation: the passage of goods is secondary to the interchange of ideas, values, and symbols: hence the leisurely comings and goings of students, artists, scientists, philosophers are more important than the quick journeys of high-pressured executives, coddling their will to power by their speedy appearance in person at distant points. Strong regional centers of culture, promoting an active and securely grounded local life, will be necessary to make possible a selective use of the goods that other peoples and cultures have to offer. If we were merely to multiply the mechanical opportunities for intercourse and interchange, without rebuilding and reinforcing such regional centers, we would only worsen the conditions from which our present megalopolitan culture already suffers: an overcrowding of sensations and stimuli would make any real organic growth impossible. Rome's original mistake would thus be repeated with equally fatal results on a worldwide scale.

The re-building of regional cultures, then, is an essential part of the new process of land utilization and land settlement. This process will give depth and maturity to the world culture that has likewise long been in the process of formation. Perhaps no contemporary artist has better exemplified the polarity between the regional and the universal, the indigenous and the human, than Waldo Frank, in his interpretations of Spain and South America. In Virgin Spain, and even more in his South American Journey, Frank has expressed the attitude and fundamental philosophy of the post-machine age: he has exemplified the organic personality who accepts all the daring technological devices that have been created during the past century, not to belittle his regional, his cultural, his human roots, but to foster those larger developments of that very humanity in which all men may eventually share. He thus continues the quest that Whitman started. In such a spirit, the century-long settlement of the planet as a whole will be finally justified; for man will be at home anywhere in the world, and all that the wide world can offer will be available, at last, at his own doorstep, or rather, around his own hearth.

5: Stabilization of Industry

The discovery and exploitation of the relatively open lands outside Europe were followed by an expansion of mechanized industry. These two movements of expansion were closely connected: one of the things that made machine industry so extraordinarily profitable, apart from the economies of standardization and power-production, was the enormous disparity in the standard of living between the colonial workers who furnished the raw materials and the classes that bought the finished products.

Within each country, the existence of an indigenous proletariat performed the same function: the high standard of living achieved by the middle classes was made possible by a low standard of living among those who did the servile work. The whole tempo of industrial expansion would have been many beats slower from the beginning if the industrial workers had been adequately fed, clothed, housed, and educated; for such a minimum standard would have put a ceiling on profits. Machines produced profits and profits were promptly plowed back into industry as capital to produce new machines wherever fresh opportunity offered, because the success of production was not gauged in terms of an adequate domestic and civic life for the population as a whole. The natural tendency of mass production to equalize the standard of life was offset by the tradition of forcing down the worker's income to the margin of subsistence.

Now, during the past generation, three important changes have taken place in industry. One is the lessening of the need for fresh capital goods in that large part of the industrial system that has already been fully mechanized. The shift from handicraft to machine production has already taken place in most parts of Western civilization: opportunities for further mechanization now occur mainly in new industries like the plane or the radio, except under the dire pressure of war. Once a railway system is built, the further demand for steel rails and locomotives remains on a replacement basis. The better the original product, the slower the tempo of replacement. This is as it should be, although the economies so effected are partly annulled by the deliberate introduction of fashion models which bring about a premature obsolescence: a perversion that has been conspicuous in the motor car industry. The accomplished success of the machine, accordingly, tends to retard its further expansion: in that sense, the machine is self-limiting, and its true economy in saving labor and conserving life can become visible only when this mature state is reached. The terms of the nineteenth century's expansion of machine industry now exist only in backward countries.

The second important change is the development of a state of chronic unemployment in the advanced industrial countries: this is the current betrayal of another good, namely, the elimination of servile human labor from the processes of mechanical production. Classic capitalism throughout the last two centuries maintained a pool of the unemployed, which was useful for the double purpose of meeting seasonal shifts without carrying a permanently large working force and for keeping down the wages of labor through unprotected competition for the same job. But the steady enlargement of this pool bears witness to another fact: the increased efficiency of the machine and the increased automatism of the process diminish the total demand for human labor. Hence the steady reduction in the hours of labor. Hence also the need to re-apportion the annual income more evenly and more equitably so that there will be a larger effective demand for the goods that the farm and factory produce.

The unemployment of labor has been accompanied by an equally significant unemployment of capital: in both cases, it would seem, because the prospects of profit no longer exist on the terms offered during the era of expansion. Neither the enterpriser nor the worker will accept the conditions that fostered expansion in the past: the first demands profits without risk; the second demands a living wage without insecurity. The concept of a living wage is an inevitable extension of the essential principles of democracy to machine industry: formal equality and liberty must now be transformed into operative equality and liberty. This is no longer the goal of a party: it is the goal of human society. Even today intelligently organized industrial corporations—especially if they are in a position to pass on the increased costs to the consumer—are ready in the interests of efficiency to grant a living wage and to carry a heavy fixed load by way of sickness benefits and retirement pensions. This is at odds with the original premises of capitalism: for every fixed charge increases the responsibility for steady production and reduces the opportunity for swift changes in either the mechanical organization or the personnel.

The desire on the part of both capital and labor to protect their status is understandable: the recurrent crises that have marked the expansion of industry have occasioned wholly rational anxieties. The private, short-sighted way of easing these anxieties is to introduce the principle of monopoly, in order to guard against sudden shifts through competition. But mark the consequences. Risk capitalism has become insurance capitalism—which is a contradiction in terms. The growth of industrial monopolies during the last fifty years, the steady intervention of the State as a participator and director in industrial enterprises, the increasing central control of the process of investment, have provided a one-sided kind of security for the favored groups at the expense of the community as a whole. For if capital need not take risks it must not expect high returns: it must consent to accept employment on the bare reward of being employable and so keeping alive the productive system itself; and capital must no longer hope for that curious form of immortality it has claimed—that of being returned intact after a period of use during which the machines and buildings it has bought have become worn out.

Industry's market now depends upon a steady rise in the annual income of the worker. This increase in consumption cannot be achieved merely by the nineteenth century method of adding to the area of the market and the number of consumers. Rather, there must be a shift in capital investments from industries promising high profits to industries promising a better fulfillment of social need: a shift in expenditure from the luxury-simulating industries to the life-maintaining industries: above all, there must be a shift in the standard of living, from one expressed in money rewards to one expressed in terms of direct biological, social, and personal satisfactions. Both the worker and the enterpriser ask for the same ultimate reward: security. And security is possible only in a stable economy: an economy in which the calculable factors outweigh the incalculable ones: in which real goods take the place of spurious ones: in which an

XV. RENEWAL OR CATASTROPHE?

The circular motion of the prisoners in van Gogh's painting epitomizes the fate of a generation that accepts its man-built walls and knows no way out. Van Gogh's painting of two walkers in the moonlight attempts to symbolize man's opening destiny—toward love, comradeship, freedom. But here the external forces of repression produce a pathological reaction: an exorbitant self-defeating vitality that obstructs the very purpose it would serve, as in the movements described in Chapter X. Van Gogh said: "The best way to know God is to love many things. Love a friend, a wife, something, whatever you like. But one must love with a lofty and serious intimate sympathy, with strength, with intelligence." One of van Gogh's last paintings, of black crows flying ominously over a yellow cornfield, shows a foreboding of his own end: insanity and suicide. Only by a great mustering of the forces of life, only by a positive renewal of the person, can our civilization escape a similar fate.

XVI. TODAY AND TOMORROW

The foreground is dark, and it will become darker before day breaks. The purging of long-accumulated poisons, the healing of ugly wounds, will not be done in a day: all this needs time, patience, resolute effort, and a willingness to forego selfish local gains for the sake of a larger common good—the unification of mankind and the replenishment of life. Nothing that is worth doing in our time will be done easily: that is, without a spiritual re-birth. Unless the blind recover their sight and the crippled learn to walk our very knowledge will slay us. No peace without struggle: no security without risk: no wholeness without simplification: no goods without measure: no love without sacrifice: no full life without the willingness to accept and transcend death in the very process of living. Those who have learned this lesson may build the City of Man.

ever larger share of the product goes into civic, rather than private, consumption.

Up to the present, this whole change has been subverted and the process of stabilization has therefore not alleviated the conditions that caused the original anxiety: never indeed have economic crises been more shattering than in the last thirty years. The reason should now be plain: all the efforts at stabilization have been framed by leaders who were attempting to maintain or restore their past scale of rewards: every gain in security, even on the part of the workers, has been conceived solely in financial terms: standard wage rates, unemployment and old age insurance, tariffs and subsidies and cartels. This financial stabilization is by nature as insecure as anything else in the world, since war and inflation or unemployment and deflation can make a mockery out of the whole house of cards that has been so delicately erected.

Stabilization cannot be achieved by private initiative, even when its agents are great corporations and great trade unions: it demands a radical change in public policy, which must be argued before an electorate and decided by the democratic process, so as to enlist the full and open participation of those most concerned. This post-capitalist economy cannot be instituted by any combination of capitalists seeking their private good, even if they are abetted by trade union leaders seeking an equally private good. Indeed, if stabilization should continue on its present pecuniary terms, of monopoly, insurance, legally enforceable class privileges, the result will be the stabilization of inequality and the underwriting of blackmail: not unlike the state created during the decay of the Roman economic order. The policy of economic appeasement, which the democratic states followed during the last generation, is as fatal to a productive economy as the policy of political appeasement was to peace. Indeed, this policy is only the more domestic, the more affable side of totalitarian absolutism. Even if the industrial structure remained outside the state, the result would be such a fossilization, such an inner deterioration, as takes place under peacetime conditions in the army—without the periodic incentive to reform that war finally brings. Appeasement is not a substitute for justice, and fossilization is not the equivalent—indeed it is the opposite—of a *dynamic* equilibrium.

The alternative to this regressive stabilization does not consist in any effort to restore free enterprise in the pattern of the mid-nineteenth century, when it was at its height: for the underlying need for stabilization remains. The conditions that favored the horizontal expansion of machine industry are all definitely over: just as a one-sided mercantile expansion is rapidly coming to an end with the building up of new centers of production and new internal markets, in regions—like the Pacific Northwest—that were once doomed to a colonial role. Expansion on past terms remains possible for only one purpose: the threatening and waging of war. This was the foundation of that spurious prosperity of which Nazism boasted before 1939: this it is that produces all the classic symptoms of expansion in every war economy: the renewed activity of the mining and smelting industries, multiplication of machine tools industries and further development of the capital goods market, vast expansions of plant and equipment, full employment of workers and maximum profit for the investors.

There is no fascist magic in that formula: every democratic country forced to meet the stresses of war has enjoyed the same dubious benefits and the same illusion of health. But the price should not be forgotten: the price is war and the product is destruction and death. War's devastating and all-devouring scale of consumption has nothing to do with the standards of a vital economy; for it rests on an exorbitant demand for machines and on a ruthless negation of non-mechanical goods, services, arts, interests.

Expansion by war or stabilization by financial insurance and corporate monopoly—is that then the only alternative? Far from it: but it is the only choice offered so long as our society clings to the ideology that fostered the age of expansion and shrinks from the democratic political efforts that will be necessary to build up a life-centered economy. The real alternative to the stoppage of land expansion and industrial expansion is a balanced economy. I shall return to that point when I have outlined the third and most important change that has taken place.

6: Population Equilibrium

The third condition for the world-wide expansion of Western civilization was the most fundamental: the increase in population. This required an enormous rise in the food supply; and it was furthered during the nineteenth century by an improvement in diet, in hygienic regimen, and in the care of children. Every new baby was a consumer; and the chief basis for an expanding economy lay in this seemingly illimitable demand. On the prospect of continued population increase, cities sprawled, urban land values rose, factories multiplied; and so long as this pressure continued, a temporary miscalculation which caused overproduction or overcapitalization would eventually be rectified by further population increase.

Around 1870 in England, somewhat earlier in France, and at various later dates in most other countries the rate of increase began to diminish and the rising curve started to flatten out. Up to 1940 most of the advanced industrial countries, with the exception of Holland, showed a strong tendency toward equilibrium: on the basis of past tendencies England, for example, would actually be losing its population by 1970. Only peasant economies and countries like Russia, still under pioneer conditions, showed any considerable lag in reaching stability. Even there the effects of a falling birthrate would have become more visible if a falling death rate had not kept pace with it.

As with industrial stabilization, there are two sides to this tendency: one socially desirable, the other dubious. On one hand, it is an example of a more general passage from quantitative to qualitative achievement: the mark of a high civilization. Intelligent people wisely prefer three children, healthfully nurtured, carefully educated, to a dozen children brought up without sufficient food or decent housing. To this extent, contraception indicates a rising standard of intelligence and civic responsibility. Aimless and uncontrolled breeding belongs to the lower orders of organic life, not to man.

But there is another side to the curbing of population growth, which comes out as soon as one relates the survival statistics to the distribution of population according to the size and nature of the habitat. This is the evident fact that fecundity is associated with rural life and rural traditions, while sterility is associated with metropolitanism. In America, cities above 50,000 do not reproduce their population, and as the size of the city increases, the rate of population increase tends to decline. Part of the curb, therefore, is due to the existence of an urban standard of expenditure and an urban routine that are hostile to reproduction: crowded residential quarters in which children are unwelcome because parents cannot afford an extra room—or in which dogs are more welcome than children: cities in which a sleek ideal of comfortable gentility has replaced the desire for the joys and anxieties of parental responsibility: social groups in which a rising standard of fashionable expenditure leaves no surplus for the birth and care of children who, if they occur at all, do so in numbers insufficient to reproduce the stock. In short, urbanism results in a decline of animal faith; and without this faith there is no urge to reproduction. Were it not for migrations from rural areas, the bigger towns would be steadily depopulated through their ineptitude for life.

When these facts are treated statistically they seem to point to a gradual tapering away of life in the more civilized countries: at best to a mere holding of their own. This fact has been pointed out repeatedly during the last half century: Emile Zola's tractarian novel, Fécondité, a somewhat wooden idyll of married love, was both a protest against an anti-social ideal and a cry of warning against its results. Those who accepted the facts as inevitable looked forward complacently to a world presided over by the aged and the prudent and the spinsterly—with no sense that such a middle-aged society would lose the vital initiative needed even to defend itself against the aggressive minorities it might harbor in its midst.

That acquiescence was premature. All the changes toward stabilization have taken place as a result of human inventions, human scientific advances, human choices; and they can be modified, or the tendencies indicated reversed, by other conditions, other inventions, other choices. No acts of man are wholly automatic until he deliberately gives himself up to automatism.

In a catastrophic period like the present one, it would be a grave sin for the peoples of the more advanced countries to permit their love of physical ease to make them lose sight of their biological responsibilities. For all its defects, their culture does in many respects represent the peak of human achievement, and to the extent that it is now threatened by barbarian forces, both within and without, it must replenish itself more vigorously at the source. To counteract deaths from warfare and disease that will soon reach dismaying proportions, to keep the balance of age groups from falling too heavily on the downward side of the life-curve, it is necessary to introduce a biological counterweight: more babies. The cult of the family is the answer to the sterile individualism that metropolitan civilization has fostered.

The desire for children, the focusing of activities on the side of child nurture and child development, are healthy responses to the dehumanization and demoralization that inevitably accompany war. Here the peoples of the United Nations, at least those that are free, have already asserted their vitality in the face of manifold counsels of prudence and discouragement: a good sign. For it is only by a fresh mobilization of vitality that Western peoples will be able to hold their own and secure for the world the real goods they have helped to create. The rational stabilization of births throughout the world must be part of an international process of resettlement and regional culture. Once this biological sphere claims precedence, our entire economic life must be redirected toward its due service and culture.

Let me sum up this general statement. The conditions for stabilization have appeared, but the institutions that will turn this process to the advantage of society have not yet been developed. The end of population expansion and the end of land expansion are the clues to the slowing-down process that has made itself felt in industry. To find new consumers and new markets, industry must raise the real standard of life: this calls for a reapportionment of its energies and its goods to the end that social need, not profit, shall become the criterion of both production and consumption. This change is already in process; but for lack of positive social adaptations, it has remained fragmentary, incomplete, abortive.

During the last generation there has been a steady shift from individual demands, satisfied mainly by machine industry as an incident in the creation of profits and dividends, to collective demands expressed in goods and services that are supplied by the community to all its citizens. This process I have elsewhere called basic communism: it applies to the whole community the standards of the household and distributes benefits according to need, not according to ability or productive contribution. Education, recreation, hospital services, public hygiene, art, have all increased in importance in every national economy: they represent collective needs that cannot be left to the automatic working out—or failure—of the laws of commercial supply and demand. Such a change in the human goals of production is essential for the full use of our natural, technical, and scientific resources.

Here is the condition forecast by Mill. "It is scarcely necessary to remark," said Mill, "that a stationary condition of capital and population implies no stationary state of human improvement. There would be as much scope as ever for all kinds of mental culture and moral and social progress; as much room for improving the Art of Living, and much more likelihood of its being improved, when minds ceased to be engrossed by the art of getting on. Even the industrial arts might be as earnestly and successfully cultivated, with this sole difference, that instead of seeking no purpose but the increase of wealth, indurstrial improvements would produce their legitimate effect, in abridging labor."

When the conditions for social equilibrium are established, when the foundations for a balanced economy are laid, there will be a transfer of energy and interest into the non-profit-making enterprises, and into those consumptive and cultural activities from which no financial return can be expected, although each year may bring steady dividends in terms of intelligence, health, and spiritual animation. In vital and essential human needs, the United States created less wealth during the boom period of the nineteen-twenties than it did in the strained years of the depression, when the public works program and the WPA cleared out slums, restored run-down lands, rehabilitated forests, and introduced art and drama into communities sunk in destitution. And historically, which has paid the greater dividends—the Cathedrals of the Middle Ages or the profit-making enterprises whose buildings and ships have long since rotted away? The true test of an economy is the ratio of consumption to creation: that is, the ratio of the life-preserving functions to the life-fulfilling functions. The balanced economy we must now seek will place its emphasis not on the horsepower it consumes but on the manpower it releases: it will translate energy into leisure and leisure into life.

So far none of the conditions for a balanced economy has been met. That is why the whole movement toward stabilization has taken place in regressive, anti-social ways; and it is why the counter-movement has stimulated barbarism and war. Meanwhile, our expansionist institutions have been steadily losing their reason for existence. Hence a hollowness, a persistent air of unreality, hangs over many parts of our culture which needed no explanation and no justification in the past. One must not be deceived by the familiar signs of accelerating mechanical progress: the inertia of a going institution is cumulative and it tends to conceal the waning of the original impulse. But the dream that man can make himself godlike by centering his energies solely on the conquest of the external world has now become the emptiest of dreams: empty and sinister. If anything should be plain by now it is the fact that man must build his culture about the complete human personality. Not only that: but he must compensate for his contemptuous neglect of the values that were not embraced by the machine by giving to his biological and psychological functions, to his values and his ideals, a fuller measure of his interest and attention.

An active knowledge of the social environment and of the behavior of men in social partnership, their needs, their drives, their impulses, their dreams, is just as indispensable for working out the new social order as reading, writing, and arithmetic were for those trained to capitalism. And so equally for the arts of society: the art of politics, the arts of enlightened behavior and orderly communication, must become the main field of new inventions. A world language is more important for mankind at the present moment than any conceivable advance in television and telephony: the pathetic provincialism of our present efforts at universal linguistics, from Esperanto to Basic English, proves the need here for moral self-examination and discipline, as well as semantic and linguistic skill. What we need today is not so much a moratorium on mechanical invention as a large-scale transfer of interest and personal talent to the fields of community and personality.

To achieve a balanced economy, to make possible a world civilization, man must understand his real condition and formulate a fresh ideal of life. It is not from machines that we can learn the purpose of machines: it is not by unlocking the power of the atom that we can learn how to make ourselves men and how to make our communities serve the purposes of men. We must create a new idolum: we must create a new super-ego: we must create a fresh plan of life, and we must educate ourselves and discipline ourselves for quite different tasks than those that commanded us during the period of expansion. In the course of this re-orientation the subjective and the objective, the primitive and the cultivated, the mechanical and the human will finally be unified in a new organic whole, which will do justice to the entire nature of man.

This brings us to the main goal of the present book: the internal crisis and the internal renewal that will enable us to carry through the external transformation I have outlined.

7: The Internal Crisis

The internal crisis in our civilization has been visible for a much longer time than the external crisis; for it grew out of the inadequacy of the New World idolum and the failure of utilitarian man to fulfill the ends of life.

The materialist creed by which a large part of humanity has sought to live during the last few centuries confused the needs of survival with the needs of fulfillment; whereas man's life requires both. For survival, the physiological needs are uppermost; and the most imperative, obviously, are the needs for air and water: then food and shelter against extremes of temperature, and so by degrees one passes to those social needs for communication and co-operation that never wholly limit themselves to life-preservation in the narrow sense. Within the life-span of a generation, the needs for sexual intercourse and parental care are as imperative as those for air and water.

In terms of life-fulfillment, however, this ascending scale of needs, from bare physical life to social stimulus and personal growth, must be reversed. The most important needs from the standpoint of life-fulfillment are those that foster spiritual activity and promote spiritual growth: the needs for order, continuity, meaning, value, purpose and design—needs out of which language and poesy and music and science and art and religion have grown. The deepest, the most organic, of these higher needs is that for love: all the stronger because it is rooted in survival. Neither group of needs is in a watertight compartment: lovers must eat and even greedy eaters have been known to share their food with the starving. Nevertheless there are conflict and tension between these two sets of needs, as there are between the primitive institutions of the tribe, seeking self-preservation, and the order of an open society, prepared to share its highest values with all other men.

Lured by his elemental needs, man tends to rest content with their satisfaction: instead of using them as the basis of the good life, he often seeks, by merely elaborating and refining them, to use them as a substitute for the good life. Here is one of the chief causes of social fixation and personal arrest. The more complicated and costly the physical and social apparatus for ensuring man's survival, the more likely will it smother the purposes for which it humanly exists. That threat was never stronger than it is today; for the very exquisiteness of our mechanical apparatus, in every department of life, tends to put the non-human process above the human end.

But no matter how primitive the community, and no matter how terrible the pressure of war, pestilence, or natural disaster, there must always be a sufficient margin of time and energy to carry forward the processes that make life-fulfillment possible. No matter how harassed a mother may be, she must give her child the gift of language as well as food. When life-fulfillment is put first, an intensification of activity takes place in all the subordinate needs, for they then have a meaning and a purpose that they do not possess in themselves: they do not merely sustain life but raise it to a higher level.

The emergence of man from his purely animal state consists in the constant increase of the ratio of higher needs to lower needs, and in the fuller contribution of his vitalities and energies to the molding of more richly endowed and more fully expressive personalities. Up to now, the fullest kind of human growth has been possible only to small groups of men: a privileged class, or at best, a city; and the fact that men as a body have not participated fully in man's own highest activities has always undermined and disordered the very growth that even the most fortunate achieved. Only now has mankind itself arrived at the point of inheriting man's whole estate. There lies the meaning and the promise of the democratic ideal.

The great gains that were made in technics during the last few centuries were largely offset by a philosophy that either denied the validity of man's higher needs or that sought to foster only that limited set of interests which enlarged the power of science and gave scope to a power personality. At a moment when a vast surplus was available for the goods of leisure and culture, the very ideals of leisure and culture were cast into disrepute—except when they could be turned to profit. Here lies the core of the inner crisis that has afflicted our civilization for at least two centuries. In the heyday of expansionism, the middle of the nineteenth century, scarcely a single humane voice could be found to defend either the means or the ideals of a power civilization. The wisdom of the race revolted against the inhuman fruits of its knowledge: Blake, Ruskin, Morris, Arnold, Emerson, Whitman, Thoreau, Melville, Dickens, Howells, Hugo, Zola, Mazzini, Tolstoy, Dostoyevsky, Ibsen—almost all the representative minds of Europe and America—denounced the human results of the whole process of mechanization and physical conquest. As with one voice, they protested against the inhuman sacrifices and brutalizations, the tawdry materialisms, the crass neglect of the human personality.

In the course of the last generation, the wisdom of this protest has become plain. As a result, many of the plans and projects that seemed like mere escapist dreams in the nineteenth century have become conditions for renewal; indeed only those who are aware of the importance of man's higher needs will be capable even of providing intelligently for bare food and shelter. This is one of those periods when only the dreamers are practical men. By the same token, the so-called practical men have become makers and perpetuators of nightmares: for it is their attempt to crawl back into the crumbled wreckage of the immediate past that has condemned our society to frustration, to sterility, to savage barbarism.

The inner crisis of our civilization must be resolved if the outer crisis is to be effectively met. Our first duty is to revamp our ideas and values and to reorganize the human personality around its highest and most central needs. If we ask ourselves as we face the future, not how to keep our old institutions and organizations running in their accustomed grooves, but how to keep life itself running, with or without the aid of these institutions, our problem immediately clarifies itself. There is no wealth, as Ruskin said, but life; and there is no consummation of life except in the perpetual growth and renewal of the human person: machines, organizations, institutions, wealth, power, culture, cities, landscapes, industries, are all secondary instruments in that process. Whatever nourishes the personality, humanizes it, refines it, deepens it, intensifies its aptitude and broadens its field of action is good: whatever limits it or thwarts it, whatever sends it back into tribal patterns and limits its capacity for human co-operation and communion must be counted as bad. Nothing that man has created is outside his capacity to change, to remold, to supplant, or to destroy: his machines are no more sacred or substantial than the dreams in which they originated.

In the end, all our contrivances have but one object: the continued growth of human personalities and the cultivation of the best life possible. What sort of personality must we now seek to foster and nourish? What kind of common life? What traits and disciplines are needed in an age of stabilization, co-operation, and balance? What is the order of value in our life needs: do we put babies above motor cars, art above plumbing, the well-being of the worker above the mechanical efficiency or cheapness of his product? If so, we must create a different ego-ideal from that which was the norm in a capitalistic and mechanical civilization: our mode of education and our plan of life must be directed to more humane ends than those that have hitherto governed us.

8: The Need for Human Balance

As our culture developed during the last five centuries, its center lay more and more outside the human personality: hence a fragment of the personality displaced the whole. In attempting to restore balance in the community and in the personality, we need not be troubled by references to the undoubted existence of individual differences or to the fact, as true in society as in the individual organism, that all equilibrium is necessarily unstable and is constantly upset by the continued act of growth. The first condition makes the effort to achieve a fuller and more balanced development necessary: the second makes it an ideal goal—one always to be aimed at but never, in the nature of things, fully achieved.

Differences in temperament, capacity, aptitude, and interest, differences that have their origin in diversities of biological inheritance, characterize all men, as they characterize the same men at successive moments in life: Who would doubt it? Who would change it? These differences are the inexhaustible source of the richness of human experience. But no man is an island: every age has a common ideal of personality which represents the goals of living toward which the whole community is more or less set. To the extent that an individual shares in this personality, he is fit for his daily tasks and can co-operate freely with his fellows and make the fullest use of his culture. The more representative the common type, the more it meets the claims of its historic moment, the fewer repressions must be exercised over those whose inner tendency is to depart from it.

If the era of stabilization is to be one devoted to the intensive but balanced cultivation of our natural and social resources, balance and intensity are equally, I believe, the key to the sort of personality that is needed to work effectively within this culture and to create the necessary changes in our disrupted institutions. The age of mechanical specialization produced a quite different ideal: that of the one-sided specialist, the piece worker, the operative conditioned by repetition and reward, as Dr. E. L. Thorndike puts it: the end product of a long period of mechanization in which one by one the higher attributes of the personality have disappeared or have been reduced to mere whims and hobbies. The fatal results of this process were pointed out by Comte a full century ago. "If we have been accustomed to deplore the spectacle, among the artisan class, of a workman occupied during his whole life in nothing but making knife handles or pinheads, we may find something quite as lamentable in the intellectual class, in the exclusive employment of the human brain in resolving equations or classifying insects. The moral effect is, unhappily, analogous in the two cases. It occasions a miserable indifference about the general course of human affairs as long as there are equations to resolve or pins to manufacture."

One of Comte's most able successors in sociology, Dr. Karl Mannheim, has carried this observation even further: he notes the growing irrationality of the personality engaged in production in proportion to the technical refinement and "rationalization" of the process. The dismembered man, whether as engineer or workman, as organizer or salesman, needs less directive insight and intelligence once he is geared to the whole machine than the carpenter or the weaver needed in his workshop. The behaviorist man, with his slot-machine mind, responding mechanically to external stimuli, passive until acted upon, incapable of taking the initiative or choosing his destination, is the typical by-product of current society: fascist minds are thus more common than the conscious philosophy of fascism. Indeed our whole civilization has put a premium upon this primitive kind of automatism and compulsion: the very humanity that quickens the life-like machine leaves the person depleted and empty.

Dr. Mannheim has well pointed out that the chief element in our inner crisis today is the disproportionate development of human faculties: "individuals as well as historical and social groups may, under certain circumstances, suffer from the danger of disintegration because their capacities fail to develop equally and harmoniously." This observation has been reinforced by an experienced psychiatrist and a profound reader of the modern soul, Dr. C. G. Jung, who has sought to combat this unfortunate lopsidedness and disparity by counseling his patients to cultivate their weaker sides. None of our dominant institutions today correct this lack of balance: on the contrary, they encourage it in the name of efficiency, an efficiency which fosters a single function at the expense of the whole life that finally supports it. Only by making the personality itself central, and by drawing forth its repressed or thwarted capacities, can this mischief be cured: balance and autonomy go together.

The ideal of balance itself is an ancient one: common to philosophers as far apart in time and culture as Confucius, Aristotle, and Spencer: the Confucian ideal of the superior man, the Greek ideal of the Golden Mean, and the renascence ideal of the gentleman all embodied this conception. Behind the notion of balance is the ethical principle laid down by Herbert Spencer: "Strange as the conclusion looks, it is nevertheless a conclusion to be drawn, that the performance of every function is, in general, a moral obligation. It is usually thought that morality requires us only to restrain such vital activities as in our present state are often pushed to excess, or such as conflict with average welfare, special or general; but it also requires us to carry on these vital activities up to their normal limits."

Spencer's doctrine of organic balance was handicapped by the same weakness that crippled Marx's socialism, a defective incarnation: his formulation was a tissue of abstractions. But it is important to realize how well the deliverances of this nonconformist and individualist expressed the mature beliefs of Marx himself. These indications are significant because the period of formulation almost always anticipates by at least half a century or more the stages of incarnation and fulfillment: so that, if we are to achieve a balanced economy and a balanced community and a balanced personality, it will be with the aid of ideas that have long been in existence: ripened sufficiently to be ready now for assimilation. Hence it is important to realize that Marx, in a brief passage in Capital, anticipated the present argument. He said: "In a socialist society, the 'fragmentary man' would be replaced by the 'completely developed individual,' one for whom different social functions are but alternative forms of activity. Men would fish, hunt, or engage in literary criticism without becoming professional fishermen, hunters, or critics."

In every department of life, man's activity is limited by his capacities for assimilation; and the greater the resources man can potentially use the more disciplined and many-sided must be his response. The difficulty our culture faces was well diagnosed by Shelley: "The accumulations of the materials of external life exceed the quantity of power of assimilating them to the internal laws of human nature." When these accumulations heap up as recklessly as they have in our time and when the internal laws and the internal capacities of human nature are disregarded, the result is to turn each potential gain *against* man: he functions as a distracted atom in a growing chaos, made poor by his wealth, made empty by his fullness, reduced to monotony by his very opportunities for variety, the victim of changes that have in themselves become fixations: all beyond his power to assimilate or control.

Civilizations do not die of old age: they die of the complications of old age. Observing this process long ago, Burckhardt predicted the coming of the "terrible simplifiers": people who would reject all the goods modern man had acquired in order to restore the capacity to act. Those terrible simplifiers have appeared. They are the barbarians who renounce every part of our culture that makes a claim upon man's higher needs: avowed barbarians like the Nazis and more insidious barbarians who, by advertising, propaganda, and education, would turn every part of our life into the mean handiwork of coachman, cook, and groom, of beauty shop, assembly-line, and roadhouse. We cannot save our culture from these barbarians, external or internal, by clinging to the habits that make us a prey to their corrupt vitality. To recover life and health again we must, like the Christians confronting the classic world, find a benign method of simplification. We must find a method that will assert the primacy of the person and that will re-endow the person with all its attributes, all its heritage, all its potentialities. But unlike the Christian, we must undertake this transformation before the barbarian has finally wrecked our civilization: only thus shall we be able to carry forward the many life-promoting activities that man has created since the breakup of the medieval synthesis.

The task for our age is to decentralize power in all its manifestations. To this end, we must build up balanced personalities: personalities that will be capable of drawing upon our immense stores of energy, knowledge, and wealth without being demoralized by them. On this point, Plato's words in The Laws cannot be improved: "If anyone gives too great power to anything, too large a sail to a vessel, too much food to the body, too much authority to the mind, and does not observe the mean, everything is overthrown, and in the wantonness of excess runs in the one case to disorders, and in the other to injustice, which is the child of excess."

If we are to control machines and organizations, then, we must make men; and our first task is that of self-examination, self-education, self-control. Those who fail at this point will be incapable of contributing to the political, economic, and social transformations that are now so long overdue.

9: The Organic Person

The ideal personality for the opening age is a balanced personality: not the specialist but the whole man. Such a personality must be in dynamic interaction with every part of his environment and every part of his heritage. He must be capable of treating economic experiences and esthetic experiences, parental experiences and vocational experiences, as the related parts of a single whole, namely, life itself. His education, his discipline, his daily routine must tend toward this wholeness. To achieve this, he must be ready to spurn the easy successes that come, in a dying culture, through self-mutilation.

Such a dynamic balance is not easily achieved: its consummations are precious and its stability is precarious: it demands a vigilance and an athletic readiness for new shifts and stresses that more specialized vocations do not habitually achieve. For balance is not a matter of allotting definite amounts of time and energy to each segment of life that requires attention: even our mechanical partition of functions does that. It means that the whole personality must be constantly at play, at least at ready call, at every moment of its existence and that no one part of life should be segregated from another part, incapable of influencing it or being influenced by it.

But qualitative balance is as important as quantitative balance: many kinds of experience have the role in life that vitamins have in the diet: quantitatively minute elements may be as important for spiritual health as the vitamins and minerals are for bodily health. Most of man's higher activities are in the latter category. No healthy person can look at pictures all day any more than he can make love all day. But for even the humblest person, a day spent without the sight or sound of beauty, the contemplation of mystery, or the search for truth and perfection is a poverty-stricken day; and a succession of such days is fatal to human life. That is why even the most superstitious forms of religion, which have at least kept alive some wraith of beauty or perfection, still contain for the mass of mankind something valuable that a bare scientific positivism has allowed to be lost both in thought and practice.

The importance of balance to both the community and the personality will come out more clearly, perhaps, if we call to mind the patent dangers that will attend stabilization: dangers that are already plainly visible in the bureaucratism and time-serving that have begun to infect every department of life: not alone government but business; and not alone business but education. Those who lack the creative capacity to establish a dynamic balance are already caught by its counterfeit and its negation: Alexandrianism or Byzantinism.

Organizations that have been stabilized for any length of time—the army is an excellent example—become embedded in routine and hostile to change: they are unable to meet fresh challenges, and their very "adjustment" becomes a profound cause of maladjustment. Scientific progress does not alter this fact, for scientific advances themselves tend to follow inflexible institutional forms, and they often seek perfection within a more and more obsolete frame of reference. Stability and security, pursued for their own sake, will result in a caste division of labor and in the denial of any changes that would upset an increasingly sessile routine: forms, precedents, stereotypes would supplant human needs, and the very attributes of life, its capacity for readjustment, for insurgence, for renewal, would be forfeited by these ill-conceived efforts to guard life more effectively.

These regressive forms of stabilization have already taken shape: they have been seized upon by Nazi philosophers and leaders as the basis for enforcing permanent caste divisions. But the danger is not confined to the conscious fascists: many of those who talk loudest about rugged individualism prove themselves in their daily practice the upholders of a Byzantine rigidity and hollowness. The standard examination papers that have appeared in so many departments of American education under the guise of progressive method would, in a short generation, paralyze the acquisition and extension of fresh knowledge: this symbolizes a much wider menace to life and thought.

Precisely because stabilization brings with it these dangers, we must introduce into our conception of the type of personality needed the ability to touch life at many points, to travel light, and to keep every part of experience in a state of constant interplay and interaction: so that fresh challenges will appear at unexpected points, in unforeseeable circumstances. For the age of balance we need a new race of pioneers, of deliberate amateurs, in order to offset the tendency to harden practice into smooth molds and to sacrifice the growing personality to the machine. Such stereotyping of activity as will free the organism for its higher functions—like those human automatisms that put a large part of the burden of behavior on the vertebral column and the cerebellum—must not halt on its way to this destination.

In this respect the varied war experiences that people in many countries have undergone, as soldiers, air raid wardens, fire fighters, nurses, and so forth, must be regarded as essential contributions to the task of peacetime co-operation: typical of a new kind of citizenship and a more vivid routine of life. But we cannot afford to promote a war every generation to break up social fixations: that is burning down the house to roast the pig. We must erect these social and personal counterpoises to rigidity and fixity as the basic requirements for a maturing personality.

The custom of our time is to think no change worth even discussing unless it can be at once organized into a visible movement: the mass enlistment of thousands, preferably millions, of men and women. The very appearance of millions of men in black shirts and brown shirts gave fascism publicity that made its rancid ideas seem important. Many of the actual movements that claim allegiance today are little better than devices of publicity: decorative devices that change nothing and move nothing. Such, even, would be a revolutionary movement, unless those who took part in it remodeled the instruments with which they work: first of all themselves.

Only in one place can an immediate renewal begin: that is, within the person; and a remolding of the self and the super-ego is an inescapable preliminary to the great changes that must be made throughout every community, in every part of the world. Each one, within his or her own field of action—the home, the neighborhood, the city, the region, the school, the church, the factory, the mine, the office, the union—must carry into his immediate day's work a changed attitude toward all his functions and obligations. His collective work cannot rise to a higher level than his personal scale of values. Once a change is effected in the person, every group will record and respond to it.

Today our best plans miscarry because they are in the hands of people who have undergone no inner growth. Most of these people have shrunk from facing the world crisis and they have no notion of the manner in which they themselves have helped to bring it about. Into every new situation they carry only a fossilized self. Their hidden prejudices, their glib hopes, their archaic desires and automatisms—usually couched in the language of assertive modernity—recall those of the Greeks in the fourth century B.C. or those of the Romans in the fourth century A.D. They are in a power dive and their controls have frozen. By closing their eyes they think they can avoid a crash.

Those who look for swift wholesale changes to take place in our institutions under-rate the difficulties we now face: the inroads of barbarism and automatism, those twin betrayers of freedom, have been too deep. In their impatience, in their despair, such people secretly long to cast the burden of their own regeneration upon a savior: a president, a pope, a dictator—vulgar counterparts of a divinity debased or a corruption deified. But such a leader is only the mass of humanity writ small: the incarnation of our resentments, hates, sadisms, or of our cowardices, confusions, and complacencies. There is no salvation through such naked self-worship: God must work within us. Each man and woman must first silently assume his own burden.

We need not wait for bombs and bullets actually to strike us before we strip our lives of superfluities: we need not wait for events to bend our wills to unison. Wherever we are, the worst has already happened and we must meet it. We must simplify our daily routine without waiting for ration cards; we must take on public responsibilities without waiting for conscription; we must work for the unity and effective brotherhood of man without letting further wars prove that the current pursuit of power, profit and all manner of material aggrandizement is treason to humanity: treason and national suicide. Year by year, we must persevere in all these acts, even though the restrictions are lifted and the urgencies of war have slackened. Unless we now rebuild our selves all our external triumphs will crumble.

There is no easy formula for this renewal. It is not enough for us to do all that is possible: we must do that which seems impossible. Our first need is not for organization but for orientation: a change in direction and attitude. We must bring to every activity and every plan a new criterion of judgment: we must ask how far it seeks to further the processes of life-fulfillment and how much respect it pays to the needs of the whole personality.

More immediately we must demand: What is the purpose of each new political and economic measure? Does it seek the old goal of expansion or the new one of equilibrium? Does it work for conquest or co-operation? And what is the nature of this or that industrial or social achievement—does it produce material goods alone or does it also produce human goods and good men? Do our individual life-plans make for a universal society, in which art and science, truth and beauty, religion and sanctity, enrich mankind? Do our public life-plans make for the fulfillment and renewal of the human person, so that they will bear fruit in a life abundant: ever more significant, ever more valuable, ever more deeply experienced and more widely shared?

If we keep this standard constantly in mind, we shall have both a measure for what must be rejected and a goal for what must be achieved. In time, we shall create the institutions and the habits of life, the rituals, the laws, the arts, the morals that are essential to the development of the whole personality and the balanced community: the possibilities of progress will become real again once we lose our blind faith in the external improvements of the machine alone. But the first step is a personal one: a change in direction of interest *towards* the person. Without that change, no great betterment will take place in the social order. Once that change begins, everything is possible.

GLOSSARY

ID, EGO, SUPER-EGO. In general, these terms are used in the sense described by Sigmund Freud in his New Introductory Lectures on Psycho-analysis, Chapter 3, "The Anatomy of the Mental Personality."

Specifically, the id denotes that part of the personality given by nature. It is the bearer of the primal energies and vitalities, and is the seat of the self-maintaining and reproductive processes in the organism. These vitalities rise to conscious expression in the ego; there they are modified, partly disguised, partly repressed, partly transformed through the development of the self in society. "Where id was," Freud observed, "there shall ego be."

Above the ego stands the super-ego. This aspect of the personality Freud tended to describe almost solely in negative terms: as the censor, the conscience, the hostile limiter of the ego's freedom. Here I have followed those psychologists like Dr. Henry A. Murray who, aware of Freud's bias here, have given due place to the super-ego as a positive force. In its positive aspect, the super-ego does not merely check the self but strengthens and enhances it: as a creator of positive standards the suger-ego nurtures the capacity for expression and life-fulfillment, through art, ethics, religion, science.

Freud avowed that the object of psycho-therapy was to "strengthen the ego and make it more independent of the super-ego." From my standpoint, the super-ego is, on the contrary, an organic part of the whole self; and the object of sound development is to effect a working harmony between the three operative parts of the personality, thus doing away with abrasive conflicts and disruptions.

Accordingly, I use the term self for the whole psychic organism, including the bodily aspects: the id represents the biological aspect, the ego the social aspect, and the super-ego the universal or personal aspect; for the highest development of personality transcends both the biological and the social conditions that underlie it. Though I have used the terminology of my contemporaries in this analysis of the self, the division is a traditional one: what are these three aspects but Aristotle's nature, habit, and reason?

IDOLUM. This term was first used in The Story of Utopias (1922) at about the same time Mr. Walter Lippmann coined the expression "pseudo-environment" for a similar fact. By idolum I do not mean either an idea or an idol: neither a concept nor a fetich nor an ideology. By idolum I indicate the existence of an ideological "field," which unites and polarizes, as it were, a number of related images, symbols, ideas, and even artifacts. Idolum is close to the German term *Weltbild* when taken in its literal sense: a picture of the world, that is, the world experienced in and through a culture, that people carry in their minds. I prefer it to the term pseudo-environment, because as such an idolum is neither fictitious nor false: it is simply the dominant mental environment of a particular culture, containing both permanently verifiable experiences and temporarily acceptable illusions.

DOMINANT, RECESSIVE, SURVIVAL, MUTATION. Used in a sociological sense, and so defined in The Culture of Cities, pages 74 and 75.

BIBLIOGRAPHY

The following list covers only a small portion of the books that might be studied with profit in dealing with this field—almost as large as human life itself. Because of the wartime need to conserve paper I have cut down my original list: only in a few cases have I noted books previously used in Technics and Civilization and in The Culture of Cities; and in addition, I have dropped many standard works known to the ordinary educated reader as well as the scholar. To the same end, I have stressed titles within the fields of religion and of ancient and medieval history, while omitting many works from the sixteenth century on that would have had a place in a more exhaustive bibliography. This sacrifice would be more painful but for my assurance that those who will get most out of The Condition of Man are not those who will be tempted to linger longest over its bibliography.

Abelard, Pierre: *The Letters of Abelard and Heloise.* Trans. by C. K. Scott Moncrieff. New York: 1933.

Adams, Henry: *The Education of Henry Adams.* New York: 1918.

The Degradation of the Democratic Dogma; with an Introduction by Brooks Adams. New York: 1919.

Contains Adams' essay on social physics on the phase rule as applied to history, which buried a profound intuition of approaching disaster beneath a pseudo-scientific structure of ideas.

Mont Saint Michel and Chartres. New York: 1913.

Agar, Herbert, Borgese, G. A., Mumford, Lewis, Neilson, William Allan, et al.: *The City of Man.* New York: 1940.

Alain de Lille: *The Complaint of Nature.* Trans. from the Latin by Douglas M. Moffat. Yale Studies in English: XXXVI. New York: 1908.

Allbutt, T. Clifford: *The Historical Relations of Medicine and Surgery to the End of the Sixteenth Century.* New York: 1905.

Greek Medicine in Rome; with Other Historical Essays. London: 1921.

Amiel, Henri-Frédéric: *Jean Jacques Rousseau.* New York: 1922.

A just and acute appraisal.

Angell, Norman: *The Great Illusion; A Study of the Relation of Military Power in Nations to Their Economic and Social Advantage.* New York: 1911.

Anglade, Joseph: *Les Troubadours; Leurs Vies, Leurs Oeuvres, Leur Influence.* Paris: 1908.

Anshen, Ruth Nanda (editor): *Science and Man.* New York: 1942.

Freedom, Its Meaning, by Benedetto Croce, Thomas Mann and Others. New York: 1940.

Ante-Nicene Fathers. 10 vols. New York: 1896.

Aquinas, Thomas: *The Summa Theologica of St. Thomas Aquinas.* (1267-73). Trans. 22 vols. London: 1912-1922.

Complete museum of the medieval mind, with all the specimens arranged and ordered in accordance with a supernatural system: no empty show-cases, no unfinished exhibits, no confused labels.

The Summa Contra Gentiles of St. Thomas Aquinas. (1258-1260). Trans. by the English Dominican Fathers. 5 vols. London: 1924.

Infinitely more satisfactory for continuous reading than the *Summa Theologica,* because of the elimination of the mechanical apparatus of proof; but less important. Neither *Summa* can be sampled at random with any profit.

Aristotle: *The Nicomachean Ethics.* Trans. by D. P. Chase. New York: 1911.

Politics. Trans. by B. Jowett. New York: 1900.

Arnold, E. Vernon: *Roman Stoicism.* Cambridge: 1911.

Augustine, Saint: *The City of God.* Introduction by Ernest Barker. New York: 1931.

Barker's introduction is excellent.

Confessions. Circa. 397 A.D. Trans. by Dr. E. B. Pusey. 1838. London: 1907.

The Writings Against the Manichaeans and Against the Donatists. Series I, Vol. IV. In *Nicene and Post-Nicene Fathers.* Buffalo: 1887.

Aurelius, Marcus: *Meditations.* Trans. by John Jackson. Oxford: 1906.

Avenel, Georges d': *La Noblesse Française sous Richelieu.* Paris: 1901.

Babbitt, Irving: *Democracy and Leadership.* Boston: 1924.

Rousseau and Romanticism. New York: 1919.

A far too unqualified picture of Rousseau's defects: yet useful as a corrective.

Bacon, Francis: *New Atlantis.* Introd. by Alfred B. Gough. Oxford: 1924.

Novum Organum. Edited by Joseph Devey. New York: 1902.

More significant, in many ways, than the better-known *Advancement of Learning.*

Of the Advancement of Learning. First ed. London: 1605.

Bacon, Roger: *The Opus Majus of Roger Bacon.* Trans. by Robert B. Burke. 2 vols. Philadelphia: 1928.

Balet, Leo (E. Gerhard, Collaborator): *Die Verbürgerlichung der deutschen Kunst, Literatur und Musik im 18. Jahrhundert.* Leiden: 1936.

Barker, Ernest: *The Crusades.* Oxford: 1923.

Barzun, Jacques: *Darwin, Marx, and Wagner; Critique of a Heritage.* Boston: 1941.

Baudrillart, J.: *Histoire du Luxe Privé et Public depuis l'antiquité jusqu'à nos jours.* 4 vols. Paris: 1880-1881.

Bax, E. Belfort: *The Social Side of the Reformation in Germany.*

Part I: *German Society at the Close of the Middle Ages.* London: 1894.

Part II: *The Peasants' War in Germany, 1525-1526.* London: 1899.

Part III: *Rise and Fall of the Anabaptists.* London: 1903.

Baxter, Richard: *Autobiography.* New York: 1931.

Self-portrait by a 17th century dissenting divine.

Beazley, C. Raymond: *Voyages and Travels; mainly during the 16th and 17th centuries.* London: 1902.

Bebel, Ferdinand August: *Woman in the Past, Present, and Future.* London: 1885.

Beers, M.: *Life and Teaching of Karl Marx.* London: 1924.

Bellamy, Edward: *Looking Backward.* Boston: 1888.

Benedict, Ruth: *Patterns of Culture.* New York: 1934.

Bentham, Jeremy: *Deontology; or, the Science of Morality; in which the Harmony and Co-incidence of Duty and Self-Interest, Virtue and Felicity, Prudence and Benevolence are Explained and Exemplified.* Two vols. London: 1834.

The title tells everything except that the explanations would not convince anyone but a Benthamite.

An Introduction to the Principles of Morals and Legislation. London: 1780.

Reprinted from new edition corrected by the author in 1823. New York: 1907.

Berdayaev, Nicolas: *The Destiny of Man.* London: 1937.

The Bourgeois Mind. New York: 1934.

Bergson, Henri: *The Two Sources of Morality and Religion.* New York: 1935.

Carries the original insight of Creative Evolution from the realm of biology to that of the personality.

Bernard, St., of Clairvaux: *The Twelve Degrees of Humility and Pride.* Clairvaux: 1127. Trans. by Barton R. V. Mills. London: 1929.

Concerning Grace and Free Will; Addressed to William, Abbot of St. Thierry. Clairvaux: 1127. Trans. by W. W. Williams. London: 1920.

Some Letters of Saint Bernard. F. A. Gasquet (editor). London: 1904.

Bett, Henry: *Joachim of Flora.* London: 1931.

Elementary introduction to this Calabrian mystic: forerunner of Campanella and Vico.

Bevan, Edwyn: *Stoics and Skeptics.* Oxford: 1913.

Beza (Bèze), Theodore: *The Life of Calvin.* Trans. Philadelphia: 1836.

Earliest life, by Calvin's successor in Geneva.

Bligh, E. W., and Stubbs, S. G. Blaxland: *Sixty Centuries of Health and Physick.* London: 1931.

Bloom, Solomon F.: *The World of Nations; a Study of the National Implications in the World of Karl Marx.* New York: 1941.

Boardman, Philip L.: *Esquisse de l'Œuvre Educatrice de Patrick Geddes.* Montpellier: 1936.

Patrick Geddes: Maker of the Future. Chapel Hill: 1944.

The best study to date.

Boehmer, Heinrich: *The Jesuits; an Historical Study.* Philadelphia: 1928.

Boëthius, Ancius Manlius Severinus: *The Consolations of Philosophy.* Trans. 1609. New York: 1926.

Theological Tractates. New York: 1926.

Booth, Arthur John: *Saint-Simon and Saint-Simonism; a Chapter in the History of Socialism in France.* London: 1871.

Borgese, G. A.: *Goliath; The March of Fascism.* New York: 1937.

Superb historical and critical analysis of the origins and the nature of fascism in Italy.

Common Cause. New York: 1943.

Recommended.

Borkenau, Franz: *Der Uebergang vom feudalen zum bürgerlichen Weltbild; Studien zur Geschichte der Philosophie der Manufakturperiode.* Paris: 1934.

Boyd, William: *The History of Western Education.* London: 1932.

Branford, Victor: *Living Religions; a Plea for the Larger Modernism.* London: 1924.

Science and Sanctity; a Study in the Scientific Approach to Unity. London: 1923.

Sometimes turgid, sometimes vague, but full of real insight into the pathology of modern life. This was to be followed by another work on the religious approach to unity.

Branford, Victor: *Interpretations and Forecasts; a Study of Survivals and Tendencies in Contemporary Society.* New York: 1914.

Branford, Victor, and Geddes, Patrick: *The Coming Polity.* London: 1919.

Our Social Inheritance. London: 1919.

Bready, J. Wesley: *England: Before and After Wesley; the Evangelical Revival and Social Reform.* London, 1938.

Copious in documentation, but with a Wesleyan bias.

Broeck, Edmond: *Le Catharisme; Etude sur les Doctrines, la Vie Religieuse et Morale, L'Activité Littéraire et les Vicissitudes de la Secte Cathare avant la Croisade.* Hoogstraten: 1916.

Brooks, Van Wyck: *The Flowering of New England.* New York: 1936.

New England: Indian Summer. New York: 1940.

Two masterly interpretations.

Bruck, Moeller van den: *Germany's Third Empire.* Trans. New York: 1934.

One of the early apologies for the group of ideas and fantasies that received their political form in the German national socialist movement. Midway between the "respectable" romantic organicism of Othmar Spann, which still has connection with the concept of mankind as an embracing unity, and the neurotic verbiage of an Alfred Rosenberg.

Burckhardt, Jacob: *The Civilization of the Renaissance in Italy.* Trans. by S. G. C. Middlemore. (From 15th German Edition.) New York: n.d.

Classic essay in cultural history; in origin a bold and valuable historic synthesis; now to be guarded against because of the errors it popularized.

Force and Freedom: Reflections on History. Edited with an introduction by James Hastings Nichols. New York: 1943.

Prophetic paper on the Crisis in History, also searching studies of other cultural-historical themes by one of the most philosophical of nineteenth century historians.

Burgess, Ernest W. (editor): *Personality and the Social Group.* Chicago: 1929.

Burke, Edmund: *A Vindication of Natural Society.* First ed. London: 1756.

Burke's early essay on Natural Society puts the great antagonist of the French Revolution on the side of Rousseau.

A Philosophical Inquiry into the Origin of Our Ideas of the Sublime and the Beautiful. In Vol. I. *Collected Works:* Boston: 1826.

Bury, J. B.: *The Idea of Progress; an Inquiry into Its Origin and Growth.* London: 1920.

Bussell, F. W.: *Religious Thought and Heresy in the Middle Ages.* London: 1918.

Encyclopedic survey of religious development, particularly in the East, with less than half the book devoted to European Middle Ages.

Butler, Dom Cuthbert: *Western Mysticism; the Teaching of Sts. Augustine, Gregory, and Bernard on the Contemplative Life.* London: 1922.

Calmette, P.: *La Société Féodale.* Paris: 1923.

Calvin, Jean: *Institutes of the Christian Religion.* First ed. 1536; final ed. 1559. Trans. from the original Latin edition and collated with the author's last edition in French, by John Allen. Preceded by a memoir of the life of Calvin by John Mackenzie. New York: 1819.

Camau, Emile: *La Provence à Travers les Siècles.* 5 vols. Paris: 1908-31.

Especially Volume III on the Crusades and the communal movement of the 13th century.

Campbell, Thomas J.: *The Jesuits; 1534-1921; a History of the Society of Jesus from Its Foundation to the Present Time.* New York: 1921.

Camugliano, Ginevra Niccolini di: *The Chronicles of a Florentine Family: 1200-1470.* Trans. London: 1933.

Cannon, Walter B.: *The Wisdom of the Body.* New York: 1932.

Study of the means whereby the body maintains constant conditions in its internal environment. The author's social allusions, at the end, have genuine significance for the sociologist.

Carr-Saunders, A. M.: *World Population; Past Growth and Present Trends.* Oxford: 1936.

Carrel, Alexis: *Man the Unknown.* New York: 1935.

Too facile generalizations, a reactionary twist.

Casanova [de Seingalt], Jacques: *The Memoirs of Jacques Casanova.*

Castiglione, Baldassare: *The Book of the Courtier.* Venice: 1528. Trans. by Thomas Hoby, 1561. Reprinted London: 1928.

Classic discussion of the ideals of courtly life in Italy, with a mixture of local citations and ideal references.

Cellini, Benvenuto: *Autobiography of Benvenuto Cellini.* Trans. by J. A. Symonds. 2 vols. London: 1888.

Chamberlain, Houston Stewart: *Foundations of the Nineteenth Century.* Berlin: 2 vols. New York: 1912.

Nothing is more astonishing about this astonishing hodge-podge of Teutonic mythology than the fact that it was taken seriously by many people who should have known better.

Chapman, (Dom) John: *Saint Benedict and the Sixth Century.* London: 1929.

Chesterfield, Lord (Stanhope, Philip Dormer): *Letters to His Son.* New York: 1929.

Chesterton, G. K.: *St. Francis of Assisi.* London: 1923.

St. Thomas Aquinas. London: 1933.

Clutton-Brock, A.: *Essays on Religion.* London: 1926.

Cochrane, Charles Norris: *Christianity and Classical Culture; A Study of Thought and Action from Augustus to Augustine.* Oxford: 1940.

Cole, Percival R.: *A Neglected Educator; Johann Heinrich Alsted.* In Records of the Education Society. No. 5. New South Wales: n.d.

Comenius, Johan Amos: *The Great Didactic; setting forth the whole art of teaching all things to all men; that the entire youth of both sexes none being excepted shall quickly, pleasantly, and thoroughly become learned in the sciences, pure in morals, trained in piety, and in this manner instructed in all things necessary for the present and for the future life.* Ed. by M. W. Keating. 2 vols. London: 1910, 1923.

Compayré, Gabriel: *Abelard and the Origin and Early History of Universities.* New York: 1893.

Comte, Auguste: *The Positive Philosophy.* Freely translated and condensed by Harriet Martineau. New York: 1856.

A work whose magistral importance is not seriously invalidated by the naïvete of certain parts of Comte's unconscious metaphysics. Outstanding in its doctrine and its exemplification of synthesis. Spencer got his Comte through Miss Martineau and then somewhat ungratefully disparaged the original source.

Early Essays on Social Philosophy. London: 1911.

Condorcet, Marie Jean A. N. C.: *Esquisse d'un Tableau Historique des Progrès de l'Esprit Humain; Ouvrage Posthume de Condorcet.* Second ed. Paris: *L'An III de la République une et indivisible.*

Conybeare, Fred. Cornwallis: *Myth, Magic, and Morals; a Study of Christian Origins.* London: 1909.

Cooke, James: *Voyages of Discovery*. First pub. 1773-1782. New York: 1902.
The first and second voyages are largely paraphrased; most of the third is given in Cook's own words. An important set of documents on the aim and method of early exploration.

Cornaro, Luigi: *The Art of Living Long*. Padua: 1558. Translated. Milwaukee (William Butler): 1905.

Coulton, George Gordon: *From St. Francis to Dante; Translations from the Chronicle of the Franciscan Salimbene (1221-1288); with notes and illustrations from other medieval sources*. Second ed. London: 1907.

Inquisition and Liberty. London: 1938.
See Lea.

Life in the Middle Ages. 4 vols. Cambridge: 1930.

Two Saints: St. Bernard and St. Francis. Cambridge: 1932.

Ten Medieval Studies; with four appendices. Third ed. Cambridge: 1930.

Five Centuries of Religion. 3 vols. Cambridge: 1923.

The Black Death. New York: 1932.
Attempts to counterbalance the exaggerated statements of the catastrophic effects of the plague. But Coulton makes an error in leaning over backwards.

Medieval Panorama. London: 1938.
One of the best pictures available, though limited by its reference to English data.

Crèvecœur, Michel Guillaume St. John de: *Sketches of Eighteenth Century America; More Letters from an American Farmer*. New Haven: 1925.

Croce, Benedetto: *Historical Materialism and the Economics of Karl Marx*. London: 1915.

The Philosophy of Giambattista Vico. Translated. New York: 1913.
Croce at his Neapolitan best. But see also Robert Flint's little study.

Philosophy of the Practical; Economic and Ethic. London: 1913.

Cumont, Franz: *The Oriental Religions in Roman Paganism*. Chicago: 1911.

The Mysteries of Mithra. Chicago: 1911.
Both these books are classics in their field. See Strzygowski for an esthetic interpretation of the same phenomena, and Spengler's *Decline of the West* for a bold generalization of these data as revealing a specific "Magian" culture.

Cyprian, Caecilius: *The Writings of Cyprian, Bishop of Carthage*. 2 vols. Edinburgh: 1868-1869.

Dante Alighieri: *The Divine Comedy*. Written 1300? First printed: 1472.
The Temple Classics edition, with the Inferno translated by Carlyle's brother, and the Italian text on facing pages, is one of the most satisfactory.

De Monarchia. Oxford: 1916.
Latin text, with good introduction by W. H. V. Reade.

Dawson, Christopher: *Beyond Politics*. New York: 1939.

Medieval Religion (The Forwood Lectures 1934) *and Other Essays*. New York: 1934.

Progress and Religion. New York: 1938.
Traces the connection between Christian religion and the idea of progress.

Deguileville, Guillaume de: *The Pilgrimage of the Life of Man*. Trans. by John Lydgate. (French, 1330, 1355, English, 1426). In Early English Text Society, Extra Series. London: 1899, 1901, 1904.

Demosthenes: *The Orations of Demosthenes*. Trans. by Thomas Leland. 2 vols. New York: 1844.

Dermenghem, Emile: *Thomas Morus et les Utopistes de la Renaissance*. Paris: 1927.

Descartes, Rene: *A Discourse on Method. The Principles of Philosophy.* Combined in the Everyman Series with an introduction by A. D. Lindsay. London: 1912.

Dewey, John: *Democracy and Education.* New York: 1916.

Experience and Nature. New York: 1925.

Human Nature and Conduct; an Introduction to Social Psychology. New York: 1930.

Reconstruction in Philosophy. New York: 1920.

Dill, Samuel: *Roman Society in Gaul in the Merovingian Age.* London: 1926.
Valuable.

Roman Society in the Last Century of the Western Empire. Second ed. rev. New York: 1905.
Indispensable.

Dopsch, Alfons: *The Economic and Social Foundations of European Civilization.* New York: 1937.

Dowden, Edward: *Michel de Montaigne.* Philadelphia: 1915.

Duchesne, Louis: *Early History of the Christian Church.* 3 vols. New York: 1923.

Dudden, F. Homes: *Gregory the Great.* 2 vols. New York: 1905.

Early English Text Society: *Queene Elizabethes Achademy, a Booke of Precedence, etc.* London: 1869.

Eastman, Max: *Marxism; Is It a Science?* New York: 1940.

Eckermann, Johann Peter: *Gespräche mit Goethe.* 2 vols. Leipzig: 1837.

Eckhard, Carl C.: *The Papacy and World Affairs.* Chicago: 1937.

Ehrenburg, Richard: *Capital and Finance in the Age of the Renaissance; a Study of the Fuggers and Their Connection.* New York: n.d.

Ellis, Havelock: *Studies in the Psychology of Sex.* 4 vols. New York: 1906-1936.
Like almost any pioneer work, of uneven merit; yet because of their original intention the studies as a unit rise above particular defects of evidence and treatment.

My Life; Autobiography of Havelock Ellis. Boston: 1939.
Revealing—and dismaying.

The Dance of Life. New York: 1923.

Emerson, Ralph Waldo: *Works.* 5 vols. Boston: 1881.

Journals. 10 vols. Boston: 1909-14.

Engel-Jánosi: *Soziale Probleme der Renaissance. In Beihefte zur Vierteljahrschrift für Sozial-und-Wirtschaftsgeschichte.* Stuttgart: 1924.

Engels, Friedrich: *Socialism: Utopian and Scientific.* New York: 1935.
Part of the Anti-Dühring; interesting for its appreciation of Fourier's dialectic of history.

Ludwig Feuerbach; and the Outcome of Classical German Philosophy. New York: undated.

Erasmus of Rotterdam: *The Manual of the Christian Knight.* London: 1533. 1905.

The Complaint of Peace. First published 1521. Chicago: 1917.

The Praise of Folly. Published 1509. London: 1913.

Eusebius: *Church History.* (In *Select Library of Nicene and Post-Nicene Fathers of the Christian Church.* Vol. I, Second Series.) New York: 1890.

Evelyn, John: *The Diary of John Evelyn.* 4 vols. London: 1879.
Valuable picture of a pious gentleman's world in 17th century England, to which Pepy's *Diary* forms a more raffish counterpart.

Fairchild, Hoxie Neale: *The Romantic Quest.* New York: 1931.

Farnell, Lewis Richard: *The Evolution of Religion; an Anthropological Study.* New York: 1905.

The Higher Aspects of Greek Religion. London: 1912.

Faure, Elie: *History of Art.* 5 vols. New York: 1921.

Over-eloquent, uneven; but often extremely perceptive.

Faÿ, Bernard: *Franklin; the Apostle of Modern Times.* Boston: 1929.

Ferrero, Guglielmo: *The Unity of the World.* London: 1931.

The Greatness and Decline of Rome. Vol. 5: *The Republic of Augustus.* New York: 1909.

Fichte, Johann Gottlieb: *Addresses to the German Nation.* Chicago: 1922.

The Vocation of Man. London: 1889.

Finkelstein, Louis: *The Pharisees; the Sociological Background of Their Faith.* 2 vols. Philadelphia: 1940-5700.

Flewelling, Ralph Tyler: *The Survival of Western Culture; an Inquiry into the Problem of Its Decline and Resurgence.* New York: 1943.

Flint, Robert: *Vico.* Philadelphia: 1884.

Fort, George F.: *Medical Economy During the Middle Ages, a Contribution to the History of European Morals from the Time of the Roman Empire to the Close of the Fourteenth Century.* New York: 1883.

Fourier, Charles François Marie: *Selections from the Works of Fourier; with an Introduction by Charles Gide.* London: 1901.

Theory of Social Organization; with an Introduction by Albert Brisbane. New York: 1876.

First edition 1822 was published under title *L'Association Domestique Agricole,* but changed in later editions to *Theory of Universal Unity.* Perhaps the best of Fourier's works in both its veritable genius and its no less veritable crotchetiness.

Frank, Waldo: *The Rediscovery of America.* New York: 1927.

Profound analysis of the inner weaknesses of modern culture.

Virgin Spain. First ed. New York: 1926. Revised ed.: 1942.

South American Journey. New York: 1943.

Both are classic studies.

Freer, Arthur S. B.: *The Early Franciscans and Jesuits.* London: 1922.

Freind, J., M.D.: *The History of Physick from the Time of Galen to the Beginning of the Sixteenth Century; Chiefly with Regard to Practice.* Third ed. London: 1727.

Of documentary importance, especially as related to baroque theories of medicine.

Freud, Sigmund: *The Future of an Illusion.* London: 1934.

Group Psychology and the Analysis of the Ego. London: 1922.

Introductory Lectures on Psycho-Analysis. London: 1936.

New Introductory Lectures on Psycho-Analysis. New York: 1933.

The Interpretation of Dreams; trans. with introduction by A. A. Brill. New York: 1913.

A book of revolutionary importance, which reopened to science man's long-closed inner world.

Friedlaender, Ludwig: *Roman Life and Manners Under the Early Empire.* 4 vols. London: 1910-1913.

Froebel, Friedrich: *The Education of Man.* Trans. New York: 1898.

Fuchs, Eduard: *Die Karikatur der Europäischen Völker.* Bd. I. *Vom Altertum bis zur Neuzeit.* Berlin: 1901. Bd. II. *Vom Jahre 1848 bis zur Gegenwart.* Berlin: 1906.

Fülop-Miller, Rene, *Leaders, Dreamers, and Rebels.* New York: 1935.

Verbose pretentious apology for the fascist attack on civilization: excellent symptom, among other things, of the prevalent barbarization of German thought.

The Power and Secret of the Jesuits. New York: 1930.

Useful, if taken with circumspection.

Furnivall, F. J. (editor): *The Babees Book.* New York: 1908.

Collection of late medieval books of manners.

Gairdner, James (editor): *The Paston Letters.* 6 vols. London: 1904.

These letters, one of the great medieval finds, were first published between 1787 and 1823.

Geddes, Patrick: *The Life and Work of Sir Jagadis C. Bose.* London: 1920.

The Masque of Learning. 2 vols. London: 1912.

Geddes, Patrick, and Branford, Victor: *The Coming Polity.* London: 1919.

Our Social Inheritance. London: 1919.

Geddes, Patrick, and Slater, Gilbert: *Ideas at War.* London: 1917.

Geddes, Patrick, and Thomson, J. Arthur: *Life; Outlines of Biology.* 2 vols. New York: 1931.

Concluding chapters contain the best brief summary of Geddes's essential theories and doctrines, together with the graphs he developed for presenting them.

Gibbon, Edward: *The Decline of the Roman Empire.* 7 vols. London: 1896-1900.

Gilson, Etienne: *The Mystical Theology of Saint Bernard.* New York: 1940.

The Spirit of Medieval Philosophy. New York: 1936.

Glover, Terrot Reaveley: *The Conflict of Religions in the Early Roman Empire.* London: 1909.

Comprehensive and excellent.

Life and Letters in the Fourth Century. Cambridge: 1901.

Godwin, William: *An Enquiry Concerning Political Justice and Its Influence on General Virtue and Happiness.* First ed. 2 vols. 1793. Edited and abridged by Raymond A. Preston. 2 vols. New York: 1926.

Goethe, Johann Wolfgang von: *Poetry and Truth.* 2 vols. London: 1872.

Wilhelm Meister's Apprenticeship and Travels. 2 vols. Boston: 1865.

Faust. Trans. by Bayard Taylor. Boston: 1870.

The Sorrows of Werther. First ed. 1774. London: 1929.

Goncourt, Edmond and Jules: *The Woman of the Eighteenth Century; Her life, from birth to death, her love and her philosophy in the worlds of Salon, Shop, and Street.* New York: 1927.

Gottfried von Strassburg: *The Story of Tristan and Iseult.* Trans. into English prose by Jessie L. Weston. Composed in 1210. 2 vols. New York: 1900.

Graves, Charles L.: *Mr. Punch's History of Modern England.* 4 vols. New York: n.d. (1920?)

Gregory the Great: *The Dialogues of Saint Gregory.* Edmund G. Gardner (editor). London: 1911.

Valuable for occasional intimate sidelights on a declining age.

Gregory of Nyssa: *Select Writings and Letters.* In a *Select Library of Nicene and Post-Nicene Fathers of the Christian Church.* Vol. 5. New York: 1893.

Haldane, J. S.: *Mechanism, Life, and Personality; an Examination of the Mechanistic Theory of Life and Mind.* New York: 1921.

Profound analysis of inadequacy of mechanism by a great experimental physiologist, not to be confused with J. B. S. Haldane.

Halévy, Elie: *The Growth of Philosophic Radicalism.* Part I. *The Youth of Bentham (1776-1789).* Part II. *The Evolution of the Utilitarian Doctrine from 1789 to 1815.* Part III. *Philosophic Radicalism.* New York: 1928.

Harington, John (translator): *The School of Salernum; Regimen Sanitatis, Salernitanun.* New York: 1920.

Baudry de Balzac states that up to 1846, 240 editions were published.

Hart, Joseph K.: *The Discovery of Intelligence.* New York: 1924.

Mind in Transition. New York: 1938.

Striking analysis of Athenian intelligence.

Harkness, Georgia: *John Calvin; the Man and His Ethics.* New York: 1931.

Harnack, Adolf: *The Expansion of Christianity in the First Three Centuries.* 2 vols. New York: 1904.

The Origin of the New Testament. New York: 1925.

Outline of the History of Dogma. New York: 1893.

Harrison, Jane: *Ancient Art and Ritual.* New York: 1913.

Haskins, Charles Homer: *The Rise of Universities.* New York: 1923.

Studies in Medieval Culture. Oxford: 1929.

Hayes, Carlton J. H.: *The Historical Evolution of Modern Nationalism.* New York: 1931.

Heard, Gerald: *Man the Master.* New York: 1941.

Narcissus; an Anatomy of Clothes. New York: 1924.

Hegel, G. W. F.: *Lectures on the Philosophy of History.* Trans. from Third German ed. London: 1888.

Hendel, Charles William: *Citizen of Geneva; Selections from the Letters of Jean-Jacques Rousseau.* New York: 1937.

Henderson, Lawrence J.: *The Fitness of the Environment.* New York: 1924.

Brilliant analysis, establishing mainly on bio-chemical grounds the special fitness of the earth's environment to maintain life. Undermines the 19th century natural theology of a hostile or indifferent nature.

Herder, Johann Gottfried: *Outlines of a Philosophy of the History of Man.* Weimar: 1784. Trans. London: 1800.

A classic: more comprehensive than Vico, if not so profound. See Vico, Hegel, Comte, Spengler, Toynbee, Kahler.

Hertzler, Joyce Oramel: *A History of Utopian Thought.* New York: 1923.

Herzen, Alexander: *My Past and Thoughts.* 6 vols. London: 1924-1927.

Himes, Norman E.: *Medical History of Contraception.* Baltimore: 1936.

Good general survey which raises many historical problems that require further research.

Hinton, James: *Chapters on the Art of Thinking; and Other Essays.* With an Introduction by Shadworth Hodgson. London: 1879.

Hippocrates: *The Genuine Works of Hippocrates.* Trans. by Frances Adams, 1849. Baltimore: 1939.

Hitler, Adolf: *Mein Kampf.* First ed.: Berlin: 1924. New York: 1941.

Turgid, incoherent, and lying, but extraordinary in its insight into the human weakness and corruption of the intellectuals and their counterparts in industry and politics. Required reading. For reference to more ideological constructions see Kolnai.

Hobbes, Thomas: *Leviathan; on the Matter, Forme, and Power of a Commonwealth, ecclesiastical and civill.* 1651. New York: 1914.

Often coupled with Machiavelli for objurgation; but in essence a more profound work. See the excellent introduction to the Everyman edition by A. D. Lindsay.

Hobson, John A.: *Wealth and Life; A Study of Values.* London: 1929.

Hocking, William Ernest: *Living Religions and a World Faith.* New York: 1940.

Holbach, Baron Paul Heinrich von: *The System of Nature; or, Laws of the Moral and Physical World.* First ed.: 1770. Two vols. in one: Boston: 1889.

Homans, George Caspar: *English Villages of the Thirteenth Century.* Cambridge, Mass.: 1941.

Admirable.

Huizinga, Johan: *Erasmus.* New York: 1924.

In the Shadow of Tomorrow. New York: 1936.

The Waning of the Middle Ages; A Study of the Forms of Life, Thought and Art in France and the Netherlands in the Fourteenth and Fifteenth Centuries. New York: 1924.

Hulme, T. E.: *Speculations: Essays on Humanism and the Philosophy of Art.* New York: 1924.

Extraordinarily prophetic essays, written just before the first world war, by one of the minds that reacted most quickly to the new philosophic and political winds that were blowing, to challenge naturalism, liberalism, and humanism with a recrudescent belief in supernaturalism, absolutism, and brute force. See Pareto, Spengler, et al. Hulme's attack has the classic clarity that sometimes characterizes a first statement.

Hume, David: *A Treatise of Human Nature; Being an Attempt to Introduce the Experimental Method of Reasoning into Moral Subjects.* Edinburgh: 1739-1740.

A revolutionary attack on reason, clothed in the vocabulary of rationalism.

An Enquiry Concerning the Human Understanding. Edinburgh: 1748.

Treatise of Morals. Edinburgh: 1751. Boston: 1893.

Jaeger, Werner: *Paideia; The Idea of Greek Culture.* Vol. I. New York: 1939. Vol. II. New York: 1943.

Demosthenes, The Origin and Growth of His Policy. Berkeley: 1938.

James, William: *The Varieties of Religious Experience.* New York: 1902.

Jarrett, Bede: *Social Theories of the Middle Ages; 1200-1500.* London: 1926.

S. Antonino and Medieval Economics. London: 1914.

Study of late medieval Catholic economic theory. See Tawney.

Jedlicka, Gotthard: *Pieter Bruegel; der Maler in seiner Zeit.* Zürich: 1938.

Jennings, H. S.: *The Biological Basis of Human Nature.* New York: 1930.

The Universe and Life. New Haven: 1933.

Jesperson, Otto: *Mankind, Nation and Individual, from a Linguistic Point of View.* Cambridge, Mass.: 1925.

John of Salisbury: *Frivolities of Courtiers and Footprints of Philosophers; Being a Translation of the First, Second, and Third Books, and Selections from the Seventh and Eighth Books of the Policraticus of John of Salisbury.* Edited by Joseph B. Pike. Minneapolis: 1938.

The Statesman's Book; Being the 4th, 5th, and 6th Books, and selections from the 7th and 8th books, of the publications. Edited by John Dickinson. New York: 1927.

Joinville, Jean de: *Memoirs of Louis IX, King of France.* In *Chronicles of the Crusades.* London: 1848.

Josephson, Matthew: *Jean-Jacques Rousseau.* New York: 1931.

Sympathetic with respect to his life; but somewhat deficient in critical analysis of Rousseau's ideas and their influence.

Zola and His Time. New York: 1928.

Victor Hugo. New York: 1942.

Jung, Carl Gustav: *Modern Man in Search of a Soul.* New York: 1934.
Psychological Types. New York: 1923.
Psychology and Religion. New Haven: 1938.

Jusserand, Jules: *Wayfaring Life in the Middle Ages.* New York: 1890.

Kahler, Erich: *Man the Measure; a New Approach to History.* New York: 1943.
Admirable.

Keating, Maurice W.: *Comenius.* New York: 1931.
Contains introduction and abbreviated translation of *The Great Didactic.*

Key, Ellen: *The Century of the Child:* New York: 1909.

Keyserling, Count Hermann (editor): *The Book of Marriage; A New Interpretation by Twenty-Four Leaders of Contemporary Thought.* New York: 1926.

Kidd, Benjamin: *Social Evolution.* New York: 1895.
Important sociological analysis of defensive role of religion. Anticipated Bergson.

Klausner, Joseph: *Jesus of Nazareth; His Life, Times, and Teaching.* New York: 1925.
A sympathetic interpretation of Jesus from the standpoint of Jewish history and Jewish religion.

Kolnai, Aurel: *The War Against the West.* New York: 1938.
Study of the ideological foundations of Nazism: scholarly and exhaustive.

Korzybski, Alfred: *Science and Sanity; an Introduction to Non-Aristotelian Systems and General Semantics.* New York: 1933.

Kropotkin, Peter: *The Great French Revolution; 1789-1798.* 2 vols. New York: 1909.
The Memoirs of a Revolutionist. Boston: 1899.
A great book.
Modern Science and Anarchism. New York: 1908.
Mutual Aid. London: 1902.

Laertius, Diogenes: *Lives of Eminent Philosophers.* Trans. by R. D. Hicks. 2 vols. New York: 1925.
A piece of hackwork, probably Third Century A.D., upon which, unfortunately, a large part of our knowledge of the Greek philosophers whose works have not themselves survived depends. Dubious but indispensable: all the more because the lack of originality in the compiler led him to rely upon earlier sources and commentators.

Langner, Suzanne K.: *Philosophy in a New Key.* Cambridge: 1942.
Admirable exposition of symbolism and semantics. Recommended.

Laski, Harold J. *Communism.* London: 1926.

Latourette, Kenneth Scott: *A History of the Expansion of Christianity.* 4 vols. New York: 1943.

Lea, Henry Charles: *An Historical Sketch of Sacerdotal Celibacy.* Philadelphia: 1867.
A History of Auricular Confession and Indulgences in the Latin Church. 3 vols. Philadelphia: 1896.
A History of the Inquisition in the Middle Ages. 3 vols. First ed. New York: 1887. Reprinted, New York: 1908.
Classic study by a great American scholar whose use of original sources has made his work necessary even to Catholic historians who seek to provide more favorable interpretations of this monstrous institution.
Materials Toward a History of Witchcraft. 3 vols. Philadelphia: 1939.

Lee, Vernon (Violet Paget): *Euphorion; Being Studies of the Antique and the Medieval in the Renaissance.* London: 1899.

Interpretations of the Renaissance which, in characterizing that phase of culture, anticipates the revisions of Burckhardt made by a later group of German scholars.

Leibnitz, Gottfried Wilhelm: *The Monadology and Other Philosophical Writings.* Oxford: 1925.

New Essays Concerning Human Understanding. Chicago: 1916.

The Philosophical Works. Trans. by George Martin Duncan. New Haven: 1890.

Lenin, Nicolai: *Marx, Engels, Marxism; a Collection of Articles.* London: 1934.

The State and Revolution. London: 1917.

Lewes, George Henry: *Problems of Life and Mind.* Vol. I. *The Foundations of a Creed.* Boston: 1874.

Liber Vagatorum. First ed. Augsburg: c. 1512. Trans. by John Camden Hotten. London: 1860.

Lippmann, Walter: *An Inquiry into the Principles of the Good Society.* Boston: 1937.

Confused and undiscriminating attack on all forms of collectivism coupled with an equally indefensible identification of freedom with the free market. The structural absurdities in Mr. Lippmann's thesis unfortunately nullify his many valid criticisms.

A Preface to Morals. New York: 1929.

Public Opinion. New York: 1922.

Lot, Ferdinand: *The End of the Ancient World and the Beginnings of the Middle Ages.* New York: 1931.

Lovett, William: *Life and Struggles of William Lovett in his pursuit of bread, knowledge, and freedom; with some short account of the different associations he belonged to and of the opinions he entertained.* Introduction by R. H. Tawney. 2 vols. New York: 1920.

Lowenthal, Marvin (editor): *The Memoirs of Glueckel of Hameln.* New York: 1932.

Loyola, Ignatius de: *Letters and Instructions.* Vol. I. 1524-1547. Selected by A. Goodier, S. J. St. Louis: 1914.

The Spiritual Exercises of S. Ignatius Loyola. With Commentary and Directory by W. H. Longridge. London: 1930.

Luther, Martin: *Conversations with Luther; Selections from Recently Published Sources of the Table Talk.* Trans. New York: 1915.

Works of Martin Luther. 4 vols. Philadelphia: 1915.

MacCurdy, Edward: *The Notebooks of Leonardo da Vinci.* New York: 1939.

The Mind of Leonardo da Vinci. New York: 1939.

An interpretation of the *Notebooks:* perhaps more useful for the ordinary student.

Mackail, J. W.: *The Life of William Morris.* 2 vols. London: 1901.

Macmurray, John: *The Clue to History.* New York: 1939.

Attempt to understand and follow the implications of the Judaeo-Christian view of life. Vitiated by a definition of religion which confines it largely to the Jews, and which fails to account for important elements nearly always associated with religion.

The Structure of Religious Experience. New Haven: 1936.

Reason and Emotion. London: 1935.

Excellent. Interprets emotion as one of the modes of reason, rather than as its opponent.

Machiavelli, Niccolo: *The Prince.* Trans. by Luigi Ricci. London: 1903.

MacKaye, James: *The Economy of Happiness.* Boston: 1906.

Mackinnon, James: *From Christ to Constantine; the Rise and Growth of the Early Church* (c. A.D. 30 to 337). New York: 1936.

Luther and the Reformation. 4 vols. New York: 1925.

Maitland, S. R.: *The Dark Ages; a Series of Essays Intended to Illustrate the State of Religion and Literature in the Ninth, Tenth, Eleventh, and Twelfth Centuries.* Sixth ed. London: 1890.

One of the earliest attempts to rectify undue disparagement of the late Dark Ages and early medieval times: valuable in its time and still interesting. See Dopsch.

Mâle, E.: *L'Art Religieux du XIIe Siècle en France.* Paris: 1922.

L'Art Religieux Après le Concile de Trente. Paris: 1932.

Malthus, T. S.: *Essay on the Principles of Population as It Affects the Future Improvement of Society.* London: 1798. Second ed. Revised; 1803. 2 vols. New York: 1927.

Mandeville, Bernard: *The Fable of the Bees: or, Private Vices, Publick Benefits.* Edited with introduction by F. B. Kaye. London: 1714. 2 vols. Oxford: 1924.

Mandonnet, Pierre: *Saint Doménique; L'Idee, L'Homme, et L'Oeuvre.* Paris: 1938.

Mann, Thomas: *The Magic Mountain.* New York: 1928.

Mannheim, Karl: *Ideology and Utopia; an Introduction to the Sociology of Knowledge.* New York: 1940.

Man and Society in an Age of Reconstruction. New York: 1940.

Important. Good exposition of the need and potentialities of democratic planning.

Marett, J. R. de la: *Race, Sex, and Environment.* London: 1936.

Maritain, Jacques: *The Angelic Doctor: The Life and Thought of Saint Thomas Aquinas.* New York: 1931.

Saint Thomas and the Problem of Evil. Milwaukee: 1942.

The Rights of Man and Natural Law. New York: 1943.

Brief but admirable attempt to give the *Rights of Man* a more organic statement.

Maritain, Jacques; Wust, Peter; Dawson, Christopher: *Essays in Order:* New York: 1940.

Marvin, F. S.: *The Century of Hope; a Sketch of Western Progress from 1815 to the Great War.* Oxford: 1919.

Marx, Karl: *Letters to Dr. Kugelmann.* New York: 1934.

Capital. Vol. I: 1867; Vol. II: 1883-1885; Vol. III: 1890-1894. Translated by Eden and Cedar Paul. New York: 1930.

Acute historical perceptions and intuitions, combined with detailed studies of the development of modern industrialism: vitiated by a scholastic theory of labor value that bears no relation to historic or economic reality. For criticism see Veblen, Thorstein: *The Place of Science in Modern Civilization.*

The Eighteenth Brumaire of Louis Bonaparte. New York: n.d.

Marx, Karl, and Engels, Friedrich: *Correspondence, 1846-1895.* New York: 1934.

Selections from the complete correspondence published under the editorship of V. Adoratsky for the Marx-Engels-Lenin Institute. Very revealing on both the biographical and historical sides.

Manifesto of the Communist Party. Moscow: 1935.

This is the English translation of a revised version of the Manifesto, issued by an official transmitter of the doctrine.

Mazzini, Joseph: *Life and Writings.* 6 vols. London: 1891.

Volume IV contains Mazzini's important address on the Duties of Man: perhaps the best statement of a humanistic nationalism in the 19th century.

Mead, George H. *Mind, Self, and Society; from the Standpoint of a Social Behaviorism.* Edited by Charles W. Morris. Chicago: 1934.

Subtle and intelligent analysis, allied to Cooley, with none of the callow dogmatism of Watson and his school.

Mead, George R. S. *Fragments of a Faith Forgotten.* Second ed. London: 1906.

Study of the gnostics, with special emphasis on their universality.

Mehring, Franz: *Karl Marx; the Story of His Life.* New York: 1935.

First published in Germany, 1918. Almost an "official" life, with the characteristic limitations of such work. See Wilson, Edmund.

Melville, Herman: *Moby Dick.* New York: 1851.

Pierre; or The Ambiguities. New York: 1852.

Mercier, Louis Sebastien: *L'An Deux Mille Quatre Quarante; Rêve s'il en fût jamais.* Londres: 1772.

Michel, André (editor): *Histoire de l'Art; Depuis les Premiers Temps Chrétiens Jusquà Nos Jours.* 8 vols. Paris: 1905-1929.

Michelet, J.: *Historical View of the French Revolution.* Trans. London: 1860.

Mill, John Stuart: *The Subjection of Women.* London: 1869.

Utilitarianism. London: 1863.

On Liberty. London: 1859.

Representative Government. With an Introduction by A. D. Lindsay.

These long essays were published together in the Everyman Series; London: 1910.

Principles of Political Economy; With Some of Their Applications to Social Philosophy. 2 vols. New York: 1874.

Montaigne, Michel de: *Essays.* 3 vols. Bordeaux: 1580-1588.

More, Louis Trenchard: *Isaac Newton; a biography; 1642-1727.* New York: 1934.

More, Paul Elmer: *The Greek Tradition from the Death of Socrates to the Council of Chalcedon,* 399 B.C. to A.D. 451. 4 vols. Princeton: 1921-1927.

Valuable.

More, Thomas: *Utopia.* Trans. by G. C. Richards. First ed.; Rotterdam: 1516. Oxford: 1923.

Morgan, C. Lloyd: *Emergent Evolution.* New York: 1923.

As a biologist turned metaphysician Morgan developed the concept of emergence in a fruitful manner, and laid the foundations for a scientific method that should be capable of dealing with those higher and more complex forms of behavior, as in the personality, whose very essence had been deliberately left out of physical science in the seventeenth century.

The Interpretation of Nature. New York: 1906.

Life, Mind and Spirit. New York: 1925.

Morley, John Viscount: *Diderot and the Encyclopedists.* 2 vols. London: 1878.

Morris, Charles: *Paths of Life; a Preface to a World Religion.* New York: 1942.

An attempt to define religion in terms of personality and to project a new religious orientation which will be favorable to the balanced personality.

Morris, William: *News from Nowhere.* London: 1891.

Hopes and Fears for Art. Boston: 1882.

Morris at his humane best.

Mounier, Emmanuel: *A Personalist Manifesto.* New York: 1938.

Mumford, Lewis: *The Social Responsibilities of Teachers and Their Implications for Teacher Education.* In *The Educational Record,* October, 1939.

Mumford, Lewis: *The Making of Men.* In *The Humanities Look Ahead; Report of the First Annual Conference Held by the Stanford School of Humanities.* Stanford University: 1943.

The Unified Approach to Knowledge and Life. In *The University and the Future of America.* Stanford University: 1941.

These three papers deal more specifically with the educational re-orientation implied, rather than fully expressed, in the final chapter of the present book.

The Story of Utopias. New York: 1922. Reprinted: 1942.

Faith for Living. New York: 1940.

Though essentially a pamphlet, written to meet the urgent needs of the moment, the last third presents a concrete discipline of life, which the author hopes to enlarge at some appropriate later day.

Herman Melville. New York: 1929.

Murray, Gilbert: *Stoic, Christian, and Humanist.* London: 1940.

Five States of Greek Religion. New York: 1930.

Murray, Henry A., and others: *Explorations in Personality; a Clinical and Experimental Study of Fifty Men of College Age by the Workers at the Harvard Psychological Clinic.* New York: 1938.

Brilliant exploratory attempt to create a substratum of solid science beneath the diverse interpretations of modern schools of psychology.

Murray, Margaret Alice: *The Witch-Cult in Western Europe; a Study in Anthropology.* Oxford: 1921.

A study whose evidence should be better known to those who still think that witches did not exist outside the diseased minds of their persecutors. See Henry Lea.

Myres, J. L.: *The Dawn of History.* New York: 1911.

The Political Ideas of the Greeks. New York: 1927.

Newman, John Henry: *On the Scope and Nature of University Education.* London: 1852.

Nice and Post-Nicene Fathers. 26 vols. New York: 1886-1895.

Niebuhr, Reinhold: *Does Civilization Need Religion?* New York: 1927.

An Interpretation of Christian Ethics. New York: 1935.

Beyond Tragedy; Essays on the Christian Interpretation of History. New York: 1937.

Moral Man and Immoral Society. New York: 1932.

The Nature and Destiny of Man; a Christian Interpretation. Vol. I: *Human Nature.* Vol. II: *Human Destiny.* New York: 1941, 1943.

A wide-ranging, subtle, acute, paradoxical re-statement of the mysteries of the Christian religion, regarded as a unique and definitive event in the life of mankind.

Nietzsche, Friedrich: *Complete Works.* New York: 1910-1927.

Nilsson, Martin P.: *Moyen Age et Renaissance.* (Vol. VI in *Norstedts Wärldshistoria.*) Paris: 1933.

Sound. Excellent appraisal of Burckhardt, Thode, Burdach, et al.

Oakeley, Hilda Diana: *History and the Self; a Study in the Roots of History and the Relations of History and Ethics.* London: 1934.

Okakura, Kakuzo: *The Ideals of the East.* New York: 1904.

Origen: *Writings.* Edited by Crombie, Frederick. Vol. I: *De Principiis;* Edinburgh: 1859. Vol. II: *Against Celsus;* Edinburgh: 1872.

Ortega y Gasset, José: *Toward a Philosophy of History.* New York: 1941.

Philosophic reflections on the State, on the meaning of technics, and on the task of human history. The view of human life as a fabrication and a drama parallels at more than one point the underlying theme of the present series.

Owen, Robert: *A New View of Society, and Other Writings.* New York: 1927.

Paine, Thomas: *Age of Reason.* New York: 1794.

Common Sense. London: 1776.

Rights of Man. London: 1791.

Panovsky, Erwin: *Studies in Iconology; Humanistic Themes in the Art of the Renaissance.* New York: 1939.

Pascal, Blaise: *Pensées.* Paris: 1670. New York: 1931.

The Provincial Letters. Translated by Rev. Thomas McCrie. Boston: 1880.

Paston Letters. See Gairdner, James.

Pater, Walter: *The Renaissance; Studies in Art and Poetry.* London: 1873.

A book that still deserves a place amid many more pretentious studies of the Renaissance, if only because Pater, in 1873, was already quite aware of the 12th century Renaissance.

Peller, Sigismund: *Studies on Mortality since the Renaissance.* In *Bulletin of the History of Medicine.* April, 1943.

Penn, William: *The Peace of Europe, the Fruits of Solitude, and Other Writings.* New York: (Everyman Edition, n.d.).

Important selection from the writings of a man whose practical historic role has overshadowed his writings.

Pepys, Samuel: *The Diary of Samuel Pepys.* First ed. 1825. 3 vols. New York: 1938.

Petrarca, Francesco: *The Life of Solitude.* Urbana: 1924.

Some Love Songs. Oxford: 1915.

Pirenne, Henri: *Mohammed and Charlemagne.* New York: 1939.

A History of Europe; From the Invasions to the 16th Century. London: 1939.

Plant, James S.: *Personality and the Cultural Pattern.* New York: 1937.

Plato: *The Republic. The Laws.* Trans. by B. Jowett. In *Plato's Works.* New York: 1937.

Both these books are fundamental developments of Athenian thoughts on ethics, politics, and religion.

Plotinus: *The Ethical Treatises.* Vol. V. In *The Library of Philosophical Translations,* edited by Stephen McKenna. 5 vols.

Plutarch: *Moralia.* Published A.D. 90-110? Translated by Philemon Holland, 1603. London: 1912.

Poole, Reginald Lane: *Illustrations of the History of Medieval Thought and Learning.* First ed. London: 1884. Second ed. Revised. New York: 1920.

Excellent pioneer study that has weathered well.

Wycliffe and the Movements for Reform. London: 1889.

Power, Eileen: *Medieval People.* London: 1924.

Studies of half a dozen medieval people, beginning with a peasant in Charlemagne's time and ending with an Essex merchant. Imaginative, scholarly, readable.

Power, Eileen (editor): *The Goodman of Paris* (*Le Ménagier de Paris.* New York: 1928.

Written around 1393. A highly informative document.

Prescott, Daniel Alfred: *Emotion and the Educative Process; a Report of the Committee on the Relation of Emotion to the Educative Process.* Washington: 1938.

Admirably conceived and extremely discerning summary.

Prestage, Edgar (editor): *Chivalry; A Series of Studies to Illustrate Its Historical Significance and Civilizing Influence.* London: 1928.

Rabelais, François: *The Lives, Heroic Deeds, and Sayings of Gargantua and His Son Pantagruel.* (1546-52). Trans. by Urquhart and Le Motteux.

An indispensable classic: both for enjoyment and the closest study.

Works. 2 vols. London: 1859.

Raleigh, Walter, and Others: *Shakespeare's England; an Account of the Life and Manners of His Age.* 2 vols. Oxford: 1916.

Raynal, Abbé: *A Philosophical and Political History of the Settlements and Trade of the Europeans in the East and West Indies.* Revised ed. 10 vols. London: 1783.

A work of indisputable merit, despite its inevitable scholarly limitations, which in addition well mirrors the pragmatic, humanitarian rationalism of the 18th century. A work that needs re-thinking and re-doing today.

Reade, Winwood: *The Martyrdom of Man.* New York: 1874.

Renan, Ernest. *Life of Jesus.* Paris: 1863.

In the Histoire des Origines du Christianisme. 8 vols. Paris: 1863-1883.

The whole work has been partly superseded by later writers in this field. See Duchesne.

Robertson, J. M.: *The Evolution of States.* London: 1912.

Robinson, Geroid Tanquary: *Rural Russia Under the Old Régime, a History of the Landlord-Peasant World and a Prologue to the Peasant Revolution of 1917.* New York: 1932.

Rocker, Rudolph: *Nationalism and Culture.* New York: 1937.

Keen criticism from the standpoint of philosophic anarchism.

Ropke, Wilhelm: *Die Gesellschaftskrisis der Gegenwart.* Erlenbach-Zürich: 1942.

Good discussion of the nature of the social crisis, critical of the giantism and centralization brought about by late capitalist economy and proposing a "third alternative." See Victor Branford.

Rosenstock-Huessy, Eugen: *Out of Revolution; Autobiography of Western Man.* New York: 1938.

Attempt at an interpretation of political development in terms of revolution and war.

Rossetti, William Michael: *Italian Courtesy-Books.* In Early English Text Society. Extra Series. No. 9. London: 1869.

Rostovtzev, M.: *A History of the Ancient World.* 2 vols. Oxford: 1933.

Rougemont, Denis de: *Love in the Western World.* New York: 1940.

Rourke, Constance Mayfield: *Audubon.* New York: 1936.

American Humor. New York: 1931.

The Roots of American Culture. New York: 1942.

These three volumes by a brave and wise spirit who died before her great task was fulfilled, are indispensable for American cultural history.

Rousseau, Jean Jacques: *Les Confessions.* 4 vols. 1782-1789.

For all its good and its bad qualities an important document.

Contrat Social, ou Principes d'art Politique. Paris: 1762.

A Discourse on the Moral Effects of the Arts and Sciences. 1750.

A Discourse on the Origin of Inequality. 1755.

A Discourse on Political Economy. 1758.

These three discourses are included in the Everyman edition of *The Social Contract.*

Emile, ou la Nouvelle Héloise. 2 vols. Paris: 1845.

The Reveries of a Solitary; with an introduction by John Gould Fletcher. London: 1927.

Citizen of Geneva; Selections from the Letters of Jean-Jacques Rousseau. Edited by Charles William Hendel. New York: 1937.

Ruehle, Otto: *Karl Marx; His Life and Work.* New York: 1929.

Ruskin, John: *Unto This Last.* London: 1862.

Munera Pulveris. London: 1872.

Russell, Bertrand: *Freedom versus Organization; 1814-1914.* New York: 1934.

Russell, Theresa Frances: *Touring Utopia; The Realm of Constructive Humanism.* New York: 1932.

Treatment by subject-matter; with an exhaustive bibliography.

Ryan, John A., and Boland, Francis J.: *Catholic Principles of Politics.* New York: 1941.

This is a revised edition of *The State and the Church.* Monsignor Ryan, a strong advocate of more humane economic practices, emphasizes the unyielding intransigence of Catholic political theory in his chapter on the Christian Constitution of States, and justifies Catholic totalitarianism when, as, and if possible.

Sabatier, Paul: *Life of St. Francis of Assisi.* New York: 1894.

Classic.

St. Bonaventure: *The Life of St. Francis of Assisi, from the Legends of Santa Francisci.* Trans. London: 1898.

Saint-Simon, Claude Henri: *De la Réorganisation de la Société Européenne.* Paris: 1914.

Du Système Industriel. Paris: 1821.

Saint-Simon, Louis de Rouvroy (Duc de): *Memoirs.* Abridged version, translated by Francis Arkwright. New York: n.d.

Invaluable for light on court life in baroque period.

Salvemini, Giovanni: *Italian Fascism.* London: 1938.

Sanctis, Francesco de: *History of Italian Literature.* New York: 1931.

Superb criticism, first published in Italy, 1870-71.

Santayana, George: *The Life of Reason; or The Phases of Human Progress.* 5 vols. New York: 1925.

A late masterpiece of classic humanism; almost a museum piece. Valuable.

Saurat, Denis: *Milton; Man and Thinker.* New York: 1925.

Schapiro, J. Salwyn: *Condorcet and the Rise of Liberalism.* New York: 1934.

Social Reform and the Reformation. New York: 1909.

Succinct, well-proportioned summary. Includes reprint of pamphlets attributed to Emperors Sigismund and Frederick, Eberlin's Utopia of Wolfaria, and The Peasants' Twelve Articles.

Schweitzer, Albert: *The Philosophy of Civilization.* Part I: *The Decay and Restoration of Civilization.* First ed. London: 1923.

Part II: *Civilization and Ethics.* First ed. 1923. Second ed. Rev.: 1929.

Seeck, Otto: *Geschichte des Untergangs der antiken Welt.* 3 vols. Berlin: 1897-1909.

Seneca, Lucius Annaeus: *Ad Lucilium Epistolae Morales.* Trans. by E. R. Gummere. 3 vols. New York: 1917.

Shaler, Nathaniel Southgate: *The Individual; a Study of Life and Death.* New York: 1901.

Sheldon, W. H.: *Psychology and the Promethean Will.* New York: 1936.

Sherrington, Charles: *Man on His Nature.* New York: 1941.

Singer, Charles: *From Magic to Science; Essays on the Scientific Twilight.* New York: 1928.

Smith, Preserved: *A History of Modern Culture.* Vol. I: *The Great Renewal: 1543-1687;* Vol. II: *The Enlightenment: 1687-1776.* New York: 1930, 1934.

Excellent: with copious bibliographies.

Smith, Preserved (editor): *Luther's Correspondence and Other Contemporary Letters.* 2 vols. Philadelphia: 1913.

Sombart, Werner: *The Jews and Modern Capitalism.* Leipzig: 1911. Trans. London: 1913.

Confused and treacherous despite Sombart's usual wealth of facts.

Sorel, Georges: *Reflections on Violence.* Paris: 1906. Translated by T. E. Hulme. New York: n.d.

The opening gun of the attack upon reason and persuasion as methods of effective government. Originally fired in the name of syndicalist freedom and direct action, it backfired, partly as the result of the influence of Pareto and Mosca, into the attack upon responsible democratic government: totalitarian absolutism and despotism.

La Ruine du Monde Antique; Conception Matérialiste de l'Histoire. First ed. Paris: 1901. Third ed. Paris: 1933.

A provocative discussion of a subject here treated in a radically different fashion.

Les Illusions du Progrès. Paris: 1908.

Sorokin, Pitirim A.: *The Crisis of Our Age.* New York: 1941.

Social and Cultural Dynamics. 3 vols. New York: 1937.

A shaky structure surrounded by a heavy scaffolding of facts.

Spencer, Herbert: *First Principles.* London: 1862.

Illustrations of Universal Progress. New York: 1883.

The Man Versus the State. New York: 1888.

The Principles of Ethics. 2 vols. New York: 1892-1893.

The crowning work of Spencer's system; sound in its basic conceptions, weak and spindly in its development.

Spengler, Oswald: *The Decline of the West.* 2 vols. New York: 1928.

The Hour of Decision. New York: 1932.

Spingarn, Joel Elias: *Bibliographical Note;* in Vossler, K.: *The Medieval Mind.* Vol. II. New York: 1929.

History of Criticism in the Italian Renaissance. Oxford: 1901.

Strieder, Jacob: *Jacob Fugger the Rich Merchant and Banker of Augsburg, 1459-1525.* Trans. New York: 1931.

Strzygowski, Josef: *Origin of Christian Church Art.* Trans. Oxford: 1923.

Stubbs, S. G. B., and Bligh, E. W.: *Sixty Centuries of Health and Physick.* London: 1931.

Sudhoff, Karl: *Essays in the History of Medicine.* New York: 1926.

Much the same as the German Skizzen, but lacking the essays on Goethe. Sudhoff was a pioneer in going to original classic and medieval sources in medicine and correcting preconceptions which even historians shared. Compare Sudhoff's informed appreciation of medieval medicine and sanitation with Coulton's lukewarmer and vaguer account.

Swabey, Marie Collins: *Theory of the Democratic State.* Cambridge, Mass.: 1937.

Taine, Hippolyte Adolphe: *The Ancient Regime.* New York: 1876.

Tarn, H. W.: *Hellenistic Civilisation.* London: 1930.

Tatham, E. H. R.: *Francesco Petrarca; The First Modern Man of Letters; His Life and Correspondence; A Study of the Early Fourteenth Century (1304-1347).* 2 vols. London: 1925.

Taylor, Henry Osborn: *Ancient Ideals.* 2 vols. New York: 1896.

The Medieval Mind; a History of the Development of Thought and Emotion in the Middle Ages. 2 vols. New York: 1911.

Thought and Expression in the Sixteenth Century. 2 vols. New York: 1920.

Taylor, Rachel Anand: *Aspects of the Italian Renaissance.* New York: 1923.
Leonardo the Florentine. New York: 1928.

Teresa, Saint: *The Life of St. Teresa of Jesus, of the Order of Our Lady of Carmel, Written by Herself.* Trans. by David Lewis. London: 1914.

Tertullianus, Quintus Septimus Florens: *Writings.* Vol. I. Edinburgh: 1859. Vols. II and III. Edinburgh: 1870.

Thomas à Kempis: *Imitation of Christ.* Printed in Latin circa 1470. Translated circa 1613.

Thompson, James Westfall: *Exploration and Discovery in the Renaissance.* In *The Civilization of the Renaissance.* Chicago: 1929.
The Literacy of the Laity in the Middle Ages. Berkeley: 1939.

Thorndyke, Lynn: *Science and Thought in the Fifteenth Century.* New York: 1929.

Tocqueville, Alexis de: *Democracy in America.* 4 vols. Paris: 1835-1840. 2 vols. New York: 1900.
A work almost beyond praise by the most profound political philosopher of the 19th century: possibly of modern times. Relatively inaccessible and too often neglected.
The State of Society in France; before the Revolution of 1789 and the Causes Which Led to That Event. Paris: 1856. Trans. London: 1873.

Tolman, Edward Chace: *Psychological Types.* In *The Journal of Social Psychology, S.P.S.S.I. Bulletin,* 1941.

Tolstoy, Leo: *Tolstoy on Art.* Edited by Aymer Maude. Oxford: 1924.
What Then Must We Do? Oxford: 1925.
War and Peace. First ed. Moscow: 1868-1869. Introduction and ed. by Aymer Maude.

Toynbee, Arnold J.: *A Study of History.* 6 vols. New York: 1934, 1938.
A large-scale analysis of the nature of civilization and the processes which lead to their integration, their fossilization, and their transformation. Obviously a product of the same conditions that gave rise to Adams' and Spengler's studies, this interpretation goes much farther both in its scholarly command of facts and in its circumspect examination of both theory and evidence. Toynbee's differentiation of civilizations is far more comprehensive than Spengler's and his understanding of human development is not marred by Spengler's Teutonic barbarisms and atavisms. Thirteen volumes are promised; and the thesis is overladen by sometimes irrelevant detail, which will require further assimilation and condensation. Vols. I and III are probably most valuable: Vol. VI comes to a curious non-sociological conclusion which gives to the Christian religion a different status from that exercised by other prophets and other churches. The whole thesis deserves close study; for its merits far outweigh its weaknesses. See Kahler, Flewelling, Sorokin.

Traill, H. D., and Mann, J. S.: *Social England; a Record of the Progress of the People; in Religion, Laws, Learning, Arts, Industry, Commerce, Science, Literature, and Manners, from the Earliest Time to the Present Day.* 6 vols. in 12. New York: 1909.

Trevelyan, George Macaulay: *England in the Age of Wycliffe.* New York: 1899.

Trever, Albert A.: *History of Ancient Civilization.* Vol. I. *The Ancient Near East and Greece.* Vol. II. *The Roman World.* New York: 1936, 1939.
The emphasis on social history gives this brief text a special value.

Troeltsch, Ernst: *Protestantism and Progress.* New York: 1912.
The Social Teaching of the Christian Churches. 2 vols. New York: 1931.
Better in its analysis of theology than in its grasp of social relations and social influences. Somewhat over-rated.

Trotsky, Leon: *The History of the Russian Revolution.* 3 vols. Trans. by Max Eastman. New York: 1932.

Unamuno, Miguel de: *The Tragic Sense of Life.* London: 1926.

Veblen, Thorstein: *The Place of Science in Modern Civilization.* New York: 1919.

An Inquiry into the Nature of Peace and the Terms of Its Perpetuation. New York: 1917.

The Theory of the Leisure Class. New York: 1899.

Perhaps the most essential of Veblen's works; to be read especially in connection with the development of European culture from the Middle Ages on.

Vico, Giovanni Battista: *Œuvres choisies de Vico; précédés d'une introduction sur sa vie et ses ouvrages par M. Michelet.* 2 vols. Paris: 1935.

Volney, C. F.: *The Ruins; or, Meditations on the Revolutions of Empires and the Law of Nature.* Paris: 1802. New York: 1890.

Voltaire, François Marie Arouet de. *Age of Louis XIV.* New York: 1926.

Useful revelation of the idola of both the 17th and 18th centuries.

Candide, ou l'Optimisme. 1759. Paris: 1921.

Vossler, Karl: *Medieval Culture; an Introduction to Dante and His Times.* Trans. by W. C. Lawton. 2 vols. New York: 1929.

Exhaustive study by a great German scholar, published in German as a study of the *Divine Comedy;* but the English title truly reveals its scope. The bibliographical note, by J. E. Spingarn, was a labor of love fully worthy of the occasion.

Waddell, Helen: *The Wandering Scholars.* New York: 1927. Seventh ed. (revised) 1937.

Wallas, Graham: *Human Nature in Politics.* New York: 1916.

Study of irrational elements in political life.

The Great Society; a Psychological Analysis. New York: 1914.

One of the best studies of the unifying processes in Western civilization. See also Marvin: *The Unity of Western Civilization.*

Our Social Heritage. New York: 1921.

Wallas's work, as a whole, contained most of what was sound in Pareto, without his bias toward those elements which finally favored outright fascism.

Warner, Wellman J.: *The Wesleyan Movement in the Industrial Revolution.* New York: 1930.

Webb, Beatrice: *My Apprenticeship.* London: 1926.

Weber, Max: *The Protestant Ethic and the Spirit of Capitalism.* London: 1930.

Weston, Jessie L. (translator): *Tristan,* by Gottfried von Strassburg. New York: 1913.

Whitehead, Alfred North: *Adventures of Ideas.* New York: 1933.

Science and the Modern World. New York: 1928.

Process and Reality: An Essay in Cosmology. New York: 1929.

Whitman, Walt: *Leaves of Grass.* Philadelphia: 1900.

Prose Works. Philadelphia: n.d.

Wilson, Edmund: *To the Finland Station; a Study in the Writing and Acting of History.* New York: 1940.

Deals with the origins of socialist ideology from Vico to Lenin; but is particularly acute in its biographical analysis of Marx. Recommended.

Wolf, A.: *A History of Science, Technology, and Philosophy in the 16th and 17th* Centuries. New York: 1935.

Wollstonecraft, Mary: *The Rights of Woman.* 1792. New York: 1929.

Woodward, E. L.: *Christianity and Nationalism in the Later Roman Empire.* New York: 1916.

Excellent. See Glover.

Woodward, William H.: *Vittorino de Feltre; and Other Humanist Educators.* Cambridge: 1905.

Includes translations of Vergerius, D'Arezzo, Aneneas Sylvius and Guarino.

Woolf, Leonard: *After the Deluge; A Study of Communal Psychology.* 2 vols. New York: 1931, 1940.

Wulf, Maurice de: *History of Medieval Philosophy.* 2 vols. trans. New York: 1935.

Zilboorg, Gregory: *Mind, Medicine, and Man.* New York: 1943.

Zimmern, Alfred: *The Greek Commonwealth.* New York: 1911.

Classic.

Nationality and Government. London: 1918.

Solon and Croesus. London: 1928.

ACKNOWLEDGMENTS

In a book that has so many diverse sources, I can hardly begin to acknowledge even a token number of debts: it would be as invidious to particularize them as it would be ungrateful to forget them.

For help in gathering reproductions I must thank the Print Room, the Photograph Reference Collection of the Metropolitan Museum of Art and of the Museum of Modern Art; for permission to use certain reproductions from their collections I must thank the Metropolitan Museum of Art, the Museum of Modern Art, the Art Institute of Chicago, the Cleveland Museum of Art, the Phillips Memorial Gallery, the Yale University Art Gallery, Mr. Walter C. Arensberg, and—not least—for the final photograph, Mr. Alfred Stieglitz. Part of the final chapter appeared in The Social Foundations of Post-War Building, in the Rebuilding Britain Series, edited by F. J. Osborn and published in London by Faber and Faber. To Mr. Malcolm Cowley and Doubleday, Doran and Company I owe the privilege of reprinting part of my essay on Spengler, which appeared originally in Books That Changed Their Minds.

In the matter of books, I must record a long-standing obligation to the New York Public Library, whose marvelous service, swift and accurate, is only rivaled by its incomparable catalog: perhaps the best in the world. But I owe thanks, too, to my Dutchess County neighbor, the Vassar College Library, for permission to use its very adequate resources. Finally, the long preparatory work on this volume would have been impossible without a John Simon Guggenheim Fellowship in 1938, and without further grants-in-aid from The Carnegie Corporation of New York: to both I owe a debt, not merely for assistance, but for the high tradition of freedom that characterizes this assistance. To the late Dr. Frederick P. Keppel's tact and understanding special acknowledgment must here, if all-too-tardily, be made. Finally, to my wife, Sophia Mumford, I owe public thanks for help not confined to the editorial preparation of the manuscript.—L. M.

INDEX

Note: Titles of books are printed in italics.

Books by Lewis Mumford
available in paperbound editions from
Harcourt Brace Jovanovich, Inc.

TECHNICS AND CIVILIZATION

THE CULTURE OF CITIES

THE CONDITION OF MAN

THE CONDUCT OF LIFE

FROM THE GROUND UP:
OBSERVATIONS ON CONTEMPORARY
ARCHITECTURE, HOUSING, HIGHWAY BUILDING,
AND CIVIC DESIGN

THE CITY IN HISTORY:
ITS ORIGINS, ITS TRANSFORMATIONS, AND
ITS PROSPECTS

THE HIGHWAY AND THE CITY

THE MYTH OF THE MACHINE
VOL. I. TECHNICS AND HUMAN DEVELOPMENT
VOL. II. THE PENTAGON OF POWER

THE URBAN PROSPECT

INTERPRETATIONS AND FORECASTS 1922–1972